Children and Same Sex Families:
A Legal Handbook

Children and Same Sex Families
A Legal Handbook

Anthony Hayden QC
St Johns Buildings, Manchester

Marisa Allman
Zenith Chambers, Leeds

Sarah Greenan
Zenith Chambers, Leeds

Elina Nhinda-Latvio
Calderdale MBC

Her Honour Judge Jai Penna
Manchester Civil Justice Centre

_fl_ Family Law

Published by Family Law
A publishing imprint of Jordan Publishing Limited
21 St Thomas Street
Bristol BS1 6JS

Whilst the publishers and the author have taken every care in preparing the material included in this work, any statements made as to the legal or other implications of particular transactions are made in good faith purely for general guidance and cannot be regarded as a substitute for professional advice. Consequently, no liability can be accepted for loss or expense incurred as a result of relying in particular circumstances on statements made in this work.

Crown Copyright material is reproduced with kind permission of the Controller of Her Majesty's Stationery Office.

British Library Cataloguing-in-Publication Data

A catalogue record for this book is available from the British Library.

ISBN 978 1 84661 319 7

Typeset by Letterpart Ltd, Reigate, Surrey

Printed in Great Britain by CPI Antony Rowe, Chippenham and Eastbourne

PREFACE

In many ways, this book feels as if it should have been written years ago and yet the simple truth is that it could not have been. Before the Human Rights Act 1998, the Adoption and Children Act 2002 and the Civil Partnership Act 2004 there would, for a start, have been a great deal less to say. Had the book been written earlier, it would, I suspect, have been a very different one, probably more agenda-driven and possibly with an authorial tone that is rather more polemical than this. That is a book that I am relieved we did not have to write, this is a book that I feel proud and privileged to have been able to have contributed to.

A society that respects diversity, values equality and promotes fairness is a healthier one for children to grow up in and a better one for us all. As I have researched my own contribution for this book and read the erudite analysis of my co-authors, what strikes me time and again is how those judges, politicians, lawyers, clergymen and others who keep these fundamental rights and liberties securely in focus are often able to move the law and social attitudes forward at a pace and with a high degree of consensus. An intuitive sense of these rights and freedoms in the past has not always found expression in the most sensitive language. It is a strange sensation in 2012 to read judgments of only a couple of decades ago that talk of homosexuals as 'abnormal' or 'unfortunate' whilst at the same time, in difficult cases involving the welfare of children, crafting analysis which is sensitive, child focused and full of integrity and fairness to a wide variety of minority groups.

Though we may sometimes be frivolous about it, in a way which is, I think, often healthy, we are nonetheless these days far more careful, considerate and thoughtful about our use of language and how it impacts upon the autonomy of others. This development, coupled with the raft of equality legislation, provides a framework for a much fairer society in the future and one in which the options for children are expanded, keeping them at the centre of the legal process. Our responsibility, be it as lawyers, parents or judges is to ensure that these opportunities for whom many fought and some died, are harnessed effectively by those charged with the responsibility to do so. This book aims to assist all of us who are engaged in that process and who want better to understand the ever-evolving concept of both parent and family.

Anthony Hayden QC
March 2012

ACKNOWLEDGMENTS

Marisa Allman

I would like to thank Charlotte Kelly for helping to prepare Chapter 4 on Private Law. I am also grateful to Neil Kelly of the British Surrogacy Centre, Anne-Marie Hutchinson, OBE, of Dawson Cornwell Solicitors and Andrew Vorizimer of Vorizimer Masserman Attorneys for sharing their experience in the field of international surrogacy, which assisted enormously in the preparation of Chapter 3 on Surrogacy. I would most like to thank my husband for almost 20 years of limitless encouragement and support, and my children for their joy and unconditional love which keep everything in perspective.

Sarah Greenan

I am grateful to my partner Christopher for his patience and forbearance during the process of writing. I would also like to thank my former pupilmaster John Morris Collins (called 1956 and still in practice) for the benefit of twenty-five years of guidance and good sense.

Elina Nhinda-Latvio

I echo the thanks to the contributors named by Marisa and would also like to thank my family Rowan, Alex and Claire for their patience and support during this process.

CONTENTS

Preface   v
Acknowledgments   vii
Table of Cases   xvii
Table of Statutes   xxv
Table of Statutory Instruments   xxxiii
Table of Abbreviations   xxxvii

Chapter 1
Parenthood   **1**
What is meant by 'parent'?   1
Biological or genetic parenthood   4
Applications for declaration as to parentage   6
Legal parentage: mother, father or parent?   7
  Terminology: mother, father, parent   9
Child of the family   12
Acquiring legal parenthood   13
  UK adoption   13
  The presumption of legitimacy   14
  Assisted reproduction   16
Tracing legal and genetic parentage   17
  Children born since the HFEA 2008 came into force on 6 April
    2009   20
  Surrogacy and parental orders   25
  Legal parenthood following surrogacy if a parental order is not
    made   29
  Effect of a parental order on legal parentage   32
Conclusions   33

Chapter 2
Parental Responsibility   **35**
Defining parental responsibility   35
Acquiring parental responsibility by agreement or order   39
  Parental responsibility agreement   39
  Application for a parental responsibility order   40
  When will the court make a parental responsibility order if it is
    disputed?   41
  Application for a residence order   43

Chapter 3
Surrogacy   **45**
What is surrogacy?   45
What is commercial surrogacy?   47
What are the routes to a commissioning parent becoming the child's
        carer following surrogacy?   55
    Need for an order   55
    What type of order?   57
Making the application for a parental order   69
    Registration of parental orders   72
Adoption   72
Guardianship   73
International surrogacy   74

Chapter 4
Private Law Applications   **81**
Scope   81
Historical background   82
The welfare principle   87
The welfare checklist   88
Parental responsibility   89
Section 8 orders   91
    Contact order   92
    Residence order   102
    Prohibited steps order   108
    Specific issue order   109
    Special Guardianship   111
    Applications   113
    Permission to apply for a section 8 order   113
Parties to private law proceedings   117

Chapter 5
Same Sex Adoption   **119**
What is the function of the Adoption Panel?   140
The constitution of the panel   140
How does the Adoption Panel work in practice?   143

Chapter 6
Gender Recognition   **145**
Meaning of 'same sex relationship' and gender recognition   145
    Introduction   145
    Trans(sexual)/transgendered people   146
Gender recognition background   147
    Development of transgender legislation   148
What is 'Gender Recognition'?   152
    Determination of applications   153
    Evidence   154
    Overseas application process   156

Successful applications 157
Consequences of issue of GRC 157
Summary 157
Registration 158
Married couples and civil partners 160
Parenthood 173
Contact with children following a breakdown of relationship in a
transgender relationship/context 174
Social security benefits, pensions and tax issues 180
Proposals for change 182

Chapter 7
Personal Protection **185**
The Family Law Act 1996 188
Cohabitants 188
Relevant children 189
Associated persons 189
Regulation of the home 190
Categories 191
Making an occupation order 194
Without notice orders 196
Transfer of tenancy 196
Breach of occupation orders 196
Non-molestation orders 197
Part IV orders: duration 198
Forced marriage 199
Protection from Harassment Act 1997 200

Chapter 8
Civil Partnership **203**
Formation and recognition of civil partnerships 203
Definition of a civil partnership 203
Is a civil partnership a marriage? 204
Civil partner or not and does it matter? 206
Registering as civil partners: procedure in England and Wales 210
Ceremony 210
Location 211
Eligibility 212
Gender change and eligibility for marriage/civil partnership 212
Pre-registration procedure 214
Registration at a British Consulate 216
Recognition of overseas relationships 218
Requirement for registration 220
Meeting of formalities 221
Capacity 222
Effect of overseas relationship being treated as a civil partnership 224
Checklist for recognition in England and Wales of overseas
relationships 225

Recognition overseas of English civil partnership   225
    International recognition generally   227
    Dissolution and the property consequences   227
Declarations as to civil partnership status   228
Civil partnership: valid, void, voidable?   230
    Grounds on which civil partnership is void   232
Breakdown of a civil partnership   235
    Application for dissolution in England and Wales   235
    Jurisdiction of the courts of England and Wales to consider an
        application for dissolution, separation or nullity   239
    Jurisdiction: applications in more than one country 240
    Recognition of dissolution, nullity and legal separation between
        different countries   242
    Recognition in the UK   245
    Ability to apply for financial provision following overseas
        dissolution   247

Chapter 9
Financial Provision on the Breakdown of Civil Partnership   **253**
Overview   253
Financial provision on dissolution for civil partners   254
    Schedule 5   254
    Provision for children of the family   256
    Matters to be taken into account   256
The general approach to applications for provision for civil partners   257
    First consideration to the children   266
    Duration of the partnership   267
    What are the partnership assets?   268
    The family home   270
    Pensions   271
Procedure   272
Consent orders   273
Financial relief in the magistrates courts   274
Alternatives to court   274
Financial relief after overseas dissolution   275

Chapter 10
Financial Provision on the Breakdown of Cohabiting Relationships   **281**
Introduction   281
The family home: occupation   283
The family home: ownership   285
The family home: the legal framework   286
    Acquisition of an interest: two legal owners   286
    No TR1 (or pre-1998 TR1) and no declaration of trust 290
    Inadequate declaration of trust   295
    Agreement to vary the declaration of trust   296
    Ownership in one name only: constructive and resulting trusts   296
    Resulting trusts   298

Proprietary estoppel 299
'Engaged' couples 299
Orders in relation to property owned by cohabitants 300
Proposals for reform 303
The family home: rented property 305
Other property issues 309
Bank accounts 309
Personal bank accounts 309
Chattels 310
Provision for children on relationship breakdown 312
Child support 312
The formula 315
Proposals for change 316
Schedule 1 Children Act 1989 316
Property transfer orders 319
Lump sum provision 320
Periodical payments 320
Big money cases 321
Procedure 321

Chapter 11
Succession **323**
Introduction 323
Property which does not pass under a will 323
Interests in real property held on a joint tenancy 323
Payments made by pension schemes and under insurance policies 325
Personal property 325
Chattels 326
The body of the deceased 326
Inheritance under a will 326
Is the will valid? 326
Gifts by will to children 328
Intestate succession 330
Inheritance on intestacy 336
Succession to tenancies 341
Rent Act tenancies 341
Assured tenancies 343
Secure tenancies 343
Inheritance and family provision 344
Civil partners 348
'Child of the deceased' 351
'Child of the family' 351
'Any person ... who immediately before the death of the deceased
    was being maintained, either wholly or partly, by the deceased' 354
What provision can be made? 356
'Reasonable financial provision' 356
Matters to which the court is to have regard 356
The approach in civil partnership cases 357

Other points in relation to the 1975 Act   358
Proposals for reform   359

Chapter 12
Welfare Benefits   **361**
Introduction   361
Background   361
Relevant legislation and effects on social security and tax credits   365
   Means-tested benefits and non-means-tested benefits   367
   Social security benefits and definitions of same sex couple   368
   Tax credits and definitions of same sex couple   368
The living together test   369
   What is meant by 'living together'   369
   Meaning of living together as husband and wife ('LTAHAW')   369
   Meaning of living together as civil partners ('LTACP')   370
   The 'living together' cohabiting same sex couples (couples who are
       unmarried and not civil partners)   370
   Same sex co-parents not living together   377
Gender recognition and implications for welfare benefits   378
   Gender recognition and the 'living together test'   378
   State pensions, benefits and tax issues   379
   Disagreement with decision maker   380
Other benefits issues relating to same sex couples   380
   Pensions provisions   380
   Tax   380
Summary   381

Appendix 1
Flowcharts Tracing Legal and Genetic Parentage   **383**

Appendix 2
Forms   **387**

Appendix 3
Material Relating to Gender Recognition   **401**

Appendix 4
Statutory Materials   **459**
Children Act 1989   460
Civil Partnership Act 2004   497
Family Law Act 1996   600
Gender Recognition Act 2004   606
Housing Act 1985   620
Housing Act 1988   621
Human Fertilisation and Embryology Act 2008   622
Inheritance (Provision for Family and Dependants) Act 1975   634
Rent Act 1977   638
Surrogacy Arrangements Act 1985   641

Trusts of Land and Appointment of Trustees Act 1996   646

Appendix 5
Useful Contacts   **649**

Index   **651**

TABLE OF CASES

References are to paragraph numbers.

A (Child of the Family), Re [1998] 1 FLR 347, [1998] 1 FCR 458, [1998]
    Fam Law 14   1.39
A and D v B and E [2003] EWHC 1376 (Fam), [2003] 2 FLR 1054   4.73
A v B and C [2012] EWCA Civ 285; [2011] EWHC 2290 (Fam)   1.2, 1.4, 1.5, 1.37, 4.15, 4.16,
     4.21, 4.37, 4.44
A v P *sub nom* A v P (Surrogacy: Parental Order: Death of Application)
    [2011] EWHC 1738 (Fam), [2011] Fam Law 1080, [2011] All ER (D)
    99 (Jul)   1.96, 3.58, 3.60
A, Re [2008] EWCA Civ 867, [2008] 2 FLR 1593   2.22
AAA v Ash (Registrar General for England and Wales intervening) [2009]
    EWHC 636 (Fam), [2010] 1 FLR 1, [2009] 4 All ER 641, [2009] 3
    FCR 95,   2.5
AB v Dobbs [2010] EWHC 497 (Fam)   11.45
Abbott v Abbott [2007] UKPC 53, [2008] 1 FLR 1451, [2008] Fam Law 215   10.56, 10.57
Agbaje v Agbaje [2010] UKSC 13, [2010] 1 AC 628, [2010] 1 FLR 1813,
    [2010] 2 All ER 877, [2010] 2 WLR 709   8.159, 8.160, 8.163, 9.67
Allardice, Re (1910) 29 NZLR 959   11.74
Alwyn (Non-Molestation Proceedings By A Child), Re [2009] NI Fam 22,
    [2010] 1 FLR 1363, [2010] Fam Law 134   7.28, 7.42
Ashby v Kilduff [2010] EWHC 2034 (Ch), [2010] 3 FCR 80, [2010] All ER
    (D) 27 (Aug)   10.20, 10.62

B (A Child) (Residence: Biological Parent), Re [2009] UKSC 5, [2010] 1
    FLR 551, [2010] 1 All ER 223, [2009] 1 WLR 2496, [2010] 1 FCR 1   4.20, 4.52
B (Adoption by One parent to Exclusion of Other), Re [2001] 1 FLR 589   5.5
B (Adoption: Natural Parent), Re [2001] UKHL 70, [2002] 1 FLR 196,
    [2002] 1 All ER 641, [2002] 1 WLR 258   1.99
B (Child: Property Transfer), Re [1999] 2 FLR 418, [1999] Fam Law 535,
    [1999] All ER (D) 460   10.133
B (Leave to Remove), Re [2006] EWHC 1783 (Fam), [2007] 1 FLR 333,
    [2006] All ER (D) 270 (Jul)   4.77
B (Parentage), Re [1996] 2 FLR 15, [1996] 3 FCR 697, [1996] Fam Law 536   1.26, 1.28, 10.126
B (Role of Biological father), Re [2007] EWHC 1952 (Fam), [2008] 1 FLR
    1015, [2008] Fam Law 411   2.18, 4.16, 4.21, 4.39
B v A (Parental Responsibility) *sub nom* Re D (Contact and Parental
    Responsibility: Lesbian Mothers and Known Father) [2006] EWHC 2
    (Fam), [2006] 1 FCR 556, [2006] All ER (D) 25 (Jan)   1.1, 1.2, 1.31, 1.39, 2.18, 4.38, 4.39
B v B (Minors) (Custody, Care and Control) [1991] 1 FLR 402, [1991] FCR
    1, [1991] Fam Law 174, FD   4.8
B v B (Occupation Order) [1999] 1 FLR 715   7.21
B v France (Application No 13343/87) (1992) 16 EHRR 1, [1992] 2 FLR
    249, [1992] Fam Law 491   6.19, 6.49
B v the UK [2000] 1 FLR 1   2.6
B, Re [2000] Ch 662, [2000] 1 All ER 665, [2000] 2 WLR 929, [2000] 1 FCR
    385   11.104

Baiai & Ors v Secretary of State for the Home Department [2008] UKHL
    53, [2009] AC 287, [2008] 2 FLR 1462, [2008] 3 All ER 1094, [2008] 3
    FCR 1   8.34
Bank of Ireland Home Mortgages Ltd v Bell [2001] 2 FLR 809, [2001]
    BPIR 429, [2001] 3 FCR 134, [2001] Fam Law 805   10.72
Baynes v Hedger [2008] EWHC 1587 (Ch), [2008] 2 FLR 1805, [2008] Fam
    Law 1087, [2008] Fam Law 952   11.86, 11.87
Beaumont, deceased, Re; Martin v Midland Bank Trust Co [1980] Ch 444,
    [1979] 3 WLR 818, [1980] 1 All ER 266, ChD   11.102
Bellinger v Bellinger [2003] UKHL 21, [2003] 2 AC 467, [2003] 2 WLR
    1174, [2003] 1 FLR 1043, [2003] UKHRR 679, [2003] 2 All ER 593,
    HL   6.26, 6.71
Benn v Dixon (1847) 16 Sim 21, 11 Jur 812, 10 LTOS 50   11.27
Birmingham City Council v R [2006] EWCA Civ 1748, [2007] 1 FLR 564   4.78
Bosch v Perpetual Trustee Co Ltd [1938] AC 463, [1938] 2 All ER 14, 107
    LJPC 53   11.74, 11.75
Boughton v Knight (1873) LR 3 P&D 64, [1861-73] All ER Rep 40, 28 LT
    562   11.73
Brighton & Hove City Council v PM and others [2011] EWCA Civ 795,
    [2011] Fam Law 1075, [2011] All ER (D) 96 (Jul)   1.12
Brock v Wollams [1949] 2 KB 388   11.64
Buchanan v Milton [1999] 2 FLR 844   11.36–11.41
Burden v The UK (Application No 13378/05) (2008) 47 EHRR 857, [2008] 2
    FLR 787, [2008] Fam Law 628, [2008] NLJR 673   8.2
Burgess v Rawnsley [1975] Ch 429, [1975] 3 All ER 142   11.8
Burrows v HM Coroner for Preston [2008] EWHC 1387 (QB), [2008] 2 FLR
    1225, [2008] Fam Law 951, [2008] Fam Law 984   11.35

C (A Minor) (Change of Surname), Re [1998] 2 FLR 656, [1998] Fam Law
    659   4.64
C (A Minor) (Residence Order: Lesbian Co-parents), Re [1994] Fam Law
    468, FD   4.12
C (Children) (Residential Assessments, Re [2001] EWCA Civ 1305, [2001] 3
    FCR 164, CA   6.98
C v C (A Minor) (Custody: Appeal) [1991] FCR 254, [1991] 1 FLR 223,
    [1991] Fam Law 175   4.7
C v C [1998] Fam 70, [1998] 1 FLR 554, [1998] 2 WLR 599   7.43
C v F (Disabled Child: Maintenance Orders) [1998] 2 FLR 1, [1999] 1 FCR
    39, [1998] Fam Law 389   10.116
Callaghan deceased, Re [1985] Fam 1, [1984] 3 WLR 1076, [1985] FLR 116,
    [1985] Fam Law 28   11.93
Carlton v Goodman [2002] EWCA Civ 545, [2002] 2 FLR 259, [2002] All
    ER (D) 284 (Apr)   10.31
Carr v Isard [2006] EWHC 2095 (Ch), [2006] All ER (D) 343 (Nov)   11.8
Ch'are Shalom Ve Tsedek v France (2000) June 27   5.13
Chalmers v Johns [1999] 1 FLR 392, [1999] Fam Law 16, CA   7.30, 7.34
Charman v Charman [2007] EWCA Civ 503, [2007] 1 FLR 1246, [2007]
    Fam Law 682, [2007] NLJR 814   9.26, 9.29
Chesterfield BC v Bailey (unreported) 22 December 2011, BAILII Citation
    Number [2011] EW Misc 18 (CC)   10.95
Churchill v Roach [2004] 3 FCR 744, [2004] 2 FLR 989   11.82
City of Westminster v IC (By His Friend The Official Solicitor) and KC and
    NN [2008] EWCA Civ 198, [2008] 2 FLR 267, [2008] Fam Law 517   8.63
Clarke v Meadus [2010] EWHC 3117 (Ch), [2010] All ER (D) 08 (Dec)   10.53
Collins's Settlement Trusts, Re, Donne v Hewetson [1971] 1 All ER 283,
    [1971] 1 WLR 37, 114 Sol Jo 936   11.50
Corbett v Corbett [1971] P 83   6.67
Cossey v United Kingdom (Application No 10843/84) (1990) 13 EHRR 622,
    [1991] 2 FLR 492, [1993] 2 FCR 97, [1991] Fam Law 362   6.18–6.20, 6.49
Crabb v Arun District Council [1976] Ch 179, [1975] 3 WLR 847, 119 Sol Jo
    711   10.62

Crake v Supplementary Benefits Commission, Butterworth v Supplementary
    Benefits Commission [1982] 1 All ER 498, (1981) 2 FLR 264   11.83, 12.30, 12.31
Croydon LBC v A [1992] Fam 169, [1992] 2 FLR 341, [1992] 3 WLR 267,
    [1992] 1 FCR 522, FD   4.69
Cyganik v Agulian [2006] EWCA Civ 129, [2006] 1 FCR 406, [2006] All ER
    (D) 372 (Feb)   3.47, 3.62

D & K (Care Plan: Twin Track Planning), Re [1999] 2 FLR 872   5.5
D (An Infant) (Adoption: Parent's Consent), Re [1977] AC 602, [1977] 2
    WLR 79, [1977] 1 All ER 145, HL   4.5
Davies v UK [2002] EHRR 720   5.8
Davis v Vale [1971] 2 All ER 1021, [1971] 1 WLR 1022, 115 Sol Jo 347   10.64
Davison, Re [1949] Ch 670, [1949] 2 All ER 551, 65 TLR 574   11.32
Dawson v Wearmouth [1999] 2 AC 308, [1999] 2 WLR 960, [1999] 2 All ER
    353, [1999] 1 FLR 1167, HL; [1998] Fam 75, [1997] 2 FLR 629,
    (1997) 94(35) LSG 34, CA   4.64
De Reneville v De Reneville [1948] P 100, III   6.59
Dödsbo v Sweden (Application No 61564/00) (2006) 45 EHRR 581, [2006]
    ECHR 61564/00   11.37
Dolan v Corby [2011] EWCA 1164   7.34
Ducksbury, Re [1966] 1WLR 1226, [1966] 2 All ER 374, 110 Sol Jo 601   11.77

E (Adoption: Freeing Order), Re [1995] 1 FLR 382   5.22
EB v France [2008] 47 EHRR 21   5.16, 5.17
Edgar v Edgar [1980] 1 WLR 1410   9.62
Edwards v Edwards [2010] EWHC 652 (Ch), [2010] All ER (D) 172 (Jun)   10.72
Elliott v Elliott [2001] 1 FCR 477   9.45
EN v Italy [2001] 31 EHRR 17   5.9
Evans v the UK (Application No 6339/05) (2006) 43 EHRR 409, [2006] 2
    FLR 172, [2006] 1 FCR 585, ECtHR   1.69

F (Children) (Paternity: Jurisdiction) [2007] EWCA Civ 873, [2008] 1 FLR
    225   4.75
F (Shared Residence Order), Re [2003] EWCA Civ 592, [2003] 2 FLR 397   4.56
F v G (Child: Financial Provision) [2004] EWHC 1848 (Fam), [2005] 1 FLR
    261   10.134, 10.141
F v the Child Support Agency, Re [1999] 2 FCR 385, [1999] 2 FLR 244,
    [1999] Fam Law 540   1.12
Fielding v Fielding [1978] 1 All ER 267, 121 Sol Jo 729   9.3
Fretté v France [2004] 38 EHRR 21   5.12, 5.14

G (A Minor) (Parental Responsibility Order), Re [1994] 1 FLR 504, [1994]
    Fam Law 372   2.14
G (Children) (Residence: Same-sex Partner), Re [2006] UKHL 43, [2006] 2
    FLR 629, [2006] 4 All ER 241, [2006] 1 WLR 2305 reversing [2006]
    EWCA Civ 372, [2006] 1 FCR 681, [2006] 2 FLR 614   1.3, 1.8, 1.9, 1.19, 1.21, 1.22, 1.103,
        2.23, 3.65, 4.18–4.21, 4.30, 4.34, 4.49, 4.52, 4.57, 4.61, 5.1, 11.35
G (Surrogacy: Foreign Domicile), Re [2007] EWHC 2814 (Fam), [2008] 1
    FLR 1047   3.33, 3.41, 3.47, 3.62, 3.106
G v F (Contact and Shared Residence: Application for Leave) [1998] 2 FLR
    799, [1998] Fam Law 587, FD   4.30, 4.53, 4.91
G v G (Occupation Order) [2009] EWCA Civ 976, [2011] 1 FLR 687   7.33, 7.34
G v G (Occupation Order: Conduct) [2000] 2 FLR 36, [2000] Fam Law 466,
    CA   7.31
Gallagher v Lawrence [2012] *The Telegraph* March 14   9.27
Ghaidan v Godin-Mendoza *sub nom* Ghaidan v Mendoza [2004] UKHL 30,
    [2004] 2 AC 557, [2004] 3 WLR 113, [2004] 2 FLR 600, [2004]
    UKHRR 827, [2004] 3 All ER 411, HL *affirming* Mendoza v
    Ghaidan [2002] EWCA Civ 1533, [2003] Ch 380   11.60, 11.87, 12.8–12.11
Gissing v Gissing [1971] AC 886, [1970] 3 WLR 255, (1970) FLR Rep 269,
    [1970] 2 All ER 780, HL   10.47

Goodwin v United Kingdom (Application No 28957/95) [2002] ECHR 588,
    (2002) 35 EHRR 18, [2002] 2 FLR 487, ECtHR   6.19, 6.21, 6.22, 6.24, 6.25, 6.49, 6.71,
                                                                                         6.78
Grant v United Kingdom (Application No 32570/03) (2006) 44 EHRR 1,
    [2006] ECHR 32570/03, [2006] All ER (D) 337 (May), ECtHR   6.49
Gray v Barr [1971] 2 All ER 949, [1971] 2 WLR 1334, [1971] 2 Lloyd's Rep
    1   11.11
Griffiths v Griffiths [1973] 3 All ER 386   10.64
Gully v Dix [2004] EWCA Civ 139, [2004] 1 FLR 918, [2004] 1 WLR 1399,
    [2004] 1 FCR 453   11.88
GW v RW (Financial Provision: Departure from Equality) [2003] EWHC
    611 (Fam), [2003] 2 FLR 108   9.24, 9.37

H (A Minor) (Section 37 Direction), Re [1993] 2 FLR 541, [1993] Fam Law
    205   3.10
H (Leave to Apply for Residence Order), Re [2008] EWCA Civ 503, [2008] 2
    FLR 848, [2008] 3 FCR 392   4.89
H (Parental Responsibility), Re [1998] 1 FLR 855, [1998] Fam Law 325   2.2
H (Prohibited Steps Order), Re [1995] 1 FLR 638, [1995] 1 WLR 667   4.69
H and A (Paternity: Blood Tests), Re [2002] EWCA Civ 383, [2002] 1 FLR
    1145, [2002] 2 FCR 469, [2002] All ER (D) 331 (Mar)   4.74
H v France [1987] 12 EHRR 74   5.8
H v H [2007] 1 FLR 1318   8.150
H v UK [1987] 10 EHRR 96   5.9
Hammersmith & Fulham LBC v Monk [1992] 1 AC 478, [1992] 1 FLR 465,
    [1992] 1 All ER 1, [1991] 3 WLR 1144, [1992] 2 FCR 129   10.95
Hapeshi v Allnatt [2010] EWHC 392 (Ch), [2010] All ER (D) 144 (Jan)   10.50
Harvell v Foster [1954] 2 QB 367, [1954] 2 All ER 736, [1954] 3 WLR 351   11.26
Hirani v Hirani (1983) 4 FLR 232   8.61
Holiday v Musa [2010] EWCA Civ 355, [2010] 2 FLR 702   3.47, 3.62
Holman v Howes [2005] EWHC 2824 (Ch), [2006] 1 FLR 1003   10.73
Hounslow v Powell [2011] UKSC 8, [2011] 2 AC 186, [2011] 2 All ER 129,
    [2011] 2 WLR 287   10.95

I v The United Kingdom (Application No 25680/94) (2002) 36 EHRR 967,
    [2002] 2 FCR 613, [2002] 2 FLR 518   6.21, 6.23–6.25
IJ (Foreign Surrogacy Agreement: Parental Order), Re [2011] EWHC 921
    (Fam), [2011] 2 FLR 646   3.56, 3.106
Ilott v Mitson [2011] EWCA Civ 346, [2011] 2 FCR 1, [2011] Fam Law 798   11.110

J (Leave to Issue Application for Residence Order), Re [2002] EWCA Civ
    1346, [2003] 1 FLR 114   4.94
J McB v LE [2011] 1 FLR   2.6
J v C (Void Marriage: Status of Children) [2006] EWCA Civ 551, [2006]
    Fam Law 742   6.70, 6.71, 6.92–6.97, 10.126
J v J (Property Transfer Application) [1993] 2 FLR 56, [1993] 1 FCR 471,
    [1993] Fam Law 461, FD   10.125, 10.126
Johansson v Norway [1997] 23 EHRR 33   5.9

K (Dec'd), Re [1986] Fam 180, [1985] 3 WLR 234, [1985] 2 All ER 833, CA,
    affirming [1985] Ch 85   11.11
K (Guardianship Order) v Sheffield City Council [2011] EWCA Civ 635   4.80
K (Minors; Foreign Surrogacy), Re [2010] EWHC 1180 (Fam), [2011] 1
    FLR 533   3.61, 3.63, 3.106
K v K (Minors; Property Transfer) [1992] 2 FLR 220, [1992] 1 WLR 530   10.133
K v K (Relocation: Shared Care Arrangement) [2011] EWCA Civ 793,
    [2011] 3 FCR 111, [2011] Fam Law 1078   4.65
Kay v Lambeth BC [2006] UKHL 10, [2006] 2 AC 465, [2006] 4 All ER 128,
    [2006] 2 WLR 570   10.95

KB v National Health Service Pensions Agency (Case C-117/01) [2004] ECR
    I-541, [2004] 1 CMLR 931, [2004] 1 FLR 683, [2004] IRLR 240,
    [2004] ICR 781, [2004] All ER (EC) 1089, ECJ   6.101, 6.102
Kellman v Kellman [2000] 1 FLR 785   8.150
Kernott v Jones [2011] UKSC 53, [2011] 2 WLR 1121   10.6, 10.36, 10.39, 10.42–10.48
Khan v Crossland (unreported) 25 November 2011   11.45
Kinch v Bullard [1998] 3 EGLR 112   11.7

L (Commercial Surrogacy), Re [2010] EWHC 3416 (Fam)   3.27–3.29, 3.56
L (Shared Residence Order), Re [2009] EWCA Civ 20, [2009] 1 FLR 1157   4.56, 4.59, 4.62
L-W (Enforcement and Committal: Contact), Re [2010] EWCA Civ 1253,
    [2011] 1 FLR 1095   4.25
Laskar v Laskar [2008] EWCA Civ 347, [2008] 1 WLR 2695, [2008] 2 FLR
    589   10.61
Leeds Teaching Hospital NHS Trust v A and B [2003] EWHC 259 (QB),
    [2003] 1 FLR 1091   1.45, 1.54, 1.68, 1.70, 1.99
Lloyds Bank v Rossett [1991] 1 AC 107, [1990] 2 WLR 867, [1990] 2 FLR
    155   10.54, 10.56, 10.57

M (Care Proceedings: Contact: Grandmother's Application for Leave), Re
    [1995] 2 FLR 86, [1995] Fam Law 540   4.94
M (Children), Re [2007] EWCA Civ 228, [2007] All ER (D) 46 (Feb)   4.73
M v H (A Child) (Educational Welfare) [2008] EWHC 324 (Fam), [2008] 1
    FLR 1400   4.73
M v M (Financial Relief: Substantial Earning Capacity) [2004] EWHC 688
    (Fam), [2004] 2 FLR 236   9.24
MA v RS (Contact: Parenting Roles) *sub nom* (1) ML (2) AR v (1) RW (2)
    SW [2011] EWHC 2455 (Fam)   1.2, 4.21, 4.42–4.44
Manoussakis v Greece [1997] 23 EHRR 387   5.13
Marshall v Marshall 1998 All England Official Transcript   11.8
Martin v Martin [1978] Fam 12   9.47, 9.48
Mesher v Mesher & Hall [1980] 1 All ER 126   9.46–9.48
Miller v Miller; Macfarlane v Macfarlane [2006] UKHL 24, [2006] 2 AC
    618, [2006] 1 FLR 1186, [2006] 3 All ER 1, [2006] 2 WLR 1283,
    [2006] 2 FCR 213   9.23–9.26, 9.40
ML v AR [2011] EWHC 2455 (Fam)   2.15

Newlon Housing Trust v Alsulaimen [1999] 1 AC 313, [1998] 3 WLR 451,
    [1998] 2 FLR 690, [1998] 4 All ER 1, HL; [1997] 1 FLR 914, CA   10.95
Noad, Re [1951] Ch 553, [1951] 1 All ER 467, 95 Sol Jo 188   11.27

O (A Child) (Contact: Withdrawal of Application), Re [2003] EWHC 3031
    (Fam), [2004] 1 FLR 1258, [2004] Fam Law 492   4.46
O (Contact: Imposition of Conditions) 1 FCR 317   4.49
Oxley v Hiscock [2004] EWCA Civ 546, [2005] Fam 211, [2004] 2 FLR 669,
    [2004] 3 WLR 715, [2004] 2 FCR 295   10.47

P (A Minor) (Custody), Re (1983) 4 FLR 401   4.6
P (Child: Financial Provision), Re [2003] EWCA Civ 837, [2003] 2 WLR
    865, [2003] 2 FLR 865, [2003] All ER (D) 312 (Jun), CA   10.134, 10.140
P (Contact: Indirect Contact), Re [1999] 2 FLR 893   4.25
P (Forced Marriage), Re [2010] EWHC 3467 (Fam), [2011] 1 FLR 2060,
    [2011] Fam Law 356   7.53, 8.60
P (Shared Residence Order), Re [2005] EWCA Civ 1639, [2006] 2 FLR 347,
    [2006] Fam Law 447   4.56
P (Surrogacy: Residence), Re [2008] 1 FLR 177, [2007] Fam Law 1135   1.99, 3.49
P and L (Contact), Re [2011] EWHC 3431 (Fam)   4.43
P v P (Inherited Property) [2004] EWHC 1364 (Fam), [2005] 1 FLR 576   9.24
P v S and Cornwall County Council (Case C-13/94) [1996] ECR I-2143,
    [1996] All ER (EC) 397, [1996] ICR 795, [1996] IRLR 347, ECJ   6.10, 6.12

Palmer (Deceased) (A Debtor), Re [1994] Ch 316, [1993] 3 WLR 877, [1993]
    4 All ER 812; reversed [1994] Ch 316, [1994] 3 WLR 420, [1994] 2
    FLR 609, [1994] 3 All ER 835, CA   11.10
Paulsen-Medalen and Svensson v Sweden [1998] 26 EHRR 260   5.8
Payne v Payne [2001] EWCA Civ 166, [2001] Fam 473, [2001] 1 FLR 1052,
    [2001] UKHRR 484   4.65, 4.77
PC, Re [1997] 2 FLR 730, [1997] Fam Law 722   4.64
Pettitt v Pettitt [1970] AC 777, [1969] 2 All ER 385, [1969] 2 WLR 966   10.64
Phillips v Peace [2005] 2 FLR 1212   10.134
Piran v France [2002] 34 EHRR 14   5.8
Porter v Porter [1969] 3 All ER 640, [1969] 1 WLR 1155, 113 Sol Jo 163   9.22
Portman Registrars & Nominees v Mohammed Latif (1987) 6 CL 217   11.65
Practice Direction (Residence and Contact Orders: Domestic Violence) (No
    2) [2009] 1 WLR 251   4.35
PV v Spain (Application No 35159/09), Press Release No 910, 30.11.2010,
    ECtHR   6.99

Qayyum v Hameed [2009] EWCA Civ 352, [2009] 2 FLR 962, [2009] Fam
    Law 811   10.52

R (IVF: Paternity of a Child), Re [2005] UKHL 33, [2005] 2 FLR 843,
    [2005] 2 WLR 1158 affirming [2003] EWCA Civ 182, [2003] 1 FLR
    1183   1.14, 1.99
R (Parental Responsibility), Re [2011] EWHC 1535 (Fam), [2011] 2 FLR
    1132   4.34, 5.1
R and F v the United Kingdom (Application No 35748/05), November 2006   6.77
R v Algar [1954] 1 QB 279, [1953] 2 All ER 1381, [1953] 3 WLR 1007   8.93
R v E and F (Female Parents: Known Father) [2010] EWHC 417 (Fam),
    [2010] 2 FLR 383   1.5, 1.37, 2.18, 4.21, 4.40
R v R [2011] EWHC 1535 (Fam)   2.17
R v Widdows [2011] EWCA Crim 1500, [2011] 2 FLR 869   7.61
Ramsay v Ramsay (otherwise Beer) (1913) 108 LT 382   9.56
Rees v United Kingdom (Application No 9532/81) (1986) 9 EHRR 56,
    [1993] 2 FCR 49, [1987] 2 FLR 111, [1993] 2 FCR 49, [1987] Fam
    Law 157   6.15, 6.18–6.20, 6.49
Richards (Sarah Margaret) v Secretary of State for Work and Pensions Case
    C-423/04 [2006] ECR I-3585, [2006] All ER (EC) 895, [2006] 2 FLR
    487, [2006] Fam Law 639   6.86, 6.103, 6.104, 6.107–6.111, 8.126
Roberts deceased, Re [1978] 1 WLR 653, 122 Sol Jo 264   11.21
Rossi v Rossi [2006] EWHC 1482 (Fam), [2007] 1 FLR 790   9.42

S (Parental Responsibility), Re [1995] 2 FLR 648, [1995] Fam Law 596   4.21
S (A Child) (Adoption Order or Special Guardianship Order), Re [2007]
    EWCA Civ 90, [2007] 1 FLR 855   4.81
S (A Child) (Residence Order: Conditions) [2002] EWCA Civ 1795, [2003] 1
    FCR 138, [2002] All ER (D) 30 (Dec)   4.60
S (Contact Application by Sibling), Re [1999] Fam 283, [1998] 2 FLR 897,
    [1998] Fam Law 581   4.92, 4.94
S (Parental Order), Re [2009] EWHC 2977 (Fam), [2010] 1 FLR 1156   3.25, 3.28, 3.29, 3.57, 3.79
Salgueiro da Silva Mouta v Portugal (Application No 33290/96) [1999]
    ECHR 176, (2001) 31 EHRR 47, ECHR   4.13, 5.14, 5.17
Salmon (deceased), Re, Coard v National Westminster Bank Ltd and Others
    [1981] Ch 167, [1980] 3 WLR 748, [1980] 3 All ER 532, ChD   11.115
Santos v Santos [1972] Fam 247, [1972] 2 WLR 889, [1972] 2 All ER 246,
    CA   11.89
Schalk and Kopf v Austria (Application No 30141/04), judgment of 24 June
    2010   8.7–8.10, 8.12, 8.64, 12.7
Schofield v Schofield [2011] EWCA Civ 174, [2011] 1 FLR 2129, [2011] Fam
    Law 570   8.165
Scotching v Birch [2008] EWHC 844 (Ch), [2008] All ER (D) 265 (Mar)   11.42–11.44

Sheffield and Horsham v United Kingdom (Application Nos 22985/93 and
  23390/94) (1998) 27 EHRR 163, [1998] 2 FLR 928, [1998] 3 FCR
  141, [1998] Fam Law 731, ECtHR   6.20, 6.49
Sheffield City Council v E and S [2004] EWHC 2808 (Fam), [2005] 1 FLR
  965   3.78, 8.62
Sibley v Perry (1802) 7 Ves 522   11.27
Southern Housing Group Ltd v Nutting [2004] EWHC 2982 (Ch), [2005]
  Fam Law 210   11.84, 11.85
ST (formerly J) v J [1998] 1 All ER 431   6.70
Stack v Dowden [2007] UKHL 17, [2007] 2 FCR 280   10.6, 10.28, 10.37–10.40, 10.42, 10.47,
       10.56, 10.61
Stockport County Council v D [1995] 1 FLR 873   5.8
Sutton v Michcon de Reya (a firm) [2003] EWHC 3166 (Ch), [2004] 1 FLR
  837, [2004] 3 FCR 142   10.10

T and M v OCC and C (a child) [2010] EWHC 964 (Fam), [2011] 1 FLR
  1487, [2011] Fam Law 337   12.31
T v B [2010] EWHC 1444 (Fam), [2010] 2 FLR 1966   1.21, 1.23, 4.32, 4.78, 5.1, 8.13, 10.126
T v T (Shared Residence) [2010] EWCA Civ 1366, [2011] Fam Law 240,
  [2010] NLJR 1718   1.5, 1.37, 2.24, 4.21, 4.41, 4.54, 4.58
T, Re [1997] SLT 724, [1996] SCLR 897, [1997] Fam Law 225, [1997] Fam
  Law 8, *Times*, August 20, 1996   5.21, 5.22
Thomson v Humphrey [2009] EWHC 3576 (Ch), [2010] 2 FLR 107, [2010]
  Fam Law 351   10.57
Timbrell v Secretary of State for Work and Pensions [2010] EWCA Civ 701,
  [2011] 1 FLR 332, [2010] Fam Law 921   6.82–6.85
Tinsley v Milligan [1994] 1 AC 340, [1993] 2 FLR 963, [1994] 2 FCR 65   10.20
TJ v CS and BA [2007] EWHC 1952 (Fam), [2008] 1 FLR 1015   1.2, 1.4, 1.39, 1.45
TT (A Child) (Surrogacy: Residence Order), Re [2011] EWHC 33 (Fam),
  [2011] 2 FLR 392, [2011] Fam Law 363   3.32, 3.48
Tuppen v Microsoft Corporation Ltd (2000) *The Times*, 15 November   7.58

V v V (Children) (Intractable Contact Dispute) [2004] EWHC 1215 (Fam),
  [2004] 2 FLR 851   4.49
Van den Boogaard v Laumen Case C220/95 [1997] QB 759, [1997] ECR
  I-1147, [1997] All ER (EC) 517, [1997] 2 FLR 399   8.143

W (Adoption: Homosexual Adopter), Re [1997] 2 FLR 406   5.20
W (Residence: Leave to Appeal) [2010] EWCA Civ 1143   4.49
W and B v H (Child Abduction: Surrogacy) [2002] 1 FLR 1008, [2002] Fam
  Law 345, FD   3.106
W and W v H (Child Abduction: Surrogacy) (No 2) [2002] 2 FLR 252,
  [2002] All ER (D) 13 (Apr)   3.106
W v W (Joinder of Trusts of Land Act and Children Act Applications)
  [2003] EWCA Civ 924, [2004] 2 FLR 321, CA   10.75
Wallbank and another v Price [2007] EWHC 3001 (Ch), [2008] 2 FLR 501   11.8
Wena and Anita Parry v the United Kingdom (Application No 42971/05),
  November 2006   6.77
Whiston v Whiston [1995] 2 FLR 268   6.70
White v White [2000] 2 FLR 981, [2000] 3 FCR 555   9.19–9.22, 9.24, 9.40, 9.43
Wilkinson v Kitzinger and Attorney General and Lord Chancellor
  intervening [2006] EWHC 2022 (Fam), [2007] 1 FLR 295   8.5, 8.6, 12.7
Williams v Williams [1882] ChD 659, ChD   11.38
Williamson v Sheikh [2008] EWCA Civ 990   10.51
Wilson v Roberts [2010] Fam CA 734   4.36

X and Y (Children), Re [2011] EWHC 3147 (Fam), [2011] All ER (D) 64
  (Dec)   3.30
X and Y (Foreign Surrogacy), Re [2008] EWHC 3030 (Fam), [2009] Fam 71,
  [2009] 2 WLR 1274, [2009] 1 FLR 733   1.45, 1.99, 1.102, 3.24, 3.26, 3.57, 3.79, 3.82, 3.106

X v The Federal Republic of Germany Application number 8741/79, 10
    March 1981, DR 24, 137   11.37
X, Y & Z v UK [1997] 2 FLR 892   6.87

Yemshaw v Hounslow London Borough Council [2011] UKSC 3, [2011] 1
    FLR 1614   7.1, 7.2, 7.29

Z v B, C and CAFCASS [2011] EWHC 3181 (Fam)   3.47, 3.62

TABLE OF STATUTES

References are to paragraph numbers.

Administration of Estates Act 1925	11.16
s 42	11.26
s 46	11.49
s 55(1)(x)	11.50
Adoption Act 1976	1.100, 5.5, 5.12, 6.93, 7.15, 11.31
s 12	2.5
s 15	5.20
s 15(1)(a)	5.20
s 15(3)	5.20
s 39	1.41, 1.52
Adoption (Scotland) Act 1978	
s 16(1)(2)	5.21
Adoption and Children Act 2002	1.28, 1.30, 1.59, 1.67, 1.100, 3.15, 3.90, 3.96, 4.14, 5.18, 5.22, 7.15, 10.115
s 1	3.23, 3.24, 3.28, 3.56, 3.57, 3.88, 12.31
s 1(2)	5.23
s 1(3)	5.5, 5.6
s 1(4)	5.6, 5.23
s 1(4)(a)–(f)	3.56
s 1(5)	5.23
s 36	3.90
s 41	3.90
s 46	2.5
s 46(3)	1.58
s 46(3)(b)	6.87
s 48	3.91
s 50	12.31
s 51	1.58, 2.5, 8.13
s 51(2)	1.41, 1.56
s 51(4)	1.99
s 52	3.74
s 52(6)	1.55
s 67	1.35, 1.41, 1.45, 1.67, 3.36, 3.54, 3.106, 11.91
s 68	1.33
s 69	1.52, 1.62
s 74	3.54, 3.106
s 83	3.106
s 83(1)(a)	3.39
s 84	3.41, 3.47, 3.62
s 85	3.41
s 88	1.43
s 92	1.80, 3.40
s 93	3.40
s 109(1)	5.6
s 111	1.57
s 144	3.98
s 144(4)	12.31

Adoption and Children Act 2002—*continued*	
s 144(4)(b)	12.31
s 144(7)	3.40
Sch 1	
para 1	3.92
Births and Deaths Registration Act 1953	1.30
s 10	6.55
s 10A	1.58
British Nationality Act 1981	3.36, 3.106
Child Abduction Act 1984	4.67
Child Maintenance and Other Payments Act 2008	10.107
Child Support Act 1991	1.24, 1.28, 10.106, 12.15
s 3(2)	10.114
s 3(3)	10.113
s 3(5)	10.114
s 4(1)	10.112
s 4(10)(aa)	10.116
s 8(1)	10.109
s 8(5)	10.116
s 8(6)	10.116
s 8(7)	10.116
s 8(8)	10.116
s 8(10)	10.116
s 26	10.115
s 26(2)	10.115
s 27	1.16
s 44	10.110
s 44(2A)	10.110, 10.116
s 54	10.115
s 55	10.111
Sch 1	
para 10C	10.117
Child Support Act 1995	12.15
Children Act 1989	1.21, 1.99, 3.56, 4.12, 4.51, 5.4, 5.5, 6.88, 6.94, 7.15, 10.74, A4.1
s 1	4.16, 4.17, 4.79, 4.92
s 1(1)	2.16, 4.16
s 1(3)	4.52, 4.65
s 1(3)(a)–(g)	4.17
s 1A(11)	4.81
s 2	2.5, 8.13
s 2(1)	2.5
s 2(1A)	2.5

Children Act 1989—*continued*

s 2(5)	2.2
s 3	6.87
s 3(1)	2.1, 4.21
s 3(4)	2.3
s 4	1.58, 1.66, 2.11, 4.21
s 4(1)	2.5
s 4(1)(a)	2.5
s 4(1)(c)	4.1
s 4(2)	2.7
s 4(2A)	2.5, 4.1
s 4A	1.39, 2.4, 2.5, 2.11, 4.84, 4.85, 6.87, 8.13
s 4A(1)	2.7
s 4A(1)(b)	2.17, 4.1
s 4A(3)	4.1
s 4ZA	2.4, 2.5, 2.11, 4.21
s 4ZA(1)(a)	2.5
s 4ZA(1)(c)	4.1
s 4ZA(5)	2.5, 4.1
s 5	3.100
s 5(1)	4.1
s 5(6)	2.5
s 5(c)	4.90
s 6(7)	4.1
s 8	3.50, 3.81, 4.1, 4.2, 4.17, 4.21–4.23, 4.26, 4.59, 4.76, 4.79, 4.83, 4.84, 4.89, 4.91–4.93, 4.95, 6.97
s 8(1)	4.24, 4.50, 4.68, 4.69, 4.71
s 8(3)	4.22, 4.83
s 8(4)	4.83
s 10	1.22, 3.47, 4.21, 4.36, 4.93, 8.13, 10.126
s 10(1)	4.22, 4.83
s 10(1)(b)	4.83
s 10(2)(b)	4.91
s 10(4)	4.21, 4.84
s 10(4)(aa)	4.85
s 10(5)	2.25, 4.78
s 10(5)–(5B)	4.86
s 10(5)(aa)	4.87
s 10(5)(b)	4.88
s 10(5)(c)	2.25
s 10(5B)	4.89, 4.91
s 10(8)	4.95
s 10(9)	2.25, 4.93
s 10(10)	4.88
s 11	4.26, 4.27
s 11(4)	3.47, 4.53
s 11(7)	4.59
s 11A	4.47
s 11A (5)(a)(i)	4.47
s 11A(5)(a)(ii)	4.47
s 11A(5)(b)	4.47
s 11J	4.48
s 11O	4.48
s 12	2.5, 3.50
s 12(2)	1.58, 2.5, 2.26, 3.47, 4.53
s 12(3)	2.5
s 13	3.50, 4.63, 4.64
s 13(1)	4.1
s 14	10.75
s 14(2)(b)	3.97
s 14A	4.2, 4.78, 8.13

Children Act 1989—*continued*

ss 14A–14G	3.96
s 14A(3)	4.78
s 14A(5)	3.98, 4.78
s 14A(6)	4.78
s 14A(7)	4.81
s 14A(7)–(11)	3.99
s 14B	3.96
s 14C	3.96, 4.2, 4.79
s 14C(1)	2.5
s 14C(3)	4.1
s 14D	4.1, 4.79
s 14D(1)	3.96
s 14D(3)	3.96
s 14D(5)	3.96
s 16	4.47
s 16(4A)	4.47
s 31(9)	7.1
s 33	2.5
s 41	8.120
s 44(4)	2.5
s 91	2.5
s 105	1.39, 4.86, 4.89
Sch A1	
para 9	4.1
Pt 2	4.1
Sch 1	1.23, 1.34, 8.13, 10.75, 10.77, 10.123, 10.124, 10.130, 10.142
para 1(2)	10.128
para 1(4)	10.131
para 5(b)	10.135
para 6	10.139
para 16	8.13, 10.125, 10.126
Children Act 2004	11.31
Children and Adoption Act 2006	4.47
Civil Partnership Act 2004	1.63, 4.14, 6.67, 6.106, 8.6, 8.20, 8.22, 8.53, 8.91, 8.112, 9.2, 10.1, 10.4, 10.77, 11.20, 11.22, 11.60, 11.79, 12.2, 12.14, 12.20, 12.25, 12.49, A4.2
Pt 2	8.1, 11.112
Pt 3	8.1, 8.35
Pt 4	8.1, 8.35
Pt 5	8.1, 8.79
s 1	8.1, 8.18, 8.24, 8.40
s 1(1)(b)	8.40
s 2	8.2, 8.16
s 2(5)	8.16
s 3	8.21, 8.97, 8.100
s 3(1)	8.2
s 6	8.18, 8.31
s 6(2)	8.20
s 6(3)	8.34
s 6(3A)(a)	8.97
s 7	8.17
s 8(1)	8.31
s 9	8.31
s 10	8.32
s 11	8.32
s 12	8.32
s 13	9.67
s 14	8.32
s 16	9.67
s 17	8.32

Civil Partnership Act 2004—*continued*

s 17(3)	8.97
s 18	8.34
s 19	8.34
s 20	8.34
s 20(5)	8.34
s 21–27	8.34
s 22	8.34
s 23	8.34
s 25	8.34, 11.81
s 37	8.51, 8.96, 8.109
s 37(1)(b)	6.87, 8.93, 8.94, 8.96
s 37(2)	8.119
s 37(3)	8.94
s 41	8.104
s 44	8.111
s 46	8.110
s 48(1)	8.119
s 48(5)	8.119
s 49	8.97, 11.21
s 49(b)	8.101
s 50	6.59, 8.27, 8.58, 8.102, 11.21
s 50(1)(d)	6.60
s 50(1)(e)	6.59, 6.68, 6.69
s 51	6.68, 8.27
s 51(1)	8.107
s 51(2)	8.105
s 51(3)	8.105
s 51(5)	6.62, 8.105
s 51(6)	6.59, 8.106
s 53	8.101
s 54	8.55, 8.58, 8.98
s 54(7)	8.95, 8.99
s 54(8)	8.55, 8.95
s 54(10)	8.55
s 56	11.50
s 58	8.51, 8.77, 8.81, 8.83
s 58(1)(a)	8.77
s 58(1)(b)	8.77
s 58(1)(c)	8.77
s 59(2)	8.76
s 59(3)	8.82
s 63	8.120
s 65	8.13, 10.63
s 66	9.3–9.6
s 66(2)	9.4
s 67	9.6
s 67(1)	9.5
s 67(4)	9.5
s 67(5)	9.5
s 68	9.6
s 72	8.13, 9.15
s 72(1)	9.1
s 72(3)	9.1
s 72(4)	9.1
s 73	7.15
s 73(3)	10.63
s 75	8.13, 9.11
s 77	1.39
s 78	1.39
s 123	8.98
s 165	8.104
s 173	8.98
s 210	8.36

Civil Partnership Act 2004—*continued*

s 211	8.4, 8.39
s 212	8.56, 8.95
ss 212–218	8.41, 8.64
s 212(2)	8.50
s 213	8.41
s 214	8.44, 8.100
s 214(a)	8.58
s 215	8.48, 8.49, 8.57, 8.100
s 215(1)	8.57
s 215(3)	8.5
s 216	8.25, 8.100
s 216(1)	8.2
s 217	8.47, 8.100
s 217(2)	8.58
s 218	8.58, 8.100
s 219	8.124, 8.148
s 221	8.71, 8.126
s 221(1)(c)	8.71
s 221(2)	6.106, 8.129
s 233	8.146
ss 233–238	8.138
s 235	8.150
ss 235–237	8.150
s 235(2)	8.151
s 235(2)(b)(ii)	8.151
s 235(2)(c)	8.151
s 235(3)	8.150
s 235(3)(b)	8.151
s 236	8.151
s 237(1)	8.150
s 237(5)	8.150
s 238	8.147
s 254	12.15, 12.46
s 259	12.15
Sch 1	8.2, 8.21, 8.58, 8.100
para 1	9.58
para 11(1)(e)	6.59
para 66	9.58
Pt 2	8.21
Sch 2	8.21, 8.27, 8.97
Pt 2	
para 6	8.21
Pt 3	8.21
Sch 4	8.13
paras 9–11	6.68
Sch 5	1.39, 8.162, 9.1, 9.7, 9.17
para 1	8.123
para 2	8.123
para 4	8.123
para 20	9.12
para 21	9.65
para 21(1)	9.67
para 21(2)	9.12
para 22(2)	9.13
para 22(3)	9.14
para 23(2)	9.9
para 38	9.10
para 46(3)	9.56
para 48	9.56
Sch 6	9.1
Sch 7	8.154, 8.157, 8.158, 9.1
para 1(1)(b)	8.155
para 1(2)	8.155

Civil Partnership Act 2004—*continued*
  Sch 7—*continued*
    para 3   8.156
    para 4   8.156
    para 4(2)   8.159, 9.63
    para 4(3)   8.156
    para 7   8.158
    para 7(1)-(5)   8.156
    para 7(2)   9.64
    para 7(3)   9.64
    para 7(4)   9.64
    para 8   8.161, 9.65
    para 8(1)   9.63
    para 8(2)   9.65
    paras 9–17   8.162
    para 11   9.67
    para 30   9.49
  Sch 20   8.4, 8.37, 8.41–8.44, 8.66
  Sch 23   8.34
  Sch 24   12.15
    para 46(3)   12.18
    para 46(5)   12.18
    para 144   12.19
Companies Act 1989   3.43
  s 2(9)   3.43
  s 66   3.43

Domestic Proceedings and
  Magistrates' Court Act 1978   9.1
Domestic Violence and Matrimonial
  Proceedings Act 1976   7.30
Domestic Violence, Crime and Victims
  Act 2004   7.15, 7.44
  s 2(2)   10.90
Domicile and Matrimonial
  Proceedings Act 1973   8.134, 8.135

Employment Act 2002   12.2
Equality Act 2010   6.13, 12.2
  s 202   6.115, 8.20
  s 202(2)   6.115
  s 202(4)   6.115
Evidence (Foreign, Dominion and
  Colonial Documents) Act 1933
  s 1   8.52

Family Law Act 1969   11.30
Family Law Act 1975 (Australia)
  s 60H   4.36
Family Law Act 1986   1.14
  s 1(1)   3.61
  s 46   8.150
  s 55   1.13
  s 55A   1.10, 1.13
  s 55A(1)   1.13
  s 55A(3)   1.16
Family Law Act 1996   7.14, 7.30, 7.36, 7.43,
          7.58, 7.60, 10.11, A4.3
  Pt IV   7.13, 7.15, 7.49
  Pt 4A   7.51
  s 30   7.17, 7.25, 8.13
  s 30(2)   7.17

Family Law Act 1996—*continued*
  s 30(4)   10.85
  s 30(5)   7.16, 10.85
  s 30(6)   7.22
  s 30(8)   7.16
  s 30(10)   7.22
  s 31   7.18
  s 33   7.20, 7.27, 7.31
  ss 33–41   7.19
  s 33(5)   7.16
  s 33(6)(a)   10.88, 10.89
  s 33(6)(b)   10.88, 10.89
  s 33(6)(c)   10.88, 10.89
  s 33(6)(f)   10.88–10.90
  s 33(6)(g)   10.88–10.90
  s 33(6)(h)   10.88–10.90
  s 33(7)   7.21
  s 35   7.23
  s 35(6)(f)   7.25
  s 35(6)(g)   7.25
  s 35(9)   7.23
  s 35(10)   7.25
  s 36   7.26, 10.93
  s 36(6)   7.26
  s 36(6)(e)   10.88–10.90
  s 36(8)   7.26
  s 36(10)   7.26
  s 36(13)   10.93
  s 37   7.27
  s 37(4)   7.27
  s 38   7.28
  s 38(4)   7.28
  s 38(5)   7.28
  s 38(6)   7.28
  s 41   10.90
  s 42   7.41
  s 42A   7.44
  s 45   7.35, 7.47
  s 46   7.46
  s 47   7.38
  s 47(7)   7.38
  s 49   7.50
  s 58   7.37
  s 62   7.4, 7.15
  s 62(1)   10.84
  s 63(1)   7.16
  s 63A   7.53
  s 63A(6)   7.53
  s 63B   7.56
  s 63C   7.54, 7.55
  s 63D   7.57
  s 63H   7.57
  s 63O   7.57
  Sch 7   10.84, 10.93, 10.94
    para 3   10.86
    para 3(1)   10.87
    para 3(2)   10.87
    para 7   10.88
    para 7(2)   10.92
    para 10   10.91
    para 10(4)   10.91
    para 10(5)   10.91
    para 14   10.92

Family Law (Scotland) Act 1985
  s 10   9.22
Family Law (Scotland) Act 2006   10.4, 10.77
Family Law Reform Act 1969
  s 20(1)   1.10, 1.11
  s 20(2)   1.10
  s 23(1)   1.12
  s 23(3)   1.12
  s 26   1.45
Family Law Reform Act 1987   1.49
  s 1   1.45
  s 1(3)   8.13
  s 27   6.70
  s 27(1)   6.70
  s 27(2)   6.70
Family Provision Act 1966
  s 1   11.49
Fatal Accidents Act 1976
  s 1   8.13
Forfeiture Act 1982   11.11
  s 2   11.11
  s 7   11.11

Gender Recognition Act 2004   6.14, 6.32,
  6.43, 6.45, 6.57, 6.59, 6.68, 6.74,
  6.77, 6.84–6.86, 6.94, 8.22, 8.58,
  8.102, 12.47, A4.4
  s 1   6.27, 8.45
  s 1(1)   6.46, 8.23
  s 1(1)(a)   6.29, 6.35
  s 1(1)(b)   6.33, 6.40
  s 1(3)   6.50
  s 2   6.34, 6.39
  s 2(1)(a)-(d)   6.31
  s 2(2)   6.29
  s 2(4)   6.33, 6.42
  s 2(a)   6.33
  s 2(b)   6.33
  s 3   6.31, 6.35
  s 3(1)   6.35
  s 3(1)(a)   6.36
  s 3(1)(b)   6.36
  s 3(2)   6.35
  s 3(2)(a)   6.37, 6.39
  s 3(2)(b)   6.37, 6.39
  s 3(3)   6.35
  s 3(3)(a)   6.37
  s 3(3)(b)   6.37
  s 3(4)   6.38
  s 3(5)   6.40
  s 3(6)   6.39
  s 3(6)(a)   6.39
  s 3(6)(b)   6.39
  s 3(6)(c)   6.39
  s 3(8)   6.39
  s 4(1)   6.46, 6.50, 8.24
  s 4(2)   6.46
  s 4(3)   6.58, 8.27
  s 5   8.28
  s 5(1)   6.64
  s 5(2)   6.66
  s 7(1)   6.28
  s 7(2)   6.28

Gender Recognition Act 2004—*continued*
  s 9   6.81, 8.24
  s 9(1)   6.47, 6.67
  s 9(2)   6.47
  s 10   6.51
  s 10(1)   6.50
  s 10(2)   6.50
  s 10(4)   6.51
  s 11   6.58
  s 12   1.38, 6.87
  s 21(3)   8.27
  Sch 1   6.27, 6.30
  Sch 2   6.58
    para 3   6.62
  Sch 3
    para 3   6.51
    para 3(1)(a)   6.52
    para 3(1)(c)   6.52
    para 3(3)   6.52
    para 3(4)   6.53
    para 3(5)   6.54
    para 3(6)   6.54
    para 3(7)   6.55
    para 3(8)   6.55
    para 3(9)   6.56
    para 3(10)   6.56
    para 4   6.51
  Sch 4   6.58
    para 1   6.73
    para 2   6.73
    para 3   6.73
  Sch 5
    para 2(1)(a)   12.48
    para 2(1)(b)   12.48
    para 2(2)(a)   12.48
    para 2(2)(b)   12.48
Guardianship of Minors Act 1971   10.133

Housing Act 1985   10.80, 10.86, A4.5
  s 91(3)(c)   11.71
Housing Act 1988   8.13, 10.80, 10.86, A4.6
  s 17   11.66
  s 94   10.82
Housing Act 1996
  Pt V   10.86
  s 177(1)   7.3
Human Fertilisation and Embryology
    Act 1990   1.34, 1.49, 1.51, 1.56, 1.69,
    3.20, 3.32, 4.76
  s 27   1.14, 1.50, 1.52, 1.55
  s 28   1.14, 1.45, 1.55, 1.99, 1.105
  s 28(1)   1.44, 1.54
  s 28(2)   1.29, 1.30, 1.50, 1.54, 1.99
  s 28(3)   1.55
  s 28(5)   1.54
  s 28(6)   1.54, 1.55, 1.70
  s 28(8)   1.54
  s 30   1.52, 1.54, 1.83, 3.22, 3.29, 3.51, 3.52
  s 30(7)   3.82
  s 42   2.5

Human Fertilisation and Embryology
    Act 2008   1.21, 1.28, 1.34, 1.51, 1.61,
        3.32, 3.63, 3.75, 3.79, 3.93, 3.94,
        4.89, 11.28, A4.7
  s 27   1.93
  s 33   1.27, 1.32, 1.62, 1.86, 1.92
  ss 33–46   10.115
  s 33(1)   3.81
  s 35 1.32, 1.44, 1.45, 1.68, 1.99, 3.40, 3.44,
        3.47, 3.65, 3.98
  ss 35–47   1.88
  s 35(1)   1.45
  s 35(1)(b)   3.65
  s 35A   1.8
  s 36   1.30, 1.32, 1.68, 1.97, 1.99, 3.65
  s 36(b)   1.72
  s 37   1.30, 1.68, 1.99, 3.65, 3.81, 4.21
  s 37(1)(a)   1.99
  s 37(1)(b)   1.99
  s 37(1)(e)   1.68, 1.72
  s 37(2)   1.72
  s 37(3)   1.72
  s 38   1.99
  s 38(1)   1.68
  s 40   1.75
  s 41   1.68, 1.75
  s 42 1.32, 1.36, 1.39, 1.45, 1.63, 1.68, 1.89,
        1.99, 3.65, 8.13, 11.33, 11.50
  s 42(1)   1.68, 1.99
  s 42(1)(b)   3.65
  s 43   1.32, 1.45, 1.65, 1.89, 2.5, 3.65, 8.13,
        11.33, 11.50
  ss 43–45   1.64
  ss 43–48   1.68
  s 43(b)   1.72
  s 44   1.65, 1.97, 3.65, 4.21
  s 44(1)(e)   1.65, 1.72
  s 44(2)   1.72
  s 44(3)   1.72
  s 45   1.99, 1.101
  s 46   1.75, 1.89
  s 47   1.62, 1.88, 1.89
  s 48   1.32, 1.45, 1.68
  s 49   1.46
  s 50   1.46
  s 54   1.62, 1.80, 1.83, 3.9, 3.19–3.21, 3.23,
        3.24, 3.28, 3.29, 3.44, 3.47,
        3.52–3.56, 3.67, 3.88, 10.115
  s 54(1)   3.56, 3.58
  s 54(1)(a)   1.91, 3.59
  s 54(1)(b)   1.87, 3.60
  s 54(2)   1.84, 1.99, 3.52, 3.58
  s 54(3)   3.61
  s 54(4)   3.58, 3.61, 3.106
  s 54(4)(b)   3.47
  s 54(5)   3.60
  s 54(6)   3.47, 3.57, 3.64, 3.73
  s 54(7)   3.35, 3.47, 3.57, 3.64, 3.71, 3.74,
        3.89
  s 54(8)   3.20–3.22, 3.24, 3.27, 3.80
  s 54(10)   3.59
  s 54(11)   1.84, 3.52, 3.81
  Sch 6   1.30

Human Rights Act 1998   5.11, 5.33, 6.26,
        6.71, 11.37, 12.7, 12.8
  s 3   5.22, 12.11
  s 3(3)(1)   6.90
  Sch 1
    Pt 1   6.89

Immigration Act 1971   3.36, 3.106
Inheritance (Family Provision) Act
    1938   11.75
Inheritance (Provision for Family and
    Dependants) Act 1975   11.16, 11.23,
        11.52, 11.72, 11.78, 11.79, 11.118,
        A4.8
  s 1   8.13, 11.80, 11.88, 11.102
  s 1(1)   11.102
  s 1(1)(c)   1.24
  s 1(1)(d)   1.24, 11.94
  s 1(1)(e)   11.102, 11.104
  s 1(1B)   11.90
  s 1(2)(aa)   11.106
  s 1(2)(b)   11.107
  s 1(3)   11.100, 11.102
  s 1(d)   1.39
  s 2   8.13, 11.80, 11.81, 11.105, 11.108,
        11.116
  s 3   11.108, 11.115
  s 3(2)   11.112
  s 9   11.116
  s 25(1)   11.91
Insolvency Act 1986
  s 335A   8.13

Jobseekers Act 1995   12.15
  s 35(1)   12.3, 12.4
  s 35(1A)   12.27

Law of Property Act 1925   11.49
  s 36(2)   11.7
Law of Property (Miscellaneous
    Provisions) Act 1989
  s 2   11.8
Local Government Act 1988
  s 28   12.13

Marriage Act 1949   6.73
Married Women's Property Act 1882
  s 17   9.3
Matrimonial and Family Proceedings
    Act 1984
  Pt III   8.157, 8.163, 9.63
  s 15   8.158
Matrimonial Causes Act 1973   6.59, 6.68,
        8.22, 9.1, 9.17
  s 1(6)   11.89
  s 5   9.16
  s 11(c)   6.26, 6.47, 6.67, 6.71
  s 12   6.58, 8.27
  s 12(g)   6.59
  ss 22–24   6.70
  s 25   6.70, 9.12, 9.15, 9.16, 9.21, 9.22
  s 25(2)   9.24

Matrimonial Causes Act 1973—*continued*
  s 25(2)(g)   6.70
Matrimonial Proceedings and Property
    Act 1970   9.16
  s 37   10.64
Mental Capacity Act 2005   3.74, 3.77

Nullity of Marriage Act 1971
  s 1(c)   6.71

Protection from Eviction Act 1977   10.18
  s 2   10.16
  s 3   10.16
Protection from Harassment Act 1997   7.61
  s 1   7.59
  s 2   7.64
  s 3   7.59
  s 3A   7.62
  s 7   7.63
  s 7(2)   7.58

Rent Act 1977   8.13, 10.80, 10.86, 10.93,
      11.60, A4.9
  Sch 1
    para 2   12.8, 12.9, 12.11
    para 2(2)   12.10
    para 3(1)   12.8
    para 6   11.61
Rent (Agriculture) Act 1976   10.81

Senior Courts Act 1981
  s 116   11.34, 11.36, 11.38, 11.44, 11.45
Sex Discrimination Act 1975   6.47
Social Security Act 1998   12.15
Social Security Administration Act
    1992   12.2, 12.15, 12.48
Social Security Administration
    (Northern Ireland) Act 1992   12.2,
      12.15, 12.48
Social Security Contributions and
    Benefits Act 1992   12.2, 12.15, 12.48
  s 39B   8.13
  s 48B   8.13
  s 111   12.46
  s 112   12.46
  s 136   12.21
  s 137   12.26
  s 137(1)   8.13, 12.3, 12.18
  s 137(1A)   12.18, 12.27
Social Security Contributions and
    Benefits (Northern Ireland) Act
    1992   12.2, 12.15, 12.48

State Pension Credit Act 2002   12.15
  s 17(1A)   12.27
  s 140   12.53
  s 142   12.53
  s 143   12.53
Supplementary Benefits Act 1976
  Sch 1
    para 3(1)(b)   12.31
Surrogacy Arrangements Act 1985   3.8, 3.29,
      3.32, A4.10
  s 1   1.49, 1.78, 3.2, 3.75
  s 1A   1.93, 3.9, 3.45
  s 2   3.12, 3.13, 3.18
  s 2(2)(a)   3.20
  s 2(2)(b)   3.20
  s 2(2A)   3.15
  s 2(2B)   3.15
  s 2(2C)   3.15
  s 2(3)   3.20
  s 2(5A)   3.15
  s 2(8A)   3.15
  s 2(8B)   3.15
  s 3   3.14
  s 4   3.12

Tax Credits Act 2002   12.2, 12.15
  s 3(5)   12.5
  s 3(5A)   12.19
  s 3(6)   12.5
  s 14(2)(b)   12.39
  s 15(2)(b)   12.39
  s 16(3)(b)   12.39
Taxation of Chargeable Gains Act
    1992
  s 58   8.13
Trusts of Land and Appointment of
    Trustees Act 1996   A4.11
  s 1   10.24
  s 6(2)   10.71
  s 14   10.65, 10.67–10.69, 10.73, 10.75
  s 15   10.69, 10.73

Welfare Reform Act 2007
  Sch 1
    para 6(5)   12.20
    para 6(6)   12.27
Wills Act 1837
  s 18B(1)   11.20, 11.21
  s 18B(3)   11.20, 11.21
  s 18C   11.22, 11.25
  s 18C(3)   11.23

TABLE OF STATUTORY INSTRUMENTS

References are to paragraph numbers.

Adoption Agencies and Independent
    Review of Determinations
    (Amendment) Regulations
    2011, SI 2011/589   5.23, 5.26
Adoption Agencies Regulations 2005,
    SI 2005/389
    Pt 4   5.23
    Pt 5   5.23
    reg 3   5.26
    reg 4   5.27
    reg 6   5.29
    reg 8   5.28
    reg 18   5.30
    reg 31   5.23
    reg 32   5.23
Allocation and Transfer of
    Proceedings Order 2008,
    SI 2008/2836   3.82

Blood Tests (Evidence of Paternity)
    Regulations 1971, SI 1971/1861   1.10

Child Support (Northern Ireland)
    Order 1991 (NI 23),
    SI 1991/2628   12.15
Child Support (Northern Ireland)
    Order 1995 (NI 13),
    SI 1995/2702   12.15
Children (Private Arrangements for
    Fostering) Regulations 2005,
    SI 2005/1533   3.43
Children (Private Arrangements for
    Fostering) (Wales) Regulations
    2006, SI 2006/940   3.43
Civil Partnership (Armed Forces)
    Order 2005, SI 2005/3188
    Pt 3   8.39
    art 2   8.39
Civil Partnership (Jurisdiction and
    Recognition of Judgments)
    Regulations 2005, SI 2005/3334   8.71,
        8.125, 8.150
    reg 1(a)-(e)   8.126
    reg 6   8.148
    reg 7   8.148
    reg 8(1)   8.149
    reg 8(2)   8.149
    reg 8(3)(a)   8.149

Civil Partnership (Jurisdiction and
    Recognition of Judgments)
    Regulations 2005,
    SI 2005/3334—continued
    reg 8(3)(b)   8.149
Civil Partnership (Pensions, Social
    Security and Child Support)
    (Consequential, etc Provisions)
    Order 2005, SI 2005/2877
    Sch 3
        para 26(6)(a)   12.17
Civil Partnership (Registration Abroad
    and Certificates) Regulations
    2005, SI 2005/2761
    reg 4   8.36, 8.37
    reg 5   8.38
    reg 9   8.38
    reg 10(2)   8.38
Civil Partnership (Registration
    Provisions) (Amendment)
    Regulations 2011, SI 2011/1171   8.15,
        8.34
Civil Partnership (Registration
    Provisions) Regulations 2005,
    SI 2005/3176   8.15, 8.34
Civil Procedure Rules 1998,
    SI 1998/3132   5.7, 7.37
    r 52.9(2)   9.67
Council Tax Benefit (Person who have
    attained the qualifying age for
    state pension credit)
    Regulations 2006, SI 2006/216
    reg 2(1)   12.27
Council Tax Benefit Regulations 2006,
    SI 2006/215
    reg 2(1)   12.27
County Court Rules 1981,
    SI 1981/1687
    Ord 29   7.37

Employment Equality (Sexual
    Orientation) Regulations 2003,
    SI 2003/1661   12.2
Employment Support and Allowance
    Regulations 2008, SI 2008/794
    reg 2(1)   12.27
    reg 119   12.17

Equality Act 2010 (Commencement
    No 4, Savings, Consequential,
    Transitional, Transitory and
    Incidental Provisions and
    Revocation) Order 2010,
    SI 2010/2317   8.20
Equality Act 2010 (Commencement
    No 8) Order 2011, SI 2011/2646 6.115
Equality Act (Sexual Orientation)
    Regulations 2007, SI 2007/1263   5.30

Family Procedure (Civil Partnership
  Staying of Proceedings) Rules
    2010, SI 2010/2986   8.134
    r 2   8.130
    r 3   8.132
    r 4   8.132
    r 5   8.135
    r 5(3)   8.131
    rr 6–9   8.135
Family Procedure Rules 2010,
    SI 2010/2955   5.7, 7.37, 8.53, 9.56,
                        9.67, 10.142
    r 1   4.97
    r 2.2   8.13
    r 2.3   8.96
    Pt 3   2.21
    r 3.1   8.51
    PD 3A   2.21
    Pt 4   3.83
    Pt 5   3.83
    r 5.3(1)   8.115
    PD 5A   2.20, 3.67, 3.84, 8.51, 8.84, 8.116
    Pt 6   3.73, 3.83, 3.85, 8.159
    r 6.47   3.73
    PD 6B   3.73, 3.85
    Pt 7   8.113
    r 7.5   8.114
    r 7.10   8.117
    r 7.10(3)   8.117
    r 7.12   8.118
    r 7.16   8.120
    r 7.19   8.120
    r 7.20   8.120
    r 7.25   8.120
    r 7.27   8.133
    r 7.28   8.121
    r 7.31   8.121
    r 7.32   8.122
    r 7.33   8.122
    PD 7A   8.51, 8.52, 8.115, 8.116
      para 2.1   8.117
    Pt 8   1.15, 8.83, 8.86
    r 8.19   8.84
    r 8.24   8.159
    r 8.25   8.159
    r 9.4   8.96
    r 10.10   7.38
    Pt 12   4.95
    r 12.2   4.1, 4.78
    r 12.3   2.10, 2.21, 4.96
    r 12.9   3.82
    r 12.11   3.82

Family Procedure Rules 2010,
    SI 2010/2955—*continued*
    r 12.19   3.83
    r 12.21   3.83
    r 13.2   3.82, 3.83
    r 13.3   3.68, 3.84
    r 13.3(4)   3.84
    r 13.4   3.86
    r 13.5   3.88, 3.90, 3.91
    r 13.7   3.73
    r 13.9(f)   3.73
    r 13.10   3.78, 3.89
    r 13.10(2)   3.89
    r 13.10(3)   3.89
    r 13.10(3)(b)   3.89
    r 13.11   3.67, 3.70
    r 13.11(4)   3.69
    r 13.12(3)   3.88
    r 13.13   3.87
    r 13.17   3.90
    r 13.21   3.92
    r 13.21(5)   3.89
    r 15   3.89
    Pt 16   3.83, 4.95
    r 16.2   4.96
    r 16.34   3.87, 3.89
    r 16.35   3.88
    PD 16A   4.96
    Pt 18   2.25, 8.159
    r 18.4   1.15
    r 18.7   1.15
    r 18.8   1.15
    PD 18A   2.25
    Pt 19   1.15, 8.86, 8.89, 8.90
    r 19.3   1.15
    r 19.5   8.88
    r 19.6   8.88
    r 19.7   1.15, 8.87
    r 19.7(3)   8.88
    r 19.8   8.89
    PD 19A   1.18, 8.86, 8.87
      para 4   8.90
    Pt 22   3.83
    Pt 23   3.83
    Pt 25   3.83, 8.90
    PD 25   8.90
    Pt 27   3.83
    r 27.4   3.73
Forced Marriage (Relevant Third
    Party) Order 2009,
    SI 2009/2023   7.54

Gender Recognition (Approved
    Countries and Territories)
    Order 2011, SI 2001/1630   A3.1

Housing Benefit (Persons who have
    attained the qualifying age for
    state pension credit)
    Regulations 2006, SI 2006/214
    reg 2(1)   12.27

Housing Benefit Regulations 2006,
  SI 2006/213
  reg 2(1)   12.27
Human Fertilisation and Embryology
  Act 2008 (Commencement No
  1 and Transitional Provisions)
  Order 2009, SI 2009/479   1.45
Human Fertilisation and Embryology
  Act 2008 (Commencement No
  3) Order 2010, SI 2010/987   1.84, 3.9,
                                               3.52
Human Fertilisation and Embryology
  (Parental Orders) Regulations
  2010, SI 2010/985   1.45, 1.62, 1.67,
      1.86, 1.100, 2.5, 3.23, 3.36, 3.52,
                                               3.56
  reg 2   11.91
  reg 5   3.106
  Sch 1   1.35, 3.54, 3.90–3.92, 3.106, 11.91
  Sch 4   3.106

Immigration (Procedure for Formation
  of Civil Partnerships)
  Regulations 2005, SI 2005/2917   8.34
Income Support (General) Regulations
  1987, SI 1987/1967
  reg 2(1)   12.27
  reg 54   12.17

Jobseeker's Allowance Regulations
  1996, SI 1996/207
  reg 1(3)   12.27
  reg 117   12.17
Jobseekers (Northern Ireland) Order
  1995 (NI 15) SI 1995/2705   12.15

Marriages and Civil Partnerships
  (Approved Premises)
  (Amendment) Regulations
  2011, SI 2011/2661
  reg 3B(7)(1B)   8.20

Non-contentious Probate Rules,
  SI 1987/2024   11.48
  r 22   11.17, 11.33, 11.36, 11.38–11.42,
                                        11.44, 11.46

Parental Orders (Human Fertilisation
  and Embryology) Regulations
  1994, SI 1994/2767   1.52, 1.100, 2.5
Parental Orders (Prescribed Particulars
  and Forms of Entry)
  Regulations 2010, SI 2010/1205   3.92
Paternity and Adoption Leave
  Regulations 2002, SI 2002/2788   12.2

Sex Discrimination (Amendment of
  Legislation) Regulations 2008,
  SI 2008/963   6.13
Sex Discrimination (Gender
  Reassignment) Regulations
  1999, SI 1999/1102   6.13
Social Security (Northern Ireland)
  Order 1998 (NI 10),
  SI 1998/1506   12.15
Special Guardianship Regulations
  2005, SI 2005/1109   4.81
State Pension Credit Regulations 2002,
  SI 2002/1792
  reg 1(2)   12.27
  reg 15(5)(d)   12.17
Statutory Paternity Pay and Statutory
  Adoption Pay (General)
  Regulations 2002, SI 2002/2822   12.2

Tax and Civil Partnerships Regulations
  2005, SI 2005/3229   8.13

TABLE OF ABBREVIATIONS

ACA 2002	Adoption and Children Act 2002
BRDA 1953	Births and Deaths Registration Act 1953
CA 1989	Children Act 1989
CCR	County Court Rules 1981, SI 1981/1687
CPA 2004	Civil Partnership Act 2004
CPR 1998	Civil Procedure Rules 1998, SI 1998/3132
CSA 1991	Child Support Act 1991
CTB (SPC 2006) Regs 2006	Council Tax Benefit (Persons who have attained the qualifying age for State Pension Credit) Regulations 2006, SI 2006/216
DPMCA 1978	Domestic Proceedings and Magistrates Court Act 1978
EqA 2010	Equality Act 2010
ESA Regs 2008	Employment Support and Allowance Regulations 2008, SI 2008/794
FLA 1986	Family Law Act 1986
FLA 1996	Family Law Act 1996
FLRA 1969	Family Law Reform Act 1969
FPR 2010	Family Procedure Rules 2010, SI 2010/2955
GPR	Gender Recognition Panel
GRA 2004	Gender Recognition Act 2004
GRC	Gender Recognition Certificate
GRR	Gender Recognition Register
HB Regs 2006	Housing Benfit Regulations 2006, SI 2006/213
HB (SPC) Regs 2006	Housing Benefit (Persons who have attained the qualifying age for State Pension Credit) Regulations 2006, SI 2006/214
HFEA 1990	Human Fertilisation and Embryology Act 1990
HFEA 2008	Human Fertilisation and Embryology Act 2008
HFE (PO) Regulations 2010	Human Fertilisation and Embryology (Parental Orders) Regulations 2010, SI 2010/985
HRA 1998	Human Rights Act 1998
IS Regs 1987	Income Support (General) Regulations 1987, SI 1987/1967
JSA 1995	Jobseekers Act 1995
JSA Regs 1996	Jobseeker's Allowance Regulations 1996, SI 1996/207
MCA 1973	Matrimonial Causes Act 1973
PD3A	FPR Practice Direction 3A – Pre-Application Protocol for Mediation Information and Assessment
PD5A	FPR Practice Direction 5A – Forms

PD7A	FPR Practice Direction 7A – Procedure for Applications in Matrimonial and Civil Partnership Proceedings
PD7D	FPR Practice Direction 7D – The Gender Recognition Act 2004
PD18A	FPR Practice Direction 18A – Other Applications in Proceedings
PD 19A	FPR Practice Direction 19A – Alternative Procedure for Applications
PHA 1997	Protection from Harassment Act 1997
SDA 1999	Sex Discrimination (Gender Reassignment) Regulations 1999, SI 1999/1102
SPCA 2002	State Pension Credit Act 2002
SPC Regs 2002	State Pension Credit Regulations 2002, SI 2002/1792
SSCBA 1992	Social Security Contributions and Benefits Act 1992
WRA 2007	Welfare Reform Act 2007

Chapter 1

PARENTHOOD

WHAT IS MEANT BY 'PARENT'?

1.1   Fifty years ago the question 'who are your parents?' was a simple one to understand, if not always simple to answer. It meant your genetic mother and father, or the people who you believed were your genetic mother and father. Since then science and society have changed the landscape of family structure. In twenty-first century Britain, the question might be met by another, more complex question, 'what do you mean by parent?', and depending on the context in which the question is asked, there might well be different answers. Does it mean the person who is named on the birth certificate, or the person with parental responsibility? The person who provided the genetic material or the person who the law recognises as the parent, or the person who nurtures the child day to day? In the case of *B and A and C and D*[1] in 2006 Mrs Justice Black observed that:

> 'the law is advancing at a pace which is probably quicker than the pace of change in the views of society in general, where new ways of living have not yet wholly crystallised and where language has not yet evolved to accommodate them.'

1.2   Since then the court has grappled with issues of what we call the biological father who is not a parenting father if not a parent, or the name for the woman or man in a same sex relationship who stands in the position of a parent but does not have a biological or legal relationship to the child of the family. In 2007 in the case of *TJ v CS and BA*[2] the court had to consider what to call the genetic father who did not have a parenting role and was also the child's uncle.[3] In 2011 in the case of *ML v AR*[4] the court began to develop the concept of 'principal parenting' and 'secondary parenting' to describe the respective roles of the women carrying out the day to day care of the child, and of the child's father and his partner.[5] However, this concept was not endorsed by the Court of Appeal in the case of *A v B and C*[6] in 2012 because 'it has the danger of demeaning the known donor and in some cases they may have an

---

[1]   [2006] EWHC 2 (Fam), [2006] 1 FCR 556.

[2]   [2007] EWHC 1952 (Fam).

[3]   In the sense of being the brother of the female step-parent who was co-parenting the child with the biological mother and regarded as a mother by the child.

[4]   [2011] EWHC 2455 (Fam).

[5]   At para 21: 'all that the picture of contact does is to establish a parenting role for all four, and to establish in the concepts that I have tried to develop in my own thinking of the role of the women as principal parenters and the role of the men as secondary parenters.'

[6]   [2012] EWCA Civ 285.

important role'. In reflecting on her judgment in the earlier case of *Re D*[7] Lady Justice Black observed that 'despite the passage of time, the courts continue to struggle to evolve a principled approach to cases such as this one'.[8]

1.3   Baroness Hale of Richmond in giving the leading judgment in *Re G (Children)*[9] explored in simple terms the various ways in which in 2006 a person could become a 'natural parent' of a child, and she included not only genetic parents and birth mothers, but also the person who is not a legal or genetic parent of a child, but is a social and psychological parent, quoting the definition:[10]

> 'A psychological parent is one who on a continuous day-to-day basis, through interaction, companionship, interplay, and mutuality, fulfils the child's psychological needs for a parent, as well as the child's physical needs.'

The Human Fertilisation and Embryology Act 2008 (HFEA 2008) has provided legal answers to some of these questions, but the language and the principles, like the law, are still evolving.

1.4   The question of 'who are your parents' is family specific and fact specific. Inevitably couples in a same sex relationship require the assistance of a third person in order to create a child. The circumstances of each child's conception and upbringing are highly individual. If assisted conception takes place through a fertility clinic the legal structure is often clearer. If a fertility clinic is not used and the arrangements for conception are informal, each of the two, three or four adults involved may have different views and expectations about their respective roles in the child's life. Some female couples will actively seek an informal arrangement with a person who they know well and which directly involves both genetic parents and psychological parents in the child's life, others will through choice or circumstance involve relative strangers and wish that person to have a limited role in the child's life. Some male couples may seek out a female couple to conceive a child with in the hope of having a fathering role without the complications of surrogacy or adoption. Reality may turn out to be rather different to expectation with the passage of time. This is new territory for families and for the courts. As Lord Justice Thorpe observed: 'what the adults look forward to before undertaking the hazards of conception, birth and the first experience of parenting may prove to be illusion or fantasy.'[11] When arrangements do not turn out as expected it has consistently been the experience of the courts that the adults involved are 'ambushed' by biology and 'that depths of emotions are engaged and feelings released that come as a surprise and a shock not only to others but also to the participants

---

[7]   [2006] EWHC 2, [2006] 1 FCR 556.
[8]   *A v B and C* [2012] EWCA Civ 285.
[9]   [2006] UKHL 43 at para 35.
[10]   Goldstein Freud and Solnit *Beyond the Best Interests of the Child* (1973).
[11]   *A v B and C* [2012] EWCA Civ 285 at para 27.

themselves'.[12] All of these factors can affect who becomes the child's family and who the child, the wider family, the law and society at large regard as the child's parents.

1.5 The diversity of alternative family structures, and the developing approach of the courts when making decisions in relation to the children who are part of them is apparent from law reports. The case of *R v E and F (Female Parents: Known Father)*[13] in 2010 concerned a 7-year-old child whose circumstances were that his home from birth had been with his genetic mother and her civil partner, but he had regular contact with his genetic father and his spouse. It was common ground that the two women had carefully chosen a good friend to be the father rather than an anonymous donor. When relations broke down the legal and genetic father sought parental responsibility. Mr Justice Bennett refused to grant parental responsibility to him and expressed the clear view that the two women were parenting the child together and although the father was a committed and loving father, he was not undertaking the role of a parent.[14] In contrast, the case of *T v T*[15] concerned children aged 10 and 7 being brought up by two women in a civil partnership. Their genetic and legal father was a man who the women met when he advertised that he would like to become a father, but by the time the matter came before the court the reality for the children was that they genuinely regarded the father as a parent and he had had parental responsibility for some time and regular overnight contact. The judge granted a shared residence order in favour of the biological mother and father which was upheld on appeal, but the biological mother's civil partner was then included in the shared residence order as a third person with whom the child was to live. The Court of Appeal observed: 'the adults may be very concerned about issues of status such as who could and should be classed as 'the parents' but those matters are not likely to be of particular concern to the children'[16] and 'in this case, three people have parental responsibility, M, F and L, and have thereby been recognised as parents; it seems to me that that probably accords with how things look at the moment from the children's point of view'.[17] Most recently the case of *A v B and C*[18] concerned a child born in circumstances where the mother and father were married because of the mother's family's difficulties in accepting the mother's sexual orientation, but the mother was in a long term relationship with a woman. The mother and father were old friends and the father offered to assist the mother and her partner to have a child. The decision in the High Court had sought to limit the father's future role in the child's life, and in the judgment of the High Court 'any benefit that accrues is likely to be outweighed by what I consider is likely to be confusion and disruption and the potential

---

[12] Per Hedley J in *TJ v CS and BA* [2007] EWHC 1952 (Fam), [2008] 1 FLR 1015 at para 15.
[13] [2010] EWHC 417 (Fam).
[14] At para 91.
[15] [2010] EWCA Civ 1366.
[16] Per Black LJ at para 13.
[17] Per Black LJ at para 23.
[18] [2012] EWCA Civ 285.

disruption of the relationship between the mothers and the child'.[19] The Court of Appeal did not accept that this determination necessarily reflected the long term best interests of the child, and considered that the father's commitment since birth suggested that he may be seeking to offer a relationship of significant value.[20] The appeal was allowed and the case returned to the High Court with indications that the court would be assisted by expert evidence, welfare reports or separate representation for the child in reaching long-term decisions about the child's welfare. The development of the law in this area continues apace.

1.6   For the family where at least one of the parents doing the parenting is genetically unrelated, or is not a legal parent, they may have difficulty in being seen as significant for the child by outsiders. For those families the possibility for legal recognition of their importance to the child may be crucial. On the other hand is the question as to whether a person's parenting role will be recognised where they are the genetic parent of a child, but are not fully involved in the child's day to day life. These issues are likely to be equally important to the legal parents, the genetic parents and those doing the day-to-day parenting.

1.7   In this part, we will explore the meaning of natural, genetic and legal parent in different factual contexts and how the particular arrangements made for the child, and at what time, impact upon legal rights, responsibilities and recognition. We will also look at the legal difference between the meaning of the terms 'mother and father' and the term 'parent', what is meant by the term 'child of the family' where and how the different types of parenthood can be accompanied by parental responsibility, and what the effect of this is. We will set out the steps by which legal parenthood and parental responsibility can be acquired and lost, and the steps which families can take to try to ensure that their wishes and the reality of their family life is respected.

BIOLOGICAL OR GENETIC PARENTHOOD

1.8   Baroness Hale in *Re G* describes genetic parenthood as 'the provision of the gametes which produce the child'[21] – the eggs and the sperm. Those who provided the gametes could be described as the genetic or biological mother and father. In the future an egg might contain the genetic material of two women in an attempt to eliminate a genetic disease, and the child would therefore have three genetic parents.[22]

1.9   Genetic parenthood is significant. Baroness Hale went on to say in *Re G* that where a person is the natural parent in every sense of the term – ie genetic,

---

[19]   [2011] EWHC 2290 (Fam) at para 37.
[20]   [2012] EWCA Civ 285 at para 24.
[21]   [2006] UKHL 43 at para 32.
[22]   In a case of mitochondrial donation which is specifically provided for in HFEA 2008, s 35A.

gestational and psychological that is an important and significant factor in determining what is best for them now and in the future.[23]

1.10 The Family Law Reform Act 1969[24] provides a procedure for determining the genetic mother or father where it is unclear or disputed.[25] Bodily samples can be taken where a person's parentage is being determined by the court,[26] and scientific tests used on those samples to ascertain whether a person is or is not the genetic father or mother of the person whose parentage is in issue. An application for scientific testing in this way cannot be free-standing, but must be made in civil proceedings in which the parentage of a person falls to be determined.[27] In other words, the court has the power to direct scientific testing if there are legal proceedings ongoing and the genetic parentage of a person is an issue in those proceedings.

1.11 The court cannot order a bodily sample to be taken for scientific testing, but can give a direction:[28]

'(a) for the use of scientific tests to ascertain whether such tests show that a party to the proceedings is or is not the father or mother of that person; and

(b) for the taking, within a period specified in the direction, of bodily samples from all or any of the following, namely, that person, any party who is alleged to be the father or mother of that person and any other party to the proceedings.'

1.12 Although the court cannot order a bodily sample to be taken without consent, if a person does not consent to a sample being taken from him/herself or a person within his/her care and control (ie the child), the court can draw inferences from this refusal.[29] The court has held that the inference which can be drawn can result in a finding that the person refusing to consent is the parent or child of another person.[30]

1.13 Scientific tests only assist with the question of whether a person is the genetic mother or father of a child, and not the question of legal parenthood, which may be governed by statute. A simple example would be an adopted

---

[23] *Re G* [2006] UKHL 43 at para 44.

[24] Section 20(1) and (2).

[25] It must be read together with the Blood Tests (Evidence of Paternity) Regulations 1971 as amended from time to time to ensure that the correct procedure for testing is followed.

[26] Pursuant to an application under FLA 1986, s 55A or in the course of proceedings for a substantive order about the child.

[27] FLRA 1969, s 20(1).

[28] FLRA 1969, s 20(1).

[29] FLRA 1969, s 23(1) and (3).

[30] *Brighton & Hove City Council v PM and others* [2011] EWCA Civ 795 per Wall P 'it is not envisaged that a sample will be taken from S without her consent. But that, of course, does not leave the court powerless, or reliant on findings of fact based on the balance of probabilities. The Statute is very clear that it is open to the court to draw an inference based on S's refusal to provide a sample' and in *Re F v the Child Support Agency* [1999] 2 FCR 385 Scott Baker J held that the putative father's refusal to submit to a test enabled an inference to be drawn that he was the father sufficiently strong to rebut the presumption of parentage.

person trying to find their biological father: the result of the genetic test does not override the fact that the child's legal parent is the adoptive mother or father. Section 55 of the Family Law Act 1986[31] provides a mechanism for an application to be made for 'a declaration as to whether or not a person named in the application is **or was** the parent of another parent so named'[32] to allow for circumstances where the parentage of a person has changed.

1.14   Parentage is not defined in the Family Law Act 1986 but the Court of Appeal specifically held in the case of *Re R (IVF: Paternity of Child)*[33] that an application for a declaration of parentage can include both genetic and legal parentage 'we agree that the term "parent" includes a person who is to be treated as a parent by virtue of s 27 or 28 of the 1990 Act'. The combination of the Family Law Reform Act and the Family Law Act mean that a person's genetic or legal parentage or both can be determined by the court, whether as a single issue or as part of an ongoing case. The case of *Re R (IVF Paternity of a Child)*[34] therefore also considered when it is appropriate for there to be a freestanding application for a declaration of parentage, and when it is appropriate merely to consider the issue within other proceedings. The circumstances in which a genetic parent is not the legal parent are many and varied – this chapter later discusses the detail of how legal parentage is acquired, and when that differs from genetic parentage.

APPLICATIONS FOR DECLARATION AS TO PARENTAGE

1.15   An application for a declaration of parentage, whether legal or genetic parentage is one of the miscellaneous applications provided for in Part 8 of the FPR 2010. The application is made on Form C63[35] and Part 19 of the FPR 2010 procedure applies. Rule 19.3 sets out the information which is required by the court when the application is made, but there is not space for all of this on the application form, so care must be taken to ensure the application has attached to it all the required information. If the applicant intends to rely on written evidence, this should be filed at the same time as the application (r 19.7). It is good practice to make an application for scientific testing at the same time if this is going to be necessary; in those circumstances a separate application form for a direction for bodily samples to be taken should be made in accordance with the Part 18 of the FPR 2010 procedure in the form of an application notice (r 18.4)[36] setting out what order the applicant seeks and briefly why the applicant is seeking the order (r 18.7). This must also be served on the respondent(s) (r 18.8) unless the application is being made without notice.

---

[31]   Section 55A: 'a person may apply to the [court] for a declaration as to whether or not a person named in the application is or was the parent of another person so named.'
[32]   Section 55A(1).
[33]   [2003] 1 FLR 1183 at para [31].
[34]   Ibid.
[35]   Per FPR 2010, PD 5A.
[36]   PD 5A describes Form FP2 as an application notice in Part 18 proceedings.

1.16 Any person may apply to the court for a declaration; this includes CMEC.[37] However, unless:

(i)   the person making the application is asking the court to decide that (s)he is a named person's parent; or

(ii)   the person making the application is asking the court to decide that a named person is his/her parent; or

(iii) the person making the application is asking the court to decide whether a named person is the other parent of the applicant's child;

the court must refuse to hear the application unless it considers that the applicant has 'sufficient personal interest' in the issue being determined.[38]

1.17 The respondent(s) to the application will be the person (child) whose parentage is in issue or any person who is alleged to be the parent of the person (child) whose parentage is in issue. The application also has to contain details of every person whose interest may be affected by the proceedings and his relationship to the applicant.[39]

1.18 The court's management of the application is governed by FPR 2010, PD 19A which allows the court to give directions immediately the application is issued or fix a hearing date at which directions may be given.[40]

LEGAL PARENTAGE: MOTHER, FATHER OR PARENT?

1.19 A legal parent is a person who is treated in law as the mother or father or parent of the child for all purposes. A person can be a legal parent whether or not they are a genetic parent, and whether the relationship between the legal parents (if there is more than one) is continuing or not. Legal parentage can operate to extinguish natural or genetic parentage. A person with two genetic parents may have one legal parent. Natural parents (as described by Baroness Hale in *Re G*[41]) who are not also legal parents are not treated by all bodies as parents for all purposes, and may find it difficult to be recognised as parents by third parties. Having a legal parent also entitles the child to refer to themselves as 'their child', which might be important in a situation where there is a trust or will referring to the 'child of' a particular person.

1.20 Parental responsibility does not define parenthood. A legal parent might or might not have parental responsibility. A person can have parental

---

[37] The Child Maintenance and Enforcement Commission which replaced the Child Support Agency, as to which see Child Support Act 1991, s 27.
[38] FLA 1986, s 55A(3).
[39] FPR 2010, r 8.20.
[40] FPR 2010, PD 19A, para 4.1.
[41] [2006] UKHL 43.

responsibility without being recognised as a legal parent. This would be the case, for example, where a person holds parental responsibility for a child as a result of a residence order in place or a step-parent agreement between civil partners. Parental responsibility is explored in detail in chapter 2.

1.21 Statutes often use the terms 'parent of' and 'child of' without defining them. The Children Act 1989 in particular does not define the term parent, but case law has consistently limited the term 'parent' in the Children Act as being referable to either a biological parent or parent by operation of law – ie the courts are clear that the term parent in the Children Act excludes purely psychological parents. Despite extensive argument on the issue of whether the term 'parent' ought to be extended to include psychological parents in the light of the HFEA 2008 and *Re G*,[42] this was rejected in the case of *T v B*.[43]

1.22 In *Re G*[44] when the birth mother and her partner separated, the partner who was the child's social or psychological mother but who was not a legal parent required the permission of the court under s 10 of the Children Act to make an application for a residence order in relation to the younger child who was not yet three.[45] A legal parent is able to make an application for a residence order as of right[46] whatever the age of the child.

1.23 In the case of *T v B*,[47] Moylan J determined that where a woman was a natural or psychological parent having parental responsibility, but was not a biological or legal parent, she did not fall within the definition of parent in Sch 1 to the Children Act 1989. This meant that she was not a person from whom the biological mother could claim financial provision for the upbringing of the child. The non-biological mother had previously had to go through lengthy court proceedings to get a shared residence order and parental responsibility because she was not a legal parent.

1.24 The Child Support Act 1991 (CSA) defines parent, for the purposes of that Act, as 'any person who is in law the mother or father of the child'.[48] The Inheritance (Provision for Family and Dependants) Act 1975 refers to 'a child of the deceased'[49] and to a 'child of the family'[50] without definition.

1.25 Legal parenthood, therefore, remains an important legal distinction despite the increased recognition of the significance which natural,

---

[42] [2006] UKHL 43.
[43] [2010] EWHC 1444 (Fam).
[44] [2006] UKHL 43.
[45] At para 11 of Baroness Hale's judgment.
[46] Section 10 of the Children Act provides that a person may make an application for a contact or residence orders – if they are a parent or guardian, hold a residence order, are a spouse or civil partner in relation to whom the child is a child of the family or have lived with the child for more than 3 years.
[47] [2010] EWHC 1444 (Fam).
[48] CSA 1991, s 54.
[49] Section 1(1)(c).
[50] Section 1(1)(d).

psychological or nurturing parents have to children. Of course, it is also an important signifier of status, and it will be important to many people involved in parenting the child to have legal recognition of their role and relationship with the child, particularly when arrangements go wrong or there is family breakdown.

Terminology: mother, father, parent

1.26 Bracewell J in the case of *Re B (Parentage)*[51] described the circumstances where a man would be recognised as a legal father when she said:

> 'I find fatherhood concerns genetics and the provision of sperm which results in the birth of a child, unless either there is a presumption of legitimacy which affects the situation or there is statutory intervention such as, for example, the change of status afforded by adoption or freeing for adoption.'

1.27 In relation to mothers, the position is made more complex by the distinction between genetic mother and birth mother where there is surrogacy or egg donation. Where the genetic mother and birth mother are not the same woman, it is the birth mother who is the legal parent unless that status is overridden by statutory intervention, namely adoption or a parental order.[52]

1.28 Since the Adoption and Children Act 2002 and the Human Fertilisation and Embryology Act 2008 came into force, a new concept of legal parenthood exists, which did not when either the CSA 1991 was enacted, or when Bracewell J heard *Re B*: namely, that of the parent who is neither mother nor father in legal terms, but is simply a 'parent'. In practice, this new category refers only to a situation where the legal parents are of the same sex.

1.29 The Human Fertilisation and Embryology Act 1990 permitted for the first time a person not genetically related to the child to be named as mother or father on the child's birth certificate and to be their legal parent.[53] One of the aims of the HFEA 1990 was to ensure that legal parentage is consistent with the assumption of all parental rights and duties with regard to the child.[54] When this legislation was reviewed, the government's approach in the Human Fertilisation and Embryology Bill 2008 was to move further towards 'a concept of parenthood as a legal responsibility rather than a biological relationship'.[55] It was a specific and hotly debated proposal of the Bill that treating fertility clinics would be required to consider the child's need for 'supportive parenting', rather than the child's need for a father as many MPs felt that the role of the father was being marginalised[56] (although there was no debate of a child's need

---

[51] [1996] 2 FLR 15.
[52] HFEA 2008, s 33.
[53] HFEA 1990, s 28(2) – unmarried man being treated together with the mother using donor sperm.
[54] Warnock Report of the Committee of Enquiry into Human Fertilisation and Embryology.
[55] HL 169/HC 630-II, Ev 07.
[56] Hansard House of Commons Debate, 12.05.08.

for a mother). The new Act makes some progress towards recognising families in all forms, but there remain some difficult areas where there is still arguably a degree of discrimination.

1.30 Where married couples are treated together to conceive a child using donor sperm, or the agreed fatherhood conditions are met, the male partner can be recognised not just as a parent but also as the legal father.[57] Where two women are treated together, however, even if they are civil partners, the woman who is not the birth mother becomes a parent but is not called a mother. There is no provision for a child in either the Adoption and Children Act 2002, or the Human Fertilisation and Embryology Act 2008, or any other statute, for a child to have two mothers or two fathers. Where they have two parents of the same sex, they simply have two parents. Where there is a parental order the statutes provide for the child to have two parents, but neither of them is called a mother or father as a matter of law. Birth certificates may now show a mother and the other female parent,[58] but not two mothers: see Appendix 2 for examples of blank birth certificates and parental orders showing how the different scenarios are registered.

1.31 Perhaps ironically, the reported decisions in cases involving two women and a known father have demonstrated the concern of the father in those cases to be not just a legal parent, specifically not just a 'donor', but to be recognised as a nurturing parent in real terms, and to have parental responsibility.[59] Those fathers may have had the legal status of parent, but little of the relationship of natural parenthood. Whereas the same sex partner was carrying out the parenting, but had no legal status as parent. Now, the same sex parent, regarded by the child as a mother or father, can be in law a parent, but neither mother or father, and the genetic father may be a natural parent but not a legal parent or a legal father.

1.32 Section 48 of the HFEA 2008 identifies 'mothers' 'fathers' and 'parents' as three distinct categories:

'48 Effect of sections 33–47

(1) Where by virtue of section 33, 35, 36, 42 or 43 a person is to be treated as the mother, father or parent of a child, that person is to be treated in law as the mother, father or parent (as the case may be) of the child for all purposes.'

1.33 This echoes s 68 of the Adoption and Children Act 2002 which deals with adoptive relatives and provides:

'(3) A reference (however expressed) to the adoptive mother and father of a child adopted by –

    (a)   a couple of the same sex, or

    (b)   a partner of the child's parent, where the couple are of the same sex is to

---

[57] HFEA 1990, s 28(2) and HFEA 2008, ss 36 and 37.
[58] BRDA 1953 as amended by Sch 6 to the HFEA 2008.
[59] For example the father in *B and A and C and D* [2006] EWHC 2 (Fam).

be read as a reference to the child's adoptive parents.'

1.34 In terms of rights, duties and obligations a legal parent is in the same position as a legal mother or father, and as a result, a good deal of primary legislation has been amended to include, where there are references to 'mother' or 'father', the term 'parent', or to specify that the term parent includes parents pursuant to the HFEA 1990 or 2008 or holders of a parental order (for example, Sch 1 to the Children Act 1989).

1.35 A parental order can be made following a surrogacy arrangement to transfer legal parentage of the child (once born) to the commissioning parents. The effect of being a legal parent by virtue of a parental order having been made is the same as being an adoptive parent – this is made clear by the Human Fertilisation and Embryology (Parental Orders) Regulations 2010[60] which provides for the Adoption and Children Act 2002 to apply as though references to adoption are replaced with references to parental orders where parental orders have been made; in fact parental orders are often referred to as 'fast track adoption'. A child who is the subject of a parental order is to be treated as though born to the holders of that order.[61] The terminology used suggests that having a parental order does not make same sex couples adoptive mothers or adoptive fathers, but instead adoptive parents.

1.36 Given the reality that the change in the law to enable two male or female (legal) parents is very recent, the vast majority of children being brought up by nurturing parents of the same sex will not have two legal parents of the same sex for some time to come. In addition, many families will continue to make informal arrangements for the conception of children to be brought up by parents of the same sex. For those families who have two parents of the same sex who are both legal parents, it is disappointing that the HFEA 2008 does not provide the opportunity for children to have three parents – a mother, a father and a second male or female parent. For example, women in a civil partnership who have conceived a baby after 6 April 2009, but who choose to conceive by artificial insemination with a known genetic father who may be a friend or relative will no longer have the option of giving their child a legal father with parental responsibility from birth by putting his name on the birth certificate – s 42 of the HFEA 2008 provides that in these circumstances 'no man is to be treated as the father of the child'. This might cause difficulties for the child later if (s)he moves to a country which does not permit same sex partnership. Two men who have the assistance of a surrogate mother, and subsequently apply for a parental order, have no route by which the surrogate mother can continue to be a legal parent. Similar difficulties may arise for that child in later life.

---

[60] SI 2010/985.
[61] ACA 2002, s 67 as read with Sch 1 to the HFE (PO) Regulations 2010.

1.37 In the light of cases such as *T v T*[62] and *R v E and F*[63] and *A v B & C*,[64] where it is apparent that the female primary carers have actively chosen a biological father who is not anonymous, and in an era when the benefits to children of the important adults in their lives cooperating and making decisions jointly are recognised, it seems a missed opportunity not to permit families to choose a legal structure which reflects the responsibility towards the children being shared by their genetic and psychological parents.[65] It also seems to make a huge assumption that same sex couples who necessarily have the assistance of a third party in the creation of a child do not want that third party to be recognised as one of the child's parents.

1.38 Note also when considering the meaning of mother, father or parent, that pursuant to s 12 of the Gender Recognition Act 2004, where a mother or father changes gender, they will remain the mother or father of the child, and not change from mother to father or father to mother. Whilst they may be able to amend their own birth certificate following a full gender recognition certificate being issued, their child's birth certificate will not be altered if they change gender after the child's birth. See chapter 6 in relation to transgendered people for a more in-depth discussion of the issue of gender and parenthood.

CHILD OF THE FAMILY

1.39 The Children Act defines this in relation to parties to a marriage or a civil partnership as a child who is the child of both of them or who has been treated by both of them as a child of their family.[66] The child in question does not have to be the genetic or legal child of either of them.[67] It is important to note that being a child of the family does not automatically give the spouse or civil partner parental responsibility for the child unless accompanied by a parental responsibility agreement or court order[68] – ie the spouse or civil partner is a step-parent. This is even the case in a situation where civil partners set out to have a child together and attended a clinic together with the intention of bringing up the child jointly. The exception to this is in relation to children conceived during the subsistence of a civil partnership post 6 April 2009 through assisted conception[69] since the HFEA 2008 provides for the other party to the civil partnership to be treated as a parent for all purposes. The

---

[62]   [2010] EWCA Civ 1366.
[63]   [2010] EWHC 417 (Fam).
[64]   [2011] EWHC 2290 (Fam) and [2012] EWCA Civ 285.
[65]   This is the author's own view, but one which is consistent with the observation by Lord Justice Thorpe in the Court of Appeal case of *A v B & C* [2012] Civ 285 in which he said that: 'it is generally accepted that a child gains by having two parents. It does not follow from that that the addition of a third is necessarily disadvantageous.' We may yet see the courts going further than Parliament in this respect.
[66]   Section 105.
[67]   *Re A (Child of the Family)* [1998] 1 FLR 347.
[68]   CA 1989, s 4A.
[69]   HFEA 2008, s 42 – note this would include children in the position of the family in *B and A and C and D* [2006] EWHC 2 (Fam) where despite the intention that the child would be brought up by two women in an enduring relationship the child was conceived by sexual

significance of being a child of the family is most likely to arise in the context of a breakdown of the relationship and the ability of the genetic parent to seek financial provision from the civil partner,[70] in relation to entitlement to apply for residence or contact orders,[71] or in the event of a need arising to seek financial provision from a deceased's estate following the death of a civil partner.[72]

ACQUIRING LEGAL PARENTHOOD

1.40 Ordinarily, but not always, a child conceived through sexual intercourse will be the legal child of both genetic parents. With assisted conception comes greater complexity. The circumstances in which there may be a difference between genetic parenthood and legal parenthood are as follows.

UK adoption

1.41 The Adoption and Children Act 2002[73] provides:

'67 Status conferred by adoption

(1) An adopted person is to be treated in law as if born as the child of the adopter or adopters.

(2) An adopted person is the legitimate child of the adopters or adopter and, if adopted by –

- (a) a couple, or
- (b) one of a couple under section 51(2),

is to be treated as the child of the relationship of the couple in question.

(3) An adopted person –

- (a) if adopted by one of a couple under section 51(2), is to be treated in law as not being the child of any other person than the adopter and the other one of the couple, and
- (b) in any other case, is to be treated in law, subject to subsection (4), as not being the child of any person other than the adopters or adopter ...'

1.42 The effect of this provision is that:

- If a person is adopted by a couple together who are neither of them the genetic parent, whether or not they are married or in a civil partnership,

---

intercourse. The method of conception was also a hotly contested issue in the case of *TJ v CV* [2007] EWHC 1952 (Fam) but not one which required resolution in that case.

[70] Schedule 5 to the Civil Partnership Act 2004 or Sch 1 to the Children Act 1989, as amended by s 78 of the Civil Partnership Act 2004.

[71] Civil Partnership Act 2004, s 77.

[72] Pursuant to s 1(d) Inheritance (Provision for Family and Dependants) Act 1975.

[73] Which replaces s 39 of the Adoption Act 1976.

of the same sex or different sexes, the adopted person is treated in law as though born to them and no other person the genetic parenthood is extinguished in law for all purposes.

• If a person is adopted by the spouse or civil partner, or partner in an enduring family relationship of the genetic mother or father, whether of the same or different sex as the genetic mother or father, the adopted person is treated in law as the child of the people in that relationship and no other person: the genetic parenthood of the biological mother or father in that relationship remains, whilst the genetic parenthood of the *other* genetic parent is extinguished in law for all purposes.

1.43 Care must be taken, however, if the adoption is an overseas adoption as such an adoption will be subject to the rules of the country in question which may not completely extinguish the genetic parents' status.[74] See chapter 5 for guidance as to the acquisition of adoptive parent status for those who are not genetic parents.

The presumption of legitimacy

1.44 A presumption of legitimacy still exists at Common Law in England and Wales. Halsbury's Laws describes the principle as follows:[75]

'At common law it is presumed that a child born to a married woman during the subsistence of her marriage is also the child of her husband. The presumption of legitimacy applies even if the child must have been conceived before the marriage, or where the child is born within the possible period of gestation after the husband's death or a final decree of divorce.'

With the presumption of legitimacy, comes a presumption of parentage: 'if a child is the legitimate child of A and B, A and B must logically be the child's parents.'[76] In cases of assisted conception, this presumption becomes statutory law.[77]

1.45 The significance of this presumption for families in a same sex relationship is that;

(1) If the birth mother was married at the time that the child was born, and donor sperm was used, even where she is separated from her husband and in a same sex relationship,[78] her husband will be presumed to be the father. This remains the position unless:

---

[74] See, for example, ACA 2002, s 88 relating to Convention Adoptions.
[75] Halsbury's Laws of England, Vol 5(3), para 94.
[76] Halsbury's Laws of England, Vol 5(3), para 94.
[77] HFEA 2008, s 35 and HFEA 1990, s 28(1).
[78] But not judicially separated.

- the child was born prior to 4 April 1988;[79]
- it can be shown that the husband did not consent to the woman's artificial insemination with that genetic father's sperm;[80] or
- the presumption is displaced[81] for example by DNA tests;[82] or
- there is a parental order or adoption order in place.[83]

(2) If the birth mother is married but separated at the time that assisted reproduction takes place, and in a same sex relationship, she cannot give legal consent for her female partner to be treated as the other legal parent unless steps are taken to first ensure that her husband is not presumed the father of the child, ie, it would have to be shown that he does not consent to her being artificially inseminated.[84]

(3) If a surrogate mother is married at the time of the birth, unless a parental or adoption order has been obtained, the mother's husband will be the legal father in the UK until it is demonstrated that he did not consent to the mother's artificial insemination by the genetic father.[85]

(4) Since s 42 of the Human Fertilisation and Embryology Act 2008 came into force on 1 April 2009, the presumption of legitimacy now also applies to women in a civil partnership following artificial insemination or assisted conception after that date.[86] If a woman was in a civil partnership at the time of the *conception* the civil partner is presumed to be the other female parent of the child, and will have parental responsibility, unless it is shown that the she did not consent to the eggs or sperm being placed in the mother or to her artificial insemination.[87] She will be treated as a parent in all situations and for all purposes.[88] The child will also have no legal father. This is not limited to assisted conception which takes place in a clinic, but will include inseminations at home as well. Whether a child was conceived via artificial insemination or sexual intercourse is likely to become an issue in some cases since the genetic father will remain the legal father where the conception arose from sexual intercourse and the child is being brought up by women in a civil partnership.[89]

---

[79] The date of commencement of the Family Law Reform Act 1987.

[80] HFEA 2008, s 35(1) or HFEA 1990, s 28.

[81] FLRA 1969, s 26 provides for the rebuttal of presumption as to legitimacy.

[82] *Leeds Teaching Hospitals NHS Trust v A and B* [2003] EWHC 259 (QB), per Butler Sloss P at para 24.

[83] ACA 2002, s 67, incorporating the HFE (PO) Regulations 2010.

[84] HFEA 2008, ss 35 and 43.

[85] See *Re X and Y (Foreign Surrogacy)* [2008] EWHC 3030 (Fam) for an example of this.

[86] Family Law Reform Act 1987, s 1 and SI 2009/479.

[87] HFEA 2008, s 42 and SI 2009/479.

[88] HFEA 2008, s 48.

[89] See for example the case of *TJ v CS* [2007] EWHC 1952 (Fam) where the mother's partner believed the child had been conceived via artificial insemination but the father alleged sexual intercourse had taken place.

1.46   Given the significance for children born through assisted conception to female civil partners, it is particularly important to establish that the registered partnership complies with all legal requirements for it to be recognised as such, whether contracted here or abroad. However, there is a degree of flexibility in that s 50 of the HFEA 2008 provides that the definition of civil partnership for the purposes of that Act includes a void civil partnership if either or both of them reasonably believed at the time when they registered as civil partners of each other that it was valid.[90] This is discussed further in chapter 8.

Assisted reproduction

1.47   For lesbian women and gay men assisted reproduction inevitably means a gamete donor, but for lesbian women in particular the choice of formal or informal routes to achieving this, and the child's date of birth, have a significant impact on the issue of whether the genetic father will also be the legal father.

1.48   The translation of natural parentage into legal parentage following assisted reproduction has been a process, and the history of this process is still reflected in the fact that a person's legal parentage following assisted reproduction will differ according to their date of birth, and the circumstances in which they were conceived.

1.49   Those born prior to the Family Law Reform Act 1987 and the HFEA 1990 are no longer minors. Unless those individuals have been adopted, or the common law presumption of legitimacy applies, their parenthood will be that of genetic parenthood.[91]

1.50   For the first time, the Human Fertilisation and Embryology Act 1990 enabled individuals to be named on a child's birth certificate and given the status of legal parent even though they had no genetic link with the child:[92]

> 'When the 1990 Act came into force ... where donated sperm or eggs are used, the birth certificate does not record the donor as a parent, and therefore is no longer a record of genetic parentage.'

This was only available to married couples or men and women being treated together, but did allow them to become not just legal parents but the legal mothers and father.[93] In 1984, the Warnock report recommended a change in the law so that the gamete donor would have no parental rights or duties in relation to the child since '[anonymity] would give legal protection to the donor but it would also have the effect of minimising the invasion of the third party

---

90   A similar provision is made in relation to marriages in HFEA 2008, s 49.
91   With the exception of birth mothers pursuant to a surrogacy arrangement using a donor egg – Surrogacy Arrangements Act 1985, s 1, or where commissioning parents are recognised as legal parents following surrogacy in another jurisdiction.
92   Per Lord Darzi of Denham, Hansard 28.01.08, col 477.
93   HFEA 1990, s 28(2).

into the family'. For the first time the 1990 Act allowed for the possibility that gamete donors might not be legal parents, and specifically provided that egg donation alone does not result in motherhood.[94]

TRACING LEGAL AND GENETIC PARENTAGE

1.51 For children born via assisted conception since the HFEA 1990 came into force on 1 August 1991, but prior to the coming into force of the HFEA 2008 on 6 April 2009, a summary of the position in respect of legal parentage is as follows:

Mother

1.52

(1) The woman who carried the child (birth mother) following the placing in her of an embryo or of sperm and eggs is to be treated as the mother.[95] This is irrespective of whether the conception took place in a UK licensed clinic or not, or whether a donor egg was used. The birth mother is the legal mother unless:

    (a) The child was adopted after birth (other than by the birth mother), and treated by law as the child of the adopter(s), in which case the adopter(s) is/are the only legal parents of the child;[96] or unless

    (b) A parental order has been made in favour of a married couple following a woman other than the wife of that couple having carried the child.[97]

Father

1.53 If assisted conception/artificial insemination took place using the sperm of the mother's spouse or partner where she was not married, the position remains straightforward – the genetic father is the legal father, unless there has since been an adoption order or parental order (see above).

1.54 Where the semen was provided by a donor, legal fatherhood is more complex:

---

[94] HFEA 1990, 27.
[95] HFEA 1990, 27.
[96] Adoption Act 1976, s 39 or ACA 2002, s 69.
[97] Pursuant to HFEA 1990, s 30 and the provisions of the Adoption Act 1976 or ACA 2002 in conjunction with the Parental Orders (Human Fertilisation and Embryology) Regulations 1994.

(1) If the sperm for conception in a UK clinic was provided by an anonymous donor and the mother was not married or being treated together with a man, there is no legal father.[98]

(2) If the child was carried by a woman who was married at the time of conception, and was conceived by the placing in her of (donor) sperm and eggs, or of an embryo, or by artificial insemination with donor sperm, the presumption of legitimacy will apply (see above) and her husband will be treated as the father unless it is shown that he did not consent to the placing in her of the eggs or donor sperm or the embryo or her artificial insemination with the donor's sperm,[99] or unless the child was subsequently adopted[100] or made the subject of a parental order.[101] This is irrespective of whether the conception takes place in an authorised clinic or whether the conception takes place in the UK.[102]

(3) If the child was carried by a woman who was married at the time of conception, and was conceived by assisted reproduction with another man's sperm, and her husband did not consent to the assisted reproduction,[103] then the presumption of legitimacy can be rebutted and the genetic father will be the legal father,[104] or, if the conception took place via a UK clinic using anonymous donor sperm provided with the appropriate consents, the child would have no legal father.[105]

(4) If the child was carried by a woman who was not married at the time of conception, significant distinctions arise depending on whether:

(a) the woman was artificially inseminated at a clinic or not;
(b) if she was, whether she was treated together with a man or not;
(c) if she was, whether she was treated with donor sperm.

---

98 HFEA 1990, s 28(6).
99 HFEA 1990, s 28(1) and (2). See however in particular *Leeds Teaching Hospital v A* [2003] EWHC 259 (QB) where it was clear that the husband had consented to artificial insemination with his own sperm, but not that of another man; the genetic father and not the spouse was the legal father.
100 HFEA 1990, s 28(5).
101 HFEA 1990, s 30.
102 HFEA 1990, s 28(8).
103 To the placing in her of the eggs or donor sperm or the embryo or her artificial insemination with the donor's sperm.
104 As in *Leeds Teaching Hospital v A* [2003] EWHC 259 (QB) or where there were informal arrangements made.
105 HFEA 1990, s 28(6).

1.55 So:

(1) If artificial insemination takes place informally or abroad: ie not 'by a person to whom a licence applies', the HFEA 1990 has no application, and the legal father will still be the genetic father.[106]

(2) If artificial insemination or assisted conception does take place at a licensed clinic, and the woman was treated together with a man, he will be the legal father.[107]

(3) If artificial insemination or assisted conception does take place at a licensed clinic but the woman was not treated together with a man, but alone using donor sperm,[108] the child will have no legal father[109] (unless one is created by adoption).

Again, all of these alternatives are subject to an adoption or parental order having been made.

1.56 The practical significance of these provisions for women hoping to parent exclusively within a same sex relationship before 2009 is that they could attend licensed clinics as a couple, but could not be treated together within the meaning of HFEA 1990. The most that could be achieved in terms of recognising their exclusive significance to the child was to create no legal father but two nurturing female parents with the potential to share parental responsibility via a joint residence order, or later adoption.[110] Since the ACA 2002 came into force, the door has been open to step-parent adoption. This is discussed further in chapter 5.

1.57 If the conception was carried out informally, the genetic father would be the legal father but if the child was born before 1 December 2003[111] the father would not have parental responsibility from birth even if he was named on the birth certificate.

1.58 For children born after 1 December 2003, if the genetic father is the legal father, the birth mother can choose whether to place his name on the birth certificate, and thereby choose whether he has parental responsibility from birth. The potential therefore still existed for the carrying mother and her female partner to agree to share parental responsibility via a joint residence order to the exclusion of the genetic father if the father was not keen to play a

---

[106] Parent means parent with parental responsibility for the purposes of giving consent to an adoption under ACA 2002, s 52(6).

[107] HFEA 1990, s 28(3).

[108] To which s 28(6) applies.

[109] Effect of HFEA 1990, ss 27 and 28.

[110] Once the Adoption and Children Act 2002 (ACA) came into force the mother's partner could apply to adopt the child under s 51(2).

[111] The date when ACA 2002, s 111 came into force.

significant role in the child's life.[112] The genetic father could still apply for parental responsibility[113] (unless the female partner had adopted the child[114] so that both women become legal parents).[115] An application for adoption does not require the involvement of the father if the father does not have parental responsibility, so the mother's decision about whether to name the father on the child's birth certificate, and the father's decision about whether to apply for parental responsibility are significant ones for the mother and her partner, for the father and for the child.[116]

Parent

1.59   Unless the child has another male or female parent as a result of adoption pursuant to the Adoption and Children Act 2002, the child will have a legal mother, and may have a legal father, but will not also have a legal same sex parent following assisted conception.

1.60   See the flow chart at Appendix 1 for the position of children born post-HFEA 1990 but pre-HFEA 2008.

Children born since the HFEA 2008 came into force on 6 April 2009

1.61   For children born since the HFEA 2008 came into force on 6 April 2009, the legal position in respect of parentage is as follows:

Mother

1.62   The woman who carried the child (birth mother) following the placing in her of an embryo or of sperm and eggs (whether in a UK clinic or not) is to be treated as the mother.[117] The birth mother is the legal mother, even where the genetic mother is the other female parent through egg donation[118] unless:

(1)   the child is adopted after birth (other than by the birth mother), and treated by law as the child of the adopter(s), in which case the adopter(s) is/are the only legal parents of the child;[119] or unless

---

[112]   Effect of CA 1989, s 12(2).
[113]   CA 1989, s 4 and pursuant to BFRA 1953, s 10A he could be re-registered as father on the birth certificate.
[114]   Under ACA 2002, s 51.
[115]   Pursuant to ACA 2002, s 46(3).
[116]   Note, however, that parental responsibility from birth is not determinative of the role which the father will or should have in the child's life, this is discussed further in chapter 4.
[117]   HFEA 2008, s 33.
[118]   HFEA 2008, s 47.
[119]   ACA 2002, s 69.

(2)   a parental order has been made in favour of a married couple or civil partners or same sex couple in an enduring relationship.[120]

If the child has been adopted by a single man or two men or women in a same sex relationship, or if there is a parental order in favour of two men or two women, the man or men or women are to be treated as the parents of the child and no other person is to be treated as the child's parent.[121] In any of those situations the child would have no legal mother, just male or female parents.

Other female parent

1.63   If at the time the child was conceived (other than by intercourse) the birth mother was in a civil partnership, the civil partner will be the other female parent (and the child will have no legal father) unless it can be shown that she did not consent to the insemination.[122] This is the position in the UK irrespective of whether the biological father is well known to the child or anonymous, whether the artificial insemination took place at home or in a clinic, in the UK or elsewhere. A civil partnership includes for these purposes a same sex partnership registered overseas falling within the definition of 'overseas relationship' in the Civil Partnership Act 2004 – see further chapter 8 in relation to overseas relationships. Men offering gametes to a female couple must be aware that if the female couple are in a civil partnership, the biological father is not the legal father and will have no legal status in relation to the child.

1.64   If the child was conceived using donor sperm at a UK licensed clinic, and the birth mother agreed to another woman who is not her civil partner being the second female parent, and the agreed female parenthood conditions are met, the other woman will be treated for all purposes as a parent of the child, and there will be no legal father.[123]

1.65   The agreed female parenthood conditions require that both women agree in writing to the other woman being treated as a parent. There are specific provisions for situations where either woman is unable to sign due to illness, injury or physical disability. The consent must not have been withdrawn.[124] The mother and the agreed female parent must not be within the prohibited degrees of relationship.[125]

1.66   It is clear then, that the only routes to both women being recognised legally as parents from the child's birth are where the women are civil partners, or the conception takes place in a UK licensed clinic. It remains open to the other nurturing parent to apply to adopt, but if the father is named on the birth

---

[120]   Pursuant to HFEA 2008, s 54 and the provision of the Adoption and Children Act 2002 in conjunction with the HFE (PO) Regulations 2010.

[121]   ACA 2002, s 69 in conjunction with the HFE (PO) Regulations 2010.

[122]   HFEA 2008, s 42.

[123]   HFEA 2008, ss 43–45.

[124]   HFEA 2008, ss 43 and 44.

[125]   HFEA 2008, s 44(1)(e).

certificate he will have parental responsibility and the right to object, and even where he does not have parental responsibility, if he is the legal father and known to the family and becomes aware of the intention to adopt, he has the right to apply for parental responsibility and object to the adoption.[126]

Father

1.67 If assisted conception/artificial insemination takes place using the sperm of the mother's spouse, or partner where the woman is not married, the position remains straightforward – the genetic father is the legal father, unless there has since been an adoption order or parental order.[127]

1.68 If the child is conceived using donor sperm, the position is more complex:

(1) If the sperm was provided by an anonymous donor and no man is treated as the father by virtue of either being the husband or meeting the agreed fatherhood conditions, there will be no legal father.[128]

(2) If the child was carried by a woman who was married at the time of an assisted conception, the presumption of legitimacy will apply (see **1.44** et seq) and her husband will be treated as the father unless it is shown that he did not consent to the sperm or eggs being placed in the woman or her artificial insemination.[129]

(3) If the woman was in a civil partnership at the time of the assisted conception, the mother's civil partner will be the other female parent[130] and there will be no legal father[131] unless it can be shown that the civil partner did not consent to the sperm or eggs being placed in the woman or her artificial insemination.[132]

(4) If the woman is not married or in a civil partnership, or if it is shown that her husband or civil partner did not consent to the assisted conception, and the treatment was carried out at a licensed clinic with donor sperm, and the woman and a man agreed to that man being treated as the child's

---

[126] Under Children Act 1989, s 4.

[127] ACA 2002, s 67 together with the HFE (PO) Regulations 2010.

[128] HFEA 2008, ss 41 and s 38(1).

[129] HFEA 2008, s 35. See however in particular *Leeds Teaching Hospital v A* [2003] EWHC 259 (QB) where it was clear that the husband had consented to artificial insemination with his own sperm, but not that of another man, the genetic father and not the spouse was the legal father.

[130] HFEA 2008, s 42.

[131] HFEA 2008, s 48.

[132] HFEA 2008, s 42(1).

father (the agreed fatherhood conditions are met), that man will be the child's father.[133] The mother and father must not be within the prohibited degrees of relationship.[134]

(5)   If the woman is not married or in a civil partnership, or if it is shown that her husband or civil partner did not consent to the artificial conception, and the agreed fatherhood conditions are not met and she was artificially inseminated using anonymous donor sperm at a UK licensed clinic, there will be no legal father.

(6)   If the child was conceived using donor sperm at a licensed clinic, and the birth mother agreed to another woman being the second female parent, and the agreed female parenthood conditions are met, the other woman will be treated for all purposes as a parent of the child, and there will be no legal father.[135]

Artificial insemination and consent

1.69   The issue of consent and withdrawal of consent is significant. First, the right to withdraw consent is absolute up to the point of implantation. In the case of *Evans v the UK*[136] the court considered the operation of the requirements in the HFEA 1990 for stored embryos to be destroyed where consent was withdrawn. The European Court found no breach and it was held that it was not a fair balance for the male party to be held to his consent even where there was no further possibility of the woman having a child without it.

1.70   Secondly, the consent must be specific. In the case of *Leeds Teaching Hospital v A*[137] where the embryo placed in the woman had through error been fertilised with the gametes of another patient instead of her husband, the court held that the woman's husband had not consented to that embryo being placed in the woman, and that her husband was therefore not the legal father. Since the man whose gametes had fertilised the embryo was not an anonymous donor but another patient being treated with his wife, he did not fall within the provisions of s 28(6) of the HFEA 1990 allowing anonymity, he was therefore declared to be the legal father until such time as the children were adopted by the mother and her husband.

1.71   Thirdly, once artificial insemination has taken place, or an embryo has been implanted in relation to treatment carried out in a UK clinic under a licence, the consent cannot be withdrawn.

1.72   Fourthly, consent to agreed fatherhood or second female parenthood is only effective if:

---

[133]   HFEA 2008, ss 36 and 37.
[134]   HFEA 2008, 37(1)(e).
[135]   HFEA 2008, ss 43–48.
[136]   Application No 6339/05 [2006] 2 FLR 172, ECtHR.
[137]   [2003] EWHC 259 (QB).

(a)   it existed at the time at which the embryo was placed in the mother, or when the mother was artificially inseminated;[138]

(b)   it is in writing and signed by the person giving consent;[139]

(c)   the implantation or artificial insemination takes place at a licensed clinic;[140]

(d)   the birth mother and agreed father or second female parent are not within the prohibited degrees of relationship.[141]

1.73 It is important to ensure, therefore, where a woman is married or in a civil partnership and she does not want her spouse or civil partner to be the child's other parent, that it is made very clear that her spouse or civil parent does not consent to the assisted conception: it is insufficient to show that the spouse or civil partner did not actively consent. It is equally important to be clear where the spouse or civil partner does consent, that the consent is to the particular conception, and that it is continuing and unqualified. It is suggested that the spouse or civil partner should sign a document indicating that they do or do not consent.

1.74 These factors are particularly important to address if home insemination is being carried out where the mother and her partner will not have the support and guidance of the clinic and the documentation used for the purposes of clarifying the issue of consent.

1.75 A further important factor for consideration in relation to consent is the question of the consequences of the death of the intended father or second female parent if (s)he should die before the child is born. This is addressed in ss 40, 41 and 46 of the HFEA 2008. Section 40 deals with a situation where a man consented to being treated as the father of the child following the woman's implantation, and also consented to this in the event of his death. Section 41 addresses a situation where the man's sperm was used after his death for a purpose to which he did not consent. Section 46 deals with a situation where a woman consented to being treated as the other female parent of the child following the mother's implantation, and also consented to this being the case in the event of her death. In relation to ss 41 and 46, these issues only arise where treatment is taking place at a clinic, and therefore the clinic will address these issues as part of the process, but in relation to s 41, this applies whether or not treatment was taking place in the UK or at a licensed clinic. The effect of this section is that if insemination takes place using donated sperm and the man dies before it was used, he is not to be treated as the father of the child.

---

[138] HFEA 2008, ss 36(b) and 43(b).
[139] Sections 37(2), (3) and 44(2), (3) unless they are unable to sign and it is given at their direction.
[140] HFEA 2008, ss 36 and 43.
[141] Section 37(1)(e) and 44(1)(e).

1.76 See Appendix 1 for a flow chart describing the position of children born post-HFEA 2008.

Surrogacy and parental orders

1.77 Chapter 3 considers surrogacy and parental orders in detail. In this chapter, we look in outline at the implications of a surrogacy arrangement for legal parentage.

1.78 What do we mean by surrogacy? The Surrogacy Arrangements Act 1985, s 1 defines a surrogate mother as:

> '(2) ... a woman who carries a child in pursuance of an arrangement –
>
> (a) made before she began to carry the child, and
> (b) made with a view to any child carried in pursuance of it being handed over to, and parental responsibility being met (so far as practicable) by, another person or persons.'

1.79 So surrogacy is an arrangement made before birth to hand a child over after the birth to someone other than the carrying mother. This definition makes no reference to artificial insemination or assisted reproduction: ie surrogacy is defined by the arrangement and not the method of conception. It also makes no reference to the father.

1.80 Where a child is conceived naturally by a husband and wife with a view to it being handed over to another person, or persons, this still constitutes a surrogacy arrangement, albeit one which creates significant difficulties for the commissioning parents since it excludes the possibility of a parental order being made,[142] and if the child is handed over this may constitute an illegal placement.[143]

1.81 The factual and genetic circumstances leading to the birth of a child pursuant to a surrogacy arrangement can be very different. The gestational mother may or may not be the genetic mother. A commissioning mother may be the genetic mother, in that she provides the egg, or she may make no contribution to the establishment of the pregnancy. The genetic mother might be a relative of the commissioning mother. The genetic father may be the spouse or partner of the commissioning mother, or of the genetic mother, or he may be an anonymous donor, or he may be a commissioning father, unconnected with the genetic mother or carrying mother and intending to be a nurturing parent.

---

[142] HFEA 2008, s 54 requires that the gamete of at least one of the applicants for a parental order was used to bring about the creation of the embryo.

[143] ACA 2002, s 92. The prohibition includes entering into an agreement with any person for the adoption of a child where no adoption agency is acting on behalf of the child, and extends to causing someone to offer a child for adoption or to offer to hand over a child.

1.82 In the UK, surrogacy arrangements are not enforceable. The carrying mother may change her mind after the birth, and the commissioning parents may be unable to have any role in the child's life if neither of them is a genetic or legal parent Additionally, orders made in other countries following a surrogacy arrangement to give parental status to the commissioning parents are not automatically recognised in the UK. In other words, it is not sufficient to secure a foreign order to regulate the relationship between child and commissioning or de facto parent here. Additionally, the routes open to a commissioning parent to secure their legal status in relation to the child will depend upon the factual and genetic circumstances leading to the birth. Before embarking upon a surrogacy arrangement it is vital to understand the different potential consequences of the various types of arrangements which might be made, and to take specialist advice, including immigration advice if the child will be born outside the UK.

1.83 Although surrogacy is not enforceable, a statutory alternative to adoption in the form of parental orders was created by HFEA 1990 to enable married couples to obtain an order which would give them parental responsibility and the status of legal parents for the child they had commissioned in certain defined circumstances. Parental orders were intended to be more straightforward than adoption.[144] They were described in the Government White Paper which led to the 2008 Act as a 'mechanism for reassigning parental status in surrogacy cases'. A Parental order is described in the 2008 Act as an order which provides for: 'a child to be treated in law as the child of the applicants.'[145]

1.84 For the first time, the HFEA 2008 extended the availability of parental orders to couples in a civil partnership or enduring family relationship (same sex or different sex)[146] in respect of children born after 6 April 2010, or applications made within 6 months of 6 April 2010 where the child was already living with the applicants.[147]

1.85 The process of application for a parental order and the circumstances in which they will or will not be granted on an application, particularly with reference to foreign surrogacy is considered in detail in chapter 3. However, here we look at surrogacy and legal parentage.

Genetics

1.86 It is the **carrying** mother (birth mother) who is the legal mother and **not** the genetic mother, without distinction as to when or where the child was conceived. The availability of a parental order is not affected by whether the

---

[144] HFEA 1990, s 30.
[145] HFEA 2008, s 54.
[146] HFEA 2008, s 54(2).
[147] Human Fertilisation and Embryology Act 2008 (Commencement No 3) Order 2010, SI 2010/987 and HFEA 2008, s 54(11).

carrying mother is a genetic mother or not. However, the genetic and/or carrying mother's status as a parent may be extinguished or superseded, either by adoption, or by a parental order.[148]

1.87 The requirement for the gametes of at least one of the applicants for a parental order to have been used in the creation of the embryo[149] means that either:

- the surrogate mother has been implanted with an embryo created with, or artificially inseminated with, sperm from an intended father who is in a relationship with someone other than the surrogate mother; or

- the surrogate mother has been implanted with an embryo created with the egg of another woman who is in an intended mother relationship with someone other than the surrogate mother.

1.88 In the situation where two women attend at a clinic for treatment together to conceive a child to be brought up by them, if one woman provides the egg which is implanted in the other woman, the legal mother will be the carrying mother and the other woman the genetic mother.[150] This is not, however, a surrogacy arrangement, but an assisted conception:[151] the child is not being handed over after birth. Egg donation does not automatically make the genetic mother a second female parent.[152]

1.89 Section 47 of the HFEA 2008 provides:

'**47 Woman not to be the other parent merely because of egg donation**

A woman is not to be treated as the parent of a child whom she is not carrying and has not carried except where she is so treated –

    (a)   by virtue of section 42 or 43, or

    (b)   by virtue of section 46 (for the purpose mentioned in subsection (4) of that section) or,

    (c)   by virtue of adoption.'

1.90 Another consideration in relation to genetics is consanguinity. It is not unusual for the surrogate mother to be implanted with an embryo using the gametes of a relative of one of the intended parents, but clearly implantation with an embryo containing gametes within the prohibited degrees of relationship will not be permitted.

---

[148] HFEA 2008, s 33 does not refer specifically to parental orders but this must be interpreted as the effect of Sch 1 to the HFE (PO) Regulations 2010 which give parental orders the same effect as adoption.

[149] HFEA 2008, s 54(1)(b).

[150] HFEA 2008, s 47.

[151] Falling within HFEA 2008, ss 35–47 which determine who the other parent is.

[152] HFEA 2008, s 47.

Method of conception

1.91　In order for a parental order to be available, the child must have been carried by a woman who was not one of the applicants for the order as a result of 'the placing in her of an embryo or sperm and eggs or her artificial insemination'.[153]

1.92　In cases where there is assisted reproduction, s 33 of the HFEA 2008 provides:

> '(1) The woman who is carrying or has carried a child as a result of the placing in her of an embryo or of sperm and eggs, and no other woman, is to be treated as the mother of the child.
>
> (2) Subsection (1) does not apply to any child to the extent that the child is treated by virtue of adoption as not being the woman's child.
>
> (3) Subsection (1) applies whether the woman was in the United Kingdom or elsewhere at the time of the placing in her of the embryo or the sperm and eggs.'

1.93　This is consistent with the definition of surrogate mother in the Surrogacy Arrangements Act 1985 (above) and with surrogacy arrangements not being enforceable[154] and is in the same terms as s 27 of the HFEA 1990 which it replaces.

1.94　In cases which do not involve assisted reproduction – e g an arrangement followed by conception through intercourse, there is no distinction between the genetic mother and the carrying mother, and the position remains as at common law until altered by adoption. The existence of surrogacy arrangement does not operate to extinguish legal motherhood.

1.95　However, the fact of conception having been arrived at following intercourse does remove the possibility of a parental order being made, and may affect legal fatherhood – see above at **1.67** et seq.

Enduring relationship

1.96　Parental orders are not available for single applicants, only to spouses, civil partners or couples in enduring relationships, same sex or opposite sex. This means that if a couple enter into a surrogacy arrangement with a woman, and their relationship breaks down before the child is born, neither of them will be able to apply for a parental order on the child's birth. Equally, if one of them dies before the child is born, or before the application is made, the surviving person will not be able to apply for a parental order. The court does, however, have a discretionary jurisdiction to confer a parental order on a surviving partner if the other person has died after the application for a parental order has been issued, but before it is made.[155]

---

[153]　HFEA 2008, s 54(1)(a).
[154]　Surrogacy Arrangements Act 1989, s 1A, as inserted by HFEA 1990.
[155]　*A v P* [2011] EWHC 1738 (Fam).

1.97 It is also important to note that it is only possible for a man or a woman to meet the agreed fatherhood or agreed female parenthood conditions where treatment takes place in a licensed UK clinic, and effective consents are operative at the time of the implantation.[156] This means that if the intended parents' relationship breaks down during the pregnancy, it will not be possible for either of them to become a parent pursuant to the agreed fatherhood or agreed second female parenthood conditions or further to a parental order. It also means that if treatment does not take place in a licensed UK clinic, neither of the intended parents can become a parent pursuant to agreed fatherhood or agreed second female parenthood conditions if the intended parents' relationship breaks down after the surrogacy agreement is reached but prior to insemination.

1.98 If one of the intended parents still wishes to parent the child following the breakdown of their relationship or death of their partner, the surviving partner still intending to parent has a number of alternatives open to him or her:

(1) Either intended parent may apply for a residence order, but if (s)he is not a legal parent (s)he would require leave to do so.

(2) A genetic father who had been intending to parent with his male partner would be a legal parent in any event of a child conceived with his gametes and would not require any form of order to confirm this.

(3) If the intended parent still wished to extinguish the birth mother's parental responsibility he or she could apply to adopt the child as a single adoptive parent.

Legal parenthood following surrogacy if a parental order is not made

1.99

(1) Legal motherhood remains with the carrying mother unless the child is adopted.

(2) If the carrying mother was married at the time of the birth of a child conceived pursuant to a surrogacy arrangement:

    (a) The presumption of legitimacy (see above) will operate.[157]

    (b) In addition, if the child was conceived using assisted conception the mother's husband will be the legal father as a matter of English law pursuant to s 28 of the HFEA 1990 or (since 6 April 2010) s 35 of

---

[156] HFEA 2008, ss 36 and 44.

[157] For example prior to the HFEA 1990 coming into force or where conception arose as a result of intercourse, or as a result of HFEA 2008, s 38 or HFEA 1990, s 28.

the HFEA 2008, even if he is not the genetic father, unless it is shown that he did not consent to the assisted conception or there has been an adoption or parental order. This can cause particular difficulties if the child is born outside the UK – as happened in the case of *Re X and Y (Foreign Surrogacy)*[158] where the child was regarded by Ukranian law as the child of the applicants, and therefore as having no status in the Ukraine, but by English law as the child of the Ukranian birth mother and her husband. Fortunately in that case problems were resolved by the birth mother's husband giving consent to the making of a parental order.

(c)   The operation of ss 28 and 35 of the HFEA 2008 to women married at the time of treatment also means specifically that if, for example, a married woman (even if separated from her husband, and pursuant to a surrogacy arrangement) agreed to assist another man to have a child by becoming artificially inseminated with his sperm in a clinic, her husband would be the child's father until it was shown that he did not consent to her insemination. It must be clear that the mother's husband did not consent to the insemination, rather than just not consenting to being the father, and some cases are reported to have run into difficulties where it is thought that the husband stated he did not consent but went along with arrangements anyway.[159]

(d)   If the carrying mother is married and it *is* shown that her husband did *not* consent to the assisted conception, then either:

(i)   the genetic father will be the legal father,[160] unless superseded by adoption or parental order; or

(ii)   if the conception was achieved with anonymous donor sperm in the course of treatment services provided by a UK Clinic and the agreed fatherhood conditions are met,[161] and the carrying mother and the man agreeing to those conditions consent to him being treated as the father,[162] that man will be the father unless superseded by adoption; or

(iii) if the conception was achieved with anonymous donor sperm (pre-HFEA 2008) and the carrying mother and a man were being treated together,[163] that man will be treated as the legal father. When considering this last scenario in the context of surrogacy arrangements, the reality is that it is likely to be difficult to demonstrate that a child conceived prior to the HFEA 2008 coming into force was conceived as a result of a woman and a gay man receiving treatment services together within the meaning of the 1990 Act, whether or not she was

---

[158] [2008] EWHC 3030 (Fam).
[159] Per Sarah Elliston, lecturer in medical law, Glasgow, 16 October 2009, Bio News.
[160] As in *Leeds Teaching Hospitals NHS Trust v A* [2003] EWHC 259 (QB).
[161] Pursuant to HFEA 2008, ss 36 and 37.
[162] HFEA 2008, s 37(1)(a) and (b).
[163] Within the meaning of HFEA 1990, s 28(2).

married. The case of *Re R (IVF: Paternity of a Child)*[164] dealt
in some detail by the issue of what is meant by the provision of
treatment services together, and explored the Code of Practice
governing the provision of treatment to people who were not
married, and the references are all to 'couples', 'cohabitants'
and 'unmarried people in stable relationships': it was clearly not
envisaged that s 28(2) might be used by an unmarried woman to
assist a gay man to have a child.

(e)   If the carrying mother is in a civil partnership at the time of conception,
and the child is born after 6 April 2009, s 42 of the HFEA 2008 provides
that that other party to the civil partnership is to be treated as a parent of
the child, unless it is shown that she did not consent to the artificial
insemination, in which case pursuant to s 45 of the HFEA 2008, the child
will have no father. The implications of this are that if a man reaches a
surrogacy arrangement with a woman who is in a civil partnership, even if
his gametes are used, and even if she is separated from her civil partner,
care must be taken to ensure that it is clear that the carrying mother's civil
partner did not consent to the assisted conception taking place in order to
ensure that the child can have a father. This is particularly the case since a
single man could not apply for a parental order.[165] It is also important to
note that the consent in issue is to the artificial insemination, not to the
issue of parenthood: it is not sufficient for the birth mother's civil partner
to declare that she does not consent to becoming the other female parent,
it must be shown specifically that she did not consent to the 'placing in
[the woman] of the embryo or the sperm and eggs or to her artificial
insemination (as the case may be)'.[166] Presumably the difficulties reported
(see above) where the surrogate mother's husband stated he did not
consent to the conception but went along with it anyway could be
replicated in the case of civil partners.

(f)   If the carrying mother is not married or in a civil partnership, then either
the genetic father is the legal father unless superseded by adoption or
parental order, or, if the conception was achieved with anonymous donor
sperm in the course of treatment services provided by a UK Clinic and the
agreed fatherhood conditions are met,[167] and the carrying mother and the
man agreeing to those conditions consent to him being treated as the
father,[168] that man will be the father (unless superseded by adoption by
someone else). In this way, ss 36 and 37 of the HFEA 2008 provide a
mechanism for a form of surrogacy by which a single gay man can become
a father, even using donor sperm. The carrying mother would still be the
legal mother unless and until adoption took place, but where the agreed
fatherhood conditions are met, it is now entirely possible that a woman

---

[164]   [2005] UKHL 33.
[165]   HFEA 2008, s 54(2).
[166]   HFEA 2008, s 42(1).
[167]   Pursuant to ss 36 and 37 of the HFEA 2008.
[168]   HFEA 2008, s 37(1)(a) and (b).

and a man can reach an agreement for the woman to undergo assisted conception and give consent to a named man who agrees to be the father becoming the legal father. Unlike the position under the 1990 Act where it would have been necessary to show that the woman and the man were being treated together, there are no requirements as to the nature of the relationship between the woman and the man. Of course, as with other surrogacy arrangements, any agreement that the man would care for the child after his or her birth rather than the mother would be unenforceable, but the man would have the legal status as parent to make an application under the Children Act 1989 for a residence order[169] and he could also apply to adopt the child if the mother died or in exceptional circumstances.[170]

Effect of a parental order on legal parentage

1.100   As set out above, the status of an adopted child, whether adopted under the Adoption Act 1976 prior to 30 December 2005 or under the Adoption and Children Act 2002 since that date is that he or she is treated in law as if he had been born a child of the adopter(s). The Schedules to the Parental Orders (Human Fertilisation and Embryology) Regulations 1994 and the Human Fertilisation and Embryology (Parental Orders) Regulations 2010 enabled the provisions of those Acts as to status to be read:

> 'A person who is the subject of a parental order is to be treated in law as not being the child of any person other than the persons who obtained the order.'

1.101   Either an adoption order or a parental order will therefore operate to extinguish the legal motherhood and parental responsibility of the carrying mother. In a situation where the holders of an adoption order or parental order are a single man (adoption) or two men (adoption or parental order), there will be no legal mother of the child. It is of note that s 45 of the HFEA 2008 specifically provides that where a woman is treated as a parent by virtue of being a civil partner of the carrying mother or where treatment is provided to a woman who agrees that the second woman is to be a parent 'no man is to be treated as father of the child', and there is no equivalent specific provision providing for no woman to be treated as mother of the child following the making of a parental order. The explanation for this would seem to be that the making of a parental order itself provides that the child is not the parent of anyone other than those holding the order.

1.102   Note that an order from another country which extinguishes the legal parenthood of the gestational mother in that country is not sufficient to extinguish the legal parenthood of the gestational mother under the law of England and Wales: it will still be necessary for the commissioning parents to

---

[169]   See for example the case of *Re P (Surrogacy: Residence)* [2008] 1 FLR 177 where a biological father and his wife who had entered into a surrogacy arrangement with the birth mother were granted residence orders.
[170]   ACA 2002, s 51(4); *Re B (Adoption: Natural Parent)* [2002] 1 FLR 196.

adopt the child or obtain a parental order in England and Wales for them to become the legal parents, or the child is in danger of having no legal parents at all.[171] The steps necessary to avoid this are discussed further in chapter 3. The procedure for obtaining parental orders is explored in detail in that chapter.

CONCLUSIONS

1.103 As a final postscript to this chapter, after reading it one might be forgiven for thinking that genetic parenthood is less important than ever. However, that would be to ignore the House of Lords decision in the case of *Re G*[172] concerning the welfare of and arrangements for children following the breakdown of their nurturing parents' same sex relationship, in which the biological mother was undoubtedly seeking to marginalise the social and psychological parent.

1.104 Lord Nicholls[173] said of the children in that case:

'Their welfare is the court's paramount consideration. In reaching its decision the court should always have in mind that in the ordinary way the rearing of a child by his or her biological parent can be expected to be in the child's best interests, both in the short term and also, and importantly, in the longer term. I decry any tendency to diminish the significance of this factor.'

1.105 This was echoed by Baroness Hale in her judgment, in which she said;

'The husband or unmarried partner of a mother who gives birth as a result of donor insemination in a licensed clinic in this country is for virtually all purposes a legal parent, but may not be any kind of natural parent: see s 28 of the 1990 Act. To be the legal parent of a child gives a person legal standing to bring and defend proceedings about the child and makes the child a member of that person's family, but it does not necessarily tell us much about the importance of that person to the child's welfare.[174]

My Lords, I am driven to the conclusion that the courts below have allowed the unusual context of this case to distract them from principles which are of universal application. First, the fact that CG is the natural mother of these children in every sense of that term, while raising no presumption in her favour, is undoubtedly an important and significant factor in determining what will be best for them now and in the future.'[175]

1.106 Whilst this decision was pre-HFEA 2008 and concerned two women, only one of whom was a legal parent, Baroness Hale clearly drew an analogy

---

[171] This happened in the case of *Re X and Y (Foreign Surrogacy)* [2008] EWHC 3030 (Fam) where the commissioning parents were the legal patents under Ukraine law, but the birth mother and her husband were the legal parents under UK law.

[172] [2006] UKHL 43.

[173] Paragraph [2].

[174] Paragraph 32.

[175] Paragraph 44.

with a traditional family situation where a child is conceived through donor insemination. It appears, therefore, that although a child may now have two legal parents of the same sex of equal legal status, 'some are more equal than others'. What, then, of the situation where one female partner donates an egg to the carrying woman and the child could be said to have a biological link to both of them? What are the implications for families where the genetic father is a known donor, but the child is being brought up by two women in a civil partnership who are the child's only legal parents? For now there are perhaps more questions than answers as families, professionals and the courts endeavour to make the right decisions for this new generation of children born of new technology and new law.

Chapter 2

PARENTAL RESPONSIBILITY

DEFINING PARENTAL RESPONSIBILITY

2.1 Parental responsibility is defined by s 3(1) of the Children Act 1989 as:

'all the rights, duties, powers, responsibilities and authority which by law a parent of a child has in relation to the child and his property.'

2.2 A person does not have to be a parent in order to hold parental responsibility. More than one person can have parental responsibility for a child.[1] In practical terms, it represents confirmation to the outside world that the holder has the right to be involved in the child's life and make significant decisions for them such as where they go to school or whether they have medical treatment. For unmarried fathers it is also a signifier of their status as the father.[2] For unmarried fathers and other people who are not in fact parents but are looking after a child day-to-day it can be crucial in the event of an emergency requiring urgent decisions when the child is with them.

2.3 The fact that a person who is a parent does not have parental responsibility for the child does not affect their statutory duty to maintain the child, or any rights which he or she may have in relation to a child's property after his death.[3]

2.4 The circumstances in which parental responsibility can be acquired are limited and restricted by statute. For children born before 6 April 2009 to families where the nurturing parents are in a same sex relationship, having parental responsibility is often the only way in which the other woman or man parenting them will be recognised as having a significant role in the child's life by third parties (unless the partner adopts the child). If the people parenting the child are married or in a civil partnership, being a 'child of the family' does not automatically confer parental responsibility[4] on the partner who is not a legal parent.

2.5 The decisions which families take about their family structure, the arrangements for conception, registration, and the status of the relationship of the adults involved is crucial to the determination of who will have parental responsibility for the children in that family. For children being brought up by

---

[1]   CA 1989, s 2(5).
[2]   *Re H (Parental Responsibility)* [1998] 1 FLR 855.
[3]   CA 1989, s 3(4).
[4]   But an application can be made under CA 1989, s 4A or 4ZA.

people in same sex relationships where there are often 3 or 4 significant adults involved, the potential range of family structures possible is wider and more complex. Wherever families have a clear view about who they want the important people in a child's life to be, there are steps they can take to achieve that goal. It is always better to tackle these questions by planning or agreement when making the decision to have a child, or when the child is born, than to try to tackle them retrospectively when a breakdown in relationship or communication has taken place. That is not to say that arrangements are set in stone, over time priorities and circumstances may change and the decisions made may have to be reviewed. Some decisions will be more permanent in effect than others. The following guidance is intended to help families make decisions about the structure which they want for their family, and to be aware of the factors they need to consider if the child is born in England or Wales:

(1)   The birth mother always has parental responsibility at birth.[5] It can only be removed by adoption or a parental order being made.

(2)   Where the birth mother is married at the time of the child's birth, irrespective of the date of birth, her husband will automatically have parental responsibility at birth if he is the legal father.[6] It can only be removed by adoption or a parental order being made.

(3)   If the child's mother and father marry after the child is born, the father will acquire parental responsibility[7] as though he always had it.

(4)   If the mother is in a civil partnership at the time of the child's conception and the child is conceived after 6 April 2009 via assisted conception, the civil partner will acquire parental responsibility for the child by virtue of being the parent and in a civil partnership.[8] It can only be removed by adoption or a parental order being made.

(5)   In relation to a child conceived after 6 April 2009, even if the birth mother subsequently enters into a civil partnership, the civil partner will only acquire parental responsibility for the child as a step-parent[9] if she was not a second female parent at the time of the birth: in other words, if two women want to have a child together and then later go through a civil partnership, the civil partner will not automatically become a second female parent or acquire parental responsibility by virtue of that ceremony.

(6)   Where the mother and father are not married to each other the father will not have parental responsibility automatically. If the child was born prior to 1 December 2003 the father will not have parental responsibility from

---

[5]   CA 1989, s 2.
[6]   CA 1989, s 2(1).
[7]   CA 1989, s 4(1).
[8]   HFEA 1990, s 42 and CA 1989, s 2(1A).
[9]   CA 1989, s 4A.

birth even where his name is on the birth certificate as the child's father. If he is the legal father and his name is on the birth certificate of a child born after 1 December 2003 he will have parental responsibility for the child.[10]

If the birth mother conceives a child informally with a known donor intending to bring the child up on her own or with a female partner who is not a civil partner or second female parent, an important choice is to be made at the time of the birth as to whether to register the father's name on the birth certificate. The birth mother must agree to the registration of the father at the time of the birth if this is to occur at that point – it cannot be imposed on her.[11] If the two women bringing up the child choose to enter into a joint residence order,[12] they can create a situation where they are the only holders of parental responsibility for the child even though the father is a legal parent. The father could, however, apply for a parental responsibility order and if he obtained it he would have the right to have the birth certificate amended[13] to show himself as the father. Equally, if the father's name is subsequently entered on the birth certificate, he will acquire parental responsibility for the child.[14]

(7) If the birth mother is not married or in a civil partnership at the time of the birth, but another woman is a second female parent having met the agreed female parenthood conditions,[15] that woman will have parental responsibility if she is also named as the second female parent on the child's birth certificate, whether at the time of the birth or subsequently.[16] Again, it is the birth mother who has control over the registration process at the time of the child's birth. If the second female parent is not named on the birth certificate at the time of the birth, she could, however, apply for a parental responsibility order and if she obtained it she would have the right to have the birth certificate amended[17] to show her as a second female parent.

(8) If the birth mother is not married or in a civil partnership with the father or second female parent, she can enter into a parental responsibility agreement with the father or second female parent, or they can apply for a parental responsibility order.[18]

(9) If a birth mother marries or enters into a civil partnership with someone who is not a parent after the child's birth, both parents with parental responsibility, with the agreement of the step-parent, may provide for the step-parent to have parental responsibility for the child, or the step-parent

---

[10] CA 1989, s 4(1)(a) but note the case of *AAA v Ash* [2010] 1 FLR 1 (FD) clarifies that the man must be both the father and on the birth certificate validly for this to be the position.

[11] BRDA 1953, s 10A.

[12] CA 1989, s 12(2).

[13] BRDA 1953, s 10A.

[14] CA 1989, s 4(1)(a).

[15] Under HFEA 2008, s 43.

[16] CA 1989, s 4ZA(1)(a).

[17] BRDA 1953, s 10A.

[18] CA 1989, ss 4A and 4ZA.

can apply for a parental responsibility order.[19] The mother, father and step-parent would then share parental responsibility. The father's partner could also acquire parental responsibility by agreement or order in the same way if the father marries or enters into a civil partnership. In this way a child conceived with a known donor could have all four adults involved in parenting him or her and sharing parental responsibility.

(10) If the court makes a residence order in respect of someone who is the unmarried father of a child, or the second female parent of a child, the court shall also grant that person parental responsibility. That parental responsibility is independent of the residence order and will endure even if the residence order does not.[20] This form of parental responsibility is, however, capable of being revoked.[21]

(11) Any other person who has a residence order in respect of a child will have parental responsibility while that residence order endures, irrespective of whether that person is a parent.[22] The scope of that parental responsibility is, however, more restricted than the parental responsibility of a parent. Their consent would not be required before an adoption could take place, for example.[23]

More than one person can hold a residence order in respect of a child, and more than one person can hold parental responsibility for a child. If, for example, the mother and (registered) father agree that the mother's civil partner should have parental responsibility, all three could hold parental responsibility together via the mother and her partner having a shared or joint residence order.

A residence order does not only arise where there is family breakdown, it can be used by agreement while partners are together to reflect that a child lives with more than one person and that the partners want both to have parental responsibility. This route has been commonly used prior to the HFEA 2008, for example where the birth mother has conceived via artificial insemination, a joint residence order obtained by agreement allows both women parenting the child to be the holders of parental responsibility.

(12) Any testamentary guardian[24] or special guardian will have parental responsibility for the child, which (s)he/they can exercise to the exclusion of the legal parent(s) but without extinguishing the parental responsibility of the legal parent(s).[25]

---

[19]   CA 1989, s 4A.
[20]   CA 1989, s 12 (1) and (1A).
[21]   CA 1989, ss 4ZA(5) and 4(2A).
[22]   CA 1989, s 12(2).
[23]   CA 1989, s 12(3).
[24]   CA 1989, s 5(6).
[25]   CA 1989, s 14C.

(13) Any adoptive parent will hold parental responsibility for a child. The adoption order will remove the parental responsibility of those who held it prior to adoption[26] unless it is a 'step-parent' adoption[27] where only the mother or father's partner adopts in which case the mother or father's parental responsibility remains intact.

(14) Anyone who holds a parental order in respect of a child will also have parental responsibility for the child, and the parental order will remove the parental responsibility of anyone who held it prior to the parental order.[28]

(15) Any holder of a care order[29] or emergency protection order[30] will also have parental responsibility. If the local authority acquires a care order, however, this will operate to extinguish any residence order, and therefore the parental responsibility of any person who has that only by virtue of the residence order.[31]

2.6 The requirement for parents who are not married or civil partnered to obtain an agreement or order, or be named on the birth certificate in order to have parental responsibility, has been accepted as a valid difference in treatment by both the European Court of Human Rights[32] and the European Court of Justice.[33]

ACQUIRING PARENTAL RESPONSIBILITY BY AGREEMENT OR ORDER

Parental responsibility agreement

2.7 The civil partner or step-parent can acquire parental responsibility by entering into a parental responsibility agreement with the birth mother, or by applying for a parental responsibility order.[34] There is a prescribed form for entering into a parental responsibility agreement which can be downloaded from the Courts Service website at www.justice.gov.uk, or should be available from the local family proceedings court or county court. It contains requirements for evidence of identity to be presented and must be officially

---

[26] Adoption Act 1976, s 12 or ACA 2002, s 46.

[27] Under ACA 2002, s 51.

[28] Also Adoption Act 1976, s 12 or ACA 2002, s 46 read in conjunction with the Parental Orders (Human Fertilisation and Embryology) Regulations 1994 or 2010.

[29] CA 1989, s 33.

[30] CA 1989, s 44(4).

[31] CA 1989, s 91.

[32] *B v the UK* [2000] 1 FLR 1.

[33] *J McB v LE* (C400/10) PU [2011] 1 FLR.

[34] CA 1989, s 4A(1).

witnessed by a justice of the peace or court clerk/court official to be valid. A parental responsibility agreement will not have effect unless it is on the prescribed form.[35]

2.8   There are 3 different forms depending on whether the agreement is for

(i)   Parental responsibility between mother and father: C(PRA1).

(ii)   Parental responsibility between mother and second female parent: C(PRA3).

(iii)   Parental responsibility for a step-parent: C(PRA2). This last requires the signatures of both parents (where there are two legal parents) and the step-parent.

There are notes for guidance which accompany the forms on the Courts Service website. Examples of the forms can be found at Appendix 2.

Application for a parental responsibility order

2.9   A parental responsibility order can be applied for quite simply by issuing Form C1 at the local court and then serving a copy on each respondent together with notice of the hearing[36] unless proceedings concerning the child are already ongoing, in which case a C2 should be used.

2.10   The application forms are also available on the Courts Service website or from the court. The respondents will be any one already having parental responsibility for the child.[37] Where the grant of parental responsibility is hotly contested by the birth mother after the breakdown of a relationship and there can be difficult court proceedings to decide the issue.

2.11   The range of people who could apply for a parental responsibility where they do not have it already order are limited by statute[38] to:

(1)   Legal fathers not married to the mother.

(2)   Legal second parents (whether male or female) not married or civil partnered to the mother.

(3)   Spouses or civil partners of either mother or father.

---

[35]   CA 1989, s 4(2).
[36]   Together with Form C1A where it is alleged that the subject child is at risk of suffering harm. Note that Part 3 of the FPR 2010 and PD 3A apply to applications for parental responsibility so that there is an obligation on the parties to attend a Mediation and Information Assessment meeting prior to issuing an application if there is a dispute as to whether the order should be made.
[37]   FPR 2010, r 12.3.
[38]   CA 1989, ss 4, 4ZA and 4A.

No other freestanding application for a parental responsibility order can be made.

2.12 Where a court makes a parental responsibility order, or there is a parental responsibility agreement, in favour of a legal parent who is not named on the child's birth certificate, acquiring parental responsibility entitles that parent to apply to the Registrar for the re-registration of the child's birth to show the other parent as a parent of the child.[39]

When will the court make a parental responsibility order if it is disputed?

2.13 The reported decisions on the acquisition of parental responsibility are at present largely focussed on considering when an unmarried father will be granted parental responsibility following breakdown of the parental relationship. These authorities may provide some guidance for same sex parents or step-parents as well in situations where the applicant for parental responsibility was in a relationship with the mother or father and bringing up the child with him or her, and that relationship has broken down.

2.14 In the case of *Re G (A Minor) (Parental Responsibility Order)* Balcolmbe LJ held:[40]

> 'the making of a parental responsibility order requires the judge to adopt the welfare principle as the paramount consideration. But having said that, I should add that, of course, it is well established by authority that, other things being equal, it is always to a child's welfare to know and, wherever possible, to have contact with both its parents, including the parent with whom it is not normally resident, if the parents have separated. Therefore, prima facie, it must necessarily also be for the child's benefit or welfare that it has an absent parent sufficiently concerned and interested to want to have a parental responsibility order. In other words, I approach this question on the basis that where you have a concerned although absent father, who fulfils the other test about which I spoke in *Re H*, namely having shown a degree of commitment towards the child, it being established that there is a degree of attachment between the father and the child, and that his reasons for applying for the order are not demonstrably improper or wrong, then prima facie it would be for the welfare of the child that such an order should be made.'

There would appear to be no reason why the same considerations would not apply to a second female parent seeking to acquire parental responsibility.

2.15 What is less settled is the court's approach to acquisition of parental responsibility by parents or step-parents who do not automatically have it in a situation where the child has more than two parents in a psychological sense, and the parents have different roles, or where the parents never intended to

---

[39] BRDA 1953, s 10A.
[40] [1994] 1 FLR 504.

parent together. Different considerations might apply when considering the grant of parental responsibility to the the civil partner of a father, for example. The concept of 'principal parents' and 'secondary parents' is starting to emerge from the case of *ML v AR*[41] but this concept has yet to be reviewed by the court of appeal.

2.16 It remains always the position than in considering a disputed application the child's welfare is paramount, and it must be better for the child for the order to be made than for no order to be made.[42]

2.17 In the recent case of *R v R*[43] the High Court held that it was not appropriate under Children Act 1989, s 4A(1)(b) for the mother's husband to be granted parental responsibility for the child whom he had initially believed to be his biological child. The court's concern was that it would be likely to lead to conflict with the mother and was not warranted by the role which the man could be expected, in that case, to have in the child's life in the future. Similar considerations might be applied if an application were made by a mother's or father's civil partner who is not the legal or biological parent of the child for parental responsibility on the breakdown of that relationship, but would be likely to depend on the significance of the particular relationship between the civil partner and the child.

2.18 In the case of *Re D*[44] in which a child was being brought up by two women and the father applied for parental responsibility, the court granted him parental responsibility but on condition that the father agreed not to contact the school or healthcare professionals involved with the child. In contrast, in the case of *R v E and F*[45] the court dismissed the biological father's application for parental responsibility. In the case of *Re B (Role of Biological Father)*[46] the court considered that notwithstanding the biological father's commitment and motivation, it was not in that child's best interests for the father, who was also his uncle in the sense of being the brother of the mother's partner, to share parental responsibility with the two women caring for him.

2.19 What is clear from the court's approach to date is that if parental responsibility is disputed in the context of an alternative family relationship where a number of different adults are involved in the legal, biological or social parentage of a child, the court is likely to have to survey the whole of the relevant adults' relationship and intentions in relation to the child as well as the course of the development of the child's relationship with each adult, and issues of parental responsibility will be considered alongside issues of residence and contact. This is discussed further in chapter 4.

---

[41]   [2011] EWHC 2455 (Fam).
[42]   CA 1989, s 1(1) and (5).
[43]   [2011] EWHC 1535 (Fam).
[44]   [2006] EWHC 2 (Fam).
[45]   [2010] EWHC 417 (Fam).
[46]   [2007] EWHC 1952 (Fam).

Application for a residence order

2.20 For those people not able to make a freestanding application for parental responsibility, it can also be acquired where the court makes a residence order, and such an order can be made by consent without the need for protracted court proceedings. Joint residence orders (a residence order in favour of two people living together) have long been used by same sex couples to ensure they both have parental responsibility for a child they are bringing up together and where they are not civil partnered. In practice, if two people who care for a child approach the court in a unified way seeking a joint residence order to ensure they both have parental responsibility, the court is almost certainly going to make the order, which would be by consent, whilst it just concerns the two of them and the child. An application for a residence order is made simply by issuing Form C100 at the local court[47] and serving a copy on each respondent.

2.21 However, if the child's father has parental responsibility (for example because he is named on the birth certificate) he will have to be given notice of the application and therefore could object.[48] If he does not have parental responsibility and wishes to object but becomes aware of the application, he could apply for a parental responsibility order and ask for this application to be joined with the mother's and partner's application for joint residence, or apply for leave to be joined as a party in the proceedings, and then still object. If it is anticipated that the application will disputed, it will be necessary to comply with the pre-action protocol which requires the parties to attend a Mediation Information and Assessment meeting prior to issue.[49]

2.22 Shared residence orders, namely a residence order in favour of two or more people who are not living together, are sometimes also made by the courts to allow people playing a parenting role in the child's life to acquire parental responsibility where there is no other route, even where the birth mother objects, if it is in the child's best interests. The case of *Re A*[50] involved an opposite sex couple in a dispute about a child where the man was not the genetic or legal father, but had parented the child and was a psychological father in all other respects. The court approved the making of a shared residence order as being the only method of enabling him to have parental responsibility and recognise his role as a nurturing and psychological parent.

2.23 A shared residence order can be appropriate in these circumstances even where the child does not spend equal time in both homes, and even when both homes are a considerable distance apart. The decision in *Re G*[51] is an example of a case where a shared residence order was made to allow the non-birth mother to have parental responsibility where she was not a legal parent and the

---

[47] FPR 2010, PD 5A together with C1A if the child is at risk of harm.
[48] FPR 2010, r 12.3.
[49] FPR 2010, Part 3 and PD 3A.
[50] [2008] 2 FLR 1593.
[51] [2006] UKHL 43.

court was concerned that her role was being marginalised by the birth mother. The birth mother had moved to Cornwall from the Midlands to try to reduce the involvement of the non birth mother in the children's lives. The Court of Appeal had provided for the children to spend the majority of their time with the non-birth mother under the terms of the shared residence order, but the House of Lords disagreed with this approach as giving insufficient weight to the importance of the genetic and gestational link of the birth mother to the children where they were, in fact, having proper time with the other mother. The House of Lords provided for the majority of the children's time to be spent instead with the birth mother in Cornwall, but the shared residence order remained in place.

2.24   In the case of *T v T*[52] the Court of Appeal made a shared residence order between the mother and the father and the mother's partner, with the effect that all 3 adults shared residence and parental responsibility.

2.25   Someone who is not a parent of a child will require the leave of the court to apply for a residence order unless they have lived with the child for 3 years[53] or have the consent of everyone who already has parental responsibility for the child.[54] Therefore, if the child's father has parental responsibility, the mother's partner will have to obtain his consent or the permission of the court to make an application for a shared residence order. If leave is required, the court will have to consider the applicant's connection with the child and any risk there might be of disrupting the child's life to the extent that he might be harmed by it when deciding whether to grant leave.[55] An application for leave is made on Form C2 and should usually be filed with a draft C100.[56]

2.26   Parental responsibility which arises as a result of a residence order only endures for as long as the residence order endures.[57] Applications for residence and contact orders are considered in more detail in chapter 4.

---

[52]   [2010] EWCA Civ 1366.
[53]   CA 1989, s 10(5).
[54]   CA 1989, s 10(5)(c).
[55]   CA 1989, s 10(9).
[56]   A leave application is a FPR 2010, Part 18 application. See PD 18A.
[57]   CA 1989, s 12(2).

Chapter 3

SURROGACY

3.1   Surrogacy is an extremely complex arena. This chapter is not a substitute for expert advice on the individual situation, and anyone contemplating becoming involved in a surrogacy arrangement in any way is advised to seek specialist advice before embarking on such involvement.

WHAT IS SURROGACY?

3.2   In English law, surrogacy is an arrangement between a person or couple, (commonly called the commissioning or intended parent or parents), and a gestational mother, which is made *before* the gestational mother begins to carry the child, with a view to the child being handed over to and cared for by someone other than the gestational mother, usually the commissioning parent(s).[1]

3.3   The key factors which make an arrangement 'surrogacy' are therefore:

- the arrangement is made before the gestational mother begins to carry the child;

- the arrangement is for the child to be handed over after the birth.

3.4   In establishing whether an arrangement constitutes 'surrogacy', it is irrelevant whether the gestational mother is genetically related to the child, or whether the commissioning parent(s) are genetically related to the child, either one or both.

3.5   In establishing whether an arrangement constitutes surrogacy for the purposes of English law, it is also irrelevant whether the child is being carried in England and Wales, or whether the arrangement is made in England and Wales.

3.6   A surrogacy arrangement may involve:

(a)   the commissioning parent or parents both being the genetic parent of the child;

---

[1]   Surrogacy Arrangements Act 1985, s 1.

(b)   neither commissioning parent or parents being genetically related to the child;

(c)   neither the commissioning parent or parents or the gestational mother being genetically related to the child;

(d)   one commissioning parent and the gestational mother being the child's genetic parent;

(f)   one commissioning parent and a donor being the child's genetic parents;

(g)   two donors being the genetic parents.

3.7   An arrangement where the birth mother is both the genetic mother and gestational mother is sometimes referred to as traditional surrogacy. Where a donated egg/embryo is implanted in the birth mother this is sometimes referred to as gestational surrogacy.[2] In this chapter the gestational mother is referred to as the surrogate mother, and the child born to her the surrogate child.

3.8   The genetic heritage of the surrogate child will have different implications for the eventual legal parentage of the child in different countries, but if the child is carried pursuant to a surrogacy arrangement it falls within the Surrogacy Act 1985 irrespective of genetic parentage. Legal parentage following surrogacy is dealt with in chapter 1.

3.9   A surrogacy arrangement is not enforceable in the UK,[3] but nor is it illegal; in fact the current legal structure in England and Wales provides a proper mechanism for commissioning parents to become the legal parents in particular circumstances. Since 2010,[4] this mechanism has included provision for same sex partners to become the legal parents of a child following surrogacy without the need to adopt. This mechanism is called a parental order[5] (see **3.51** below). Commercial surrogacy is, however, illegal. This is discussed further below.

3.10   If the arrangement in question is not made before the pregnancy begins, it is not surrogacy. It does sometimes happen that arrangements are made for a child to be handed to someone other than the gestational mother *after* the child is conceived,[6] for example:

---

[2]   These terms are used by Stonewall in their 'Guide for Gay Dads'.
[3]   Surrogacy Arrangements Act 1985, s 1A.
[4]   HFEA 2008, s 54 came into force on 6 April 2010: see SI 2010/987.
[5]   HFEA 2008, s 54.
[6]   *Re H (A Minor) (Section 37 Direction)* [1993] 2 FLR 541 is an example of a case where a married couple agreed early in their pregnancy to allow two women to care for their child after it was born.

(a) an arrangement is made by a genetic and gestational mother who is already carrying a child to hand her child to someone else (who might be the child's father or not) after the birth because she can not care for it;

(b) an embryo is placed in a gestational mother in error by a clinic which is not her genetic child, and the child is handed to the genetic parents to care for after the birth (sometimes confusingly called 'unintentional surrogacy');

3.11 These scenarios are not 'surrogacy' and are outside the scope of this section. However, scenario (a) may fall within the definition of a 'commercial adoption' and therefore fall within the Convention on Protection of Children and Co-operation in Respect of Intercountry Adoption 1983.

WHAT IS COMMERCIAL SURROGACY?

3.12 Commercial surrogacy is not legal in the UK; in particular it is a criminal offence[7] to *make* or *negotiate* a commercial surrogacy agreement in the UK, or initiate or take part in any such negotiations.[8]

3.13 A surrogacy arrangement acquires a 'commercial' element if someone other than the surrogate mother receives a *payment* in respect of making, or negotiating or facilitating the making of, any surrogacy arrangement, or does those things with a view to receiving payment, in the UK.[9]

3.14 The law is intended to discourage and deter commercial surrogacy agencies, and advertising commercial surrogacy in the UK is illegal, including advertising for prospective surrogates, advertising that a person is looking for a surrogate mother, or advertising that a person is willing to negotiate or facilitate a surrogacy arrangement.[10]

3.15 Not for profit organisations do not commit offences in carrying out these acts, provided that any payment to that organisation does not exceed their reasonable costs of doing it.[11]

3.16 Clearly the fact that commercial surrogacy is prohibited in the UK makes it more difficult for prospective commissioning parents to enter into surrogacy arrangements in the UK, to find surrogate mothers, and to have all necessary safeguards in place around the surrogacy arrangement. The illegality of commercial surrogacy in the UK leaves UK surrogacy unregulated in the sense that:

---

[7] Surrogacy Arrangements Act 1985, s 4.
[8] Surrogacy Arrangements Act 1985, s 2.
[9] Surrogacy Arrangements Act 1985, s 2.
[10] Surrogacy Arrangements Act 1985, s 3.
[11] Sections 2(2A), (2B), (2C), (5A), (8A), (8B) inserted by the ACA 2002.

- there is no legal framework for screening or assessment of donors, gestational mothers or intended parents;

- there is no binding contract or legal status in place to protect intended parents or gestational mothers until a parental order, residence or adoption order is made some time after the birth;

- there are no legal requirements for intended parents to make provision for the children born pursuant to surrogacy arrangements in the event of their deaths.

3.17   On one view, this places intended surrogate parents in the same position as any parent who conceives a child naturally or informally via artificial insemination, perhaps with someone they do not know very well. There are many working within the surrogacy field, however, who feel strongly that the complexity of the arrangements needed to get from 'A' to 'P' (agreement to parental order), the potential for things to go wrong when a child is being carried by someone who never intended to bring that child up, the implications for the children born if the surrogacy arrangement fails or breaks down or the intended parents die, and the added layer of complexity for a surrogate child's sense of (legal and personal) identity mean that there should be proper regulation and thorough screening.

3.18   Commercial surrogacy arrangements made in other countries are not illegal in the UK in the sense that a UK national does not commit an offence by entering into or negotiating a commercial surrogacy arrangement abroad. Section 2 of the Surrogacy Arrangements Act 1985 sets out in detail the acts which are prohibited, and provides specifically that;

> 'No person shall on a commercial basis do any of the following acts in the United Kingdom.'

3.19   In other words, the prohibited acts are only offences if they are done in the United Kingdom. This is significant because it opens up the potential for parental orders to be made in the UK following a commercial surrogacy arrangement entered into outside the UK, and provided that the provisions of the s 54 of the HFEA 2008 are complied with and public policy is not offended, parental orders are available in the UK in respect of children born pursuant to a commercial surrogacy arrangement made in another country.

3.20   Considerable care must be taken to ensure that the provisions of s 54 of the HFEA 2008 are complied with and public policy not offended. In the context of the illegality of commercial surrogacy in this country, the HFEA 2008, and the HFEA 1990 Act before it, make a key distinction between payments of 'reasonable expenses' and other payments, whether to the surrogate mother, the applicants or someone else, and only allows reasonable expenses to be paid. Whilst the Surrogacy Act 1985 does not make a payment to or for the benefit of a surrogate mother or prospective surrogate mother illegal,[12] the prohibition on payments in s 54(8) of the HFEA 2008 firmly includes payments to the surrogate mother, so:

- whilst a surrogate mother is not liable to prosecution for receiving a payment; and

- an intended parent is not liable to prosecution for making a payment;[13]

- any third party involved in negotiating or facilitating that in the UK will be liable;[14] and

- the intended parents will not be able to secure a parental order if they make a payment to the surrogate mother or anyone else beyond reasonable expenses.

3.21 Section 54(8) of the HFEA 2008 does not apply solely to money or benefits given or received in the UK. The restrictions on payments of money or other benefits in s 54 apply equally to surrogacy arrangements made in the UK and to those made overseas following which an application for a parental order is made in the UK.

3.22 Section 54(8) of the HFEA 2008[15] provides that before making a parental order:

'The court must be satisfied that no money or other benefit (other than for expenses reasonably incurred) has been given or received by either of the applicants for or in consideration of –

(a) The making of the order,
(b) Any agreement [to the making of the order],
(c) The handing over of the child to the applicants, or
(d) The making of arrangements with a view to the making of the order,

unless authorised by the court.'

3.23 In addition to the provisions of s 54 of the HFEA itself, the child's welfare throughout its life is also the court's paramount consideration when considering an application for a parental order,[16] and the court must have regard to the matters set out in s 1 of the Adoption and Children Act 2002.

---

[12] Surrogacy Arrangements Act 1985, ss 2(2)(a) and 2(3).
[13] Surrogacy Arrangements Act 1985, s 2(2)(b).
[14] Unless they fall within the exceptions available for not-for profit organisations in the Surrogacy Arrangements Act.
[15] Which replaced s 30 of the HFEA 1990.
[16] The Human Fertilisation and Embryology (Parental Orders) Regulations 2010, SI 2010/985 imports the provisions of s 1 of the Adoption and Children Act 2002 (as well as other sections of that Act) into s 54 so that whenever the court considers an application for a parental order the welfare of the child throughout his/ her life will be paramount and the welfare checklist will apply.

3.24   In these two provisions, the legislation endeavours to strike a balance between recognising that the surrogate mother will inevitably incur expenses and require some financial support as a result of the pregnancy following a lawful surrogacy arrangement, and being concerned not to endorse a commercial surrogacy which contravenes public policy. Much of the case law since 1990 concerning whether a surrogacy arrangement can be converted into a parental order is therefore concerned with what constitutes 'reasonable expenses'. The legislation also recognises the horrendous implications for a surrogate child of being parentless or stateless if the surrogate mother does not wish to bring up the child, or is not recognised as the legal parent in her own country, and if the intended parents cannot secure an appropriate order to enable them to parent the child in the UK. The final line of s 54(8) of the HFEA 2008 therefore permits, in appropriate circumstances, the court to give retrospective authorisation to payments where they exceed reasonable expenses, and the provisions of s 1 of the ACA 2002 read together with s 54 of the HFEA 2008 require the court to make the order which best meets the child's welfare throughout his life. Mr Justice Hedley in the case of *Re X and Y*[17] said this of the competing considerations:

> 'I feel bound to observe that I find this process of authorisation most uncomfortable. What the court is required to do is to balance two competing and potentially irreconcilably conflicting concepts. Parliament is clearly entitled to legislate against commercial surrogacy and is clearly entitled to expect that the courts should implement that policy consideration in its decisions. Yet it is also recognised that as the full rigour of that policy consideration will bear on one wholly unequipped to comprehend it let alone deal with its consequences (ie the child concerned) that rigour must be mitigated by the application of a consideration of that child's welfare. That approach is both humane and intellectually coherent. The difficulty is that it is almost impossible to imagine a set of circumstances in which by the time the case comes to court, the welfare of any child (particularly a foreign child) would not be gravely compromised (at the very least) by a refusal to make an order.'

3.25   In the case of *Re S*[18] Mr Justice Hedley further considered the particular difficulty of cases where intended parents enter perfectly lawfully into surrogacy arrangements abroad, and then seek approval of those arrangements by applying for a parental order here subsequently. He considered that this raises matters of public policy and highlighted three particular public policy objectives in any case of this nature:

> '(1) To ensuring that commercial surrogacy agreements are not used to circumvent childcare laws in this country, so as to result in the approval of arrangements in favour of people who would not have been approved as parents under any set of existing arrangements in this country.

---

[17]   [2008] EWHC 3030 (Fam), [2009] 1 FLR 733.
[18]   [2009] EWHC 2977 (Fam).

(2) The court should be astute not to be involved in anything that looks like the simple payment for effectively buying children overseas. That has been ruled out in this country and the court should not be party to any arrangements which effectively allow that.

(3) The court should be astute to ensure that sums of money which might look modest in themselves are not in fact of such a substance that they overbear the will of a surrogate.'

3.26 In the earlier case of *Re X and Y*[19] Mr Justice Hedley also identified three questions which the court should ask itself in relation to public policy issues:

'(i)   was the sum paid disproportionate to reasonable expenses?
(ii)   were the applicants acting in good faith and without "moral taint" in their dealings with the surrogate mother?
(iii) were the applicants party to any attempt to defraud the authorities?'

In relation to the first question the answer may vary considerably depending upon the particular circumstances of the case and where the surrogacy arrangement was made:[20]

'The whole basis of assessment will be quite different in say urban California to rural India.'

3.27 In the recent case of *Re L (Commercial Surrogacy)*[21] Mr Justice Hedley was again faced with a situation where the applicants for a parental order had clearly made payments of more than 'reasonable expenses' to the surrogate mother. He said in that case:

'This case relates to a commercial surrogacy agreement made in Illinois, USA. There is no doubt that the agreement was wholly lawful under the law of Illinois just as there is no doubt that it would continue to be unlawful under the 2008 Act in this country. The reason is simple: no payments other than reasonable expenses are lawful here whereas no such restriction applies in Illinois. It is clear to me that payments in excess of reasonable expenses were made in this case. Accordingly no parental order can be made unless those expenses are authorised retrospectively by the court pursuant to s 54(8) of the 2008 Act.'

3.28 Mr Justice Hedley did, in fact give retrospective authorisation in both *Re S* and *Re L* and parental orders were made. He also made it plain in *Re L* that the matters which he had highlighted as being public policy concerns in *Re S*[22] still apply, but the effect of the importation of s 1 of the ACA 2002 into the provisions of s 54 of the HFEA 2008 is that the balance between the child's

---

[19]   [2008] EWHC 3030 (Fam), [2009] 1 FLR 733.
[20]   *Re X and Y* at para 22 of the judgment.
[21]   [2010] EWHC 3416 (Fam) at paras 3 and 4.
[22]   [2009] EWHC 2977 (Fam).

welfare and public policy is now weighted decisively in favour of welfare, albeit that the court should continue to scrutinise and police[23] the public policy issues identified in *Re S.*[24] He held in *Re L*:[25]

> 'It must follow that it will only be in the clearest case of the abuse of public policy that the court will be able to withhold an order if otherwise welfare considerations support its making.'

3.29 The Surrogacy Arrangements Act 1985 does not make it illegal for payment to be made to the surrogate mother, in fact, in s 2(3) which defines when a person does an act on a 'commercial basis', it is provided specifically that 'In this subsection "payment" does not include payment to or for the benefit of a surrogate mother or prospective surrogate mother'. However *Re L (Commercial Surrogacy)*[26] is clear guidance that payments beyond reasonable expenses to the surrogate mother are 'unlawful' under s 54 of the HFEA 2008 even where they are made outside the UK. The burden will be on the applicants for a parental order to satisfy the court that any money or benefits given or received by either of them does not contravene s 54.[27] Also, following *Re L*,[28] any payment described as 'compensation' or similar is likely initially to be treated as going beyond reasonable expenses.

It is advisable for anyone intending to apply for a parental order to keep detailed records of the expenses for which payments are made with receipts if possible.

3.30 The most recent decision on the issue of whether commercial surrogacy arrangements entered into abroad should be retrospectively authorised here by the making of parental orders is *In the Matter of X and Y (Children)*,[29] where the President of the Family Division, Sir Nicholas Wall approved the judgments given by Mr Justice Hedley in this arena. He also approved, in that case, the making of parental orders in relation to children born in India pursuant to surrogacy arrangements where there were undoubtedly payments made beyond merely reasonable expenses. He accepted that the payments were nonetheless made in good faith, the authorities not defrauded, and the payments were 'not so disproportionate that the granting of a parental order would be an affront to public policy'.[30]

3.31 The prohibition against commercial surrogacy in the UK does not mean that a surrogacy arrangement in the UK has to be made between individuals who are known to each other. Surrogacy is often referred to as 'altruistic surrogacy' if the arrangements are made informally or the carrying mother is

---

23   *Re L* at para 12 of the judgment.
24   [2009] EWHC 2977 (Fam).
25   [2010] EWHC 3416 (Fam) at para 10 of the judgment.
26   [2010] EWHC 3416 (Fam).
27   Per Hedley J in relation to s 30 of the HFEA 1990 in *Re S* [2009] EWHC 2977.
28   [2010] EWHC 3416 (Fam) at para 7 of the judgment.
29   [2011] EWHC 3147 (Fam).
30   At paras 33 and 40.

known to or comes to know the commissioning parent(s) and offers to carry the baby out of a desire to assist the commissioning parent(s) to have a child. This is not the only alternative to commercial surrogacy in the UK. Despite the restrictions on commercial surrogacy, there are a number of legitimate organisations which offer valuable support to people wishing to enter into a surrogacy arrangement and who are careful to do so within the law in the UK, and enable surrogates, donors and intended parents to find each other, access support and share information. Some are not-for-profit organisations and therefore not offering services on a commercial basis. Others manage the restrictions partly by having their centre of interests outside the UK. Some UK based agencies, whilst not advertising for surrogates, keep a database of egg donors and gestational surrogates who have volunteered their assistance, and who are likely to have been screened and assessed by the agency.

The advice, counselling and experience which can be offered by the most experienced agencies cannot be overstated, but the quality of advice can vary significantly in this unregulated sector.

3.32 In the recent case of *TT*[31] Mr Justice Baker encouraged those considering surrogacy to seek the support of experienced and established agencies. In that case the intended parents, Mr and Mrs W, had registered on a number of surrogacy websites with a view to finding a surrogate mother, and the birth mother made contact with them. Mr W provided the sperm for inseminating the birth mother, but the arrangements between them broke down during the pregnancy. When the baby was 7 days old Mr W made an application for a residence order, and this was opposed by the birth mother. The case came to court as a contested application for residence of the child when the child was 5 months old, and had been living with the birth mother for that period. He found that both the birth mother and the intended parents had a lack of insight into the child's needs, and that their 'close involvement with the internet may inadvertently lead them to introduce their children to risk'. He ultimately concluded that the birth mother was, on balance, better able to meet the child's emotional needs, and made a residence order in her favour. But, of the way in which the birth of the child had come about he said this:

'In this country Parliament has passed a series of statutes governing surrogacy – see the Surrogacy Arrangements Act 1985, the Human Fertilisation and Embryology Act 1990 and most recently the Human Fertilisation and Embryology Act 2008. Amongst the guiding principles underpinning the legislation is the rule that no money or other benefit (other than expenses reasonably incurred) may be paid to the surrogate. Negotiating a surrogacy arrangement on a commercial basis is a criminal offence in this country. A number of agencies have been set up to facilitate surrogacy arrangements by making appropriate introductions, and providing advice and counselling to the parties. Those agencies have to be careful to ensure that the rules prohibiting commercial transactions are respected. Inevitably, however, the advent of the internet has facilitated the making of

---

[31]   [2011] EWHC 33 (Fam).

informal surrogacy arrangements between adults. In such cases, those entering the arrangement do not have the advantage of the advice, counselling and support that the established agencies provide.'

3.33 Conversely, the case of *Re G (Surrogacy: Foreign Domicile)*[32] provides a startling example of intended parents being seriously ill-advised by a well meaning surrogacy agency with expensive and complex consequences. In that case it emerged that a particular agency had advised dozens of parents domiciled abroad that they could obtain parental orders in England and Wales. In the case in question, the costs of unravelling this incorrect advice ran to £35,000. Mr Justice McFarlane observed:

> 'The court's understanding is that surrogacy agencies such as COTS are not covered by any statutory or regulatory umbrella and are, therefore, not required to perform to any recognised standard of competence. I am sufficiently concerned by the information uncovered in these two cases to question whether some form of inspection or authorisation should be required in order to improve the quality of advice that is given to individuals who seek to achieve the birth of a child through surrogacy. Given the importance of the issues involved when the life of a child is created in this manner, it is questionable whether the role of facilitating surrogacy arrangements should be left to groups of well-meaning amateurs. To this end, a copy of this judgment is being sent to the Minister of State for Children, Young People and Families for her consideration.'

3.34 Many surrogacy agencies feel strongly that they have a duty to offer a high level of support to intended parents, egg donors and gestational mothers to protect the children born following surrogacy arrangements. For them, this involves rigorous screening and careful legal, and, where appropriate, immigration, preparation and implementation, but the level of support and guidance which they provide can vary enormously. The requirements of donors, surrogates and intended parents can include:

- The egg donor to have medical, legal and psychological screening.

- The surrogate (and her partner) to have medical and legal screening, and the surrogate to have medical examinations and psychological screening.

- The intended parents to have medical and legal screening, and home visits from the social work team.

- The intended parent(s) to demonstrate their financial stability, and that they have made wills appointing a guardian(s) for the child(ren) in the event of their death(s).

- A contract to have been signed between the surrogate and intended parents even if the surrogacy takes place wholly in the UK on a non-commercial basis.

---

[32] [2007] EWHC 2814 (Fam).

WHAT ARE THE ROUTES TO A COMMISSIONING PARENT BECOMING THE CHILD'S CARER FOLLOWING SURROGACY?

Need for an order

3.35 It is vitally important that following a surrogacy arrangement, the legal status of the commissioning parents and their relationship to, and parental responsibility for, the child are established as quickly as possible. It is also vitally important that the route to doing this in each individual case is established and prepared for before the surrogate mother begins to carry the child, even though UK orders cannot be obtained until 6 weeks after the child is born.[33]

3.36 In England and Wales, the status of legal parenthood for a child is significant in wide ranging situations. It is also the case that legal parenthood in one country does not automatically result in recognition of that parenthood in other countries, whether the legal parenthood arises as a result of genetic parenthood or a court order. This is discussed in more detail in chapter 1.[34] The circumstances in which parents and non-parents can acquire parental responsibility for a child are discussed in detail in chapter 2.

3.37 The lack of cross-border recognition of legal parenthood can mean that a child's legal parents are different according to the laws of different countries; this is a particularly significant issue in the context of international surrogacy. The significance is not only important to the child; where it is particularly important to English intended parents that they are recognised as the legal parents here, it may be equally important to the overseas surrogate mother that she is not regarded as the legal mother there. It may therefore be necessary for there to be orders relating to parenthood in more than one jurisdiction.

3.38 Whilst it will often be in the child's best interests for those caring for him to become his or her legal parents under the law of England and Wales following surrogacy, or at least acquire parental responsibility, this is not always possible and there are particular perils and pitfalls following a surrogacy arrangement which require careful consideration, and which will apply at the very least in the period until the arrangements for the child's care can be formalised by a legal order.

---

[33] HFEA 2008, s 54(7) provides that any agreement given to a parental order in the first 6 weeks is not effective.

[34] Note that for immigration purposes, ACA 2002, s 67 which confers status on a person who is the subject of a parental order as though born to the holders of the parental order, by virtue of Sch 1 of the HFE (PO) Regulations 2010, does not apply for the purposes of the British Nationality Act 1981 or the Immigration Act 1971.

3.39   First, there are criminal sanctions attached to bringing a child into the UK for the purposes of adoption if statutory requirements have not been complied with.[35]

3.40   Secondly, there are legal restrictions in place to prevent anyone who is not an adoption agency offering a child for adoption, or handing a child over for the purposes of adoption, to someone other than an adoption agency or the child's parent, relative or guardian or partner of a parent of the child[36] (ie the parent and the partner are a couple[37]). Breach of the restrictions is a criminal offence.[38] When considering whether the proposed adopter is a parent of the child, it will be particularly important to establish that they are the legal parent, and not simply a genetic parent. For example where the surrogate mother is married and conceives a child via artificial insemination with a man not her husband who proposes to adopt the child, she and the prospective adopter would both be committing a criminal offence if the baby is simply handed over to the genetic father after birth.[39]

3.41   Thirdly, it is an offence for a person to remove a child from the UK for the purpose of an adoption unless the requirements of s 85 of the Adoption and Children Act 2002 are complied with.[40] So, for example, if foreign nationals enter into a surrogacy arrangement in the UK and the child is born in the UK, they cannot remove the child from the UK without first making an application under s 84 of the Adoption and Children Act for parental responsibility for this purpose.[41]

3.42   Fourthly, if a child is 'placed with' ie living with, people who are not the legal parents of the child, with the agreement of the mother, but not with a view to adoption, this may constitute a private fostering arrangement, even if one of the people with whom the child is placed is a genetic parent (see chapter 1 for discussion of legal and genetic parenthood).

3.43   Where a child[42] is cared for by and accommodated in the home of a person who is not a parent, person with parental responsibility or relative for more than 28 days, this amounts to a private fostering arrangement.[43] This means it is a placement subject to regulation, which in England means the

---

[35]   ACA 2002 – eg s 83(1)(a) which makes it a criminal offence for a person habitually resident in the UK to bring a child habitually resident elsewhere, into the UK for the purposes of adoption.

[36]   ACA 2002, s 92. The prohibition includes entering into an agreement with any person for the adoption of a child where no adoption agency is acting on behalf of the child, and extends to causing someone to offer a child for adoption or to offer to hand over a child.

[37]   ACA 2002, s 144(7).

[38]   ACA 2002, s 93.

[39]   The legal father will be the mother's husband unless it can be shown that he did not consent to the artificial insemination: s 35 of the HFEA 2008.

[40]   This also involves acquiring parental responsibility under ACA 2002, s 84.

[41]   See in particular *Re G (Surrogacy: Foreign Domicile)* [2007] EWHC 2814 (Fam).

[42]   Under 16, or if disabled under 18.

[43]   CA 1989, s 66.

Children (Private Arrangements for Fostering) Regulations 2005 are applicable, and in Wales, the Children (Private Arrangements for Fostering) (Wales) Regulations 2006. A private fostering arrangement in respect of a child does not confer parental responsibility on the carer,[44] even if they are a genetic parent. The regulations impose a number of requirements on people privately fostering children, notably the duty to notify the local authority of the arrangement and provide particular information.

3.44 In the context of a UK surrogacy, the subsequent care of the child is most likely to fall within the definition of a private fostering arrangement where either:

- a single person, or a couple who are not genetically related to the child, and therefore are not eligible to apply for a parental order[45] care for a child following a surrogacy agreement being implemented; or

- the surrogate mother is married and it cannot be demonstrated that her husband did not consent to the artificial insemination, and therefore he remains the legal father of the child, even though the commissioning parent is a genetic parent;[46] or

- the father is not in a marriage or civil partnership with his partner, but the child lives with the father's partner some of the time.

What type of order?

Residence orders

3.45 Residence orders do not change legal parentage, and do not operate to extinguish the gestational mother's parental responsibility. However, in the context of surrogacy they have an important role because:

- surrogacy arrangements are not enforceable in the UK;[47]

- any agreement to hand over the baby to the intended parent(s) sometimes breaks down before legal parentage has been changed;

- parental or adoption orders may not be available in the circumstances of the case.

3.46 The procedure for applications for residence orders, and the effect of making a residence order are considered in more detail in chapter 4 relating to private law applications. A residence order is sometimes the only route by which a person who is not a legal parent or step-parent can acquire parental

---

[44]   CA 1989, s 2(9).
[45]   HFEA 2008, s 54 requires at least one applicant to be the genetic parent of the child.
[46]   HFEA 2008, s 35.
[47]   Surrogacy Arrangements Act 1985, s 1A.

responsibility for a child. Legal parentage is considered in detail in chapter 1 and parental responsibility in chapter 2.

3.47 Examples of scenarios in which a residence order might be particularly important.

(a)   If the surrogate mother was married but separated, her husband would still be the child's legal father until such time as either a declaration of parentage displaces s 35 of the HFEA 2008 or the presumption of parentage, or a parental order is made if one is available, or the child is adopted (see chapter 1). In the meantime, if the genetic father was caring for the child he would be doing so without legal parentage or parental responsibility. A residence order would both provide him with parental responsibility[48] and ensure that child's residence with him is not a private fostering arrangement (see **3.44** above). If he is not the child's legal father he would require leave to apply for such an order.[49] Since a residence order can be made in favour of more than one person,[50] the genetic father and his partner could both potentially apply for residence orders if they are caring for the child together.

(b)   Although there is no such order as an 'interim residence order', in reality residence orders endure until they are changed by further order, and this might be for a short or long period. If it were necessary to secure parental responsibility for the child (following surrogacy) in the short term whilst an application for a parental order was pending, or whilst a declaration of parentage was being obtained, a residence order could be used to secure the child's welfare in the interim. They are also available immediately from birth.

(c)   If two men entered into a surrogacy arrangement with a woman and their relationship broke down before a parental order was made, a parental order would not be available to them.[51] The court could make a residence order in favour of either or both of them, whether or not they are living together,[52] to secure the arrangements as to with whom the child is to live.

(d)   If neither of the intended parents is domiciled in the UK, the court cannot make a parental order or adoption order in favour of them.[53] It may be that both intended parents are resident here and intending to live here for some time, but retain domiciles of origin in another country. A

---

[48]   CA 1989, s 12(2).
[49]   CA 1989, s 10.
[50]   CA 1989, s 11(4).
[51]   HFEA 2008, s 54 requires the applicants to be married, civil partners or in an enduring relationship.
[52]   CA 1989, s 11(4).
[53]   HFEA 2008, s 54(4)(b).

residence order could secure the child's residence with them until such time as they either return to their domicile of origin or demonstrate a change of domicile.[54]

(e)   A parental order is only available where both the surrogate mother, and any other person who is the parent of the child, but is not one of the applicants, freely, and with full understanding of what is involved, agree to the making of the order.[55] This is the corollary of surrogacy arrangements being unenforceable. If the surrogate mother does not hand the baby over, a parental order is no longer an option, but a residence order might be.

3.48   In the most recent decision concerning the breakdown of a surrogacy arrangement in the UK, *Re TT (A Minor)*[56] Mr Justice Baker refused the intended parents' application for a residence order. The arrangement had broken down whilst the mother was still carrying the child, the commissioning father was also the genetic father and he was married to the commissioning mother. The final hearing took place when the child was 5 months old. The judge applied the test as to which home the child was most likely to mature into a happy and balanced adult and achieve his fullest potential. There were concerns about the behaviour of both the mother and of the commissioning parents, but on balance the judge decided that the mother was better able to meet the whole of the child's needs and refused the residence application.

3.49   An earlier decision of Mr Justice Coleridge, *Re P (Surrogacy: Residence)*[57] concerned a child born further to a UK surrogacy arrangement in circumstances where the judge found that the mother had never intended to hand over the baby and had set out to deliberately deceive the commissioning parents. The judge carefully balanced all of the factors relevant to the question of in which home the child was most likely to mature into a happy and balanced adult and achieve his fullest potential, and made a residence order in favour of the commissioning parents. The mother's appeal was dismissed by the Court of Appeal.[58]

---

[54]   For a discussion as to domicile of origin and domicile of choice see recent Court of Appeal cases *Holiday v Musa* [2010] EWCA Civ 355, [2010] 2 FLR 702 and *Cyganik v Agulian* [2006] EWCA Civ 129. In *Re G (Surrogacy: Foreign Domicile)* [2007] EWHC 2814 (Fam) both parents were domiciled in Turkey but the child was born here pursuant to a surrogacy arrangement; in that case McFarlane J made an order pursuant to s 84 of the ACA 2002 giving the intended parents parental responsibility on the basis that the court was satisfied that they intended to apply to adopt the child in Turkey. In the case of *Z v B, C and CAFCASS* [2011] EWHC 3181 (Fam) the intended parents had arrived from Israel 2 years before the child's birth. The court accepted that they had acquired a domicile of choice in England.

[55]   HFEA 2008, s 54(6), unless one of those people cannot be found or is incapable of giving agreement per s 54(7).

[56]   [2011] EWHC 33 (Fam).

[57]   [2008] 1 FLR 177.

[58]   [2007] EWCA Civ 1053.

Effect of a residence order

3.50 Where a residence order is made parental responsibility is shared with the mother and anyone else holding parental responsibility. That parental responsibility will endure until revoked if made in favour of the legal father or parent, but will end with the ending of the residence order otherwise.[59] Whilst it is in force, no one can cause the child to be known by a new surname, or remove the child from the UK for more than 28 days.[60] The court may make a contact order requiring the person or people with whom the child lives to allow the child to visit or stay with or have contact with the mother or someone else.[61]

Parental orders

3.51 Since the HFEA Act 1990, it has been possible for a married couple to apply for a 'parental order' if either or both of them were the genetic parents of the child and it had been carried by a surrogate mother, so as to make the married couple the legal parents of the child,[62] provided the provisions of s 30 of the HFEA 1990 were complied with.

3.52 Since s 54 of the HFEA Act 2008 came into force on 6 April 2010,[63] it repealed and replaced s 30 of the HFEA 1990. For the first time, the HFEA Act 2008 extended the availability of parental orders to couples (but not single applicants) in a civil partnership or enduring family relationship (same sex or opposite sex)[64] in respect of children born after 6 April 2010, or applications made within 6 months of 6 April 2010 where the child was already living with the applicants.[65]

3.53 The availability of parental orders for 6 months after 6 April 2010 enabled children who had been living with same sex commissioning parents, for example pursuant to a residence order, to become the legal child(ren) of their de facto parents provided the criteria in s 54 of the HFEA 2008 were fulfilled. Since that 6 month period has now passed, there is no longer any mechanism for children who have been living with same sex parents pursuant to a surrogacy arrangement since before the HFEA 2008 came into force to become the subject of parental orders. This section is therefore confined to guidance relating to future applications in relation to children not yet born or not yet 6 months old.

3.54 The legal effect of a parental order is similar to the legal effect of adoption: it allows the holders of the order to be treated as a matter of law as

---

[59]   CA 1989, s 12.
[60]   CA 1989, s 13.
[61]   CA 1989, s 8.
[62]   Per s 30 of the HFEA 1990.
[63]   HFE (PO) Regulations 2010.
[64]   HFEA 2008, s 54(2).
[65]   Human Fertilisation and Embryology Act 2008 (Commencement No 3) Order 2010, SI 2010/987 and s 54(11) of the HFEA 2008.

the parents of the child for all purposes, and means that no other person is, in law, the parent of that child.[66] Legal parenthood is discussed in more detail in chapter 1 and adoption in chapter 5.

3.55 An application for a parental order is attractive to many because it is a more straightforward process than adoption, and does not require, for example, that the applicants for a parental order be assessed as prospective adopters by the local authority. The circumstances in which a parental order can be applied for and made are set out in s 54 of the HFEA 2008, and require a number of very specific criteria to be met. If they are not met, then a parental order is not available.

3.56 If they are met, a parental order is not inevitable. Section 54(1) makes it clear that these are the circumstances in which a parental order *may* be made, not shall be made, and as such there is an element of discretion. In addition to the provisions of s 54 of the HFEA itself, the child's welfare throughout its life is also the court's paramount consideration when considering an application for a parental order,[67] and the court must have regard to the matters set out in s 1 of the Adoption and Children Act 2002 when considering whether to make a parental order. These matters are (in general terms):

(a)   the child's ascertainable wishes and feelings (which can realistically only be by inference given that the child must be less than 6 months old);

(b)   the child's particular needs;

(c)   the likely effect on the child throughout his or her life of having ceased to be a member of his or her original family and becoming a person who is the subject of a parental order;

(d)   the child's age, sex, background and relevant characteristics;

(e)   any harm (within the meaning of the Children Act 1989) which the child has suffered or is at risk of suffering;

(f)   the relationship (not limited to legal relationships) which the child has with relatives and any other person who has a relevant relationship with the child.

---

[66]   An application for a parental order is described in s 54 of the HFEA 2008 as an order providing for the child to be treated in law as the child of the applicants. It is to be read together with s 67 of the Adoption and Children Act 2002 which applies where a parental order is made pursuant to the HFE (PO) Regulations 2010, Sch 1 to provide that a person who is the subject of a parental order is to be treated in law as if born as the child of the persons who obtained the order. Subject however to ACA 2002, s 74.

[67]   The HFE (PO) Regulations 2010 imports the provisions of s 1 of the ACA2002 (as well as other sections of that Act) into s 54 so that whenever the court considers an application for a parental order the welfare of the child throughout his/ her life will be paramount and the welfare checklist will apply.

This last provision specifically requires the court to consider the likelihood of the child's relationship with a relative continuing, the ability and willingness of any of the child's relatives to provide him or her with a secure environment in which (s)he can develop and otherwise meet his needs, and the wishes and feelings of any of the child's relatives.[68] This must be particularly relevant in a surrogacy situation if the child's surrogate mother and her husband/civil partner (if she has one) cannot offer the child a home and are not willing to do so. Indeed there may be situations in which they cannot do so as under the law of their country they are not the legal parents and the child is not a citizen of that country.[69] In any balancing situation, it must be the welfare of the child which carries the greatest weight,[70] and this must involve careful scrutiny of the alternatives for the child if the order is not made.

3.57 When considering s 1 of the ACA 2002 and carrying out the balancing exercise, and given that agreement of the surrogate mother and any other legal parent is one of the criteria for the making of a parental order,[71] the court would have to have a high level of concern about the child's welfare before refusing to make a parental order where there is agreement to it. One scenario in which this might occur is where the payment to the surrogate mother was so disproportionate as to be said to have overborne her free will in deciding whether to give agreement to it.[72]

The necessary criteria for the making of a parental order

Applicants

3.58 There must be two applicants who are either married, civil partners, or living as partners in an enduring family relationship.[73]

The relevant time for determining whether there are two applicants satisfying these criteria will normally be at the time of making the application and the order – in particular there is also a requirement for the child's home to be with the applicants at the time of the application *and* the order, under s 54(4), but in exceptional circumstances the court can make a parental order where the criteria were satisfied at the time of the application – in particular in the case of

---

[68] See ACA 2002, s 1(4)(a)–(f), as amended by the the HFE (PO) Regulations 2010.

[69] This situation arose in the case of *Re IJ (Foreign Surrogacy Agreement: Parental Order)* [2011] EWHC 921 (Fam), [2011] 2 FLR 646 when the child was born further to a commercial surrogacy arrangement in the Ukraine, and under the law of the Ukraine the birth mother and her husband were not the child's legal parents, the applicants were. Unless the court retrospectively sanctioned payments in excess of reasonable expenses and made a parental order, the child would be parentless and stateless.

[70] Per Hedley J in *Re L* [2010] EWHC 3146 (Fam).

[71] HFEA 2008, s 54(6) unless she is incapable of giving agreement or cannot be found per s 54(7).

[72] This being one of the factors which the court should take into account when considering whether to retrospectively authorise payments in excess of reasonable expenses per Hedley J in *Re S* [2009] EWHC 2977 (Fam) as approved by Wall P in *In the matter of X and Y* [2011] EWHC 3147 (Fam).

[73] Which is not within the prohibited degrees of relationship; i e two sisters or brothers cannot apply, or father and son etc; s 54(1) and (2).

A, A v P, P, B[74] where the husband had died between the making of the application and the making of the order the court still had jurisdiction to make the order and did so where the welfare of the child required it and could not be secured in any other way.[75]

Conception

3.59 The child must have been conceived via assisted conception or artificial insemination.[76] A parental order is not available where the child has been conceived through intercourse. The conception need not take place in a licensed clinic or in the UK,[77] it can be a home insemination.

3.60 A couple can only apply for a parental order where at least one of them is the genetic parent of the child.[78] If both intended parents have fertility difficulties and both a donor egg or the surrogate's own egg and donor sperm are used, a parental order will not be available. At the time that the order is made, both of the applicants must be over the age of 18.[79]

Timing

3.61 The application for the order must have been made within 6 months of the day when the child was born,[80] and both at the time of making the application and at the time of the making of the order, the child's home must be with the applicants.[81] In other words, such orders are only available where the child has lived with the applicants since (s)he was less than 6 months old and is living with them on the date when the order is to be made. If the child is born abroad, this means that the applicants must travel to be with the child from shortly after the birth. It is not a requirement of the 2008 Act that either the child or the parents are present or resident in the UK at the time of making the order.[82]

Domicile

3.62 At the time of the application, and at the time of the making of the order, either or both of the applicants must be domiciled in the UK or in the Channel Islands or the Isle of Man.[83]

---

[74] [2011] EWHC 1738 (Fam).
[75] But note that this decision was on the particular facts of this case and Theis J particularly observed that the decision was not to be taken as creating a precedent whereby single applicants could defeat the intention behind the legislation.
[76] HFEA 2008, s 54(1)(a).
[77] HFEA 2008, s 54(10).
[78] HFEA 2008, s 54(1)(b).
[79] Section 54(5) but note *A v P* [2011] EWHC 1738 (Fam) where the intended father was deceased.
[80] HFEA 2008, s 54(3).
[81] HFEA 2008, s 54(3) and (4).
[82] The Family Law Act 1986 Part I does not apply to applications for a parental order, per s 1(1) of that Act but see *Re K (Minors; Foreign Surrogacy)* [2011] 1 FLR 533.
[83] For a discussion as to domicile of origin and domicile of choice see recent Court of Appeal cases *Holiday v Musa* [2010] EWCA Civ 355, [2010] 2 FLR 702 and *Cyganik v Agulian* [2006]

In the most recent decision on parental orders and domicile, *Z and B and C v CAFCASS*,[84] Mrs Justice Theis held that the applicant fathers had changed their domicile of origin in Israel to a domicile of choice in the UK. As a prime example of the potential complexity of international surrogacy arrangements, the children were conceived as a result of a surrogacy agreement between the applicants and a clinic in India, arranged through a surrogacy agency based in Israel. The surrogate mother was Indian, both applicants were of Israeli origin, one of the applicants is the biological father and the egg donor originated from South Africa. The applicants had moved to the UK in 2008, largely because of the difficulties of openly conducting a committed same sex relationship in Israel, and intended to remain in the UK. The issue of domicile was heard as a preliminary issue, but the children had Israeli passports and had still not been granted leave to enter the UK by the UK Borders Agency. The particular concern of the judge was to ensure that the applicants had not asserted a domicile of choice in the UK in order to gain some advantage such as being entitled to apply for a parental order. In the circumstances she was satisfied that the applicants were genuine in their change of domicile.

3.63 The HFEA 2008 does not require the child to be present in the UK at the time of making the order, or the applicants to be resident in the UK. However, Hedley J in the case of *Re K (Minors; Foreign Surrogacy)*[85] felt unable to progress the application for a parental order whilst the children were still in India, and queried whether he had jurisdiction over them whilst they were not habitually resident in this country.

Agreement

3.64 The court must be satisfied that both the woman who carried the child and any other person who is a parent of the child but is not one of the applicants, have freely, and with a full understanding of what is involved, agreed unconditionally to the making of the order, unless the person cannot be found or is incapable of giving agreement.[86]

Whose agreement?

3.65 The agreement of the woman who carried the child, the surrogate mother is always required. If the woman who carried the child was married or in a civil partnership at the time that she was inseminated or the eggs and sperm or embryo placed in her, her husband or civil partner will be the child's other legal parent, irrespective of whether the surrogate mother was in the UK

EWCA Civ 12. In the case of *Re G (Surrogacy: Foreign Domicile)* [2007] EWHC 2814 (Fam) both parents were domiciled in Turkey but the child was born here pursuant to a surrogacy arrangement and therefore a parental order was not available. In that case McFarlane J made an order pursuant to ACA 2002, s 84 giving the intended parents parental responsibility on the basis that the court was satisfied that they intended to apply to adopt the child in Turkey.

84   [2011] EWHC 3181 (Fam).
85   [2011] 1 FLR 533.
86   HFEA 2008, s 54(6) and (7).

at the time that the eggs or sperm or embryo were placed in her[87]. In those circumstances, whether or not the surrogate mother and/or her husband's or civil partner's gametes were used, the agreement of the mother and of her husband/civil partner, or any other legal parent[88] will be required to the parental order, unless it can be shown in relation to the husband/civil partner that (s)he did not consent to the gametes or embryo being placed in her.[89] It will therefore be crucially important to establish whether the surrogate mother is married or in a registered partnership before she conceives, and if so to establish that her husband or registered partner will agree to the making of a parental order. If a long-lost husband emerges after the baby is born and refuses to agree there is no route to overriding that refusal.

Agreement to what

3.66 Note firstly that it is the making of the order that each relevant person must agree to, not simply to the intended parents caring for the child. Since, in English law, the parental order has the effect of removing the surrogate mother's status as mother (and if relevant, her husband's / civil partner's status as parent), it will be necessary to demonstrate that the surrogate mother (and any other legal parent) agreed to an order being made in England and Wales which means she is no longer the child's mother in this jurisdiction.

Agreement in what form

3.67 Unless the court directs otherwise, the agreements required must be given in Form A101A as prescribed by the Family Procedure Rules 2010.[90] Form A101A states clearly that 'If a parental order is made in respect of my child, I understand that I will no longer legally be treated as the parent and that my child will become a part of the applicants' family' in order to fulfill the requirements of s 54 of the HFEA 2008 (see the forms in Appendix 2).

3.68 Additionally, there is a requirement in r 13.3 of the FPR 2010 for any woman who carried the child, the other parent, if any, any person in whose favour there is provision for contact, and any other person with parental responsibility for the child, to be respondents to the application for a parental order (see below further in relation to procedure).

3.69 When entering into a surrogacy arrangement with a view to a parental order being made, therefore, the surrogate mother and any other person who is a legal parent of the child, or anyone else with parental responsibility should expect to cooperate to the extent of recording their agreement on the correct

---

[87] HFEA 2008, ss 35 and 42.

[88] For example if there was a parent pursuant to the agreed fatherhood or agreed female parenthood conditions per HFEA 2008, ss 36, 37, 43 and 44.

[89] Sections 35(1)(b) and 42(1)(b), the statutory presumption of legitimacy can be rebutted by showing that the spouse or civil partner did not consent to the treatment or insemination. Note that 'did not consent' is different to 'has not consented' per McFarlane J in *Re G* ibid.

[90] Rule 13.11 provides that agreement shall be given in the form required by PD 5A, which specifies Form A101A.

form, and should expect to be a respondent in the parental order proceedings. Rule 13.11(4) provides that any form of agreement executed outside the UK must be witnessed by:

(a)   any person authorised to administer an oath in the country where the agreement is to be executed;

(b)   a British consular officer;

(c)   a notary public; or

(d)   an officer holding commission in the armed forces if the person signing the document is serving in the armed forces.

If the person executing the agreement does not read or write or speak English, the court is also likely to require an appropriately notarised certificate of translation.

Form A101A also specifically requires the person signing it to indicate either that they have had legal advice, or have been advised to do so and have declined.

3.70   Rule 13.11 does allow the court to authorise the agreement in another form than Form A101A (provided it is to like effect). If Form A101A is not used, and the people whose agreement is required do not respond to the proceedings, it is likely to be difficult to persuade a court that unconditional agreement to the making of the order had been freely given with full understanding.

When

3.71   There is no specific time at which the agreement must be given, however, it is specifically provided that the agreement of the woman who carried the child is ineffective if it is given by her less than 6 weeks after the child's birth.[91] If the country where the child was born required consent before or at birth in order to allow the child to be handed over to the intended parents, it will still be necessary for agreement to be executed again at a later date in the correct form.

3.72   Any intended parent would be well advised to ensure that Form A101A is completed by any person whose agreement is required as soon as the child is 6 weeks old to avoid a situation arising whereby some intervening event takes place between that date and the application for a parental order being made or heard. This reduces the potential for a person to become incapable of giving agreement or of being found in the intervening period.

3.73   Provided the agreement has been given in the correct form at the correct time, and provided that service of the application, a form for acknowledging

---

[91]   HFEA 2008, s 54(7).

service and notice of the proceedings and of the hearing on the respondents can be demonstrated, the court is not prevented from making the parental order if for some reason the respondents do not respond to or become involved in the proceedings.[92] It may become difficult to demonstrate service if the person cannot be found, but the provisions of s 54(6) clearly envisage that the court can make a parental order even without agreement if the person cannot be found or is incapable of giving agreement. Inevitably if a person cannot be found it will be difficult to demonstrate service on them. It is to be expected, therefore, that if agreement has been given in the correct form, the court might dispense with service[93] if satisfied agreement was given, in circumstances where the person who had given it has disappeared since it was given.

Incapable of giving agreement or cannot be found

3.74 Section 54(7) provides that the Act does not require the agreement of a person who cannot be found or is incapable of giving agreement. There are a number of different ways in which a person might be incapable of giving agreement. It is significant that the wording of the HFEA 2008 does not mirror the wording of s 52 of the ACA 2002 which provides that:

> 'The court cannot dispense with the consent of any parent or guardian of a child to the child being placed for adoption or to the making of an adoption order in respect of the child unless the court is satisfied that –
>
> (a)   The parent or guardian cannot be found or lacks capacity (within the meaning of the Mental Capacity Act 2005) to give consent, or
> (b)   The welfare of the child requires consent to be dispensed with.'

3.75 First, the language of the HFEA 2008 mirrors the basis for surrogacy itself: surrogacy is an arrangement made before the child is born,[94] and not simply the actions of one person with the consent of another. The welfare of the child is not a ground for making a parental order in the absence of agreement, unless the lack of agreement falls within the statutory exceptions. Adoption is primarily about child welfare and child protection, whereas surrogacy is primarily an arrangement between consenting adults to create a child who would not otherwise exist.

3.76 Secondly, the agreement is required of persons who may not have been involved in the making of the arrangement at all whose circumstances restrict

---

[92]   Part 6 of the FPR deals with demonstrating service and in particular Chapter 4 and PD 6B deal with service out of the jurisdiction and requires service in accordance with methods permitted by the country where the document is to be served. Rule 6.47 requires service accompanied by a translation in the official language of the country to be served. Rule 13.7 requires an acknowledgement of service to be filed and served within 7 days, subject to the provisions of PD 6B. Rule 27.4 enables the court to proceed in the absence of parties provided it is proved to the satisfaction of the court that the respondent received reasonable notice of the date of the hearing.

[93]   Under r 13.9(f).

[94]   Surrogacy Arrangements Act 1985, s 1.

them from making such an agreement. For example, if the surrogate mother is married, but her husband has had his liberty deprived and is not entitled to enter into such an agreement.

3.77 Thirdly, there may be difficulties with evidencing that a third party who lives in another country satisfies the definitions of the Mental Capacity Act 2005; although it is to be expected that there will need to be medical evidence if the reason for which the person is incapable of giving agreement relates to their mental health.

3.78 It will be necessary for the court to make a determination as to whether a person whose agreement is required is incapable of giving the agreement or cannot be found in any case in which this is asserted. Rule 13.10 of the FPR 2010 provides a specific procedure for such cases, including requiring the applicants to provide a statement of facts to satisfy the court that the woman who carried the child or other parent cannot be found or is incapable of giving agreement. The court may appoint a litigation friend to represent that person's interests if it considers that (s)he is incapable of giving agreement.[95] It is to be remembered that capacity is issue specific; the issue will be whether the person in question is incapable of giving agreement to the making of a parental order.[96]

3.79 Although the 2008 Act does not make any distinction between a surrogate mother who is incapable of giving agreement and another parent incapable of giving agreement, the UK public policy in relation to surrogacy and commercial surrogacy is relevant here. In particular, the court will be concerned to ensure that a vulnerable surrogate mother has not been taken advantage of by the commissioning parents or her husband or a surrogacy agency. The public policy considerations identified in *Re X and Y*[97] and *Re S*[98] apply. If the surrogate mother was incapable of giving agreement to being a surrogate mother at the time that she was artificially inseminated or the embryo/eggs and sperm were placed in her, the court is likely to exercise its discretion to refuse to make a parental order. This situation can be distinguished from a situation where she has become incapable at some later date, perhaps through injury or illness.

Payment of not more than reasonable expenses

3.80 This is dealt with at **3.12** et seq above relating to commercial surrogacy. Section 54(8) prohibits not only payments by intended parents to surrogate mothers, but generally prohibits the *giving or receiving* of money by the applicants for a parental order, irrespective of who the payment is made from or to. This includes prohibiting paying any one in return for a parental order being made, paying an agency or anyone else for making surrogacy

---

95   Rule 13.10(b).
96   *Sheffield City Council v E and S* [2004] EWHC 2808 (Fam).
97   [2009] 1 FLR 733.
98   [2009] EWHC 2977 (Fam).

arrangements, paying a parent for giving their agreement, or paying anyone for handing over the child, all with the exception of reasonable expenses.

A note on single parents

3.81 A single applicant cannot apply for a parental order.[99] However, there is nothing to prevent a woman and a man who are not in a relationship from having a child through assisted reproduction, and agreeing that the child will be brought up by the genetic or legal father. If the agreement is reached prior to the child being carried it would fall within the definition of a surrogacy arrangement. Provided the mother is not married, whether the father is the genetic father, or complies with the agreed fatherhood conditions provided for in s 37 of the HFEA Act 2008 he will be the legal father (see chapter 1 for further discussion of legal and genetic parenthood). This arrangement differs in effect from a parental order because even if the gestational mother is not the genetic mother, she will remain the legal mother.[100] She will therefore retain parental responsibility and the right to apply for a residence order or other s 8 Children Act order unless there is subsequently an adoption. As with any surrogacy arrangement, it is not binding on her.

MAKING THE APPLICATION FOR A PARENTAL ORDER

3.82 An application for a parental order must be made in the family proceedings court in the first instance.[101] However, as Hedley J observed in the case of *Re X and Y (Foreign Surrogacy)*:[102]

'Domestic surrogacy applications frequently pose no problems and can be dealt with [in the Family Proceedings Court] (especially where as at Inner London there is current experience and expertise) or in the county court. However, overseas surrogacy agreements potentially raise much more difficult issues and will often merit transfer to a county court perhaps even to the relevant international adoption centre. Where there is a commercial element to the surrogacy, it will usually require careful consideration as to why it should not be transferred to the High Court. Certainly any case which involves a significant conflict of private international law or which may require authorisation to be given under s 30(7) of the Act should, in my view, be so transferred.'

Rules 12.9 and 12.11 of the FPR 2010 apply concerning transfers from the family proceedings court.[103]

3.83 Part 13 of the Family Procedure Rules 2010 deals with the procedure specific to parental order applications, and must be read together with the other parts of the FPR 2010 which apply to all applications, in particular:

---

[99]   HFEA 2008, s 54(11).
[100]   HFEA 2008, s 33(1).
[101]   Allocation and Transfer of Proceedings Order 2008, SI 2008/2836, as amended.
[102]   [2008] EWHC 3030 (Fam), [2009] 1 FLR 733 at para [28].
[103]   FPR 2010, r 13.2.

- Part 4 concerning the court's case management powers;

- Part 5 which specifies the appropriate forms for commencing proceedings;

- Part 6 concerning service out of the jurisdiction (if the respondents are in another country);

- Rules 12.19 and 12.21 relating to evidence and hearings apply by virtue of r 13.2;

- Part 16, Chapter 3 which makes provision relating to parental order reporters;

- Parts 22 and 23 concerning evidence;

- Part 25 concerning experts if there is any issue of foreign law involved requiring an expert;

- Part 27 concerning hearings and directions appointments.

3.84 The application for a parental order is made on Form C51.[104] The respondents are:[105]

(a)   the woman who carried the child;

(b)   any other (legal) parent;

(c)   any person in whose favour there is provision for contact;

(d)   any other person or body with parental responsibility at the date of the application.

The court can add additional respondents, or remove someone as a respondent.[106]

3.85 All of the respondents must be served by the applicant with:

(a)   the application;

(b)   a form for acknowledging service;

(c)   a notice of proceedings.

And if the respondents are not in England and Wales, Chapter 3 of Part 6 and Practice Direction 6B to the FPR 2010 apply. If a respondent is to be served in

---

[104]   FPR 2010, PD 5A.
[105]   FPR 2010, r 13.3.
[106]   FPR 2010, r 13.3(4).

a member state of the European Union, the provisions of Council Regulation (EC) No 1393/2007 apply. Note that Part 6 and the EU service regulation both have requirements as to translation of documents. Additionally, if it is necessary to serve the respondents through a foreign central authority or consular, judicial authority or government, the foreign authority can take a considerable period of time to effect service, and to notify that they have effected service.

3.86 In identifying respondents, note that r 13.4 requires the applicants, at any stage of the proceedings, to give notice of the proceedings to anybody who they are aware of who holds, or is believed to hold, parental responsibility for that child in a Member State which is signatory to the 1996 Hague Convention, if they are not already a respondent.

3.87 When giving notice to a person whose agreement to the parental order is required, the notice shall notify that person of the date and place where the application will be heard, and of the fact that unless the person wishes or the court requires, that person need not attend the hearing.[107] The appointment of a parental order reporter to prepare a report is mandatory.[108]

3.88 As soon as practicable after the application is issued, the court will list the matter for a first directions hearing and appoint a parental order reporter, unless the court considers it appropriate to give directions without a hearing.[109] The directions will include directions relating to the parental order report.[110] The reporter must investigate the criteria for the making of a parental order in s 54 of the HFEA 2008, and any other matter which seems relevant to the parental order reporter, and advise the court as to the welfare considerations in s 1 of the ACA 2002 as they relate to the child in question.[111] The court is required to consider which of the parties the report should be disclosed to, and has power to direct that the report shall not be disclosed to a party.[112] The court may deem it inappropriate, for example for the surrogate mother's husband who has not been party to the surrogacy arrangements to have intimate information about the applicants for a parental order.

3.89 There are specific procedural requirements in r 13.10 which apply where the applicants stated that the agreement of the mother or other parent of the child is not required to the making of the parental order because (s)he is incapable of giving agreement or cannot be found.[113] In particular, a statement of facts is required from the applicants, which will also be sent to the mother or other parent, unless they cannot be found, and which will be sent to the

---

[107] FPR 2010, r 13.13.
[108] FPR 2010, r 16.34.
[109] FPR 2010, r 13.5.
[110] FPR 2010, r 13.9.
[111] FPR 2010, r 16.35.
[112] FPR 2010, r 13.12(3).
[113] Pursuant to HFEA 2008, s 54(7).

parental order reporter.[114] The issue of whether the mother or other parent is incapable of giving agreement or cannot be found is one of the matters for investigation by the parental order reporter.[115] If the applicants consider that the mother or other parent is incapable of giving agreement, the court will consider whether to appoint a litigation friend for that person,[116] and r 15 of the FPR 2010 applies. The court has a discretion not to send interim orders to all parties to the proceedings.[117]

3.90   Whilst the proceedings are pending, the applicants for a parental order are protected from unauthorised removals of the child(ren) from their care. Only the local authority or a person who has the court's leave may remove the child from the applicants' care once the application has been made.[118]

3.91   If the application is refused, the court may not hear another application for a parental order by the same applicants in relation to the same child unless there has been a change in circumstances or the court considers it is proper to do so for some other reason. The court will consider this on issue of the second application.[119]

Registration of parental orders

3.92   If the application is granted, and a parental order made, the court is required to send a copy of the order to the applicants, the Registrar General and any respondent. The court also has a discretion to send it to others.[120] The order must direct the Registrar General to make an entry in the parental order register in the correct form.[121] A copy of the Form of Entry in the Parental Order Register appears at Appendix 2.

ADOPTION

3.93   Prior to the HFEA 2008 coming into force, adoption was the only route by which a same sex couple could become the legal parents of a child following a surrogacy arrangement.

---

[114]   FPR 2010, r 13.10(2) and (3).

[115]   FPR 2010, r 16.34.

[116]   FPR 2010, r 13.10(3)(b).

[117]   FPR 2010, r 13.21(5).

[118]   ACA 2002, ss 36 and 41 apply to applications for a parental order by virtue of Sch 1 to the HFE (PO) Regulations 2010 and per FPR 2010, r 13.5. Rule 13.17 of the FPR 2010 provides the relevant procedure for making an application for a recovery order if the child has been unlawfully removed from the applicants' care.

[119]   ACA 2002, s 48 as applicable to parental orders by virtue of Sch 1 to the HFE (PO) Regulations 2010 and per FPR 2010, r 13.5.

[120]   FPR 2010, r 13.21.

[121]   Per ACA 2002, Sch 1, para 1 as applicable to parental orders by virtue of Sch 1 to the HFE (PO) Regulations 2010. The Parental Orders (Prescribed Particulars and Forms of Entry) Regulations 2010, SI 2010/1205 also apply.

3.94 Since the coming into force of the HFEA 2008 the circumstances in which adoption may particularly be considered, instead of a parental order following surrogacy, are likely to be when a parental order is not available, for example the child is now too old, or the intended parents are no longer together and one of them wishes to apply to become the child's sole legal parent.

3.95 Whilst a single person can apply to adopt a child carried by a surrogate mother, particular caution needs to be taken to ensure that the arrangement for the intended parent to care for the child following birth complies with the legal requirements for a placement for adoption if the person is not the legal father of the child. In particular, see **3.43** above in relation to private fostering arrangements and illegal adoption placements, and chapter 5 in relation to adoption.

GUARDIANSHIP

3.96 Special guardianship is perhaps half way between a residence order and an adoption or parental order. It does not extinguish the parental status of the legal parent(s) but it gives the special guardian parental responsibility and allows a special guardian to exercise parental responsibility to the exclusion of any other person with parental responsibility (except another special guardian).[122] It also allows the court to give permission for the child to be known by a new surname.[123] It also requires any parent or anyone else having parental responsibility for the child to obtain the permission of the court before being able to make any application to vary or discharge the special guardianship, and the court may not give leave unless there has been a significant change in circumstances since the special guardianship order was made.[124] Special guardianship is a relatively new concept inserted into the CA 1989[125] by the provisions of the ACA 2002.

3.97 Its application in same sex family situations to the problem of co-parenting is, however, limited by the fact that a special guardian must not be a (legal) parent of the child in question.[126] It cannot, therefore be used to allow one parent to exercise their parental responsibility to the exclusion of the other. Nor can it be used to establish, for example, a father and his male partner as primary parents to the exclusion of the surrogate mother, because the fact of a special guardianship order being made in favour of the male partner would entitle him to exercise parental responsibility to the exclusion of the father also.

3.98 Circumstances in which a special guardianship order might prove useful, however, are if a single man enters into a surrogacy arrangement with a woman who is married. Unless it can be demonstrated that her husband did not

---

[122] CA 1989, s 14C.
[123] CA 1989, s 14B.
[124] CA 1989, s 14D(1), (3), (5).
[125] CA 1989, ss 14A–14G.
[126] CA 1989, s 14(2)(b).

consent to her being artificially inseminated with the man's gametes, her husband will be the legal father.[127] The genetic father, who is not the legal father in those circumstances, could not apply for a parental order as a single man, but he could apply for a special guardianship order. If he entered into a relationship later on, both men could be special guardians. In this situation, unless the person applying for a special guardianship order:

- already held a residence order; or

- was already a legal guardian for the child; or

- the child had been living with him for more than 3 years; or

- has the consent of the people having parental responsibility for him; or

- if the child is in care, has the consent of the local authority; or

- is a relative[128] of the child or a local authority foster carer and the child has been living with him for more than a year;

he will require the leave of the court to apply for a special guardianship order.[129]

3.99 Note that any application for a special guardianship order requires notice to be given to the local authority in the area where the individual ordinarily resides, and the local authority will be required to conduct an investigation and prepare a report for the court dealing with the suitability of the applicant to be a special guardian.[130]

3.100 A legal guardian who is not a special guardian may only be appointed where the child has no parent with parental responsibility for him, or a residence order has been made with respect to a child in favour of a parent, guardian or special guardian who has died while the order was in force, or the child's only special guardian has died.[131]

INTERNATIONAL SURROGACY

3.101 Of all the legal aspects of surrogacy, this is by far the most difficult. Any person contemplating a surrogacy arrangement which is reached outside England and Wales or involves:

---

[127] HFEA 2008, s 35.
[128] Per the definition in s 144 of the ACA 2002 as applicable to parental orders by virtue of Sch 1 to to the HFE (PO) Regulations 2010.
[129] CA 1989, s 14A(5).
[130] CA 1989, s 14A(7)–(11).
[131] CA 1989, s 5.

- a surrogate mother resident or domiciled outside England and Wales;

- a legal parent resident or domiciled outside England and Wales;

- the child being born outside England and Wales;

- the intended parents not being resident or not being domiciled in England or Wales;

- the intended parents intending to reside outside England and Wales in the future,

would be strongly advised to seek highly specialist advice before embarking on such an arrangement, in particular;

- as to immigration issues in respect of all of the countries concerned;

- as to the law of the country/State where the surrogate mother resides or will give birth or is domiciled;

- as to the law of the country/State where the donor lives if she is not the surrogate mother;

- as to the law of the country/State where any other legal parent or person with parental responsibility resides;

- as to the law of the country/State where the intended parents intend to live with the child;

- as to the law of the country/State where the arrangement is to be made;

- as to the law of any country where the child might be intended to have citizenship in due course;

- as to the law of England and Wales.

3.102 There is no Private International Law consensus in relation to surrogacy, and the stance of individual countries / States varies from permitting and legalising commercial surrogacy, to permitting and legalising non-commercial surrogacy, being neutral and unregulated on the issue of surrogacy, to permitting it for opposite sex couples but outlawing it for same sex couples, to making any form of surrogacy arrangement at all unlawful.

3.103 Particularly for those countries which tolerate, permit or retrospectively endorse surrogacy under certain conditions, there is currently a significant impetus to explore the possibilities for and ramifications of international surrogacy arrangements.

3.104   In July 2010, the Nuffield Foundation awarded a grant to the School of Law, University of Aberdeen to conduct a study into private international law aspects of international surrogacy arrangements to explore possible types of international regulation of surrogacy arrangements, and to prepare a document that could assist in the process of preparation of a possible future international Convention on surrogacy.[132]

3.105   In April 2011, the Hague Conference on Private International Law's Council on General Affairs and Policy invited its Permanent Bureau to intensify its work on the broad range of issues arising from international surrogacy arrangements.[133]

3.106   It is outside the scope of this text, and outside the scope of the perspective of a lawyer practising solely in England and Wales to seek to offer guidance as to the law in other countries or states relating to surrogacy. It is also outside the scope of this text to provide guidance as to immigration law. However, it will be apparent from much of what has been said already in this chapter that there are a number of potential difficulties and pitfalls arising in cases of international surrogacy which impact upon the decisions to be taken by individuals here and the orders which can be made in England and Wales. In addition to the guidance set out above, some of the potential difficulties are therefore highlighted here both to emphasise the importance of seeking specialist advice in the relevant countries and to highlight that those embarking on surrogacy arrangements may well run into difficulties which they had never anticipated, and the reasons for the need for specialist advice in respect of the circumstances of each individual family:

(1)   The issue which pervades all international surrogacy is immigration, not only at the moment of bringing the baby home to the intended parents, but also for the long term future. The lack of international consensus, or even European or United States Federal consensus, around the status of individuals in relation to each other can cause difficulties for freedom of movement in later life for a child born of surrogacy. Specialist immigration advice is essential.

It is vital that preparations are made to ensure that a child who it born elsewhere but who it is intended to live in England and Wales will be able to legally enter the UK, ie obtain Entry Clearance prior to travel here. *Re K (Foreign Surrogacy)*[134] is an example of a case where the parents and children effectively became stranded in India, with the UK court unable to progress the application for a parental order without the children in this jurisdiction and Entry Clearance had not been granted.

A copy of the 'Intercountry surrogacy and the Immigration Rules' is available to download on the Home Office website,[135] it bears detailed reading <u>before</u> making any surrogacy arrangements. This guidance makes

---

[132]   Text taken from The University of Aberdeen website.
[133]   Hague Conference on Private International Law Press Release.
[134]   [2010] EWHC 1180 (Fam).
[135]   See www.ukba.homeoffice.gov.uk: Form MN1.

it plain, in particular, that the routes to immigration are a good deal simpler if the child already has a legal parent who is a British Citizen. Realistically in a surrogacy situation this only arises where the genetic father is also the legal father and one of the intended parents, and the surrogate mother is not married. Note that there are slight differences as to who the legal parents are for the purposes of the British Nationality Act which affect immigration.

(2) The issue of immigration is not only relevant to freedom of movement but also relevant to the issue of citizenship, and the countries for which a child born of surrogacy will be able to apply for citizenship in due course. The question of what is recorded on the child's birth certificate can have implications for the child's citizenship in some countries.

In relation to British Citizenship, the ACA 2002,[136] provides an exception to the rule that an adopted person is to be treated in law as if born as the child of the holders of the parental order. In particular, this rule does not apply for the purposes of the British Nationality Act 1981, the Immigration Act 1971, or other regulations which determine British Citizenship.

However, once a parental order is made, if at least one of the applicants is a British Citizen, the child will become a British Citizen.[137] This led Hedley J to consider in the case of *Re IJ (Foreign Surrogacy Agreement: Parental Order)*[138] whether it is necessary to give notice to the Home Office of the intention to bring a child into the UK for a parental order to be made. He reached the conclusion that it is not because of the degree of involvement of the UK Borders Agency in any such process.

(3) There are restrictions imposed on people who are habitually resident in the British Isles bringing a child who is habitually resident outside the British Isles into the UK for the purposes of making a parental order.[139] It is a criminal offence to fail to comply with the requirements.

(4) The homophobic attitude to same sex relationships and surrogacy in some countries or states can result in a child born of same sex surrogacy or his parents being at some risk if their parentage becomes known. In some US states a child born of surrogacy can be issued with more than one birth certificate because of the consequences for that child if (s)he intends to move to a state or country which does not tolerate surrogacy. A child who is the subject of a parental order in the UK will have a birth certificate showing the legal mother and father at birth and a parental order certificate (see the forms in Appendix 2) which will show details of the

---

[136] ACA 2002, ss 67 and 74 are applicable to parental orders by virtue of Sch 1 to the HFE (PO) Regulations 2010.

[137] HFE (PO) Regulations 2010, reg 5, Sch 4 which amends the British Nationality Act 1981.

[138] [2011] EWHC 921 (Fam).

[139] ACA 2002, s 83 which applies to those causing a child to be brought into the UK for the purposes of making a parental order by virtue of the Sch 1 to the HFE (PO) Regulations 2010.

child's birth and who the two parents are without reference to the sex of the parents or the existence of a parental order.

(5)   The lack of international consensus on the status of individuals relating to each other can mean that a child born following a surrogacy arrangement can become parentless and stateless, effectively falling through the cracks in International Private Law. The case of *Re X and Y (Foreign Surrogacy)*[140] involved precisely this scenario, with a child being neither the legal child of the birth mother and her husband in the Ukraine, nor of the intended parents in England.

(6)   The lack of international consensus on the status of individuals relating to each other can mean that more than one order is required in different countries or different states to enable freedom of movement.

(7)   The question of in which countries orders to recognise parenthood can be obtained is complex. For example, parental orders can only be obtained in the UK where at least one of the applicants is domiciled here.[141] This can give rise to a situation where foreign nationals are habitually resident here, and enter into a surrogacy arrangement here, but cannot secure a parental order here.

(8)   The lack of international consensus or even European or Federal consensus about the enforceability of surrogacy arrangements can lead to a woman who has changed her mind about handing over the baby leaving a state where an enforceable surrogacy arrangement has been signed, or pre-birth order been made, for a state where surrogacy is either not enforceable or not permitted.

(9)   The lack of enforceability of surrogacy arrangements in some jurisdictions, including the UK, means that if there is a breakdown in relationship between the mother and the intended parents, the case can turn into a child abduction matter. In the case of *W and B v H (Child Abduction: Surrogacy)*[142] the surrogate mother and the intended parents had entered into a binding surrogacy arrangement in California, and the genetic and legal father had obtained a pre-birth order in California. The mother, however, changed her mind, and came to the UK to have the children. The father alleged that there had been a child abduction. Hedley J found the position to be that:

    •   in Californian law, the mother was not a legal parent;
    •   in English law, the mother was a legal parent;

---

[140]   [2008] EWHC 3030 (Fam), [2009] 1 FLR 733.
[141]   HFEA 2008, s 54(4). See also *Re G (Surrogacy: Foreign Domicile)* [2007] EWHC 2814 (Fam), [2008] 1 FLR 1047.
[142]   [2002] 1 FLR 1008.

- the father was the legal father in both jurisdictions, and the court could find that he had parental responsibility in California, but did not have parental responsibility in English law;
- the children did not have a habitual residence. They were present here with the legal mother in the eyes of English law, but it had always been intended that they would live in America.

Whilst Hedley J found that in those circumstances there had not been an abduction of the child, he described it as a 'pyrrhic victory' on the part of the mother, since it was open to him to determine that the more appropriate forum for determining welfare matters relating to the children was California, where undoubtedly the children were the legal children of the intended parents.[143]

(10) The lack of enforceability of surrogacy arrangements in some jurisdictions, including the UK, can mean that if the relationship between the surrogate mother and the intended parents breaks down, there can be a dispute as to which is the most appropriate country to make decisions about the children, or there can be conflicting decisions about the children in different countries.[144]

(11) The lack of international regulation of surrogacy can lead to some surrogate mothers being extremely vulnerable to the avarice of others. There have been reports in India, for example, of women being made available for surrogacy essentially as a form of prostitution. Well intentioned intended parents have a responsibility to ensure that the surrogate mother is not being exploited by someone else.

---

[143] Indeed, in the sequel to this case *W and W v H (Child Abduction: Surrogacy) (No 2)* [2002] 2 FLR 252 Hedley J went on to determine that the case should be heard in California and ordered the summary return of the children to California.

[144] As in *W and W v H (Child Abduction: Surrogacy) (No 2)* [2002] 2 FLR 252.

Chapter 4

PRIVATE LAW APPLICATIONS

SCOPE

4.1   The term private law is used to define the legal framework within which the court resolves the arrangements for children. Most commonly this arises where the adults in their life cannot agree the arrangements but it may also arise where there is agreement but the parties want the agreement endorsed by the court, in particular in order to be able to demonstrate their relationship with the child(ren) to people outside the family. As set out in r 12.2 of the Family Procedure Rules 2010 the scope is broad:

12.2 Interpretation

'In this part "private law proceedings" means proceedings for –

- (a)   a section 8 order except a residence order under section 8 of the 1989 Act relating to a child who is the subject of a care order;
- (b)   a parental responsibility order under sections 4(1)(c), 4ZA(1)(c) or 4A(1)(b) of the 1989 Act or an order terminating parental responsibility under sections 4(2A), 4ZA(5) or 4A(3) of that Act;
- (c)   an order appointing a child's guardian under section 5(1) of the 1989 Act or an order terminating the appointment under section 6(7) of that Act;
- (d)   an order giving permission to change a child's surname or remove a child from the United Kingdom under sections 13(1) or 14C(3) of the 1989 Act;
- (e)   a special guardianship order except where that order relates to a child who is subject of a care order;
- (f)   an order varying or discharging such an order under section 14D of the 1989 Act;
- (g)   an enforcement order;
- (h)   a financial compensation order;
- (i)   an order under paragraph 9 of Schedule A1 to the 1989 Act following a breach of an enforcement order;
- (j)   an order under Part 2 of Schedule A1 to the 1989 Act revoking or amending an enforcement order; or
- (k)   an order that a warning notice be attached to a contact order.'

4.2   Subsections (a), (d) and (g)–(k) deal with the group of orders which a court can make under s 8 of the Children Act 1989 (CA 1989) and sections supplemental to that. The majority of this chapter will be devoted to exploring the role and effect of these orders, which regulate with whom the child is to live, who that child is to have contact with and decide specific issues within the child's life, and which represent the backbone of private law relating to children. Subsection (b) is given a fuller treatment in chapter 2 on parental responsibility, but also has a role in the context of private law proceedings which will be discussed in this chapter. Subsections (c), (e) and (f) relating to guardianship are also discussed in chapter 3 on surrogacy because an application for a special guardianship order cannot be made by a parent, and special guardianship operates to limit the exercise of parental responsibility by a parent.[1]

HISTORICAL BACKGROUND

4.3   Any lawyer advising same gender couples will benefit by understanding the historical context for their situation. Until comparatively recently, attitudes to non-heterosexuals were radically different from those accepted as the norm and experienced today. For that reason, this chapter will begin by giving that context as it is important to understand what the fears and misapprehensions of the people involved may be.

4.4   To summarise and simplify a lengthy and painful history, until the early 1990s a parent who left a heterosexual relationship into which children had been born, and who was unable to agree arrangements for them with their former partner, could expect to lose the children if the case came to court and they had established a relationship with a same gender partner.

4.5   For example, in *Re D (An Infant)*[2] a father's consent to adoption was dispensed with on the basis of his sexuality, despite his acknowledged love and concern for his son.

4.6   Lesbian mothers were allowed to retain custody (as it then was) if there was no viable alternative for the child, although the courts were not necessarily comfortable with this option:[3]

> 'This is neither the time nor place to moralise about sexual deviance and its consequences by those who practise it, but the possible effect on a young child living in proximity to that practice is of crucial importance to that child and to the public interest. I accept that it is not right to say that a child should in no circumstances live with a mother who is carrying on a lesbian relationship with a woman who is also living with her, but I venture to suggest that it can only be countenanced by the court when it is driven to the conclusion that there is in the interests of the child no other acceptable alternative form of custody.'

4.7   By late 1990s the Court of Appeal was expressing itself in rather more circumspect terms:[4]

---

1   CA 1989, ss 14A and 14C.
2   [1977] AC 602.
3   Per Watkins LJ in *Re P (A Minor) (Custody)* (1983) 4 FLR 401 (in this case the child remained with her mother, subject to a supervision order.)
4   Per Glidewell LJ in *C v C (A Minor) (Custody: Appeal)* [1991] FCR 254.

'Despite the vast change over the past 30 years or so in the attitudes of our society generally to the institution of marriage, to sexual morality and to homosexual relationships, I regard it as axiomatic that the ideal environment for the upbringing of a child is the home of loving, caring and sensible parents, her father and her mother. When the marriage between father and mother is at an end, that ideal cannot be attained. When the court is called upon to decide which of two possible alternatives is then preferable for the child's welfare, its task is to choose the alternative which comes closest to that ideal.

Even taking account of the changes of attitude to which I have referred, a lesbian relationship between two adult women is an unusual background in which to bring up a child. I think that the mother herself recognises this, because the judge recorded her as saying that she was sensitive to the problems that could arise, and did not flaunt the sexual nature of her relationship.

The judge had no evidence, and thus we have none, about the effect on a young child of learning the nature of a lesbian relationship and of her friends learning about it. Nevertheless, it seems that the judge accepted, and it is certainly my view, that it is undesirable that this child should learn or understand at an early age the nature of her mother's relationship ...

... he seems to have disregarded the effect on C of her school friends learning of the relationship. If or when they do, she is bound to be asked questions which may well cause her distress or embarrassment. If she is at school in Shrewsbury, living in a heterosexual household, it is much less likely that she will be exposed to this.

... That the nature of the relationship is an important factor to be put into the balance seems to me to be clear.'

A joint custody order was made and the matter remitted to a judge of the Family Division for determination of care and control, which, in the event, was awarded to the mother. This remained the leading case at the time the Children Act came into force.

4.8   In *B v B (Minors) (Custody, Care and Control)*[5] the court had available to it the expert assistance of Professor Derek Russell-Davis, an eminent consultant psychiatrist and chartered psychologist and Emeritus Professor of Mental Health at Bristol University.

'His opinion and advice basically are that one has to assess the problems of lesbianism and children being brought up in such households under two heads: the sexual identity of the child being brought up in such a household and the stigmatisation. It is very much the same thing as talking about corruption on the one hand and reputation on the other.

The professor came to the conclusion that ... there is not an increased incidence of homosexuality among the children of homosexual parents ... there is no evidence that lesbian mothers tend to prejudice the differentiation of roles during early childhood, and he specifically says that he has examined this particular mother

---

[5]   [1991] 1 FLR 402.

and that lesbian mothers almost without exception express a wish, as does this mother, that the sexual orientation of their children should be heterosexual.

Let me say immediately, on the question of stigmatization, the professor indicated quite plainly that children tend to be teased about matters about which they show sensitivity, and the professor indicated that most of his cases in his experience, and he has made a special study of this, of, for example, nicknaming of children and teasing of children, relate to the child personally, and that those stigmatisations that arise do so from features such as large ears, noses, smell or conduct of the child, and that in his experience it is very rare for children to show an interest in the background of the parents of other children and that, in fact, children are far more tolerant of their classmates' background and parents than most people give them credit for.

Professor Russell-Davis has said that the fears of psychosexual development being distorted if a child is reared in a lesbian household, or that he will be subjected unduly to taunts and teasing or be ostracised, find no support in the systematic evidence that he has looked at ... such stigmatisation, said the professor, as there is tends to come from the minority of adults, only exceptionally from peers, and the children are largely unaware of it and unaffected by it ... the dangers to the child in living in a lesbian household tend to be overestimated and there are, of course, widespread prejudices about lesbianism.'

4.9   Judge Callman (sitting as a deputy High Court judge in this case) distinguishes this mother from 'militant lesbians who try to convert others to their way of life'. Interestingly, in his paper on this subject as revised in April 1992, Professor Russell-Davis expresses doubt as to the prevalence in lesbian households of attitudes which are extravagantly feminist or openly hostile to men, and points out that such attributes are also met in heterosexual households.

4.10   Over time the courts with the assistance of research have left behind the assumptions that being raised in same gender parented households would incur social disadvantage or distortion in the child's developing sexuality.

4.11   Recent research by the Williams Institute at UCLA School of Law[6] illustrated the importance to children of same sex couples of a legal framework that endorses the familial relationships:

'To the best of our knowledge, the current study is the first to provide empirical longitudinal data on parental relationship dissolution in planned lesbian families. Our findings show that nearly all breakups occurred before the former couples could have obtained the legal equivalent of same sex marriage in their state of residence. At the age of 17, most offspring rated their satisfaction with life relatively high, and most mothers considered the communication with their ex-partners cordial. Separated mothers were significantly more likely to share custody if the co-mother had legally adopted the offspring.

---

[6]   Gartrell N, Bos H, et al, *Family Characteristics, Custody Arrangements and Adolescent Psychological Well-being After Lesbian Mothers Break Up* Family Relations 60 (December 2011), pp 572–586.

The percentage of adolescents reporting closeness to both mothers was significantly higher in families with co-parent adoption. As legal co-custody and guardianship becomes more universally available, regardless of a parent's sexual orientation or biological connection to the child, future studies will continue to expand our understanding of family dynamics when same sex parents break up.'

4.12 In England and Wales, the coming into force of the Children Act 1989 offered a new opportunity for the sharing of parental responsibility for a child by those who were not both genetic parents. This opportunity was taken in 1994 when a joint residence order was made in favour of a female same sex couple thereby giving them shared parental responsibility in *Re C*.[7] Following the reporting of this case the making of joint residence orders as a route to sharing parental responsibility became more common and for some years remained the only option available to same gender couples who wanted to share legal status for the children they were raising. Such applications initially attracted concern from the courts as to welfare issues (in some cases the Official Solicitor was invited to act for the child or children, or a welfare report was ordered) but with time such steps were less common and such orders came to be made by consent at the first hearing unless the case gave rise to obvious welfare issues.

4.13 In 2000 the European Court of Human Rights (ECtHR) gave judgment that a father's Art 8 rights to family life had been infringed where parental responsibility had been granted to the mother by reason that he was in a same sex relationship with another man. In the case of *Salgueiro Da Silva Mouta v Portugal*[8] the court further held that there had been unlawful discrimination against the father on grounds of his sexual orientation.

4.14 Shortly after the ECtHR made the position clear in this case, the options available to same sex couples in England and Wales wanting to have their relationship to the children to be recognized, expanded considerably; first with the introduction of the ability to register same gender relationships in the Civil Partnership Act 2004, followed by the wholesale revision of adoption law by the Adoption and Children Act 2002 (implemented in 2005); and most recently by the major leap forwards in the law when the Human Fertilisation and Embryology Act 2008 came into force in 2009 thereby allowing two parents of the same sex to be a child's legal parents and named on the birth certificate from birth or from the granting of a parental order. With the expansion of options comes an equivalent expansion in the variety of family structures which can be endorsed by the court, and in the wake of these comes a flurry of reported cases endeavouring to resolve disputes between adults who have been unable to agree arrangements for the children in their lives.

4.15 Many of the reported cases have arisen in circumstances where the significant adults in a child's life have differing perspectives on their roles in relation to the children. One strategy which can reduce the potential for a

---

[7]   [1994] Fam Law 468.

[8]   (Application No 33290/96).

breakdown in communication of relationships between the adults is to try to reach cooperative parenting agreements before embarking on the arrangements to conceive a child. When discussing a parenting agreement potential problems or misunderstandings can be flagged up before the child is conceived, which may help to ensure that all the adults involved have the same understanding, and thereby reduce the opportunity for misunderstandings. Recent proposals by the government in their response to the Family Justice Review indicate that for all families there will be increased encouragement to reach parenting agreements in the future.[9] It will also be apparent from the cases discussed below that the courts have encouraged parenting agreements. Although pre-conception intentions should not be determinative, and are not binding, and although what is in the children's best interests will change over time, it is sensible for people to 'spell out in as much detail as they can what they contemplate will be the arrangements for the care and upbringing of their child'.[10] Key questions to consider pre-conception are:

- Who are to be the legal parents?

- Who is to have parental responsibility?

- Who is to have a parenting role?

- Who will the child live with?

- Which country will the child live in?

- Do all concerned understand the significance of these decisions?

- What day-to-day role will all of the significant adults for the child have?

- What are the expectations around contact?

- What are the expectations for making important decisions in the child's life?

- What will the child be told about their relationship with each of the significant adults?

- What name and surname(s) will the child have?

- How will disagreements about the child's upbringing be resolved in the future?

---

[9]   Ministry of Justice and Department for Education: Government Response to the Family Justice Review February 2012: 'It is our intention that parents will be supported to reach [parenting] agreements through dispute resolution services, including targeted parenting programmes, so that as many disputes as possible can be resolved without the need for court intervention'.

[10] Per Black LJ in *A v B and C* [2012] EWCA Civ 285 at para 44.

The guidance in this chapter can be used to help families consider all the important issues at the outset and to develop the agreement, as appropriate, as the child grows up. Inevitably, people, feelings and relationships change over time, and disputes can arise nonetheless, or may already have arisen for some families. Therefore guidance in this chapter also addresses the role of the court and court orders in that situation.

THE WELFARE PRINCIPLE

4.16 Section 1 of the CA 1989 makes it clear that, in deciding all applications relating to a child's upbringing 'the child's welfare shall be the court's paramount consideration'.[11] The effect of the application of this paramountcy principal will be different in different cases to take account of the particular circumstances of the particular child. In the case of *Re B (Role of Biological Father)*[12] the child's biological father was also the co-parent's brother, and therefore a form of uncle. It had been agreed before the child was conceived that the child would grow up in a nuclear family unit which consisted of him and the two women parenting him, but which would not include his biological (and legal) father. Precisely what the father's role was to be, however, was perceived differently on each side. After the child's birth the father sought a more significant role in the child's life. This substantially unsettled the child's nuclear family unit and resulted in the estrangement of the father from the family unit. Despite the judge's sympathy for the father he stressed that the child's welfare must be the paramount consideration and that welfare was best met by limited contact between the child and his father which reflected the child's need to know his genetic parents, but which did not advance his parental status. He refused the father's application for parental responsibility and stated:

> 'I am satisfied that it would be wholly contrary to the best interests of BA [the child] to grant TJ [the biological father] parental responsibility. TJ would undoubtedly seek to exercise it and forcefully to advance his views. CV and S [the two women parenting BA] would feel assailed and undermined in their status as parents. The inevitable resulting conflict would bode ill for BA.'

More recently in the case of *A v B and C*[13] the Court of Appeal reiterated both that 'the only principle is the paramountcy of child welfare', and that 'this is an area of family law in which generalised guidance is not possible'.[14] In that case in which the father appealed the limitation of his role in the child's life imposed by the High Court, Lord Justice Thorpe held in allowing the appeal that the women 'may have had the desire to create a two parent lesbian nuclear family completely intact and free from fracture resulting from contact with the third

---

[11] CA 1989, s 1(1).
[12] [2007] EWHC 1952 (Fam), [2008] 1 FLR 1015.
[13] [2012] EWCA Civ 285 per Lord Justice Thorpe at para 23.
[14] Per Lady Justice Black at para 39.

parent. But such desires may be essentially selfish and may later insufficiently weigh the welfare and developing rights of the child that they have created'.[15]

THE WELFARE CHECKLIST

4.17   Section 1(3) of the Children Act sets out a checklist of factors to which in all contested section 8 applications the court must have reference. These factors, while not defining 'welfare', are the matters which must be considered[16] when assessing what is best for the welfare of the child. These factors are:[17]

'(a)   the ascertainable wishes and feelings of the child concerned (considered in the light of his age and understanding);

(b)   his physical, emotional and educational needs;

(c)   the likely effect on him of any change in his circumstances;

(d)   his age, sex, background and any characteristics of his which the court considers relevant;

(e)   any harm which he has suffered or is at risk of suffering;

(f)   how capable each of his parents, and any other person in relation to whom the court considers the question to be relevant, is of meeting his needs;

(g)   the range of powers available to the court under this Act in the proceedings in question.'

4.18   It is helpful, particularly where alternative family arrangements may arise, for the judge to formally assess each factor in the list in the course of the judgment, though not obliged to do so. The factors are not in any way ranked and each must be considered by the court.[18]

4.19   It is also significant to note the link between genetic parentage and the child's welfare. Baroness Hale in *Re G (Children)*[19] held that whilst psychological parents have an important contribution to make to a child's welfare, in the overall welfare judgment, biological parentage must count for something in the vast majority of cases:[20]

'Of course, in the great majority of cases, the natural mother combines all three. She is the genetic, gestational and psychological parent. Her contribution to the welfare of the child is unique.'

Baroness Hale equally recognised that genetic parentage, or even legal parentage alone, 'does not necessarily tell us much about the importance of that person to the child's welfare'.[21]

---

[15]   At para 27.

[16]   CA 1989, s 1(3) is mandatory, the court shall have regard to these factors.

[17]   CA 1989, s 1(3)(a)-(g).

[18]   *Re G* [2006] UKHL 43.

[19]   [2006] UKHL 43 at paras 37 and 38.

[20]   [2006] UKHL 43 at at para 36.

[21]   [2006] UKHL 43 at para 32.

4.20   Following the decision in *Re G*, the Supreme Court again considered the link between genetic parenthood and welfare, on that occasion in the context of a disagreement between a father and a grandparent regarding the arrangements for the child. In particular, in the case of *Re B (A Child)*[22] the Supreme Court considered the observations of Lord Nicholls in *Re G*, that 'in the ordinary way' the rearing of a child by his or her biological parent can be expected to be in his or her best interests. Lord Kerr reiterated:[23]

> 'All consideration of the importance of parenthood in private law disputes about residence must be firmly rooted in an examination of what is in the child's best interests. This is the paramount consideration. It is only as a contributor to the child's welfare that parenthood assumes any significance. In common with all other factors bearing on what is in the best interests of the child, it must be examined for its potential to fulfil that aim. There are various ways in which it may do so, some of which were explored by Baroness Hale in *In Re G*, but the essential task for the court is always the same.'

In that case, it was in the child's best interests to be brought up in the care of his grandmother who had cared for the child for most of his life, notwithstanding that the father could provide good enough care.

PARENTAL RESPONSIBILITY

4.21   Parental responsibility must be the starting point for any consideration of the legal position since it is not only all the rights, duties, powers, responsibilities and authority which by law a parent of a child has,[24] but it also reflects the 'status of parenthood' beyond genetic or legal parentage.[25] In the context of same sex families and private law matters the particular significance of parental responsibility arises:

- In conferring the 'status of parenthood' on a committed legal parent not automatically having parental responsibility by virtue of a marriage or civil partnership. In particular, a person who is a legal parent by virtue of satisfying the agreed fatherhood conditions[26] or the agreed female parenthood conditions[27] can apply for parental responsibility[28] where the mother does not agree that (s)he should have it.

---

[22]   [2009] UKSC 5.
[23]   At para 37.
[24]   CA 1989, s 3(1).
[25]   *Re S (Parental Responsibility)* [1995] 2 FLR 648 'It is wrong to place undue and therefore false emphasis on the rights and duties and the powers comprised in 'parental responsibility' and not to concentrate on the fact that what is at issue is conferring upon a committed father the status of parenthood for which nature has already ordained that he must bear responsibility.'
[26]   Within the meaning of HFEA 2008, s 37.
[27]   Within the meaning of HFEA 2008, s 44.
[28]   Pursuant to CA 1989, ss 4 and 4ZA.

- In determining whether a person has the right to apply for orders relating to a child, even if they are not a parent.[29] For example, if two people in a civil partnership co-parent a child, and the relationship breaks down, step-parent parental responsibility entitles the non-legal parent to apply for any section 8 order.[30]

- In demonstrating to the outside world that a non-legal parent has the right to make significant decisions relating to the child. For example, if two people co-parent a child, and are not civil partners, and the relationship breaks down, the court in granting a shared residence order can confer parental responsibility on the non-legal parent so that (s)he has the right to receive information from school or to consent to emergency medical treatment.[31]

- In defining and restricting the role of the biological father in the child's life where the child is being brought up by two female parents; for example *Re B (Role of Biological Father)*[32] referred to above where Hedley J refused the father parental responsibility because of the impact on the child's nuclear family. In the case of *R v E and F (Female Parents: Known Father)*[33] Bennett J similarly refused to grant parental responsibility to the biological father in a case where there was no evidence that the child regarded the father as having a parental role in relation to him.

- Where two women have a child with the assistance of a man, they have a fundamental choice to make about whether to place that man's name on the birth certificate at the time of the child's birth, and thereby confer parental responsibility on him. If they choose not to do so, he can still apply for a parental responsibility order at a later stage,[34] giving rise to the issue for the court already referred to. If they choose to do so, then:

    (a) they will be required to make him a respondent to any application which they make for a section 8 order, for example if they applied for a shared residence order in order to confer parental responsibility on the non-biological mother, and,

    (b) the fact of parental responsibility may carry some weight if the court is charged with determining what is in the best interests of the child. In the case of *MA v RS (Contact: Parenting Roles) sub nom (1) ML*

---

29 CA 1989, s 10 requires those without parental responsibility, or those who have parental responsibility but are not parents, to apply for leave to make an application for a section 8 order

30 CA 1989, s 10(4).

31 The case of *Re G (Children)* [2006] UKHL 43, in the Court of Appeal at [2005] EWCA Civ 462 is an example of this step being taken, and the Court of Appeal observed per curiam that there was little doubt that if the applicant had been an unmarried father parental responsibility would be likely to be granted.

32 [2007] EWHC 1952 (Fam), [2008] 1 FLR 1015.

33 [2010] EWHC 417 (Fam).

34 Pursuant to CA 1989, s 4.

(2) AR v (1) RW (2) SW[35] two women had a child with the assistance of the genetic father and his partner, both of whom had a significant role in the child's life by agreement. When relationships broke down, and the extent of the role of the father and his partner in the child's life could no longer be agreed, it was a significant factor that the genetic father held parental responsibility. However, his and his partner's secondary parenting role in the child's life was regulated by other section 8 orders.[36]

Parental responsibility is explored more fully in chapter 2.

SECTION 8 ORDERS

4.22 Many circumstances may arise where an individual might want to consider applying for a section 8 order. It might be that a dispute has arisen regarding with whom the child or children are to live, or with whom the child is to have contact, or the role of particular adults in a child's life. It might be that there is disagreement regarding a specific issue in the child's life. Equally it is possible that a family might wish to consider seeking a section 8 order in amicable circumstances where they have reached an agreement, regarding for instance sharing residence to secure parental responsibility, and want that agreement to be endorsed by the court. The court may make a section 8 order not only where it is applied for, but also in any family proceedings in which a question arises with respect to the welfare of the child, if the court considers that the order should be made.[37] Therefore, once the court is concerned with determining an aspect of a child's upbringing, it can make whichever orders are necessary to secure the welfare of the child even if those are not the orders applied for by any party.[38]

4.23 Under section 8 of the CA 1989[39] a court may make, vary or discharge the following orders:

- a contact order;

- a residence order;

---

[35] [2011] EWHC 2455 (Fam).

[36] Note however the Court of Appeal decision in *A v B and C* [2012] EWCA Civ 285 in which the court of appeal did not endorse Hedley J's concept of principal and secondary parents. From that case and the earlier Court of Appeal case of *T v T* [2010] EWCA Civ 1366 it is clear that the care which the father provides and the child's perception of his role is likely to carry greater weight than whether he has parental responsibility.

[37] CA 1989, s 10(1).

[38] Family proceedings as defined in CA 1989, s 8(3).

[39] Note that the government is currently considering replacing contact and residence orders with child arrangements orders to adjust the focus from perceived parental rights to practical arrangements. Ministry of Justice and Department of Education response to the Family Justice Review, February 2012.

- a prohibited steps order;

- a specific issue order.

In this section we look at the particular relevance for children being brought up by people in same sex relationships of these different types of orders.

Contact order

4.24 A 'contact order' means 'an order requiring the person with whom a child lives, or is to live, to allow the child to visit or stay with the person named in the order, or for that person and the child otherwise to have contact with each other'.[40]

4.25 Contact has a broad meaning and may encompass both direct contact (physical visits) and indirect contact such as exchange of letters.[41] Note that a contact order is an order which imposes the obligation on the person with whom the child is living or to live, not an order which imposes an obligation on a person to have contact. The wording of the precise obligation is significant in determining what the resident parent is required to do: 'To "allow" is to concede or to permit; to "make available" is to put at one's disposal or within one's reach', but it does not require a parent to physically force a child who genuinely refuses to attend.[42]

4.26 The terms of any contact order can be wide. Section 11 of the Children Act 1989 provides that a section 8 order may:

'(a)   Contain directions about how it is to be carried into effect;
(b)   Impose conditions which must be complied with by any person –
    (i)   In whose favour the order is made
    (ii)   Who is a parent of the child concerned
    (iii) Who is not a parent of his but who has parental responsibility for him; or
    (iv) With whom the child is living
    and to whom the conditions are expressed to apply
(c)   Be made to have effect for a specified period;
(d)   Make such incidental, supplemental or consequential provision as the court thinks fit.'

4.27 Section 11 conditions are used to effect in a wide variety of situations where there is a dispute as to the contact which a person shall have. Commonly, a contact order may:

- define frequency and duration;

---

[40]   CA 1989, s 8(1).
[41]   *Re P (Contact: Indirect Contact)* [1999] 2 FLR 893.
[42]   *Re L-W (Enforcement and Committal: Contact)* [2011] 1 FLR 1095.

- impose a condition of supervision, or contact taking place in a particular venue, if there are welfare concerns;

- require a child to be dropped off or collected from a particular venue;

- specify who may and who may not attend contact;

- specify the places that the child may or may not be taken to.

Such conditions, if imposed, form part of the order.

4.28 In cases between mothers and fathers who have been in a relationship with each other, the courts have taken the approach that a full relationship with both parents is usually in the child's best interests unless there are welfare or safety concerns which mean a child's contact with one parent needs to be restricted or curtailed. This is likely to be formally reinforced in legislation, the government has recently stated:[43]

'Both Governments believe that children benefit from both parents being as fully involved as possible in their child's upbringing, unless there are safety or welfare concerns ... The Government believes that there should be a legislative statement of the importance of children having an ongoing relationship with both their parents after family separation, where that is safe, and in the child's best interests.'

In the context of same sex relationships, the court's approach to an application for contact where it is disputed will need to reflect not only any welfare or safety concerns, but also the particular family structure for that child, and the nature of the relationship between the adults in dispute and between the applicant and the child. This is an area of law currently rapidly evolving as the courts endeavour to meet the best interests of the child in a wide variety of factual circumstances. What is emerging is an approach which focuses on the importance of a particular relationship to the child rather than the biological or legal significance of a relationship.

Contact between same sex parents and their child following the breakdown of their relationship

4.29 An application for contact by a parent, whether legal or psychological, following the breakdown of a same sex relationship holds many similarities with applications for contact by parents (usually fathers) following the breakdown of opposite sex relationships in which the courts have overwhelmingly endeavoured to promote the fullest contact possible where it is safe to do so.

---

[43] Ministry of Justice and Department of Education response to the Family Justice Review, February 2012.

4.30   In recent years, the increasing tendency of the court has been to make a shared residence order in favour of both natural parents[44] after the breakdown of a same sex relationship because of the lack of alternative means for conferring parental responsibility on someone who is going to have the child in their care for substantial periods of time and may need to be able to take decisions in relation to them. An early example of this can be found in the case of *G v F*[45] which concerned the breakdown of a same sex relationship. The approach taken by Bracewell J in that case to the issue of making a shared residence order was later endorsed by the decisions of the Court of Appeal and in the House of Lords in *Re G*.[46] In the case of *Re G*, the county court had made a residence order in favour of the biological mother and contact order in favour of the non-biological mother. On appeal from that decision, the Court of Appeal made a shared residence order defining the time that the children would spend in each household, and imposed a condition requiring the biological mother to remain in the Leicestershire area.[47] The link between the ordering of shared residence and parental responsibility was clear. Lord Justice Thorpe held:

'[27] But perhaps more crucial for me was the judge's finding that between the first and second days of the hearing the mother had been developing plans to marginalise Miss W. In that context it is relevant to refer to the publication in July 2004 of the Government's Green Paper in relation to contact difficulties. That Green Paper has led to the relatively recent publication of the draft Children (Contact) and Adoption Bill. The Government has, by its consultation paper and its subsequent proposed bill, highlighted the very great social problems that have been developing over the last few years as a consequence of an increased tendency for primary carers to ignore, or to observe only in the letter, court orders designed to guarantee contact to the absent parent. The whole purpose of the Bill is to introduce new powers and management techniques for judges to combat such adult manipulation. The CAFCASS officer had expressed a clear fear that, unless a parental responsibility order was made, there was a real danger that Miss W would be marginalised in the children's future. I am in no doubt at all that, on the judge's finding, the logical consequence was the conclusion that the children required firm measures to safeguard them from diminution in, or loss of, a vital side of family life — not only their relationship with Miss W, but also with her son. The parental responsibility order was correctly identified by the CAFCASS officer as the appropriate safeguard. The judge's finding required a clear and strong message to the mother that she could not achieve the elimination of Miss W, or even the reduction of Miss W from the other parent into some undefined family connection. It may be that the mother's own needs and emotions drove her in that direction, but that road had to be sealed off for, if not sealed off, it would be taken at a real cost to the children. I do not think that that factor was sufficiently identified by the judge.

[28] For all those reasons I would allow the appeal and grant the joint residence order that the judge refused.'

---

44   In the sense defined by Baroness Hale in *Re G*.
45   [1998] 2 FLR 799.
46   [2006] UKHL 43.
47   *Re G (Residence: Same-Sex Partner)* [2005] EWCA Civ 372.

4.31 Following the biological mother's breach of the condition as to residence, the High Court retained the shared residence order but changed the times that the children were to spend in each household so that the non-biological mother became the primary carer. In the appeal from that decision, in both the Court of Appeal[48] and the House of Lords,[49] the shared residence order was confirmed. The issue was as to how that was to operate in terms of time spent with each parent, and who was to be their primary carer. Ultimately the House of Lords allowed the appeal against the non-biological parent being the primary carer.

4.32 The county court similarly made a shared residence order in the case of *T v B*[50] prior to the biological mother issuing an application for financial provision. The making of a shared residence order had been opposed by the biological mother in that case, and lengthy court proceedings were necessary to secure the order so that the non-biological mother could have parental responsibility for the child who was spending half of the week with her.

4.33 In both of these cases the biological mother had questioned the importance of the non-biological mother in the children's lives, and the child's perception was that both of the women were natural parents and of equal importance to them.

4.34 In contrast, the recent High Court decision in *Re R (Parental Responsibility)*[51] concerned a heterosexual relationship where the man brought the child up as his own, he and the mother were married, and after separation the mother told him that he was not in fact the father. The court refused the application for parental responsibility, and placed considerable weight on the fact that he was not the biological father, citing *Re G*. Albeit that was not a contact application, the court observed that the man was not likely to have such a significant role in the child's future development that it warranted investing him with equal status.

4.35 The question of what contact with a co-parent is in the child's best interests will undoubtedly be affected by any domestic violence in the relationship. *Practice Direction (Residence and Contact Orders: Domestic Violence) (No 2)*[52] sets out what should be the court's approach in cases where domestic violence has been raised as an issue. Where domestic violence is disputed the first role of the court is to consider whether to hold a fact-finding hearing to make a determination of whether and/or to what extent domestic violence has occurred. Where domestic violence has occurred the court should take steps to obtain a report by a CAFCASS officer regarding the local facilities available to support or assist any party and whether any party would benefit from support or counselling before a decision is made on whether to

---

48 [2006] EWCA Civ 372, [2006] 2 FLR 614.
49 [2006] UKHL 43.
50 [2010] EWHC 1444 (Fam).
51 [2011] EWHC 1535 (Fam).
52 [2009] 1 WLR 251.

grant a contact order. Where domestic harm has occurred the court 'should in every case consider any harm which the child has suffered as a consequence of that violence and any harm which the child is at risk of suffering if an order for residence or contact is made and should only make an order for contact if it can be satisfied that the physical and emotional safety of the child and the parent with whom the child is living can, as far as possible, be secured before during and after contact.'[53] If after applying the welfare checklist the court decides that direct contact is in the child's best interest it can decide to impose directions as to how the contact is to proceed, for instance that the contact be supervised.

Contact between the biological father and the child of a same sex relationship

4.36   The court has relatively recently had to grapple with the question of what role should be played in a child's life by his or her biological father where the child is being brought up by his or her mother and her partner in a same sex relationship. Part of this may concern the grant or refusal of parental responsibility, discussed at **4.21** et seq, but in addition to parental responsibility, the court can regulate his role in a child's life utilising contact orders and conditions attached to those orders. No English cases have yet been reported which concern an application by a genetic father who is not the legal father in the context of a child being brought up by two female parents. It will undoubtedly arise in due course that the court will be asked to consider such an application where two female civil partners have created a child which legally they are the sole parents of using donated gametes through informal at-home insemination and the genetic father later seeks contact. He will have to apply for leave to make such an application in accordance with s 10 of the Children Act 1989, and it will be interesting to see whether the court grants leave in such circumstances. The outcome is likely to depend, in part, on whether the genetic father has had any part to play in the child's life beyond donating gametes, and whether there was any agreement as to the genetic father's role. This has been the approach of the Australian High Court within their similar statutory framework.[54] The Australian case of *Wilson v Roberts*[55] concerned a child born to two female parents following sperm being donated by a man who was also in a same sex relationship. It was agreed before the child was born that the genetic father and his partner would have a significant role in the child's life, but it was the women who were the child's only legal parents. This was the reality for the child for the first year before the relationship between the adults broke down. The genetic father and his partner were permitted to make applications relating to the child, and the court order provided for them to have contact at a level which did not disrupt the family unit, but permission was given for the child and her parents to re-locate abroad.

---

[53]   [2009] I WLR 251 at [26].
[54]   Section 60H of the Australian Family Law Act 1975.
[55]   [2010] Fam CA 734.

In 2009 the Irish Supreme Court considered this issue in the case of *McD v L and Another*[56] where the father applied for contact and a guardianship order. The child was being brought up by two women in a civil partnership. The Irish Supreme Court considered that it was in the child's best interests to know his father through the medium of contact, but refused the application for guardianship, which would have had an effect similar to conferring parental responsibility on the father. The court considered that the effect on the child's nuclear family unit would have been caused detriment by granting the father guardianship.

4.37 In the courts of England and Wales there has been a line of authority developing in recent years culminating in the landmark Court of Appeal decision in the case of *A v B and C*[57] in March 2012, and it is plain from that decision that the law is still evolving.

4.38 In *Re D (Contact and PR: Lesbian Mothers and Known Father)* (2006)[58] the situation arose that a female same sex couple had advertised for a male sperm donor with the intention that he would play a role within the child's life (the exact nature of that role was not fully explored and led to difficulties after the child's birth regarding parental responsibility). As regards contact it was noted by Mrs Justice Black that contact between the child and the child's father had the potential to help the child by allowing her father to answer the questions she would have about him. Against this had to be weighed the potential disruption of contact to the same sex couple. In the event a contact order was made as it 'would contribute greatly to her self esteem to know that she has a father who loves her and to see him from time to time'.[59]

4.39 In *Re B (Biological Father)* (2008)[60] occurred in similar circumstances to *Re D*, in that a father who had donated his sperm to a female same sex couple now sought to be more involved in the life of the child. There was in this case a greater degree of animosity between the couple and the father, who in this instance was also the brother of the non-biological mother and therefore also had an avuncular role. The court was asked to decide upon whether a contact order should be granted in circumstances where the same sex couple wanted the father's role to be limited to a purely avuncular one and the father wanted a more substantial relationship. A contact order was made but only for contact four times a year, this being seen to balance the need on one hand for the child to have the opportunity to ask questions which might arise but on the other hand also to ensure that the contact order was not seen as granting parental status and did not undermine the role of the women parenting the child.

---

[56]   [2009] IESC 81.
[57]   [2012] EWCA Civ 285.
[58]   [2006] EWHC 2 (Fam).
[59]   [2006] EWHC 2 (Fam) at [10].
[60]   [2007] EWHC 1952 (Fam), [2008] 1 FLR 1015.

4.40   In *R v E and F (Female Parents: Known Father)* (2010)[61] the child, then nearly 7, was being parented by two women in a civil partnership. The child's father was also in a civil partnership (US marriage) and lived in America. The parents had been friends since before the child was born, and the father and his partner had been involved with the child throughout his life. Unfortunately relations broke down and the father applied for contact and shared residence. At that time the child had never spent a night away from his mothers, although the families had holidayed together. The psychological evidence demonstrated that although the child loved his father he did not perceive his father as having a parenting role in relation to him. Mr Justice Bennett limited contact to 50 days per year.

4.41   The case of *T v T* (2010)[62] concerned children aged 10 and 7 being brought up by two women in a civil partnership. Their genetic and legal father was a man who the women met when he advertised that he would like to become a father, but by the time the matter came before the court the reality for the children was that they genuinely regarded the father as a parent and he had had parental responsibility for some time and regular overnight contact. The judge granted a shared residence order in favour of the biological mother and father which was upheld on appeal, and the birth mother's civil partner was then included in the shared residence order as a third person with whom the child was to live.[63] The court was keen to emphasise in this case, that the child's perception of the importance of the particular adults involved to them was more important than the labels, which were essentially adult issues.

4.42   In the recent case of *ML & AR v RW & SW* (2011)[64] Hedley J introduced the concept of 'principal and secondary parenting' into a contact dispute between two same sex couples. The circumstances were that a female same sex couple – the respondents – had advertised for man to donate gametes. They had been contacted by the first applicant who was in a long-term same sex relationship with the second applicant and was also seeking to become a parent. The mother was inseminated with the sperm of the first applicant, which lead to the birth of two children. He was the legal father and had parental responsibility. Evidence from letters exchanged by the two couples before conception showed that a role within the children's lives had definitely been envisaged for the father and his partner though it was recognised that the female same sex couple would hold the principal parenting role.

4.43   Noting that existing legal language struggled to describe the present scenario he suggested that the female same sex couple should be thought of as the 'principal parenters'. The father and his partner should be thought of as the 'secondary parenters', not taking day-to-day decisions for the children or

---

[61]   [2010] 2 FLR 383.
[62]   [2010] EWCA Civ 1366.
[63]   Per Black LJ at para 47: 'I would still not have treated [the position should the mother die] as sufficient to interfere with the Recorder's order had it not been for F's offer to agree to a residence order that includes L as well as M and himself'.
[64]   [2011] EWHC 2455 (Fam).

providing primary care but acting to give the children a sense of their identity, providing a male component to their upbringing and a 'more general level of benign involvement'.[65] The court in trying to uphold that important role refused the father's application for residence but granted a contact order to the male same sex couple enabling them to have contact with the younger child for two nights a month, acknowledging the importance of the children seeing all four parents, including the father's partner. Unfortunately, the older child had suffered significant emotional harm as a result of the breakdown in the relationship between the parents to the extent that she was now refusing contact with her father, and the sequel to this decision is the case of *Re P and L (Contact)*.[66]

4.44 Hot on the heels of this decision by Mr Justice Hedley came the case of *A v B & C* in the High Court[67] (2011) which on appeal became the landmark Court of Appeal decision of the same name (March 2012).[68] The facts of that case were different again to the other cases which had been considered by the court in the context of regulating the relationship between a child and his or her biological father. In this case the mother and father were in fact married, although both of them were in same sex relationships with other people, and as good friends they had married for reasons relating to the mother's family's cultural expectations. The consequence, however, was that the father was indeed a legal father sharing parental responsibility, whilst the child was being parented by the mother and her partner, who was not a legal parent, and it had always been intended that this should be so. The mother, father and mother's partner were agreed that father should have a role in the child's life, but had differing expectations of the extent of that role. When the relationship between the adults broke down when the child was about 18 months old, the father applied for shared residence. The women were particularly concerned about the marginalisation of the non-biological mother and what should happen if the birth mother died. Despite the father's unusual status as a father married to the mother where there had never been anything like a marital relationship between the parents, HHJ Jenkins sitting as a deputy judge of the High Court held that it was completely inappropriate to treat this as a situation analogous to a divorce, and that to do so would not be in the best interests of the child as it would threaten the stability of his primary parenting unit.

The father appealed, not particularly because of the terms of the contact order, but because in the course of his judgment HHJ Jenkins indicated that the father's role in the child's life for any foreseeable future should be secondary; enough for the child to know who his father was but not so much as to fracture the nuclear family. In allowing the appeal, the Court of Appeal, whilst declining to give generalised guidance, or make a welfare decision for this child:

---

[65] [2011] EWHC 2455 (Fam) at [17].
[66] [2011] EWHC 3431 (Fam).
[67] [2011] EWHC 2290 (Fam).
[68] [2012] EWCA Civ 285.

(a)   Did not endorse Mr Justice Hedley's formulation of 'principal' and 'secondary' parents in the case of *ML & AR v RW & SW* (2011)[69] (albeit acknowledging that at that time the father was providing only secondary care to the child).

(b)   Did not endorse the idea of a 'general rule' to be applied in cases where there is a dispute with a known father and reiterated that welfare is the only principle.

(c)   Indicated that the question of whether the child's relationship with his father should be encouraged to thrive and develop had to be decided in stages in the light of accumulating evidence (as to the child's welfare).

(d)   Opened the door to a 'three parents and two homes' regime in appropriate cases.

(e)   Indicated that the long term advantages to a child of having a relationship with his or her father must be weighed against short term distress caused to the mother.

(f)   Confirmed that the child's source of nurture, security and stability is likely to be important in deciding what is best for the child.

(g)   Endorsed intended parents planning in as much detail as they can what they contemplate will be the arrangements for the care and upbringing of the child, whilst also rejecting the notion that such agreements will or should be determinative.

The Court of Appeal also suggested that expert evidence may be appropriate in this case, to guide the court, and it is therefore to be expected that the jurisprudence will develop further.

Enforcement of the contact order

4.45   The making of a contact order alone may not always mean that contact takes place as set out in it. The reasons for this are manifold; there may be a significant breakdown in communication, it may be that the adult responsible for facilitating contact is actively obstructing contact due to antagonism towards the other party, or that the resident parent has genuine concerns about contact or it may be that the party in whose favour the contact order has been made is somehow not complying with it. It may also be the cause of the breakdown of contact lies with the child him or herself due to apprehension about contact which may be the child's own fears or the fears of the resident parent which have been projected onto the child. In alternative family structures the legal mother or father is perhaps not a person known very well by the day-to-day parents, and there may be a heightened lack of trust and an added dynamic which may not present in traditional family structures.

---

[69]   [2011] EWHC 2455 (Fam).

4.46 Wall J in *Re O (A Child) (Contact: Withdrawal of Application)*[70] acknowledged that disputes about contact post contact orders are some of the hardest cases which family judges have to deal with. He urged parties if possible to try to come to a reconciliation if that was a suitable alternative[71] rather than pursue their dispute through the courts.

4.47 In the past the court's powers to enforce contact orders were largely limited to punitive measures against the non-co-operating party. Whilst these powers continue they have now been supplemented by the Children and Adoption Act 2006. The measures contained in the Children and Adoption Act 2006, as inserted into the CA 1989, allow the court to make a contact activity direction in connection with a contact order.[72] Contact activity directions are not only enforcement mechanisms, but can be made for the purposes of trying to address the underlying issues such as poor communication between the parents. A contact activity direction can be made not only in respect of the resident parent, but also the parent in whose favour the contact order is made. The direction may require any person who is party to the proceedings to attend classes or programmes either to 'assist a person as regards establishing, maintaining or improving contact with a child'[73] or 'by addressing a person's violent behaviour, enable or facilitate contact with a child'.[74] A person may also be required to attend information sessions to help them achieve better contact.[75] The court may seek reports on compliance with contact order directions or monitoring of the contact by a CAFCASS officer.[76] In practice, the facilities currently available as contact activity directions are limited to domestic violence programmes and parenting information programmes. However, the court can also make a family assistance order[77] where appropriate requiring an officer of CAFCASS or social worker to 'advise, befriend and assist' the people named in the order for up to 12 months, and often CAFCASS or the named social worker can offer some valuable support to the family during that time which enables contact to progress more smoothly. The court can provide specifically, when making a family assistance order and a contact order, for the CAFCASS officer or social worker to give advice and assistance as regards establishing, improving and maintaining contact to persons named in the order.[78] This can be a particularly useful tool where there are extended family relationships to consider which affect the contact arrangements. It may be that this is an order which is well suited to working with the complicated extended family dynamics which can arise where a child is being parented by people in a same sex relationship and where there is a breakdown in the adult relationships which are of significance to the child.

---

[70]   [2003] EWHC 3031 (Fam), [2004] 1 FLR 1258.
[71]   In cases of suspected domestic violence a reconciliation might well be inappropriate.
[72]   CA 1989, s 11A.
[73]   CA 1989, s 11A (5)(a)(i).
[74]   CA 1989, s 11A(5)(a)(ii).
[75]   CA 1989, s 11A(5)(b).
[76]   CA 1989, ss 11G–11H.
[77]   CA 1989, s 16.
[78]   CA 1989, s 16(4A).

4.48 Where contact orders have been breached the court may impose an 'enforcement order' which imposes an unpaid work requirement[79] or require the non-co-operating party to provide compensation for the breach of the contact order – for instance the cost of travel for a parent with a contact order who travelled to the appointed place for contact only to find that their child was not there.[80]

4.49 As a last resort the court may commit a person who repeatedly breaches a contact order to prison.[81] Residence can also be transferred to the person in whose favour the contact order has been made as a mechanism of enforcement although such a significant step can only be taken when it is in the best interests of the child's welfare and should not be taken to punish a parent.[82] It is recognised in the cases between mothers and fathers that the child's welfare includes the need for a child to have a relationship with both parents, and if it is necessary to transfer residence from one parent to another in order to ensure that this happens, the court will sometimes do so.[83] The case of *Re G*[84] concerned not a contact order, but breach of the terms of a shared residence order which prohibited relocation when the biological mother moved the children to Cornwall. The Court of Appeal changed the arrangements so that the non-biological mother cared for the children most of the time having regard to the 'real risk' that the biological mother would marginalise the non-biological mother (as discussed a **4.30** above), but this was overturned on appeal by the House of Lords. It was a significant factor in that case, however that the non-biological mother was still being afforded good contact time with the children.

Residence order

4.50 A 'residence order' means 'an order settling the arrangements to be made as to the person with whom a child is to live'.[85]

4.51 A residence order determines the practical arrangements for the child. The only criteria for the court in making the decision as to where the child is to live is the child's welfare: the test in s 1 of the CA 1989 applies.

4.52 There is no legal presumption that it is in a child's best interests that (s)he is brought up by a biological parent.[86] As set out above (see **4.20**), biological

---

[79] CA 1989, s 11J.

[80] CA 1989, s 11O.

[81] *Re O (Contact: Imposition of Conditions)* 1 FCR 317.

[82] *V v V (Children) (Intractable Contact Dispute)* [2004] EWHC 1215 (Fam) at [48], [2004] 2 FLR 851.

[83] *Re W (Residence: Leave to Appeal)* [2010] EWCA Civ 1143. Transfer of residence following frustration of contact. Not appropriate to change a child's residence in order to punish the mother for failure to obey court orders. But in this case there was ample material on which the court could say the child would continue to suffer harm if she stayed with the mother.

[84] [2006] UKHL 43.

[85] CA 1989, s 8(1).

[86] *Re B* [2009] UKSC 5.

parentage is, however one of the factors to be taken into account when considering what order is in a child's best interests, and must not be overlooked. In the case of *Re B*[87] referred to above, the child had lived with his maternal grandmother since birth – he was at that time three years old. His biological father applied to remove the child from his grandmother's care. Lord Kerr in discussing the interpretations of the decision in *Re G*[88] said that: 'For a proper understanding of the view that he [Lord Nicholls] expressed, it is important at the outset to recognise that Lord Nicholls' comment about the rearing of a child by a biological parent is set firmly in the context of the child's welfare'. This he identified as 'the court's paramount consideration'. 'It must be the dominant and overriding factor that ultimately determines disputes about residence and contact'.[89] Lord Kerr explained that the sense of Lord Nicholls' comment should be that, in the ordinary case of things, one could expect a child to do best with their biological parents. However, disputes over residence often occurred far outside the ordinary case of things and thus it should always be born in mind that the child's welfare as set out in s 1(3) of the Children Act was the primary concern not biological connection. In the context of alternative family relationships where it might arise that the adults best able to provide for the child's welfare were not the child's biological parents this is a decision of some importance.

4.53 The key things to note about a residence order in the context of same sex relationships are:

- It confers parental responsibility on whomever it is made in favour of[90] but it does not confer any sort of status on a parent or anyone else (it should be noted that this parental responsibility lasts only as long as the residence order is in place).[91]

- It does not need to be made in favour of a parent.[92]

- It can be made in favour of more than one person.[93]

- Where the court makes a residence order in favour of more than one person, it may specify the periods during which the child(ren) are to live in the households concerned.[94]

---

[87] [2009] UKSC 5.
[88] [2006] UKHL 43.
[89] [2009] UKSC 5 at [34], [2010] 1 FLR 551.
[90] CA 1989, s 12(2).
[91] CA 1989, s 12(2).
[92] *G v F (Contact and Shared Residence: Applications for Leave)* [1998] 2 FLR 799: There is statutory endorsement of the fact that the persons do not have to be mother and father and neither do they have to be equal periods in respect of the time spent in the different households.
[93] CA 1989, s 11(4).
[94] CA 1989, s 11(4).

4.54 Commonly, a residence order made in favour of two people who are living together is referred to as a joint residence order, and where it is made in favour of two or more people who are not living together it is referred to as a shared residence order. The former allows same sex couples who are still in a relationship to both have parental responsibility for the children they are bringing up without entering into a civil partnership and where they are not both legal parents. It also clarifies the immediate arrangements for the child in the event that the legal parent dies. A shared residence order is more commonly used following the breakdown of a relationship, whether between the same sex couple themselves, or between the couple and a third party such as the genetic father.[95]

4.55 The importance of a residence order therefore extends outside simply deciding with whom the child is to live; it can also act as a medium to grant parental responsibility where there is no other means of doing so; it can act as a signifier of the importance of a parent to a child; and it can be made so as to reduce the opportunity for a parent to be marginalised – this is discussed further above with reference to the decision of the Court of Appeal in the case of *Re G*.[96]

4.56 A shared residence order does not require exceptional circumstances and the Court of Appeal has held that where a child is spending broadly equal periods of time in each home, good reasons are required if a shared residence order is not to be made.[97] Even where the child is not spending equal amounts of time in each home, a shared residence order can properly be made. In *Re L (Shared Residence Order)*[98] Lord Justice Wall reiterated clearly: 'There is no doubt that a shared residence order can properly be made where there is a substantial geographical distance between the parties: see, for example, the decision of this court *Re F (Shared Residence Order)*,[99] in which the mother was planning to relocate to Edinburgh, a considerable distance from where the father lived'. Furthermore, shared residence orders are sometimes made as an important way of emphasising the fact that both parents are equal in the eyes of the law, and that they have equal duties and responsibilities as parents.[100]

4.57 In *Re G*[101] itself provides an example of a case involving a same sex couple who had been in a relationship and where a shared residence was made in circumstances where the children were not anticipated to spend equal amounts of time with both parties or even live in close proximity to each other.

---

[95] In the case of *Re TT* [2010] EWCA Civ 1366 there was a joint residence order in favour of three people, the mother and her female partner who remained in a relationship, and the genetic father.

[96] [2005] 2 FLR 957.

[97] *Re P (Shared Residence Order)* [2005] EWCA Civ 1639.

[98] [2009] EWCA Civ 20, [2009] 1 FLR 1157.

[99] [2003] EWCA Civ 592, [2003] 2 FLR 397.

[100] *Re P (Shared Residence Order)* [2005] EWCA Civ 1639.

[101] [2006] UKHL 43, [2006] 2 FLR 629.

4.58 In the leading case of *T v T*[102] a three-way residence order was made between a mother, her female partner and the child's biological father. The children were primarily living with the two women, but knew their father as a father and were spending considerable periods of time with him: '[The] children genuinely regarded F as their parent, wanted to spend time in both homes and would be spending a significant portion of the year with F'. It was observed by Lady Justice Black in upholding the shared residence order which extended to the father, that the three-way order which extended to the non-biological mother would not have been made had it not been consented to by the biological mother and father. It is not clear why the court at first instance should have been reluctant to include the non-biological mother (who was involved in the day-to-day parenting for the child) in the shared residence order. However, the Court of Appeal endorsed the sharing of residence between the 3 adults, and in particular it was significant for the child that in the event of the birth mother dying unexpectedly, the co-parenting mother sharing a residence order as well as parental responsibility should serve to reduce anxiety about where the child should live.

Conditions

4.59 It may be the case that the court attaches conditions to a residence order[103] containing directions on how it is to be carried out or applying restrictions or specific conditions to it. However, instances in which the court will do so are rare because, per Lord Justice Wall in the case of *Re L (Shared Residence Order)*:[104]

> 'the imposition of restrictions is likely to have an adverse effect on the welfare of the children indirectly through the emotional and psychological disturbance caused to the primary carer by denial of the freedom to exercise reasonable choice.'

4.60 *S (A Child) (Residence Order: Conditions)*[105] is an example, in the context of a mother and father who had previously been in a relationship, of an exceptional case where conditions were placed on a residence order which restricted the mother from moving with the child away from London, where her father lived, to Cornwall. Baroness Hale in giving judgment did stress, in cases where the adult with the residence order was providing suitable care, that conditions would only be imposed in exceptional circumstances. In the case of *S (A Child) (Residence Order: Conditions)* those exceptional circumstances were that the child in question had Down's Syndrome and so would be unable to comprehend such major changes in her life or why she could no longer see her father regularly after she moved to Cornwall.

---

[102] [2010] EWCA Civ 1366.
[103] Indeed conditions may be attached to any section 8 order – CA 1989, s 11(7).
[104] [2009] EWCA Civ 20, [2009] 1 FLR 1157.
[105] [2002] EWCA Civ 1795.

4.61   The Court of Appeal in the case of *Re G*[106] made a shared residence order and imposed on the biological mother a condition that she reside in Leicestershire. Although this condition was not appealed, when the mother moved to Cornwall in breach of the condition, and the High Court granted the non-biological mother the primary parenting role under the auspices of the shared residence order, and the Court of Appeal endorsed that approach, the House of Lords allowed the appeal against that decision. The effect of this was to allow the biological mother to continue to reside in Cornwall with the children.

4.62   In the ordinary way, a condition as to where a parent should live if the child is living with them is an 'unwarranted imposition' on the right of a parent to choose where (s)he will live in the UK.[107] The existence of a shared residence order does, of itself, mean that one parent will not be allowed to re-locate within the UK in such a way as to make the existing shared care arrangements unworkable:[108]

> 'There may be cases in which it is determinative of welfare, but there will be others where it will plainly be in the best interests of the child to relocate, notwithstanding the existence of a shared residence order. Simply to distinguish the case on the basis of a shared residence order is, in my judgment, to run the risk of making it determinative in all cases and of distorting the welfare balancing exercise.'

Effect of a residence order

4.63   Section 13 of the CA 1989 sets out two specific consequences of a residence order namely:[109]

> '(1) Where a residence order is in force with respect to a child, no person may –
>
> (a)   cause the child to be known by a new surname; or
> (b)   remove him from the United Kingdom;
>
> without either the written consent of every person who has parental responsibility for the child or the leave of the court.'

Change of name

4.64   The requirement that the child's surname cannot be changed without either consent of every person with parental responsibility or the leave of the court is fairly straightforward. In the event that all those with parental responsibility consent to the changing of the name this can be simply evidenced by executing a change of name deed. In the event that all those with parental responsibility do not consent then an application for leave must be made to the court. The court has also indicated that it is good practice for the mother to apply to the court for permission to change a child's surname even where there

---

[106]   [2002] EWCA Civ 1795.
[107]   *Re L* [2009] EWCA Civ 20, [2009] 1 FLR 1157.
[108]   Per Wall LJ at para 52.
[109]   CA 1989, s 13(1).

is no residence order in force or the father does not hold parental responsibility.[110] There is as yet no reported authority on the issue of a biological mother or father changing the surname of a child brought up in a same sex relationship with a co-parent, or the extent to which the principles normally applied as between a mother and a father[111] apply in those circumstances. In the context of same sex relationships, if the child is being brought up by two people with parental responsibility, and not by the biological mother or father, pursuant to s 13 CA 1989, the consent of the biological mother or father would still be required before the child could be 'known' by a different name to that on his or her birth certificate. This would include the child being known by a different name without it being formally changed by a change of name deed.

Removal from the jurisdiction

4.65 If the parent with residence wishes to remove the child from England and Wales for more than one month, then, either permission must be granted by every person with parental responsibility or an application for leave must be made to the court. It is outside the scope of this work to explore in detail the law pertaining to applications for leave to remove a child permanently from the jurisdiction for the purposes of relocation in another country, save to note in the context of the increased tendency to grant shared residence orders to same sex parents in cases where this is the only means of ensuring both have parental responsibility, the case of *K v K (Relocation: Shared Care Arrangement)*[112] confirms that the court's approach where there is no 'primary carer' is necessarily different to those cases where there is a clear primary carer. The Court of Appeal also made it plain that the question of whether there is more than one primary carer is not dependent on the existence of a shared residence order:

> 'What is significant is not the label "shared residence" because we see cases in which for a particular reason the label is attached to what is no more than a conventional contact order. What is significant is the practical arrangements for sharing the burden of care between two equally committed carers. Where each is providing a more or less equal proportion and one seeks to relocate externally then I am clear that the approach which I suggested at para [40] in *Payne v Payne* [2001] EWCA Civ 166, [2001] Fam 473, [2001] 1 FLR 1052, [2001] UKHRR 484 should not be utilised. The judge should rather exercise his discretion to grant or refuse by applying the statutory checklist in s 1(3) of the CA 1989.'

4.66 In that case the Court of Appeal overturned the decision of the High Court to allow the mother to relocate to Canada. It is of note that the court refers to 'carers' rather than parents, but of course it must be borne in mind that biological parentage is one of the factors in determining welfare.

---

[110] *Re PC* [1997] 2 FLR 730; *Re C* [1998] 2 FLR 656.
[111] Per the decision in *Dawson v Wearmouth* 1999] 1 FLR 1167.
[112] [2011] EWCA Civ 793.

4.67   It is also worth noting particularly in the context of children being brought up by same sex parents, if they are a couple and hold a shared residence order for the purposes of conferring parental responsibility, the residence order will prevent them from removing the child from the jurisdiction for more than a month without the permission of a parent with parental responsibility – for example a father to a child born after 3 December 2003 and named on the birth certificate. The co-parenting women would then have to make an application for leave to remove the child from the jurisdiction even for the purposes of taking a holiday for longer than a month. Holders of a residence order should be aware that a breach of this statutory restriction on removing the child from the jurisdiction for more than a month without the written consent of all persons holding parental responsibility or order of the court may constitute an unlawful removal from the jurisdiction and an offence of child abduction,[113] even where the other person holding parental responsibility has a limited role in the child's life.

Prohibited steps order

4.68   A 'prohibited steps order' means an order that 'no step which could be taken by a parent in meeting his parental responsibility for a child, and which is of a kind specified in the order, shall be taken by any person without the consent of the court'.[114]

4.69   A prohibited steps order may be made against a person (not necessarily a person with parental responsibility) in order to prohibit any act 'which could be taken by a parent in meeting his parental responsibility'.[115] In practice this means that an order could be made to prohibit a person, even if they did not have parental responsibility, from seeking contact with a child where that person posed a risk to the child.[116]

4.70   A prohibited steps order may be made to prevent a person from removing a child from the care of another person or from places such as school outside agreed or ordered contact arrangements. A prohibited steps order is also commonly made to prohibit a parent from removing a child from the jurisdiction where there is a fear of abduction, although the prohibited steps order of itself is not sufficient to prevent an abduction and urgent specialist advice should be taken if the risk of abduction is a concern, including contacting Reunite International for guidance and information.[117] It is outside the scope of this work to explore the law relating to international child abduction.

---

[113]   The Child Abduction Act 1984 makes it an offence for a parent to remove a child from the UK without the appropriate consents.

[114]   CA 1989, s 8(1).

[115]   CA 1989, s 8(1).

[116]   *Re H (Prohibited Steps Order)* [1995] 1 FLR 638.

[117]   Their child abduction prevention pack can be downloaded from their website and contains useful information for parents concerned about the possibility of child abduction.

Specific issue order

4.71 A 'specific issue order' means 'an order giving directions for the purpose of determining a specific question which has arisen, or which may arise, in connection with any aspect of parental responsibility for a child'.[118]

4.72 This is similar to the prohibited steps order in that it relates to the exercise of parental responsibility on a particular issue. Unlike a prohibited steps order however it can require positive action as well as mandate against action being taken.

4.73 A specific issue order, much like a prohibited steps order, may be made to resolve specific issues including where the child should go to school[119] (this may be of particular importance to a child being brought up by same sex parents if they hold fears regarding how the child's circumstances would be perceived in a particular school), medical treatment[120] and permission to take the child out of the country on holiday.[121]

4.74 A specific issue order is sometimes used where there is a lack of agreement about what a child should be told of his or her parentage. This has historically been the case most usually where a parent has changed gender, or a child has been brought up believing that a step-parent is his or her natural parent. It is perhaps to be expected that issues of this nature will arise in some same sex families because of the necessity for third party involvement, and that this may increase following the change of the law to allow two female parents. Should a child be told that his social uncle is in fact his genetic father, for instance? Does the answer to this change depending on whether the uncle is also a legal parent? What should a surrogate child be told about their genetic mother or gestational mother? This is a particular area in which the legal landscape is still evolving, and of course the decision in any case will be fact specific. The courts have made it clear in the context of children conceived within opposite sex relationships that scientific certainty is preferable to legal presumption.[122] It is less clear what the courts will determine a child should be told of his or her biological parentage where he or she has two legal parents of the same sex.

4.75 In *F (Children) (Paternity: Jurisdiction)*[123] a mother in an opposite sex relationship appealed against the court's decision to make a specific issue order compelling her to tell her children about their true paternity. The circumstances were that they were being raised by another man with whom their mother was in a relationship and they believed this man to be their natural father. The appeal was dismissed and it was found that it was within the court's jurisdiction

---

[118] CA 1989, s 8(1).
[119] *M v H (A Child) (Educational Welfare)* [2008] EWHC 324 (Fam), [2008] 1 FLR 1400.
[120] *A and D v B and E* [2003] EWHC 1376 (Fam), [2003] 2 FLR 1054.
[121] *Re M (Children)* [2007] EWCA Civ 228.
[122] *Re H and A (Paternity: Blood Tests)* [2002] EWCA Civ 383.
[123] [2007] EWCA Civ 873, [2008] 1 FLR 225.

to require children to be told of their true paternity. In that case, the applicant was the child's legal and biological father.

4.76 In the earlier case of *J v C*[124] the applicant was neither the legal or biological father, having changed gender from a woman to a man without the mother's knowledge, and the child having been conceived via an assisted conception. The applicant was not the mother's husband within the meaning of the HFEA 1990 because he could not contract a lawful marriage with the mother whilst he remained in law a woman. He therefore had no legal or biological status in relation to the child. The children believed the applicant was their father, and he issued an application for a prohibited steps order to prevent them from being told of their true parentage without the input of a particular doctor, and for a specific issue order to require the mother to take professional advice before informing the children of their origins. The mother undertook to take this advice in any event, and so the court found it unnecessary to grant him leave to apply for a section 8 order, and considered that he could not have hoped to have achieved more even if he had been granted leave. The applicant in that case did not have a current relationship with the children.

4.77 An application for permission to remove a child from the jurisdiction for more than a month, or permanently, is an application for a specific issue order for the purposes of procedure. An example of such an application in the context of same sex family relationships is the case of *Re B (Leave to Remove)*[125] which concerned a long dispute between the mother who was caring for the child with her female partner, and the father, also in a same sex relationship. It was a case in which the parents had been unable to agree what the father's role in relation to the child would be. The father had been granted parental responsibility by the court at one stage in the proceedings. The mother applied for permission to relocate to the USA and the father had made a cross application for residence. The court in considering the mother's application for permission to relocate to the USA applied the same legal test, namely that in the case of *Payne v Payne*,[126] as in cases between mothers and fathers who had previously been in heterosexual relationships. The court when granting permission to the mother to relocate observed:

> '[171] The seeds of this disastrous situation were sown before P was born. The agreement between all three of them was that the father was to play the role of an uncle. No one had anticipated the strong emotional effect on the father of having a son. He was unable to keep to the agreement. That had a significance which became far more profound. It involved his sister and her relationship with the mother.
>
> [172] His assertion of a paternal role, whilst most understandable, threatened their plans to be joint parents, and in the end was a major factor in the termination of their relationship. It is no surprise with the father's new found role, the accusations

---

[124]   [2006] EWCA Civ 551.
[125]   [2006] EWHC 1783 (Fam), [2007] 1 FLR 333.
[126]   [2001] EWCA Civ 166, [2001] Fam 473, [2001] 1 FLR 1052.

made against him and the battle to establish contact on the one hand, and the mother's upset at his aggressive and threatening behaviour and the effect on her relationship with L, that there should be lasting conflict.

[173] That conflict does not permit of a shared residence order at this time and prevents or substantially reduces the prospect of a developing role for the father here. The adverse effect on P who has already been affected is too serious. The unanimous opinion of the experts is so well founded that it cannot be ignored; it is ultimately decisive. But this does not address the mother's application in the form which Thorpe LJ put forward in *Payne v Payne*.'

Special Guardianship

4.78 An application for a special guardianship order is a private law application, except where it is made in relation to a child who is already the subject of a care order.[127] It cannot be made in favour of a child's legal parent.[128] There is nothing, however, to prevent a psychological or social parent of the child, or person having a parenting role, from making such an application. Any legal guardian or anyone already holding a residence order in respect of a child can apply for such an order without leave,[129] as can any relative who has lived with the child for more than one year, or any person who has lived with the child for more than 3 years, or has the consent of all those with parental responsibility for the child or holding a residence order for the child.[130] Other persons can apply for the leave of the court to make a special guardianship application,[131] but until they have obtained the leave of the court they can neither issue an application for a special guardianship order or give notice of their intention to do so.[132] Special guardianship orders are also included within the range of orders that a court can make of its own motion in family proceedings concerning that child if the court considers that such an order should be made.[133]

4.79 Special guardianship is a sort of half-way house between residence and adoption. It has the effect of giving the special guardian parental responsibility which (s)he is entitled to exercise to the exclusion of any other holder of parental responsibility (except another special guardian), but does not extinguish the parental responsibility of a parent.[134] A special guardian may not, however, cause the child to be known by a new surname or remove the child from the UK for more than 3 months without the written consent of every person having parental responsibility for him or her, or the leave of the

---

[127] FPR 2010, r 12.2.
[128] CA 1989, s 14A: note the term parent in the Children Act means legal parent: *T v B* [2010] EWHC 1444 (Fam).
[129] CA 1989, s 14A(5).
[130] CA 1989, ss 14A and 10(5).
[131] CA 1989, s 14A(3).
[132] *Birmingham City Council v R* [2007] 1 FLR 564.
[133] CA 1989, s 14A(6).
[134] CA 1989, s 14C.

court.[135] Following the making of a special guardianship order, parental rights are curtailed to the extent that a parent or step-parent requires the leave of the court before (s)he can make an application for a section 8 order.[136] When considering whether to make a special guardianship order, s 1 of the Children Act applies, and the welfare of the child is paramount.

4.80   In the context of same sex families, the need for a special guardianship order might arise, for example:

- Where the child's legal parent has died, and the other person parenting the child needs to secure their status as the primary carer and decision-maker for the child as against a genetic parent who has very little to do with the child, or as against the deceased's extended family.

- Where a child's legal parent is unable to care for the child, whether through ill health, inadequate parenting, imprisonment or other obstacle, and the other person parenting the child needs to secure their status as the primary carer and decision-maker for the child as against a genetic parent who has very little to do with the child, or as against the deceased's extended family.

- Where the child's genetic and known father is not a legal father, and the mother(s) are unable to care for the child.

- Where the child's parents are unable to care for the child, whether through ill health, inadequate parenting, imprisonment or other obstacle, and a relative steps in to offer a home, as in the case of *K (Guardianship Order) v Sheffield City Council*[137] where the child's grandmother and her female partner became the child's special guardians.

4.81   Because the effect of a special guardianship order is to allow a non-parent to exercise parental responsibility to the exclusion of a parent, the provisions of the Children Act create a role for the local authority in cases where there is an application for a special guardianship order, or where a special guardianship order is made, and the Special Guardianship Regulations 2005 apply. The court may not make a special guardianship order unless it has received a report from the local authority,[138] and therefore there is a requirement that anyone intending to apply for a special guardianship order must give 3 months' notice to the local authority for the area in which the proposed applicant ordinarily resides.[139]

---

[135]   CA 1989, s 14C.
[136]   CA 1989, s 14D.
[137]   [2011] EWCA Civ 635.
[138]   CA 1989, s 1A(11) and *Re S* [2007] 1 FLR 855.
[139]   CA 1989, s 14A(7).

Applications

4.82 Note in particular that the pre-application protocol for Mediation, Information and Assessment applies to all private law applications, and requires all intended applicants to attempt to mediate before issuing a private law application, unless they fall within one of the exceptions.[140]

Permission to apply for a section 8 order

4.83 The court can exercise its power to make a section 8 order in one of two circumstances:

(a) First, of its own motion, under s 10(1)(b) of the Children Act 1989 the court may make any section 8 order in the course of family proceedings where a 'question arises with respect to the welfare of any child'.[141] The effect is that a section 8 order may be in the course of family proceedings,[142] though no party has applied for one. As to the meaning of family proceedings this is defined in s 8(3)–(4), a long list of possible proceedings which is likely to cover most family law proceedings where a child could be affected. This only arises where there are already proceedings before the court.

(b) Secondly, on the application of a person who asks the court to make a section 8 order.

4.84 As to those who can apply for a section 8 order, the first class of applicants are those who are entitled to apply for any section 8 order. These are:[143]

> '(a) any parent, guardian or special guardian of the child;
> (aa) any person who by virtue of section 4A has parental responsibility for the child;
> (b) any person in whose favour a residence order is in force with respect to the child.'

4.85 Much of this is self-evident. Any parent may apply for any order (see chapter 1 for a full discussion of the meaning of parent). Any person with a residence order in force in respect of the child may also apply for any order; this is consistent with the fact that with a residence order comes parental responsibility and so the need may arise for the exercise of that responsibility in the form of seeking an order. Section 10(4)(aa) refers to a person who has acquired parental responsibility as a step-parent as set out in s 4A. Further details of how a step-parent may gain parental responsibility can be found in chapter 2. It is worth noting that step-parent can include those who are in a civil partnership with the child's parent. There is nothing to prevent a legal

---

[140] FPR 2010, PD 3A.
[141] CA 1989, s 10(1).
[142] As defined in CA 1989, s 8(3).
[143] CA 1989, 10(4).

parent from applying for an order that residence be granted, either jointly or solely, in another person's favour: it is not necessary for the applicant for a joint residence order, for example, to be the person who needs the order to be made in order to acquire parental responsibility.

4.86 There then exist the class of persons who can apply for residence and contact orders, but not as of right for specific issue and prohibited steps orders. These are:[144]

'(a) any party to a marriage (whether or not subsisting) in relation to whom the child is a child of the family;

(aa) any civil partner in a civil partnership (whether or not subsisting) in relation to whom the child is a child of the family;

(b) any person with whom the child has lived for a period of at least three years;

(c) any person who –

(i) in any case where a residence order is in force with respect to the child, has the consent of each of the persons in whose favour the order was made;

(ii) in any case where the child is in the care of a local authority, has the consent of that authority; or

(iii) in any other case, has the consent of each of those (if any) who have parental responsibility for the child.

(5A) A local authority foster parent is entitled to apply for a residence order with respect to a child if the child has lived with him for a period of at least one year immediately preceding the application.

(5B) A relative of a child is entitled to apply for a residence order with respect to the child if the child has lived with the relative for a period of at least one year immediately preceding the application.'

4.87 It is worth noting that anyone who is or has been in a civil partnership in which a child was treated as a 'child of the family' will be entitled to apply for a residence and contact order even if that civil partnership has ended.[145]

4.88 Also anyone who has lived with a child for three out of the past five years (which need not be continuous but must not have ended more than three months before the date of the application)[146] may apply for a residence or contact order. For those who are or have very recently been in same sex cohabiting relationships of some duration this may act as a means to apply for a residence or contact order. Clearly this is not possible where the child is under the age of 3.

4.89 Any relative who lived with the child during the year immediately preceding the application may apply as of right for a residence order,[147] but would need leave to apply for any other section 8 order, unless they also fell within one of the other categories. Whilst relative is defined in s 105 of the

---

[144] CA 1989, s 10(5)–(5B). Relative is defined in s 105 of the CA 1989.
[145] CA 1989, s 10(5)(aa).
[146] CA 1989, s 10(10), (5)(b).
[147] CA 1989, s 10(5B).

Children Act, it is important to remember that this definition relates to the legal relationship of the person to the child, rather than the social or psychological relationship, or even the genetic relationship where this has been superseded by a legal relationship. In principle, this includes genetic siblings or half siblings. However, in the case of *Re H (Leave to Apply for Residence Order)*[148] the court granted leave to the applicants, who were the adoptive parents of the child's half sibling to make an application for a residence order. Despite the fact that the applicants' child was to be treated in law as though he had been born to the applicants by virtue of his adoption, the court had regard to the relationship of half sibling between the subject child and the applicants' adoptive child, and considered the principle that wherever possible siblings should be brought up together. It is significant that in that case the subject child could not be brought up by his own parents, but it raises a question as to how the court would approach an application by a genetic half sibling for a section 8 order where the legal relationship had been extinguished by the making of a parental order or by the operation of the Human Fertilisation and Embryology Act 2008.[149]

4.90 Section 5(c) sets out another possible route by which someone may have standing to apply for a residence or contact order, namely with the consent of either all those who have parental responsibility or, if a residence order is in place, all those in whose favour the residence order is made. As such its use is effectively limited to situations where an amicable relationship is maintained between those with parental responsibility and the person seeking the residence order. It would be excluded for instance in situations where a same sex partner sought a joint residence order in respect of her partner's biological children where the children's other biological parent had parental responsibility and was opposed to such an order.

4.91 Finally there are those who are in none of the categories of person set out above. They require leave to apply.[150] This would include any sibling or half sibling who has not lived with the child for a period of at least 1 year immediately preceding the application in the case of a residence application, or any sibling making an application for any other order unless (s)he had lived with the child for at least 3 years.[151] Note also that if a child has two legal parents of the same sex, the other genetic parent is no longer a legal parent and has no right to apply for a section 8 order in respect of the child (see chapter 1 on legal parentage). A genetic parent in that situation could, however, apply for leave to apply for a section 8 order. Whether the court granted leave would depend on an application of the relevant criteria. In practice, in situations where a child has been brought up by two people in a same sex relationship, and one of them is not a legal parent and requires leave to apply for a section 8 order, the court readily grants leave.[152]

---

[148] [2008] 2 FLR 848.
[149] Eg if the genetic father was not a legal father but had a child to another relationship.
[150] CA 1989, s 10(2)(b).
[151] CA 1989, s 10(5B).
[152] An early case is that of *G v F* [1998] 2 FLR 799.

4.92   An application for leave to apply for a section 8 order is not a question with respect to the upbringing of a child within the meaning of s 1 of the Children Act, and the child's welfare is not, therefore, the court's paramount concern when considering whether to grant leave.[153]

4.93   In the case of applications by those other than the child concerned, s 10 of the Children Act sets out the criteria to be considered by the court when determining whether to grant leave:[154]

> 'the court shall, in deciding whether or not to grant leave, have particular regard to –
>
> (a)   the nature of the proposed application for the section 8 order;
> (b)   the applicant's connection with the child;
> (c)   any risk there might be of that proposed application disrupting the child's life to such an extent that he would be harmed by it; and
> (d)   where the child is being looked after by a local authority –
>   (i)   the authority's plans for the child's future; and
>   (ii)   the wishes and feelings of the child's parents.'

4.94   The section does not provide that the court may not have regard to any other factors, nor prevent appropriate consideration of the child's welfare (which the court is always likely to have regard to). The court should also have regard to the overall merits of the application,[155] though it has been established that a party seeking leave to apply does not have to prove that their substantive application is bound to succeed, simply that it is not devoid of any chance of success or vexatious.[156] *Re J (Leave to Issue Application for Residence Order)*[157] stressed that the court should make full enquiry before dismissing an application for leave.

4.95   It is also possible for the child who is or would be the subject of the order to apply for leave. In this case 'the court may only grant leave if it is satisfied that he has sufficient understanding to make the proposed application for the section 8 order'.[158] The test of that understanding is not the child's age but rather a specific enquiry into whether the child has sufficient maturity to understand the issues in the proceedings. Where any application is made by a child the relevant Family Procedure Rules apply and the child must make the application through a litigation friend.[159]

---

[153]   *Re S (Contact Application by Sibling)* [1998] 2 FLR 897.
[154]   CA 1989, s 10(9).
[155]   *Re S (Contact Application by Sibling)* [1998] 2 FLR 897.
[156]   *Re M (Care Proceedings: Contact: Grandmother's Application for Leave)* [1995] 2 FLR 86.
[157]   [2002] EWCA Civ 1346, [2003] 1 FLR 114.
[158]   CA 1989, s 10(8).
[159]   See Part 16 of the FPR 2010 and Part 12 of the FPR 2010 in particular.

PARTIES TO PRIVATE LAW PROCEEDINGS

4.96 The court may at any time direct that any person be made a party to private law proceedings.[160] Anyone with parental responsibility for a child, or anyone who was previously a party to proceedings concerning the child as a result of which an order was made which it is sought to vary, extend or discharge will automatically be a respondent to private law applications. In addition, if the application is for a special guardianship order, anyone holding a residence order must be a respondent.[161] The people whom the court can join as a party are not limited, but the court may only make a child a party to the proceedings where it is in the best interests of that child to do so.[162]

4.97 A number of particular points arise in the context of same sex relationships:

- The significance of parental responsibility, and in particular the decision to be made regarding whether the father is named on the child's birth certificate.

- A same sex couple wishing to confer parental responsibility or joint residence on the non-legal co-parent will need to name anyone with parental responsibility as a respondent to that application, irrespective of their actual relationship with the child.

- If a father or mother holding parental responsibility wishes to make an application in relation to the child, (s)he is not obliged to name as a respondent the other parent's partner who may be caring for the child. In practice, however, the court would be likely to join that person as a party.

- The court can make all of the significant adults in a child's life parties to the proceedings if it considers it to be necessary and appropriate having regard to the court's overriding objectives in family cases.[163] This can include extended family members or other persons, whether or not they have a legal or genetic relationship with the child.

---

[160] FPR 2010, r 12.3.
[161] FPR 2010, r 12.3.
[162] FPR 2010, r 16.2. See also PD 16A for guidance as to when it will be in a child's best interests to be made a party.
[163] FPR 2010, r 1.

Chapter 5

SAME SEX ADOPTION

5.1 One of the great challenges facing the family lawyer is the elusive nature of some of the concepts we try to deal with. The definition of 'parent', as we have seen elsewhere in this book, is by no means as straightforward as many members of the public might think.[1] Similarly, defining the 'family' can be equally fraught. From the child's perspective, the core function of a family must be to provide a stable, secure and loving environment in which the child has the opportunity to reach his or her potential. It is interesting that nowhere in the legislative framework relating to children is any definition formulated either of family or parent. Either the legislators considered the words too obvious to require description or they had the foresight to recognise that they were too fluid to capture adequately. Attempts to define these concepts are also rather prone to causing offence. The family is as much an emotional construction as a biological one it is also required to absorb change rapidly. As recently as the 1950's most would have included marriage as integral to the concept of family, these days most would, I suspect, place little emphasis on it. Developments in medical science, changes to the social and cultural composition of society, advances in technology, divorce, each, in different ways, has an impact, not only on how families function but on what they become. Various though families can be few cause greater interest or controversy than the adoptive one. Given adoption in fact affects so few children[2] this is perhaps rather surprising. It is not always easy to get reliable comparative statistics from other jurisdictions about adoption, we are often looking at different systems with a variety of traditions, cultural norms and religious influences. That said, many European lawyers seem to regard the UK approach to adoption as essentially quite draconian in its nature. The essence of our adoption law is that it involves complete legal transference of parental responsibility from one set of parents, 'the birth parents', to another, 'the adoptive parents'. All legal ties between the child and the birth family are severed, usually permanently. The child becomes a member of a new family. Whether this model will survive a generation immersed in social networking via the internet is unclear. It is ironic that a society that seeks to protect concepts of privacy more vigorously now than in any other generation is also happy to waive that privacy fragrantly in internet communications. All this has a direct impact on adopted children whose curiosity in adolescence about their birth family can be satisfied, sometimes by the most rudimentary investigations on a laptop in their own bedroom.

---

[1] *Re G (Children) (Residence: Same Sex Partner)* [2006] UKHL 43, [2006] 1 WLR 2305; *Re R (Parental Responsibility)* [2011] 2 FLR 1132; *T v B* [2011] 1 ALL ER 17.

[2] In 2010–2011 3,050 children were adopted – Department of Education Adoption Statistics for England and Wales.

5.2   This is no place for an exegesis of the evolution of adoption, but our understanding of it requires rooting in at least a rudimentary knowledge of its history. In Roman law adoption was largely concerned with ancestral honour, inheritance and succession[3] and the major crucial function of adoption was until recent times rooted in balancing shortage of human labour, rather than motivated by welfare considerations.[4] It only became a legal construct in the United Kingdom in the aftermath of World War I and the subsequent flu epidemic which left many children without parents. Section 5(1) of the Adoption and Children Act 1926 encapsulates the guiding philosophy of the legislation, the spirit of which still holds under the Adoption and Children Act 2002. It vested rights in the adoptive parents 'as though the adopted child was born to the adopter in lawful wedlock'. That phrase, 'lawful wedlock' cast a long shadow over the development of the law of adoption, confining it, inevitably, not only to heterosexual couples but to those who were married. This reflected the prevailing public attitude of society, probably until the mid-60's, ie that a married couple presented not only the best chance for children who could not remain within their birth families but, in effect, the only secure option.

5.3   The Adoption and Children Bill emerged largely in consequence of the review initiated in February 2000 by the then Prime Minister Tony Blair. The uncovering of institutional abuse, particularly the North Wales Inquiry, invigorated the drive to find permanent secure families for children who could not grow up within or be part of their own birth families. The main objectives of the bill were described by the Department of Health in 2002 as:

(a)   Placing the needs of the child at the centre of the adoption process, by aligning adoption law with the Children Act 1989, to make the child's welfare the paramount 'consideration' in all decisions until the adoption.

(b)   To encourage more people to adopt children by helping to ensure the support they need and by placing new clear duties on local authorities to provide an Adoption Support Service and a new right for people affected by adoption to request and receive an assessment of their needs for adoption services.

(c)   To help cut harmful delays in the adoption process by legally underpinning the Adoption and Children Act Register, to suggest matches between children and approved adopters, and to provide measures requiring courts to draw up timetables for adoption.

(d)   To support the Government's efforts in building confidence in the adoption process and encouraging more people to come forward to adopt,

---

[3]   WW Bookland & AD McNair *Roman Law and Common Law – A Comparison in (Outline)* (Cambridge University Press, 1952).

[4]   B Tizard *Adoption: A Second Chance* (Open Books, 1977).

by enabling the Secretary of State to establish an Independent Review Mechanism for applicants who considered they were being turned down unfairly.

(e)   To provide a more consistent approach to access to information held in Adoption Agency records, the aim of which was to ensure that the release of identifying information about adoptive people and birth families happened in an appropriate manner, taking account of their views wherever possible.

(f)   To strengthen and safeguard adoption by improving the legal controls relating to inter-country adoption, arranging adoptions and advertising children for adoption.

5.4   Avoidance of delay was, in 2000 and remains today, one of the chief imperatives for those concerned in providing an effective framework for moving children on to adoption. The avoidance of delay as a statutory obligation was one of the central innovations of the Children Act 1989. This book is written for both lawyers and non-lawyers and this chapter, in particular, aims to embrace same sex couples wishing to understand how the UK law has adapted to harness the opportunities they offer to children. As with any prospective adopter the emphasis is placed on the opportunity such families provide for permanency, ie a family to which children will belong all their lives.

5.5   Hale LJ has observed:[5]

> 'in the right circumstances adoption is the most valuable way of supplying a child with the "family for life" to which everyone ought to be entitled and of which some children are most tragically deprived.'

The objective of permanency fits seamlessly with the major theme motivating the reforms, namely the recognition of unacceptable numbers of children languishing for far too long within the care system. This is not the place to comment on how effective the new legislation has been in avoiding delay but merely to identify the centrality of the principle in the new legislation. It recognises as Bracewell J observed, now over 10 years ago:[6]

> 'Children deprived of permanent parenting grow up with unmet psychological needs and far too many have to wait too long before permanent families are found for them when they cannot return to their natural families. The longer the delay, the more difficult it is to place children who often become progressively more disturbed in limbo, thereby rendering the task of identifying suitable adoptive families a lengthy and uncertain process. The older the child, the greater the risk of breakdown in an adoptive placement. It is therefore incumbent on local

---

[5]   *Re B (Adoption by One Parent to Exclusion of Other)* [2001] 1 FLR 589, the observation was obiter.
[6]   *Re D & K (Care Plan: Twin Track Planning)* [1999] 2 FLR 872 at 875.

authorities and guardians to seek to prevent these delays by identifying clearly the options available for the court by twin track planning as opposed to sequential planning.'

Prior to the ACA 2002 practitioners had recognised the dissonance between the Adoption Act 1976 and the Children Act 1989. The latter placed the child's welfare as the paramount consideration wherever a question of the upbringing of a child was being considered by the courts, the Adoption Act 1976 had required that 'welfare' be merely the first consideration in adoption proceedings. Undoubtedly the developing case-law had done much to merge the distinction but one of the key objectives of the ACA 2002 was to align its philosophy with that of the Children Act 1989 putting 'the needs of the child at the centre of the process'.[7] An understanding of this rationale is central when considering the approach of the legislation to same sex couples.

Section 1(3) provides:

> 'The Court or Adoption Agency must at all times bear in mind that, in general, any delay in coming to the decision is likely to prejudice the child's welfare.'

The obligation here is an overarching one, applying across all decisions relating to the adoption of a child. The words 'any delay' serve to enhance even the emphasis given to the principle in the Children Act 1989 and incorporate the obligation upon the court to bear in mind the consequences of delay 'at all times'. The section recognises that some delay might be purposive but should be confined to exceptional circumstances.[8]

5.6   The provision is, of course, linked to Art 6(1) of the European Convention on Human Rights which requires that cases be heard within a reasonable time and underlines the importance of rendering justice without delay which might jeopardise its effectiveness and credibility. Section 109(1) of the ACA buttresses the general avoidance of delay principle in s 1(3) by imposing an obligation on the court to draw up a timetable with a view to determining the question of whether an adoption order or a placement order should be made without delay and to give appropriate directions to ensure that the timetable is adhered to. Section 1(4) of the Adoption and Children Act 2002 takes its starting point as s 1(3) of the Children Act 1989 by providing a checklist of welfare factors (non-exhaustive) that have to be taken into account, not only by the court but also by the Adoption Agency:

> 'The Court or Adoption Agency must have regard to the following matters (amongst others) –
>
> (a)   The child's ascertainable wishes and feelings regarding the decision (considered in the light of the child's age and understanding);
> (b)   The child's particular needs;
> (c)   The likely effect on the child (throughout his life) having ceased to be a member of the original family and become an adoptive person;

---

[7]   PIU Report (July 2000), para 8.2.
[8]   HL Official Report 24 June 2002, CWH 19–20 per Lord Hunt of Kingsmead.

(d)   The child's age, sex, background and any of the child's characteristics which the Court or agency considers relevant;

(e)   Any harm within the meaning of the Children Act 1989 which the child has suffered or is at risk of suffering;

(f)   The relationship with the child has with relatives, and with any other person in relation to whom the Court or Agency considers the question to be relevant, including –

    (i)   The likelihood of any such relationship continuing an the value to the child of its doing so;

    (ii)   The ability and willingness of any child's relatives, or any such person to provide the child with a secure environment in which the child can develop otherwise to meet the child's needs;

    (iii)   Wishes and feelings of any of the child's relatives, or any such person regarding the child.'

5.7   In addition the scheme is regulated rigorously by the Family Procedure Rules 2010. They provide a unifying code applied throughout the entire family court system (ie High Court, county court and magistrates' court) and mirroring the Civil Procedure Rules 1998 contain Practice Directions which have mandatory force:

'The overriding objective

1.1 (1) These rules are a new procedural code with the overriding objective of enabling the court to deal with cases justly, having regard to any welfare issues involved.

(2) Dealing with a case justly includes, so far as is practicable –

(a)   ensuring that it is dealt with expeditiously and fairly;

(b)   dealing with the case in ways which are proportionate to the nature, importance and complexity of the issues;

(c)   ensuring that the parties are on an equal footing;

(d)   saving expense; and

(e)   allotting to it an appropriate share of the court's resources, while taking into account the need to allot resources to other cases.

Application by the court of the overriding objective

1.2 The court must seek to give effect to the overriding objective when it –

(a)   exercises any power given to it by these rules; or

(b)   interprets any rule.

Duty of the parties

1.3 The parties are required to help the court to further the overriding objective.

Court's duty to manage cases

1.4 (1) The court must further the overriding objective by actively managing cases.

(2) Active case management includes –

(a)   encouraging the parties to co-operate with each other in the conduct of the proceedings;

(b)   identifying at an early stage –
        (i)   the issues; and
        (ii)   who should be a party to the proceedings;

(c)   deciding promptly –
        (i)   which issues need full investigation and hearing and which do not; and
        (ii)   the procedure to be followed in the case;

(d)   deciding the order in which issues are to be resolved;

(e)   encouraging the parties to use an alternative dispute resolution procedure if the court considers that appropriate and facilitating the use of such procedure;

(f)   helping the parties to settle the whole or part of the case;

(g)   fixing timetables or otherwise controlling the progress of the case;

(h)   considering whether the likely benefits of taking a particular step justify the cost of taking it;

(i)   dealing with as many aspects of the case as it can on the same occasion;

(j)   dealing with the case without the parties needing to attend at court;

(k)   making use of technology; and

(l)   giving directions to ensure that the case proceeds quickly and efficiently.'

5.8   Avoiding delay, however, often represents a complex and multi-faceted challenge to lawyers, judges and social workers, the difficulties of which are not easily apparent to members of the public or politicians. It is perhaps best illustrated by example. Whilst it is easy to see how a 3 year old child who cannot live within his family should be found an adoptive placement as quickly as possible, the position becomes rather more complex if one of the most significant people to that child is his 9 year old sister and adoption might involve the severance of that relationship. Nine year olds do not fare particularly well, either in finding adoptive placements or thriving within them. There is a balance to be struck between properly recognising the corrosive effects of delay and making a fetish of its avoidance. The reasonableness of the length of the proceedings always has to be assessed in the light of the particular circumstances. Both the UK courts[9] and the European Court[10] have recognised that departure from the avoidance of delay principle should be exceptional. European case-law provides some guidance as to what might constitute 'exceptional' and has emphasised that it should be assessed in the light of:

(a)   the complexity of the case;

(b)   the conduct of the applicant;

(c)   the relevant authorities;

(d)   the importance of what is at stake for the applicant in the litigation.[11]

---

9   *Stockport County Council v D* [1995] 1 FLR 873.
10   *H v France* [1987] 12 EHRR 74, *Paulsen-Medalen and Svensson v Sweden* [1998] 26 EHRR 260.
11   *Piran v France* [2002] 34 EHRR 14 at para 54; *Davies v UK* [2002] EHRR 720 at para 26.

5.9   In the context of adoption cases and indeed in all cases relating to children's welfare, emphasis is properly placed on the importance of what is at stake for the applicant in the proceedings in question: *H v UK*[12] emphasises that particular celerity is required in cases concerning the custody of a child:[13]

> '85. In the present case, the Court considers it right to place special emphasis on the importance of what was at stake for the applicant in the proceedings in question. Not only were they decisive for her future relations with her own child, but they had a particular quality of irreversibility, involving as they did what the High Court graphically described as the "statutory guillotine" of adoption (see paragraph 28 above).

> In cases of this kind the authorities are under a duty to exercise exceptional diligence since, as the Commission rightly pointed out, there is always the danger that any procedural delay will result in the de facto determination of the issue submitted to the court before it has held its hearing. And, indeed, this was what happened here.'

5.10   The sensible recognition that delay will usually be inimical to the welfare of the child was the central factor driving the debate in the passage of the Bill. The exclusion of 'unmarried' couples from a potential pool of adopters had long before the beginning of the twenty-first century become manifestly unsustainable. Recruitment for adopters had fallen out of step with the way in which a great many people lived their lives in the United Kingdom. Excluding unmarried couples from the catchment of prospective adopters inevitably reduced the families available and consequently therefore added to delay in finding families. Though the passage of the Bill saw contrary arguments advanced by those who, for religious and other reasons, saw the proposals as an erosion of the status of marriage, the force of the argument from the perspective of children waiting to be adopted was difficult to resist. By emphasising the 'delay' arguments, those supporting the Bill (it was eventually a 'free vote') took the spotlight off the concept of 'appropriate' placements, in itself a loaded and somewhat judgmental concept, inconsistent with a scheme in which the welfare of the individual child became the paramount consideration. The Government's legislative campaign was a masterpiece of tactic. Once the argument in favour of expanding the pool of adopters to the unmarried was carried, the prospect of a human rights challenge was perceived as looming large if the resultant legislation were then to go on to discriminate against categories of unmarried. In the slipstream of the argument for more adopters 'gay adoption' arrived.

5.11   In the UK in 2000, human rights were enjoying their moment in the sun, even if it was a typical English summer rather than a Mediterranean one. Human rights had 'come home' as the Prime Minister heralded in the passage of the Human Rights Act 1998. The political landscape was, at that particular moment in history at its most receptive to the absorption of Convention rights.

---

[12]   *H v UK* [1987] 10 EHRR 96 at para 70.
[13]   See also *Johansson v Norway* [1997] 23 EHRR 33; *EN v Italy* [2001] 31 EHRR 17.

What was notably absent from debate in the passage of the Bill, however, was any vibrant ideological assertion of 'Gay Rights to Adoption'. The emphasis focused unwaveringly on the avoidance of delay, expanding the pool of families with an implicit, if not entirely well-founded threat that any discriminatory legislation based on sexual orientation would be given short shrift by Europe.

5.12   In fact, the ECtHR had held, by 4 votes to 3, the ban on adoption by lesbian and gay people was not a violation of Art 14, the non-discriminatory provision of the ECHR (read as it must be in conjunction with Art 8):

The relevant Articles in question provide:

'Article 14

> The enjoyment of the rights and freedoms set forth in [the] Convention shall be secured without discrimination on any grounds such as sex ...

Article 8

> **1** Everyone has the right to respect for his private and family life ...
>
> **2** There shall be no interference by a public authority with the exercise of this right except such as is in accordance with the law and is necessary in a democratic society ... for the protection of health or morals, or for the protection of the rights and freedom of others.'

The European Court emphasised, once again, that Art 14 complements the other substantive provisions of the Convention and its protocol. It has no independent existence since it has effect solely in relation to the 'enjoyment of the rights and freedoms' safeguarded by those provisions. Although the application of Art 14 does not presuppose a breach of those provisions – and to this extent it is autonomous – there can be no room for its application unless the facts at issue fall within the ambit of one or more of the provisions of the Convention. The Court found that the State was entitled to draw a distinction between homosexuals and others in the adoption process. It was noted, in the judgment, that generally, as exemplified by the Adoption Act 1976, the majority of contracting States did not specifically exclude homosexuals from adoption when permitting unmarried individuals to adopt, but there was, significantly, from the perspective of the European Statutes and jurisprudence, a considerable variety of opinion on what were perceived to be controversial questions throughout the member States. The Court emphasised, as it had done previously, that the Convention did not guarantee the right to adopt as such.[14] Moreover, the right to family life presupposes the existence of a family and does not safeguard the mere desire to found a family. In the instant case the Court found the decision to dismiss the application for authorisation as an adopter could not be considered to have infringed the applicant's rights to the free expression and development of his personality or the manner in which he led his life, in particular his sexual life. The Court nonetheless recognised that under French domestic law, all single persons were able to apply for adoption,

---

[14]   *Fretté v France* [2004] 38 EHRR 21.

provided that they were granted 'prior authorisation' (under the provisions of the domestic legislation) to adopt children in State care (or foreign children). The applicant maintained that the French authority's decision to reject his application had been based implicitly on his sexual orientation alone. The Court had to determine therefore whether, as the applicant maintained, his homosexuality had a decisive influence on the decision.

5.13 The Court recognised that the reason given by the French administrative and judicial authorities for the decision was the applicant's 'choice of lifestyle' although the Authority had never made any explicit reference to his homosexuality. The ECHR's survey of the case files revealed however that that criterion had implicitly yet undeniably made the applicant's homosexuality the decisive factor and accordingly Art 14 of the Convention, taken in conjunction with Art 8 was applicable. The majority judgment concluded:

> '[39] The right not to be discriminated against in the enjoyment of the rights guaranteed in the convention is also violated when States without an objective and reasonable justification fail to treat differently persons whose situations are significantly different.[15]

> However, the contracting States enjoy a certain margin of appreciation in assessing whether and to what extent differences in otherwise similar situations justify a different treatment in law. The scope of the margin of appreciation will vary according to the circumstances, the subject matter and its background; in this respect, one of the relevant factors is the existence or non-existence of common ground between the laws of the contracting States.'[16]

Having evaluated the ambit of the margin of appreciation the Court considered whether there was any emerging consensus in relation to same sex couples in the arena of adoption. In 2002 the picture was not at all clear:

> 'It is indisputable that there is no common ground on a question. Although most of the contracting States do not expressly prohibit homosexuals from adopting where single persons may adopt, it is not possible to find in the legal and social orders of the contracting States uniform principles on the social issues on which opinions within a democratic society may reasonably differ widely. The Court considers it quite natural that the national authorities, whose duty it is in a democratic society also to consider, within the limits of their jurisdiction, the interests of society as a whole, should enjoy a wide margin of appreciation when they are asked to making rulings on such matters. By reason of their direct continuous contact with the vital forces of their countries, the national authorities are in principle, better placed than an international Court to evaluate local needs and conditions. Since the delicate issues raised in the case, therefore, touch on areas where there is little common ground amongst the member States of the Council of Europe and, generally speaking, the law appears to be in a transitional stage, a wide margin of appreciation must be left to the authorities of each State.[17]

---

[15] See *Thlimmenos v Greece* 44.

[16] See *Manoussakis v Greece* [1997] 23 EHRR 387 para 44.

[17] See *mutatis mutandis, Manoussakis v Greece* [1997] 23 EHRR 387 at para 44 and Application No 27417/95, *Ch'are Shalom Ve Tsedek v France* (2000) June 27 at para 84.

This margin of appreciation should not, however, be interpreted to grant the State arbitrary power, and the authority's decision remains subject to review by the Court for conformity with the requirement of Article 14 of the Convention.'

The Court gave emphasis to the French Government's submission that this case identified competing interests between the Applicant who sought authorisation to adopt and children who were eligible for adoption. The fact that under the French procedure being considered, no particular child had been identified, did not mean that there was no competing interest to be balanced:

'Adoption means "providing a child with a family, not a family with a child", and the State must see to it that the persons chosen to adopt are those who can offer the child the most suitable home in every respect.'

In the view of this author no passage better illuminates the correct approach to family finding, including families with same sex parents than does this one.

5.14 It is impossible to comment on *Fretté* without considering the joint (partly) dissenting opinions of Sir Nicholas Bratza and Judges Fuhrmann and Tulkens:

'We are unable to share the view of the majority that there has been no violation of Article 14 of the Convention, read in conjunction with Article 8 ...

...

We have no difficulty in accepting the European Commission on Human Rights' consistently expressed opinion that Article 8 of the Convention does not guarantee a right to adoption as such. We also accept that Article 8, which guarantees the right to respect for family life, may not be interpreted to safeguard the mere desire to found a family, whether by adopting or any other means. In this connection, there is a distinction between the instant case and the *Salgueiro da Silva Mouta v Portugal* case, in which there was already an established family life between the applicant and his daughter and the decision of the Lisbon Court of Appeal to award parental authority over the child to the applicant's ex-wife constituted a clear infringement of his right ... within the scope of Article 8.'

However, these Judges went on to conclude that a finding to the effect that the difference in treatment between the applicant and others was not discriminatory within the meaning of Art 14 of the Convention was 'contrary in fact and in law to the requirement of Art 14 of the Convention as interpreted by the Court's case-law'.[18]

'As far as the constituent elements of discrimination are concerned, we must therefore examine in turn whether there is a difference in treatment in the instant case and, if so, whether it pursues a legitimate aim and there is a proportionate relationship between the aim pursued and the methods used. Not every difference in treatment is prohibited by Article 14 of the Convention, only those which

---

[18]   [2004] 38 EHRR 21 469, 0-112.

amount to discrimination. According to the Court's established case-law, the principle of equality of treatment is infringed if the difference ascertained has no "objective and reasonable justification".

(a) To determine whether there was a difference in treatment, it is necessary to place oneself in the domestic-law context once again. Prior authorisation to adopt is a procedure whose aim is to take a decision not in relation to a child but in relation to a potential parent and check that there is nothing to indicate that he or she would be unsuitable to adopt. Thereafter, it is for the civil courts to weigh up the interests of the parties when the adoption plans are formalised and in particular to assess whether the child's real interests are fully respected.

In the instant case, prior authorisation to adopt, which may be requested by any single person, was refused to the applicant solely because of his "choice of lifestyle" and not because this choice would pose any actual threat to a child's interests. Unless it is held that homosexuality – or race for example – is in itself an objection, the refusal of authorisation could only have been justified by Mr Fretté's homosexuality if it had been combined with conduct that was detrimental to a child's upbringing, and that was not the case here. In addition, in the applicant's case, as he moreover acknowledged himself, even if authorisation had been granted, it was not certain that a child would have been placed with him. Conversely however, if he had been a heterosexual or if he had concealed his homosexuality, he would certainly have obtained authorisation because his personal qualities were acknowledged throughout the proceedings.

Because the sole ground given for the refusal of authorisation was the applicant's lifestyle, which was an implicit yet undeniable reference to his homosexuality, the right guaranteed by Article 343-1 of the Civil Code was infringed on the basis of his sexual orientation alone (see, *mutatis mutandis*, *Smith and Grady v the United Kingdom*, nos. 33985/96 and 33986/96, ECHR 1999-VI, and *Lustig-Prean and Beckett v. the United Kingdom*, nos. 31417/96 and 32377/96, § 71, 27 September 1999).

(b) Is this difference in treatment justified by a legitimate aim? As the Court has repeatedly pointed out "very weighty", "particularly serious" or "particularly convincing and weighty reasons" are needed for a difference in treatment on the ground of sex to be regarded as compatible with the Convention (see *Smith and Grady*, cited above, § 90, and *Lustig-Prean and Beckett*, cited above, § 82).

As the Government submitted, the decision to refuse the applicant authorisation stemmed from a desire to protect the rights and freedoms of the child who might have been adopted. In itself this aim may of course be legitimate, and in fact would even be the only legitimate aim. In the instant case, however, it has to be observed that the applicant's personal qualities and aptitude for bringing up children were emphasised on a number of occasions. The *Conseil d'Etat* even specified in its Statement of reasons that there was no reference in the case file "to any specific circumstance that might pose a threat to the child's interests". The legitimate aim was not therefore effectively established in any way.

In their general and abstract wording, the reasons given by the judicial authorities for their decision to refuse the applicant authorisation are based solely on the applicant's homosexuality and therefore on the view that to be brought up by homosexual parents would be harmful to the child at all events and under any circumstances. The *Conseil d'Etat* failed to explain in any way, by referring for example to the increasing range of scientific studies of homosexual parenthood in recent years, why and how the child's interests militated in the instant case against the applicant's application for authorisation.'

Addressing the 'proportionality' and 'margin of appreciation' factors that had led the majority to conclude that there had not been discrimination within Art 14, the dissenters, in two very powerful paragraphs, discounted that as taking the protection of fundamental rights in a 'backwards' direction and emphasised the obligation on the European Court to secure rights where they are guaranteed by the Convention.

'(c) Finally, on the question of proportionality, we might conceivably accept the Government's view that some margin of appreciation should be afforded to States in the sensitive area of adoption by homosexuals. It is not for the Court to take decisions (or pass moral judgment) instead of States in an area which is also a subject of controversy in many Council of Europe member States, especially as the views of the French administrative courts also seem to be divided. Neither is it for the Court to express preference for any type of family model. On the other hand, the reference in the present judgment to the lack of "common ground" in the contracting States or "uniform principles" on adoption by homosexuals (see paragraph 41 of the judgment), which paves the way for States to be given total discretion, seems to us to be irrelevant, at variance with the Court's case-law relating to Article 14 of the Convention and, when couched in such general terms, liable to take the protection of fundamental rights backwards.

It is the Court's task to secure the rights guaranteed by the Convention. It must supervise the conditions in which Article 14 of the Convention is applied and consider therefore whether there was a reasonable, proportionate relationship in the instant case between the methods used – the total prohibition of adoption by homosexual parents – and the aim pursued – to protect children. The *Conseil d'Etat*'s judgment was a landmark decision but it failed to carry out a detailed, substantive assessment of proportionality and took no account of the situation of the persons concerned. The refusal was *absolute* and it was issued without any other explanation than the applicant's choice of lifestyle, seen in general and abstract terms and thus in itself taking the form of an irrebuttable presumption of an impediment to any plan to adopt whatsoever. This position fundamentally precludes any real consideration of the interests at stake and the possibility of finding any practical way of reconciling them.

At a time when all the countries of the Council of Europe are engaged in a determined attempt to counter all forms of prejudice and discrimination, we regret that we cannot agree with the majority.'

5.15 The dissenters had emphasised the importance of establishing 'very weighty', 'particularly serious' or 'particularly convincing' reasons to be required when seeking to justify discriminatory treatment. The majority also recognise that throughout the European member States social attitudes on same sex parenting were undergoing a period of 'transition'. The stage was set for change.

5.16 Four years later the ECtHR came to consider the case of *EB v France*.[19] The applicant had been in a long-term same sex relationship. She decided to attempt to adopt a child and the relevant Social Services Department advised that her request be refused on the grounds that 'her partner was not adequately committed to raising a child' and her family situation 'failed to provide adequate safeguards for the child's stable and well-adjusted development, in particular, the absence of male role models'. The Social Services Department recommendation was followed and the applicant was refused permission to adopt. The applicant complained of a violation of Arts 8 and 14 of the Convention.

5.17 The Court unanimously held that the application was admissible, and by 10 votes to 7 it held that there had been a violation of Art 14 taken with Art 8. By 11 votes to 6 the respondent was to pay a sum of money in respect of non-pecuniary damage, costs and expenses:

> 'The Court considers that the reference to the applicant's homosexuality was, if not explicit, at least implicit. The influence of the applicant's avowed homosexuality on the assessment of her application has been established and, having regard to the foregoing, was a decisive factor leading to the decision to refuse her authorisation to adopt (see, *mutatis mutandis*, *Salgueiro da Silva Mouta*, cited above, § 35).

> 90. The applicant therefore suffered a difference in treatment. Regard must be had to the aim behind that difference in treatment and, if the aim was legitimate, to whether the different treatment was justified.

> 91. The Court reiterates that, for the purposes of Article 14, a difference in treatment is discriminatory if it has no objective and reasonable justification, which means that it does not pursue a "legitimate aim" or that there is no "reasonable proportionality between the means employed and the aim sought to be realised" (see, inter alia, *Karlheinz Schmidt*, cited above, § 24; *Petrovic*, cited above, § 30; and *Salgueiro da Silva Mouta*, cited above, § 29). Where sexual orientation is in issue, there is a need for particularly convincing and weighty reasons to justify a difference in treatment regarding rights falling within Article 8 (see, *mutatis mutandis*, *Smith and Grady v. the United Kingdom*, nos. 33985/96 and 33986/96, § 89, ECHR 1999-VI; *Lustig-Prean and Beckett v. the United Kingdom*, nos. 31417/96 and 32377/96, § 82, 27 September 1999; and *S.L. v. Austria*, no. 45330/99, § 37, ECHR 2003-I).

> 92. In that connection the Court observes that the Convention is a living instrument, to be interpreted in the light of present-day conditions (see, *inter alia*, *Johnston and Others*, cited above, § 53).

> 93. In the Court's opinion, if the reasons advanced for such a difference in treatment were based solely on considerations regarding the applicant's sexual orientation this would amount to discrimination under the Convention (see *Salgueiro da Silva Mouta*, cited above, § 36).

---

[19]   [2008] 47 EHRR 21.

94. The Court points out that French law allows single persons to adopt a child (see paragraph 49 above), thereby opening up the possibility of adoption by a single homosexual, which is not disputed. Against the background of the domestic legal provisions, it considers that the reasons put forward by the Government cannot be regarded as particularly convincing and weighty such as to justify refusing to grant the applicant authorisation.

95. The Court notes, lastly, that the relevant provisions of the Civil Code are silent as to the necessity of a referent of the other sex, which would not, in any event, be dependent on the sexual orientation of the adoptive single parent. In this case, moreover, the applicant presented, in the terms of the judgment of the *Conseil d'Etat*, "undoubted personal qualities and an aptitude for bringing up children", which were assuredly in the child's best interests, a key notion in the relevant international instruments (see paragraphs 29-31 above).

96. Having regard to the foregoing, the Court cannot but observe that, in rejecting the applicant's application for authorisation to adopt, the domestic authorities made a distinction based on considerations regarding her sexual orientation, a distinction which is not acceptable under the Convention (see *Salgueiro da Silva Mouta*, cited above, § 36).

97. Consequently, having regard to its finding under paragraph 80 above, the Court considers that the decision in question is incompatible with the provisions of Article 14 taken in conjunction with Article 8.

98. There has accordingly been a breach of Article 14 of the Convention taken in conjunction with Article 8.'

5.18 Before leaving the European case-law it is important to consider the European Convention on the Adoption of Children 1967, ratified by the United Kingdom on the 21 December 1967. This Convention regulates the adoption of children throughout the member states and endeavours to harmonise differences in procedures for adoption. In 2005 the United Kingdom denounced the 1967 Convention on the basis it did not guarantee same sex couples the same rights to adopt as had now been afforded in domestic law, ie under the ACA 2002. In this it was following Sweden which had acted similarly in 2002. This led to the Convention being revised, which occurred on the 27 November 2008. Article 7 now states:

'*Article 7*
Conditions for adoption

> (1) The law shall permit a child to be adopted –
>> (a) by two persons of different sex –
>>> (i) who are married to each other, or
>>> (ii) where such an institution exists, have entered into a registered partnership together;
>> (b) by one person.

(2) States are free to extend the scope of this Convention to same sex couples who are married to each other or who have entered into a registered partnership together. They are also free to extend the scope of this Convention to different sex couples and same sex couples who are living together in a stable relationship.'

5.19 As we have seen above, during the passage of the Adoption and Children Act Bill the 'characteristics' of prospective adopters were given relatively modest attention beyond whether they were married or not. The arguments against 'gay adoption' were predicated on the assertion that unmarried and same sex couples were more likely to separate than married couples and that it followed that such couples were less likely to provide children with the stability they needed. Some suggested that children placed with same sex couples would also be stigmatised by their peers. The arguments advanced in favour, somewhat ambitiously, sought to establish that by excluding same sex couples the pool of prospective adopters would be needless be decreased. It was insinuated that adoption agencies might well hold a 'traditional preference' for heterosexual married couples in any event when assessing the needs of the individual children and that, by implication, the Act was not going to make much difference on the ground as far as any increase in the number of same sex couples adopting was concerned. It is often forgotten that under the Adoption Act 1976, whilst a joint application for adoption order could only be made by a married couple, it did not prevent single people being granted adoption orders. The courts came to approach this anomaly purposively, often by making an adoption order in favour of one member of a married couple and frequently buttressing it by the making of a joint residence order (see *AB*[20]).

5.20 In *Re W (Adoption: Homosexual Adopter)*,[21] Singer J was considering an application by a Local Authority under s 18 of the Adoption Act 1976 for an order freeing the child J for adoption. J had been made subject to a care order on the basis that he had suffered significant harm as a result of being neglected. After a series of placements, J was placed with a woman L who was 49 years of age and had lived with her lesbian partner S for over 10 years. The placement had been made with a view to adoption and the child had manifestly thrived within the family. The view of all concerned was that the child should remain with L and S permanently. The parents did not consent to the freeing order, and the court was invited to find that the withholding of consent was 'unreasonable' and to dispense with the requirement for it. The mother had played a particularly active part in opposing the application and contended that an adoption order or an order freeing for adoption in favour of a single woman living in a lesbian relationship should not be permitted and that the Adoption Act 1976 should be construed, 'as a matter of necessary implication' so as to exclude the power to make an order in such circumstances. Alternatively, it was contended that, if on its true construction, the statute permitted such an order, public policy issues dictated that it should never be made. Singer J found that the relevant words of the statute falling for consideration were those set out in s 15(1)(a) of the Adoption Act 1976:

---

[20]   [1996] 1 FLR 27.
[21]   [1997] 2 FLR 406.

'An Adoption Order may be made on the application of one person where he has attained the age of 21 years and is not married.'

The judge observed:

> 'Section 15(3) of the Adoption Act 1976 imposes certain requirements upon a court considering an individual adoption application made by one of the child's parents. Section 15(1)(i) of the Act of 1976 provides for the case of one party to a subsisting marriage who makes an individual application to adopt. In such a case the court before making an order must be satisfied that the marriage relationship although subsisting at law is not viable in fact. Thus the court must be satisfied either that the applicant's spouse cannot be found; or that the spouses have separated and are living apart in circumstances such that the separation is likely to be permanent; or that the applicant's spouse is incapable of making an adoption application by reason of physical or mental ill-health. The policy G behind this provision is clearly to avoid creating limping relationships within marriage whereby as a result of an individual adoption order the child would become for all purposes a child of one spouse but not at all of the other. Apart however from those situations for which specific provision is made as just described by section 15(1)(6) and section 15(3) of the Adoption Act 1976, and apart from in the ordinary case a domicile requirement, the words of the statute relevant for present purposes are simply those contained in section 15(1)(a), namely that "an adoption order may be made on the application of one person where he has attained the age of 21 years and is not married." At first sight, it may well be thought, those words are plain and their intention is unambiguous, reading as one must "she" for "he" in the case of an individual female applicant. There is A no hint in those words that an individual applicant should not be able to apply for and obtain an adoption order because of circumstances specific to the individual such as their sexual orientation and/or whether they live in cohabitation with someone of the same or of the other gender.'

Later the judge went on to recognise that though the framers of the legislation may not have contemplated a single homosexual applicant might apply for and obtain an adoption order and indeed 'were such an applicant's orientation to be known, they may well have thought it implausible that he or she would be successful whether living alone or in cohabitation' nonetheless the reason for that would not have been the wording of the Adoption Act 1976 which the court found contained no prohibition against such an application, but because arrangements for the adoption of children and the placement of children for adoption were broadly the responsibility of adoption agencies.

> 'The likely attitude of adoption agencies, for the most part local authorities, would, again I am prepared to accept, 20 years ago have been to withhold approval from would-be applicants whose homosexual orientation was made clear. But since then times, and the attitude of adoption agencies, have clearly changed, and whereas it has not been commonplace for children to be placed in the care of homosexual carers whether for fostering or prospective adoption purposes, it is by no means unknown. That this has become the case, so far as adoption is concerned, can be gathered as a matter of inference from relevant paragraphs of the consultation document issued by the Department of Health and the Welsh Office in October 1992 and entitled "Review of Adoption Law: Report to

Ministers of an Inter-departmental Working Group." Paragraph 5 of the foreword is to this effect: "The Working Group has not proposed any additional rules by which the suitability of prospective adoptive parents should be judged. Nor has any change been proposed as regards the eligibility of single adopters." In the body of the report, paragraphs 26.9 to 26.11 consider whether it would be appropriate to allow an unmarried couple to adopt jointly, but for the reasons there stated make no such recommendation. Paragraphs 26.13 and 26.14 read:

> "We do not propose any changes to the law relating to single applicants, including lesbians and gay men. There are examples of extremely successful adoptions, particularly of older children and children with disabilities by single adopters. Some children are only able to settle in single-parent households as a result of experiences in their early lives.

> Some agencies may place a child with a single applicant who is living with a partner. As a matter of practice, to safeguard the child, they also assess the suitability of the partner. We have suggested above that an unmarried couple should not be allowed to adopt jointly, i.e. that it should not be possible for them to have the same legal relationship towards the child which they would have if they were a married couple adopting together. We do not feel that this is necessarily incompatible with allowing a single person who has a partner to adopt. We recommend that, where assessing a single applicant, agencies should have a duty to assess any other person who is likely to act in a parental capacity towards the adopted child."

The gender-neutral language of the second of these two paragraphs leads me to believe that the working group members had in contemplation the possibility that an adopter's partner might be of the same sex. The earlier of the two paragraphs clearly indicates, that by 1992, and after "wide consultation with voluntary and professional organisations and with interested individuals" (see the foreword), the working group members had evidence of and expressed no reservations about adoption by individual homosexuals, both male and female. This spectrum of approach over a relatively short span of years warns me clearly how unruly is the horse of public policy which I am asked to mount, and upon what shifting sands I would be riding if I did so. I have formed the firm conclusion not only that the Adoption Act 1976 cannot be construed in so restricted and discriminatory a fashion as is proposed, but also that public policy considerations should not fall within the province of judges to define within this sphere. If there is to be a line drawn as a matter of policy to prevent homosexual cohabiting couples or single persons with homosexual orientation applying to adopt, then it is for Parliament so to conclude and with clarity to enact. But at the moment the Act of 1976 is drawn in words so wide as to cover all these categories. If that conceals a gap in the intended construction of the Act then it is for Parliament and not the courts to close it.'

5.21 Singer J was following a similar approach to that pursued in the case of *Re T*[22] in the Scottish Court of Session, arising from the Adoption (Scotland) Act 1978, s 16(1)(2). The issue being whether the mother's consent was being unreasonably withheld. T was a 6 year old boy with a number of disabilities (a

---

[22] Inner House, First Division [1997] SLT 724, [1996] SCLR 897, [1997] Fam Law 225, [1997] Fam Law 8, *The Times*, August 20, 1996.

recurring scenario in same sex adoption). T had been in the care system since birth, his mother had health difficulties of her own and was unable to care for him. The male prospective adopter (A) lived in a stable relationship with another man and had professional experience of nurturing and helping people with disabilities. A petition for adoption and all reports and investigations conducted in the proceedings endorsed the placement as serving the best interests of the child. The mother disengaged from the court proceedings and did not oppose the petition. The Lord Ordinary who considered the case refused the petition on the grounds that it had not been demonstrated that the birth mother had withheld her consent unreasonably and that the application raised 'fundamental questions of principle as to whether the court ought to sanction adoption where it was expressly proposed that a child should be brought up by a carer in a homosexual relationship'. The statutory provisions being considered very much mirror the provisions of the Adoption Act 1976. The Lord President (Hope) concluded that as there was no express prohibition on homosexual carers within the Act, it could not be said that a point of 'fundamental principle' arose at all. Effectively, the sexual orientation of the carer, the judge considered, was but one factor in assessing the carer's capacity to meet the child's needs:[23]

> 'There can be no more fundamental principle in adoption cases than that it is the duty of the Court to safeguard and promote the welfare of the child throughout his childhood. Issues relating to the sexual orientation, lifestyle, race, religion or other characteristics of the parties involved must, of course, be taken into account as part of the circumstances but they cannot be allowed to prevail over what is in the best interests of the child. The suggestion that it is a fundamental objection to an adoption that the proposed adopter is living with another in a homosexual relationship finds no expression in the language of the statute, and in my opinion it conflicts with the rule in Section 6 of the Act.'

Lord Hope found considerable support for his analysis in a much earlier judgment:

> 'If further guidance was needed on this matter it was, I believe to be found, in the speech of Lord Kilbrandon in *Re D (Adoption: Parents' Consent)* [1977] AC PP641 G-642B where he said "it could easily be productive of injustice if one were to attempt any hard and fast rule as to the attitude which the Courts ought to adopt, in custody, access or adoption matters, towards those whose sexual abnormalities have denied them the possibility of a normal family life". This is because it is not possible to generalise about homosexuals, or fair to treat them as other than personalities demanding the assessment appropriate to their several individualities in exactly the same way as each heterosexual member of society must be regarded as a person, not as a member of a class or herd. Naturally, in a family law context the fact of homosexual conduct cannot be ignored, but no more can the consequences of taking it into account be standardised. The kind of influence, in this type of problem, which the fact may have will be infinitely variable. I can see no trace, in the present case, of the Learned Judges having tried to make any rule about what view the Court should take about the position of a

---

[23] At p 732, para B.

homosexual spouse in an application for adoption; on the contrary, the decision at which he arrived plainly rests upon a careful and detailed examination of problems as it affected this father, this trial and this family. Any other approach would have been wrong.'

5.22 It is important that the language here quoted from Lord Kilbrandon does not obscure either the sensitivity of the decision or the rigour of the forensic analysis. With some refining of the language to reflect our advanced understanding of diversity, the judge in effect foreshadowed the present approach of the courts by some 30 years. It is notable too that Lord Hope whilst concluding that there was no ambiguity in the legislation he was considering, expressed the clear view that had there been so, he would have resolved that in an ECHR compatible manner:

'It is, however, now an integral part of the general principles of European Community Law that fundamental human rights must be protected, and that one of the sources to which regard may be made for an expression of these rights, is International Treaties for the Protection of Human Rights on which member States have collaborated or of which they are signatories: see Stair Memorial Encyclopaedia Vol 10, "European Community Law," [95] ... In my opinion the Courts in Scotland should apply the same presumption as that described by Lord Bridge, namely that, when legislation is found to be ambiguous in the sense that it is capable of a meaning which either conforms to or conflicts with the Convention, Parliament is to be presumed to have legislated in conformity with the convention not in conflict with it.'

That approach is now given statutory force by the interpretive provisions of s 3 of the Human Rights Act 1998. In *Re T* above the subject child had, as we have seen, a range of disabilities. It is a feature of the case-law, that homosexual adopters have frequently been selected for children with disabilities or children who would otherwise, for a variety of reasons, have been difficult to place. In *Re E (Adoption: Freeing Order)*,[24] E, a young girl of 12½ years had lived with parents who had a led a chaotic lifestyle, characterised by high levels of domestic violence. At 2 years of age she had experienced 18 moves within the care system and, perhaps unsurprisingly, had developed attachment difficulties and significant behavioural problems for which she was receiving help. Having been received into care she proved a challenging child to look after and experienced broken placements and a period in residential care too. Miss A responded to an advertisement to care for E. Miss A is described in the Law Reports as 'an experienced social worker of mature years'. She had professional experience of working with children with behavioural difficulties and was assessed to care for E. Included within the assessment was consideration of the relevance of Miss A's sexuality and the fact that she was a single carer. The assessment was resoundingly positive and Miss A was approved by the Adoption Panel. E was shortly thereafter placed into her care. E's behaviour in placement was, as it had been for some time, extremely difficult to manage, though Miss A was reported as having shown 'strong commitment.' Application was made by the local authority to free E for adoption. It was

---

[24]   [1995] 1 FLR 382.

opposed by the mother on the basis that the withholding of her consent was not unreasonable given the lesbian orientation of the adoptive mother. The judge at first instance received evidence from Professor Golambok, whose research continues to remain some of the most highly regarded in this field. The first instance judge expressed his conclusion in clear and unambiguous terms:

> 'Prima facie it is undesirable that E had gone to a lesbian ... but this case is a special one. E is a special girl who has a specially unhappy past and has a unique opportunity now'.

No doubt Miss A was pleased with the outcome and there can be little doubt the judge got the right result for the child. The case is 17 years old now and again the language quoted above and the sentiments underpinning the judgment must be viewed in the context of their time. Society's understanding of diversity issues has progressed dramatically in the intervening years. This case, however, remains significant for two reasons. Firstly because it articulates the view that homosexual adopters might really only have a role with children who otherwise may find themselves adrift in the care system and secondly, because it identifies (unambiguously) a view that for children looking to be placed for adoption, the heterosexual couple represents the 'gold standard' with same sex carers to be regarded as second best. The case went to the Court of Appeal, which upheld the first instance judge, but it did so on the basis that the overwhelming force of the advantages of the adoption would have been recognised by the reasonable parent and the parents' refusal to consent in such circumstances would logically therefore be unreasonable. There was, of course, no need, given the ambit of the appeal, to make any comment on the proposition expressed by the judge that 'prima facie it is undesirable that E should have gone to a lesbian.' Indeed, had the Court of Appeal done so, it would have, for the reasons looked at earlier, been trespassing into an area of public policy which is probably the province of Parliament and not that of the court. Now that same sex couples can adopt following the enactment of the Adoption and Children Act 2002, it is relevant to ask whether such couples fall to be considered on equal terms to their heterosexual counterparts or whether it remains the position that they will only usually be considered as suitable for children for whom the 'gold standard' of the heterosexual couple cannot be realised. It is the view of this author that this question that was largely circumvented in the passage of the Adoption and Children Act 2002. Some commentators plainly believe that very little has changed. The reality is that at the moment it is difficult to evaluate how same sex prospective adopters are likely to fare in the system. In practice, once a court approves a care plan endorsing a plan for adoption, the selection process is devolved to the Adoption Panel for the relevant Local Authority.

5.23 The panel is regulated by the Adoption Agencies Regulations 2005.[25] These Regulations are of great significance to prospective adopters. Save in the

---

[25] SI 2005/389, as amended by the Adoption Agencies and Independent Review of Determinations (Amendment) Regulations 2011, SI 2011/589.

context of financial provision, not within the scope of this chapter, these Regulations have not been subjected to a great deal of scrutiny in reported cases. For that reason it is perhaps helpful to consider some of the provisions in detail. Part 4 sets out the 'duties of the Adoption Agency in respect of prospective adopters'. It emphasises:

(a)   The requirement to provide counselling and information to prospective adopters (information must include for example, details of the procedure and the legal implications of adoption).

(b)   The requirement to consider an application for an assessment of suitability to adopt a child. The Agency must set up a case record in respect of the prospective adopter (the Prospective Adopter's Case Record) and consider his suitability to adopt a child. It is important to note that the Adoption Agency may ask the prospective adopter to provide any further information in writing which the agency may **reasonably require.** It must place on the prospective adopter's case record the application by the prospective adopter for an assessment of his suitability to adopt a child.

(c)   The information reports obtained by the Agency by virtue of this part.

(d)   The prospective adopter's report and his observations **on that report**.

(e)   The written records of the proceedings of the Adoption Panel under reg 26 ... the record of the agency's decision ... notification to the prospective adopter as soon as possible, where it is determined that he cannot be considered to adopt a child.

(f)   The Agency is required to provide preparation for adoption.

5.24   Part 5 concerns the duties the Adoption Agency in respect of proposed placements of a child with prospective adopters. Of particular importance is reg 32:

'32 Function of the Adoption Panel in relation to Proposed Placement

(1) The adoption panel must consider the proposed placement referred to it by the adoption agency and make a recommendation to the agency as to whether the child should be placed for adoption with that particular prospective adopter.

(2) In considering what recommendation to make the adoption panel shall have regard to the duties imposed on the adoption agency under section 1(2), (4) and (5) of the Act (considerations applying to the exercise of powers in relation to the adoption of a child) and

(a)   must consider and take into account all information and the reports passed to it in accordance with regulation 31;

(b)   may request the agency to obtain any other relevant information which the panel considers necessary; and

(c)   may obtain legal advice as it considers necessary in relation to the case.

(3) the adoption panel must consider –

  (a)   in a case where the adoption agency is a local authority, the authority's proposals for the provision of adoption support services for the adoptive family;

  (b)   the arrangements the adoption agency proposes to make for allowing any person contact with the child; and

  (c)   whether the parental responsibility of any parent or guardian or the prospective adopter should be restricted and if so the extent of any such restriction.'

WHAT IS THE FUNCTION OF THE ADOPTION PANEL?

5.25 Adoption Panels provide independent recommendations to the Housing and Social Services Department about whether:

(a)   adoption is in the best interests of children;

(b)   people who have applied to be adoptive parents are suitable to undertake the task of adoption;

(c)   the child's best interests are served by linking the child to an identified and approved adoptive parent.

THE CONSTITUTION OF THE PANEL

5.26 In addition to the recommendations about adoption for a child, the suitability of adoptive parents and the linking or matching of children, the panel also advises the Department about the legal steps that may need to be taken with a particular child. The 2011 amendments[26] now provide for a 'central list' ensuring the panel is constituted by individuals 'suitable to be members of an adoption panel'.

'The central list

3 (1) Subject to regulation 5, an adoption agency must maintain a list of persons who are considered by it to be suitable to be members of an adoption panel ("the central list"), including –

  (a)   one or more social workers who have at least three years' relevant post-qualifying experience, and

  (b)   the medical adviser to the adoption agency (or at least one if more than one medical adviser is appointed).

(2) A person who is included in the central list may at any time ask to be removed from the central list by giving one month's notice in writing.

---

[26]   SI 2011/589.

(3) Where the adoption agency is of the opinion that a person included in the central list is unsuitable or unable to remain in the list the agency may remove that person's name from the list by giving them one month's notice in writing with reasons.'

5.27 Panels will usually consist of approximately 10 people, chaired by an independent person with a vice chair who is also independent. The 2011 amendments now provide as follows:

'Constituting an adoption panel

4 (1) The adoption agency must constitute one or more adoption panels, as necessary, to perform the functions of an adoption panel under these Regulations and must appoint the panel members from the persons in the central list including –

    (a)   a person to chair the panel, being an independent person, who has the skills and experience necessary for chairing an adoption panel, and

    (b)   one or two persons who may act as chair if the person appointed to chair the panel is absent or that office is vacant ("the vice chairs").

(2) The adoption agency must ensure that an adoption panel has sufficient members, and that individual members have between them the experience and expertise necessary to effectively discharge the functions of the panel.

(3) Any two or more local authorities may jointly constitute an adoption panel ("a joint adoption panel") in which case the appointment of members must be by agreement between the authorities.

(4) A local authority may pay to any member of an adoption panel constituted by it such fee as it may determine, being a fee of a reasonable amount.

(5) Any adoption panel member may resign at any time by giving one month's notice in writing to the adoption agency which appointed them.

(6) Where an adoption agency is of the opinion that any member of the adoption panel appointed by it is unsuitable or unable to continue as a panel member, it may terminate that member's appointment at any time by giving the member notice in writing with reasons.

(7) A person ("P") is not an independent person for the purposes of this regulation and regulation 6 if –

    (a)   in the case of a registered adoption society, P is a trustee or employee of that society, or

    (b)   in the case of a local authority, P –

        (i)   is an elected member of that authority, or

        (ii)   is employed by that authority for the purposes of the adoption service or for the purposes of any of that local authority's functions relating to the protection or placement of children, or

    (c)   P is the adoptive parent of a child who was –

        (i)   placed for adoption with P by the adoption agency ("agency A"), or

        (ii)   placed for adoption with P by another adoption agency where P had been approved as suitable to be an adoptive parent by agency A, unless at least 12 months has elapsed since the adoption order was made in respect of the child.'

5.28   In practice panels will usually consist of:

(a)   An experienced social worker from the Adoption Team, and a Deputy Team Manager in childcare;

(b)   A medical advisor, now based on a much clearer footing as a consequence of the amended Regulations;

'Requirement to appoint an agency adviser and a medical adviser

8 (1) The adoption agency must appoint a senior member of staff, or where local authorities agree to constitute joint adoption panels as necessary appoint a senior member of staff of one of them, (referred to in this regulation as the "agency adviser") –

> (a)   to assist the agency with the maintenance of the central list and the constitution of adoption panels,
> (b)   to be responsible for the induction and training of persons in the central list,
> (c)   to be responsible for liaison between the agency and an adoption panel, monitoring the performance of persons in the central list and members of the adoption panel and the administration of adoption panels, and
> (d)   to give such advice to an adoption panel as the panel may request in relation to any case or generally.

(2) The agency adviser must be a social worker and have at least five years' relevant post-qualification experience and, in the opinion of the adoption agency, relevant management experience.

(3) The adoption agency must appoint at least one registered medical practitioner to be the agency's medical adviser.

(4) The medical adviser shall be consulted in relation to the arrangements for access to, and disclosure of, health information which is required or permitted by virtue of these Regulations.'

(c)   An elected member from the Council's Social Services Committee;

(d)   Four other people, both professional and lay people, two of whom have direct experience of fostering or adoption.

The panel also has a legal advisor and social advisor who are not members of the panel. In addition it has an administrator responsible for taking minutes at the meeting and for circulating the relevant documents to panel members. Adoption panels recognised the importance of ensuring that they are representative of the communities they serve and as such will try to include:

(a)   Members of ethnic minority;

(b)   A balance of men and women;

(c)   People who have direct experience of fostering and adoption.

HOW DOES THE ADOPTION PANEL WORK IN PRACTICE?

5.29   The panel usually meets monthly and by the time adoptive applicants are being considered by the panel, they will have attended adoption preparation training sessions led by a social worker. The amended Regulations put this on a clearer procedural foundation.

'Meetings of adoption panel

6 (1) No business may be conducted by an adoption panel unless at least the following meet as the panel –

  (a)   either the person appointed to chair the panel or one of the vice chairs,
  (b)   one person falling within regulation 3(1)(a),
  (c)   three, or in the case of an adoption panel established under regulation 4(3) four, other members and where the chair is not present and the vice chair is not an independent person, at least one other panel member must be an independent person.

(2) An adoption panel must make a written record of its proceedings, its recommendations and the reasons for its recommendations.'

The social worker will complete a home study report which will be submitted to the panel. Adoptive applicants will have seen the report written by the social worker and will have had the opportunity to make any further comments they wish. The panel will then move to consider the reports and contributions made by the applicants and make a recommendation to the Department about the suitability of the particular individual or couple to be adoptive parents. The applicants may attend the panel meeting, though they are not compelled to do so. The reports written by the social worker remain the main source of information upon which the panel makes its recommendation. Where applicants do attend they will be present for part of the discussion and will meet the chair of the panel prior to being brought to the meeting. Applicants are present usually when their social worker asks questions about their application and also may ask any questions they have about the panel process. Having withdrawn to consider its decision, the panel will make a recommendation and the applicants, if present, will be told of the panel's decision immediately by their social worker. The ultimate decision-maker, though this is sometimes controversial in practice, is the 'Agency Decision-maker' who is the Assistant Director of Childcare. If the panel decide an applicant should not be approved as an adoptive carer, the applicant is then given 28 days from the date of that decision in which to notify the Department that they wish their application to be reconsidered, alternatively they can choose to refer the matter to the Independent Review Mechanism.

5.30   In addition to the many specific provisions which we have looked at above designed to ensure that the decision making processes of the panel are rational, respect the rules of natural justice, procedurally fair and Convention compliant all of which protect same sex prospective adopters (as well as other minority interests). The process must now also comply with the Equality Act (Sexual Orientation) Regulations 2007.[27] These Regulations have specific provision for adoption and fostering agencies:

'Adoption and fostering agencies

15 (1) Paragraph (2) applies to a voluntary adoption agency or fostering agency that is an organisation of the kind referred to in regulation 14(1), or acts on behalf of or under the auspices of such an organisation.

(2) Subject to paragraph (3), during the period from the commencement of these Regulations until 31st December 2008, nothing in these Regulations shall make it unlawful for such a voluntary adoption agency or fostering agency to restrict the provision of its services or facilities to a person on the grounds of his sexual orientation.

(3) If such a voluntary adoption agency or fostering agency restricts the provision of those services or facilities as mentioned in paragraph (2), it must at the same time refer the person seeking them to another person who the agency believes provides similar services or facilities to persons of his sexual orientation.

(4) Paragraph (2) permits a restriction only if imposed if it is necessary to comply with the doctrine of the organisation, or so as to avoid conflicting with the strongly held religious convictions of a significant number of the religion's followers.'

5.31   What emerges from a consideration of the developments in this area of law in the last 20 years is a system which, whilst it now embraces diversity of options for children, places the welfare of a child awaiting an adoptive placement above any rights based agenda. There is a real understanding that adoption truly means providing a child with a family not a family with a child.

5.32   The Adoption Panel procedures are much improved and transparent. Their legitimacy is buttressed by the Independent Review Mechanism and the availability of minutes and written reasons for the decisions.

5.33   There is no evidence, either substantially or anecdotally which points to gay and lesbian prospective adopters feeling grievance about the process or that they are discriminated against. That said, those putting themselves forward as prospective adopters often feel highly vulnerable, recognising that their 'suitability' to adopt is under scrutiny. The desire to parent adoptive children is often every bit as consuming as any desire to parent and for some applicants it will be the final stage of a painful journey. This is not an easy position from which to launch a challenge to the process. That said, the mechanisms are in place, these are 'public bodies' making decisions which are required to be 'rational' in administrative law terms and human rights compatible under the Human Rights Act 1998. As such they remain susceptible to challenge in the future.

---

[27]   SI 2007/1263.

Chapter 6

GENDER RECOGNITION

MEANING OF 'SAME SEX RELATIONSHIP' AND GENDER RECOGNITION

Introduction

6.1   Although this book is about children and same sex families, a section on transsexual/gender identity has been included because, unless the gender of all the people involved is clear, it cannot be certain whether the family includes a same sex relationship. This is because some same sex relationships are created as a result of gender change or reassignment. It is therefore important to discuss how those relationships are created and how they affect the children raised in them.

Lord Nicholls said the following about gender reassignment in the case of *Bellinger v Bellinger*.[1]

> '... In this country, as elsewhere, classification of a person as male or female has long conferred a legal status. It confers a legal status, in that legal as well as practical consequences follow from the recognition of a person as male or female. The legal consequences affect many areas of life, from marriage and family law to gender-specific crime and competitive sport. It is not surprising, therefore, that society through its laws decides what objective biological criteria should be applied when categorising a person as male or female. Individuals cannot choose for themselves whether they wish to be known or treated as male or female. Self-definition is not acceptable. That would make nonsense of the underlying biological basis of the distinction.

> This approach did not give rise to legal difficulty before the advent of gender reassignment treatment. This was noted by Lord Reed in his article "Splitting the difference: transsexuals and European Human Rights law" (September 2000). Gender identity disorder seems always to have existed. But before the advent of gender reassignment treatment a claim by a transsexual person to be recognised in his or her self-perceived gender would have been hopeless. The anatomy of his or her body of itself would have refuted the claim.

> The position has now changed. Recognition of transsexualism as a psychiatric disorder has been accompanied by the development of sophisticated techniques of medical treatment. The anatomical appearance of the body can be substantially altered, by forms of treatment which are permissible as well as possible. It is in

---

[1]   [2003] 2 All ER 593 at paras 28–32.

these changed circumstances that society is now facing the question of how far it is prepared to go to alleviate the plight of the small minority of people who suffer from this medical condition. Should self-perceived gender be recognised?

Recognition of gender reassignment will involve some blurring of the normally accepted biological distinction between male and female. Some blurring already exists, unavoidably, in the case of inter-sexual persons. When assessing the gender of inter-sexual persons, matters taken into account include self-perception and style of upbringing and living. Recognition of gender reassignment will involve further blurring. It will mean that in law a person who, unlike an inter-sexual person, had all the biological characteristics of one sex at birth may subsequently be treated as a member of the opposite sex.

Thus the circumstances in which, and the purposes for which, gender reassignment is recognised are matters of much importance. These are not easy questions. The circumstances of transsexual people vary widely. The distinction between male and female is material in widely differing contexts. The criteria appropriate for recognising self-perceived gender in one context, such as marriage, may not be appropriate in another, such as competitive sport.'

6.2   Sexual orientation is understood to refer to each person's capacity for profound emotional, affectional and sexual attraction to, and intimate and sexual relations with, individuals of a different gender or the same gender or more than one gender.[2]

6.3   Gender identity is understood to refer to each person's deeply felt internal and individual experience of gender, which may or may not correspond with the sex assigned at birth, including the personal sense of the body (which may involve, if freely chosen, modification of bodily appearance or function by medical, surgical or other means) and other expressions of gender, including dress, speech and mannerisms.[3]

Trans(sexual)/transgendered people

6.4   The terms 'trans people' and 'transgender people' are both often used as umbrella terms for people whose gender identity and/or gender expression differs from their birth sex, including transsexual people (those who intend to undergo, are undergoing or have undergone a process of gender reassignment to live permanently in their acquired gender), transvestite/cross-dressing people (those who wear clothing traditionally associated with the other gender either occasionally or more regularly), androgyne/polygender people (those who have non-binary gender identities meaning they do not identify as male or female), and others who define as gender variant.[4]

---

[2]   The Yogyakarta Principles on the Application of International Human Rights Law in Relation to Sexual Orientation and Gender Identity (March 2007).
[3]   The Yogyakarta Principles on the Application of International Human Rights Law in Relation to Sexual Orientation and Gender Identity (March 2007).
[4]   Trans Research Review – Equality and Human Rights Commission.

6.5 The term transsexualism does not indicate, or refer to, sexual orientation, ie a person's preference for a sexual partner of the opposite, or of the same sex/gender. Trans people may identify as straight, gay, lesbian, bisexual, or asexual. Some trans people say that, until the process of transition is complete, they cannot tell what their future sexual preference will be. It may remain the same; it may change. A trans person who has always been attracted to women may remain so. Or not. A trans person who has always been attracted to men, may remain so. Or not. During the process of transition, the issue of sexual orientation may be of little interest to the individual concerned, since the issue of gender identity is uppermost in his or her mind.[5]

6.6 Although the number of transgender persons is small, it should be pointed out that the transgender community is very diverse. It includes pre-operative and post-operative transsexual persons, but also persons who do not choose to undergo or do not have access to operations. They may identify as female-to-male (FTM) or male-to-female (MTF) transgender persons, and may or may not have undergone surgery or hormonal therapy. The community also includes cross-dressers, transvestites and other people who do not fit the narrow categories of 'male' or 'female'. Many legal frameworks only seem to refer to transsexual persons, leaving out a decisive part of the community.[6]

6.7 This chapter relates to the group of people referred to as 'transgender' or 'transsexual' and throughout this book the terms 'transsexual' and 'transgender' will be used when referring to the widest range of possible gender identities and will use more specific terminology such as trans men, trans women, transsexual people, polygender people and so on when referring to particular sub-sections of this diverse population. It is however acknowledged that the term 'transsexual' is not universally accepted as appropriate and that the term 'transgender' might be preferable.[7]

GENDER RECOGNITION BACKGROUND

6.8 Gender identity is one of the most fundamental aspects of life. The sex of a person is usually assigned at birth and becomes a social and legal fact from there on. However, a relatively small number of people experience problems with being a member of the sex recorded at birth. This can also be so for intersex persons whose bodies incorporate both or certain aspects of both male and female physiology, and at times their genital anatomy. For others, problems arise because their innate perception of themselves is not in conformity with the sex assigned to them at birth.[8]

---

[5]   Gires – Gender Variance (Dysphoria) 2008.

[6]   Commission for Human Rights – Human Rights and Gender Identity – Issue Paper by Thomas Hammarberg, Council of Europe Commissioner for Human Rights, Strasbourg, 29 July 2009 (CommDH/IssuePaper(2009)2).

[7]   See Glossary at Appendix 3 for further terms and definitions.

[8]   Commission for Human Rights – Human Rights and Gender Identity – Issue Paper by Thomas Hammarberg, Council of Europe Commissioner for Human Rights, Strasbourg, 29 July 2009 (CommDH/IssuePaper(2009)2).

6.9   The human rights situation of transgender persons has long been ignored and neglected, although the problems they face are serious and often specific to this group alone. Transgender people experience a high degree of discrimination, intolerance and outright violence. Their basic human rights are violated, including the right to life, the right to physical integrity and the right to health.[9]

6.10   The case of *P v S and Cornwall County Council*[10] opened the door for the inclusion of trans people under EU gender equality legislation.[11] In this case, P (the applicant) was a British transsexual woman who had been dismissed while on sick leave recovering from her gender reassignment surgery. She claimed that she had been discriminated against on the ground of sex. The domestic judge referred the case to the European Court of Justice for a preliminary ruling in order to find out whether Art 2(1) prohibiting discrimination on grounds of sex, and Art 5(1) applying equal treatment in employment conditions (including dismissal) of Directive 76/207/EEC, were to be interpreted so as to include the dismissal of a transsexual person with reference to her gender reassignment.

6.11   The court established that the scope of the Directive, as far as the concept of discrimination on grounds of sex was concerned, was not limited to discrimination based on the fact that the individual is of one sex or the other. In fact, the court ruled that the Directive also extended to discrimination based on the sex of the person, thus including the case of dismissal of a transsexual person related to her/his gender reassignment.

6.12   *P v S* was a landmark case, not only because it represents a precedent on which the European Court of Justice has constructed solid jurisprudence, but also because it constitutes the foundation on which gender reassignment was included in the scope of subsequent gender equality Directives. It was then followed by other important decisions of the court that reinforced its rationale, expanding it to other pieces of European legislation.[12]

Development of transgender legislation

6.13   During the last decade or so a number of equality laws have been implemented to protect transsexual people from discrimination and accord rights. Key amongst these were the Sex Discrimination (Gender Reassignment) Regulations 1999, SI 1999/1102 (SDA 1999), the Gender Recognition Act 2004 (GRA 2004) and the Equal Treatment Directive (2004/113/EC), leading to the

---

[9]   Commission for Human Rights – Human Rights and Gender Identity – Issue Paper by Thomas Hammarberg, Council of Europe Commissioner for Human Rights, Strasbourg, 29 July 2009 (CommDH/IssuePaper(2009)2).

[10]   Case C-13-94 (1994).

[11]   Equal Treatment Directive 76/207/EEC which is stated in Art 1 to put into effect the principle of equal treatment for men and women as regards access to employment etc.

[12]   Transgender People and the Gender Recast Directive Implementation Guidelines written by Stefano Fabeni & Silvan Agius December 2009 for The European Region of the International Lesbian, Gay, Bisexual, Trans & Intersex Association ILGA).

Sex Discrimination (Amendment of Legislation) Regulations 2008, SI 2008/963 and now the Equality Act 2010 (EqA 2010). These acts and regulations collectively give a statutory requirement to examine whether people who were undergoing, planning to undergo, or who had undergone gender reassignment treatment, were receiving recognition of their acquired or chosen gender identity and protection from discrimination in employment, and more recently, protection from discrimination in the provision of goods, facilities and services.

6.14 Prior to the GRA 2004, transsexual people were not recognised in their acquired gender under the law of any part of the United Kingdom. Although transsexual people could obtain some official documents in their new name and gender, they could not obtain new birth certificates or enjoy any rights confined by law to people of the gender to which they feel they belong. For example, they could not marry in their acquired gender.[13] Over a number of years test cases have been taken before the European Court of Human Rights which objected to the requirement that a couple end their marriage in order for one of the partners to be recognised in their acquired gender. The development of the law can be grasped from the following cases.

6.15 In *Rees v United Kingdom*,[14] the applicant was a female-to-male transsexual who claimed that UK legislation relating to the registration of births and marriages violated Arts 8 and 12 of the Convention. The court held that:

- although the essential object of Art 8 is to protect the individual against arbitrary interference by public authorities, there may also be positive obligations inherent in an effective respect for private life, albeit subject to a State's margin of appreciation;

- the mere refusal to alter an original entry, or to issue a new birth certificate in corrected terms, could not be regarded as such an interference;

- the notion of 'respect' for private life, particularly with regard to positive obligations, was not clear cut, and having regard to the diversity of practices throughout the Contracting States, the requirements will vary from case to case;

- this diversity of practice was evidenced by the fact that, via legal, judicial and/or administrative practices, many States had a system whereby transsexuals could align their personal status with their acquired status. However, the conditions under which this could be done were also quite variable. As a result, there was little common ground in this area and so the 'margin of appreciation' was wide;

---

[13] These issues were first considered by an Interdepartmental Working Group (on Transsexual People) convened on 14 April 1999 by the Secretary of State for the Home Department.

[14] *Rees v United Kingdom* (1986) 9 EHRR 56.

- in deciding whether or not a positive obligation exists, regard must be had to the fair balance which must be struck between the general interest of the community and the interest of the individual.

6.16 The court noted that the authorities had endeavoured to meet the practical needs of the applicant in a reasonable way and did not consider that the United Kingdom should be asked to adopt a new system of registration. Accordingly, it found that there was no violation of Art 8.

6.17 In relation to Art 12, the court held that the right to marry, as provided for in that Article, referred to the traditional marriage between persons of the opposite biological sex. It thus found that there was no violation of Art 12.[15]

6.18 In *Cossey v United Kingdom,*[16] comparable issues to *Rees* were addressed. The applicant, a male-to-female transsexual, complained that the failure to permit her to marry a male constituted a violation of Arts 8 and 12. The court followed its earlier decision in *Rees*. Whilst the court noted some developments since *Rees*, these were not such as to reveal any real common ground on the issue between Contracting States. A considerable diversity of practice still existed. In such circumstances, it considered that a departure from its decision in *Rees* would not be justified.

6.19 Until the court's decision in *Goodwin v United Kingdom*[17] discussed below, the case of *B v France*[18] provided the only instance where the court found a violation of Art 8 in respect of transsexual persons. The court distinguished *Rees* and *Cossey* on the grounds that the French system impugned in this case was significantly different to that at issue in *Rees* and *Cossey*. However, because of the particular features of the French system at issue (for example, birth certificates could be amended by court order, the applicant was not permitted by law to change her forename and she experienced frequent difficulties on production of official documents), this case did not have a widespread impact on the position of transsexuals in other States.

6.20 In *Sheffield and Horsham v United Kingdom,*[19] the court was again invited to find that the United Kingdom, by not recognising the applicants' new gender, had failed to comply with its positive obligations to ensure respect for the applicants' private lives. However, the court refused to overturn *Rees* and

---

[15]   Note that the ECtHR has more recently adjusted its view of the operation of Art 12 in relation to same sex couples in the case of *Schalk and Kopf v Austria* (Application No 30141/04). The ECtHR held: '[The] Court would no longer consider that the right to marry enshrined in Article 12 must in all circumstances be limited to marriage between two persons of the opposite sex. Consequently, it cannot be said that Article 12 is inapplicable to the applicants' complaint. However, as matters stand, the question whether or not to allow same sex marriage is left to regulation by the national law of the Contracting State'.

[16]   *Cossey v United Kingdom* (1991) 13 EHRR 622.

[17]   (Application No 28957/95).

[18]   *B v France* (1992) 16 EHRR 1.

[19]   *Sheffield and Horsham v United Kingdom* (1998) 27 EHRR 163.

Cossey, finding that there had been no significant developments in the area of medical science in the previous 10 years, which would justify a departure from their previous decisions. The court also found that an examination of legislative trends across Europe did not establish the existence of any common European approach to the problems created by the recognition in law of post-operative gender status. The court did reiterate, however, the need for States to keep this area under review.

6.21 In the cases of *Goodwin v The United Kingdom*[20] and *I v The United Kingdom*,[21] the applicants both complained about the lack of legal recognition of their post-operative sex and about the legal status of transsexuals in the United Kingdom. They complained, in particular, about their treatment in relation to employment, social security and pensions and their inability to marry either as a man or a woman. They both relied on Art 8 (right to respect for private and family life), Art 12 (right to marry and to found a family) and Art 14 (prohibition of discrimination) of the European Convention on Human Rights. Ms Goodwin also relied on Art 13 (right to an effective remedy).

Goodwin v The United Kingdom

6.22 Christine Goodwin, born in 1937, claimed that she had problems and faced sexual harassment at work during and following her gender re-assignment. Most recently, she experienced difficulties concerning her national insurance (NI) contributions. As legally she is still a man, she has to continue to pay NI contributions until the age of 65. If she had been recognised as a woman, she would have ceased to be liable at the age of 60 in April 1997. She has had to enter into a special arrangement to continue paying her NI contributions directly herself to avoid questions being raised by her employers about the anomaly. She also alleges that the fact that she keeps the same NI number has meant that her employer has been able to discover that she previously worked for them under another name and gender, with resulting embarrassment and humiliation.

I v The United Kingdom

6.23 I, who used to work as a dental nurse, claims that she was unable to obtain admittance to a nursing course, as she refused to present her birth certificate. Since 1988 it appears that she has not worked and that she is living on a disability pension due to ill-health.

6.24 In giving judgment on 11 July 2002 in *Goodwin v The United Kingdom* and *I v The United Kingdom* the European Court of Human Rights found that the UK had breached the Convention rights of these two transsexual people, under Arts 8 (the right to respect for private life) and 12 (the right to marry).

---

[20] (Application No 28957/95) [2002] ECHR 588, (2002) 35 EHRR 18.
[21] (Application No 25680/94) (2002) 36 EHRR 967, [2002] 2 FCR 613, [2002] 2 FLR 518.

6.25   It was quite clear from the emerging ruling from the European Court of Human Rights that the UK government has a positive obligation under international law to secure the Convention rights and freedoms and must rectify these ongoing breaches. Therefore even before final judgment in *Goodwin* and *I* the government started getting transgender issues considered by an Interdepartmental Working Group convened in 1999. Therefore as a result of these cases and others, the UK government announced its intention to bring forward legislation in this area. The government introduced the Gender Recognition Bill.[22]

6.26   On 10 April 2003, the House of Lords gave judgment in the case of *Bellinger v Bellinger*.[23] Mrs. Bellinger, a male-to-female transsexual person, was seeking legal recognition of her 1981 marriage to a man. Although their Lordships were sympathetic to Mrs Bellinger's plight, they ruled that the marriage was void. They declared that s 11(c) of the Matrimonial Causes Act 1973 was incompatible with the Human Rights Act 1998. The result of this was that legislation was needed to enable transsexual people to marry in their acquired gender. Consequently the Gender Recognition Act became law.

WHAT IS 'GENDER RECOGNITION'?

6.27   The GRA 2004[24] provides transsexual[25] people with legal recognition of their acquired gender (as members of the sex appropriate to their gender whether it is male or female). The Act sets out who may apply for a gender recognition certificate and who determines that application.

'1 Applications

(1) A person of either gender who is aged at least 18 may make an application for a gender recognition certificate on the basis of –

    (a)   living in the other gender, or

    (b)   having changed gender under the law of a country or territory outside the United Kingdom.

(2) In this Act "the acquired gender", in relation to a person by whom an application under subsection (1) is or has been made, means –

    (a)   in the case of an application under paragraph (a) of that subsection, the gender in which the person is living, or

    (b)   in the case of an application under paragraph (b) of that subsection, the gender to which the person has changed under the law of the country or territory concerned.

(3) An application under subsection (1) is to be determined by a Gender Recognition Panel.

---

[22]   On 13 December 2002. A draft Bill was published on 11 July 2003, and underwent pre-legislative scrutiny by the Joint Committee on Human Rights.

[23]   [2003] 2 All ER 593.

[24]   Came into force on 4 April 2005.

[25]   See Glossary in Appendix 3 for definition of transsexual.

(4) Schedule 1 (Gender Recognition Panels) has effect.'

6.28 An application[26] to the Gender Recognition Panel (GRP) must be made in a form and manner specified by the Secretary of State after consultation with the Scottish Ministers and the Department of Finance and Personnel in Northern Ireland.[27] Consequently the Secretary of State can specify the form and manner of applications to the Gender Recognition Panel, for example how and where the application is to be made (see Appendix 3 for an example of the current form for an application for a Gender Recognition Certificate and guidance notes for an application to the Gender Recognition Panel). The applicant may be required to pay a non refundable fee[28] for the application and the fee may differ according to individual circumstances.[29]

6.29 Therefore an application for a Gender Recognition Certificate (GRC) may be made by any person of either gender who is aged at least 18 on the basis of:

- living in the other gender;[30] or

- having changed gender in another jurisdiction.[31]

Where an applicant has been recognised under the law of another country or territory as having changed gender, the panel need only be satisfied that the country or territory in question has been approved.[32] A list of approved countries or territories can be found at Appendix 3.

6.30 Schedule 1 (Gender Recognition Panels) set out the requirements for making an application and the criteria by which the panels will decide applications.

Determination of applications

6.31 The criteria for determination of the application are covered by s 2(1)(a)–(d) of the GRA. Therefore before issuing a certificate, the GRP must be satisfied that the applicant:

---

[26] Application packs are available from www.grp.gov.uk or direct from the Gender Recognition Panel by contacting: Gender Recognition Panel PO BOX 9300 Leicester LE1 8DJ Tel: 0300 123 4503 (Between 9:00 and 17:00, Monday to Friday) E Mail: grpenquiries@hmcts.gsi.gov.uk.
[27] GRA 2004, s 7(2).
[28] The maximum fee for applying for a Gender Recognition Certificate is £140. By law, certain applicants are eligible for a reduced fee or are exempt from paying altogether. The amount applicable will be prescribed by order by the Secretary of State.
[29] GRA 2004, s 7(1). A person is not required to pay a fee if applying to the Gender Recognition Panel for: (i) a *full* Gender Recognition Certificate, if an *interim* Gender Recognition Certificate has already been granted; (ii)a correction has to be made to a Gender Recognition Certificate that the panel has already issued.
[30] GRA 2004, s 1(1)(a).
[31] GRA 2004, s 1(1)(a).
[32] GRA 2004, s 2(2).

- must have, or have had, gender dysphoria;[33]

- have lived in the acquired gender for at least two years before making the application;

- intends to continue to live in the acquired gender for the rest of his or her life; and

- provides the evidence required by or under s 3.

6.32   The GRA therefore requires applicants to have transitioned two years before a certificate is issued. However, it makes no requirement for sex reassignment surgery to have taken place, although such surgery could be accepted as part of the supporting evidence for a case where it has taken place.

6.33   Section 2(2)(a) and (b) provides that applications made under s 1(1)(b) must be granted if the evidence requirements are met and if the panel is satisfied that the gender change occurred under the law of an approved country or territory. Therefore those who have obtained legal recognition in approved overseas jurisdictions may obtain recognition under GRA with much-reduced evidence requirements; for example such applicants are not required to have transitioned two years before or to be resident overseas. Section 2(4) provides the Secretary of State with the power to prescribe what is an approved country or territory for this purpose (see Appendix 3 for the current list of approved countries and territories namely the Gender Recognition (Approved Countries and Territories) Order 2011.[34] This power will be used to prescribe those countries that have recognition criteria which are at least as rigorous as those in the Act.

Evidence

6.34   The Gender Recognition Panel reviews applications from transsexual people who want to legally change their gender. In effect, as described in s 2 of the GRA, two types of applications are considered by the panel and applicants who wish to legally change their gender must provide evidence to the panel demonstrating that:

- they are at least 18 years of age or more, have or had gender dysphoria and must also have lived in the new gender for two years and intend to live permanently in their acquired gender; or

- changed gender legally in another country.

---

[33]   Gender Dysphoria is the term used in the UK legislation to denote Gender Identity Disorder.
[34]   SI 2011/1630.

6.35 Section 3 of the GRA stipulates what evidence must be submitted as part of an application[35] for a GRC. Section 3(1)–(3) set out what medical evidence is needed for an application on the basis of 'living in the other gender'.[36]

6.36 There must be a report from a registered medical practitioner, or a chartered psychologist, either of whom must be practising in the field of gender dysphoria.[37]

6.37 The report must include details of diagnosis.[38] The second report need not be from a medical professional practising in the field of gender dysphoria, but could be from any registered medical practitioner or chartered psychologist.[39] At least one of the reports must include details of any treatment that the applicant has undergone, is undergoing or that is prescribed or planned, for the purposes of modifying sexual characteristics.[40]

6.38 An application must also include a statutory declaration by the applicant, stating that the applicant meets the conditions as to having lived in the acquired gender for at least two years and intends to continue to do so.[41]

6.39 Some of the evidential provisions are shared by both types of application, and these are set out in s 3(6). It stipulates that an application must include a statutory declaration as to whether or not the applicant is married.[42] It also provides the Secretary of State with the power to specify, in effect, the further content of an application form.[43] For instance, an application will need to include details of name, date of birth, and correspondence address. This will be done by way of an order. The GRP has the flexibility to specify other evidence that will enable them better to determine whether the applicant meets the criteria for a successful application.[44] The panel is required to provide reasons for requiring any further information or evidence.[45] The applicant is also given a right to supply other evidence pertaining to the criteria. There are also notes for applicants clarifying what evidence the panel will regard as useful for satisfying the criteria set out in s 2.

---

[35] See Appendix 3 for an example of an Application for a GRC to the Gender Recognition Panel and the Guidance Notes for the Application.
[36] GRA 2004, s 1(1)(a).
[37] GRA 2004, s 3(1)(a) and (b). The GRP provides a list of approved practitioners.
[38] GRA 2004, s 3(2)(a) and (b).
[39] GRA 2004, s 3(2)(b).
[40] GRA 2004, s 3(3)(a) and (b).
[41] GRA 2004, s 3(4).
[42] GRA 2004, s 36(a).
[43] GRA 2004, s 3(6)(b).
[44] GRA 2004, s 3(6)(c).
[45] GRA 2004, s 3(8).

Overseas application process

6.40 Evidence of change of gender[46] is also required for applications under the category of 'having changed gender under the law of another country or territory'.[47]

6.41 Many other countries and territories now make provision in their law for transsexual people to change gender (a list of such countries can be found at Appendix 3 titled table of gender recognition schemes in countries and territories that have been approved by the Secretary of State). Having obtained legal recognition for their change of gender in a country or territory outside of the UK, they may then wish to have that gender change recognised in the UK. For example, they may wish to marry or enter into a civil partnership with someone here, or they may be living or working here.

6.42 Except where the original change of legal gender took place within the European Union (EU) or European Economic Area (EEA), the Gender Recognition Act 2004 does not provide for overseas gender changes to be automatically recognised in the UK. However, it does allow a person whose change of gender has been recognised overseas to apply for a gender recognition certificate on the basis of a simplified procedure,[48] provided the country or territory in question is one which has been approved for this purpose by the Secretary of State.[49]

6.43 Overseas applicants must therefore demonstrate that they are recognised in their acquired gender in a country or territory that is on the panel's approved list.[50] In addition, the applicant will be required to comply with appropriate rigorous requirements, such that the UK can be satisfied there has been a proper assessment of the permanence of the gender change. This is to reflect the guiding principle fundamental under the Gender Recognition Act that an individual must have taken decisive steps to live fully and permanently in their acquired gender.

6.44 The precise requirements applied in the overseas country vary. In most cases this will have involved gender reassignment surgery, but in some cases other evidence of permanence may have been involved (just as in the UK surgery is not a requirement of gender recognition). In most cases there will have been a long period living in the acquired gender. The precise requirements

---

[46] GRA 2004, s 3(5).

[47] Under GRA 2004, s 1(1)(b).

[48] Details of the procedures can be found at http://www.justice.gov.uk/downloads/guidance/courts-and-tribunals/tribunals/gender-recognition-panel/overseas-application-process/guidance-application-gender-recognition-certificate10052011.pdf.

[49] Section 2(4) provides the Secretary of State with the power to prescribe what is an approved country or territory for this purpose. This power will be used to prescribe those countries that have recognition criteria which are at least as rigorous as those in the Act.

[50] A list of approved countries can be found at Appendix 3.

are a matter for the country concerned, and the requirement to provide evidence of having lived in the acquired gender for two years does not apply to such cases.

6.45 A country or territory which is not included in the subordinate legislation is not an approved country or territory. Applications in these circumstances must be made on the basis of having lived for a period of two years or more in the acquired gender to be eligible to apply using the standard application process for a Gender Recognition Certificate. Whichever application process is relevant, the procedures that are followed to make an application will be the same.[51]

Successful applications

6.46 If the GRP grants an application under s 1(1) it must issue a Gender Recognition Certificate (GRC) to the applicant[52] and unless the applicant is married, the certificate is to be a full gender recognition certificate.[53]

Consequences of issue of GRC

6.47 Once a full gender recognition certificate is issued to an applicant, the person's gender becomes for all purposes the acquired gender, so that an applicant who was born a male would, in law, become a woman for all purposes. She would, for example, be entitled to protection as a woman under the Sex Discrimination Act 1975; and she would be considered to be female for the purposes of s 11(c) of the Matrimonial Causes Act 1973, and so able to contract a valid marriage with a man.[54]

Recognition of one's gender is not retrospective, therefore a certificate cannot rewrite the gender history of the transsexual person.[55]

Summary

6.48 A full gender recognition certificate, will afford the applicant the right to:

• marry or enter into a civil partnership in their acquired gender (as discussed below);

---

[51] The GRP has provided an Explanatory leaflet – A guide for users Gender Recognition Act 2004. Application for a Gender Recognition Certificate Overseas Track Application can be found at http://www.justice.gov.uk/downloads/guidance/courts-and-tribunals/tribunals/gender-recognition-panel/overseas-application-process/guidance-application-gender-recognition-certificate10052011.pdf.

[52] GRA 2004, s 4(1).

[53] GRA 2004, s 4(2).

[54] GRA 2004, s 9(1).

[55] GRA 2004, s 9(2).

- obtain a birth certificate that recognises the acquired gender (as discussed below under Registration heading);

- acquire benefits and state pension just like anyone else of that gender (as discussed later).

REGISTRATION

6.49   Birth certificates are one of the matters of most concern to transsexual people, because birth certificates are frequently required as proof of identity or age or place of birth.

Article 8 of the European Convention states that 'everyone has the right to respect for his private and family life, his home and his correspondence'. The European Court of Human Rights has ruled that failure of a state to alter the birth certificate of a person to the preferred gender constitutes a violation of Art 8 of the Convention.[56] Member states are thus required to legally recognise the gender change of transsexual people.

6.50   In the UK legal recognition follows from the issue of a GRC[57] by a GRP.[58] A person who has received recognition in the acquired gender and who has a UK birth register entry will have new entries created to reflect the acquired gender.[59]

6.51   Under Sch 3 to the GRA successful applicants are entered on the Gender Recognition Register (GRR), held by the Registrar General for England and Wales, similar in operation to the Adoptions Register for those who have been adopted.[60] Schedule 3[61] requires the Registrar General for England and Wales to create a Gender Recognition Register (GRR). The Register is not open to the public for inspection or search.[62] An application can be made to the Registrar General for a new birth certificate in the new name and gender. The new birth certificate is created from a new record from the GRR. The new birth certificate will be indistinguishable from other birth certificates and will not refer to the Gender Recognition Register.

6.52   The issuing of a gender recognition certificate obliges the Registrar General to make an entry in the GRR and to mark the original entry referring

---

[56]   See ECtHR, *B v France* judgment of 25 March 1992 (Series A No 232-C) (distinguishing the *Rees* and *Cossey* judgments), ECtHR, *Sheffield and Horsham v the United Kingdom* judgment of 30 July 1998, ECtHR, *Christine Goodwin v the United Kingdom*, Application No 28957/95, judgment of 11 July 2002. ECtHR (4th sect), *Grant v the United Kingdom*, Application No 32570/03, judgment of 23 May 2006.

[57]   GRA 2004, s 4(1).

[58]   GRA 2004, s 1(3).

[59]   GRA 2004, s 10(1), (2).

[60]   GRA 2004, s 10 deals with registration.

[61]   Section 10(4) brings Sch 3 into effect.

[62]   Schedule 3, paras 3, 4.

to the birth (or adoption) of the transsexual person to show that the original entry has been superseded.[63] This should ensure that caution is exercised when an application is received for a certificate from the original birth (or adoption) record. Therefore should an applicant for a birth certificate provide details of the name recorded on the birth certificate, he or she will be issued with a certificate from the birth record and where an applicant supplies the details recorded on the GRR, they will receive a certificate compiled from the entry in the GRR. The mark linking the two entries is chosen with care to ensure that the fact that an entry is contained in the GRR is not apparent.[64] The mark will not be included in any certificate compiled from the entries on the register.[65]

6.53 The annual index to birth records will include entries relating to the GRR.[66] Such entries will be recorded in the index in the year in which the new record is created. The entry for a transsexual person's birth record will remain in the index for the year in which the birth was originally registered. The index will not disclose the fact that an entry relates to a record in the GRR.

6.54 There are provisions for certified copies to be made of any entry in the GRR and to be issued to anyone who would be entitled to a certified copy of the original entry relating to the transsexual person.[67] This ensures that it is not apparent from the certified copy that it is compiled from the GRR. Such certificates will look the same as any other birth (or adoption) certificate.[68]

6.55 The Registrar General has the same power to re-register a birth recorded in the GRR to show a person as the father, as a registrar would have under s 10 of the Births and Deaths Registration Act 1953.[69] The Registrar General also has a power to correct an entry in the GRR in the same way as the original entry could be corrected.[70]

6.56 Provisions have also been made for any entry in the GRR, or mark relating to that entry in the original register, to be cancelled if the gender recognition certificate is revoked.[71] A certified copy of an entry in the GRR will have the same evidential value as a certified copy of the entry in the original register.[72]

6.57 Whilst it is possible to re-register one's own certificate, the GRA does not provide provision for a child's birth certificate to show their parent's new acquired gender. This means that the child's birth certificate would still show their parent's pre-acquired gender.

---

[63] Schedule 3, para 3(1)(a).
[64] Schedule 3, para 3(1)(c).
[65] Schedule 3, para 3(3).
[66] Schedule 3, para 4(1).
[67] Schedule 3, para 5.
[68] Schedule 3, para 6.
[69] Schedule 3, para 7.
[70] Schedule 3, para 8.
[71] Schedule 3, para 9.
[72] Schedule 3, para 10.

Married couples and civil partners

6.58 If an applicant for a GRC is married or in a civil partnership, they will be issued with an Interim Gender Recognition Certificate (IGRC).[73] Schedule 2[74] of the GRA deals with interim certificates and Sch 4[75] amends s 12 Matrimonial Causes Act 1973 (MCA). The MCA is amended as follows:

> In section 12 (grounds on which a marriage celebrated after 31st July 1971 is voidable), after paragraph (f) insert –
>> "(g) that an interim gender recognition certificate under the Gender Recognition Act 2004 has, after the time of the marriage, been issued to either party to the marriage;
>> (h) that the respondent is a person whose gender at the time of the marriage had become the acquired gender under the Gender Recognition Act 2004".

6.59 The law requires parties to a marriage, and now a civil partnership, to comply with the correct formalities and to have the legal capacity to contract a marriage or civil partnership. The formalities in respect of civil partnership are discussed in chapter 8. If there are any irregularities in the legal capacity, a party to the marriage or civil partnership may seek a decree of annulment. A distinction is drawn between those marriages or civil partnerships that the law consider as **void** and those it regards as **voidable**. The distinction between void and voidable marriages was explained by Lord Greene MR in *De Reneville* v *De Reneville*:[76]

> 'A void marriage is one that will be regarded by every court in any case in which the existence of the marriage is in issue as never having taken place and can be so treated by both parties to it without the necessity of any decree annulling it; a voidable marriage is one that will be regarded by every court as a valid subsisting marriage until a decree annulling it has been pronounced by a court of competent jurisdiction.'

Section 50 of the Civil Partnership Act 2004 is the equivalent provision which deals with grounds under which a civil partnership is voidable. Therefore a civil partnership will be voidable where the respondent had obtained a GRC[77] prior to the ceremony and the petitioner was unaware of it[78] (please refer to chapter 8 on civil partnership for a detailed analysis).

The interim certificate may then be used by either party to the marriage as evidence in support of an application to annul the marriage under s 12(g) of, or para 11(1)(e) of Sch 1 to, the Matrimonial Causes Act 1973 or s 50 of the Civil

---

[73] GRA 2004, s 4(3).
[74] Brought into effect by GRA 2004, s 4(3).
[75] Brought into effect by GRA 2004, s 11.
[76] *Reneville v De Reneville* [1948] P 100, III.
[77] Civil Partnership Act 2004, s 50(e).
[78] Civil Partnership Act 2004, s 51(6).

Partnership Act 2004 ('that an interim gender recognition certificate has, after the time of the marriage, been issued to either party to the marriage').[79]

6.60   This means in effect that, in England, Wales and Northern Ireland, the fact that an interim gender recognition certificate has been issued to either party to a marriage or civil partnership is a ground (the first new ground of nullity) for that marriage or civil partnership being voidable.[80]

6.61   When the applicant receives an IGRC it will have the effect of making the marriage or civil partnership voidable on the application to the court by either party to the marriage or civil partnership. This is because current law does not recognise marriages between individuals of the same sex. Either party to the marriage or civil partnership can, following the grant of an interim certificate, make an application to court for the marriage or civil partnership to be annulled.

6.62   Proceedings for nullity on this basis must be made within six months of the issue of the interim certificate.[81] Without this time limit an interim certificate could be used to annul a new marriage entered into in the future. If proceedings for nullity have not been issued within six months the interim certificate will lapse and a fresh application supported by evidence would have to be made to the GRP as described above.

6.63   Therefore an interim certificate is issued only for the purpose of annulling a marriage or a civil partnership to allow the issuing of a full certificate. Different rules will apply for couples whose marriage or civil partnerships are not registered in the United Kingdom.[82]

6.64   If a court annuls a marriage on the ground that an interim gender recognition certificate has been issued to one party, it must, on doing so, issue a full gender recognition certificate to that party and send a copy to the Secretary of State.[83] This is the only known example where the law requires someone to relinquish one right (the right to remain married to their partner) in order to access another (the right to be recognised in the acquired gendered as afforded by the GRA).

6.65   Following the legal recognition, the former spouses or civil partners are then able to contract a civil partnership or marriage as their circumstances would allow for their respective legal genders, which reflects their acquired gender.

---

[79]   PD 7D – The Gender Recognition Act 2004, para 1.1.
[80]   CPA 2004, s 50(1)(d).
[81]   GRA 2004, Sch 2(3). Note that in Scotland, on account of differences in marriage law, the grant of an interim certificate will provide a ground for divorce, rather than make the marriage voidable.
[82]   Refer to guidance for CP and married couples overseas applications at http://www.justice.gov.uk/guidance/courts-and-tribunals/tribunals/gender-recognition-panel/overseas-application-process.htm.
[83]   GRA 2004, s 5(1).

6.66 If the marriage is dissolved or annulled on some other ground than issue of an IGRC, in proceedings started within six months of the grant of an interim gender recognition certificate, or if the spouse of the person to whom an interim certificate has been issued dies within this period, a full gender recognition certificate is not automatic on annulment but the person with the interim certificate may apply again to the panel within six months of the date on which the marriage comes to an end and the panel must issue a full certificate if satisfied that the applicant is no longer married.[84]

6.67 Once a full gender recognition certificate is issued to an applicant, the person's gender becomes for all purposes the acquired gender, so that an applicant who was born a male would, in law, become a woman for all purposes.[85] She would be considered to be female for the purposes of s 11(c) of the Matrimonial Causes Act 1973, and so able to contract a valid marriage only with a man. She may also enter into a civil partnership only with a woman.[86] This is because under the laws of the UK, a marriage may only be contracted by two people of opposite genders and a civil partnership may only be registered between two people of the same sex.[87] A leading case on the ability of transsexuals to marry was *Corbett v Corbett*[88] where the respondent was born biologically a male. Experiencing psychological difficulties as a male, he underwent a sex change operation and, being now known as April Ashley, 'she' went through a marriage with the petitioner, a male. His case was brought under the premise that, as Ashley was born male (and should therefore be treated as male in perpetuity despite her change of sex) the marriage was illegal. At the time, medical opinion on transsexuality was divided and no consensus on whether Ashley should be legally seen as male or female could be reached.

Ormrod J held that the sex of a party to a marriage was a matter to be determined in accordance with biological and not psychological criteria. Ormrod J suggested that sex is determined by biology whereas gender, and the perception of oneself, is determined by psychology and as he points out: 'Marriage is a relationship which depends on sex and not on gender'. On that basis the marriage between the petitioner and April Ashley was void.

6.68 Section 12(h) of the Matrimonial Causes Act 1973 is also amended so that if at the time of a marriage one party to the marriage did not know that the other was previously of another gender, the former may seek to annul the marriage.[89] Equivalent provisions are made for Northern Ireland in paras 9–11[90] unlike in Scotland where they do not have the same concept of voidable marriage. Similarly, the Civil Partnership Act 2004, ss 50(1)(e) and 51

---

[84] GRA 2004, s 5(2).
[85] GRA 2004, s 9(1).
[86] CPA 2004.
[87] Refer also to chapter 8 on civil partnership.
[88] [1971] P 83.
[89] GRA 2004, Sch 4, paras 4–6.
[90] GRA 2004, Sch 4.

provide that a civil partnership is voidable where the respondent (to an application for nullity) had an acquired gender at the time of registration provided proceedings are instituted within 3 years, and provided the applicant had not led the respondent to believe he would not do so.

6.69 This is in effect a second ground of nullity which exists where the other party to a civil partnership was at the time of the civil partnership a person whose gender had become the acquired gender[91] (that is someone to whom a full certificate has been issued) and that fact was unknown to the other party to the civil partnership at the time of the civil partnership.

6.70 If a person marries and is not aware at the time of the marriage that their partner was of the opposite gender at birth, as was the case in *ST (Formerly J) v J*[92] and later reported as *J v C (Void Marriage: Status of Children)*,[93] they are able to seek an annulment of the marriage. The reason behind this provision is that it is expected that this is the type of personal discussion that would take place prior to marriage. In *J v C (Void Marriage: Status of Children)*, Mr J and Mrs C went through a ceremony of marriage on 17 July 1977. At that point, Mrs C was a spinster aged 20. Mr J was 30, and suffering from gender dysmorphia. Although living as a man since approximately the age of 17, he had been registered on the day after his birth as a female, and, at the date of the ceremony of marriage was, both in fact and in law a woman. This was something he knew, and which he concealed both from Mrs. C and from the priest who conducted the ceremony.

Thereafter Mr J and Mrs C lived together for many years as though husband and wife. Mrs C remained in ignorance of the fact that Mr J was a woman. Their children, C and E, were conceived by means of AID in 1986 and 1991 respectively. Although what Mr J said to the clinic which provided the treatment has never been the subject of judicial investigation, it is plain that he did not disclose the fact that he was a woman to anybody involved in the process.

The relationship between Mr J and Mrs C broke down in 1994 and Mrs C filed a petition for divorce on 22 April of that year. During the divorce proceedings she saw a copy of Mr J's birth certificate and realised (for the first time) that Mr J was a woman.

On 26 May 1994 the divorce petition was dismissed, and proceedings taken for nullity of marriage. On 19 August 1994, a decree nisi of nullity was pronounced in undefended proceedings in the county court, and was 'pronounced and declared to have been by law void because at the date of the said ceremony the parties were not respectively male and female'. That decree nisi was made absolute on 10 October 1994. In fact the court took the view that by purporting to marry Mrs C, Mr J had committed perjury.

---

[91]   CPA 2004, s 50(1)(e).
[92]   [1998] 1 All ER 431.
[93]   *J v C (Void Marriage: Status of Children)* [2006] EWCA Civ 551.

Lord Justice Richards at para 45 observed that:

> '"the parties to that marriage" within FLRA 1987 section 27(1) include, by section 27(2), parties to a void marriage; the grounds on which a marriage celebrated after 31 July 1971 shall be void are set out in MCA 1973 section 11 and include, by section 11(c), "that the parties are not respectively male and female", so that section 27 extends on the face of it to a marriage celebrated between a woman and another woman. I am satisfied, however, that that cannot be the correct construction. If one stands back and looks at the statute in its context and against the background of the Warnock report to which Wall LJ has referred (and passages from which were cited to us, in particular from the section at paras 4.17-4.28), I think it plain that the legislative intention must have been for the provisions to apply only to a marriage in the sense of a union between a woman and a man, and that "marriage" in section 27 must be read accordingly.'

Originally the case of *ST (Formerly J) v J* concerned an application for financial relief following the annulment of a marriage and non-disclosure of gender prior to marriage. The Court of Appeal judgment[94] indicated that, the court was entitled, in exercising its discretion in accordance with s 25 of the Matrimonial Causes Act 1973, to take account of the fact that the applicant had practised a grave deception on the other party at the time of the marriage and ought as a matter of public policy to be refused relief. The court also noted that the effect of non-disclosure on a genetic wife, ST, who had stated that she 'was not into women,' had been 'catastrophic and that she [had] been traumatised by the experience'.[95]

Lord Justice Neill said there was sufficient evidence to justify the judge's conclusion that the defendant knowingly made a false declaration when getting married that there was no hindrance to the marriage, and had therefore committed the offence of perjury.

The court's power to grant ancillary relief on the grant of a decree of divorce or nullity, under ss 22–24 of the Matrimonial Causes Act 1973, was discretionary. In exercising it, the court was required by section 25(2)(g) to have regard to 'the conduct of each of the parties, if that conduct is such that it would in the opinion of the court be inequitable to disregard it'.

In this case the judge decided that the defendant was barred in limine from pursuing his application. He took into account that the defendant had committed a serious crime against the plaintiffs, and applied the principal of public policy explained in *Whiston v Whiston*[96] (in which it was held that since bigamy undermined the fundamental notions of marriage, a bigamist should be barred from claiming ancillary relief).

This court was bound by the decision in *Whiston*, but it was not necessary to treat it as laying down an inflexible rule that, even where the court was

---

[94] By Lord Justice Neill, Lord Justice Ward, Lord Justice Potter.
[95] [1998] 1 All ER 431, 439 and 456.
[96] [1995] 2 FLR 268.

exercising a discretionary jurisdiction to grant ancillary relief, the fact that the marriage was contracted in circumstances involving the commission of a serious crime debarred the guilty party in limine from making a claim.

But it was legitimate to take account of principles of public policy as a guide to the exercise of the court's discretion under the 1973 Act. The fact that the applicant had been guilty of a serious crime and had practised grave deception on the other party to the marriage were clearly relevant circumstances, which in this case fully justified refusing relief.

Accordingly the Court of Appeal dismissed an appeal by the defendant, against a preliminary ruling of Mr Justice Hollis on 25 January 1996 that the defendant be debarred from pursuing a claim for ancillary relief against the plaintiff, following the annulment of their marriage.

6.71 The case of *Bellinger v Bellinger*[97] more specifically, questioned whether the petitioner, Mrs Elizabeth Bellinger, had validly been married to Mr Michael Bellinger. On 2 May 1981 Mr and Mrs Bellinger went through a ceremony of marriage to each other. Section 1(c) of the Nullity of Marriage Act 1971, re-enacted in section 11(c) of the Matrimonial Causes Act 1973, provides that a marriage is void unless the parties are 'respectively male and female'. The question is whether, at the time of the marriage, Mrs Bellinger was 'female' within the meaning of that expression in the statute. In these proceedings she sought a declaration that the marriage was valid at its inception and was subsisting. The trial judge, Johnson J, refused to make this declaration;[98] so did the Court of Appeal, by a majority of two to one.[99]

In an alternative claim, advanced for the first time before the House of Lords, Mrs Bellinger sought a declaration that s 11(c) of the Matrimonial Causes Act 1973 was incompatible with Arts 8 and 12 of the European Convention on Human Rights. The Lord Chancellor intervened in the proceedings as the minister with policy responsibility for that statutory provision.

For as long as she could remember, Mrs Bellinger felt more inclined to be female although correctly classified and registered as male at birth. She had an increasing urge to live as a woman rather than as a man. Despite her inclinations, and under some pressure, in 1967 she married a woman. She was then twenty one. The marriage broke down. They separated in 1971 and were divorced in 1975.

Since then Mrs Bellinger dressed and lived as a woman and underwent treatment. Unlike in the case of *J v C (Void Marriage: Status of Children)* when she married Mr Bellinger he was fully aware of her background. He had throughout been entirely supportive of her. She was described on her marriage

---

[97] [2003] UKHL 21, [2003] 2 All ER 593.
[98] See [2001] 1 FLR 389.
[99] See [2001] EWCA Civ 1140, [2002] 2 WLR 411; the majority comprised Dame Elizabeth Butler-Sloss P and Robert Walker LJ. Thorpe LJ dissented.

certificate as a spinster. Apart from that, the registrar did not ask about her gender status, nor did Mrs Bellinger volunteer any information. Since their marriage Mr and Mrs Bellinger have lived happily together as husband and wife, and had presented themselves in this way to the outside world.

Lord Nicholls states at para 46-49:

> 'even in the context of marriage, the present question raises wider issues. Marriage is an institution, or relationship, deeply embedded in the religious and social culture of this country. It is deeply embedded as a relationship between two persons of the opposite sex. There was a time when the reproductive functions of male and female were regarded as the primary raison d'être of marriage. The Church of England Book of Common Prayer of 1662 declared that the first cause for which matrimony was ordained was the "procreation of children". For centuries this was proclaimed at innumerable marriage services. For a long time now the emphasis has been different. Variously expressed, there is much more emphasis now on the "mutual society", help and comfort that the one ought to have of the other.

> Against this background there are those who urge that the special relationship of marriage should not now be confined to persons of the opposite sex. It should be possible for persons of the same sex to marry. This, it is said, is the appropriate way to resolve problems such as those confronting Mrs Bellinger.

> It hardly needs saying that this approach would involve a fundamental change in the traditional concept of marriage. Here again, this raises a question which ought to be considered as part of an overall review of the most appropriate way to deal with the difficulties confronting transsexual people.

> For these reasons I would not make a declaration that the marriage celebrated between Mr and Mrs Bellinger in 1981 was valid. A change in the law as sought by Mrs Bellinger must be a matter for deliberation and decision by Parliament when the forthcoming Bill is introduced.'

Mrs Bellinger claimed in the alternative for a declaration that in so far as s 11(c) of the Matrimonial Causes Act 1973 makes no provision for the recognition of gender reassignment it is incompatible with Arts 8 and 12 of the Convention. Mrs Bellinger's claim was advanced on the footing that, although she and Mr Bellinger celebrated their marriage long before the Human Rights Act 1998 came into force, and although the *Goodwin* decision dealt with the human rights position as at the date of the judgment (July 2002), the non-recognition of their ability to marry continues to have adverse practical effects. The statute continues to prevent them marrying each other.

Following the decision in *Goodwin v United Kingdom*,[100] in which the European Court held unanimously that the United Kingdom was in breach of Arts 8 and

---

[100]   (2002) 35 EHRR 18.

12. The House of Lords held that in the present case s 11(c) of the Matrimonial Causes Act 1973 remains a continuing obstacle to Mr and Mrs Bellinger marrying each other.

6.72 There is a school of thought that is of the view that transgendered people who have been issued with a GRC and wish to enter into a marriage or civil partnership should not have to disclose their past gender history to the intended spouse or civil partner. Professor Alex Sharp[101] has recently argued in an article[102] that the provisions referred to at **6.68** above which impose a specific legal obligation on transgender people who intend to marry or enter into a civil partnership are discriminatory and encroach on the right to privacy, breaching Arts 14 and 8 of the European Convention on Human Rights.

Professor Sharp contends that the enactment of the gender history ground for nullity matters because it impacts negatively on transgender people in a number of ways:

'First, implicit in the creation of the gender history ground is the legal and broader cultural assumption that non-disclosure of gender history to a prospective marriage partner constitutes some form of harm.

Second, the gender history ground singles out gender as the slice of subjectivity in relation to which disclosure of historical "facts" must be made. It is not entirely clear why gender is singled out. There are no corresponding legal obligations in the MCA pertaining to, for example, race, disability or sexuality. Moreover, and significantly, the gender history ground does not apply to all persons intending to marry. Rather, it is confined to transgender people as a specific class. That is to say, it is only transgender people who are required to disclose their gender history. In this respect, the gender history ground appears to be discriminatory and therefore in conflict with Article 14 of the European Convention on Human Rights.

Third, the requirement to disclose gender history constitutes a significant and illegitimate invasion of privacy and therefore of personal autonomy. In this respect, it conflicts with Article 8 of the European Convention on Human Rights, which guarantees the right to respect for private and family life.

Fourth, ... that non-disclosure of gender history is in some way unethical or fraudulent. In this respect, ... law constructs "truth" around the facts it demands be disclosed. Non-compliance with the gender history provision may also lead to a finding of inequitable conduct barring ancillary relief under the MCA, s 25(2)(g).'

Professor Sharp argues that the provision represents transgender people as sexually harmful, gender ambiguous and deceptive. Sexually harmful: because inadvertent sexual contact with a transgender person is scripted as harmful. Gender ambiguous: because the gender history ground implies some 'truth'

---

[101] Professor of Law at Keele Univeristy, Director of the Gender, Sexuality & Law LLM Programme.

[102] Transgender Marriage and the Legal Obligation to Disclose Gender History by Professor Alex Sharpe (2012) MLR 33–53.

about (trans)gender that is inconsistent both with the fact of legal recognition and the prior gender experiences of many transgender people. Deceptive: because this is precisely what non-disclosure is presumed to be.

At p 43 of the article she states that:

> 'there is no such requirement in relation to, for example, race, physical disability or sexuality. Thus a person is not, prior to marriage, required to disclose the fact that s/he used to identify as lesbian, gay or bisexual and/or that s/he has engaged in same gender sexual relations. Equally, in the context of a civil partnership ceremony, a person is not required to disclose the fact that s/he used to identify as heterosexual or bisexual or that s/he has engaged in opposite gender sexual relations.'

Professor Sharp explains that the main legal difficulty here is not that gender, as distinct from sexuality, race or disability, exhausts legal desire for historical knowledge. Rather, it is the fact that while gender is singled out it is not gender at large with which law is concerned. Rather, the legal obligation to disclose gender history applies only to transgender persons legally capable of marrying or entering into a civil partnership. She gives several examples, for instance non-transgender women and men choosing to marry are not generally required to disclose personal facts that relate to their gender pasts. Thus, for example, non-transgender women and men are not required to disclose the fact that in childhood they were considered tomboys or sissies and perhaps enjoyed these gender roles. Rather, it is a particular kind of gender experience with which law is concerned.

She concludes at pp 52–53 of the article that:

> 'By virtue of the MCA, as amended by the GRA, transgender people living in the UK are, prior to going through a marriage ceremony, expected to disclose information about their gender pasts. Failure to do so enables the other party to exit the marriage in an accelerated fashion. She argues that the legislative provision is objectionable in a number of respects. First, it is discriminatory, and therefore contrary to Article 14 of the European Convention on Human Rights, in that it targets transgender people as a class in a way that encroaches upon their Article 8 and 12 rights. There is no corresponding legal obligation placed on non-transgender people to disclose information about gender history. Second, it represents an encroachment upon the right to privacy guaranteed by Article 8 of the Convention, one that is not easily justified within the ambit of Article 8(2). Third, the logic of a contrary finding would involve a conclusion that sexual contact with transgender people is potentially harmful. This is a view that should not be given any legal oxygen in normative terms. It is a view that runs contrary to the spirit of transgender law reform and indeed the GRA itself. Further, the assumption of harm is premised on the claim that gender history is a material fact. This claim has been rejected. However, if gender history were to be considered a material fact, either in some general normative sense or from the perspective of the other marriage party, this should not serve to vitiate consent because a right to

know in these circumstances ought to be trumped by considerations of justice, legal consistency and a public policy concern to limit transphobia.'[103]

It is clear from case law and subsequent legislation that there is in effect a requirement on transgender people to disclose their 'gender history' to the other party to a marriage or civil partnership prior to the marriage or civil partnership ceremony. Failure to do so would enable the other party to exit the relationship through nullity proceedings.

Restrictions on marriage or civil partnership for married and civil partnered couples when one of them transitions or acquires a new gender

6.73 The Marriage Act 1949[104] has been amended to provide an additional exception to the obligation on clergy in the Church of England and the Church in Wales to solemnise marriages.[105] A clergyman will not be obliged to marry a person he reasonably believes to have changed gender under the Act.[106] No such provision is needed for Northern Ireland or Scotland as there is no obligation to solemnise marriages on the clergy of churches in those jurisdictions.

6.74 As explained in detail in chapter 8, the right to marry is subject to national laws regulating marriage, and in the UK at present the right to marry is restricted to persons of opposite gender[107] and a civil partnership is restricted to people of the same gender.

As a result the GRA does not allow a full Gender Recognition Certificate to be issued where there is still a pre-existing marriage. The marriage has to be annulled first. The GRA as an alternative permits the issue of an Interim Gender Recognition Certificate. The Interim Certificate creates a rapid means for the applicant's marriage or civil partnership to be annulled, whereupon full legal recognition follows. If a full GRC is obtained whilst an applicant is still married or in a civil partnership, this will invalidate the marriage or civil partnership and any rights or benefits arising in the acquired gender. Same sex marriage is only possible in six member states of the Council of Europe.[108]

---

[103] Transgender Marriage and the Legal Obligation to Disclose Gender History by Professor Alex Sharpe (2012) MLR 33–53.

[104] There are, for example, restrictions on marriage between a woman and her ex-husband's father. The adjustments made here will mean that where one party to the marriage is regarded as being of the acquired gender, the restrictions cover relationships flowing from any previous marriage in the birth gender, i.e. a woman who is a male-to-female transsexual person may not marry her ex-wife's father.

[105] GRA 2004, Sch 4, paras 1, 2.

[106] GRA 2004, Sch 4, para 3.

[107] Section 11(c) Matrimonial Causes Act 1973.

[108] Belgium, Netherlands, Spain, Norway, Sweden and Portugal.

The case of *Corbett*[109] remains authoritative as far as restriction on marriage to persons of opposite gender is concerned. That case is supported by other decisions of the European Court of Human Rights discussed earlier in the chapter. The first of these was *Rees v United Kingdom*[110] which ruled that the failure of English law to recognise the right of transsexuals to marry did not constitute a violation of the right to marry guaranteed by Art 12 of the European Convention on Human Rights. This was again confirmed in *Cossey v United Kingdom*[111] although such a claim has been successful in the context of French law (see *B v France*).[112] These principles were further applied in *Sheffield and Horsham v UK*.[113] In all of the UK cases, however, the court stressed the need for member states to keep their law under review, suggesting a general relaxation in attitudes towards transsexuals. In light of this review there were a number of cases looking at the status of *Corbett*. See *W v W* [2001] 1 FLR 324 and *Bellinger v Bellinger* [2001] 2 FLR 1048. Although in *Bellinger* the House of Lords followed the position in *Corbett* they did declare, under s.4 HRA 1998, that s 11(c) MCA was incompatible with Arts 8 and 12 of the European Convention on Human Rights, in accordance with s 4 of the Human Rights Act 1998. They felt it was up to Parliament to change the law.

6.75 An apparent lacuna in law exists in a situation where a transsexual person has remained in a marriage or civil partnership contracted with someone prior to their gender transition and legal recognition. This has led to some transsexual people deciding not to use the Gender Recognition process, as they argue their marriage vows were for life and they object to the idea that their partner (by remaining with them and true to those vows) would be unfairly treated by dissolving their original vows.

6.76 Therefore the prerequisite to annul an existing marriage or civil partnership before a grant of a full gender recognition certificate is one of the factors that may prevent some people applying for a GRC. A civil partnership is not viewed as fully equal with marriage by some in that same sex couples cannot legally be married in a religious ceremony. Some trans people have therefore been reluctant to apply for a GRC because they do not feel morally able to divorce their partners, or annul their marriage and register for a civil partnership. Further, divorce/annulment is the breaking of a relationship and legal contract which neither partner may wish to break. The couple may not themselves identify as a same sex couple in sexual orientation terms, since their relationship was founded on the basis of the trans person's previous gender.[114] Furthermore, changing a marriage to a civil partnership is not straightforward

---

[109] *Corbett v Corbett* [1971] P 83.
[110] *Rees v United Kingdom* (1987) 9 EHRR 56.
[111] *Cossey v United Kingdom* (1991) 13 EHRR 622.
[112] *B v France* (1992) 16 EHRR 1.
[113] *Sheffield and Horsham v UK (1991) 27 EHRR 163.*
[114] Equality and Human Rights Commission, Trans Research Review by Martin Mitchell and Charlie Howarth (2009).

and it will impact on matters such as state benefits, property ownership, pensions and inheritance[115] (as discussed in chapter 8 on civil partnership).

6.77 The requirement for persons who seek to have a full GRC to be single at the time has been a contentious issue for many years and it remains so to date. As a result test cases have been taken to the European Court of Human Rights to object to the requirement that a couple end their marriage in order for one of the partners to be recognised in their acquired gender and be granted a GRC. However, the European Court has found in the United Kingdom government's favour and held that it is within its rights ('margin of appreciation') to not provide for same sex marriage and noted instead that there is a civil partnership arrangement available for such couples. An example of some of those cases are *Wena and Anita Parry v the United Kingdom*[116] and *R and F v the United Kingdom,*[117] where the applicants were respectively married and had children. In each case, one of them underwent gender reassignment surgery and remained with his/her spouse as a married couple. Following the introduction of the Gender Recognition Act 2004, the applicants who had undergone gender reassignment surgery made an application for the issue of a Gender Recognition Certificate, which could not be obtained unless they terminated their marriage. The applicants complained in particular under Arts 8 (right for respect to private and family life) and 12 (right to marry) that they had been unable to obtain legal recognition of their acquired gender without terminating their marriage.

6.78 Their applications were declared inadmissible (rejected as manifestly ill-founded). The applicants were requested to annul their marriage because same sex marriages were not permitted under English law. The United Kingdom had not failed to give legal recognition to gender re-assignment and the applicants could continue their relationship through a civil partnership which carried almost all the same legal rights and obligations. The court observed that, when the new system was introduced following the Christine Goodwin judgment, the legislature was aware of the fact that there were a small number of transsexuals in subsisting marriages but deliberately made no provision for those marriages to continue in the event that one partner made use of the gender recognition procedure. The court found that it could not be required to make allowances for that small number of marriages.[118]

6.79 The decision effectively leaves married couples in a forced divorce situation which is usually against the explicit will of the married couple, who may wish to remain a legally recognised family unit, especially if they have children in their care. Indeed, forced divorce may have a negative impact on the children in the marriage. In several countries the parent who has undergone the gender change will lose custody rights of the children. In other states ambiguous legislation is in place and hardly any attention is given to the best

---

[115] Refer to section on state benefits and pensions.
[116] Application No 42971/05 (November 2006).
[117] Application No 35748/05 (November 2006).
[118] European Court of Human Rights Press Unit Factsheet – Transsexual Rights (June 2011).

interests of the child. This can lead to hardship as in the case where both spouses wished to remain married so that the non-transsexual male partner would not lose custody of the child and could continue to receive state benefits in addition to his part-time work, in order to support his disabled, and now transsexual, spouse in providing care for the joint child.[119]

6.80 It follows that with a couple, where one partner to a marriage or civil partner is living in their acquired gender and chooses to remain in that legal relationship, without obtaining a full GRC, then the person in the acquired gender will remain legally identified according to their original birth certificate and their legal status remains unchanged and therefore their children, state benefits, property ownership, pensions and inheritance will be unaffected.

6.81 However, some couples, where one partner to a marriage or civil partnership is living in their acquired gender, choose to annul their marriage or civil partnership because of the need to have legal recognition of their acquired gender. This is so that the person who is living in their acquired gender may obtain a GRC which will lead to the re-issue of a new birth certificate, passport, diving licence etc. In those circumstances, the couple could then enter into a civil partnership if their acquired gender is the same as that of their partner,[120] or marriage if they are of opposite gender.

6.82 In the recent case of *Timbrell v Secretary of State for Work and Pensions*,[121] Ms Christine Timbrell was born a male on 17 July 1941. From her teenage years she felt that she should have been a girl. In her twenties she met Joy and they were married and had two children. Ms Timbrell became an accountant. In the late 1990s Ms Timbrell took advice from a consultant psychiatrist and she was treated for gender dysphoria. Then in October 2000, with the full knowledge and consent of Joy, Ms Timbrell underwent gender reassignment surgery. Joy and Ms Timbrell decided to continue to live together as a married couple. They remain so.

6.83 On 17 July 2001 Ms Timbrell reached her 60th birthday. Just over a year later, on 6 August 2002, Ms Timbrell applied to the Inland Revenue National Insurance Contributions Office to receive her state pension, which she asked to be back-dated to her 60th birthday.

6.84 The Secretary of State rejected her claim, stating that she was not entitled to her pension until she reached the age of 65, the age of entitlement for men. In particular, the Secretary of State purported to rely on the Gender Recognition Act 2004 which requires transsexuals to divorce before the Government will recognise their acquired gender. Ms Timbrell and her wife, who have been married for more than 40 years, did not wish to divorce.

---

[119] Human Rights and Gender Identity, Issue Paper by Thomas Hammarberg, Council of Europe Commissioner for Human Rights.
[120] GRA 2004, s 9 in conjunction with the CPA 2004 which came into force law in December 2005.
[121] *Timbrell v Secretary of State for Work and Pensions* [2010] EWCA Civ 701.

6.85 On 22 June 2010, the Court of Appeal unanimously held that the Secretary of State was wrong to treat Christine Timbrell, a male to female transsexual, as a man for state pension purposes. Aikens LJ, with whom the other members of the court agreed, held that EU law discrimination law conferred a directly effective right on Ms Timbrell to be treated as a woman and consequently to receive her pension from the age of 60. The Gender Recognition Act had not been in force at the time that Ms Timbrell had made her claim and the Secretary of State could not rely on its provisions either directly or indirectly. The court consequently allowed Ms Timbrell's appeal against the decision of the Upper Tribunal which had upheld the Secretary of State's decision.

6.86 The ruling has been described by some as creating confusion[122] because it suggests that a transgender woman need not have to divorce to have her gender legally reassigned, as required by the GRA. It is unlikely that this ruling will be treated as causing confusion because a distinguishing feature in this case is the fact that the decision to refuse to treat Ms Timbrell as a woman was made before the GRA was enacted and was made in line with the judgment of *Sarah Margaret Richards v Secretary of State for Work and Pensions*.[123] In *Richards,* the applicant, a post-operative transsexual woman, had argued that the provision of the United Kingdom Gender Recognition Act 2004 establishing in certain cases a pensionable age based on the gender of birth (in her case 65 years like men, instead of 60 years for women) constituted a violation of Directive 79/7/EC implementing the principle of equal treatment between men and women in social security. In this case the court also ruled that domestic legislation establishing unfavourable retirement conditions for individuals on the basis of their gender reassignment, breached the principle of equal treatment in the field of social security.

PARENTHOOD

6.87 The issue of parenthood in a transgender context was discussed in the case of *X, Y & Z v UK*[124] which was decided before the GRA 2004. In that case the UK government followed the traditional view that a legal father must have been registered male at birth and that parenthood is gender-specific as there can only be one father and mother and not two of the same sex. In this case the European Court held that a refusal to allow a child born to a transsexual 'man's' partner to have the 'father's' name was a breach of Art 8, but that there was no breach in English law in denying 'him' parental rights (parental responsibility).

Section 12 of the GRA provides that though a person is regarded as being of the acquired gender, the person will retain their original status as either father

---

[122] Janet Scott representing transgender support group the Beaumont Society – Uncertainty After Court of Appeal Ruling on Transgender Pension Rights, LNB News 05/07/2010 44.

[123] Case C-423/04 (2006).

[124] *X, Y & Z v UK* [1997] 2 FLR 892.

or mother of a child. Therefore the fact that a GRC has been issued will not change a parent's parental responsibility[125] in respect of their child and the transgender person's status in relation to any children remains unchanged. The continuity of parental rights and responsibilities is thus ensured. Therefore if you are the birth mother and are now legally a man under the GRA, as above, you retain parental responsibility. If you then enter a civil partnership with your ex-husband, both of you retain parental responsibility in respect of your child. If you enter into a civil partnership with a man who is not the child's parent, or you marry a woman, either of these partners may obtain parental responsibility as a step-parent without extinguishing[126] your parental responsibility, in accordance with the mechanisms outlined in chapter 1.

(a) If you are the transgender partner who is the legal father of the child having acquired a new gender as a woman under the GRA, you remain the child's father and it is the same for mothers under s 12 of the GRA.

(b) If as the child's father you have annulled your marriage to the child's mother, you retain parental responsibility, whether you enter into a civil partnership with your ex-wife or with another woman, or you marry a man. The same scenario would apply if the situation were reversed.

(c) If you are a step-parent and have gained parental responsibility under s 4A of the Children Act 1989 and your marriage or civil partnership is annulled you retain parental responsibility unless the court rules otherwise.

(d) If you are a transgender partner who is the legal mother of the child, and you have parental responsibility, you will retain this even if your ex-husband has a new partner who obtains parental responsibility.

Contact with children following a breakdown of relationship in a transgender relationship/context

6.88 Proceedings to end a marriage or a civil partnership and cases involving children, are usually dealt with at the same time in the county court or the magistrates' court (Family Proceedings Court).[127] Although the first principle of the Children Act 1989 (CA 1989) is that 'the child's welfare shall be the court's paramount consideration', meaning that it is usually regarded as in the child's best interests to have a relationship with both parents, historically trans parents have experienced difficulties in maintaining contact with their children following a breakdown of their former relationship, the most common reason being their change of gender identity or acquired gender.

---

[125] CA 1989, s 3.
[126] ACA 2002, s 46(3)(b).
[127] For details about making these applications, see chapter 4 and chapter 8.

6.89 The principle that the child's welfare is paramount has to be balanced against Art 8 of the Human Rights Act 1998 (HRA 1998)[128] the right to respect for private and family life which gives greater rights to parents. Article 8[129] of the Act states:

'1. Everyone has the right to respect for his private and family life, his home and his correspondence.

2. There shall be no interference by a public authority with the exercise of this right except such as is in accordance with the law and is necessary in a democratic society in the interests of national security, public safety or the economic well-being of the country, for the prevention of disorder or crime, for the protection of health or morals, or for the protection of the rights and freedoms of others.'

6.90 The Human Rights Act places a duty on all courts and tribunals in the UK to interpret legislation so far as possible in a way compatible with the rights laid down in the European Convention on Human Rights (ECHR).[130] Therefore the UK legislation has to be interpreted, if at all possible, in such a way that it is compliant with the Convention and if such an interpretation proved impractical, the UK government is under an obligation to change its legislation so that it is compliant with the ECHR.

6.91 Although Art 8 enhances the rights of trans parents, it is a qualified right, not an absolute right; therefore, it would be possible, to derogate from it for instance if it is in accordance with the law and is necessary in a democratic society in the interests of national security, public safety or the economic well-being of the country, for the prevention of disorder or crime, for the protection of health or morals, or for the protection of the rights and freedoms of others. This qualified right has no doubt been used in argument by antagonistic parents, on the ground that it is *necessary for the protection of health or morals* of a child concerned to refuse contact with the natural parent in his or her acquired gender. Whilst this would not be accurate, transgender parents facing acrimonious family breakdown need to be aware that such arguments may be made and be ready to counter them when they arise, by bringing expert opinion to give an informed view and to reassure the court of the effect on a child of having a trans parent. There is a wide range of research which could outline the innate biological nature of the condition, which is also supported by NHS leaflets and studies/research[131] on Transgender Experiences.

6.92 Despite the above however, it is still unfortunately reported that there are some instances where a parent who has undergone the gender change will lose custody rights of the children. An example of this can be found in the case of *J*

---

[128] Enacted on 2nd October 2000.
[129] HRA 1998, Sch 1, Part 1.
[130] HRA 1998, s 3(3)(1).
[131] NHS leaflet Transgender Experience information, Trans, a practical Guide for the NHS.

v C (Void Marriage: Status of Children)[132] discussed earlier. Following a finding that his marriage to Mrs C was void, Mr J applied to have contact with the children C and E. The court dismissed Mr J's application for both direct and indirect contact with C and E. No contact between E and Mr J had taken place since the divorce in 1994. Subsequent applications were made in respect of ancillary relief in the nullity proceedings and were dismissed.

6.93   In April 1996, Mr and Mrs C married. On 25 April 1997, Sir Stephen Brown P dismissed a renewed application by Mr J for contact with the two children. In April 1999, Mr and Mrs C issued adoption proceedings in relation to the children. On 19 April 1999, the President of the Family Division, Dame Elizabeth Butler-Sloss gave directions for the trial of a preliminary issue as to whether Mr J was to be regarded as a parent of either child within the meaning of the Adoption Act 1976. In September 1999, however, Mr and Mrs C withdrew the application.

6.94   On 1 June 2005, Mr J obtained a Gender Recognition Certificate (GRC) under GRA 2004. This shows (1) his gender to be male, and (2) that he is, from 1 June 2005 'of the gender shown'. He has also obtained a fresh birth certificate, giving his sex at birth as male. The relief sought by Mr J in the CA 1989 proceedings was as follows.

6.95   A prohibited steps order that the children should not be informed of:

- their parentage, and

- the reasons for the breakdown in relationships and in particular Mr J's gender save at such times and in a manner advised by Dr E (a consultant psychiatrist) or such other consultant child psychiatrist as may be agreed;

- a specific issue order that Mrs C seek the advice of Dr E; and

- an order that Mrs C swear an affidavit setting out whether she intended to proceed in accordance with a letter dated 6 November 2002 (the letter was from Mr J's solicitors to Mrs C's solicitors setting out Mr J's view of the manner in which both children should be informed of their respective histories).

6.96   At para 39, the court said 'Mr J is not, and never was, E's parent. The fact that he acted as such for a short period of her childhood does not, as a matter of law, enable him to claim the status of parenthood'. The declaration made by the judge was correct in law under the HFEA 1990. The court found that the two children were conceived by donor insemination during the course of the purported marriage which was subsequently declared void. Section 27 of the Family Law Reform Act 1987 applied in this case. In order to be a parent of a child born through artificial insemination by a donor (AID), the mother's

---

[132]   *J v C (Void Marriage: Status of Children)* [2006] EWCA Civ 551.

partner had to be the other party to a marriage with the mother. Where the mother's partner was another woman, there could be no marriage, and the partner could not be the child's parent.

6.97 At paras 41–42 of the judgment LJ Thorpe states:

'Whilst the question of Mr J's status is plainly a matter of importance to him, the real question in the case is how both C and E are to be informed about their respective origins. This is a highly sensitive matter, but it does not seem to me to be one which is ultimately justiciable by way of orders under CA 1989 s 8. What Mrs C says to C and E is, in my judgment, a matter for her, and not for the court to determine. There is a limit to which the court can and should seek to govern parental behaviour.

In my judgment Mrs C has sensibly agreed to take the advice of Dr E before telling either C or E about their respective backgrounds. I do not think the court can, or should, ask her to do any more. Thus, in my judgment, Mr J, by securing Mrs C's undertaking, had achieved all he could reasonably expect to have achieved in the proceedings under CA 1989, and their prosecution could only have served unnecessarily to prolong what has already been an unduly extended court involvement.'

The court took the view that the relevant undertaking by Mrs C to take advice from an expert before informing E and C about Mr J was sufficient.

6.98 In the matter of *Re C (Children)*,[133] the parents had been married for 7 years before separation, and the father's contact with the C ceased following his decision to live as a woman. F started contact proceedings, which were delayed while he underwent gender re-assignment. A report was commissioned from a medical expert, which explained the complex issues arising from the father's gender re-assignment and the professional support and assistance required by the mother's reaction. The expert recommended that NYAS be asked for assistance. The judge determined that the mother did not require the recommended assistance, and instead imposed a 20-month moratorium, allowing the father to send cards only.

The father appealed on the grounds that the judge had erred in dismissing the doctor's recommendations, and that it was in the C's best interests to know of the gender re-assignment sooner rather than later, in case they found out for themselves and suffered irreparable damage.

The Court of Appeal held that the critical issue was identified by the doctor that the C must understand the truth about their father, and the judge was wrong to reject the doctor's recommendations. The order denied the C the crucial assistance they required, and the appeal was allowed.

---

[133] *Re C (Children)* [2007] 1 FLR 1642.

6.99 A recent European Court judgment on a transgendered parent in the process of transitioning was also made in the case of *PV v Spain*.[134] The applicant, PV, is a Spanish national who was born in 1976 and lives in Lugo (Spain). She is a male-to-female transsexual who, prior to her gender reassignment, had a son with PQF in 1998. When they separated in 2002 the judge approved the amicable agreement they had concluded, by which custody of the child was awarded to the mother and parental responsibility to both parents jointly. The agreement also laid down contact arrangements for the applicant, who was to spend every other weekend and half of the school holidays with the child.

In May 2004 PQF applied to have PV deprived of parental responsibility and to have the contact arrangements and any communication between the father and the child suspended, arguing that the father had shown a lack of interest in the child and adding that PV was undergoing hormone treatment with a view to gender reassignment and usually wore make-up and dressed like a woman. PQF's application was dismissed in respect of the first point.

As regards the contact arrangements, the judge decided to restrict them rather than suspend them entirely. Since ordinary contact arrangements could not be made on account of PV's lack of emotional stability, a gradual arrangement was put in place, initially involving a three-hour meeting every other Saturday 'until [PV] undergoes surgery and fully recovers her physical and psychological capacities'. The judge pointed out that PV had begun the gender-reassignment process only a few months earlier and that it entailed far-reaching changes to all aspects of her life and her personality and hence emotional instability, a characteristic noted by the psychologist in her report.

That decision was upheld by the Audiencia Provincial, which reiterated that ordinary contact arrangements could undermine the child's emotional stability. The child would have to come to terms gradually with his father's decision, which he was in the process of doing since they enjoyed a good emotional relationship. As regards the applicant's objection to the psychologist who had drawn up the report, the Audiencia Provincial held that it had not been raised in time.

The contact arrangements were extended in February 2006 to five hours every other Sunday and subsequently, in November 2006, to every other Saturday and every other Sunday, for approximately eight hours each time.

In December 2008 an *amparo* appeal by the applicant was dismissed. The Constitutional Court held that the ground for restricting the contact arrangements had not been PV's transsexualism but her lack of emotional stability, which had entailed a real and significant risk of disturbing her son's emotional well-being and the development of his personality, in view of his age

---

[134] Application No 35159/09 (the judgment is available only in French, reported only on 30.11.2010).

– he had been six years old at the time of the expert report – and the stage of his development at that time. The court held that in reaching that decision, the judicial authorities had taken into account the child's best interests, weighed against those of the parents, and not PV's status as a transsexual.

Complaints and procedure

Relying on Art 8 (right to respect for private and family life) taken in conjunction with Art 14 (prohibition of discrimination), the applicant complained about the restrictions ordered by a judge on the arrangements for contact with her son, on the ground that her lack of emotional stability following her gender reassignment was liable to upset the child, who had been six years old at the time. The application was lodged with the European Court of Human Rights on 18 June 2009.

Decision of the court

The European Court of Human Rights agreed that once they had learned of PV's gender emotional instability, the Spanish courts had adopted contact arrangements that were less favourable to her than those laid down in the separation agreement.

The ECtHR emphasised that, although no issue of sexual orientation arose in the applicant's case, transsexualism was a notion covered by Art 14, which contained a non-exhaustive list of prohibited grounds for discrimination.

While emotional disturbance had not been considered a sufficient reason for restricting contact, the decisive ground for the restriction had been the risk of jeopardising the child's psychological well-being and the development of his personality. In addition, PV's lack of emotional stability had been noted in a psychological expert report which she had had the opportunity to challenge.

Rather than suspending contact entirely, the judge had made a gradual arrangement, whereby he would review the situation on the basis of a report submitted every two months. From a three-hour meeting every two weeks under professional supervision, the contact arrangements were eventually extended to eight hours every other Saturday and every other Sunday. The overriding factor in that decision had been the child's best interests and not the applicant's transsexualism, the aim being that the child would gradually become accustomed to his father's gender reassignment. The court further noted that the contact arrangements had been extended although there had been no change in the applicant's gender status during that period.

The court therefore considered that the restriction of the contact arrangements had not resulted from discrimination on the ground of the applicant's transsexualism and concluded that there had been no violation of Art 8 taken in conjunction with Art 14.

SOCIAL SECURITY BENEFITS, PENSIONS AND TAX ISSUES

6.100 As indicated earlier a full GRC is only issued to an applicant if unmarried and if the applicant is married an interim GRC is issued pending a divorce. Following a divorce it is then expected that the couple enter into a civil partnership which is not straightforward as this would impact on matters such as state benefits, property ownership, pensions and inheritance. The principle is that state pensions and benefits will be paid according to the acquired gender.

6.101 Indeed the impact on pensions was argued in the case of *KB v National Health Service Pensions Agency*.[135] The applicant was a woman living in a long-term relationship with a transsexual man. She worked for 20 years for the NHS and was a member of the NHS Pension Scheme. The NHS Pensions Agency informed the applicant that as she and her partner were not married, she would not be able to receive a widower's pension if she were to predecease her partner. She went to court to try to secure her right to marry him in order that he could inherit her pension if she died. The Court of Appeal referred the case to the European Court of Justice.

6.102 The applicant claimed that the United Kingdom's denial of widower's pension scheme to her partner in case of her death constituted a breach of Art 141 of the EC Treaty that established the principle of equal pay between men and women, as well as Directive 75/117/EEC on the implementation of such a principle in the national law of Member States. She supported her argument by the fact that in the United Kingdom transsexuals were not allowed to marry even following gender reassignment. The European Court of Justice ruled that, although pension schemes constitute a payment under the scope of the above-mentioned principle, Art 141 had been breached because the domestic legislation precluded transsexual individuals from the right to marry,[136] in violation of a judgment of the European Court of Human Rights (ECtHR). Member States had to determine the conditions under which legal recognition was given to the change of gender of a person. It is thus for the national court to determine whether the applicant could rely on Art 141 in order to gain recognition of her right to nominate her partner as the beneficiary of a survivor's pension. *KB* also established that individuals are protected on their gender role, and not only the sex given to them at birth.

6.103 The inclusive interpretation of the European Court of Justice went further in *Sarah Margaret Richards v Secretary of State for Work and Pensions.*[137] Following gender reassignment surgery, Ms Richards applied for a retirement pension at the age of 60, the legal retirement age for women in the

---

[135] Case C-117/01 (2004) or Case C-117/01, *KB v National Health Service Pensions Agency, Secretary of State for Health* [2004].

[136] Article 12 of the European Convention on Human Rights states that: 'Men and women of marriageable age have the right to marry and to found a family, according to the national laws governing the exercise of this right'.

[137] Case C-423/04 (2006).

United Kingdom. The Department for Work and Pension refused the claim
and the case was taken to the European Court of Human Rights.

6.104 Given the refusal by the Secretary of State, she referred the matter to
the Social Security Commissioner, who asked the European Court of Justice to
examine the compatibility with Community law[138] of legislation which refuses
to award a retirement pension to a male-to-female transsexual until the age of
65 when she would have been entitled to such a pension at the age of 60 had she
been held to be a woman. Her appeal to the Social Security Commissioner
claimed that, the refusal to pay her a retirement pension as from the age of 60
was a breach of Art 8 of the European Convention, as well as discrimination
contrary to Art 4 of Directive 79/7.

6.105 Article 4(1) of Directive 79/7 provides:

> 'The principle of equal treatment means that there shall be no discrimination
> whatsoever on ground of sex either directly, or indirectly by reference in particular
> to marital or family status, in particular as concerns:
>
> • the scope of the schemes and the conditions of access thereto,
> • the obligation to contribute and the calculation of contributions,
> • the calculation of benefits including increases due in respect of a spouse and
>   for dependants and the conditions governing the duration and retention of
>   entitlement to benefits.'

6.106 Article 7(1) of Directive 79/7 allows Member States to determine the
pensionable age for the purposes of granting old-age and retirement pensions.

6.107 The Secretary of State for Work and Pensions submitted that 'the claim
by the appellant in the main proceedings did not fall within the scope of
Directive 79/7. According to him, Community law provides only for a measure
of coordination for old-age benefits but does not confer a right to receive such
benefits. Moreover, Ms Richards had not been discriminated against having
regard to those who constitute the correct comparator, namely men who have
not undergone gender reassignment surgery.'

6.108 The case was subsequently referred to the European Court, which
rejected the Secretary of State's argument stating:

> 'Article 4(1) of Council Directive 79/7/EEC of 19 December 1978 on the
> progressive implementation of the principle of equal treatment for men and
> women in matters of social security is to be interpreted as precluding legislation
> which denies a person who, in accordance with the conditions laid down by
> national law, has undergone male-to-female gender reassignment entitlement to a

---

[138] Council Directive 79/7/EEC of 19 December 1978 on the progressive implementation of the
principle of equal treatment for men and women in matters of social security [1979] OJ L6,
pp 24–25.

retirement pension on the ground that she has not reached the age of 65, when she
would have been entitled to such a pension at the age of 60 had she been held to be
a woman as a matter of national law.'

6.109   The court pointed out that it was for the Member States to determine
the conditions under which legal recognition is given to gender reassignment.
But it underlined the fact that Directive 79/7 is the embodiment in the field of
social security of the principle of equal treatment of men and women, which is
one of the fundamental principles of Community law.

6.110   In view of its purpose and the nature of the rights which it seeks to
safeguard, the scope of that Directive applies not only to discrimination based
on the fact that a person is of one or other sex, but also to discrimination
arising from the gender reassignment of the person concerned. The court
accordingly reached the conclusion of discrimination by comparing the
situation of a transsexual who has become a woman with that of women 'who
were always women' (paras 29 and 30 of the judgment), thereby undertaking a
comparison of 'between women'.

6.111   As the unequal treatment at issue was based on Ms Richards' inability
to have the new gender which she acquired following surgery recognised for the
purposes of pensions legislation, this must be regarded as discrimination
prohibited by the Directive.

In this context, the court pointed out that in the absence of harmonisation at
Community level it is for the legislation of each Member State to determine,
first, the conditions governing the right or duty to be insured with a social
security scheme and, second, the conditions for entitlement to benefits.
Nevertheless, the Member States must comply with Community law when
exercising that power. The United Kingdom's argument that no Community
right had been breached by the decision of 12 March 2002 refusing to award
Ms Richards a pension, as entitlement to a retirement pension derived only
from national law, was rejected by the court. The judgment was, in substance, in
line with the observations submitted by the Commission.[139]

PROPOSALS FOR CHANGE

*The current government proposal for same sex marriage and transgender
equality*

6.112   On 17 March 2011 the Equality and Human Rights Commission
Scotland launched a new Report: Equal Access to Marriage – ending the
segregation of same sex couples and transgender people in Scotland[140] calling
for access to equal marriage for same sex couples in Scotland. Scotland
currently has a segregated system of family law. This means that same-sex

[139]   EU – LEX Judgment of the Court (First Chamber) of 27 April 2006.
[140]   Equality and Human Rights Commission (EHRC) Scotland, report: Equal Access to Marriage

couples do not have the legal right to marry and are restricted to civil partnership and at the same time the law excludes heterosexual couples from civil partnership. The position is the same for the rest of the UK, the proposals made in the report apply to England and Wales only.[141]

6.113 In its report the Commission states that current legislation in Scotland discriminates against same sex couples and transgender people and this, the report claims, has significant detrimental impacts:

- same sex couples cannot involve their faith in the process for formalising their relationships;

- transgender people are required to divorce if they wish to gain full gender recognition, as the law does not allow same sex marriage or a mixed-sex civil partnership;

- evidence suggests that civil partnerships are seen as having less value and status than marriage;

- same sex couples do not have the same choices as mixed sex couples.

The report presents a series of recommendations for making equal access to marriage 'a reality' while also taking into consideration possible religious implications.

6.114 Recommendations include:

- in order to uphold religious freedom for all, an opt-out 'conscience clause' is proposed for religious bodies and celebrants not wishing to perform same sex marriages;

- in order to ensure the widest choice, civil partnership should be retained and legislation should be introduced to allow same sex couples to marry;

- following the election in May 2011 an Equal Access to Marriage (Scotland) Bill should be brought before the Scottish Parliament that would allow same sex marriage in Scotland.

6.115 In England and Wales, on 5 December 2011, the Marriages and Civil Partnerships (Approved Premises) (Amendment) Regulations 2011 came into force[142] which allows specific religious premises to apply for approval as a place of registration of civil partnership; along with s 202 of the Equality

---

- Ending the segregation of same sex couples and transgender people in Scotland can be found at http://www.equalityhumanrights.com/uploaded_files/Scotland/Projects_and_Campaigns/pdf_final_2.pdf.
[141] It is hoped that the report will provide a springboard to moving this issue on in Scotland.
[142] SI 2011/2661.

Act 2010,[143] which came into force pursuant to the Equality Act 2010 (Commencement No 8) Order 2011, SI 2011/2646. In particular:

- Section 202(2), which removes from the Civil Partnership Act 2004 (CPA 2004) the prohibition preventing civil partnerships from being registered on religious premises.

- The remainder of s 202(4) inserts a new provision into the CPA 2004 to make it explicit that nothing in the CPA 2004 obliges religious organisations to host civil partnerships if they do not want to do so.

6.116 On 17 September 2011, Lynne Featherstone MP, Minister for Equalities, announced that the government intends to consult on opening up civil marriage to same sex couples and civil partnership to mixed-sex couples. A public consultation began in March 2012 with a view to changing the law ahead of the next general election scheduled for May 2015.

6.117 The government has also recently published 'Advancing transgender equality: a plan of Action'.[144] The document lays out the government's vision and the focus for the government's commitment to deliver greater equality for transgender people. In the Ministerial foreword, the government's position is expressed by Rt Hon Theresa May MP, Home Secretary and Minister for Women and Equalities and Lynne Featherstone MP, Minister for Equalities, as follows:

> 'We do not underestimate the challenges transgender people face and the actions in this document are just the first steps towards achieving this vision. It will take all of us working together to make this the era where we consign transphobia to the past, and build a strong, modern and fair Britain for all.'

Amongst the many commitments referred to in the publication, from October 2011 until June 2012, the Government Equalities Office (GEO) will work with the transgender community to ensure that everyone with an interest has the opportunity contribute to government's work on equal civil marriage and that their needs are considered as part of this work.

---

[143] The Government published a consultation document on 31 March 2011, seeking views on the practical arrangements necessary to implement this change. The consultation ran until 23 June 2011.

[144] December 2011.

Chapter 7

PERSONAL PROTECTION

7.1 The term 'domestic violence' includes 'physical violence, threatening or intimidating behaviour and any other form of abuse that directly or indirectly might give rise to the risk of harm'.[1] Harm to a child means 'ill treatment or the impairment of health or development including, for example, impairment suffered from seeing or hearing the ill-treatment of another'.[2] The witnessing by a child of domestic violence, as defined here, is therefore 'harm'.

7.2 This definition of domestic violence was endorsed by the Supreme Court in the *Yemshaw*[3] case, which concerned the question of whether a woman and her children were 'homeless', and therefore not entitled to priority housing. This turned on the issue of whether it was reasonable for the woman and her children to return to the marital home, in circumstances where she was alleging domestic abuse falling short of physical violence. The family were residing in local authority accommodation. The woman reported to housing officers that '[She] is scared that if she confronts him he may hit her. [However her] husband has never actually threatened to hit her.' She went on to complain of his shouting in front of the children, so that she retreated to her bedroom with them, not treating her 'like a human', not giving her any money for housekeeping, being scared that he would take the children away from her and say that she was not able to cope with them, and that he would hit her if she returned home.' The housing officers decided that she was not 'homeless' in that it was reasonable for her to return home, that this behaviour was not domestic violence.

7.3 Lord Brown defined the issue for the court in this way:

> 'Section 177(1) of the [Housing Act 1996] provides:
>
>> "It is not reasonable for a person to continue to occupy accommodation if it is probable that this will lead to domestic violence or other violence against him ..."
>
> The issue identified by the parties for the court's determination on this appeal is:

---

[1]   *Yemshaw v Hounslow London Borough Council* [2011] UKSC 3 [2011] 1 FLR 1614 and *Practice Direction (Residence and Contact Orders: Domestic Violence) (No 2)* [2009] 1 WLR 25.

[2]   CA 1989, s 31(9).

[3]   CA 1989, s 31(9).

"Is the concept of "domestic violence" in section 177(1) of the Act limited to actual physical violence or is it capable of extending to abusive psychological behaviour which could reasonably be described as "violence"?'

7.4 The court considered in particular the difference between 'domestic' violence and other violence and concluded that the term 'domestic' applies if it is from a person who is 'associated with' the victim, a term also used in the Family Law Act 1996, and which includes people not only having a formal relationship, but also who 'have or have had an intimate personal relationship with each other which is or was of significant duration', and people who 'live or have lived in the same household, otherwise than merely by reason of one of them being the other's employee, tenant lodger or boarder',[4] or where two people both have parental responsibility for a child. The Supreme Court allowed the appeal, and referred the case back to the Housing Authority.

7.5 It is clear, therefore, that the legal definitions of behaviour which constitutes domestic violence or abuse, and of the relationships which give rise to it being categorised as 'domestic' in nature, are wide enough to include all forms of physical, sexual or emotional abuse in heterosexual, transgendered or same sex relationships involving cohabitation, shared parental responsibility or an intimate relationship of significant duration.

7.6 A study conducted by the University of Sunderland and the University of Bristol in 2006 'Comparing Domestic Abuse in Same Sex and Heterosexual Relationships'[5] reached the conclusion that domestic abuse is an issue for a considerable number of people in same sex relationships in the UK, particularly in an individual's first same sex relationship. They included in this both abuse taking place during a relationship and post separation, and abuse that is emotional, physical, sexual. They highlighted the often hidden nature of domestic violence, particularly for people in same sex relationships, because of misconceptions about what constitutes domestic abuse, and how and between whom it occurs:

'Domestic abuse is understood in Britain and by our respondents as a problem largely of heterosexual women being physically abused by their male partners. In consequence, most respondents had not understood their experience at the time as domestic abuse and it had not occurred to most of them to report their experiences to any agency.

On top of their own lack of naming of their experience as abuse, most respondents using a heterosexual model of domestic violence in which the (female) survivor is understood as the physically smaller and therefore more vulnerable person against the physically stronger and more powerful (male) perpetrator, did not think that they would be believed, taken seriously or understood if they presented as a survivor.'

7.7 What was also clear from the study is that:

---

4   The full list appears at FLA 1996, s 62 discussed at **7.15** below.
5   Hester, Holmes and McCarry 2006.

'many police, domestic abuse agencies, GPs and LGBT services do not have coordinated responses for responding to domestic abuse in same sex relationships even though some individual practitioners within them may respond sympathetically and be of great support.'

7.8   A similar study carried out in Australia in 2005[6] referred to earlier research which exposed a number of misconceptions about domestic violence and same sex relationships, namely:

(a)   an outbreak of gay male domestic violence is logical (because all or most men are prone to violence), but lesbian domestic violence does not occur (because women are not prone to violence);

(b)   same sex partner violence is not as severe as when a woman is abused by a man;

(c)   because the partners are of the same gender, it is mutual abuse, with each perpetrating and receiving 'equally';

(d)   the perpetrator must be the 'man' or the 'butch' and the victim must be the 'woman' or the 'femme' in emulation of heterosexual relationships.

7.9   Chan observed:

'Misconceptions such as these, also derivative of homophobic assumptions, can contribute to the isolation of abused gay and lesbian people by masking the realities of domestic violence in same sex relationships and placing the safety of the abused person at continued risk. Victims may be reluctant to call the police or seek legal help due to fears that the violence would be dealt with as 'mutual battering' and fear that they may get arrested.'

The Australian study also identified that, perhaps due to these misconceptions, victims of domestic violence in same sex relationships were having difficulty in accessing refuges and other forms of support for victims of domestic violence, a finding which the Bristol study echoed.

7.10 The research suggests that people in same sex relationships or transgendered people may have additional barriers to overcome in protecting themselves from an abusive partner or former partner. Broken Rainbow UK is a registered charity funded by the Home Office who offer advice, support and referral services to LGBT people experiencing homophobic, transphobic and same sex domestic violence.[7] If a person in, or separating from, a same sex relationship seeks out professional advice and support, the legal framework is

---

[6]   *Domestic Violence in Gay and Lesbian Relationships:* Carrie Chan, Senior Researcher, Australian Domestic and Family Violence Clearinghouse.

[7]   See www.broken-rainbow.org.uk.

available and intended to protect them and any relevant children from experiencing further violence in the same way as any heterosexual victim of domestic violence.

7.11 Note that the availability of legal funding for victims of domestic violence is wider than in any other situation. Often solicitors will offer an initial half hour appointment without charge to consider eligibility for public finding of legal fees.

7.12 The key elements of this protective framework in a same sex family law context are considered here.

THE FAMILY LAW ACT 1996

7.13 Part IV of the Family Law Act is entitled 'Family Homes and Domestic Violence'. There are three ways in which the Family Law Act 1996 offers protection from domestic violence:

(1) by regulating occupation and tenancy of the home;

(2) by making non-molestations orders, breach of which is an arrestable offence;

(3) by making forced marriage protection orders for the purposes of preventing a person from any attempt to be forced into a marriage.[8]

These are considered in turn below.

7.14 In the context of same sex relationships the most significant element of the Family Law Act 1996 is its definitions and applicability: no distinction is made at all between men and women, or same sex and opposite sex relationships. Not does the language of the 1996 Act discriminate between traditional and less traditional family circumstances, children of their legal parents and children living with a person under whatever arrangements.

7.15 In particular many of the provisions of Part IV of the Act refer to spouses or civil partners or former civil partners, cohabitants or former cohabitants, associated persons, and relevant children. Section 62 Family Law Act 1996 provides the following definitions:

Cohabitants

(1) For the purposes of this Part –

---

8   There is no equivalent protection to prevent a person from being forced into a civil partnership, but the provisions are included in this chapter in particular because one form of domestic abuse might be a family member seeking to force a person into a marriage because of their sexuality.

(a)   "cohabitants" are two persons who are neither married to each other nor civil partners of each other but are living together as husband and wife or as if they were civil partners; and[9]

(b)   "cohabit" and "former cohabitants" are to be read accordingly, but the latter expression does not include cohabitants who have subsequently married each other or become civil partners of each other.

This definition was specifically amended by the Domestic Violence Crime and Victims Act 2004 to include cohabitants of the same sex.

Relevant children

(2) In this Part, "relevant child", in relation to any proceedings under this Part, means –

(a)   any child who is living with or might reasonably be expected to live with either party to the proceedings;

(b)   any child in relation to whom an order under the Adoption Act 1976, the Adoption and Children Act 2002 or the Children Act 1989 is in question in the proceedings; and

(c)   any other child whose interests the court considers relevant.

This definition clearly does not turn on legal parentage, and is wide enough to encompass all of the children living with or who might be expected to live with either party, irrespective of the precise legal relationship between them.

Associated persons

(3) For the purposes of this Part, a person is associated with another person if –

(a)   they are or have been married to each other;

(aa)   they are or have been civil partners of each other;

(b)   they are cohabitants or former cohabitants;

(c)   they live or have lived in the same household, otherwise than merely by reason of one of them being the other's employee, tenant, lodger or boarder;

(d)   they are relatives;

(e)   they have agreed to marry one another (whether or not that agreement has been terminated);

(eza)   they have entered into a civil partnership agreement (as defined by section 73 of the Civil Partnership Act 2004) (whether or not that agreement has been terminated);

(ea)   they have or have had an intimate personal relationship with each other which is or was of significant duration;

(f)   in relation to any child, they are both persons falling within subsection (4); or

(g)   they are parties to the same family proceedings (other than proceedings under this Part).

(4) A person falls within this subsection in relation to a child if –

---

[9]   See chapter 11 on succession for a discussion on the law relating to living together as spouses or civil partners, and chapter 12 in relation to welfare benefits.

(a)   he is a parent of the child; or

(b)   he has or has had parental responsibility for the child.

(5) If a child has been adopted or falls within subsection (7), two persons are also associated with each other for the purposes of this Part if –

(a)   one is a natural parent of the child or a parent of such a natural parent; and

(b)   the other is the child or any person –

   (i)   who has become a parent of the child by virtue of an adoption order or has applied for an adoption order, or

   (ii)   with whom the child has at any time been placed for adoption.

REGULATION OF THE HOME

7.16   The first part of Part IV is merely declaratory, in that it sets out the rights of spouses and civil partners to occupy a house[10] which has at some point been, or was intended to be, a 'marital home' or 'civil partnership home' of theirs.[11] The rights only exist for so long as the marriage or civil partnership exists unless the court orders otherwise.[12]

7.17   Essentially, s 30 FLA 1996 provides that if one spouse or civil partner is entitled to occupy a property (whether because they own it or are a tenant of it, or have a statutory entitlement to live there), by virtue of the marriage or civil partnership the other spouse or civil partner also has a right not to be evicted or excluded from the dwelling house. If they have been excluded or have never actually lived there, they also have a right to return to it or move into it with the leave of the court.[13] These rights are collectively referred to as 'matrimonial home rights'.

7.18   Matrimonial home rights also operate as a charge on the estate which should be registered with the land charges registry as soon as possible to prevent the other spouse or civil partner disposing of their interest in the land to a third party whether by sale, transfer or mortgage.[14]

7.19   Sections 33–41 of the FLA 1996 then provide for the court to regulate occupation of the dwellinghouse in different circumstances: 'occupation orders'. The court's powers and the factors which the court must take into account vary depending on the nature of the relationship between the occupants, and the nature of the occupation of the dwelling house. There are 5 different categories in which a person can make an application for an occupation order.

---

[10]   Including a boat or caravan: FLA 1996, s 63(1).

[11]   FLA 1996, s 30(5).

[12]   FLA 1996, ss 30(8) and 33(5).

[13]   FLA 1996, s 30(2).

[14]   FLA 1996, s 31.

Categories

7.20 Section 33 applies where:

- the applicant for an order is entitled to occupy the dwelling house, whether because of matrimonial home rights or his/her own interest in the property;

- the respondent to the application is 'associated with' the applicant; and

- the dwelling house is, or has been, or was intended to be the home of the applicant and the person he is 'associated with'.

Ie anyone who has an entitlement to occupy a dwelling house in which they live or intended to live with someone associated with them can apply for an order to restrict or exclude the associated person's occupation of that dwelling house.

7.21 In that situation the applicant can apply for an order to:

(a) enforce the applicant's entitlement to remain in occupation as against the other person ('the respondent');

(b) require the respondent to permit the applicant to enter and remain in the dwelling-house or part of the dwelling-house;

(c) regulate the occupation of the dwelling-house by either or both parties;

(d) if the respondent is entitled as mentioned in subs (1)(a)(i), prohibit, suspend or restrict the exercise by him of his right to occupy the dwelling-house;

(e) if the respondent has home rights in relation to the dwelling-house and the applicant is the other spouse or civil partner, restrict or terminate those rights;

(f) require the respondent to leave the dwelling-house or part of the dwelling-house; or

(g) exclude the respondent from a defined area in which the dwelling-house is included.

An order is mandatory under this section if it appears to the court that a relevant child is likely to suffer significant harm attributable to the conduct of the respondent if the order is not made, unless the child would also suffer equivalent or greater harm if the order is made.[15]

---

[15] FLA 1996, s 33(7). See *B v B (Occupation Order)* [1999] 1 FLR 715 for an example of a case where the father's conduct and the effect of it undoubtedly justified an order, but the harm to

7.22 If a relevant child is not at risk of significant harm there is a balancing exercise to be carried out by the court which must take into account the housing needs and housing resources of the parties, the financial resources of each of the parties, the effect of refusing the application on the health, safety or wellbeing of either party or a relevant child, and the conduct of the parties in relation to each other.[16] The order can be for such period as the court specifies.[17]

7.23 Section 35 operates specifically to protect former spouses or former civil partners who have no independent right to occupy the dwelling house in question, although this does not include circumstances where the applicant is a former spouse or civil partner because the other spouse or civil partner is deceased.[18]

7.24 If one former spouse or former civil partner has a right to occupy a dwelling house which was or was intended to be their marital or civil partnership home, and the other former spouse or former civil partner does not, the former spouse or former civil partner can apply for an order to restrict or exclude the entitled former spouse or former civil partner's occupation of the property.

7.25 This provision differs from s 30 in three key respects:

- the order can only be made for 6 months in the first instance, although it can be extended for 6 months;[19]

- the court must consider additionally the length of time that has elapsed since the parties ceased to live together, and since the marriage or civil partnership was annulled or dissolved;[20] and

- the court must also consider the existence of other relevant pending proceedings between the parties.[21]

7.26 Section 36 operates specifically in relation to cohabitants and former cohabitants with no right to occupy the property, where the respondent is so entitled. The effect of the provision is that if a couple lived together as spouses or civil partners, or intended to do so, in a dwelling house which one of them is entitled to occupy but the other is not, the cohabitant who is not entitled to occupy the property can apply for an order restricting the other cohabitant's occupation of the property. Again, the court can only make an order under this

---

the child he was caring for would have been greater if he were evicted than the harm which would have been caused to the mother and baby if they had to remain in their temporary accommodation.

[16] FLA 1996, s 30(6).
[17] FLA 1996, s 30(10).
[18] FLA 1996, s 35(9).
[19] FLA 1996, s 35(10).
[20] FLA 1996, s 35(6)(f).
[21] FLA 1996, s 35(6)(g).

section for a 6 month period, but it can be extended for one further 6 month period.[22] The key difference in this section from ss 33 and 35 is the balance of harm test. The court is required to have regard to additional factors relating to the nature of the parties' relationship and in particular the level of commitment involved in it, the length of time during which they have cohabited, and whether there are or have been any children of both parties or for who both parties have had parental responsibility.[23] This would not include a child who both parties had brought up as their own in circumstances where one cohabitant was not a legal parent of the child and did not have parental responsibility for the child, although the court is not precluded from taking this into consideration since the court is required to have regard to all of the circumstances, and the list in s 36(6) is not exhaustive. The court is still required to consider whether any 'relevant child' is likely to suffer significant harm attributable to the conduct of the respondent, but is not obliged to make an order under this section even if satisfied as to this fact.[24]

7.27 Section 37 applies where the applicant and respondent are spouses or civil partners or former spouses or civil partners, and neither of them is entitled to occupy the property. This section is rarely used because it is not often that spouses or civil partners live together in a property which neither of them has any legal entitlement to occupy. However, it might arise, for example where the couple are living in a relative's property without a formal tenancy, or are squatting. The balance of harm test is the same as for s 33 applications, but the court may only make an order for 6 months, and may only extend it on one occasion for 6 months.[25]

7.28 Section 38 applies where the applicant and respondent are cohabitants and former cohabitants and neither is entitled to occupy the property. Again, this will occur relatively infrequently. In this scenario the court is still required to consider whether any 'relevant child' is likely to suffer significant harm attributable to the conduct of the respondent, but is not obliged to make an order under this section even if satisfied as to this fact.[26] The court must consider the effect of not making an order on the welfare of any relevant child.[27] The court may only make an order for 6 months, and may only extend it on one occasion for 6 months.[28] A child may not apply for an occupation order, not being a person who is 'entitled' to occupy a property, or a spouse, civil partner, or cohabitant, or formerly so.[29]

---

22 FLA 1996, s 36(10).
23 FLA 1996, s 36(6)(e), (f) and (g).
24 FLA 1996, s 36(8).
25 FLA 1996, ss 37(4) and (5).
26 FLA 1996, s 38(5).
27 FLA 1996, s 38(4).
28 FLA 1996, s 38(6).
29 *Re Alwyn (Non-Molestation Proceedings By A Child)* [2010] 1 FLR 1363.

Making an occupation order

7.29   An order which requires a person to leave their home or intended home, an occupation order, has been repeatedly described by the courts as a 'draconian order'. The bar is set high for applicants for such an order. Notwithstanding the wide definition of domestic violence (as accepted by the Supreme Court in the *Yemshaw*[30] case), the courts are reluctant to exclude a person from the home unless there has been the use or threat of physical violence, and otherwise will often prefer to regulate occupation of the home by restricting the use of the rooms within the home, combined with a non-molestation order to prohibit any form of abusive conduct.

7.30   The key principles are clearly stated in the case of *Chalmers v Johns*[31] as follows:

'The gravity of an order requiring a respondent to vacate a family home, an order overriding proprietary rights, was recognised in cases under the Domestic Violence and Matrimonial Proceedings Act 1976 and a string of authorities in this court emphasise the Draconian nature of such an order, and that it should be restricted to exceptional cases. I do not myself think that the wider statutory provisions contained in the Family Law Act 1996 obliterate that authority. The order remains Draconian, particularly in the perception of the respondent. It remains an order that overrides proprietary rights and it seems to me that it is an order that is only justified in exceptional circumstances. Of course there will be cases where the character of the violence or the risk of violence and the harm to the victim or the risk of harm to the victim is such that the Draconian order must be made, must be made immediately, and must be made at the earliest interlocutory stage. But I simply do not see this case on its facts approaching anywhere near that category. Conventionally the court has given careful consideration to the control of domestic disharmony by the imposition of injunctive orders before resorting to the Draconian order.'

7.31   In *G v G (Occupation Order: Conduct)*[32] the court considered the requirement for the court to make an order where a child is at risk of significant harm attributable to the conduct of the respondent, and in particular whether that conduct had to be 'intentional' before the obligation to make an order came into play. In that case the children had undoubtedly suffered harm in consequence of the breakdown of the relationship and witnessing unpleasantness between their parents, the fault lay with both parents, but the court did find the conduct of the respondent proved. The judge did not make an occupation order excluding the father from the home but did regulate occupation of the property. The Court of Appeal held:

'Plainly, the court's concentration must be upon the effect of conduct rather than on the intention of the doer. Whether misconduct is intentional or unintentional is not the question. An applicant under s 33 is entitled to protection from unjustifiable conduct that causes harm to her or the children of the family. The

---

[30]   *Yemshaw v Hounslow London Borough Council* [2011] UKSC 3, [2011] 1 FLR 1614.
[31]   [1999] 1 FLR 392.
[32]   [2000] 2 FLR 36.

effect is what the judge must assess. Tiny wounds may be inflicted with great malice: great blows may be struck unintentionally. Of course, lack of intent might support a plea of accidental injury. But where something is not done accidentally it is not to be dismissed on the grounds that it was not done deliberately.'

7.32 The Court went on to say:

'This was not a case in which the wife had suffered any violence at the hands of the husband. It has been said time and time again that orders of exclusion are draconian and only to be made in exceptional cases. Add to that the judge's assessment that the friction between the parties was only the product of their incompatible personalities and the heightened tensions that any family has to live with whilst the process of divorce and separation is current, and the judge's conclusion is plainly justified.'

The appeal was not allowed.

7.33 In *G v G (Occupation Order)*[33] the Court of Appeal observed:

'An occupation order is always serious, and no doubt can sometimes be particularly serious when it relates to a spouse's removal from what one might almost call his ancestral home. But the occupation order is likely to carry its greatest level of seriousness when it is made against a spouse to whom alternative accommodation is not readily available.'

In that case an order was made excluding the husband, against which he appealed, in the absence of physical violence having taken place. The order was upheld on appeal, primarily on grounds that it was a very short term order, and the husband had readily available to him alternative accommodation.

7.34 In the recent case of *Dolan v Corby*[34] the Court of Appeal did uphold the making of an occupation order where there had been no physical violence, but where there had been abusive behavior towards a vulnerable woman. Lady Justice Black held;

'I do not read *Chalmers v Johns* or *G v G* as saying that an exclusion order can only be made where there is violence or a threat of violence. That would be to put a gloss on the statute which would be inappropriate. *Chalmers v Johns* and *G v G* stress that it must be recognised that an order requiring a respondent to vacate the family home and overriding his property rights is a grave or draconian order and one which would only be justified in exceptional circumstances, but exceptional circumstances can take many forms and are not confined to violent behaviour on the part of the respondent or the threat of violence and the important thing is for the judge to identify and weigh up all the relevant features of the case whatever their nature.'

---

[33]   [2009] EWCA Civ 976, [2011] 1 FLR 687.
[34]   [2011] EWCA Civ 1664.

Without notice orders

7.35   The court can make an occupation order without the respondent having been given notice of the application for an occupation order, taking into account any risk of significant harm to the applicant or a relevant child if the order is not made immediately. If the court does so it must give the respondent the opportunity to contest the order at a full hearing of which (s)he is notified.[35]

Transfer of tenancy

7.36   The Family Law Act 1996 also includes provisions to enable the court to transfer statutory, protected or local authority tenancies as between spouses/civil partners where a decree nisi/conditional decree is granted, or on the separation of cohabitants in relation to a property in which they lived together. This is considered further in chapters 9 and 10.

Breach of occupation orders

7.37   Breach of an occupation order is a contempt of court, punishable by imprisonment for up to two years.[36] There are two mechanisms for enforcing breach of an occupation order, depending on whether a power of arrest has been attached to the order.

7.38   If the court makes an occupation order, and it appears to the court that the respondent has used or threatened violence against the applicant or a relevant child, the court must attach a power of arrest to the order unless the court is satisfied that the applicant or child will be adequately protected without a power of arrest.[37] If the court attaches a power of arrest, the order must be delivered to the applicant's local police station.[38] This enables the order to be enforced by officers arresting the respondent[39] and then being brought before the court within 24 hours of his arrest[40] and the court hearing the allegations of breach.

7.39   If the court does not attach a power of arrest, or if the occupation of the property is regulated by way of the respondent giving an undertaking (a binding promise to the court) in the appropriate form, breach of the order or undertaking is still a contempt of court, but the respondent cannot be arrested for the breach (unless the nature of the breach amounts to a criminal offence in its own right). However, the applicant may issue proceedings for the respondent to be committed to prison for contempt of court.

---

[35]   FLA 1996, s 45.
[36]   FLA 1996, s 58 and CCR Ord 29 as incorporated into the CPR 1998 and FPR 2010.
[37]   FLA 1996, s 47.
[38]   FPR 2010, r 10.10.
[39]   Provided it can be demonstrated that the order has been properly served on him.
[40]   Interpreted in accordance with FLA 1996, s 47(7).

7.40 There are very strict and detailed requirements imposed by statute and practice directions which must be complied with in cases of contempt of court, and which are outside the scope of the general guidance in this chapter as to the available protection.

NON-MOLESTATION ORDERS

7.41 A non-molestation order is an order prohibiting a person, who is the respondent to the application, from molesting a relevant child or another person who is 'associated with' the respondent.[41] The definition of 'associated with' is the same as for occupation orders – see **7.15** above.

7.42 A child under the age of 16 can only make an application for a non-molestation order with the leave of the court, which will only be given in exceptional circumstances. An adult can, however, apply for a non-molestation order to prevent the respondent from molesting a relevant child.[42]

7.43 There is no definition of molestation in the 1996 Act. Commonly, a non-molestation order will prohibit the respondent from:

- using or threatening violence against the applicant or relevant child, whether by himself or by instructing another to do so;

- communicating with the applicant, whether by letter, text, email, phone or any other means than through solicitors.

However, the jurisdiction is wide enough to allow the court to prohibit any form of conduct which amounts to pestering, harassing, vexing or interfering in an unwanted way.[43] In recent years courts have been willing to include in non-molestation orders prohibitions on internet bullying and postings on social networking sites.

7.44 What is key, is that the terms of the behaviour which the respondent is prohibited from doing must be sufficiently specific that it will be clear to him or her what it is that he or she must not do, and so that it will be clear to a police officer or the court when the order has been breached. Breach of a non-molestation order is a criminal offence, which will be dealt with by the police like any other criminal offence, imprisonable for up to 12 months.[44]

7.45 If a non-molestation injunction is made pursuant to the respondent giving an undertaking not to molest a person or persons named in the

---

[41] FLA 1996, s 42.
[42] *Re Alwyn (Non-Molestation Proceedings By A Child)* [2010] 1 FLR 1363.
[43] See *C v C* [1998] 1 FLR 554. It implies some quite deliberate conduct which is aimed at a high degree of harassment of the other party. There has to be some conduct which clearly harasses and affects the applicant to such a degree that the intervention of the court is called for.
[44] FLA 1996, s 42A, inserted by the Domestic Violence, Crime and Victims Act 2004.

undertaking, there is no power of arrest, and breach is not an offence, but the applicant may issue proceedings for the respondent to be committed to prison for contempt of court in the event of a breach. There are very strict and detailed requirements imposed by statute and practice directions which must be complied with in cases of contempt of court, and which are outside the scope of the general guidance in this chapter as to the available protection.

7.46 The court may not accept an undertaking not to molest in any case where it appears to the court that the respondent has used or threatened violence against the applicant or a relevant child, or where for the protection of the applicant or child it appears to the court that it is necessary for there to be an order, breach of which would be an arrestable offence.[45] A person cannot be punished by both the criminal court and the civil court for the same breach.

7.47 The court can make a non-molestation order without the respondent having been given notice of the application for a non-molestation order, taking into account any risk of significant harm to the applicant or a relevant child if the order is not made immediately. If the court does so it must give the respondent the opportunity to contest the order at a full hearing of which (s)he is notified.[46]

7.48 The court can make a non-molestation order without making an occupation order: ie the court can and often does refuse an application for an order excluding the respondent from the home, but at the same time make an order preventing the respondent from, for example, entering the applicant's bedroom, using foul or abusive language to the applicant, speaking derogatorily to the applicant or about the applicant to a relevant child or other person.

Part IV orders: duration

7.49 Whilst a non-molestation order can be made 'until further order', very often Part IV orders are used as a holding position until the parties to a relationship which has come to an end establish separate homes and move on. In other cases, where there is repeated domestic violence during or after the end of a relationship, non molestation orders are made repeatedly, and there are repeated breaches resulting in criminal sanctions. Occupation orders are in the main of a more temporary nature, and except in the case of an applicant who is entitled to occupy the property in question, an occupation order can be in place for no more than 12 months in any case.

7.50 Occupation or non-molestation orders can be varied or discharged during the currency of the order on the application of either party.[47]

---

[45]   FLA 1996, s 46.
[46]   FLA 1996, s 45.
[47]   FLA 1996, s 49.

FORCED MARRIAGE

7.51 Part 4A of the Family Law Act 1996 gives the court power to make an order for the purposes of protecting a person from being forced into a marriage or from any attempt to be forced into a marriage, or where they have been forced into a marriage.

7.52 It is outside the scope of this work to consider the law relating to forced marriage in detail. As indicated above, however, a brief discussion of the court's powers is included here because it is a form of domestic abuse, and an issue which might arise in a range of circumstances including where a person's family are uncomfortable with that person's sexuality, or in a culture where homosexuality is perceived as unacceptable, to be feared, or contrary to the person's religious beliefs or their family's religious beliefs.

7.53 A person is forced into a marriage if another person forces them into a marriage without their free and full consent.[48] Force includes coercion by threats or other psychological means.[49] It is not necessary for the individual who the person being forced into the marriage is marrying, or has married, to be either the person doing the forcing, or aware that the person has been or is being forced into the marriage;[50] ie the force can come from a third party, not necessarily one of the intended spouses.

7.54 The court can make a forced marriage protection order on the application of the person to be protected by the order, or a relevant third party, or, with leave, any other person can apply.[51] In some situations the police will apply for an order if they are informed of the concerns.

7.55 The court can also make an order where specified family proceedings are before the court and the court considers that such an order should be made to protect a person, even though there has been no application for it, provided that *one* of the people who would be a respondent (whether the person to be protected or some other person) in any proceedings for a forced marriage protection order is a party to those family proceedings.[52]

7.56 The order, when made, can be wide in scope. It can restrict conduct out of the jurisdiction, and it can apply to people who may become involved in the forced marriage in other respects. It can be made without notice. It can restrict any behaviour which might amount to aiding, abetting, procuring or encouraging another person to force or attempt to force a person into a marriage, or which constitutes conspiring to force a person into a marriage.[53]

---

[48]   FLA 1996, s 63A.
[49]   FLA 1996, s 63A(6).
[50]   *Re P (Forced Marriage)* (2010) [2010] EWHC 3467 (Fam) (Baron J) 20/9/2010.
[51]   FLA 1996, s 63C. Relevant third party is proscribed by the Forced Marriage (Relevant Third Party) Order 2009, SI 2009/2023 to mean a local authority.
[52]   FLA 1996, s 63C.
[53]   FLA 1996, s 63B.

7.57   The order can be made without notice[54] to the respondent(s) and can have a power of arrest attached.[55] Breach of an order is a contempt of court and can be punished accordingly.[56]

PROTECTION FROM HARASSMENT ACT 1997

7.58   An alternative to proceedings under the Family Law Act 1996, perhaps where the circumstances are such that two people are not 'associated persons', is the reporting of an offence of breach of the Protection from Harassment Act 1997 (PHA 1997), or a civil claim for breach of the Protection from Harassment Act 1997. This Act is sometimes colloquially referred to as the Prevention of Stalking Act because in the case of *Tuppen v Microsoft Corporation Ltd*[57] the court held that a proper construction of the 1997 Act confined the breaches of the Act giving rise to a civil remedy to those arising in cases of stalking, anti-social behaviour by neighbours and racial harassment. By analogy, it is likely that a civil claim for breach of the 1997 Act could equally be founded on homophobic harassment. Harassment includes alarming a person or causing distress.[58]

7.59   Any person who is the victim of a course of conduct by another person which amounts to harassment and which that person ought to know amounts to harassment of the victim can bring a civil claim for breach of s 1 of the Protection from Harassment Act 1997.[59]

7.60   This allows a person to take action against another person who is harassing them, even where they do not know that person or know them only slightly: ie they do not have to have a sufficient degree of relationship to fall within the definition of associated persons in the Family Law Act 1996.

7.61   Indeed, the PHA 1997 is not to be used in circumstances where a non-molestation order might be more appropriate. The criminal courts have consistently held, most recently in the case of *R v Widdows*:[60]

> 'The section is not normally appropriate for use as a means of criminalising conduct, not charged as violence, during incidents in a long and predominantly affectionate relationship in which both parties persisted and wanted to continue.
>
> Description of a number of acts of violence spread over 9 months during a close and affectionate relationship does not satisfy the *course of conduct* requirement or the requirement that it is conduct amounting to harassment.'

---

[54]   FLA 1996, s 63D.
[55]   FLA 1996, s 63H.
[56]   FLA 1996, s 63O.
[57]   (2000) *The Times*, 15 November.
[58]   PHA 1997, s 7(2).
[59]   PHA 1997, ss 1 and 3.
[60]   [2011] EWCA Crim 1500, [2011] 2 FLR 869.

7.62   The remedies which the court can grant under the Act to a person who is or may be a victim of the course of conduct in question includes issuing an injunction to the person for the purposes of restraining them from pursuing any conduct which amounts to harassment.[61]

7.63   The words 'course of conduct' are defined in s 7 of the Act. Specifically, in order for it to be a 'course' it must involve conduct on at least 2 occasions. The definition is drafted widely enough to allow a course of conduct to be established if there is more than one person carrying out the conduct on separate occasions, or if conduct is by a third person at the instigation of the person who is the subject of the application.

7.64   More commonly, where a person has been subjected to harassment within the meaning of the PHA 1997, they will report this to the police who will issue a warning to the perpetrator initially. Additionally, any person who pursues a course of conduct in breach of the PHA 1997 is guilty of an offence.[62] A person cannot be prosecuted and the subject of a civil claim for the same course of conduct.

---

[61]   PHA 1997, s 3A.
[62]   PHA 1997, s 2.

Chapter 8

CIVIL PARTNERSHIP

FORMATION AND RECOGNITION OF CIVIL PARTNERSHIPS

Definition of a civil partnership

8.1   The Civil Partnership Act 2004 defines a civil partnership as follows:

'1 Civil partnership

(1) A civil partnership is a relationship between two people of the same sex ("civil partners") –

    (a)   which is formed when they register as civil partners of each other –
        (i)   in England or Wales (under Part 2),
        (ii)   in Scotland (under Part 3),
        (iii)   in Northern Ireland (under Part 4), or
        (iv)   outside the United Kingdom under an Order in Council made under Chapter 1 of Part 5 (registration at British consulates etc or by armed forces personnel), or
    (b)   which they are treated under Chapter 2 of Part 5 as having formed (at the time determined under that Chapter) by virtue of having registered an overseas relationship.'

8.2   The moment at which two people become civil partners is the moment of signing the 'civil partnership document'.[1] The status of civil partnership is restricted to:

- Same sex relationships, irrespective of whether the partnership was registered in a country or State which makes no distinction between marriage of a man and a woman and marriage between two people of the same sex.[2]

- People who are not related within the 'prohibited degrees of relationship.[3]

---

[1]   CPA 2004, s 2.

[2]   CPA 2004, s 216(1).

[3]   CPA 2004, s 3(1) as specified in Sch 1 to the CPA 2004. In the case of *Burden v the United Kingdom* (13378/05) [2008] 2 FLR 787 the applicant sisters argued that they were discriminated against as cohabiting sisters not able to enjoy the exemptions from inheritance tax available to spouses or civil partners. This was rejected by the European Court of Human Rights.

Is a civil partnership a marriage?

8.3   English law is presently clear that a civil partnership is not a marriage irrespective of where and when it takes place. The Parliamentary Under Secretary for Equalities has announced that a formal consultation on whether to grant same sex couples in England and Wales the same legal rights to marry as opposite couples will be launched in March 2012. At the time of publication, however, the guidance in this chapter remains correct.

8.4   The definition of civil partnership includes not only relationships formed by registration under UK law, but also overseas relationships registered outside the UK which either feature on the list in Sch 20 to the Civil Partnership Act 2004, or meet certain conditions called 'the general conditions'.[4] The types of registered overseas relationships recognised in Sch 20 ranges from 'significant relationships' (Australia) to marriage (Spain, Netherlands, Belgium, Canada, and Massachusetts USA),[5] but all of those relationships fall within the definition of Civil Partnership when given recognition in the UK. The government is currently in the process of updating the Sch 20 list, with a new list planned for December 2012.[6]

8.5   This means that where two people of the same sex celebrate a marriage abroad which is a valid marriage in that country, it will be treated as a civil partnership in England and Wales.[7] This is in contrast to a marriage between a man and a woman formed abroad which will be recognised as a marriage in England and Wales.[8] If the couple married abroad prior to the Civil Partnership Act 2004 coming into force in England and Wales, their prior marriage will be afforded recognition as a Civil Partnership in England and Wales from the date of the CPA 2004.[9] Not all countries which enable same sex marriage or civil partnership now extend that status to relationships registered prior to the statute which made it possible for same sex couples to marry or enter a civil partnership in that country.

8.6   The English Parliament's purpose in making a distinction between civil partnership and marriage was discussed in the case of *Wilson v Kitzinger*,[10] which concerned a couple who had entered into a same sex marriage in Canada. Lord Justice Potter rejected the application for a declaration that the

---

[4]   Special provisions apply in relation to Armed Forces personnel; see CPA 2004, s 211.

[5]   Schedule 20 has not been updated since 2005 and there are now more overseas territories which recognise same sex marriage, and which are capable of being recognised if the general criteria are met, but which are not yet on the list. This is discussed further below in the section of this chapter on overseas relationships.

[6]   Government Equalities Office publication.

[7]   *Wilkinson v Kitzinger and Attorney General and Lord Chancellor intervening* [2006] EWHC 2022 (Fam).

[8]   Dicey & Morris *The Conflict of Laws* (14th edn), Chapter 17 (subject to meeting the requirements as to form for it to be valid at all).

[9]   CPA 2004, s 215(3). Provided the formalities and legal requirements were complied with and it would have fallen within the definition of an 'overseas relationship' in the CPA 2004.

[10]   [2006] EWHC 2022 (Fam) at paras [49] and [50].

women were married as a matter of English Law, and described the intended purpose and effect of the provisions of the Civil Partnership Act 2004:

'In the course of the passage of the CPA, Parliament closely re-examined the complex problems involved if recognition were to be given to same sex marriages. The solution which it reached was that there should be statutory recognition of a status and relationship closely modelled upon that of marriage which made available to civil partners essentially every material right and responsibility presently arising from marriage, with the exception of the form of ceremony and the actual name and status of marriage ... [The] intention of the government in introducing the legislation was not to create a "second class" institution, but a parallel and equalising institution designed to redress a perceived inequality of treatment of long-term monogamous same sex relationships, while at the same time, demonstrating support for the long-established institution of marriage.'

8.7 Potter LJ went so far as to suggest that to permit marriage between two people of the same sex would be contrary to the rights enshrined in Art 12 of the European Convention on Human Rights and Fundamental Freedoms, which provides:

'Men and women of marriageable age have the right to marry and found a family, according to the national laws governing exercise of this right.'

At that time the European Court of Human Rights (ECtHR) had not specifically considered this issue or the question of whether signatory states can refuse same sex partners the right to marry. That question was considered for the first time in the case of *Schalk and Kopf v Austria*.[11]

8.8 In giving judgment on 24 June 2010 in *Schalk v Kopf v Austria* the ECtHR held that whilst the European convention does not limit marriage to partnerships between a man and a woman, the question of whether to allow couples of the same sex to marry remains one for the discretion of national government, not Europe.[12] In large part this conclusion was reached because there is, as yet, no European consensus on same sex partnership and marriage. The court observed that at that time only 6 out of 47 Member States granted same sex couples equal access to marriage.

8.9 In giving judgment, the ECtHR held:

'61. [The] Court would no longer consider that the right to marry enshrined in Article 12 must in all circumstances be limited to marriage between two persons of the opposite sex. Consequently, it cannot be said that Article 12 is inapplicable to the applicants' complaint. However, as matters stand, the question whether or not to allow same sex marriage is left to regulation by the national law of the Contracting State.

---

[11] (Application No 30141/04).
[12] Para [61] of the judgment.

62. In that connection the Court observes that marriage has deep-rooted social and cultural connotations which may differ largely from one society to another. The Court reiterates that it must not rush to substitute its own judgment in place of that of the national authorities, who are best placed to assess and respond to the needs of society (see *B and L v the United Kingdom*, cited above, § 36).

63. In conclusion, the Court finds that Article 12 of the Convention does not impose an obligation on the respondent Government to grant a same sex couple like the applicants access to marriage.

64. Consequently, there has been no violation of Article 12 of the Convention.'

8.10 The European Court in *Schalk and Kopf v Austria*[13] also clarified that where a State provides same sex couples with an alternative means of registration of their relationship, it is not obliged to ensure that the alternative means of recognition corresponds with marriage in each and every respect. The question of the exact status of the registered relationship remains a matter for individual States.

8.11 States may also make a distinction between unions formed in their own territory and unions formed abroad in terms of effect. In Spain and Portugal, no distinction is made between same and different sex marriages, but civil partnerships formed in other countries are not automatically afforded the status of marriage and different consequences arise.[14]

8.12 The prohibition on marriage for same sex couples, and the restriction of civil partnership to same sex couples, nevertheless remains a contentious point for many people, and in spite of the decision in *Kopf v Austria*, in December 2010 eight couples attempted to register marriages or civil partnerships in England which they were not entitled to register as a springboard for launching a further claim in the European Court of Human Rights.

Civil partner or not and does it matter?

8.13 The question of whether two people are treated by law as civil partners is an important one. Being able to demonstrate the current or former existence of a valid civil partnership is a gateway to a number of significant aspects of family life and financial remedies or entitlements. In particular:

(a) On relationship breakdown, it enables an application for **a financial remedy**[15] to be made against the other civil partner: s 72 of the Civil Partnership Act 2004 makes provision for financial relief in connection with a civil partnership.

---

[13] (Application No 30141/04) at para 108.
[14] Legal Recognition of Same Sex relationships in Europe: Southern Jurisdictions Outline Cristina González Beilfuss Universitat de Barcelona, April 2011.
[15] As defined in FPR 2010, r 2.2.

(b)   It affects whether a person can be ordered to make **financial provision for a child** who is not their legal or biological child.[16] A parent, guardian, or person holding a residence order in respect of a child can make an application for an order requiring either or both of a child's parents to make financial provision for him or her under Sch 1 to the Children Act 1989. In this context parent is specifically defined to include a civil partner[17] where the child has been treated as a child of the family within that partnership;[18] eg one civil partner can make an application for financial provision from the other civil partner in respect of their biological child, the other civil partner's step-child, irrespective of whether there is an ongoing relationship or has been a dissolution of that partnership.

(c)   In some circumstances, it affects whether the civil partner is treated as a **legal parent** of a child.[19] In particular, s 42 of the HFEA 2008 provides for the civil partner of a woman artificially inseminated to be the other female parent of a child born after 1 April 2009.

(d)   It affects whether a person has or may apply for **parental responsibility** in respect of a child. In particular, if a woman is the 'other female parent' of a child,[20] and the civil partner of the mother of the child at the time of the child's birth,[21] she will automatically have parental responsibility.[22] The civil partner of a child's parent can acquire parental responsibility for a child by agreement or by court order, even where they are not a legal parent of the child.[23]

(e)   It affects the person's legal relationship **with wider family members**. Part 6 of the Civil Partnership Act deals with relationships arising through civil partnership and includes a comprehensive list. For example, 'brother-in-law' includes civil partner's brother, 'daughter-in-law' includes daughter's civil partner. This can be particularly important when interpreting the effect of wills or trust documents.

(f)   It affects what applications a person may make without the court's permission for **orders in relation to a child**. In particular, a person in a current or former civil partnership can apply for a residence order, contact order, or special guardianship order in respect of a child who has been

---

[16]   *T v B* [2010] EWHC 1444 (Fam).
[17]   Paragraph 16 to Sch 1 of the CA 1989.
[18]   CPA 2004. s 75 'child of the family' includes any child treated by both of them as a child of their family.
[19]   See chapter 1 for a detailed discussion on legal parenthood and civil partnership.
[20]   As a result of HFEA 2008, s 43 where the agreed female parenthood conditions are met – this is discussed in more detail in chapter 1.
[21]   Or at any time between artificial insemination and birth: HFEA 2008, s 43 and Family Law Reform Act 1987, s 1(3).
[22]   CA 1989, s 2 and Family Law Reform Act 1987, s 1(3).
[23]   CA 1989, s 4A.

treated as a child of the family by the partners in that civil partnership,[24] whether or not the applicant has parental responsibility for that child, and whether or not they have lived with that child for 3 years.

(g)   It affects **whether a person can apply to adopt a child**. Section 51 of the Adoption and Children Act 2002 provides that an adoption order can only be made on the application of one person (rather than by a couple) if that person is not married or a civil partner, unless the civil partner cannot be found, is incapacitated, or they have separated and the separation is likely to be permanent.

(h)   It can affect **property ownership**. For example, where a person makes a substantial contribution in money or money's worth to property owned by their civil partner,[25] they will be treated as having acquired a 'beneficial interest' in that property.[26] This may be particularly significant if, for example, one civil partner is made bankrupt, the extent of the bankrupt's estate acquired by the trustee in bankruptcy may be limited by this provision.

(i)   It determines whether a person who does not hold a legal title to or beneficial interest in land has **'home rights'** in respect of a house which is, has been or was intended to be a home of the civil partners. Home rights are rights not to be evicted or excluded from the dwelling-house or any part of it by the other civil partner except with the leave of the court, or, if not in occupation, a right with the leave of the court to enter into and occupy the house.[27]

(j)   **Welfare benefits and tax credits** are sometimes affected by the question of whether a person is the spouse or civil partner of another. Whilst two people are treated as a couple for the purposes of means-tested benefits if they are of the same sex and living as civil partners in the same household,[28] bereavement benefits are payable to surviving civil partners[29] and not simply cohabitants.

(k)   **Housing:** The question of whether two people are civil partners may affect the rights of one of them not to be evicted from a property, or to succeed under a private sector tenancy under the Rent Act 1977 or a public sector tenancy under the Housing Act 1988. The issue might be particularly crucial if the partners are not living together at the time but had not dissolved the civil partnership.

---

24   CA 1989, ss 10 and 14A. This is discussed in more detail in chapter 4.
25   Or potentially by someone who agreed to become their civil partner, similar to engagement.
26   CPA 2004, s 65. The detail of this provision and its effects is discussed further below in chapter 10.
27   Family Law Act 1996, s 30.
28   Social Security Contributions and Benefits Act 1992, s 137(1).
29   Social Security Contributions and Benefits Act 1992, s 39B.

(l)   **Inheritance:** Civil partners are entitled to inherit the estate of their deceased civil partner under the intestacy rules. Wills are revoked automatically by the testator becoming a civil partner unless made in contemplation of the civil partnership.[30] Civil partnership also affects the question of whether a person is able to make an application for financial provision out of another person's estate on their death. Specifically if a civil partner dies without making provision for their civil partner, the surviving civil partner will fall within the class of people who may apply to the court for an order for financial provision from the deceased's estate.[31]

(m)   **Fatal accident claims**: The executors of a deceased's estate can bring legal proceedings for damages for a wrongful act causing death on behalf of a civil partner or former civil partner.[32]

(n)   **Pensions:** Whether a person is a surviving civil partner or not may affect their ability to claim death in service benefits from a private or occupational pension scheme of which the deceased civil partner was a member depending on the rules of the scheme. In respect of state pensions, whether the surviving person was a civil partner will affect the question of whether they are entitled to a state pension equal to the deceased partner's.[33]

(o)   **Taxation:** Whether a couple are civil partners affects their taxation position. For example, for capital gains tax purposes transfers between spouses or civil partners (not separated) are treated as being at no gain, no loss, and therefore no capital gains tax is payable.[34]

(p)   **Insolvency:** Whether a person is the civil partner of someone who has been made bankrupt will affect their position vis à vis the partner's trustee in bankruptcy. For example, the extent to which the court has to take into account the civil partner's needs and resources when being asked to order a sale of a property.[35] It may also affect the extent of the equity in a property which can be treated as part of the bankrupt's estate.[36]

(q)   **Immigration:** The question of whether a couple are civil partners may affect the ability of a partner who is not an EEA national to live and work in the UK.

(r)   **Freedom of movement:** Civil partnership will affect the question of whether an EU citizen can bring their non-EU citizen partner to the UK.

---

[30]   CPA 2004, Sch 4.
[31]   Inheritance (Provision for Family and Dependants) Act 1975, ss 1 and 2.
[32]   Fatal Accidents Act 1976, s 1.
[33]   SSCBA 1992, s 48B.
[34]   Taxation of Chargeable Gains Act 1992, s 58, as amended by SI 2005/3229.
[35]   Insolvency Act 1986, s 335A.
[36]   For example pursuant to CPA 2004, s 65.

The rights of citizens of the European Union and their family members to move and reside freely in and between the Member States includes 'the partner with whom the Union citizen has contracted a registered partnership if the legislation of the host Member State treats registered partnerships as equivalent to marriage'.[37]

8.14   This list is not exhaustive but rather illustrative of the need to be clear about whether a relationship meets the statutory requirements for a civil partnership. The differing positions of civil partners and non-civil partners in respect of these various aspects of family rights and responsibilities are discussed in detail in the chapters on personal safety, breakdown of civil partnerships and cohabiting relationships, parentage, succession and welfare benefits and housing.

REGISTERING AS CIVIL PARTNERS: PROCEDURE IN ENGLAND AND WALES

8.15   All of the relevant forms appear in the schedule to the Civil Partnership (Registration Provisions) Regulations 2005[38] and some are reproduced in the Appendix 2.

Ceremony

8.16   Civil partnership is formed by the signing of a civil partnership document by two people in the presence of a civil partnership registrar, each other, and two witnesses. Both of the witnesses and the registrar must also sign the document in the presence of each other and the couple.[39] Beyond this the CPA 2004 does not make any specification about a ceremony of civil partnership, but it does provide that no religious service is to be used while the civil partnership registrar is officiating at the signing of a civil partnership document.[40] The guidance from the General Register Office goes further than this and specifies that a civil marriage ceremony cannot have any religious content, specifically no religious music or religious readings.[41] The restrictions on religious content may change, following a government consultation issued on this subject during 2011. The proposals would allow a religious service to be held, but the registration would remain secular. The consultation on same sex marriage being launched in 2012 will also consider this issue.

8.17   The civil partnership document which the civil partners sign is called a 'Civil Partnership Schedule'[42] (in place of a marriage certificate); see an example at Appendix 2. The word 'condition' on the form refers to the required

---

[37]   Directive 2004/38/EC.
[38]   As amended by SI 2011/1171 in respect of parties subject to immigration control.
[39]   CPA 2004, s 2.
[40]   CPA 2004, s 2(5).
[41]   At www.directgov.uk/Governmentcitizensandrights.
[42]   CPA 2004, s 7 – unless using the special procedure.

information about whether the proposed civil partner is single, widowed or has had a previous marriage or civil partnership dissolved.

Location

8.18 The place where the civil partnership is registered is the place where the civil partnership document is signed.[43] This must be in England or Wales and (save for the defined circumstances discussed below) must be open to anyone wishing to attend, and must be agreed with the registration authority in whose area that place is located.[44] It must take place on approved premises.

8.19 The place of registration can be the local register office or other approved premises. Couples can ask the local registrar for details of already-approved premises or search for already-approved premises on the General Register Office's website.[45] Owners or trustees of premises can apply to the local registration authority to have their premises registered for civil partnerships.[46]

8.20 The CPA 2004 prohibited civil partnerships from taking place on religious premises, which includes buildings which have historically mainly been used for religious purposes and have not mainly been used for other purposes since.[47] However, on 5 December 2011 the Marriages and Civil Partnerships (Approved Premises) (Amendment) Regulations 2011 came into force[48] which allows specific religious premises to apply for approval as a place of registration of civil partnership. Section 202 of the Equality Act 2010 was brought into force to amend the CPA 2004 and enable this to take place.[49] The types of religious premises are:[50]

(a) a church or chapel of the Church of England or Church of Wales;

(b) a place of meeting for religious worship included in the list of certified places maintained by the Registrar General;

(c) a Jewish synagogue;

(d) a place of meeting for members of the Society of Friends.

Unless further changes are made as a result of the consultation being launched in 2012, the registration of civil partnerships would remain secular, despite taking place on religious premises.

---

[43] CPA 2004, ss 1 and 6.
[44] CPA 2004, s 6.
[45] At www.gro.gov.uk.
[46] Marriages and Civil Partnerships (Approved Premises) Regulations 2005.
[47] CPA 2004, s 6(2).
[48] SI 2011/2661.
[49] SI 2010/2317 brought it into force on 1 October 2010.
[50] SI 2011/2661, reg 3B(7)(1B) which also sets out the procedure for application.

Eligibility

8.21 The civil partnership will only be valid if the two people signing the civil partnership document are eligible to register as the civil partners of each other. To be eligible they must be of the same sex, not already a civil partner or lawfully married, over 16, and not closely related to each other – ie not within the prohibited degrees of relationship.[51] The full list of relationships which are within prohibited degrees is contained in Sch 1 to the CPA 2004, and includes relatives of former spouses and of former civil partners as 'qualified prohibitions' rather than absolutes,[52] which means that an application can be made to the High Court for a declaration that the couple can enter into civil partnership notwithstanding the degree of relationship.[53]

If either person proposing to enter into a civil partnership has previously been married or a civil partner, they will need to provide evidence to the registrar that the marriage or civil partnership has been dissolved. If one of the proposed civil partners is under 18, consent is required from the people having parental responsibility for that person.[54] It is possible for a person whose consent is required to forbid the minor to enter into the civil partnership, in which case all civil partnership proceedings will be void.[55] This is different from refusing to give consent, or being unable to give consent, in which circumstances it is possible to apply to the court for consent to be given by the court.[56]

Gender change and eligibility for marriage/civil partnership

8.22 For a person who is living in an acquired gender, the question, in England and Wales, of whether they are eligible to marry or enter a civil partnership by reference to their sex is governed by the provisions of the Gender Recognition Act 2004 in conjunction with the Matrimonial Causes Act 1973 and the Civil Partnership Act 2004.

8.23 A person may apply to the Gender Recognition Panel for a Gender Recognition Certificate where they have changed gender, either as a result of living in a new gender or as a result of acquiring a changed gender under the law of another country.[57]

8.24 If the person is not married or a civil partner and their application succeeds, they must be issued with a full gender recognition certificate.[58] If their

---

51 CPA 2004, s 3
52 There is also an additional form to complete (Form 8) to declare that the younger of the proposed civil partners has not at any time been a child of the family in relation to the other where the relationship falls within qualified prohibitions.
53 Schedule 1, Part 2, para 7(1) to the CPA 2004.
54 A list is contained in Sch 2 to the CPA 2004.
55 Paragraph 6 of Sch 2 to CPA 2004.
56 Part 3 of Sch 2 to CPA 2004.
57 GRA 2004, s 1(1).
58 GRA 2004, s 4(1).

acquired sex is different to that of their partner, they may then marry that person.[59] If their acquired sex is the same as that of their partner, then they are eligible to enter into a civil partnership with that person.[60]

8.25 If a couple wish to enter into a civil partnership or same sex marriage overseas, and one of them has changed gender, the overseas relationship will not be recognised under UK law as a civil partnership unless, at the time of registering the partnership, the partners were recognised as being of the same sex under UK law.[61] In other words, changing sex overseas and then registering a same sex relationship overseas is not sufficient to create a valid civil partnership: the acquired gender must also be the partner's legal gender in English law at the time of registration for the same sex relationship to be recognised.

8.26 It is equally the case that acquiring recognition of acquired gender here, followed by marriage or civil partnership in the acquired gender is not given automatic recognition outside the UK.

8.27 If the person is married or a civil partner at the time of their application for a gender recognition certificate, and the application succeeds, the Gender Recognition Panel must issue an interim gender recognition certificate.[62] This has the immediate effect of making a marriage or civil partnership voidable[63] for a period of time.[64] However, if a person enters in to a foreign post-operative marriage abroad, and subsequently is issued with a full gender recognition certificate here, the foreign marriage will no longer be void on grounds that the parties were of the same sex at the time of marriage.[65] See **8.91** below for further discussion in relation to void and voidable marriage and civil partnership.

8.28 If the marriage or civil partnership is annulled as a result of an interim gender recognition certificate having been issued, the court annulling the relationship must also then issue a full gender recognition certificate.[66] This then leaves the person who has changed sex free to enter into a further marriage or civil partnership with a person of the opposite/same sex respectively.

8.29 The effect is, therefore, that a person cannot finally, legally, acquire a new gender during the currency of a marriage or civil partnership without affecting the status of that marriage or civil partnership. This is consistent with the continued distinction between marriage for different sex couples and civil partnership for same sex couples. There is nothing to prevent a married couple

---

[59] Effect of GRA 2004, s 9 in conjunction with the English common law in relation to marriage.
[60] Effect of GRA 2004, s 9 in conjunction with s 1 of the CPA 2004.
[61] CPA 2004, s 216.
[62] GRA 2004, s 4(3).
[63] CPA 2004, s 50; MCA 1973, s 12.
[64] But a decree of nullity may only be granted if proceedings were instituted within 6 months of the interim gender recognition certificate being granted: GRA 2004, Sch 2 and CPA 2004, s 51.
[65] GRA 2004, s 21(3).
[66] GRA 2004, s 5.

from annulling their marriage and then entering into a civil partnership, or annulling a civil partnership and then marrying, where a full gender recognition certificate is granted on annulment. Gender change is discussed in more detail in chapter 6.

Pre-registration procedure

8.30 Before a civil partnership can take place, there is a pre-registration procedure which must be followed for the registration to be valid.

8.31 The standard procedure involves giving notice of the proposed civil partnership to a registration authority, and requires that both proposed civil partners must have resided in England or Wales for at least 7 days immediately before giving the notice.[67] The form for notice is Form 1 at Appendix 2.[68] The registrar can require evidence of any of the information given in the notice.[69] The notice has to specify where the civil partnership is going to take place and that place must be agreed with the registration authority in that area.[70]

8.32 Once notice has been given to the registration authority, the proposal for a civil partnership between the people giving notice has to be publicised for 15 days not only in the area of the registration authority that notice has been given to, but also in the area where the civil partnership is to take place and the area where the proposed civil partners have been residing for 7 days before the notice.[71] This 15 day period is called the waiting period, and it can be shortened on application.[72] Once the waiting period is complete the registrar will give the parties a partially completed civil partnership schedule for signature at the registration (provided there have been no objections to the proposed civil partnership).[73] The parties have 12 months from the date of issue of the schedule in which to register a civil partnership.[74] If the parties change their minds about where they want to have their civil partnership ceremony during the 12 months it is not clear from the regulations whether the notice can be amended.

8.33 Steps:

• 7 days of residence;

• give notice;

---

[67] CPA 2004, s 8(1).
[68] Or Form 2 if one party is a minor, or Form 3 if one party is subject to immigration control, or Form 5 if one party is a minor and one party is subject to immigration control.
[69] CPA 2004, s 9.
[70] CPA 2004, s 6.
[71] CPA 2004, s 10.
[72] CPA 2004, ss 11 and 12.
[73] By any person, including the registrar if (s)he believes there is a 'lawful impediment' to the partnership – CPA 2004, s 14.
[74] CPA 2004, ss 14 and 17.

- agree location;

- publicise the proposed partnership;

- register the partnership.

8.34 Alternative pre-registration procedures exist to provide for the circumstances where:

- One of the parties is **house bound**, in which case the procedure is the same as the standard procedure except a certificate from a medical practitioner is required, and the civil partnership has to take place within 3 months of the schedule being issued.[75] It is not stated explicitly that this procedure allows the registrar to authorise the civil partnership to take place in the house bound person's home, but by virtue of not being a standard procedure registration, the requirement is removed for the place where the registration is to take place to be open to the public or agreed with the registration authority.[76]

- One of the parties is **detained in a hospital or prison**, in which case the procedure is the same as the standard procedure, except that the hospital manager or prison governor has to provide a supporting statement stating that they have no objection to the prison or hospital being the place at which the detained person is to register as a civil partner.[77]

- One of the parties is **seriously ill and not expected to recover**, in which case the 'special procedure' applies instead, which is provided for in ss 21–27 of the CPA 2004. This requires a different, more detailed notice document,[78] and provides for the civil partnership document to be a Registrar's Licence rather than a Civil Partnership Schedule.[79] There is no requirement for a waiting period or for the proposed civil partnership to be publicised under the special procedure, and the only visible difference between a schedule and a licence is that the licence makes no reference to the waiting period. The special procedure does however require a certificate from a registered medical practitioner stating that one of the proposed civil partners is seriously ill and not expected to recover, and that the person who is ill understands the nature and effect of registering a civil partnership by signing the licence.[80]

- One of the parties is **resident in Scotland or Northern Ireland or is serving overseas in HM Armed Forces** in which case the party resident here can give the relevant notice, and it is not necessary for the other party to have

---

[75] CPA 2004, s 18.
[76] CPA 2004, s 6(3).
[77] CPA 2004, s 19.
[78] Form 5 attached to SI 2005/3176.
[79] CPA 2004, s 25.
[80] CPA 2004, ss 22 and 23.

been resident in England or Wales for the 7 days prior.[81] Other modifications to the standard procedure are that the person residing outside England and Wales must obtain a certificate from the District Registrar (Scotland), or Prescribed Registrar (Northern Ireland) or from their Commanding Officer (Armed Forces) that there is no impediment to the civil partnership.[82] Once the civil partnership schedule has been issued it is only valid for 3 months if the party is serving overseas.[83]

• One party to the proposed civil partnership is subject to **immigration control**. Schedule 23 to the Civil Partnership Act 2004 makes provision for certain procedures to be followed where a civil partnership is to be formed in the United Kingdom. These procedures are additional to the standard procedures to be followed by all couples prior to formation of a civil partnership. They require that the notice of proposed civil partnership must be given to a specified registration authority[84] and must be delivered to the relevant individual *in person by the two proposed civil partners*.[85] The Regulations contain a table of the specified registration authority for each district, and this information will otherwise be available at the local register office.

8.35 The procedural requirements for registration of civil partnerships in Scotland and Northern Ireland are different and are provided for in Parts 3 and 4 of the Civil Partnership Act 2004 and other statutory instruments enacted under those parts. A detailed analysis of Scottish or Northern Irish law relating to the formation of civil partnerships is outside the scope of this work.

Registration at a British Consulate

8.36 A civil partnership may be registered under UK law at a British Consulate outside the UK provided that at least one party is a UK National.[86] The relevant procedural requirements are contained in the Civil Partnership (Registration Abroad and Certificates) Regulations 2005.[87] The partnership can be registered by a British Consular Officer, also called a Civil Partnership Officer. The regulations[88] provide that:

---

[81]   CPA 2004, s 20.
[82]   CPA 2004, ss 20, 97, 150, 239.
[83]   CPA 2004, s 20(5).
[84]   Or in Scotland the relevant district registrar, or in Northern Ireland the prescribed registrar: SI 2005/2917, explanatory notes.
[85]   Immigration (Procedure for Formation of Civil Partnerships) Regulations 2005, SI 2005/2917, explanatory notes. The requirement for permission from the Secretary of State for a person subject to immigration control had to be removed following the declaration of the House of Lords in *Baiai & Ors v Secretary of State for the Home Department* [2008] UKHL 53 that the regulations were incompatible with the Human Rights Act, resulting in SI 2011/1171 and a new Form 3.
[86]   CPA 2004, s 210.
[87]   SI 2005/2761.
[88]   SI 2005/2761, reg 4.

(2) A civil partnership officer is not required to allow two people to register before him as civil partners of each other unless he is satisfied that the following conditions are met –

(a)   at least one of the proposed civil partners is a United Kingdom national,

(b)   the proposed civil partners would have been eligible to register as civil partners of each other in the relevant part of the United Kingdom,

(c)   the authorities of the country or territory in which it is proposed that they register as civil partners will not object to the registration, and

(d)   insufficient facilities exist for them to enter into an overseas relationship under the law of that country or territory.

8.37   What are insufficient facilities within the meaning of this regulation? This categorisation will definitely not apply if the country in question is one of those named in Sch 20 to the CPA,[89] in which case the partnership will have to proceed in accordance with the law of the country in question. In respect of other countries some enquiries will be necessary to establish whether the local law would enable a partnership registered there to be recognised as an overseas relationship under English Law. In other words, couples cannot bypass the requirement to ensure that a partnership entered into abroad fulfils the criteria for recognition of overseas relationships under the Civil Partnership Act simply by choosing to register the relationship at a British Consulate. It will be necessary to first establish whether it would be possible for them to enter into a registered partnership under the local law which is capable of being recognised by the provisions of the Civil Partnership Act, and only if the country in question cannot facilitate this does the option of registering at the British Consulate arise. The requirements for recognition of an overseas relationship registered in accordance with the local law of the country in question is discussed further below at **8.40**.

8.38   The detailed procedural requirements for registration at a British Consulate abroad include that the proposed civil partners must have resided in the country 7 days before giving notice, and notice must be given at least 14 days prior to registration. The civil partnership must be formed within 3 months of giving notice.[90] Two people can only register as civil partners of each other in the presence of the civil partnership officer at his official house in the presence of two witnesses, at a time to be set by the civil partnership officer between the hours of 8 am and 6 pm (local time).[91]

Armed forces personnel

8.39   A civil partnership may also be registered overseas under UK law where at least one of the proposed civil partners is a member of HM Armed Forces serving in the country or territory in question.[92] The countries where this may

---

[89]   SI 2005/2761, reg 4(4).
[90]   SI 2005/2761, regs 5 and 9.
[91]   SI 2005/2761, reg 10(2).
[92]   CPA 2004, s 211.

take place are limited.[93] Separate provision is also made for Officers, Seamen and Marines at sea.[94] The Civil Partnership (Armed Forces) Order 2005 contains detailed provisions as to notice, residence, and publicising the proposed partnership.

RECOGNITION OF OVERSEAS RELATIONSHIPS

8.40   The definition of Civil Partnership in s 1 of the CPA 2004 includes 'a relationship between two people of the same sex ... which they are treated ... as having formed by virtue of having registered an overseas relationship'.[95]

8.41   Sections 212–218 of the CPA 2004 set out the meaning of and requirements for an overseas relationship to be treated in England and Wales as a civil partnership. As set out above, the Civil Partnership Act envisages automatic recognition of certain overseas relationships as creating civil partnerships; Sch 20 to the CPA 2004 (see Appendix 4) lists these, they are called 'specified relationships'.[96]

8.42   The types of specified relationships recognised in Sch 20 ranges from 'significant relationships' (Australia) to marriage (Spain, Netherlands, Belgium, Canada, and Massachusetts USA),[97] but all of those relationships fall within the definition of civil partnership in the UK. Some countries, such as Canada and the Netherlands allow marriage and civil partnership between same sex couples; either would have the status of civil partnership in England.

8.43   The government is currently in the process of updating the Sch 20 list, with a new list planned for December 2012.[98] There are a number of countries not currently on the Sch 20 list in which a same sex marriage can be registered, such as Mexico (Mexico City only), Argentina, South Africa and Portugal. In addition New York is the most recent US state to permit same sex marriage. There are also a great many more countries in which a same sex partnership can be registered including most recently Austria, Brazil and Ireland. This is an area of law which is rapidly evolving worldwide. At present there are no cases which have been reported in England determining whether a same sex partnership registered overseas meets the criteria for recognition in the UK, and it remains to be seen which of the countries which have permitted same sex marriage or civil partnership will make it on to the updated Sch 20.

---

[93]   Civil Partnership (Armed Forces) Order 2005, SI 2005/3188, art 2
[94]   Civil Partnership (Armed Forces) Order 2005, SI 2005/3188, Part 3.
[95]   CPA 2004, s 1(1)(b).
[96]   CPA 2004, s 213.
[97]   Schedule 20 has not been updated since 2005 and there are now more overseas territories which recognise same sex marriage, and which are capable of being recognised if the general criteria are met, but which are not yet on the list. This is discussed further below in the section of this chapter on overseas relationships.
[98]   Government Equalities Office publication.

8.44 However, the relationships which are recognised as a civil partnership in the UK are not limited to those listed on Sch 20. In addition to the Sch 20 relationships, *a relationship may also be an 'overseas relationship' treated as a civil partnership in the UK if it meets the 'general conditions'.* These relate to the laws of the country where the relationship is to be registered; 'the relevant country' and are set out in s 214 of the CPA 2004. In essence, the law for that country must provide for the relationship to result in the parties being treated as married or as a couple, and provide for the key two elements which are associated with a marriage, including not being bigamous or capable of being bigamous[99] and being of indeterminate length.

8.45 In addition, the Civil Partnership Act is clear[100] that only relationships of people of the same sex are to be treated as civil partnerships in England and Wales; a couple registering an opposite sex partnership of whatever kind overseas will not be treated as civil partners in England and Wales.

214 The general conditions

The general conditions are that, under the relevant law –

    (a)   the relationship may not be entered into if either of the parties is already a party to a relationship of that kind or lawfully married,

    (b)   the relationship is of indeterminate duration, and

    (c)   the effect of entering into it is that the parties are –

        (i)   treated as a couple either generally or for specified purposes, or

        (ii) treated as married.

8.46 Being treated 'as a couple' is not further defined, nor is the extent of the 'specified purposes'. This raises firstly the potential for there to be an issue about whether the extent to which registered partners are treated as a couple in the country of registration is sufficient to satisfy the general conditions (eg is it sufficient that they are treated as a couple for tax purposes but no other purposes?).

8.47 Secondly, it raises an issue about the nature of the relationship. Whilst the partnership will not be treated as a civil partnership if the partners are too closely related and either of them was domiciled in England and Wales,[101] where *neither* of them was domiciled in England & Wales, there is no bar to a relationship being treated as a civil partnership due to them being too closely related. For example, if a country or territory allows siblings living together to register a partnership for the purposes of claiming benefits as a couple, arguably they could be treated as civil partners here if neither of them is domiciled in the UK.

8.48 It is significant that the Civil Partnership Act specifically provides for overseas relationships which were entered into before the Civil Partnership Act

---

[99] No separate word yet having been recognised for entering into two civil partnerships or a marriage and then a civil partnership.

[100] Section 1.

[101] CPA 2004, s 217.

came into force to be recognised – for all those couples who went abroad to register their same sex union in the absence of provision in English law for their relationship to be recognised, the partnership became automatically recognised in England and Wales when the CPA 2004 came into force,[102] provided the registration met the requirements for overseas relationships in the CPA.

8.49 Requirements which must be satisfied in order for an overseas relationship to be treated as a civil partnership are set out in s 215 of the CPA 2004:

> (1) Two people are to be treated as having formed a civil partnership as a result of having registered an overseas relationship if, under the relevant law, they –
>
> (a)   had capacity to enter into the relationship, and
> (b)   met all requirements necessary to ensure the formal validity of the relationship.

Requirement for registration

8.50 The first point of note is that the relationship must be registered according to the relevant law (the law of the country where it is registered[103]) – ie it must be registered and that registration must be according to the relevant law. Different countries will have different requirements as to what constitutes registration, but there must have been a registration, and in reality this means there must be a document issued in the relevant country evidencing the registration, or an entry in the public register of that country.

8.51 A party seeking a dissolution of a civil partnership is required by the application form (Form D8) to attach to the application a certified copy of their civil partnership certificate. Likewise, a party seeking a declaration under s 58 of the CPA as to their Civil Partnership Status is required by the application form (Form 70) to attach a certified copy of their civil partnership certificate.[104] Practice Direction 7A to the Family Procedure Rules 2010[105] provides that when making an application for a civil partnership order,[106] and where the validity of the civil partnership is not disputed, the civil partnership will be proved by the application being accompanied by a certificate of civil partnership or similar document issued in the country where the registration took place or a certified copy of such certificate or document.[107]

8.52 If the existence of the civil partnership is in dispute and there is no certificate, the validity of the overseas relationship may still be proved using the provisions of the Evidence (Foreign, Dominion and Colonial Documents)

---

[102]   CPA 2004, s 215.
[103]   CPA 2004, s 212(2).
[104]   Both of these forms are specified by FPR 2010, PD 5A.
[105]   Rule 3.1.
[106]   A decree of dissolution, nullity, separation or presumption of death pursuant to CPA 2004, s 37.
[107]   Where it is not in English the there must also be a translation certified by a notary or accompanied by a statement of truth: PD 7A, para 3.1(b).

Act 1933.[108] This Act allows copies of public registers kept in the relevant country to be admitted in evidence to the court. That is not to say that the register operates as proof of the existence of the civil partnership, but rather that the entry may be admitted in evidence of the fact of the registered partnership.[109]

Meeting of formalities

8.53 The requirements for registration and for the meeting of formalities is one area in which the law relating to overseas civil partnerships differs from the law relating to overseas marriage. It is clear from the Civil Partnership Act that there must have been a registration, and the provisions of the Family Procedure Rules 2010 set out above are indicative of the nature and degree of the proof of registration that will be required for an overseas relationship to be treated as a civil partnership. It is also specifically stated that all of the requirements necessary to ensure the formal validity of the relationship in the relevant country must be met.

8.54 In contrast, marriage does not have a statutory definition requiring registration where it takes place overseas, and whilst in general private international law operates to provide that a marriage which complies with local requirements as to ceremony and form will be formally valid in England and Wales,[110] there is a legal presumption in English common law which operates to create a valid marriage even where the necessary formalities have not been complied with:[111]

'6. Presumption from cohabitation without ceremony

Where a man and woman have cohabited for such a length of time, and in such circumstances, as to have acquired the reputation of being man and wife, a lawful marriage between them will be presumed, even if there is no positive evidence of any marriage ceremony having taken place, particularly where the relevant facts have occurred outside the jurisdiction; and this presumption can be rebutted only by strong and weighty evidence to the contrary.'

8.55 There is no such legal presumption in respect of civil partnership and it is doubtful, in the light of the extensive statutory requirements for an overseas relationship to be recognised as a civil partnership set out in the Civil Partnership Act 2004 that there will be any scope for treating an overseas relationship as a civil partnership under English law, where it has not been registered in accordance with local law or has not met all of the requirements necessary in that country to ensure the formal validity of that relationship. Section 54 of the Civil Partnership Act 2004 does however give some scope for

---

[108] FPR 2010, PD 7A, para 3.5.
[109] Section 1 of the Evidence (Foreign, Dominion and Colonial Documents) Act 1933. Proof and effect of foreign dominion and colonial registers and certain official certificates.
[110] Dicey & Morris *Conflict of Laws* (14th edn), Chapter 17.
[111] Halsbury's Laws of England Volume 72 (2009) 5th edn Matrimonial and Civil Partnership Law, para 6.

an overseas relationship being treated as a 'voidable' civil partnership in England and Wales if it would be 'voidable' under the law of the country in which it is was registered.[112]

8.56 There is clearly a high degree of responsibility placed on couples seeking to formalise same sex relationships abroad to ensure that all necessary formalities required by the law of the relevant country are complied with, and to ensure that the laws of that country meet the 'general conditions' required by s 212 of the CPA 2004. In all cases it would be advisable to seek guidance from a local matrimonial lawyer and the official registration body before embarking upon registration overseas to ensure that the law and procedural requirements of that country are complied with.

Capacity

8.57 Section 215 of the CPA 2004 provides that an overseas relationship is only to be treated as a civil partnership if both people entering into it had capacity to do so under the 'relevant law' – ie the law of the country where the relationship is to be registered. This contrasts with marital law – the issue of capacity is to be determined by reference to English law rather than the law of the country in which the civil partnership was registered.[113] This variation arises because the Civil Partnership Act codifies the law relating to civil partnerships whereas matrimonial law is largely common law.

- If there is a potential issue regarding capacity, it will be essential to take advice from a lawyer in the relevant country as to whether the parties have capacity.

- Capacity relates to not only the mental capacity to enter into the relationship, but also factors such as degrees of consanguinity and affinity.

- The starting point then is that the couple must have capacity, of whatever kind, under the law of the country where they are to register the partnership.[114]

8.58 In addition:

- The relationship must meet the general conditions set out above, which mean the relationship must not be bigamous or capable of being bigamous under the local law.[115]

---

[112] CPA 2004, s 54(8) 'The Civil Partnership is voidable if the overseas relationship is voidable under the relevant law'. Section 54(10) 'relevant law means the law of the country or territory where the overseas relationship is registered'.

[113] Dicey & Morris *Conflict of Laws* (14th edn), Chapter 17.

[114] CPA 2004, s 215(1).

[115] CPA 2004, s 214(a).

- If either party is domiciled in England and Wales, neither of them must be under 16.[116]

- If either party is domiciled in England and Wales, they must not be within the degree of relationship prohibited by Sch 1 of the CPA 2004.[117]

- Section 54 together with s 50 of the CPA 2004 provide an overriding provision that any civil partnership registered overseas is voidable in England & Wales if:

  (a) either of them did not consent to its formation (whether as a result of duress, mistake, unsoundness of mind or otherwise);

  (b) at the time of its formation either of them, though capable of giving a valid consent, was suffering (whether continuously or intermittently) from mental disorder of such a kind or to such an extent as to be unfit for civil partnership;

  (c) at the time of its formation, the respondent was pregnant by some other person than the applicant [for a decree of nullity];

  (d) an interim gender recognition certificate under the Gender Recognition Act 2004 (c 7) has, after the time of its formation, been issued to either civil partner;

  (e) the respondent is a person whose gender at the time of its formation had become the acquired gender under the 2004 Act.

- There is also an overriding and general provision in relation to all overseas relationships in s 218 of the CPA 2004 that:

  'Two people are not to be treated as having formed a civil partnership as a result of having entered into an overseas relationship if it would be manifestly contrary to public policy to recognise the capacity, under the relevant law, of one or both of them to enter into the civil partnership.'

8.59 In respect of capacity and in particular issues such as whether a person consented to the civil partnership being registered or was suffering from a mental disorder to such an extent as to be unfit for civil partnership, the law relating to capacity to marry is likely to be treated as providing guidance. Cases of significance are as follows.

Re P (Forced Marriage)[118]

8.60 Baron J found that the wife's free will was overborne because she was isolated and ostracised by her own family. She was made to feel that she was letting her parents down by her attitude and that she was not behaving honourably. Her travel documents and phone had been removed and she was effectively marooned in Pakistan. As such she had no effective choice but to

---

[116] CPA 2004, s 217(2).
[117] CPA 2004, s 217(2).
[118] [2011] EWHC 3467 (Fam).

follow the wishes of her family. Therefore, she did not give a valid consent to this marriage which was forced upon her. Hers was not reluctant consent. It was no consent at all. A decree of nullity was granted.

Hirani v Hirani[119]

8.61 The wife sought a degree of nullity on the ground that she had entered into the marriage under duress. The Court of Appeal held that the crucial question was whether the threats or pressure were such as to overbear the will of the individual and destroy the reality of consent; duress, whatever form it took, was a coercion of the will so as to vitiate consent

Sheffield City Council v E and S[120]

8.62 The appropriate test is whether the party has the capacity to understand what a contract of marriage is and the duties and responsibilities normally attached to a marriage in general. The issue is not whether a person has the capacity to understand the consequences of marriage to a particular individual.

City of Westminster v IC (By His Friend The Official Solicitor) and KC and NN[121]

8.63 The court refused to recognise the marriage of a vulnerable adult who was functioning at the level of a 3-year-old. He had married by telephone whilst in England to a woman in Bangladesh and the marriage was capable of being valid in Bangladesh but was not entitled to recognition here. There was an issue in that case, the marriage having been conducted by telephone, as to which country the marriage took place in, but in any event, if it was conducted in England it did not comply with the requirements of English law and if it was conducted in Bangladesh there were powerful public policy grounds for refusing recognition.

Effect of overseas relationship being treated as a civil partnership

8.64 If an overseas relationship is treated as a civil partnership as a result of the provisions of ss 212–218 of the Civil Partnership Act, in terms of legal rights and responsibilities arising from the relationship, they will be no different to a civil partnership registered in England and Wales, and in reality no different to a marriage entered into in England and Wales. This is not the same for all of the other countries which permit civil partnerships to be registered; there may be a very limited number of consequences arising from registering a civil partnership in some countries. The European Court of Human Rights in the case of *Schalk and Kopf v Austria*[122] recognised that different States afford different degrees of legal recognition for registered partnerships between same sex couples, and held that the signatory States 'enjoy a certain margin of

---

[119] (1983) 4 FLR 232.
[120] [2004] EWHC 2808 (Fam).
[121] [2008] EWCA Civ 198.
[122] Application No 30141/04 Judgement 24 June 2010.

appreciation as regards the exact status conferred by alternative means of recognition'. In other words it is permissible for signatory states to differentiate between the rights afforded to a same sex couple in a registered partnership and a married couple in a way that the UK does not. In 'Central Europe' the UK, Germany, Austria, Ireland and The Netherlands, allow a registered partnership an equal degree of protection as marriage. Belgium, Switzerland, Luxembourg and France currently offer registration of same sex partnerships without affording the couple the same degree of protection as a marriage.[123]

8.65 It is particularly significant for foreign nationals or residents who entered into a civil partnership overseas to be aware that whatever the limited rights and obligations arising from that relationship in the country of registration, in the UK they will be treated as having entered into a civil partnership carrying all the rights and responsibilities afforded by UK law to that relationship.

Checklist for recognition in England and Wales of overseas relationships

8.66 The relationship was registered:

- in a country on the Sch 20 list; or

- in a country which recognises same sex unions and:

  (a) does not allow the registration if either party is married or already a registered partner; and
  (b) provides for the registration to endure indefinitely; and

- is between 2 people of the same sex who are not within the prohibited degrees of relationship; and

- both people had the capacity to enter the relationship under local law; and

- local requirements for formalities were complied with.

RECOGNITION OVERSEAS OF ENGLISH CIVIL PARTNERSHIP

8.67 There is no uniformity of approach overseas to civil partnerships registered in the UK. This includes no uniformity of approach within the European Union. EC Council Regulation 2201/2003 concerning jurisdiction and the recognition and enforcement of judgements in matrimonial matters and the matters of parental responsibility (BIIR) specifically provides that it

---

[123] Swennen & S Eggermont (2011) Legal Recognition of Same Sex Couples in Central Europe.

does not apply to questions linked to the status of persons,[124] ie it does not provide for recognition and enforcement of decisions as to status within the European Union.

8.68 Within the European Union, Council Regulation (EC) No 4/2009 covers all maintenance obligations arising from a family relationship, parentage or affinity in order to guarantee equal treatment of all maintenance creditors.[125] However, it is also made clear in the regulations that it determines only the law applicable to maintenance obligations and does not determine the law applicable to the establishment of the family relationships are based, which continues to be covered by the national laws of the Member States.[126]

8.69 The one area in which there is some degree of cross border recognition of same sex relationships is that of freedom of movement. The Citizenship (Free Movement) Directive[127] which concerns the rights of citizens of the Union and their family members to move and reside freely within the territory of the Member States of the European Union provides:

> 'The right of all Union citizens to move and reside freely within the territory of the Member States should, if it is to be exercised under objective conditions of freedom and dignity, be also granted to their family members, irrespective of nationality. For the purposes of this Directive, the definition of "family member" should also include the registered partner if the legislation of the host Member State treats registered partnership as equivalent to marriage.'

8.70 In effect, this directive attempts to guarantee the rights of civil partners or those in same sex marriages to reside in the same country as their spouse or civil partner within the European Union even if they are not European citizens. The rights extend to the position of the non-citizen spouse or civil partner in the event of the EU citizen's death or the divorce of the spouses or partners.[128] An unmarried or unregistered partner does not automatically fall within these provisions, the status of the relationship will therefore be important.

8.71 The lack of an international approach causes particular difficulty when considering where a civil partnership can be dissolved. If the couple enter into civil partnership in the UK but move to a country where it is not recognised they are likely to be unable to dissolve their partnership in the country of habitual residence. In recognition of this difficulty, in addition to the ordinary rules of jurisdiction to determine an application for dissolution of a civil partnership,[129] s 221 of the CPA 2004 opens up the possibility of the courts of England and Wales hearing an application for dissolution where the two people concerned registered as civil partners of each other in England or Wales and

---

[124] Recital 10 to the Regulation.
[125] Recital (11) EC 4/2009.
[126] Recital (21) EC 4/2009.
[127] 2004/38/EC.
[128] Articles 12 and 13 Directive 2004/38.
[129] Provided for in the Civil Partnership Jurisdiction and Recognition of Judgments) Regulations 2005.

fall outside the ordinary rules if it appears to be in the interests of justice for the court to assume jurisdiction.[130] This issue is discussed further below in relation to dissolution of civil partnership.

International recognition generally

8.72 In relation to civil partnerships registered overseas, problems may still arise for a couple if they no longer reside in the country where the partnership was registered, do not habitually reside in England and Wales, and do not reside in a country where their partnership is recognised. They may find themselves unable to obtain dissolution without at least one of them returning to live in the country where they registered the civil partnership, or without becoming habitually resident in the UK. If this is impossible for immigration reasons, they may find themselves unable to legally separate or claim financial provision from each other.

8.73 This is an important consideration to bear in mind if planning a civil partnership overseas. The parties planning a civil partnership who may move internationally should consider in particular how they own their property and whether their partnership should be supported by executing a trust.

8.74 If the civil partners are considering entering into an agreement making provision in the event of breakdown of their relationship, including an agreement as to the country which would have jurisdiction to deal with an application for dissolution, nullity or separation, it would be necessary to take legal advice to ensure that jurisdiction could be accepted by the country of choice.

Dissolution and the property consequences

8.75 The lack of uniformity in recognition of civil partnerships gives rise to further difficulties about where the property consequences of the dissolution of a civil partnership can be resolved, and about cross border recognition of decisions relating to the property consequences of dissolution. Within the European Union there is currently a draft council regulation to provide for the applicable law and the recognition of property consequences of registered partnerships intended to address these issues.[131] This is discussed further below in relation to dissolution of civil partnership, but this lack of uniformity is a further reason for choosing carefully where to register a civil partnership, and whether that civil partnership should be backed up by specific arrangements being made in relation to the ownership of property during the relationship.

---

[130] CPA 2004, s 221(1)(c).
[131] 2011/0060 (CNS).

DECLARATIONS AS TO CIVIL PARTNERSHIP STATUS

8.76   If there is a question as to whether a registered civil partnership is valid, or was valid on a particular date, an application can be made for a declaration as to the validity of the civil partnership. This includes civil partnerships entered into in other countries. If a declaration is made it is binding on 'Her Majesty and all other persons'.[132]

8.77   Section 58 of the CPA of the 2004 allows any person with sufficient interest to make an application for a declaration that the civil partnership in question:

(a)   was valid at the moment when it was created;[133]

(b)   was in existence on a particular date;[134]

(c)   was not in existence on a particular date.[135]

8.78   By this mechanism even a civil partnership which no longer exists or may no longer exist, but the existence of which at a particular time is crucial, can be declared to have been a valid civil partnership at the relevant time. This situation might arise, for example, if one of the parties to the civil partnership is deceased and the other party is seeking to secure provision from the deceased civil partner's estate.

8.79   In determining the validity at a particular time under the law of England and Wales of a civil partnership entered into overseas, it will be necessary for the court to consider the requirements for overseas relationships to be treated as a civil partnership in Part 5 of the CPA 2004 which is discussed above at **8.40** et seq.

8.80   In seeking to determine whether a civil partnership remains in existence, the question of whether it has already been dissolved in another country might arise. This could be significant, for example, to determine whether an application for financial provision could be issued in England and Wales. It sometimes occurs that one party makes an application for divorce or dissolution, intending also to make an application for financial provision, and the answer to the application states that the marriage or civil partnership has already been dissolved in another country.

8.81   Section 58 of the CPA 2004 also allows any person with sufficient interest to make an application for a declaration that either:

'(a)   A dissolution, annulment or legal separation obtained outside England and Wales is entitled to recognition in England and Wales, or

---

[132]   CPA 2004, s 59(2).
[133]   Section 58(1)(a) 'at its inception valid'.
[134]   Section 58(1)(b) 'subsisted on a date specified in the application'.
[135]   Section 58(1)(c) 'did not subsist on a date so specified'.

(b)   A dissolution, annulment or legal separation obtained outside England and Wales is not entitled to recognition in England and Wales.'

8.82 If an overseas dissolution, separation or nullity is not entitled to recognition, then this suggests that the civil partnership still exists under the law of England and Wales. However, it does not automatically follow that the court can then make a declaration that the civil partnership is valid; the court cannot make a declaration which has not been applied for when dismissing an application for a declaration which has.[136] If the respondent to an application for a declaration that a civil partnership has been dissolved overseas requires a declaration that the civil partnership remained in existence at a certain date, then they will also need to issue an application for the declaration which they ask the court to make.

8.83 An application for a declaration as to civil partnership status must be made in accordance with the provisions of the FPR 2010. In particular, Part 8 of the FPR 2010 contains the procedure for 'miscellaneous applications', specifically Chapter 5 of Part 8 applies to applications for declarations made in accordance with s 58 of the CPA 2004.

8.84 Form D70 is used to commence the application,[137] which may be made in the High Court or a county court.[138] The respondent(s) to the application will be just the other civil partner if the application is made by one of the civil partners, or both civil partners if the application is made by an interested third party.[139]

8.85 Whilst the rules say that the application should contain details of every person whose interest may be affected by the proceedings, there is no guidance as to what this might mean. It is to be expected that it means legal interest rather than emotional interest. An obvious example might be other beneficiaries under a will or other family members if the application is being made with a view to establishing the status of the civil partnership at the time of the death of one of the civil partners for the purposes of entitlement to inheritance or family provision. In that situation, if it was not made explicit to the court at the outset that the declaration was being sought for the purposes of establishing entitlement to an inheritance, the declaration might be rendered vulnerable if granted without the other beneficiaries being given notice.

8.86 By default, the Part 19 of the FPR 2010 procedure applies to applications for declarations of status, although this is not obvious from Part 8 or Part 19. The application form D70 is not particularly well tailored to the Part 19 procedure which makes particular provision for the contents of the application and the filing and serving of written evidence. The notes to *The*

---

[136]   CPA 2004, s 59(3).
[137]   FPR 2010, PD 5A.
[138]   FPR 2010, r 8.19.
[139]   FPR 2010, r 8.20.

Family Court Practice 2011 under Part 8 of the FPR 2010 are particularly useful in bringing together the requirements of Part 8, Form D70, Part 19 and PD 19A.

8.87   Any written evidence on which the applicant seeks to rely should be filed at the same time as the application.[140] PD 19A of the FPR 2010 gives further guidance as to the filing and serving of written evidence, in particular the requirement for a statement of truth if the evidence is not in the form of a statement or affidavit. The requirements elsewhere in the FPR 2010 regarding written evidence and statements of truth must be complied with.

8.88   Particularly of note for respondents to an application for a declaration are the provisions of rr 19.5 and 19.6 of the FPR 2010 which state expressly that if a respondent fails to file an acknowledgement of service within 14 days of the application being served on him or her, the respondent may not take part in the hearing of the application unless the court gives permission. There is also a requirement for the respondent to file their written evidence at the same time as the acknowledgement of service and serve it on the other party.[141]

8.89   If either party has not filed and served their written evidence in accordance with the provisions of Part 19, they may be prevented from relying on that evidence at the final hearing.[142]

8.90   In addition to the general provisions of Part 19 the court may give other case management directions when the application for a declaration is issued and fix a hearing date.[143] These directions might include provision for further evidence if necessary or appropriate, and if the issue relates to the validity of an overseas civil partnership or dissolution, nullity or separation this may include provision for expert evidence as to the law and formalities of that jurisdiction as they relate to civil partnership. Part 25 of the FPR 2010 and PD 25A must be followed carefully if expert evidence is required.

CIVIL PARTNERSHIP: VALID, VOID, VOIDABLE?

8.91   For all of the consequences of civil partnership to flow, it must either be validly registered according to the law of England and Wales, or treated as a civil partnership by virtue of being validly registered overseas. If the requirements of the Civil Partnership Act 2004 are not complied with then either:

(a)   the civil partnership will be void;

(b)   the civil partnership will be voidable;

---

[140]   FPR 2010, r 19.7.
[141]   FPR 2010, r 19.7(3).
[142]   FPR 2010, r 19.8.
[143]   PD 19A, para 4.

(c)   the relationship will not be treated as a civil partnership.

This part aims to explain the differences between and the consequences of each of these possibilities.

8.92   Where the requirements for formation of a civil partnership set out above have not been followed, both in terms of eligibility and/or procedure, this may render the civil partnership void or voidable. There are also other specified circumstances in which a civil partnership is void or voidable. The importance of meeting all of the statutory requirements cannot, therefore be overstated.

8.93   A **void** civil partnership is one which is treated as though it never took place and never existed and by analogy with a void marriage does not need any form of order or decree to dissolve or annul it in order for it to be non-existent.[144] However, the court may grant a decree of nullity in respect of a void civil partnership.[145]

8.94   A **voidable** civil partnership is one which can be annulled, and which a court will treat as existing and having existed[146] until it is annulled. The court may grant a decree of nullity in respect of a voidable civil partnership.[147]

8.95   An overseas relationship may be void or voidable,[148] or it may simply not be treated as any civil partnership at all if it does not fall within the definition of overseas relationship in s 212 of the CPA 2004, for example it was not registered. In those circumstances there is **no recognition** of the existence that relationship, it is not treated as a civil partnership, and no legal rights or responsibilities flow in England and Wales and no decree may be granted in respect of it.

8.96   The extent of the financial remedy which a court would grant in the exercise of its discretion if a civil partnership is void is unclear because of lack of judicial precedent to date, but it is unlimited by statute. Rule 2.3 of the FPR 2010 defines a civil partnership order means 'one of the orders mentioned in s 37 of the 2004 Act'. Section 37 provides for dissolution orders, nullity orders, presumption of death orders and separation orders. A civil partnership order would include a nullity order which annuls a civil partnership which is void.[149] Rule 9.4 of the FPR 2010 provides that an application for a financial order may be made in an application for a civil partnership order as defined in r 2.3. The court can therefore make a financial order on granting any of the orders in s 37 of the CPA 2004.

---

[144]   *R v Algar* [1954] 1 QB 279 at 287.
[145]   CPA 2004, s 37(1)(b).
[146]   CPA 2004, s 37(3).
[147]   CPA 2004, s 37(1)(b).
[148]   CPA 2004, s 54(7) and (8).
[149]   CPA 2004, s 37(1)(b).

Grounds on which civil partnership is void

8.97 Section 49 of the CPA provides:

'Where two people register as civil partners of each other **in England and Wales**, the civil partnership is void if –

    (a)   at the time when they do so, they are not eligible to register as civil partners of each other under Chapter 1 (see section 3),

    (b)   at the time when they do so they both know –

        (i)   that due notice of proposed civil partnership has not been given,

        (ii)   that the civil partnership document has not been duly issued,

        (iii)   that the civil partnership document is void under section 17(3) or 27(2) (registration after end of time allowed for registering),

        (iv)   that the place of registration is a place other than that specified in the notices (or notice) of proposed civil partnership and the civil partnership document, ...

        (v)   that a civil partnership registrar is not present, or

        (vi)   that the place of registration is on premises that are not approved premises although the registration is purportedly in accordance with section 6(3A)(a), or

    (c)   the civil partnership document is void under paragraph 6(5) of Schedule 2 (civil partnership between child and another person forbidden).'

8.98 In addition, where two people register as civil partners in Scotland or Northern Ireland, the civil partnership is void if it would be void in Scotland under s 123 of the CPA or in Northern Ireland under s 173 of the CPA.[150] In Scotland a civil partnership is void if they were not eligible or did not consent, and in Northern Ireland, if they were not eligible or the necessary formalities not complied with.

8.99 Where two people have registered an apparent or alleged relationship overseas, it will be void if it does not fall within the definition of an overseas relationship, or the parties are not treated as having formed a civil partnership under Chapter 2 of Part 5.[151]

8.100 In essence, this means that the civil partnership **will be void** if:

• the people were not of the same sex according to English law at the time of registering the civil partnership;[152]

• either of the two people was already in a civil partnership or marriage at the time of registration;[153]

---

[150] CPA 2004, s 54.

[151] CPA 2004, s 54(7).

[152] CPA 2004, s 3 and s 216 unless a full gender recognition certificate is issued to a person who has registered an overseas relationship s 216 of the CPA 2004.

[153] CPA 2004, s 3.

- the civil partnership was registered in the UK, or was registered overseas but either of them was domiciled in England and Wales, and either of them was under 16;[154]

- the civil partnership was registered in the UK, or was registered overseas but either of them was domiciled in the UK, and their relationship is within the prohibited degrees of relationship (ie they are relatives in a relationship appearing on the list in Sch 1 to the CPA);[155]

- the procedural formalities have not been complied with[156] wherever it took place;

- the civil partnership was registered overseas, but in a country which allows civil partnership to take place even where one of the parties is already in a marriage or civil partnership;[157]

- the civil partnership was registered overseas, but the law of the country where it was registered did not provide for the relationship created to treat the parties as married or a couple for indeterminate duration;[158]

- the civil partnership was registered overseas and either one of the parties did not have capacity to register it under the law of the country where it was registered[159] or it would be contrary to public policy to recognise the capacity of one or both of them to register it.[160]

8.101 The Lord Chancellor has the jurisdiction to validate a void civil partnership where it was registered in England or Wales if there has been some error of procedure relating to the registration itself,[161] but not otherwise.

8.102 Section 50 of the CPA provides:

'50 Grounds on which civil partnership is voidable in England & Wales

(1) Where two people register as civil partners of each other in England and Wales, the civil partnership is voidable if –

    (a) either of them did not validly consent to its formation (whether as a result of duress, mistake, unsoundness of mind or otherwise);

---

[154] CPA 2004, s 3 and s 217.
[155] CPA 2004, s 3 and s 217.
[156] As set out in Chapter 1 of the CPA 2004 or if it was registered overseas if the partners did not meet all the requirements necessary to ensure the formal validity of the relationship in the relevant country per s 215 of the CPA.
[157] CPA 2004, s 214.
[158] CPA 2004, s 216.
[159] CPA 2004, s 215.
[160] CPA 2004, s 218.
[161] CPA 2004, s 53 and s 49(b).

(b)   at the time of its formation either of them, though capable of giving a valid consent, was suffering (whether continuously or intermittently) from mental disorder of such a kind or to such an extent as to be unfitted for civil partnership;

(c)   at the time of its formation, the respondent was pregnant by some person other than the applicant;

(d)   an interim gender recognition certificate under the Gender Recognition Act 2004 (c 7) has, after the time of its formation, been issued to either civil partner;

(e)   the respondent is a person whose gender at the time of its formation had become the acquired gender under the 2004 Act.'

8.103 These grounds do not include one of the key grounds for nullity in relation to a marriage, that of non-consummation. In other words, it will not be open to a civil partner to seek to annul a civil partnership on the grounds that the other civil partner has not engaged in sexual relations with them since the partnership were registered. There are evidently issues of definition surrounding what constitutes non-consummation of a same sex relationship which are different to those affecting a relationship between two people of different sexes. It remains to be seen whether this distinction is retained if the law is changed to allow two people of the same sex to marry.

8.104 In reality, if a civil partnership is voidable, the only persons who this needs to concern are the parties to the civil partnership. If neither of them seeks a nullity order, then it will not affect their status vis a vis each other or third parties. The status of 'voidable' is rather like a separate ground for bringing the civil partnership to an end which does not depend on meeting the grounds for dissolution. The primary significance of being able to seek to annul the civil partnership instead of dissolving it is that a court can annul (but not dissolve) a civil partnership during the first year of the partnership.[162]

8.105 In line with this there are time bars placed on seeking to annul a civil partnership.

• 	If it is sought to annul it on grounds that either partner was suffering from a mental disorder, or either of them did not validly consent to its formation, or the respondent was pregnant by some other person, then the nullity proceedings must be started within 3 years of the registration.[163]

---

[162] CPA 2004, s 41 but note that s 165 of the CPA 2004 imposes a time bar so that no application for a dissolution order may be made before the end of the period of 2 years from the date of formation of the civil partnership in Northern Ireland.

[163] CPA 2004, s 51(2) unless leave has been granted to extend the 3 year period on grounds that the applicant has during the 3 year period suffered from a mental disorder – s 51(3) of the CPA 2004.

- If it is sought to annul it on grounds that an interim gender recognition certificate has been issued, the proceedings must be instituted within 6 months of the issue of the certificate.[164]

8.106 In addition, the court cannot annul a civil partnership on grounds that the respondent was pregnant by another person or had changed gender prior to the civil partnership unless the court is satisfied that the applicant did not know about these things at the time of the formation of the civil partnership.[165]

8.107 The court is also prohibited from making a nullity order if the respondent to the application for the order satisfies the court that the applicant led them to reasonably believe that they would not seek a nullity order.[166]

8.108 In reality, therefore, the court is only likely to make a nullity order within the 1 year period during which dissolution is prohibited if something emerges post registration of which the applicant was not aware at the time of the civil partnership.

BREAKDOWN OF A CIVIL PARTNERSHIP

Application for dissolution in England and Wales

8.109 There are four different orders which a court can make to bring an end to a civil partnership:[167]

(a) a dissolution order on the ground that the civil partnership has broken down irretrievably;

(b) a nullity order where the civil partnership is void or voidable (discussed above);

(c) a presumption of death order which dissolves a civil partnership on grounds that one of the civil partners is presumed to be dead;

(d) a separation order which provides for the separation of the civil partnership.

Collectively, these are called civil partnership orders.

Grounds for dissolution

8.110 Where the civil partnership has irretrievably broken down, this is the only ground for seeking dissolution. If the civil partnership has not

---

[164] CPA 2004, s 51(5).
[165] CPA 2004, s 51(6).
[166] CPA 2004, s 51(1).
[167] CPA 2004, s 37.

irretrievably broken down, the court can still make a separation order and then go on to make a dissolution order at a later date.[168] A separation order is still a 'civil partnership order' which allows the court to make financial provision. A further application for financial provision could be made if there were a later application for dissolution, but the financial order made on separation would carry considerable weight. Financial provision on separation and dissolution is discussed in chapter 9.

8.111   Where the court is asked to dissolve a civil partnership, there is additionally a requirement in s 44 of the CPA 2004 to satisfy the court of particular facts in support of the contention that it has broken down, and the court must not grant the dissolution unless the facts are demonstrated:

(a)   that the respondent has behaved in such a way that the applicant cannot reasonably be expected to live with him or her;

(b)   that the partners have lived continuously apart for at least 2 years immediately preceding the application and the respondent consents to the partnership being dissolved;

(c)   that the partners have lived continuously apart for the 5 years immediately preceding the application;

(d)   that the respondent has deserted the applicant for a continuous period for at least 2 years immediately pre-ceding the making of the application.

8.112   The question of what constitutes separation or unreasonable behaviour will be the same as for divorce, since the provisions in the CPA 2004 mirror the provisions of the MCA 1974 in this respect. The only distinction is that adultery is not a fact on which an applicant can rely in asserting that a relationship has broken down for the purposes of obtaining a dissolution. However there is nothing to prevent the formation by one party of an intimate relationship with another person being cited as evidence of unreasonable behaviour.

Application procedure

8.113   Part 7 of the FPR 2010 sets out the procedure for applications for any civil partnership order for dissolution, nullity or separation and bears detailed reading to ensure all procedural requirements are complied with. The rules for starting proceedings are the same for civil partnership orders as they are for matrimonial orders.

8.114   Provided the courts of England and Wales have jurisdiction to entertain an application for a civil partnership order (see **8.124** below), civil partnership

---

[168]   CPA 2004, s 46.

proceedings may be started in any court which is designated as a 'Civil Partnership Proceedings County Court'.[169] It does not have to be a court near to where either of the parties live.

8.115 Civil partnership proceedings, like other family proceedings, are started when the court issues an application at the request of the applicant.[170] The application is started by using form D8 for dissolution or separation, D8D for presumption of death and dissolution and D8N for nullity.[171]

8.116 Form D8 replaced the divorce petition when the FPR 2010 came into force in April 2011 and the same form is used whether the application is for a matrimonial order or civil partnership order. The form must contain sufficient particulars of the facts on which the applicant relies to demonstrate the grounds for a civil partnership order for the court to be satisfied that the criteria are met. It must be accompanied by a copy of the civil partnership certificate.[172]

8.117 In an application for a civil partnership order, the only respondent will ordinarily be the other partner[173] since adultery is not a ground for dissolution. If there is an intimate relationship with a third party it is not necessary or indeed possible to rely on grounds of adultery in order to cite that relationship as evidence of the breakdown of the parties' relationship. It is not necessary to name the third party on the application for dissolution or separation, but r 7.10(3) of the FPR 2010 allows for the possibility that a person named as having formed an 'improper association' with the respondent could become a party to the application. The naming of third parties in this way is generally discouraged by the court and by PD 7A, para 2.1 unless the applicant believes that the respondent is likely to object to the application for separation or dissolution: ie if the relationship is likely to be denied and it becomes necessary to prove it.

8.118 A respondent wishing to make a cross application for a civil partnership order, say on different grounds, may do so pursuant to r 7.12 of the FPR 2010.

8.119 Every dissolution, nullity or presumption of death order made is, in the first instance, a conditional order[174] and cannot be made final before 6 weeks have passed from the making of the conditional order unless the court orders a shorter period.[175] A conditional order is the civil partnership equivalent of a decree nisi in matrimonial proceedings.

---

[169] FPR 2010, r 7.5.
[170] FPR 2010, r 5.3(1).
[171] FPR 2010, PD 5A.
[172] PD 5A and PD 7A.
[173] FPR 2010, r 7.10.
[174] CPA 2004, s 37(2).
[175] CPA 2004, s 48(1) and (5).

8.120 An application may be made to the court to make a conditional order or separation order at any time after the time for filing an acknowledgement of service or answer has expired provided the other party has not indicated an intention to defend the application.[176] If the court is satisfied that the applicant is entitled to the conditional order or decree of separation, and it is not defended, the court will certify this and list the application before a district judge for the decree or conditional order to be made in open court.[177] If it is defended then the court will list it for case management and give directions.[178] Before the court grants a conditional decree, it must consider the arrangements for the children of the family, and consider in particular whether it should make arrangements for the child to be represented.[179]

8.121 Once the court has made a conditional order, either civil partner may apply to the court for that order to be rescinded on grounds that the parties have reconciled.[180] A party may also apply to the court for an order that the conditional order should not be made final.[181] This latter is more appropriate to be used not where the parties have reconciled, but where there is real prejudice to the applicant arising from the making of a final order such as loss of entitlement to a widow(ers) pension on dissolution pending financial provision being made.

8.122 The civil partner who obtained the conditional order can give notice to the court that (s)he wishes it to be made final, and r 7.32 of the FPR 2010 applies. If the notice is given more than 12 months after the conditional order is made there are additional requirements for information to be provided to the court.[182] The other partner may make an application to the court for the conditional order to be made final if the applicant for the conditional order has not done so.[183]

8.123 Only on the making of the final dissolution or nullity order does the civil partnership cease to exist, and only on the making of the final dissolution, separation or nullity order can an order for financial provision be effective.[184] However, an order for financial provision can be made following a conditional order, and orders for interim periodical payments or an interim lump sum for the benefit of a child can be made even prior to a conditional order.[185] This is discussed further below in chapter 9 in relation to financial provision.

---

[176] FPR 2010, r 7.19.
[177] FPR 2010, rr 7.16 and 7.20.
[178] FPR 2010, r 7.20.
[179] FPR 2010, r 7.25 and CPA 2004, s 63 and CA 1989, s 41: in practice this would be a extremely rare course for the court to take.
[180] FPR 2010, r 7.28.
[181] FPR 2010, r 7.31.
[182] FPR 2010, r 7.32(3).
[183] FPR 2010, r 7.33.
[184] CPA 2004, Sch 5, paras 1 and 4.
[185] CPA 2004, Sch 5, paras 1 and 2.

Jurisdiction of the courts of England and Wales to consider an application for dissolution, separation or nullity

8.124 The provisions of Council Regulation EC 2201/2003 (BIIR) do not apply on the breakdown of a civil partnership to regulate the country in which a civil partnership can be dissolved. The question of whether the courts of England and Wales have jurisdiction to entertain an application for dissolution is therefore governed solely by domestic law in the form of s 219 of the CPA 2004 and the regulations made under that section. However, the same jurisdictional basis as for applications on the breakdown of marriage have been adopted by the UK government[186] so that the provisions of EC 2201/2003 BIIR are effectively adopted for civil partnerships for the purposes of determining when the courts of England and Wales have jurisdiction.

8.125 The regulations provide:[187]

'1 The courts in England and Wales shall have jurisdiction in relation to proceedings for the dissolution or annulment of a civil partnership or for the legal separation of civil partners where –

(a)   both civil partners are habitually resident in England and Wales;

(b)   both civil partners were last habitually resident in England and Wales and one of the civil partners continues to reside there;

(c)   the respondent is habitually resident in England and Wales;

(d)   the petitioner is habitually resident in England and Wales and has resided there for at least one year immediately preceding the presentation of the petition; or

(e)   the petitioner is domiciled and habitually resident in England and Wales and has resided there for at least six months immediately preceding the presentation of the petition.'

8.126 If the civil partners do not fall within reg 1(a)–(e) above but one of the civil partners is domiciled in England and Wales, or the civil partnership was registered in England and Wales and the court considers it is in the interests of justice for the court to assume jurisdiction, then the court can deal with an application for dissolution.[188]

8.127 This provision is intended to deal with the situation where the civil partners cannot get a dissolution in the country in which they are now living, but they have sufficient links with this jurisdiction, either because one (or both) of them is domiciled here or because they registered the partnership here, to make it in the interests of justice that the courts of England and Wales should be able to dissolve the partnership.

8.128 This provision is only necessary because of the lack of cross border recognition for civil partnerships which leaves some people in the position of

---

[186]   Pursuant to CPA 2004, s 219.

[187]   Civil Partnership (Jurisdiction and Recognition of Judgments) Regulations 2005, SI 2005/3334.

[188]   CPA 2004, s 221.

not being able to dissolve their civil partnership at all because no country has jurisdiction to entertain the application if they are no longer living in the country where they registered the partnership. If the partnership was not registered in England and neither party is domiciled in England, some partners will still find themselves in the position of having a civil partnership which is incapable of dissolution.

8.129   In addition, in cases of application for nullity, if the civil partner who was domiciled in this country or habitually resident here has died, the court may have jurisdiction.[189]

Jurisdiction: applications in more than one country

8.130   As a result of EC Council Regulation 2201/2003 not being applicable to civil partnerships, a further issue arises, namely which court has jurisdiction if proceedings for dissolution have been issued in more than one country? The Family Procedure (Civil Partnership: Staying of Proceedings) Rules 2010 have been implemented to address this situation. The applicant for a civil partnership order (dissolution, nullity, separation) is under a duty to provide the court with information about any proceedings in another jurisdiction which are capable of affecting the validity or substance of the civil partnership[190] – this would include ongoing proceedings for dissolution, nullity or separation ongoing in another jurisdiction.

8.131   Firstly, the rules provide for the proceedings in England and Wales to be mandatorily stayed (on the application of one of the parties) if there are already proceedings for dissolution ongoing in another country and that is the country where the parties last lived together at the date the proceedings were issued, or before the proceedings were issued and either of them had been habitually resident there for a year prior.

> **'Obligatory stays of civil partnership proceedings**
>
> **3** (1) Paragraph (2) applies if, in proceedings for a dissolution order, a party to the civil partnership applies before the beginning of the trial for an order that the proceedings be stayed.
>
> (2) Subject to rule 5(3), the court will order that the proceedings be stayed if it appears to the court that –
>
> > (a)   in respect of the same civil partnership, proceedings for the dissolution or annulment of the civil partnership are continuing in a related jurisdiction;
> > (b)   the parties to the civil partnership have lived together after its formation;
> > (c)   the place where they lived together –
> > (i) on the date when the proceedings before the court were begun, or
> > (ii) if they did not live together at that date, where they last lived together before those proceedings were begun, is in that jurisdiction; and

---

[189]   CPA 2004, s 221(2).

[190]   Family Procedure (Civil Partnership: Staying of Proceedings) Rules 2010, SI 2010/2986, reg 2.

(d)   either of those parties was habitually resident in that jurisdiction throughout the year ending with the date on which they last lived together before the proceedings before the court were begun.

(3) This rule applies to proceedings only so far as they are for a dissolution order.'

8.132 Where the case does not fall within the category of requiring an obligatory stay under r 3, the court may order a stay nonetheless on the application of one of the parties where fairness demands, under the provisions of r 4:

Discretionary stays of civil partnership proceedings

'4(1) Paragraph (2) applies, subject to paragraph (5), where, before the beginning of the trial in any civil partnership proceedings, it appears to the court that –

(a)   any relevant proceedings are continuing in another jurisdiction, and
(b)   the balance of fairness (including convenience) as between the parties to the civil partnership makes it appropriate for the proceedings in that jurisdiction to be disposed of before further steps are taken –
  (i)   in the proceedings before the court, or
  (ii)   in those proceedings so far as they are a particular kind of civil partnership proceedings

(3) In considering the balance of fairness and convenience for the purposes of paragraph (1)(b), the court will have regard to all factors appearing to be relevant, including the convenience of witnesses and any delay or expense which may result from the proceedings being stayed, or not being stayed.'

8.133 The court may also make directions of its own motion if it considers that the issue of granting a stay ought to be considered by the court in circumstances where proceedings are pending in another jurisdiction.[191]

8.134 The provisions of the Family Procedure (Civil Partnership: Staying of Proceedings) Rules 2010 largely mirror the provisions of the Domicile and Matrimonial Proceedings Act 1973 (which have long governed the issue of matrimonial proceedings in competing jurisdictions in cases which are not governed by EC Regulation 2201/2003 (BIIR) and therefore similar considerations are likely to apply where the court has a discretion whether to grant a stay. However, there may be an added dimension in civil partnership cases attributable to the lack of uniformity between states and countries as to the legal rights and responsibilities arising from being in a civil partnership as compared to a marriage, and it remains to be seen whether this issue will feature in the court's assessment of the balance of fairness.

8.135 Also similarly to the provisions of the Domicile and Matrimonial Proceedings Act 1973, the Family Procedure (Civil Partnership: Staying of Proceedings) Rules 2010 make provision for interim financial orders in specified circumstances even whilst the proceedings in England and Wales are

---

[191]   FPR 2010, r 7.27.

stayed.[192] The stay may be discharged on application where the proceedings in the other jurisdiction have concluded or are not being proceeded with promptly.[193]

8.136   Although the law of England and Wales provides for circumstances in which an application for a stay can be made if proceedings are ongoing in another jurisdiction, other jurisdictions may not provide equivalent provisions. Council Regulation EC 2201/2003[194] provides for the court second seised of matrimonial proceedings to grant an automatic stay, which does not apply to civil partnerships. If there are civil partnership proceedings ongoing in two jurisdictions, the other jurisdiction may not have a mechanism for staying civil partnership proceedings ongoing here, or the case may not fall within their mechanisms. This gives rise to the potential for conflicting orders in different jurisdictions, and further issues as to which jurisdiction should deal with issues of financial provision following the dissolution, nullity or separation.

Recognition of dissolution, nullity and legal separation between different countries

8.137   As indicated above, there is little uniformity between countries regarding the status and effect of registered same sex partnerships ranging from illegality through partial recognition to complete assimilation of same sex partnership and marriage, even within Europe. As a result, there is a corresponding lack of uniformity regarding the status and effect of dissolution of same sex partnership and marriage, and for dealing with the property consequences of registered partnerships.

8.138   Sections 233–238 of the CPA 2004 deal with the issue of recognition of orders for dissolution, annulment and separation in terms of:

- recognition between the different parts of the UK of orders dissolving, annulling or legally separating parties obtained in the UK;

- recognition in the UK of orders dissolving, annulling or legally separating parties obtained outside the UK.

8.139   The law of England and Wales cannot make provision for the recognition in other countries of orders obtained in the UK,[195] and there is as yet no EC uniformity. In particular, EC law does not presently provide for:

- the status of a registered same sex partnership to be recognised;

---

[192]   SI 2010/2986, regs 6–9.
[193]   SI 2010 /2986, reg 5.
[194]   Article 17.
[195]   Unless it enters into an international treaty or convention with another country.

- a regime for determining which member states have jurisdiction to dissolve, annul or legally separate a same sex partnership which is not a marriage;

- cross border recognition of dissolution, annulment or legal separation orders between EU states;

- a regime for determining which member states have jurisdiction to deal with the property consequences of same sex partnerships and the dissolution, annulment or legal separation of registered partners.

8.140 In fact, the provision for cross border recognition in Europe differs from the position in relation to marriage only in that EC Regulation 2201/2003 makes specific provision for which member states have jurisdiction to deal with an application for divorce, legal separation or marriage annulment. The regulation only applies to the 'dissolution of matrimonial ties' and not with issues such as the grounds for a divorce or property consequences of divorce.[196] The regulation is also not concerned with 'questions linked to the status of persons',[197] ie the issue of whether two people are married at all is a question for individual member states, and not within the scope of this regulation.

8.141 It is to be remembered that presently in England and Wales a same sex marriage contracted in another country is recognised only as a civil partnership here. Therefore, the fact that a same sex couple has entered into a Netherlands same sex marriage does not mean EC Regulation 2201/2003 entitles them to apply for a divorce in England if, for example, they are habitually resident here. Equally, if same sex marriage becomes valid in the UK, it will not necessarily be recognised as a marriage elsewhere.

8.142 However, the EC Maintenance Obligations Regulation 4/2009[198] does provide for cross border recognition of decisions and court settlements as to maintenance obligations arising from family relationships in general without specifically providing for the recognition of the relationships themselves, and without distinction as to what the nature of that relationship is:[199]

'**Article 22**
No effect on the existence of family relationships

The recognition and enforcement of a decision on maintenance under this Regulation shall not in any way imply the recognition of the family relationship, parentage, marriage or affinity underlying the maintenance obligation which gave rise to the decision.'

---

[196] Paragraph 8 of the preamble to EC Regulation 2201/2003.
[197] Paragraph 10 of the preamble to EC Regulation 2201/2003.
[198] [2009] OJ L7/1.
[199] EC Regulation 4/2009 has been in force in the UK since 20/6/11 and relates to decisions or authentic instruments from that date. Decisions prior to that date remain within the regime of Brussels I: EC Regulation 44/2001.

The EU maintenance regulation 4/2009[200] also determines which member states have jurisdiction to deal with an application for maintenance arising from a relationship, parentage, marriage or affinity.

8.143 The particular impact of EC Regulation 4/2009 in the context of same sex partnerships is:

(a) If a UK court makes an order for periodical payments,[201] or an order which otherwise falls within the definition of 'maintenance'[202] requiring one partner to make provision for the other or for a child of the family, this will fall within EC Regulation 4/2009 and be enforceable in another member state, even if that member state does not recognise the same sex relationship, legal parenthood or dissolution of civil partnership which underlies the UK decision. An order for periodical payments on dissolution of a civil partnership in England would therefore be enforceable in Greece even if Greece does not recognise the civil partnership.

(b) The Regulation allows[203] parties who are not spouses to agree in writing that the court in which one of them is habitually resident, or of which one of them is a national, shall have jurisdiction to settle any disputes as to maintenance obligations.[204] Obviously that would be dependent upon the member state which the parties agree should have jurisdiction having provision within its national law to deal with the issues at large. But if, for example, one civil partner is English and the other is German they could enter into a pre-nuptial agreement to the effect that Germany will be the jurisdiction to deal with disputes as to maintenance between them on dissolution.

(c) The Regulation sets out which member states shall have jurisdiction to deal with matters relating to maintenance obligations.[205] There might be more than one country having jurisdiction in that civil partnership. Dissolution may have been obtained in England, but the paying party is

---

[200] [2009] OJ L7/1.

[201] Or if there is an administrative decision, or separation agreement or other 'authentic instrument' within the meaning of Art 48 EC Reg 4/2009.

[202] The definition of maintenance is not confined to orders for periodical payments: *Van den Boogaard v Laumen* Case C220/95 [1997] 2 FLR 399 at para 22: '[If] a provision awarded is designed to enable one spouse to provide for himself or herself or if the needs and resources of each of the spouses are taken into consideration in the determination of its amount, the decision will be concerned with maintenance. On the other hand, where the provision awarded is solely concerned with dividing property between the spouses, the decision will be concerned with rights in property arising out of a matrimonial relationship and will not therefore be enforceable under the Brussels Convention. A decision which does both these things may, in accordance with Art 42 of the Brussels Convention, be enforced in part'.

[203] But not in relation to children who are under the age of 18: Article 4(3) EC Regulation 4/2009.

[204] Article 4(1)(a) and (b) EC Regulation 4/2009.

[205] Article 3 EC Regulation 4/2009.

habitually resident in Germany, under the regulation both countries would have jurisdiction to deal with the maintenance obligations arising as a result of the relationship.

8.144 There is currently a proposal for a council regulation on jurisdiction, applicable law and the recognition and enforcement of decisions regarding the property consequences of registered partnerships pending.[206] The aim of the proposal is to 'establish a comprehensive set of rules of international private law applicable to the property consequences of registered partnerships'.[207] This proposal makes reference to a separate proposal pending to deal with the recognition and enforcement of decisions in matters of matrimonial property regimes.

8.145 Key aspects of the proposed regulation if it comes into force are:

- The applicable law in determining the property consequences of registered partnerships would be the law of the country where the partnership is registered (proposed Art 15).

- One member state should have jurisdiction to deal with all aspects of the partners' separation (proposed Art 4).

- A member state should not be able to refuse to recognise a decision dealing with the property consequences of a registered partnership on grounds that the state does not recognise the partnership itself (Preamble to the proposed regulation).

Recognition in the UK

8.146 A dissolution, annulment or separation of a civil partnership obtained in one part of the UK is to be recognised throughout the UK.[208]

8.147 The Civil Partnership Act 2004 specifically provides that the fact that a dissolution or annulment granted in the UK would not be recognised outside the UK does not prevent the parties from forming a subsequent marriage or civil partnership within the UK.[209] In other words, dissolving here a civil partnership which was entered into in another jurisdiction allows the ex-civil partners to form new civil partnerships here without that being bigamous even if the country in which they entered into the first civil partnership does not recognise that it has been dissolved by the English court. However, the new civil partners may find that their relationship is not recognised in another country which does not recognise the dissolution of the first civil partnership.

---

[206] Brussels 16.3.11 COM (2011) 127 Final.
[207] Paragraph 3.1 of the explanatory memorandum to the proposal.
[208] CPA 2004, s 233, subject to the validity of the civil partnership itself being established and subsisting.
[209] CPA 2004, s 238.

8.148   An order for the dissolution or annulment of a civil partnership or the legal separation of civil partners in Belgium, Cyprus, Czech Republic, Denmark, Germany, Greece, Spain, Estonia, France, Hungary, Ireland, Italy, Latvia, Lithuania, Luxembourg, Malta, Netherlands, Austria, Poland, Portugal Slovakia, Slovenia, Finland and Sweden can be recognised in the UK without special formality.[210]

8.149   The courts of England and Wales can, however, refuse to recognise the dissolution or annulment or legal separation:

- if the validity of the civil partnership itself is in issue, or if it was no longer in existence at the time of the apparent dissolution, annulment or separation;[211]

- if one of the civil partners was not given proper notice of the proceedings or a proper opportunity to participate in the proceedings;[212]

- if there is no official document certifying that the judgement is effective under the law of the country where it was obtained, or under the law of the country where either civil partner was domiciled.[213]

8.150   If there has been a dissolution, annulment or legal separation in another country outside the UK not in the list above appearing in the Civil Partnership (Jurisdiction and Recognition of Judgements) Regulations 2005, then ss 235–237 of the Civil Partnership Act 2004 apply to determine whether the dissolution, annulment or legal separation will be recognised.

- If a dissolution, annulment or legal separation has been obtained outside the UK by means of proceedings[214] whether judicial or other proceedings,[215] it is to be recognised if;

- it is effective under the law of the country in which it was obtained;[216] and

---

[210] Civil Partnership (Jurisdiction and Recognition of Judgments) Regulations 2005, SI 2005/3334, regs 6 and 7. The regulations are made under s 219 of the CPA 2004.

[211] Regulation 8(1) and (2) of SI 2005/3334.

[212] Regulation 8(3)(a) of SI 2005/3334.

[213] Regulation 8(3)(b) of SI 2005/3334.

[214] CPA 2004, s 235 largely mirrors s 46 of the Family Law Act 1986 in respect of recognition of an overseas divorce, annulment or legal separation. The relevant jurisprudence regarding what constitutes a divorce, annulment or separation obtained 'by proceedings' and whether it is 'effective under the law of the country in which it was obtained' is likely to be applied to determine whether dissolution, annulment or legal separation of a civil partnership fulfils the same criteria.

[215] CPA 2004, s 237(5). See in particular *H v H* [2007] 1 FLR 1318 regarding the meaning of proceedings.

[216] See in particular *Kellman v Kellman* [2000] 1 FLR 785 for the meaning of 'effective'.

- at the date of the proceedings commencing[217] one of the civil partners was either habitually resident, domiciled[218] in or a national of the country in which it was obtained.

8.151 If the dissolution, annulment or legal separation was not obtained by proceedings, then it may still be recognised[219] if:

- it is effective under the law of the country in which it was obtained; and

- either both civil partners were, at the date of the dissolution, annulment or legal separation[220], domiciled in the country where it was obtained, or one of them was and the other was domiciled in a country which recognises it as valid;[221] and

- neither of them was habitually resident in the UK for 1 year prior to the dissolution, annulment or legal separation.[222]

These provisions for cross border recognition are all subject to the validity of the civil partnership itself, and its continuance until the date when the dissolution annulment or legal separation to be recognised was effective.[223]

8.152 What will be apparent from these provisions is that it is not open to civil partners who are UK nationals and habitually resident here to go an obtain a dissolution in another country not on the approved list and then ask for it to be recognised in England and Wales: there is scope for cross border recognition only where the dissolution, annulment or legal separation is obtained in a country with which the partners have a close connection of residence, nationality or domicile or it is an approved country.

Ability to apply for financial provision following overseas dissolution

8.153 Where the courts of England and Wales do recognise a divorce, annulment or dissolution obtained outside the UK, a secondary issue often arises as to which country should deal with the financial consequences of the breakdown of that relationship. As discussed above, there are proposals but currently no uniformity for regulating that situation. England and Wales has its own domestic provisions for determining, however, when the courts of England and Wales will entertain an application for financial provision following an overseas dissolution, annulment or legal separation.

---

[217] CPA 2004, s 235(3).
[218] Domicile is to be determined by the law of the country or part of the UK in question: CPA 2004, s 237(1).
[219] CPA 2004, s 235(2).
[220] CPA 2004, s 235(3)(b).
[221] CPA 2004, s 235(2)(b)(ii).
[222] CPA 2004, s 235(2)(c).
[223] CPA 2004, s 236.

8.154 Schedule 7 to the Civil Partnership Act 2004 sets out the framework for financial relief in England and Wales after overseas dissolution, annulment or legal separation of a civil partnership.

8.155 First, the provisions only apply if the overseas dissolution, annulment or legal separation are entitled to recognition in England and Wales.[224] Interestingly, the provisions also apply even if the dissolution, annulment or legal separation was obtained before the Civil Partnership Act came into force.[225]

8.156

- Either civil partner can make an application for financial relief in England and Wales, even if an order has been made in another country requiring one of the civil partners to make a payment or transfer of property to the other,[226] provided that:

- the applicant has not entered into a new civil partnership or marriage with someone else;[227] and

- the court has given leave for the application to be made;[228] and[229]

- either one of the civil partners was domiciled in England and Wales on the date when leave was applied for or on the date when the overseas dissolution, annulment or separation took effect in that country; or

- either of the civil partners was habitually resident in England and Wales throughout the period of one year ending on the date when leave was applied for, or ending with the date when the overseas dissolution, annulment or separation took effect in that country; or

- either or both of the civil partners had a beneficial interest in a dwelling house in England and Wales at the date when leave was applied for, and it was a house which was at some time the home of the civil partners.

8.157 In imposing a requirement for leave to be obtained, Sch 7 of the CPA 2004 mirrors the provisions of Part III of the Matrimonial and Family Proceedings Act 1984 which deals with applications for financial provision after overseas divorce, annulment or legal separation of a marriage.

8.158 Insofar as an application for financial provision following an overseas dissolution, divorce or annulment or legal separation relates to maintenance

[224] CPA 2004, Sch 7, para 1(1)(b).
[225] CPA 2004, Sch 7, para 1(2).
[226] CPA 2004, Sch 7, para 4(3).
[227] CPA 2004, Sch 7, para 3.
[228] CPA 2004, Sch 7, para 4.
[229] CPA 2004, Sch 7, para 7(1)–(5)

obligations, then the jurisdiction of the court to entertain the application pursuant to the provisions of Sch 7 to the CPA 2004 must be considered together with the provisions of EC Regulation 4/2009. The Matrimonial and Family Proceedings Act 1984, s 15 (which is the counterpart of para 7 in Sch 7 to the CPA 2004) states explicitly that the fact that England and Wales has jurisdiction pursuant to Council Regulation EC 44/2001, which was superseded by Regulation EC 4/2009 in matters relating to maintenance obligations obviates the need for the requirements of s 15 to be satisfied. Schedule 7 to the CPA 2004 is silent on this issue. By analogy, it would appear that if England and Wales has jurisdiction to hear matters relating to maintenance obligations between civil partners as a result of the operation of EC Regulation 4/2009, then the domestic tests as to jurisdiction in para 7 of Sch 7 to the CPA 2004 are automatically met or superseded. Equally, the scope and extent of orders for financial provision which the court of England and Wales can make may be limited by a pre-existing decision in respect of maintenance made in another Member State which falls within EC Regulation 4/2009.

8.159 The procedure for applications for leave to apply for orders for financial provision is the same whether based in divorce or dissolution, namely in accordance with Chapter 6 of Part 8 of the FPR 2010. The application must be made to the Principal Registry in accordance with Part 18 procedure[230] and the application for leave may be made without notice to the other civil partner.[231] The court must not grant leave to apply unless it considers that there is a 'substantial ground'[232] for the making of the application for such an order.[233]

8.160 If leave is granted, the respondent can apply to set aside the grant of leave, but by analogy with the provisions of the MFPA, an application to set aside will only succeed if the applicant for an order setting aside the leave 'can deliver a knockout blow'.[234]

8.161 Even if leave is granted, however, the court can decline to exercise its discretion to make an order for financial relief at all. Paragraph 8 of Sch 7 to the CPA 2004 imposes a duty on the court to consider whether England and Wales is the appropriate venue for the application, and the court is required by that provision to have regard to:

(a) the connection which the civil partners have with England and Wales;

(b) the connection which they have with the country where the civil partnership was dissolved annulled or separated;

---

[230] FPR 2010, r 8.24.
[231] FPR 2010, r 8.25.
[232] The UKSC Held in the case of *Agbaje v Agbaje* [2010] UKSC 13 the principal object of the filter mechanism is to prevent wholly unmeritorious claims being pursued to oppress or blackmail a former spouse. The threshold is not high, but is higher than 'serious issue to be tried' or 'good arguable case' found in other contexts. It is perhaps best expressed by saying that in this context 'substantial' means 'solid'.
[233] CPA 2004, Sch 7, para 4(2).
[234] *Agbaje v Agbaje* [2010] UKSC 13 per Lord Collins.

(c)   the connection which they have with any other country outside England and Wales;

(d)   any 'financial benefit' which the applicant or a child of the family has received or is likely to receive in a country outside England and Wales as a result of the dissolution, annulment or legal separation;

(e)   any financial relief order already made in another country and the extent to which it is likely to be complied with;

(f)   any right of the applicant to apply for financial relief in any other country and the reasons for which they have not exercised that right;

(g)   the availability of property in England in relation to which orders could be made;

(h)   the enforceability of any order made here under Sch 7;

(i)   the length of time since the dissolution, annulment or separation.

8.162 If the court does exercise its discretion to make financial provision, then paras 9–17 of Sch 7 set out the orders which the court can make and the factors which the court must take into account when considering which orders to make, corresponding with Sch 5 to the CPA 2004, which is discussed in more detail below in the chapter dealing with financial provision.[235]

8.163 It is to be expected that the court in applications for financial provision following overseas dissolution, annulment or separation will exercise its discretion to grant leave or make provision in line with the existing jurisprudence relating to Part III of the Matrimonial and Family Proceedings Act 1984. However, there is an added dimension in civil partnership cases because of the lack of uniformity of approach to civil partnerships worldwide, and the lack of provision for international recognition. The ability of either civil partner to apply for or enforce financial relief in another country may well be more circumscribed than if they were married, and this may impact upon the court's assessment of whether to grant leave or whether to make an order taking into account the hardship which might otherwise ensue and having regard to the principles in the Supreme Court decision in the case of *Agbaje*.[236]

8.164 Whilst the jurisdiction to make financial orders following overseas divorce or dissolution operates on the basis that there is to be respect for overseas orders, and comity between international jurisdictions, the court will exercise its discretion where otherwise injustice would occur.

---

[235] Note that the jurisdiction to make Sch 5 orders is more circumscribed where the court only has jurisdiction because of a dwelling house in this country: CPA 2004, Sch 7, para 9.
[236] [2010] UKSC 13.

8.165 One example of a recent matrimonial case in England and Wales where financial provision after a German divorce was granted is the case of *Schofield v Schofield*[237] in which relief was granted on appeal because the German Court which had dealt with the divorce had been unable to make a pension sharing order in relation to one spouse's substantial UK army pension. The German court had implicitly invited the English court to deal with this aspect of the family financial provision. It could be inferred from this decision that if financial provision on dissolution of a civil partnership in another country were limited by reason of a distinction between the rights of married couples and civil partners in that country, the English court might well entertain an application for financial provision here.

---

[237] [2011] EWCA Civ 174.

Chapter 9

FINANCIAL PROVISION ON THE BREAKDOWN OF CIVIL PARTNERSHIP

OVERVIEW

9.1 The Civil Partnership Act 2004 (CPA 2004) makes provision for financial relief on the breakdown of civil partnerships which corresponds to the relief available to married parties under the Matrimonial Causes Act 1973 (MCA 1973) and the Domestic Proceedings and Magistrates Court Act 1978 (DPMCA 1978). The 2004 Act does this expressly: s 72(1) of the Act sets out that Sch 5 of the Act 'makes provision for financial relief in connection with civil partnerships that corresponds to provision made for financial relief in connection with marriages by Part 2' of the MCA 1973. Section 72(3) deals with Sch 6 and states that it provides relief that corresponds to that made in connection with marriages by the DPMCA 1978. Section 72(4) refers to Sch 7 to the CPA 2004, which sets out the relief available when a civil partnership has been brought to an end by an order made overseas.

9.2 These Schedules provide the framework for financial provision which is intended as the main form of remedy when a civil partnership has come to an end. The CPA 2004 does however permit the courts to make some decisions in relation to civil partnership property outside that framework.

9.3 Section 66 of the CPA 2004 makes provision for the court (High Court or county court) to have jurisdiction 'in any question between the civil partners in a civil partnership as to title to or possession of property'. This section is the CPA's equivalent of s 17 of the Married Women's Property Act 1882 which gives the courts a similar jurisdiction in the case of husband and wife. Neither section gives the court any power to transfer property from one partner to the other; it simply permits the court to declare what the partners' rights are in relation to a particular property issue.[1] Section 17 should not be used in a case where the proper course is to apply for financial relief under the MCA 1973: *Fielding v Fielding*.[2] The same principle applies to s 66.

9.4 If a situation arises where civil partners need to obtain a declaration from the court as to strict property rights between themselves, s 66 provides a procedure for obtaining such a declaration. If an application is made under

---

[1] '... the question for the court was – "Whose is this" and not – "To whom shall this be given."' per Lord Morris in *Pettitt v Pettitt* [1969] 2 All ER 385.

[2] [1978] 1 All ER 267.

s 66 the court has the power, in addition to making a declaration as to ownership, to order the return or restitution of property to the civil partner who is declared to be the owner. The court also has the power to order the sale of property.[3]

9.5   Section 66 extends not just to real property but also covers chattels and property held in the form of money. Section 67(1) of the CPA 2004 permits application to be made in relation to money or other property to which the applicant is beneficially entitled. This includes money which has arisen as the proceeds of sale of property in which the applicant has an interest. If the court finds that the partner holding the money has not made to the applicant 'such payment or disposition as would have been appropriate in the circumstances' the court can make an order for payment by the other party to the applicant of such sum in respect of the money or of the value of the property as the court considers appropriate.[4]

9.6   Sections 66 and 67 apply to the partners to an existing civil partnership. Section 68 permits applications can be made under ss 66 and 67 by former civil partners (whose partnership has been dissolved or annulled) provided that the application is made within three years of the dissolution or annulment.

FINANCIAL PROVISION ON DISSOLUTION FOR CIVIL PARTNERS

Schedule 5

9.7   The financial relief available to a civil partner under Sch 5 falls into two categories: that which can be granted by the court 'on making a dissolution, nullity or separation order' or at any time thereafter; and that which can be granted before an order has been made.

9.8   The orders which can be made on making an order for dissolution, nullity or separation or at any time thereafter are:

(a)   An order that one civil partner make periodical payments to the other.

(b)   An order that one civil partner make secured periodical payments to the other.

(c)   An order that one civil partner pay a lump sum to the other.[5]

(d)   A property adjustment order – this includes: an order that one civil partner transfer property to the other civil partner, to a child of the family, or to any person for the benefit of a child of the family; an order

---

3   CPA 2004, s 66(2).
4   CPA 2004, s 67(4) and (5).
5   Which may be made payable by instalments.

for the settlement of property for the benefit of the other civil partner or for a child of the family, or both; an order varying a relevant settlement for the benefit of the civil partners or a child of the family, or extinguishing the interest or either of the civil partners under a relevant settlement.[6]

(e) An order for the sale of property in which either of the civil partners has a beneficial interest; the court has the power to make other directions in relation to the sale to determine matters such as which partner has conduct of the sale, and to establish if necessary a price-fixing mechanism.

(f) A pension sharing order providing for one civil partner's shareable rights under a pension scheme to be transferred, wholly or in part, to the other partner. Such an order can be made in relation to shareable rights under an occupational pension scheme, a personal pension scheme, a retirement annuity contract, and an annuity which has been purchased to give effect to rights under an occupation or personal pension scheme, and the state pension scheme.

(g) A pension compensation sharing order; this order may be made if one civil partner has received shareable rights to Pension Protection Fund Compensation.

If any of the above orders is made on the making of a conditional order for dissolution or nullity, it does not take effect until the order is made final.

9.9 If the court makes an order against one civil partner in favour of the other civil partner it is required to consider 'whether it would be appropriate to exercise those powers in such a way that the financial obligations of each civil partner towards the other will be terminated as soon after the making of the dissolution or nullity order as the court considers just and reasonable.'[7] In addition if the court makes a periodical payments order against one civil partner in favour of the other civil partner it is required to consider 'whether it would be appropriate to require the payments to be made or secured only for such term as would in its opinion be sufficient to enable [the recipient] to adjust without undue hardship to the termination of [the recipient's] financial dependence on the other civil partner.' If a court dismisses an application for periodical payments the court may dismiss the application and direct that the applicant is not entitled to make any application for periodical payments in future.

---

[6] 'Relevant settlement' is defined by Sch 5, para 3 as a settlement made on the partners during the subsistence of the civil partnership or in anticipation of the partnership being entered into. The ability to vary settlements is therefore limited; the court cannot use this provision to attack pre-existing family trusts, for example.

[7] CPA 2004, Sch 5, para 23(2).

9.10   Similar provisions exist in the MCA 1973.[8] The court has the power, on an application by either party, to make provision for the payment of periodical payments on an interim basis, pending the making of an order for dissolution, nullity or separation.[9]

Provision for children of the family[10]

9.11   The court can make any of the following orders in relation to a child of the family at any time after proceedings for dissolution, separation or nullity have commenced:

(a)   An order that one of the civil partners make periodical payments to the child of the family or to another person for the benefit of a child of the family.

(b)   An order that one of the civil partners make secured periodical payments to the child of the family or to another person for the benefit of a child of the family.

(c)   An order that one of the civil partners pay a lump sum[11] to a child of the family or to another person for the benefit of a child of the family.

Matters to be taken into account

9.12   In deciding whether to make any of the above orders and what order to make the court 'must have regard to all the circumstances of the case, giving first consideration to the welfare, while under 18, of any child of the family who has not reached 18'.[12] After that, the court 'must in particular have regard to':[13]

'(a)   the income, earning capacity, property and other financial resources which each civil partner –
(i)   has, or
(ii)   is likely to have in the foreseeable future,
including, in the case of earning capacity, any increase in that capacity which it would in the opinion of the court be reasonable to expect a civil partner in the civil partnership to take steps to acquire;
(b)   the financial needs, obligations and responsibilities which each civil partner has or is likely to have in the foreseeable future;

---

[8]   MCA 1973, s 25A.
[9]   CPA 2004, Sch 5, para 38.
[10]   CPA 2004, s 75 provides that a 'child of the family' for the purposes of the Children Act and the CPA, in relation to 'two people who are civil partners of each other, means – (a) a child of both of them, and (b) any other child, other than a child placed with them as foster parents by a local authority or voluntary organisation, who has been treated by both of them as a child of their family.'
[11]   Which may be made payable by instalments.
[12]   CPA 2004, Sch 5, para 20.
[13]   CPA 2004, Sch 5, para 21(2).

(c)   the standard of living enjoyed by the family before the breakdown of the civil partnership;

(d)   the age of each civil partner and the duration of the civil partnership;

(e)   any physical or mental disability of either of the civil partners;

(f)   the contributions which each civil partner has made or is likely in the foreseeable future to make to the welfare of the family, including any contribution by looking after the home or caring for the family;

(g)   the conduct of each civil partner, if that conduct is such that it would in the opinion of the court be inequitable to disregard it;

(h)   in the case of proceedings for a dissolution or nullity order, the value to each civil partner of any benefit which, because of the dissolution or annulment of the civil partnership, that civil partner will lose the chance of acquiring.'

These criteria are in the same terms as those contained in s 25 of the MCA 1973 and references in the case law to 'the section 25 criteria' must be construed accordingly as applying to the criteria in para 21 of Sch 5.

9.13   In considering whether to exercise any of its powers relating specifically to children the court 'must have particular regard to':[14]

'(a)   the financial needs of the child;

(b)   the income, earning capacity (if any), property and other financial resources of the child;

(c)   any physical or mental disability of the child;

(d)   the way in which the child was being and in which the civil partners expected the child to be educated or trained;

(e)   the considerations mentioned in relation to the civil partners in paragraph 21(2)(a), (b), (c) and (e).'

9.14   If the court is considering making an order in relation to a child against a civil partner who is not the parent of that child, the court must additionally have regard to:[15]

'(a)   whether A has assumed any responsibility for the child's maintenance;

(b)   if so, the extent to which, and the basis upon which, A assumed such responsibility and the length of time for which A discharged such responsibility;

(c)   whether in assuming and discharging such responsibility A did so knowing that the child was not A's child;

(d)   the liability of any other person to maintain the child.'

THE GENERAL APPROACH TO APPLICATIONS FOR PROVISION FOR CIVIL PARTNERS

9.15   The MCA 1973 and the CPA 2004 set out what orders the court can make and what matters should be taken into account, but they do not specify what the court is trying to achieve by making any of the orders. Section 72 gives

---

[14]   Schedule 5 para 22(2).
[15]   Schedule 5, para 22(3).

the court the power to make orders for 'financial relief' but this term is not defined. This gap has had to be filled by the courts.

9.16 The forerunner to the MCA 1973, the Matrimonial Proceedings and Property Act 1970, set out a similar list of criteria to those contained in s 25 of the MCA 1973, but contained in s 5(1) a direction that the court was to exercise its powers under that Act so '… as to place the parties, so far as it is practicable and, having regard to their conduct, just to do so, in the financial position in which they would have been if the marriage had not broken down and each had properly discharged his or her financial obligations and responsibilities towards the other.' That requirement was omitted from the MCA 1973 and nothing inserted in its place.

9.17 A series of cases decided by the higher courts since 2000 has sought to clarify what the court is trying to achieve by making an order under the MCA 1973 and the same principles apply to orders under Sch 5 of the CPA 2004. It appears from those cases that the court should seek to ensure fairness between the parties. This is not a synonym for equality. The court has to make an order which ensures that the parties are, at the end of their partnership, on a footing which does not discriminate between them. So if one partner has stayed at home and devoted himself to looking after the home and the children, and the other has advanced his career, they will be in very different positions when the relationship ends and the court will make different provision to reflect that.

9.18 Although many of the cases in which these principles have been considered in the last decade are 'big money' cases where the assets are far removed from those dealt with by the county courts on a day to day basis the basic approach is the same in all cases.

9.19 The starting point for this decade of debate was the decision of the House of Lords in *White v White*.[16] This case concerned a married couple who had spent the thirty years of their relationship running a farm. Their children were independent adults by the time the marriage came to an end. Their farming assets were in part acquired by purchase but in part derived from funds and assets made available by the husband's family. The principal farming asset was owned jointly by the husband and wife and they were partners in the business which ran it. Initially the wife was awarded a lump sum of £980,000, which was slightly more than one-fifth of the total assets. This provided her with funds to purchase a substantial house, with stabling and land for her horses, and left sufficient after the purchase of that property to provide her with an income for life of about £40,000 per annum. She was required to transfer her share in all the jointly owned assets to the husband. She appealed successfully to the Court of Appeal, who awarded her an additional £700,000. Her husband appealed to the House of Lords, and Mrs White cross-appealed seeking a half share in all the assets. Both appeals were dismissed.

---

[16]   [2000] 2 FLR 981, [2000] 3 FCR 555.

9.20 Lord Nicholls, giving the principal judgment, noted that there were no children requiring assistance and that the Whites were in the fortunate position of having more than enough assets to provide both of them with a home and income. Two other features were in his view notable: first, that there was an equality of contribution between Mr and Mrs White. She had brought up the children but also worked in many different ways on the farm. He had been a hard-working farmer. They had both been partners in the business partnership. Second, some of the assets had been purchased with the assistance of the husband's family.

9.21 Lord Nicholls noted the lack of any wording in s 25 of the MCA 1973 to guide the court as to the outcome it should be trying to achieve. He referred to the wording used in the legislation which preceded the MCA 1973 and said that:

'Implicitly, the objective must be to achieve a fair outcome. The purpose of these powers is to enable the court to make fair financial arrangements on or after divorce in the absence of agreement between the former spouses ... The powers must always be exercised with this objective in view, giving first consideration to the welfare of the children.'

9.22 He continued:

'Self-evidently, fairness requires the court to take into account all the circumstances of the case. Indeed, the statute so provides. It is also self-evident that the circumstances in which the statutory powers have to be exercised vary widely ... [T]he statutory jurisdiction provides for all applications for ancillary financial relief, from the poverty stricken to the multi-millionaire. But there is one principle of universal application which can be stated with confidence. In seeking to achieve a fair outcome, there is no place for discrimination between husband and wife and their respective roles. Typically, a husband and wife share the activities of earning money, running their home and caring for their children. Traditionally, the husband earned the money, and the wife looked after the home and the children. This traditional division of labour is no longer the order of the day. Frequently both parents work. Sometimes it is the wife who is the money-earner, and the husband runs the home and cares for the children during the day. But whatever the division of labour chosen by the husband and wife, or forced upon them by circumstances, fairness requires that this should not prejudice or advantage either party when considering para (f), relating to the parties' contributions. This is implicit in the very language of para (f): "... the contribution which each has made or is likely ... to make to the welfare of the family, including any contribution by looking after the home or caring for the family". If, in their different spheres, each contributed equally to the family, then in principle it matters not which of them earned the money and built up the assets. There should be no bias in favour of the money-earner and against the home-maker and the child-carer.

A practical consideration follows from this. Sometimes, having carried out the statutory exercise, the judge's conclusion involves a more or less equal division of the available assets. More often, this is not so. More often, having looked at all the circumstances, the judge's decision means that one party will receive a bigger share than the other. Before reaching a firm conclusion and making an order along these lines, a judge would always be well advised to check his tentative views against the yardstick of equality of division. As a general guide, equality should be departed from only if, and to the extent that, there is good reason for doing so. The need to consider and articulate reasons for departing from equality would help the parties and the court to focus on the need to ensure the absence of discrimination.

This is not to introduce a presumption of equal division under another guise. Generally accepted standards of fairness in a field such as this change and develop, sometimes quite radically, over comparatively short periods of time. The discretionary powers, conferred by Parliament 30 years ago, enable the courts to recognise and respond to developments of this sort. These wide powers enable the courts to make financial provision orders in tune with current perceptions of fairness. Today there is greater awareness of the value of non-financial contributions to the welfare of the family. There is greater awareness of the extent to which one spouse's business success, achieved by much sustained hard work over many years, may have been made possible or enhanced by the family contribution of the other spouse, a contribution which also required much sustained hard work over many years. There is increased recognition that, by being at home and having and looking after young children, a wife may lose for ever the opportunity to acquire and develop her own money-earning qualifications and skills. In *Porter v Porter* [1969] 3 All ER 640, 643–644, Sachs LJ observed that discretionary powers enable the court to take into account "the human outlook of the period in which they make their decisions". In the exercise of these discretions "the law is a living thing moving with the times and not a creature of dead or moribund ways of thought".

Despite these changes, a presumption of equal division would go beyond the permissible bounds of interpretation of s 25. In this regard s 25 differs from the applicable law in Scotland. Section 10 of the Family Law (Scotland) Act 1985 provides that the net value of matrimonial property shall be taken to be shared fairly between the parties to the marriage when it is shared equally or in such other proportions as are justified by special circumstances. Unlike s 10 of the Family Law (Scotland) Act 1985, s 25 of the 1973 Act makes no mention of an equal sharing of the parties' assets, even their marriage-related assets.[17] A presumption of equal division would be an impermissible judicial gloss on the statutory provision. That would be so, even though the presumption would be rebuttable.'

9.23 The question of the overall approach was considered again by the House of Lords in *Miller v Miller; Macfarlane v Macfarlane*[18] where appeals in two cases were heard together. The facts of both cases are far removed from everyday experience. *Miller* concerned a short childless marriage where at the time of the marriage the husband earned £1 million per annum and the wife about £85,000. During the marriage the wife gave up work to concentrate on running their two homes, and the husband changed jobs so that his salary reduced substantially but he acquired very valuable shares in his new firm. The

---

[17]   It should be noted that in the case of *Miller; Macfarlane* (see below) the Scottish Law Lord, Lord Hope, commented that the Scottish scheme for financial provision on divorce discriminated against partners who had given up their careers in favour of their families and required urgent reconsideration.

[18]   [2006] UKHL 24.

wife was awarded a lump sum of £5 million, the judge finding that the husband could not rely on the short (3 year) duration of the marriage because it was his bad behaviour which had caused it to end, and that the wife had an expectation of affluence. In *Macfarlane* the parties were married for 16 years and had three children. Both husband and wife were highly qualified professionals and earned about the same until the birth of the second child, when the wife stopped working in order to look after the children. The husband continued to advance in his career and his salary increased. There was insufficient capital to provide the wife with a clean break, so she was awarded periodical payments of £250,000 per annum on a joint lives basis,[19] amounting to one-third of the husband's net salary, although her income needs were about £128,000 per annum. This disparity was justified by the argument that the wife should have a share of the husband's future earning because they resulted from her efforts in looking after the family and supporting his career.

9.24 In *Miller* the husband appealed unsuccessfully to the Court of Appeal, and then to the House of Lords. In *Macfarlane*, there was an appeal from a district judge to a judge, who reduced the wife's periodical payments to £180,000. The wife appealed to the Court of Appeal who restored the award of £250,000 per annum but limited the order to a period of 5 years, after which the wife would have to reapply. The wife appealed to the House of Lords. Lord Nichols, again giving the lead judgment, set out some general principles:

'[4] Fairness is an elusive concept. It is an instinctive response to a given set of facts. Ultimately it is grounded in social and moral values. These values, or attitudes, can be stated. But they cannot be justified, or refuted, by any objective process of logical reasoning. Moreover, they change from one generation to the next. It is not surprising, therefore, that in the present context there can be different views on the requirements of fairness in any particular case.

[5] At once there is a difficulty for the courts. The Matrimonial Causes Act 1973 (the 1973 Act) gives only limited guidance on how the courts should exercise their statutory powers. Primary consideration must be given to the welfare of any children of the family. The court must consider the feasibility of a "clean break". Beyond this the courts are largely left to get on with it for themselves. The courts are told simply that they must have regard to all the circumstances of the case.

[6] Of itself this direction leads nowhere. Implicitly the courts must exercise their powers so as to achieve an outcome which is fair between the parties. But an important aspect of fairness is that like cases should be treated alike. So, perforce, if there is to be an acceptable degree of consistency of decision from one case to the next, the courts must themselves articulate, if only in the broadest fashion, what are the applicable if unspoken principles guiding the court's approach.

[7] This is not to usurp the legislative function. Rather, it is to perform a necessary judicial function in the absence of parliamentary guidance ...

---

[19] Until either of the parties should die, or until the court, on an application by either party, varies or discharges the order.

[8] For many years one principle applied by the courts was to have regard to the reasonable requirements of the claimant, usually the wife, and treat this as determinative of the extent of the claimant's award. Fairness lay in enabling the wife to continue to live in the fashion to which she had become accustomed. The glass ceiling thus put in place was shattered by the decision of your Lordships' House in the *White* case. This has accentuated the need for some further judicial enunciation of general principle.

[9] The starting point is surely not controversial. In the search for a fair outcome it is pertinent to have in mind that fairness generates obligations as well as rights. The financial provision made on divorce by one party for the other, still typically the wife, is not in the nature of largesse. It is not a case of "taking away" from one party and "giving" to the other property which "belongs" to the former. The claimant is not a supplicant. Each party to a marriage is entitled to a fair share of the available property. The search is always for what are the requirements of fairness in the particular case.

[10] What then, in principle, are these requirements? The statute provides that first consideration shall be given to the welfare of the children of the marriage. In the present context nothing further need be said about this primary consideration. Beyond this several elements, or strands, are readily discernible. The first is financial needs. This is one of the matters listed in s 25(2) of the 1973 Act, in para (b): "the financial needs, obligations and responsibilities which each of the parties to the marriage has or is likely to have in the foreseeable future".

[11] This element of fairness reflects the fact that to greater or lesser extent every relationship of marriage gives rise to a relationship of interdependence. The parties share the roles of money-earner, home-maker and childcarer. Mutual dependence begets mutual obligations of support. When the marriage ends fairness requires that the assets of the parties should be divided primarily so as to make provision for the parties' housing and financial needs, taking into account a wide range of matters such as the parties' ages, their future earning capacity, the family's standard of living, and any disability of either party. Most of these needs will have been generated by the marriage, but not all of them. Needs arising from age or disability are instances of the latter.

[12] In most cases the search for fairness largely begins and ends at this stage. In most cases the available assets are insufficient to provide adequately for the needs of two homes. The court seeks to stretch modest finite resources so far as possible to meet the parties' needs. Especially where children are involved it may be necessary to augment the available assets by having recourse to the future earnings of the money-earner, by way of an order for periodical payments.

[13] Another strand, recognised more explicitly now than formerly, is compensation. This is aimed at redressing any significant prospective economic disparity between the parties arising from the way they conducted their marriage. For instance, the parties may have arranged their affairs in a way which has greatly advantaged the husband in terms of his earning capacity but left the wife severely handicapped so far as her own earning capacity is concerned. Then the wife suffers a double loss: a diminution in her earning capacity and the loss of a share in her husband's enhanced income. This is often the case. Although less marked than in

the past, women may still suffer a disproportionate financial loss on the breakdown of a marriage because of their traditional role as home-maker and childcarer.

[14] When this is so, fairness requires that this feature should be taken into account by the court when exercising its statutory powers . . .

[15] Compensation and financial needs often overlap in practice, so double-counting has to be avoided. But they are distinct concepts, and they are far from co-terminous. A claimant wife may be able to earn her own living but she may still be entitled to a measure of compensation.

[16] A third strand is sharing. This "equal sharing" principle derives from the basic concept of equality permeating a marriage as understood today. Marriage, it is often said, is a partnership of equals ... This is now recognised widely, if not universally. The parties commit themselves to sharing their lives. They live and work together. When their partnership ends each is entitled to an equal share of the assets of the partnership, unless there is a good reason to the contrary. Fairness requires no less. But I emphasise the qualifying phrase: "unless there is good reason to the contrary". The yardstick of equality is to be applied as an aid, not a rule.

[17] This principle is applicable as much to short marriages as to long marriages . . . A short marriage is no less a partnership of equals than a long marriage. The difference is that a short marriage has been less enduring. In the nature of things this will affect the quantum of the financial fruits of the partnership.

[18] A different approach was suggested in *GW v RW (Financial Provision: Departure from Equality)* [2003] EWHC 611 (Fam), [2003] 2 FLR 108 at 121–122. There the court accepted the proposition that entitlement to an equal division must reflect not only the parties' respective contributions "but also an accrual over time": at 122, para [40]. It would be "fundamentally unfair" that a party who has made domestic contributions during a marriage of 12 years should be awarded the same proportion of the assets as a party who has made the domestic contributions for more than 20 years: para [43]. In *M v M (Financial Relief: Substantial Earning Capacity)* [2004] EWHC 688 (Fam), [2004] 2 FLR 236, at 252, para [55](7), this point was regarded as "well made".

[19] I am unable to agree with this approach. This approach would mean that on the breakdown of a short marriage the money-earner would have a head start over the home-maker and childcarer. To confine the *White* approach to the "fruits of a long marital partnership" would be to re-introduce precisely the sort of discrimination the *White* case was intended to negate.

[20] For the same reason the courts should be exceedingly slow to introduce, or re-introduce, a distinction between "family" assets and "business or investment" assets. In all cases the nature and source of the parties' property are matter to be taken into account when determining the requirements of fairness. The decision of Munby J in *P v P (Inherited Property)* [2004] EWHC 1364 (Fam), [2005] 1 FLR 576 regarding a family farm is an instance. But 'business and investment' assets can be the financial fruits of a marriage partnership as much as "family" assets.

The equal sharing principle applies to the former as well as the latter. The rationale underlying the sharing principle is as much applicable to "business and investment" assets as to "family' assets".'

9.25 The appeal in *Miller* was dismissed: although this was a short marriage the wife was entitled to some share in the assets, but she received significantly less than half because the assets had grown because of the husband's contacts and capacities. The appeal in *Macfarlane* was allowed and the five year period imposed on the periodical payments order by the Court of Appeal removed: the burden was on the husband to justify any reduction in the order. This was a 'paradigm case' for compensation because the wife had given up an established and highly paid career to devote herself to the family. The husband had surplus income after supporting himself, the wife, and their children, and she was entitled to an ongoing share in it, there being insufficient capital to buy out her entitlement.

9.26 Not long after the decision in *Miller; Macfarlane* another 'big money' case in which the principles the court applies were to be considered made its way to the Court of Appeal. In *Charman v Charman*[20] the parties had been married for 28 years and had two adult children. They had started the relationship without capital assets but the husband had been an exceptionally successful businessman and by the time of separation were about £131 million, including £68 million in an off-shore discretionary trust of which the husband was the beneficiary during his lifetime. The wife had not worked after their first child was born. She was awarded 35.5% of the assets; the husband appealed on the basis inter alia that this did not take into account sufficiently his extraordinary contribution to the acquisition of their fortune. In a lengthy judgment Sir Mark Potter, then President of the Family Division, suggested that the courts had moved since the decision in *White* only seven years previously from 'the yardstick of equality' to a principle that property should be shared equally unless there was a good reason to depart from it. The court suggested that the law in this area was in need of modernisation in the light of social and other changes and of the experience of applying it in practice.

9.27 In view of the fact that the legislation providing for financial relief on the ending other than by death of a civil partnership takes the same form as that providing for financial relief on divorce, it has been anticipated that the courts will broadly take the same approach in same-sex cases as has developed over the years in divorce cases. Anecdotal evidence suggests that this has generally been the position. As this work goes to press the decision of the Court of Appeal in *Gallagher v Lawrence* is awaited. The case concerns the ending of the partnership between a successful financial analyst and an actor whose work was intermittent and who during the relationship played the role of a homemaker to a large extent. The civil partnership lasted only seven months but there was a lengthy period of settled cohabitation beforehand bringing the total length of the relationship to 11 years. At first instance Parker J had included in the parties' assets a flat acquired by the financial analyst before the

---

[20]   [2007] EWCA Civ 503.

relationship began, which had substantially increased in value since it was purchased. This brought the parties' joint assets up to about £4 million, only £40,000 of which had been contributed by the actor (his life's savings). He received an award worth about £1.7 million. The analyst had contended that the previously acquired property should be excluded and that his former partner should have received only a share of the remaining assets, worth about £650,000, and he appealed the against Parker J's decision. One argument advanced before the Court of Appeal[21] was that same sex relationships are less likely to result in children and should therefore be treated as 'dual career' cases (it was conceded that where there were children the approach should be no different to that adopted in opposite sex cases.) It is anticipated that the Court of Appeal will clarify whether the approach in civil partnership cases is or is not identical to that in divorce cases and give some general guidance as to the proper approach.

9.28   Those cases which make their way into the law reports involving financial relief after the end of a marriage or civil partnership are usually those where significant amounts of money are involved and the parties have the incentive and the means to litigate matters in the High Court and thereafter on appeal. Although the same statutory criteria apply in every case regardless of the sums involved the assistance which can be derived from such cases when litigating the typical financial remedy application where there is insufficient income and capital to support two households is limited.

9.29   The broad nature of the court's discretion in these cases and the fact that what is being aimed at is 'fairness' in a general sense makes it very difficult for any lay person to have an idea as to how the assets should be divided at the end of a civil partnership. As Coleridge J said in one of the hearings in the lower courts in *Charman*: 'In a field as discretionary as this one, it is often hard to provide real guidance'.[22] Predicting what a court might do is an art rather than a science. Lawyers who practice in the field are through experience able to indicate the parameters within which a court is likely to make an award. Despite this uncertain framework the majority of people whose marriages or civil partnerships end in divorce or dissolution manage to divide their assets without the help of lawyers: in cases where there are no assets of substance there is nothing to argue about; where there are no children and the relationship has lasted for some time it may be easy for the parties to agree that equal division is a fair outcome. In other cases the lack of funds to litigate may force a solution which is not necessarily fair upon the parties.

---

[21]   Reported in *Daily Telegraph* 14 March 2012.

[22]   See also the comments of the national chair of Resolution (the solicitor's family law association) in March 2007 Fam Law, where he characterised the exercise as playing a board game where your entire assets and your children's futures are at stake, but where the rules are to be found on 'several tatty bits of paper with holes, blanks, crossings out and addendums, all made during the past 33 years' and that the 'while the game is in play, new rules will be made up'.

9.30 In every case the outcome will depend on how the court assesses the case against the criteria set out above, with first consideration being given to any children of the family. Subject to that, there are some areas where general guidance can be given.

First consideration to the children

9.31 Child support in the form of periodical payments will ordinarily be calculated in accordance with the child support formula and either paid voluntarily or dealt with through CMEC. The basis for this and the exceptions when periodical payments will be payable are dealt with in chapter 10.

Although there is a power to award a lump sum to or for the benefit of a child this will rarely be exercised; capital provision for children will only be ordered in exceptional cases.

9.32 The court's focus in any claim for a financial remedy where there are children to consider is to ensure that they are provided with suitable accommodation, that the person who has day to day care of them has sufficient to provide for their everyday needs (and for himself to the extent that his needs must be met in order for him to look after the children), and that there is some degree of security provided for them in that whatever arrangements are put in place should be capable of being maintained in at least the medium term.

9.33 In practical terms this is likely to result in a civil partner who has day to day care of the children being given priority in relation to the retention of housing. If there is a family home which is owned by one or both partners, but there is insufficient capital to rehouse both from that property, the partner with the children may, at least until the children reach their majority, be permitted to retain occupation of the property. If the partner with whom the children live has insufficient income to provide for the children, and cannot reasonably be expected to acquire additional income by working (for example, because the children are of pre-school age), the court will have to consider whether the other partner has the means to make periodical payments to alleviate the situation. The interaction between means-tested benefits, tax credits, income from part-time work, and periodical payments[23] complicates the position.

9.34 The statute requires first consideration to be given only to children of the family who have not reached the age of eighteen. Once the children have attained that age the court may regard them as being part of the 'circumstances' which have to be taken into account, or, if they are still dependent, as being one of the 'responsibilities' of one or both civil partners as set out in the criteria. In practice the courts are likely to take into account the fact that children may need to be supported financially and housed at least until completing a first degree. If a child in this position is a child of both civil partners, or has been treated as a child of the family for a lengthy period, this is

---

[23]   Benefits are discussed in detail in chapter 12.

likely to be regarded as a joint responsibility. Where this is the position and one civil partner is having to bear the responsibility without assistance from the other (and this imbalance is not justified by the other partner's finances), the court may make allowance for this in the orders which it makes between the civil partners.

9.35 The extent to which the court will make allowance in this way for adult children will also vary in accordance with the pressure that there is upon the civil partners' finances. If there is insufficient capital to rehouse both partners, the presence in the household of one partner of a young adult child, even if that adult child is likely to have difficulties finding his own accommodation, is unlikely to be considered a relevant factor in deciding how such capital as there should be shared out.

9.36 The courts are not insensitive to changing economic conditions and it is possible that the current high level of unemployment among young people, including higher education leavers, will have some impact on the approach to cases where one partner asks the court to take into account the fact that they have a moral and practical obligation to a child of the family.

Duration of the partnership

9.37 This is one of the factors to be taken into account under the criteria. The longer the partnership, the more likely it is that the court will aim at equality and that capital brought in by either partner at the start will not be the subject of any ring-fencing. The question arises as to how the courts will view a civil partnership which began in December 2005 but was preceded by many years of cohabitation beforehand. In matrimonial cases seamless pre-marital cohabitation will be taken into account when considering the issue of duration: *GW v RW (Financial Provision: Departure From Equality)*.[24] This is the position even though the parties could have married before they chose to do so. It is likely that the courts will regard pre-registration cohabitation, where in other respects the arrangements are the same as would be expected if a civil partnership had been entered into, as highly relevant to the issue of the duration of the relationship.

9.38 If the pre-registration cohabitation was of an unstable nature, involved the maintenance of separate homes (unless there was a particular reason for this; for example, geographical separation for work), or was otherwise contingent, it may not be treated as seamless. Each such case will turn on its own facts.

---

[24]   [2003] 2 FLR 108.

What are the partnership assets?

9.39 The line of cases referred to above where the overall approach to financial relief was reviewed by the courts also involved consideration of what assets should be regarded as those which might be made the subject of an order.

9.40 Particular consideration was given to this issue in *Miller*, where Lord Nichols said:

> '[22] This does not mean that, when exercising his discretion, a judge in this country must treat all property in the same way. The statute requires the court to have regard to all the circumstances of the case. One of the circumstances is that there is a real difference, a difference of source, between: (1) property acquired during the marriage otherwise than by inheritance or gift, sometimes called the marital acquest but more usually the matrimonial property; and (2) other property. The former is the financial product of the parties' common endeavour, the latter is not. The parties' matrimonial home, even if this was brought into the marriage at the outset by one of the parties, usually has a central place in any marriage. So it should normally be treated as matrimonial property for this purpose. As already noted, in principle the entitlement of each party to a share of the matrimonial property is the same however long or short the marriage may have been.
>
> [23] The matter stands differently regarding property ("non-matrimonial property") the parties bring with them into the marriage or acquire by inheritance or gift during the marriage. Then the duration of the marriage will be highly relevant. The position regarding non-matrimonial property was summarised in the *White* case, at 610 and 994 respectively:
>
>> "Plainly, when present, this factor is one of the circumstances of the case. It represents a contribution made to the welfare of the family by one of the parties to the marriage. The judge should take it into account. He should decide how important it is in the particular case. The nature and value of the property, and the time when and circumstances in which the property was acquired, are among the relevant matters to be considered. However, in the ordinary course, this factor can be expected to carry little weight, if any, in a case where the claimant's financial needs cannot be met without recourse to this property."
>
> [24] In the case of a short marriage, fairness may well require that the claimant should not be entitled to a share of the other's non-matrimonial property. The source of the asset may be a good reason for departing from equality. This reflects the instinctive feeling that parties will generally have less call upon each other on the breakdown of a short marriage.
>
> [25] With longer marriages the position is not so straightforward. Non-matrimonial property represents a contribution made to the marriage by one of the parties. Sometimes, as the years pass, the weight fairly to be attributed to this contribution will diminish, sometimes it will not. After many years of marriage the continuing weight to be attributed to modest savings introduced by one party at the outset of the marriage may well be different from the weight attributable to

a valuable heirloom intended to be retained in specie. Some of the matters to be taken into account in this regard were mentioned in the above citation from the *White* case. To this non-exhaustive list should be added, as a relevant matter, the way the parties organised their financial affairs.'

9.41   In most cases where a relationship comes to an end the assets and income are insufficient, or barely sufficient, to support the former partners on separation and the issue of needs will outweigh any consideration of where property originally came from. Even if the court takes the view that some property which is owned by one of the partners is not a partnership asset, this property is one of the resources available to him and is not excluded from consideration under the criteria.

9.42   Property brought into the marriage by one party is not quarantined but in short marriage cases it is less likely to be taken into account:[25]

'The non-matrimonial property is not quarantined and excluded from the court's dispositive powers. It represents an unmatched contribution by the party who brings it to the marriage. The court will decide whether it should be shared and, if so, in what proportions. In so deciding it will have regard to the reality that the longer the marriage the more likely non-matrimonial property will become merged or entangled with matrimonial property. By contrast, in a short marriage case non-matrimonial assets are not likely to be shared unless needs require this.'

Inherited property

9.43   Inherited property is not part of the family assets and also requires some separate consideration:[26]

'Plainly, when present, this factor is one of the circumstances of the case. It represents a contribution made to the welfare of the family by one of the parties to the marriage. The judge should take it into account. He should decide how important it is in the particular case. The nature and value of the property, and the time when and circumstances in which the property was acquired, are among the relevant matters to be considered. However, in the ordinary course, this factor can be expected to carry little weight, if any, in a case where the claimant's financial needs cannot be met without recourse to this property.'

9.44   The greater the time which passes between the inheritance and the end of the partnership, the more likely it is to be regarded as a partnership asset. If the inheritance is mingled with partnership assets, it may be treated as such an asset. If one partner came into the relationship with a substantial inherited fortune, or acquired it during the relationship, this is more likely to justify a departure from equality when the assets are divided. If a partner inherits £30,000 from an aunt, the money is put into the partnership home, and the partners separate ten years later, that inheritance is likely to be treated as part of the matrimonial assets.

---

[25]   *Rossi v Rossi* [2007] 1 FLR 790.
[26]   Lord Nichols in *White*, see above.

The family home

9.45   The property which has been the joint home of the civil partners and which has been acquired through their joint efforts will usually be treated as a joint asset, regardless of whose name it is vested in. If one party's efforts have not been financial but have consisted of looking after the home, this will not affect this principle. In a case where the home is the only asset (other than pension provision) the court will be slow to deprive either party of their share in the home: in *Elliott v Elliott*[27] the Court of Appeal upheld a judge's decision to permit a husband to retain a 45% interest in a property purchased by the wife as a substitute for the former matrimonial home on the basis that he had a 'reasonable entitlement to deploy capital to house himself at the end of a long marriage during which he has worked hard, mainly in the police service, and has contributed his earnings to the building of family capital'.

9.46   The court has a range of options in considering what order to make in relation to the family home. They include immediate sale, deferred sale, and transfer by one partner of his share to the other, with or without payment of a lump sum to the partner who is deprived of his share in the property. If there is a need to preserve it as a home for the children until they reach adulthood, there is the particular option of a *Mesher* order, whereby the property is transferred into the name of the partner with whom the children live, but with a legal charge back in favour of the other partner for a fixed percentage of the net proceeds of sale.[28] That charge will only be enforceable on the happening of the earliest of certain events: usually the formation of a civil partnership (or marriage) by the partner who remains in the property; cohabitation with another person for more than 6 months; death; voluntary sale; or the youngest child attaining a particular age (usually somewhere between 16 and 21). The effect of such an order is that the partner with whom the children live, provided he survives and does not introduce a new partner into the household, can remain in the property without the threat of sale until the children are adults. The property is then sold and the proceeds split in accordance with the percentage specified in the charge. The court can regulate the issue of who pays the mortgage and other outgoings on the property by requiring as a pre-condition to such an order that the occupying partner give undertakings to the court to pay them, and to indemnify the other partner against any failure to do so. The court may also make provision for who pays for repairs during the period of retention of the property: usually the partner in residence is expected to deal with day to day repairs, wear and tear, and decoration, but the cost of major repairs needed to preserve the value of the property may be split in accordance with the percentages which the parties will eventually receive.

9.47   There is a variant of a *Mesher* order, known as a *Martin* order, whereby one partner remains in the home, subject to a charge, until death, voluntary sale, or the formation of a new partnership/enduring cohabitation. Such orders

---

[27]   [2001] 1 FCR 477.
[28]   After deduction of any mortgage in existence at the time of the order, and the costs of selling the property.

are uncommon but have a role in some cases. For example, where the partners are relatively elderly, one has remained in the home on separation, and the other has secured affordable accommodation elsewhere, the court may be reluctant to make an order for sale which makes an older person homeless, but may not wish to deprive the other partner permanently of his share in the sale proceeds. A practical solution may be a *Martin* order with an enhanced share of the proceeds for the partner who is kept out of the property (or for his estate if he dies first).

9.48   If one partner is to remain in the family home, whether on the basis of a *Mesher* order or a *Martin* order, and there is an existing mortgage, the other partner may require that his liability under that mortgage be extinguished so that he can obtain mortgage finance elsewhere to purchase another property. The court can make it a condition of an order that the occupying partner obtains the release of the other from his liability under the mortgage[29] with a default provision requiring the property to be sold if this is not done within a fixed period of time. How long the occupying party will be given to arrange this will depend on both parties' circumstances.

Pensions

9.49   Since 2000 the court has had the power to make an order sharing the pension of one party to a marriage with the other party, or to transfer a pension outright from one party to the other, and the same power has existed from the start of the civil partnership regime.[30] The same criteria apply to the issue of pension sharing as to any other form of financial relief. Pensions are therefore an asset which must be taken into account by the court and by parties seeking to make their own arrangements without the assistance of the court. An up to date transfer value is needed for each pension which is in existence when the parties separate (unless it has been taken out so recently and has had so few contributions that its value is nominal).

9.50   The court also has the power to 'earmark' a pension. This permits a range of orders including requiring part of the pension, when payment begins to be made, to be paid to the other partner, payment of part of any lump sum received from the pension to the other partner, an order for commutation of a lump sum, and orders for payment of death in service benefits to the other partner. This power was given to the courts in 1995, and formed a half way house between the previous position, where the court could not make orders directly against pensions, and the current position, where pensions can be shared or transferred.

9.51   Under a pension sharing order the part of any pension transferred becomes the pension of the recipient, who receives all the benefits which attach

---

[29]   The mechanics of this are in the hands of the mortgage lender. Some insist on a complete remortgage; others will vary the existing mortgage so that there is only one borrower.

[30]   Similar provisions exist in relation to compensation provided by the Pension Protection Fund: CPA 2004, Sch 7, para 30.

to the scheme, including the income for life once the pension is payable. The receiving partner has the option of keeping the transferred pension within the original scheme or transferring it out to another scheme, including an existing scheme of his own. Once made, a pension sharing order cannot be varied.

9.52 Where an earmarking order is made the pension remains the property of the other partner, a clean break between the parties is not brought about, and the order can be varied by the courts on application by either party. In practice such orders are rarely made.

9.53 In many cases although pensions are an issue, a pension sharing order is not required. The partners' shares in the currently available capital can be adjusted to take into account any future imbalance in pensions. Where the pension provision available to both parties is relatively modest, another factor which must be taken into account is the cost of making a pension sharing order. This varies between pension providers but can be several thousand pounds,[31] a prohibitive figure if the pension has a modest transfer value.

9.54 Pensions transfer values are not treated simply as another capital asset because the benefits which they yield may be many years away. If a pension has a transfer value of £50,000 and is to be retained by the partner to whom it belongs, the court will not award the other partner an extra £50,000 of any available capital when the order is made to offset that asset. The amount needed to offset the retention of that pension will be discounted to reflect the fact that the person with the pension will have to wait to receive it. There is no set rule about how that discount should be calculated and in practice it will depend on what other capital is available and the application of the statutory criteria.

9.55 Pensions are a long term investment and a court will be less willing to make pension sharing orders after short civil partnerships. The younger the parties, the less significant pensions will be, if both will have the opportunity to make pension provision in future.

PROCEDURE

9.56 In 2011 the Family Procedure Rules modified the procedure for applications for a financial remedy/financial order in all the courts. There must be an application for a dissolution, a nullity order, or a separation order before the court before an application for financial relief can be made.[32] The order for financial relief can be made at the same time as the order for dissolution, nullity or separation, or at any time thereafter. Entry into a subsequent civil

---

[31] The National Association of Pension Funds publishes a table of recommended charges for processing a pension sharing order which vary between £1,350 and £3,000 depending on the type of pension and whether the transfer is within the scheme or out of the scheme.

[32] CPA 2004, Sch 5, para 46(3).

partnership bars the right to apply for financial relief;[33] an applicant for an order must ensure that a final order is in place before entry into a new partnership. In most cases both parties to an application for a financial order are seeking relief from the court, and both must wait until matters conclude before they form a new partnership.

An application can be made for financial relief even if the civil partnership is being brought to an end on the basis that it was void from the start.[34]

The majority of applications for financial relief begin in the county court. The party who wishes to make an application issues a Form A, which starts the procedure. Both parties are then required to file detailed forms (Form E) setting out their financial positions fully and attaching relevant documentation. There is a duty of full and frank disclosure on each party throughout the proceedings and the Form E contains a warning of possible prosecution if this is not complied with. The matter proceeds to court for a First Directions Appointment where the court will give directions for further disclosure if it is required, for valuations, if not agreed, of the family home and of relevant business interests and other assets, and may permit each party to ask written questions of the other in relation to financial matters.

9.57 Thereafter the case is listed for a Financial Dispute Resolution Appointment where the parties appear before a judge who will be familiar with the case, having read the documents filed with the court, and will attempt to give the parties some idea of what order might be made at a final hearing. The purpose of this hearing is for discussion and negotiation and the court will be informed of any offers made by either party. The parties are required to file details of their legal costs to date, and the likely costs if the matter proceeds to a contested final hearing. If the matter does not resolve at that stage, the court will list it for such a hearing.

CONSENT ORDERS

9.58 If at any stage after issue of an application, the parties succeed in reaching an agreement, the approval of the court will be required before the terms of that agreement become an order binding on the parties. This will require an application to the court for approval of a consent order. Even if the parties have reached agreement without litigation, it is often necessary to obtain a court order to ensure finality and to avoid the risk of any future claims. The court will make such an order on the basis of relatively limited information[35] in the form of what is known as a 'Statement of Information' summarising each parties' income and capital position, where the parties and their children will live, whether either has formed a new relationship, and confirming that notice has been given to the mortgagee of any property which

---

[33] CPA 2004, Sch 5, para 48.
[34] *Ramsay v Ramsay (otherwise Beer)* (1913) 108 LT 382.
[35] CPA 2004, Sch 1, para 66.

is the subject of the order, and to any pension provider upon who a pension sharing order will be served. Either both parties must complete the same statement of information and sign it to confirm that its contents are true, or they must complete separate forms which must be signed by the other party to confirm that their contents are true. The court is not a rubber stamp, and the draft order and the statement(s) of information are put before a judge who considers the order before making it. Generally, provided what is proposed comes within the parameters of what a court might be expected to do on those particular facts before it, the order will be approved. If one party is represented, and the other is not, the court will scrutinise the order particularly carefully. If both parties are unrepresented, the court will have to consider whether the order which they have drafted is in fact capable of forming an order of the court: it is not easy for litigants in person to draft financial provision orders. The court will provide assistance, but judges will not generally completely redraft orders for unrepresented parties.

FINANCIAL RELIEF IN THE MAGISTRATES COURTS

9.59 Under Sch 6 of the Act application may be made to the magistrates' court for certain types of order if:[36]

> (a) has failed to provide reasonable maintenance for the applicant,
> (b) has failed to provide, or to make a proper contribution towards, reasonable maintenance for any child of the family,
> (c) has behaved in such a way that the applicant cannot reasonably be expected to live with the respondent, or
> (d) has deserted the applicant.

The orders which can be made are:

(a) an order for payment of a lump sum limited to £1,000;

(b) an order for periodical payments.

The order may be made in favour of the applicant, or in favour of the child, or for the applicant for the benefit of the child.

ALTERNATIVES TO COURT

9.60 Civil partners who cannot between themselves resolve financial matters at the end of their partnership have a number of options open to them before they embark on the expensive process of litigation. They can seek the assistance of a trained family mediator, who will work with both of them over a series of meetings to reach a solution acceptable to both. Lawyers are not normally be involved for either party during mediation, although in many cases one or both

---

[36] CPA 2004, Sch 6, para 1.

partners will have taken some initial legal advice and the referral to mediation will have been made or recommended by one or both parties' solicitors.

9.61 If more in the way of legal input is needed, but both parties are committed to avoiding litigation, representation of both parties by collaboratively trained lawyers may be the way forward. The collaborative process involves the parties and their lawyers signing up at the outset to an agreement not to go to court: if one party changes their mind about this, both have to start afresh with new lawyers who have not been involved in the collaborative process. Once the possibility of going to court has been excluded, the parties and their lawyers meet face to face on two or more occasions with a view to establishing priorities, building trust, and reaching an agreement about finances. Sometimes outside professionals, such as financial advisors, are brought in to advise both parties. The aim of collaborative law is to resolve family disputes without the damaging side-effects consequent on litigation and to allow the parties and their at the end of the process to move forward with dignity and with functioning relationships established for the future.

9.62 If an agreement is reached following mediation or by the use of the collaborative process, it may be necessary to make an application to the court for financial relief in order to have a consent order approved (see **9.58**). If there is no application before the court for a dissolution, separation or nullity, the question arises as to how the parties can record their agreement so as to prevent future difficulty. The correct approach is to record what is agreed in written form signed by the parties and expressed to be binding on them. The agreement should not seek to oust the jurisdiction of the court. If the agreement has been reached with legal advice on both sides, the court will be likely to uphold it provided there has been no abuse of a dominant position, undue influence, or failure to make propery disclosure.[37]

FINANCIAL RELIEF AFTER OVERSEAS DISSOLUTION

9.63 Schedule 7 of the CPA 2004 permits the court to grant financial relief where a civil partnership has been dissolved, annulled, or the subject of a separation order overseas, and the dissolution, annulment or separation order is entitled to be recognised as valid in England and Wales.[38] Permission from the court to make an application for financial relief is required in these circumstances: this is an additional hurdle which does not exist where the application follows a dissolution in England and Wales. The court will only give permission to make an application if it considers that 'there is substantial ground for the making of an application for such an order'.[39] The fact that there has already been an order in another country requiring payment by one civil partner, or transfer of property, to the other, is not a bar on the granting of

---

[37] *Edgar v Edgar* [1980] 1 WLR 1410.
[38] There is equivalent provision for married couples in the Matrimonial and Family Proceedings Act 1984, Part III and case law under that Act will guide the interpretation of Sch 7.
[39] CPA 2004, Sch 7, para 4(2).

permission. When considering whether or not to grant permission the court must consider whether 'in all the circumstances of the case it would be appropriate for an order of the kind applied for to be made by a court in England and Wales'.[40] If the court is not satisfied it would be appropriate, the application must be dismissed: the onus is therefore on the applicant to show that it would be appropriate.

9.64 There are certain jurisdictional pre-requisites before the court can entertain an application for permission to apply for financial relief. The applicant must satisfy at least one of them. First, at least one of the civil partners must have been domiciled in England and Wales either on the date when the application for permission was made or on the date when the dissolution, annulment or separation order took effect in the jurisdiction where it was granted.[41] Second, one of the civil partners must have been habitually resident in England and Wales for a year ending with the date on which permission was applied for or for a year ending with the date on which the dissolution, annulment or separation order took effect in the overseas jurisdiction.[42] Third, one or both of the civil partners had, at the date when permission was applied for, a beneficial interest in a dwelling house situated in England and Wales which at some time during the partnership was the home of the civil partners.[43].

9.65 Even where permission to apply is granted, that is not the end of the matter. The court is still required to consider before granting the application for financial relief, whether England and Wales is the appropriate venue for the application.[44] In making this decision, the court is required in particular to have regard to the following matters:[45]

> '(a)   the connection which the civil partners have with England and Wales;
> (b)   the connection which the civil partners have with the country in which the civil partnership was dissolved or annulled or in which they were legally separated;
> (c)   the connection which the civil partners have with any other country outside England and Wales;
> (d)   any financial benefit which, in consequence of the dissolution, annulment or legal separation –
>   (i)   the applicant, or
>   (ii)   a child of the family,
>   has received, or is likely to receive, by virtue of any agreement or the operation of the law of a country outside England and Wales;
> (e)   in a case where an order has been made by a court in a country outside England and Wales requiring the other civil partner –
>   (i)   to make any payment, or
>   (ii)   to transfer any property,

---

40   CPA 2004, Sch 7, para 8(1).
41   CPA 2004, Sch 7, para 7(2).
42   CPA 2004, Sch 7, para 7(3).
43   CPA 2004, Sch 7, para 7(4).
44   CPA 2004, Sch 7, para 8.
45   CPA 2004, Sch 7, para 8(3).

for the benefit of the applicant or a child of the family, the financial relief given by the order and the extent to which the order has been complied with or is likely to be complied with;

(f)   any right which the applicant has, or has had, to apply for financial relief from the other civil partner under the law of any country outside England and Wales and, if the applicant has omitted to exercise that right, the reason for that omission;

(g)   the availability in England and Wales of any property in respect of which an order under this Schedule in favour of the applicant could be made;

(h)   the extent to which any order made under this Schedule is likely to be enforceable;

(i)   the length of time which has elapsed since the date of the dissolution, annulment or legal separation.'

Assuming that the court decides that England and Wales is the appropriate venue, the criteria which apply on deciding whether or not to make an order for financial relief are the same as the criteria in Sch 5, para 21.

9.66   The initial application for permission to make a claim for relief after overseas dissolution is normally made and dealt with by the court without notice to the other side. Once the permission is granted and the other party becomes aware of the application, he can apply to set it the grant of permission.

9.67   The correct approach in cases of this nature was considered by the Supreme Court in *Agbaje v Agbaje*.[46] The parties were originally from Nigeria and were married for thirty-two years. They spent most of this period living in the Nigeria, but also spent some time in London, where the husband owned a property. They had dual Nigerian/UK nationality. On separation they had about £700,000 in assets, of which £530,000 was represented by two properties in London, and the remainder by assets in Nigeria. The husband sought and obtained a divorce in Nigeria, and a Nigerian court granted the wife a life interest in the former matrimonial home in Nigeria (worth £86,000) and ordered the husband to pay her a lump sum of £21,000. The wife sought permission to make an application for ancillary relief in the English courts. By this time she was living in one of the London properties. She obtained an order whereby she would receive £275,000 from the sale proceeds of the property she was living in. The husband appealed successfully to the Court of Appeal, which took the view that the trial judge had attached insufficient weight to the Nigerian aspect of the case, and found that the order made in Nigeria did not effect any real injustice. The wife appealed successfully to the Supreme Court. Lord Collins, giving the judgment of the court, made the following observations:

'In the present context the principal object of the filter mechanism is to prevent wholly unmeritorious claims being pursued to oppress or blackmail a former spouse. The threshold is not high, but is higher than "serious issue to be tried" or

---

46   [2010] 1 FLR 1813.

"good arguable case" found in other contexts. It is perhaps best expressed by saying that in this context 'substantial' means "solid". Once a judge has given reasons for deciding at the ex parte stage that the threshold has been crossed, the approach to setting aside leave should be the same as the approach to setting aside permission to appeal in the Civil Procedure Rules 1998 (the CPR), where (by contrast with the FPR) there is an express power to set aside, but which may only be exercised where there is a compelling reason to do so: r 52.9(2) of the CPR ... In an application under s 13, unless it is clear that the respondent can deliver a knock-out blow, the court should use its case management powers to adjourn an application to set aside to be heard with the substantive application.

Once the court has decided that England and Wales is the appropriate venue, it has to consider whether to make an order, and what order to make. The court has broadly the same powers as if the application had been made following dissolution in England and Wales, and the criteria under Schedule 5 para 21(2) apply.[47] The court also has to consider whether to impose a clean break. The criteria which are relevant to the question of venue are not also the criteria which determine whether or not an order shall be made.

The legislation does not mention hardship and it is not necessary to show it, although if there will be hardship if no order is made, this is a relevant factor.

It is not the purpose of Part III to allow a spouse (usually, in current conditions, the wife) with some English connections to make an application in England to take advantage of what may well be the more generous approach in England to financial provision, particularly in so-called big-money cases. There is no condition of exceptionality for the purposes of s 16, but it will not usually be a case for an order under Part III where the wife had a right to apply for financial relief under the foreign law, and an award was made in the foreign country. In such cases mere disparity between that award and what would be awarded on an English divorce will certainly be insufficient to trigger the application of Part III. Nor is hardship or injustice (much less serious injustice) a condition of the exercise of the jurisdiction, but if either factor is present, it may make it appropriate, in the light of all the circumstances, for an order to be made, and may affect the nature of the provision ordered. Of course, the court will not lightly characterise foreign law, or the order of a foreign court, as unjust.

The amount of financial provision will depend on all the circumstances of the case and there is no rule that it should be the minimum amount required to overcome injustice. The following general principles should be applied. First, primary consideration must be given to the welfare of any children of the marriage. This can cut both ways as the children may be being supported by the foreign spouse. Second, it will never be appropriate to make an order which gives the claimant more than she or he would have been awarded had all proceedings taken place within this jurisdiction. Third, where possible the order should have the result that provision is made for the reasonable needs of each spouse. Subject to these principles, the court has a broad discretion. The reasons why it was appropriate for an order to be made in England are among the circumstances to be taken into account in deciding what order should be made. Where the English connections of the case are very strong there may be no reason why the application should not be

[47]   See **9.11**.

treated as if it were made in purely English proceedings. The full procedure for granting ancillary relief after an English divorce does not apply in Part III cases. The conditions which can be attached to leave, together with the court's case management powers, can be used to define the issues and to limit the evidence to be filed, as was done by Munby J in this case. This enables the jurisdiction to be tailored to the needs of the individual case, so that the grant of leave does not inevitably trigger a full blown claim for all forms of ancillary relief.'

The court's powers are restricted in cases where the only reason the court is able to entertain an application is that the family home was in England and Wales. In that case the court can make a lump sum order (payable to the partner or to a child of the family) a property transfer order, requiring one partner to transfer all or part of his interest in the house to the other partner or to a child of the family, an order for sale of the house, and certain types of orders for settlement and variation in relation to the house.[48] If the court makes a lump sum order, the sum is limited to the value of the paying party's interest in the property, or proceeds of sale thereof.

---

[48] CPA 2004, Sch 7, para 11.

Chapter 10

FINANCIAL PROVISION ON THE BREAKDOWN OF COHABITING RELATIONSHIPS

INTRODUCTION

10.1 'Cohabitation' is used in this part of this work as referring to same sex partners engaged in an intimate relationship whose principal home is in the same household. Until the coming into force of the Civil Partnership Act 2004 same sex couples had no method of gaining legal recognition of their relationship, and public acknowledgment of their cohabitation was the primary form of recognition by society of such relationships. Cohabitation remains for many same sex couples a preferred method of arranging their lives without subjecting themselves to the formality of civil partnership and the legal consequences which accompany it.

10.2 The same is true of heterosexual couples. Cohabitation without marriage has been a growing phenomenon in recent decades: in 1986 11% of unmarried men and 13% of unmarried women aged 16 to 59 were cohabiting; by 2004, the figures were 24% and 25%.[1] The 2001 Census shows that 1,278,455 children were dependant on a cohabiting couple.

10.3 The Office for National Statistics predicts that by 2031, 3,793,000 couples will be living in relationships of cohabitation, an increase of 62% from in 2008, when the estimated figure was 2,340,000.[2]

10.4 Against this background it might be expected that some attempt would be made by government to provide a practical legal framework for cohabitation, and in particular to assist couples whose relationships break down in managing their financial and property affairs. As we have seen, the Civil Partnership Act 2004 provides a detailed scheme for resolving issues arising on the breakdown of civil partnerships. There have been a number of attempts to introduce legislation which would provide such a scheme for cohabitants.[3] Legislation was introduced in Scotland in 2006 which gives some

---

[1] Office for National Statistics, Social Trends 35 and 36. These figures include same sex couples.
[2] 2008 Marital Status Predictions, Office of National Statistics.
[3] For example, Lord Lester's Cohabitation Bill in 2009. The Bill received a Second Reading but did not proceed beyond the Committee stage because the government did not make time available for it to do so. Lord Lester also introduced the Civil Partnership Bill in 2002, which aimed to introduce civil partnership for same sex and opposite sex couples.

financial protection to cohabitants.⁴ Recently, the Law Commission has provided very detailed recommendations for reform⁵ but there appears to be little prospect of those reforms being implemented in the foreseeable future.

10.5 The current position however is that the law grants only limited recognition to relationships of cohabitation:

(a)   Legislation dealing with domestic abuse protects cohabitants in broadly the same way as it does parties to a marriage. This legislation gives the court the power to regulate occupation of the family home in the short term.⁶

(b)   The court has the power to transfer tenancies between cohabitants.⁷

(c)   The court has the power to make some financial provision for the children of a cohabitual relationship.⁸

(d)   If a cohabitual relationship is ended by death, rather than separation, the survivor may have a right to apply to the court for provision from the deceased's estate.⁹

10.6   The court has no power to grant any general financial relief to the adult parties on the ending of a cohabitual relationship. Where a cohabitating couple separate, their property rights are governed by the general law relating to property. The Supreme Court has in recent cases encouraged the development of an approach which sees cases involving the family home as a particular type of property dispute where the court may take a more 'holistic' approach,¹⁰ but this falls far short of the power to transfer property between parties and in some cases to achieve equality which is available on the ending of a civil partnership.

10.7   Not only is there no legal remedy tailored to cohabitants, but the application of the general law in such cases is uncertain and can produce results which are arbitrary and unfair. This uncertainty makes the giving of advice to the parties to such disputes difficult (for lawyers) and causes their resolution to be on many occasions protracted and expensive.¹¹

---

⁴   Family Law (Scotland) Act 2006.
⁵   See **10.76–10.78**.
⁶   See chapter 9 for more detail.
⁷   See **10.79–10.95**.
⁸   See **10.123** onwards.
⁹   See chapter 11.
¹⁰   See in particular *Stack v Dowden* and *Kernott v Jones*, discussed in more detail below.
¹¹   See Law Commission Consulatation Paper 179, *Cohabitation: the financial consequences of relationship breakdown*: 'The formulation of a claim based on these rules is time-consuming and expensive, and the nature of the inquiry before the court into the history of the relationship results in a protracted hearing for those disputes that are not compromised. The inherent uncertainty of the underlying principles makes effective bargaining difficult to achieve as parties will find it hard to predict the outcome of contested litigation.'

10.8 There is widespread ignorance among the general public of the lack of legal protection given to cohabitants. There is a widespread belief (at least among opposite sex couples) that living together for a certain period results in 'common law marriage'. This concept has not been known to English law since 1753.[12] A study carried out in the late 1990s indicated that 56% of the general population believe that living together for a period confers such rights.[13]

10.9 It may be that same sex couples are less likely to believe that there is such a concept as 'common law civil partnership'.[14] Civil partnership does not come with the historical baggage of marriage and same sex couples may have a lesser expectation that the law will give them protection. Same sex couples may however share the reluctance of opposite sex couples to give any detailed consideration to their legal position until forced to do so by a relationship breakdown. A study of cohabitating couples[15] found that very few had a clear understanding of their legal position and that most regarded such considerations as 'antithetical to the nature of a trusting, loving relationship'. There is no reason why same sex couples should be immune from this tendency to allow the romantic impulse to outweigh the practicalities.

10.10 One course of action which does permit cohabiting couples some degree of certainty is to enter into a written cohabitation agreement. Such an agreement can have whatever content the couple feel it should have; some agreements concentrate primarily on the family home and what should happen to it if the relationship comes to an end; others deal additionally with joint bank accounts, other joint assets, and personal property; it is also possible to include more personal matters such as the parties' intentions towards and expectations of one another. Attempting to express or regulate a sexual relationship by such a deed should be avoided as it is likely to render it unenforceable.[16]

THE FAMILY HOME: OCCUPATION

10.11 The Family Law Act 1996 permits the court to regulate occupation of the family home on a short term basis. This is discussed more fully in chapter 7.

10.12 Subject to that legislative protection, mere cohabitation does not given the cohabitant who occupies a property in which he has no legal or beneficial interest any continuing right to occupy the property on the breakdown of that relationship. If a same sex cohabitant occupies with his partner a property in

---

[12] When it was abolished by the Clandestine Marriages Act.

[13] A Barlow, S Duncan, G James and A Park, 'Just a Piece of Paper? Marriage and Cohabitation in Britain' in A Park, J Curtice, K Thomson, I Jarvis and C Bromley, C (eds) British Social Attitudes: The 18th Report, (Sage, 2000).

[14] The extent to which same sex couples' knowledge of their legal rights may differ from that of opposite sex couples does not appear to have been the subject of any research.

[15] C Smart and P Stevens, Cohabitation breakdown (Family Policy Studies Centre/Joseph Rowntree Foundation, 2000).

[16] *Sutton v Michcon de Reya (A Firm)* [2004] 3 FCR 142.

which he has asserts no claim to any legal interest, he has in law no more than a bare licence to occupy. He occupies the property with the permission of the owner, which can be withdrawn at any time. Once that permission is withdrawn, the cohabitant has no right to remain.

10.13   The practical arrangements made by cohabitants vary. In some cases a cohabitant may have his own room, which he is entitled to occupy to the exclusion of the other party. That is perhaps a less common arrangement where the parties have set up home together in the ordinary course of events, but may occur if the relationship has begun as that of landlord and tenant, but developed into something more intimate.

10.14   Even if the cohabitant has his own room, if the other partner/landlord retains a general right of management over the property, including a right to enter the cohabitant's room, the cohabitant does not have exclusive occupation of his own room and remains no more than a lodger.

10.15   The non-rent paying cohabitant's position is less favourable than that of a paying lodger. A lodger, that is a person sharing accommodation with his landlord and paying rent, has a contractual licence to occupy the property and is entitled to reasonable notice from the landlord before he can be required to leave the property. A person sharing a house on an informal basis, without payment of rent, does not have a contractual licence and can be required to leave at any time.

10.16   Even if the cohabitant has exclusive occupation of some part of the premises, the protection afforded to him if he is required by the landlord to leave is limited. The Protection from Eviction Act 1977 prevents a landlord recovering possession of a property in which a person is lawfully residing other than by court proceedings.[17] This protection does not extend to persons who share accommodation with their landlord, if that accommodation forms part of the landlord's principal home:

'(2) A tenancy or licence is excluded if –

(a)   under its terms the occupier shares any accommodation with the landlord or licensor; and

(b)   immediately before the tenancy or licence was granted and also at the time it comes to an end, the landlord or licensor occupied as his only or principal home premises of which the whole or part of the shared accommodation formed part.'

10.17   A landlord is therefore not required to obtain a court order prior to evicting a cohabitant with whom he has been sharing accommodation. He is of course subject to the ordinary provisions of the criminal law and the use of force to eject an estranged cohabitant might well bring him into conflict with

---

[17]   Protection from Eviction Act 1977, ss 2 and 3.

that. The cohabitant is entitled to recover his possessions on departure and the wrongful retention of those would constitute the civil wrong of interference with goods.

10.18 This is the position in any case where a cohabitant shares accommodation with his landlord, who is the other party to the relationship. If the cohabitant has exclusive accommodation of some part of the property, and makes some payment to the other party in respect of that accommodation, he may be able to establish that he has a tenancy of that part, but that tenancy will not fall within the provisions of the Protection From Eviction Act 1977 because the cohabitant is sharing accommodation with the landlord. If he pays rent to the landlord, he may have a contractual licence. In either case he will be entitled to be given reasonable notice by the landlord before being required to depart. How long would constitute reasonable notice will depend on the facts of each case. If the cohabitant is paying rent, the notice period is likely to be the period for which each rent payment is made. If no rent is being paid, it may be no more than a few days. In any event it is unlikely to be more than twenty-eight days. Even this protection is of limited practical utility as the landlord is not required to get a court order to recover possession.

THE FAMILY HOME: OWNERSHIP

10.19 As was discussed above, English law has yet to make proper legal provision for the joint ownership of property by people living in an intimate relationship. If cohabitants acquire a property in which both have, or may have, an interest, the creation of that interest, and disputes arising from it, particularly on the ending of the relationship, are determined by the law relating to property, with some modification to take into account the particular nature of such relationships. This however is the regime within which cohabitants have to operate.

10.20 There are few reported cases concerning the family home where the partners were a same sex couple. Those that have occurred suggest that the legal approach will be the same as for heterosexual unmarried couples. In *Ashby v Kilduff*[18] a male same sex couple parted, and litigation ensued about various joint properties; the approach taken by the Deputy High Court judge did not vary from that which would apply in the case of a heterosexual couple. Similarly in *Tinsley v Milligan*[19] the case of a female same sex couple was analysed in three courts (county court, Court of Appeal, and House of Lords) on the same basis as if they had been heterosexual cohabitants (although the reference in the Court of Appeal to the parties having been 'to use the [county court] judge's expression, lovers for about 4 years' suggests a degree of unfamiliarity with such relationships).

---

[18]   [2010] EWHC 2034 (Ch).
[19]   [1994] 2 FCR 65.

THE FAMILY HOME: THE LEGAL FRAMEWORK

10.21 In order to understand the framework within which the law operates it is necessary for cohabitants to grasp that in English law there are two 'levels' of property ownership. First, there is the issue of legal ownership: who has their name on the title to the property, or the 'deeds' as many people will still refer to them. Second, who owns the beneficial interest in the property, or 'the equity'. Any textbook on land law, or equity and the law of trusts, will contain detailed discussion of the meaning of and distinctions between this type of ownership. For practical purposes, the easiest explanation is perhaps that legal ownership determines who is the public owner of the property and entitled to deal with it in relation to third parties, whereas the beneficial owner(s) are those who are entitled to benefit from the value in the property, whether by occupying it or by receiving part of the proceeds if it is sold.

10.22 In discussion of concepts of legal and beneficial ownership the owners are often referred to as 'tenants'. This is highly confusing for the non-lawyer who understandably assumes that the expression 'tenant' refers to a person who pays rent to a landlord. Unfortunately it is not possible to avoid this terminology.[20]

10.23 The legal title to property is either held by a single owner or by up to four owners. If there is more than one owner, the owners are referred to as joint tenants in law. It is not possible to hold the legal title to a property as tenants in common. Every legal title (unless held by a sole owner) is held by legal joint tenants/owners.

10.24 The beneficial interest[21] in property where there is more than one person with an interest is held by the owners of the legal title on a 'trust of land' for the benefit of the beneficial owners.[22] The beneficial interest may be held by the beneficial owners as joint tenants or as tenants in common.[23]

10.25 The easiest way for an interest to be acquired in a property is by or on transfer. However, an interest in the beneficial ownership of a property may arise as a result of the behaviour or conduct of parties to a relationship. This is discussed in more detail in **10.54–10.59** below.

Acquisition of an interest: two legal owners

10.26 If two people purchase a property together in their joint names, the law's starting point is that they intend to own the property jointly and that each will have some beneficial interest in the property. This will be the position even

---

[20] The use of the word 'tenant' is based on the concept that all land ultimately belongs to the Crown and that all landowners are ultimately tenants of the Crown.

[21] Also known as the equitable interest.

[22] Trusts of Land and Appointment of Trustees Act 1996, s 1.

[23] For more detailed discussion of the difference between beneficial joint tenancy and tenancy in common; see also chapter 11, at **11.4** et seq and **10.31–10.35** below.

if the documentation which they sign at the point of purchase is entirely silent as to the beneficial interest in the property and deals solely with the legal title.

10.27 In practice it is unusual at the present time for a purchase of property not to contain some reference to the beneficial as well as the legal ownership. Since 1925 England and Wales have been moving to a system of compulsory land registration whereby all property is registered and recorded by the Land Registry and all transfers of property are carried out via the Land Registry. The vast majority of property in urban areas is already registered. Unregistered property is required to be registered whenever a transfer takes place.

10.28 The Land Registry uses a standard form of transfer document for all land known as a TR1. This form which must be completed and signed by the vendors and purchasers whenever a sale of land takes place, contains a section (Box 10) which requires the purchasers to set out the basis on which they own the land. Use of this form has been compulsory since April 1998.[24] However, there is no requirement on the purchasers to complete Box 10. If they do not, the Land Registry will enter a restriction which simply indicates that there is no evidence of a joint tenancy.[25] It does not determine what the parties' interests are.

---

10   Declaration of trust. The transferee is more than one person and

☐ they are to hold the property on trust for themselves as joint tenants

☐ they are to hold the property on trust for themselves as tenants in common in equal shares

☐ they are to hold the property on trust:

10.29 In 2009 the Land Registry set up a working party to consider whether the wording of the TR1 should be changed or a new form introduced. It recommended that joint purchasers should be required either to make a declaration of trust on the form they use to buy the property, or should execute a separate declaration of trust. If neither was done, the Land Registry would refuse to register the purchase and would send the documentation back to the purchasers' solicitors. In 2011 the Land Registry's director of legal services informed the working party that the intention was to implement this recommendation but also that this proposal is the subject of a government moratorium on new domestic regulation. The Land Registry is now considering whether a voluntary approach might achieve the same aim.[26] There seems no prospect of any imminent change.

---

[24] See *Stack v Dowden per* Baroness Hale at para 52.

[25] Known as a Form A restriction, this requires any subsequent transfer of the property to be signed by both parties.

[26] There is an informative article on this subject by a member of the working party, Professor

10.30 It can be seen that the form gives three alternatives: ownership as joint tenants in equity; ownership as tenants in common in equal shares; ownership as tenants in common in shares set out by the parties.

10.31 These are important distinctions, but it is apparent that those purchasing properly are on many occasions not given adequate advice by conveyancers about the different forms of ownership.[27] The principal characteristics of the different forms of tenancy are as follows:

10.32   Joint tenancy in law and equity

(a)   Subject to what is said below, the owners own the legal and beneficial interest in the property in equal shares, regardless of what contribution they have made to the purchase price, whether by providing initial capital or by paying the mortgage.

(b)   If the relationship comes to an end, on sale the proceeds of sale, after deduction of the costs of sale and any mortgage, will be divided equally. Again this is the position regardless of the contributions the parties have made to the purchase.

(c)   On death, the survivor will inherit the share of the deceased, regardless of whether or not the deceased has made a will or what it says.[28] His share in the property does not form part of his estate and does not pass under his will.

10.33   Joint ownership in law and tenancy in common in equity in equal shares

(a)   Subject to what is said below, the owners own the legal and beneficial interest in the property in equal shares, regardless of what contribution they have made to the purchase price, whether by providing initial capital or by paying the mortgage.

Elizabeth Cooke, at [2011] FLJ 1142. She comments that the proposed amendment 'could have saved hundreds of thousands of pounds in legal and litigation costs, and the unquantifiable financial cost to those for whom the absence of a declaration of trust may have meant the loss of a contribution made to the purchase of a property ... It would have ensured, in effect, that clients would not be able to say 'I don't want to know'; in order to purchase their property they would have to address the issue of beneficial ownership'.

27   See the comments of Ward LJ in *Carlton v Goodman* [2002] EWCA Civ 545: 'I ask in despair how often this court has to remind conveyancers that they would save their clients a great deal of difficulty if only they would sit the purchasers down, explain the difference between a joint tenancy and a tenancy in common, ascertain what they want and then expressly declare in the conveyance or transfer how the beneficial interest is to be held ... This court has urged that time after time. Perhaps conveyancers do not read the law reports. I will try one more time: ALWAYS TRY TO AGREE ON AND THEN RECORD HOW THE BENEFICIAL INTEREST IS TO BE HELD.'

28   For a fuller discussion of the position on death, please see chapter 11.

(b) If the relationship comes to an end, on sale the proceeds of sale, after deduction of the costs of sale and any mortgage, will be divided equally. Again this is the position regardless of the contributions the parties have made to the purchase.

(c) On death, the deceased's share forms part of his estate and passes under his will (or on intestacy if he has made no will); it will not pass to the surviving owner.

10.34 Joint ownership in law and 'tenancy' in specified shares in equity: equitable 'tenancy in common'

(a) The owners own the legal title to the property in equal shares.

(b) The owners own the equitable interest in the property in the shares which they have specified in the TR1 or in some other trust deed.

(c) On sale, the proceeds after deduction of the costs of sale and any mortgage, will be divided in accordance with those shares.

(d) On death, the deceased's share (as specified in the TR1 or other trust deed) forms part of his estate and passes under his will (or on intestacy if he has made no will); it will not pass to the surviving owner.

The scheme set out above assumes that there is a TR1 and it has been properly completed, thus settling the question of the parties' interests.

10.35 The parties may select the 'tenancy in common' option on the TR1 but rather than specifying their shares in the document itself, execute a trust deed setting out those shares. That deed should be referred to in the TR1. If the parties have adopted this course, a court is likely to accept that the interests set out in that deed represent the parties' intention as to how they should own the property. Unfortunately there is no guarantee that such deeds will be skilfully drafted and on occasions they may be difficult to interpret.

10.36 Various different scenarios can arise in which the position is not as clear:

(a) The purchase may have taken place before 1998 when an earlier version of the TR1 which did not contain an express declaration of trust was in use.

(b) The parties may not have completed Box 10 of the TR1. Normal Land Registry Practice as described above is to send the TR1 back to the purchaser's solicitors if that part is not completed with a request that it should be. If no adequate response is received, the Land Registry will go ahead and register the transaction on the basis that there is no evidence that the parties are joint tenants. That registration is not binding on the parties, but if a dispute arises, a court will have to decide what they intended when they purchased the property.

(c)   The parties may have completed Box 10 but have received no adequate explanation as to what its significance is. In that case, there is some doubt as to whether or not it is binding. As is suggested at **10.31** above, conveyancers do not give adequate advice on this issue. Often a letter setting out the difference is sent by the conveyancer to the parties and they are asked to tick which form of ownership they prefer. No independent advice is given to a party who may be disadvantaged by this; for example, if they have contributed the majority of the purchase price. There is no face to face contact with the solicitor/conveyancer. The contents of the letter may not explain the differences fully: for example, the letter may explain survivorship on death, but not what happens if the relationship ends and a sale becomes necessary.

(d)   The parties may have executed a separate trust deed, but its meaning may not be clear.

(e)   The parties may have behaved in such a way after acquisition that a court would infer that they intend to vary their interest in the property.[29]

(f)   The parties may have attempted expressly to vary their interests.

No TR1 (or pre-1998 TR1) and no declaration of trust

10.37   The legal position in such cases was considered in detail by the House of Lords in *Stack v Dowden*.[30] This case concerned an unmarried couple who purchased a house together in their joint names. They had previously lived in a property owned in the sole name of the female cohabitant (Ms Dowden), although there was some evidence that the male cohabitant had contributed to the purchase price. They purchased the joint home, in Willesden, in 1993. The purchase was made using the form of TR1 then in use, which did not contain a box dealing with the issue of joint ownership. The purchase was funded by a mixture of capital from Ms Dowden's building society account (part of which consisted of the proceeds of sale of the previous property, and part being savings of her own) and a mortgage in the parties' joint names. The male cohabitant paid from the date of purchase the mortgage instalments and the payments due under linked endowment policies. In addition both repaid lump sums off the mortgage. Generally during the relationship Ms Dowden earned more than Mr Stack.

---

29   *Kernott v Jones.*
30   [2007] UKHL 17.

10.38 Nine years after the purchase the parties separated. Mr Stack moved out and Ms Dowden remained in the house with their four children. He then began proceedings seeking a sale of the property and equal division of the proceeds.

10.39 His claim was successful in the county court. The trial judge took a very 'broad brush' approach to the claim and made numerous references in his judgment to the idea that the parties' financial arrangements were a partnership. He said:

> 'It seems to me, although the defendant has been the bigger wage-earner over this very long association between the parties, they have both put their all into doing the best for themselves and their family as they could. In these circumstances after such a very long relationship a 50/50 share is . . . an appropriate division of the net proceeds of sale.'

Ms Dowden appealed to the Court of Appeal, who found that the she was entitled to 65% of the net proceeds of sale and Mr Stack to 35%. Mr Stack then appealed to the House of Lords. This decision was keenly awaited by lawyers as it was hoped that it might clarify the law, but it did not do so: if anything, the area has become more complex following *Stack* and the more recent decision in *Kernott v Jones*.

10.40 In summary *Stack* decided the following:

(a)   A couple who purchase a property in their joint names as a home for themselves, without any declaration of trust, ordinarily own the legal and beneficial interest jointly in equal shares:

> '... the starting point where there is sole legal ownership is sole beneficial ownership, the starting point where there is joint legal ownership is joint beneficial ownership. The onus is upon the person seeking to show that the beneficial ownership is different from the legal ownership.[31]
>
> For the reasons already stated, at least in the domestic consumer context, a conveyance into joint names indicates both legal and beneficial joint tenancy, unless and until the contrary is proved.'[32]

(b)   However, the court has to consider the joint intention of the parties at the time they purchased the property. If the parties have made their intentions clear (but not executed a declaration of trust) they will own the beneficial interest in accordance with their intentions;

(c)   If the parties have not made their intentions clear, the court may nonetheless infer their intention from their conduct generally:[33]

---

[31]   Baroness Hale at para 56 of *Stack v Dowden*.
[32]   Baroness Hale at para 58 of *Stack v Dowden*.
[33]   Baroness Hale at para 69–70 of *Stack v Dowden*.

'In law, "context is everything" and the domestic context is very different from the commercial world. Each case will turn on its own facts. Many more factors than financial contributions may be relevant to divining the parties' true intentions. These include: any advice or discussions at the time of the transfer which cast light upon their intentions then; the reasons why the home was acquired in their joint names; the reasons why (if it be the case) the survivor was authorised to give a receipt for the capital moneys; the purpose for which the home was acquired; the nature of the parties' relationship; whether they had children for whom they both had responsibility to provide a home; how the purchase was financed, both initially and subsequently; how the parties arranged their finances, whether separately or together or a bit of both; how they discharged the outgoings on the property and their other household expenses. When a couple are joint owners of the home and jointly liable for the mortgage, the inferences to be drawn from who pays for what may be very different from the inferences to be drawn when only one is owner of the home. The arithmetical calculation of how much was paid by each is also likely to be less important. It will be easier to draw the inference that they intended that each should contribute as much to the household as they reasonably could and that they would share the eventual benefit or burden equally. The parties' individual characters and personalities may also be a factor in deciding where their true intentions lay. In the cohabitation context, mercenary considerations may be more to the fore than they would be in marriage, but it should not be assumed that they always take pride of place over natural love and affection. At the end of the day, having taken all this into account, cases in which the joint legal owners are to be taken to have intended that their beneficial interests should be different from their legal interests will be very unusual.

This is not, of course, an exhaustive list. There may also be reason to conclude that, whatever the parties' intentions at the outset, these have now changed. An example might be where one party has financed (or constructed himself) an extension or substantial improvement to the property, so that what they have now is significantly different from what they had then.'

(d)   In some circumstances, if there is no evidence from which their intentions can be inferred, the court may imply an intention that they should own the property in such shares as would be considered fair:[34]

'The law has indeed moved on in response to changing social and economic conditions. The search is to ascertain the parties' shared intentions, actual, inferred *or imputed*, with respect to the property in the light of their whole course of conduct in relation to it.'

10.41   This decision was widely criticised for failing to clarify the law and for potentially encouraging the courts in a case where there was no express declaration of trust to engage in an investigation into the parties' conduct and contributions (the 'holistic' approach suggested by Baroness Hale).

---

[34]   Baroness Hale at para 60 in *Stack v Dowden*.

10.42 A particular concern arising out of the decision in *Stack* was that it appeared to open up the possibility of the parties' interests in a property changing over time, without clarifying in what circumstances this could occur. Lord Hoffman, one of the judges involved in the decision in the House of Lords, had referred when the case was being argued before the court, to the possible existence of an 'ambulatory constructive trust'.[35] This led to the Supreme Court again considering the relevant law in the case of *Kernott v Jones*.[36]

10.43 *Kernott* involved a situation which has occurred very commonly from about 1990 onwards, but may become less frequent as UK house prices become static. Ms Jones and Mr Kernott purchased a property together in Benfleet in Kent. It was bought in 1985 in their joint names without any express declaration of trust. The purchase price was £30,000; Ms Jones contributed £6,000 and the balance was obtained by a mortgage in their joint names. After they had moved in Mr Kernott built and paid for an extension to the property, which increased the value of it by nearly half. They had two children.

10.44 In 1993 the couple separated and Mr Kernott moved out. They cashed a life insurance policy and divided the proceeds: this was primarily so that Mr Kernott had a sufficient deposit to purchase his own property, which he did. Ms Jones thereafter paid the mortgage and all the outgoings on the property from the date of his departure. She also did not seek to pursue child maintenance claims against him.

10.45 By 2008 Mr Kernott's new property was worth about £205,000 with a mortgage of £38,000. The former cohabitual home was worth £245,000 with a mortgage of just under £27,000. At that stage Mr Kernott sought an order for sale of the former home, with the sale proceeds to be divided equally. Ms Jones opposed this: she argued that the court could infer, on the basis of arrangements since the separation, including the surrender of the life policy, that they intended to vary their interests in the property so that she owned the equity outright.

10.46 The parties had the misfortune to go through no fewer than four hearings, commencing with a trial in the county court, followed by appeals to the High Court, Court of Appeal, and Supreme Court. The judge in the county court found that the parties' interests had been varied, and that they owned the beneficial interest on trust as to 90% for Ms Kernott and 10% for Mr Jones. That decision was upheld in the High Court, but reversed in the Court of Appeal where it was found that they owned the property jointly. That decision was reversed again in the Supreme Court where the original decision was restored (albeit without the members of that court necessarily agreeing with the original judge's reasoning).

---

[35] Referred to by Baroness Hale in para 62 of her judgment.
[36] [2011] UKSC 53.

10.47 Baroness Hale and Lord Walker, giving the main judgment of the court, made the following observations:

'(1) The starting point is that equity follows the law and they are joint tenants both in law and in equity.

(2) That presumption can be displaced by showing (a) that the parties had a different common intention at the time when they acquired the home, or (b) that they later formed the common intention that their respective shares would change.

(3) Their common intention is to be deduced objectively from their conduct: "the relevant intention of each party is the intention which was reasonably understood by the other party to be manifested by that party's words or conduct notwithstanding that he did not consciously formulate that intention in his own mind or even acted with some different intention which he did not communicate to the other party" (Lord Diplock in *Gissing v Gissing* [1970] 2 All ER 780 at 790, [1971] AC 886 at 906). Examples of the sort of evidence which might be relevant to drawing such inferences are given in *Stack v Dowden* [2007] 2 FCR 280 at [69], [2007] 2 All ER 929.

(4) In those cases where it is clear either (a) that the parties did not intend joint tenancy at the outset, or (b) had changed their original intention, but it is not possible to ascertain by direct evidence or by inference what their actual intention was as to the shares in which they would own the property, "the answer is that each is entitled to that share which the court considers fair having regard to the whole course of dealing between them in relation to the property": Chadwick LJ in *Oxley v Hiscock* [2004] 2 FCR 295 at [69], [2004] 3 All ER 703. In our judgment, "the whole course of dealing ... in relation to the property" should be given a broad meaning, enabling a similar range of factors to be taken into account as may be relevant to ascertaining the parties' actual intentions.

(5) Each case will turn on its own facts. Financial contributions are relevant but there are many other factors which may enable the court to decide what shares were either intended (as in case (3)) or fair (as in case (4)).'

10.48 In addition they observed:

'where the parties already share the beneficial interest, and the question is what their interests are and whether their interests have changed, the court will try to deduce what their actual intentions were at the relevant time. It cannot impose a solution upon them which is contrary to what the evidence shows that they actually intended. But if it cannot deduce exactly what shares were intended, it may have no alternative but to ask what their intentions as reasonable and just people would have been had they thought about it at the time. This is a fallback position which some courts may not welcome, but the court has a duty to come to a conclusion on the dispute put before it.'

10.49 What can the cohabitant contemplating a house purchase draw from this confusing situation? As is set out in **10.10** above, the preferred method of achieving certainty on the joint purchase of a property is to draw up a trust deed which deals with ownership issues including contribution to the purchase price, responsibility for paying the mortgage, and contains a mechanism for what should happen on dissolution. In the absence of such an agreement, a basic declaration of trust in the current version of the TR1 may at least deal with the issue of equitable ownership of the property at the time of the purchase. As can be seen below, this may not be the end of the story.

Inadequate declaration of trust

10.50 Even if the TR1 contains a declaration of trust, this will not necessarily be binding on the parties if its significance was not adequately explained to them. In *Hapeshi v Allnatt*[37] an elderly mother and one of her sons (M) signed a transfer indicating that they intended to purchase a property as joint tenants in law and equity. They were sent a letter by the conveyancing solicitors explaining briefly the difference but nothing to suggest that any attempt had been made to check that this was understood. The mother died and another son (K) argued that there had been an agreement that the equitable interest would be owned jointly by his mother, the other legal purchaser, and himself, on the basis that the benefit would accrue to the brothers on the death of their mother. In reliance on this he had made occasional mortgage payments. M died first, the mother dying some six years later. A deputy High Court judge accepted that there had been such an agreement and on that basis adopted a holistic approach to the quantification of the parties' interests. The judge found that the mother and M had owned the property as joint tenants in law but held it on trust for themselves and K as equitable tenants in common. On that basis K had a 25% interest.

10.51 The judge was dismissive of the statement in the transfer document that the deceased and M intended to hold the property on trust for themselves as joint tenants. The conveyancing solicitors had sent out a standard form letter explaining the difference between joint tenancy and tenancy in common in which the purchasers were requested to tick which option they preferred and return the document. Although no copy of the completed letter was located (the complete conveyancing file was not available twenty years after the purchase) the inference was that this had been returned with the joint tenancy option indicated as the preference, because the transfer document indicated that the parties were joint tenants. At the time the document was executed the deceased could not read English at all and spoke only a few words of the language, and there was no evidence that anyone had explained to her what the difference was between tenancy in common and joint tenancy. The judge stated:

> 'True it is that in the transfer [the mother] and [M] declared that they held as beneficial joint tenants, but it is quite clear that [the mother] could not understand written English. It is quite clear from [the conveyancer's] evidence that Mrs Hapeshi never received any explanation direct from [the conveyance] as to the basis on which the property should be held. It is quite clear that she would not have understood (if she had been shown it) the document that [she was] sent enquiring whether it should be held as beneficial joint tenants or tenants in

---

[37] [2010] EWHC 392 (Ch).

common. So even if that document was returned, it does not indicate or connote an understanding and intention on Mrs Hapeshi's part that the property should necessarily be held in that way.'

In *Hapeshi* there was nothing to suggest that the mother had intended to hold the property on trust for herself and M and joint tenants. A declaration of trust drawn up by the parties, but left unsigned, may still be useful evidence of their intentions.[38]

Agreement to vary the declaration of trust

10.52   If the parties can determine their interest by a trust deed, they can also agree to vary it. In *Qayyum v Hameed*[39] a husband executed a trust deed whereby he held the whole of his interest in a jointly owned property on trust for the wife. Subsequently the wife agreed that they could again become joint beneficial owners of the property and a mortgage was raised against it in their joint names. The husband became bankrupt and the wife sought to argue that the trust deed still applied and that the subsequent oral agreement was ineffective. The court found that a constructive trust arose in the husband's favour and the beneficial interest was held jointly (and therefore fell into the hands of his trustee in bankruptcy).

10.53   In *Clarke v Meadus*[40] the court had to consider complicated family property arrangements arising out of a scheme to reduce the payment of inheritance tax. There was an express declaration of trust but a High Court judge found that it was arguable that this had been overridden by an interest arising under a proprietary estoppel and/or a constructive trust.[41] This was a decision on a preliminary application; not a final determination of the case.

Ownership in one name only: constructive and resulting trusts

10.54   A constructive trust may arise in circumstances where it is inequitable to permit the legal owner to continue to assert his beneficial ownership of the property. In the case of ownership of the family home, this is most likely to occur where there is a common intention to share the ownership of the home, even though the legal title is held in the name of one party only, and the other party acts to his detriment in reliance on that. In *Lloyds Bank v Rossett*[42] the House of Lords suggested that this might occur in two ways:

---

[38]   *Williamson v Sheikh* [2008] EWCA Civ 990.
[39]   [2009] EWCA Civ 352.
[40]   [2010] EWHC 3117 (Ch).
[41]   'It cannot, in my judgment, sensibly be argued that once beneficial interests have been declared in a formal document, those interests become immutable and incapable of being affected by a proprietary estoppel ... So far as the claim based on constructive trust is concerned, the position is more difficult. That claim seems to rely on a remedial constructive trust, a juridical beast which English case law has set its face against. Perhaps the attitude of the courts is changing' – Warren J.
[42]   [1991] 1 AC 107.

'The first and fundamental question which must always be resolved is whether, independently of any inference to be drawn from the conduct of the parties in the course of sharing the house as their home and managing their joint affairs, there has at any time prior to acquisition, or exceptionally at some later date, been any agreement, arrangement or understanding reached between them that the property is to be shared beneficially. The finding of an agreement or arrangement to share in this sense can only, I think, be based on evidence of express discussions between the partners, however imperfectly remembered and however imprecise their terms may have been. Once a finding to this effect is made it will only be necessary for the partner asserting a claim to a beneficial interest against the partner entitled to the legal estate to show that he or she has acted to his or her detriment or significantly altered his or her position in reliance on the agreement in order to give rise to a constructive trust or a proprietary estoppel.

In sharp contrast with this situation is the very different one where there is no evidence to support a finding of an agreement or arrangement to share, however reasonable it might have been for the parties to reach such an arrangement if they had applied their minds to the question, and where the court must rely entirely on the conduct of the parties both as the basis from which to infer a common intention to share the property beneficially and as the conduct relied on to give rise to a constructive trust. In this situation direct contributions to the purchase price by the partner who is not the legal owner, whether initially or by payment of mortgage instalments, will readily justify the inference necessary to the creation of a constructive trust. But, as I read the authorities, it is at least extremely doubtful whether anything less will do.'

10.55   The position in law following that decision was that a cohabitant or partner could gain an interest in the family home even if there had been no express discussion on the subject by direct contribution to the purchase price (including by way of mortgage repayments) but not by reliance on other acts (for example, contributions towards repairs,[43] or payments towards household expenses). If there had been a discussion that the ownership should be shared, even if such a discussion was highly informal, any form of reliance on that discussion might suffice provided the person claiming the interest can show that he had acted to his detriment.

10.56   More recently the Privy Council has suggested that the law has moved on. In *Abbott v Abbott*[44] the courts of Antigua and Barbuda had applied the *Lloyds Bank v Rosset* test in a case in which a property asset was in the sole name of the husband, but the wife claimed an interest. Baroness Hale, giving judgment in this case, referred to her own judgment in *Stack v Dowden* and said:

'Lord Walker, Lord Hoffmann and Lord Hope of Craighead all agreed with my own opinion, in which I summed the matter up thus at para 60:

---

[43]   But see **10.63** for the position in relation to engaged couples.
[44]   [2007] UKPC 53.

"The law has indeed moved on in response to changing social and economic conditions. The search is to ascertain the parties' shared intentions, actual, inferred or imputed, with respect to the property in the light of their whole course of conduct in relation to it.'"

10.57   What *Abbott* fails to do is to clarify how this exercise should be undertaken. In some cases decided after *Abbott*, the court appears still to apply the approach taken in *Lloyds Bank plc v Rossett*. In *Thomson v Humphrey*[45] Warren J commented that:

'Accepting that matters have moved on since Lord Bridge of Harwich's restrictive requirement that there needs to be a direct contribution in terms of the mortgage payments, it is not sensible to attempt to say what will and will not be enough. There will be cases which, on any view, fall from the claimant's point of view on the wrong side of the line, wherever that line is to be drawn. Each case is to be viewed on its facts, but one can obtain a flavour of the correct approach from the reported cases.'

10.58   Examples of such cases would in his view include: looking after the family home and children, paying some utility bills, and purchasing some household items, which was insufficient to give rise to an interest; looking after the house, entertaining clients, and supervising building works, which were similarly insufficient; helping run a business including undertaking heavy physical work, also insufficient.

10.59   These are of course activities of a type which many non-working partners will engage in, particularly if childcare is one of their responsibilities. A cohabitant should not assume that making contributions of this kind will assist him in obtaining an interest in a home in the sole name of his partner, unless there has been some clear discussion between them to this effect.

Resulting trusts

10.60   A resulting trust arises by operation of law where a trust is imposed on the parties. In the context of family relationships this is most likely to occur where one of two partners pays money to the other to be used for the purchase of a property. In those circumstances there is no presumption that the money was intended as a gift and the property will be held on trust for the parties in the proportions in which they supply the funds. Thus if A provides B with £100,000 to use towards the purchase of a property in B's sole name which costs £200,000, the property will be held on trust by B for himself and A jointly. In this situation the property will almost certainly be held by B on trust for himself and A as tenants in common in shares proportionate to their contribution.

10.61   The courts have been increasingly reluctant to apply resulting trust principles to situations where the parties purchase a property in which to live

---

[45]   [2009] EWHC 3576 (Ch).

together.[46] However this approach will be taken if parties purchase a property as an investment. In *Laskar v Laskar*[47] a mother and daughter joined forces to purchase the mother's council house. The property was purchased partly with a joint mortgage, partly by capital contributions from mother and daughter; however, the biggest contribution came from the mother's right to buy discount. There was no declaration of trust and the transfer document did not set out the parties' interests. The mother moved out shortly after the purchase and the property was let as an investment property. Disputes arose between mother and daughter and the daughter sought a declaration that she had a half interest in the property on the basis that the purchase in joint names gave rise to a presumption that the beneficial interest was held equally. The court held that the approach taken in *Stack* did not apply in a 'commercial context' and found that the property was held on the basis that the resulting trust presumption applied and the discount should be treated as the mother's contribution to the purchase price (together with her capital contribution and one half of the joint mortgage).

Proprietary estoppel

10.62   A non-owner may also acquire an interest in a property by proprietary estoppel. This arises where the non-owner acts in a belief that he is acquiring an interest in a property, and the owner permits or even encourages him to act on that belief. The principle distinction between proprietary estoppel and constructive trust is that in the latter case, the person claiming the right acquires a beneficial interest in the property as a result of the operation of the trust. In the case of proprietary estoppel, the person claiming the right acquires a right to seek relief from the court, which will grant such relief on the basis that it should do no more than is needed to give effect to the estoppels.[48] In some cases that may involve a transfer of an interest in the property which is the subject of the dispute; in others, it may involve payment of a sum of money.[49]

'Engaged' couples

10.63   Where a couple have agreed to enter into a civil partnership,[50] s 65 of the Civil Partnership Act applies to their property:

'(1) This section applies if –

(a)   a civil partner contributes in money or money's worth to the improvement of real or personal property in which or in the proceeds of sale of which either or both of the civil partners has or have a beneficial interest, and

---

[46]   See the judgment of Baroness Hale in *Stack v Dowden*, op cit, at paras 58–60.
[47]   [2008] EWCA Civ 347.
[48]   *Crabb v Arun DC* [1976] Ch 179.
[49]   For an example, see *Ashby v Kilduff*, op cit, where the judge considered that the claim in relation to one of the properties could be satisfied either by payment of a lump sum or by an order permitting one party to live in the property rent free for a period.
[50]   An agreement to enter into a civil partnership: CPA 2004, s 73(3).

(b)   the contribution is of a substantial nature.

(2) The contributing partner is to be treated as having acquired by virtue of the contribution a share or an enlarged share (as the case may be) in the beneficial interest of such an extent –

(a)   as may have been then agreed, or
(b)   in default of such agreement, as may seem in all the circumstances just to any court before which the question of the existence or extent of the beneficial interest of either of the civil partners arises (whether in proceedings between them or in any other proceedings).

(3) Subsection (2) is subject to any agreement (express or implied) between the civil partners to the contrary.'

10.64 A similar provision applies in the case of engaged opposite sex couples.[51] There are few reported cases dealing with the application of that earlier legislation, but the following propositions can be deduced from them:

(a)   the contribution must be substantial, not just general DIY;[52]

(b)   contributions to the initial purchase price will be treated as giving the parties such beneficial interest as seems just in all the circumstances;[53]

(c)   making household contributions which free up the other's partner's income for mortgage payments will be taken into account;[54]

(d)   the court will take a broad approach as to what amounts to an improvement.[55]

Orders in relation to property owned by cohabitants

10.65 Section 14 of the Trusts of Land and Appointment of Trustees Act 1996 permits 'any person who is a trustee of land or has an interest in a property subject to a trust of land' to make an application to the court for an order as to the trustees' exercise of their functions and to make a declaration as 'to the nature or extent of a person's interest in property subject to the trust'.

10.66 This gives the court the power to declare on what basis the owners own a property. In the case of a sole legal owner where another person is claiming an interest in the property, the court can make a finding as to whether or not that person has an interest, and as to its nature and extent. It can also appoint him a joint trustee of the property (together with the existing legal owner) so that he becomes one of the legal owners of the property. If the property is

[51]   Matrimonial Proceedings and Property Act 1970, s 37.
[52]   *Pettitt v Pettitt* [1970] AC 777.
[53]   *Davis v Vale* [1971] 2 All ER 1021.
[54]   *Davis v Vale* [1971] 2 All ER 1021.
[55]   *Griffiths v Griffiths* [1973] 3 All ER 386.

owned by two or more legal owners, the court can determine whether they hold the beneficial interest as joint tenants, or as tenants in common, and, if the latter, in what shares.

10.67 What the court cannot do under s 14 is to transfer one owner's beneficial interest in the property to the other. It can make a declaration as to the existing state of the beneficial ownership of the property, but cannot alter that ownership.

10.68 Section 14 also permits a court to make an order that a property be sold and to give directions to permit that sale to proceed in a sensible manner. These can include:

(a)   which of the owners should be involved in instructing estate agents (usually known as 'having conduct of the sale');

(b)   who the agents should be;

(c)   which solicitor/conveyancer should carry out the conveyancing on the sale;

(d)   how viewings of the property should be handled;

(e)   how the sale price should be determined, including setting a sale price if the parties cannot agree.

Section 14 also gives the court the power to determine when a property should be sold. This may be a particular problem if a relationship has come to an end but the children of that relationship continue to live at the property with one or both of the partners.

10.69 In considering the exercise of its powers under s 14 of the Act the matters which the court is required to have regard to include the following:[56]

      (a)   the intentions of the person or persons (if any) who created the trust,
      (b)   the purposes for which the property subject to the trust is held,
      (c)   the welfare of any minor who occupies or might reasonably be expected to occupy any land subject to the trust as his home, and
      (d)   the interests of any secured creditor of any beneficiary.

10.70 In addition in cases where an application is made relating to the exercise of the trustees' powers to exclude or restrict a beneficiaries' right of

---

[56]   Trusts of Land and Appointment of Trustees Act 1996, s 15.

occupation,[57] the circumstances and wishes of each of the beneficiaries who is or would be entitled to occupy the land will be taken into account.

10.71 In the case of any other application,[58] the court will also have regard to the circumstances and wishes of any beneficiaries of full age and entitled to an interest in possession in the property or (in case of dispute) the majority (according to the value of their combined interests).

10.72 There are few reported cases about applications under the 1996 Act where the issue is the timing of any sale. Those that have been reported are mostly cases where the applicant is a financial institution which has acquired an interest in the property by lending on it as security, the borrower has failed to pay, and the borrower's former partner who remains in the home with the children is seeking to delay sale. The case law indicates that the court is to have regard to all the circumstances of the case: the list set out in **10.69** above is not exhaustive – *Edwards v Edwards*.[59] Where there is such a creditor, the best that can be hoped for is that the sale will be postponed, rather than refused.[60]

10.73 *Holman v Howes*[61] is an interesting example of how the court will apply ss 14 and 15. The parties had been a married couple, but divorced. Following the divorce they attempted reconciliation and purchased a property, each contributing about half the cost. The purchase was in the sole name of the former wife. She alleged that it had always been intended that the beneficial interest would be solely hers. The court rejected this argument, and found that she held the property on trust for herself and the former husband jointly. However the judge accepted that the intention of the purchase was to provide her with a home for as long as she wished to occupy it. The intention of the persons who created the trust were to provide the wife with a home for as long as she wished to occupy it, and likewise the purpose of the trust was to provide her with such a home. On this basis the court declined to make an order for sale.

10.74 The welfare of children who might be expected to occupy the property as their home is a factor to be taken into account, but their welfare is not paramount as it is in applications under the Children Act 1989.

10.75 It is possible for applications under the Trusts of Land and Appointment of Trustees Act 1996 to become coupled with an application under Sch 1 of the Children Act 1989.[62] The scenario where this may occur is where one cohabitant leaves the property and the other remains in it with the

---

[57] Under s 13 of the Trusts of Land and Appointment of Trustees Act 1996.
[58] Any application which is not one to exclude or restrict a beneficiary's right of occupation and which is also not one relating to the power of trustees to convey the land to the beneficiaries under s 6(2) of the Trusts of Land and Appointment of Trustees Act 1996.
[59] [2010] EWHC 652 (Ch).
[60] *Bank of Ireland Home Mortgages Ltd v Bell* [2001] 3 FCR 134.
[61] [2006] 1 FLR 1003.
[62] See below at **10.123**.

children. The departing cohabitant applies for an order for sale; the one who remains in the property seeks provision for the children under Sch 1 of the Children Act. A good example of this can be seen in *W v W (Joinder Of Trusts Of Land Act And Children Act Applications)*.[63] In that case an unmarried couple owned a property jointly and occupied it with their children. On separation M, who expected that the children would live with her, issued an application under s 14 of the 1996 Act to defer F's realisation of his half share until the youngest child reached eighteen. F opposed this application on the basis that the property should be sold immediately. There were proceedings in relation to the children and the court decided that they should live with F. He then sought to defer the sale whereas M pressed for an immediate sale. F issued an application under Sch 1 of the Children Act 1989 for a transfer of M's interest during the children's minority. The matter was heard in the county court and the judge decided to deal with the TLATA application first, adjourning the Children Act application. He then made an order for sale. F appealed. The Court of Appeal found the judge's approach to be wrong in principle. The two applications should have been heard together. As a matter of good practice it would have also been preferable if the judge who had heard the proceedings in relation to the children's residence had also dealt with the property matters as he had a greater degree of insight into the family dynamics.[64] Any cohabitant with children who is seeking to fend off an application for an order for sale should give consideration to whether an application under Sch 1 is advisable.

Proposals for reform

10.76 In July 2007 the Law Commission produced proposals to provide some financial protection for cohabitants whose relationship breaks down. The key features of the scheme were:

(a) It would apply only to cohabitants who had a child together or who had lived together for a minimum period (which the Law Commission suggested should be no less than two and no more than five years).

(b) The definition of cohabitant would be wide and would include same sex couples and cohabitants who were still the civil partners of a third party but were cohabiting with someone else. It would also be possible to cohabit with more than one person at the same time.

(c) An eligible cohabitant would have to show that on separation the other cohabitant had retained a benefit, or that the applicant had suffered an economic disadvantage, as a result of qualifying contributions made by the applicant.

---

[63] [2004] 2 FLR 321.
[64] The Court of Appeal however held that the judge's decision regarding an order for sale had been correct, because F could downsize with the children to a smaller property.

(d)   Qualifying contributions would include not only financial contribution but also contribution by looking after the home and children.

(e)   An economic disadvantage would include a loss of future earnings or future earning capacity; a retained benefit would include income, capital and earning capacity retained or enhanced;

(f)   The court could make an order adjusting any retained benefit taking into account the following discretionary factors:

   (i)   the welfare while a minor of any child of both parties who has not attained the age of eighteen;
   (ii)   the financial needs and obligations of both parties;
   (iii) the extent and nature of the financial resources which each party has or is likely to have in the foreseeable future;
   (iv)   the welfare of any children who live with, or might reasonably be expected to live with, either party; and
   (v)   the conduct of each party, defined restrictively but so as to include cases where a qualifying contribution can be shown to have been made despite the express disagreement of the other party.

   Of those factors the welfare of any minor would have first consideration.

(g)   The court would have the power to transfer property, order the payment of lump sums, make orders for sale and transfer pensions.

(h)   Cohabitants would be able to opt out of the scheme.

10.77   The approach involves a more structured decision process than the making of an order for a financial remedy under the Civil Partnership Act. The Law Commission suggested that the scheme would achieve the following:

> 'We consider that a scheme based on these principles would provide a sound basis on which to address the hardship and other economic unfairness that can arise when a cohabiting relationship ends. It would respond, more comprehensively than the current law can, to the economic impact of the contributions made by parties to their relationship, and so to needs which arise in consequence. Where there are dependent children, the scheme would enable a remedy to be provided for the benefit of the primary carer, and so better protect those children who share their primary carer's standard of living. By making adequate provision for the adult parties, the scheme would give more leeway to the court than it currently has to apply Schedule 1 to the Children Act 1989 for the benefit of the parties' children.'

On 6 September 2011 the government announced that it did not intend to implement the reforms within the lifetime of the current government. It put forward two reasons for doing this: first, that research into the effect of the Family Law (Scotland) Act 2006 did not justify the implementation of reform in England and Wales; second, that the family justice system was under review with major changes on the horizon. As the Family Justice Review[65] did not include the position of cohabiting couples within its terms of reference it is difficult to see why this was a justification for delay. Research into the Family Law (Scotland) Act (which provides some financial protection for cohabitants on separation) suggested the take up of the rights granted by the Act was lower than expected, but the research was carried out when the Act had only been in force for three years. The suspicion among lawyers is that the government sees the implementation of cohabitation reform as a 'vote loser'.[66]

10.78   It seems unlikely that there will be any attempt to change the law for the foreseeable future. The Law Commission recommended that, if its proposals were implemented, there should be a period before the provisions took effect during which couples would have an opportunity to opt out.

THE FAMILY HOME: RENTED PROPERTY

10.79   Where cohabitants occupy rented property as their home there are two issues to consider at the outset: first, is the tenancy in joint names or the sole name of one of them; second, what is the nature of the tenancy.

10.80   Rented property in England and Wales will in most cases be held under one of three forms of tenancy:

(a)   A tenancy under the Rent Act 1977.
      No new tenancies under this Act have been created since 15 January 1989, when the Housing Act 1988 came into force.

(b)   An assured or assured shorthold tenancy under the Housing Act 1988.

(c)   A secure tenancy pursuant to the provisions of the Housing Act 1985.

10.81   Property which is occupied by an agricultural worker is likely to be subject to an assured agricultural occupancy or to be held as a statutory tenancy pursuant to the Rent (Agriculture) Act 1976.

10.82   Secure tenancies are the default form of tenure for the tenants of local authority landlords. Tenants of local authority properties whose home was transferred to a housing association via a stock transfer will retain their secure tenancy status.[67] New tenants of housing associations which have taken over local authority housing stock will usually be assured tenants. Tenancies granted

---

[65]   The Family Justice Review was published on 3 November 2011. The Review was chaired, inevitably, by a businessman (a director of Marks and Spencer) rather than a lawyer.

[66]   Because it will annoy traditional conservatives who will see it as eroding the institution of marriage, without being sufficiently popular to gain many votes. The right wing research institute Civitas has been pushing an anti-cohabitation agenda – see *Marriage-Lite* by Patricia Morgan *Civitas* (2000).

[67]   Housing Act 1988, s 94.

by registered social landlords are generally assured tenancies. Most landlords in the private sector use assured shorthold tenancies, which can be determined on two months' notice by the landlord.

10.83 The tenancy agreement (assuming there is a written agreement) is the first place to look to ascertain the nature of the tenancy.

10.84 On the breakdown of a relationship the court has the power under Sch 7 of the Family Law Act 1996 to transfer a tenancy from one cohabitant to another. 'Cohabitants' in this context are defined as 'two persons who are neither married to each other nor civil partners of each other but are living together as husband and wife or as if they were civil partners'.[68]

10.85 It should be noted that occupation by one cohabitant is not treated as occupation by both[69] and a cohabitant who is not a tenant but who remains in the property alone after the departure of the other is not entitled as of right to pay the rent or other outgoings. The position is different for civil partners.[70]

10.86 Pursuant to para 3 of Sch 7:

'(1) This paragraph applies if one cohabitant is entitled,[71] either in his own right or jointly with the other cohabitant, to occupy a dwelling-house by virtue of a relevant tenancy.[72]

(2) If the cohabitants cease [to cohabit], the court may make a Part II order.'

10.87 The court may not make an order under Sch 7 unless the property was one in which the parties cohabited.[73] The court has the power to make such an order if only one of the parties is the tenant[74] and they have ceased to cohabit.

10.88 Under para 7 of the Schedule the court may order that the interest of one partner in the property be transferred to the other partner from a date specified in the order. In considering whether to make such an order the court shall:

'have regard to all the circumstances of the case including –

(a)   the circumstances in which the tenancy was granted to either or both of . . . the cohabitants or, as the case requires, the circumstances in which either or both of them became tenant under the tenancy;

---

68   FLA 1996, s 62(1).
69   FLA 1996, s 30(4).
70   FLA 1996, s 30(5).
71   A cohabitant is treated as having such a right 'whether that entitlement is in his own right or jointly with the other ... cohabitant.'
72   In this context a relevant tenancy includes: a tenancy under the Rent Act 1977; a secure tenancy under the Housing Act 1985; an assured tenancy under the Housing Act 1988; an introductory tenancy under the Housing Act 1996 Part V; and certain types of agricultural tenancy.
73   FLA 1996, Sch 7, para 3(2).
74   FLA 1996, Sch 7, para 3(1).

(b)   the matters mentioned in section 33(6)(a), (b) and (c) and, where the parties are cohabitants and only one of them is entitled to occupy the dwelling-house by virtue of the relevant tenancy, the further matters mentioned in section 36(6)(e), (f), (g) and (h); and

(c)   the suitability of the parties as tenants.'

10.89   The matters mentioned in s 33(6)(a), (b) and (c) are as follows:

'(6) In deciding whether to exercise its powers under subsection (3) and (if so) in what manner, the court shall have regard to all the circumstances including –

(a)   the housing needs and housing resources of each of the parties and of any relevant child;

(b)   the financial resources of each of the parties;

(c)   the likely effect of any order, or of any decision by the court not to exercise its powers under subsection (3), on the health, safety or well-being of the parties and of any relevant child.'

10.90   The matters referred to in s 36(6)(e), (f), (g) and (h) are:

'(d)   the conduct of the parties in relation to each other and otherwise;

(e)   the nature of the parties' relationship and in particular the level of commitment involved in it;[75]

(f)   the length of time during which they have cohabited;

(g)   whether there are or have been any children who are children of both parties or for whom both parties have or have had parental responsibility;

(h)   the length of time that has elapsed since the parties ceased to live together.'

10.91   On making an order transferring a tenancy to a cohabitant, the court can order payment by the transferee of a sum to the transferor (whether the tenancy was held jointly or separately).[76] In deciding whether to make such a payment the court will have regard to:[77]

'(a)   the financial loss that would otherwise be suffered by the transferor as a result of the order;

(b)   the financial needs and financial resources of the parties; and

(c)   the financial obligations which the parties have, or are likely to have in the foreseeable future, including financial obligations to each other and to any relevant child.'

This payment may be postponed or deferred if the balance of hardship requires it.[78]

---

[75]   This part of the Schedule has an interesting legislative history. The wording was originally found in s 41 of the 1996 Act, and required the court in considering any question under the Act, to have regard to the unmarried status of cohabitants, apparently to meet a criticism that the 1996 Act, as originally drafted, equated marriage with cohabitation. The section was repealed by the Domestic Violence, Crime and Victims Act 2004, s 2(2), and the current wording of s 36(6)(e) introduced as a replacement.

[76]   FLA 1996, Sch 7, para 10.

[77]   FLA 1996, Sch 7, para 10(4).

[78]   FLA 1996, Sch 7, para 10(5).

10.92 On the making of a transfer order, any liabilities arising out of any covenant or obligation in the tenancy agreement cease to have effect against the party from whom the tenancy is transferred from the date of the transfer.[79] The landlord of the property has a right to be heard on such an application.[80]

10.93 Difficulties can arise if the tenancy has come to an end prior to the making of an order under Sch 7. A statutory tenancy under the Rent Act 1977 can be ended without an order of the court if the tenant gives up possession. If the tenant cohabitant leaves such a property, not intending to return, while the non-tenant cohabitant remains in residence, the latter's occupation is not automatically treated as occupation by the former, and the tenancy may be treated as having ended. The non-tenant cohabitant can protect his position in the short term by applying for an occupation order under s 36 of the Family Law Act 1996.[81] Such an order, while it remains in force, has the effect of causing the non-tenant's occupation to be treated as occupation by the tenant.[82] This will prevent the landlord seeking possession on the basis that the tenant has given up possession. Alternatively, the non-tenant cohabitant can apply for an order under Sch 7, provided he does so before the tenant cohabitant can be treated as having given up possession permanently.

10.94 If the non-tenant cohabitant fails to take either of these steps, there is a risk that the tenancy may be regarded as being at an end. This would prevent an application under Sch 7, as that of course only applies to existing tenancies.

10.95 A further problem area is the effect of a notice to quit if given by one of two joint tenants. Such a notice will serve to terminate the tenancy of both: *Hammersmith & Fulham LBC v Monk*[83] (secure tenancy) and *Newlon Housing Trust v Alsulaimen*[84] (assured tenancy). The usual approach to possession proceedings following such an event is that they will be conducted in accordance with domestic law and that arguments about rights to family life pursuant to Art 8 of the ECHR will not prevail provided the correct procedure is followed.[85] However a recent unreported decision involving a case in which a husband gave a notice to quit and the local authority subsequently sought possession of the former matrimonial home from the wife suggests that some judges will be willing to listen to Art 8 arguments in this situation.[86] Such arguments can only be used where the landlord is a public body.

---

[79] FLA 1996, Sch 7, para 7(2).
[80] FLA 1996, Sch 7, para 14.
[81] See chapter 9 for more detail on occupation orders under s 36.
[82] Section 36(13).
[83] [1992] 1 All ER 1.
[84] [1998] 4 All ER 1.
[85] *Kay v Lambeth BC* [2006] UKHL 10.
[86] *Chesterfield BC v Bailey* BAILII Citation Number: [2011] EW Misc 18 (CC) applying *Hounslow v Powell* [2011] UKSC 8.

OTHER PROPERTY ISSUES

Bank accounts

10.96   Money held in a joint account is not inevitably joint property, although if a dispute arises the court will start from the position that such funds are joint unless one party can show that there was an intention that the position should be otherwise. In *Jones v Maynard*[87] a husband and wife operated a joint bank account into which both paid their earnings. The husband was much the larger earner. He drew money from the account to buy investments in his sole name. On separation, the wife was entitled to half the funds in the account and half the value of the investments, because they were bought with joint funds. Vaisey J said:

> 'In my judgment, where there is a joint purse between husband and wife—a common pool into which they put all their resources—it is not consistent with that conception that the joint account should thereafter (in this case in the event of a divorce) be divided up with reference to the respective contributions of husband and wife, crediting the husband with the whole of his earnings and the wife with the whole of her dividends. I do not believe that when once the joint pool has been formed it ought to be, and can be, dissected in any such manner. I take the view that when spouses have a common purse and a pool of their resources, the husband's remuneration is earned on behalf of them both, and the idea that years afterwards one can dissect the contents of the pool by taking an elaborate account as to how much was paid in by the husband and how much was paid in by the wife is not consistent with the original fundamental idea of a joint purse or a common pool. When the money goes into the pool it is there as joint property.'

10.97   If one party provides all the funds in a joint account, and the account is held on this basis purely as a matter of administrative convenience, the funds will be the property of the provider: *Heseltine v Heseltine.*[88]

10.98   In any case concerning a joint bank account the court will have to consider the parties' intentions as to the funds. If there is no clear intention, it is likely that a joint account will be treated as a joint fund.

Personal bank accounts

10.99   Similarly a personal bank account in the name of one party is the property of that party unless there is evidence to the contrary. In *Paul v Constance* a cohabitant opened an account in his sole name, but told his partner that the money in the account (much of which came from a substantial personal injury award made to the male cohabitant) was as much hers as his, and gave her authority to draw on it. He said this repeatedly, and other moneys, including joint bingo winnings, were paid into the account. He died intestate.

---

[87]   [1951] Ch 572.
[88]   [1971] 1 All ER 952.

The court accepted that his assertions about the ownership of the account constituted a declaration of trust, and his partner was entitled to a half share in the account.

Chattels

10.100 In disputes between cohabitants questions of the ownership of personal possessions present particular difficulties. There is often no clear answer to the question of who owns a particular item acquired during the relationship. The difficulty can be seen when considering who owns property purchased with funds from a joint bank account. *Jones v Maynard*[89] suggests that investments purchased in the name of a husband with monies drawn from a joint account are to be treated as joint property. However, in *Re Bishop deceased*[90] a husband and wife had a joint bank account to which both contributed and on which both drew. Monies were drawn from the account for investment purposes: some investments were bought in the name of the husband and some in the name of the wife. There was no particular pattern. After the husband's death a dispute arose about what property fell into his estate, and the court was required to determine whether Mrs Bishop had any interest in shares bought in the husband's name with monies from the joint account, what interest she had in shares bought in her name with monies from the joint account, and what interest she had in the sum remaining in the joint account. Stamp J expressed the following view:

> 'Where a husband and wife open a joint account at a bank on terms that cheques may be drawn on the account by either of them, then, in my judgment, in the absence of facts or circumstances which indicate that the account was intended, or was kept, for some specific or limited purpose, each spouse can draw upon it not only for the benefit of both spouses but for his or her own benefit. Each spouse, in drawing money out of the account, is to be treated as doing so with the authority of the other and, in my judgment, if one of the spouses purchases a chattel for his own benefit or an investment in his or her own name, that chattel or investment belongs to the person in whose name it is purchased or invested: for in such a case there is, in my judgment, no equity in the other spouse to displace the legal ownership of the one in whose name the investment is purchased. What is purchased is not to be regarded as purchased out of a fund belonging to the spouses in the proportions in which they contribute to the account or in equal proportions, but out of a pool or fund of which they were, at law and in equity, joint tenants. It also follows that if one of the spouses draws on the account to make a purchase in the joint names of the spouses, the property purchased, since it is purchased in joint names, is, prima facie, joint property and there is no equity to displace the joint legal ownership. There is, in my judgment, no room for any presumption which would constitute the joint holders as trustees for the parties in equal or some other shares.'

10.101 The two decisions are not easy to reconcile. In both cases the outcome was determined largely on the basis of the parties' intentions and the way in

---

[89]   See para 1 above.
[90]   [1965] Ch 450.

which they saw the account and its use. In *Jones v Maynard* the parties viewed the account as containing joint funds, and by extension, the investments made from it were regarded as joint. In *re Bishop* the account was opened in part in order to allow investments to be made in the names of the parties and they did not regard the account as containing joint savings, so each was entitled to draw on it for their own benefit.

10.102   It follows that the fact that a chattel or an investment was bought with funds from a joint account does not automatically result in its being a joint asset.

10.103   Similar difficulties can arise when a household item is purchased by one party and a dispute arises as to its ownership. Consider the position if A buys a three piece suite with his own money for use by both parties in their joint party. At around the same time his partner B, also with his own money, pays for a good holiday for them both; and A and B, from their joint account, buy two mountain bikes. All three items of expenditure are of around the same value. Is the three piece suite any less joint property than the bikes? And how does the holiday fit in?

10.104   In practice every dispute about chattels will turn on its own facts. The following guidance may assist:

(a)   Items purchased with joint funds will usually be treated as joint property unless clearly intended only for the use of one party (e g the electric guitar bought where only one partner can play it).

(b)   Items purchased with the funds of one party which are intended for joint use will probably be treated as joint property unless there is evidence of an agreement or understanding between the parties that, on separation, each would retain what he had purchased.

(c)   If partners put all their income into a joint account, the court will more readily regard purchases from that account as being the property of the purchaser (on the basis that, where there is only one account, and that is joint, the purchaser has no option about where to get the money from).

(d)   If partners maintain a joint account for joint expenses, but separate accounts for receipt of income and payment of personal expenses, feeding the former from the latter, purchases from the joint account will usually be regarded as joint.

(e)   Gifts from one partner to the other will usually be regarded as the property of the recipient.

10.105   Litigating about chattels is likely to cost more than the items are worth. Judges, if asked to decide disputes about chattels, may threaten to order them sold by house clearance agents and the proceeds divided between the parties: this is intended to encourage the parties to avoid such litigation.

PROVISION FOR CHILDREN ON RELATIONSHIP BREAKDOWN

Child support

10.106 Prior to the coming into force of the Child Support Act 1991 the courts were in a position to determine levels of periodical payments for children in cases where those who were responsible for supporting them could not agree on the appropriate level of support. The Child Support Act 1991 was intended:[91]

(a) to simplify the provision of maintenance for children;

(b) to reduce the cost to the public of collecting such maintenance;

(c) to reduce the number of children living in families whose primary source of income was state benefits;

(d) to discourage parents in receipt of state benefits from refusing to name the other parent in order to prevent them having to make payments which reduced the state's liability to support the family while at the same time providing little or no cash benefit for the recipient.

10.107 The Act was a failure. In particular, the number of children living in families supported by state benefits where the absent parent made no contribution did not decrease following implementation of the Act. The original formula for calculation of the amount due from the absent parent was difficult to implement. The Child Support Agency was ineffective: it failed to assess child support accurately, and, where it had been assessed, failed to collect it. The Child Support Agency was been abolished and replaced by the Child Maintenance and Enforcement Commission (CMEC).[92]

10.108 There have been regular amendments to the child support legislation since it was first introduced and what follows is a statement of the current position.

10.109 Section 8(1) of the Child Support Act 1991 ousts the court's jurisdiction in the majority of cases. It provides that:

'(1) This subsection applies in any case where the Commission would have jurisdiction to make a maintenance calculation with respect to a qualifying child and an a non-resident parent of his on an application duly made by a person entitled to apply for such a calculation with respect to that child.

---

[91]　See Select Committee on Social Security 10th report.
[92]　By the Child Maintenance and Other Payments Act 2008.

(3) [I]n any case where subsection (1) applies, no court shall exercise any power which it would otherwise have to make, vary or revive any maintenance order in relation to the child and non-resident parent concerned.'

10.110 Section 44 of the Act provides that:

'(1) The Commission shall have jurisdiction to make a maintenance calculation with respect to a person who is –

(a)   a person with care;

(b)   a non-resident parent;[93] or

(c)   a qualifying child,

only if that person is habitually resident in the United Kingdom, except in the case of a non-resident parent who falls within subsection (2A).'

Non-resident parents against whom a maintenance calculation can be made include those serving overseas in the armed forces and persons working for the civil service abroad.[94]

10.111 Section 55 of the Act defines a qualifying child as follows:

'(1) In this Act, "child" means (subject to subsection (2) a person who –

(a)   has not attained the age of 16, or

(b)   has not attained the age of 20 and satisfies such conditions as may be prescribed.

(2) A person who is or has been party to a marriage or civil partnership is not a child for the purposes of this Act.

(3) For the purposes of subsection (2), "marriage" and "civil partnership" include a void marriage and a void civil partnership respectively.'

10.112 An application for a maintenance calculation can be made in accordance with the following provision:[95]

'(1) A person who is, in relation to any qualifying child or any qualifying children, either the person with care or the non-resident parent may apply to the Commission for a maintenance calculation to be made under this Act with respect to that child, or any of those children.'

10.113 Section 3(3) of the Act provides that:

'(3) A person is a "person with care", in relation to any child, if he is a person –

(a)   with whom the child has his home;

(b)   who usually provides day to day care for the child (whether exclusively or in conjunction with any other person); and

(c)   who does not fall within a prescribed category of person.'

10.114 More than one person may be the 'person with care': s 3(5). Section 3(2) of the Act defines 'non-resident parent' as:

---

[93]   Referred to hereafter as a NRP.

[94]   CSA 1991, s 44(2A).

[95]   CSA 1991, s 4(1).

'(2) The parent of any child is an "absent parent" [a "non-resident parent"], in relation to him, if –

(a)   that parent is not living in the same household with the child; and
(b)   the child has his home with a person who is, in relation to him, a person with care.'

10.115 'Parent' is defined by s 54 of the Act as 'any person who is in law the mother or father of the child'. This definition includes a 'parent' within the meaning of the Human Fertilisation and Embryology Act 2008 or the Adoption and Children Act 2002. Disputes about parentage can be resolved by the Commission under s 26 of the Act. In the case where a person is alleged to be a biological parent, failure to comply with scientific testing entitles the Commission to make a maintenance calculation against that person on the assumption that he is a parent of the child: s 26(2). The Commission can also make a maintenance calculation on that basis if the alleged parent is a parent with the meaning of ss 33–46 or s 54 of the Human Fertilisation and Embryology Act 2008. A parent who has acquired that status by the making of a parental order therefore falls within the Act, as does a parent who has become a parent by way of assisted reproduction under Part 2 of the 2008 Act.

10.116 Cases where the court retains jurisdiction to set maintenance for children include:

(a)   Cases where the child, or the NRP are abroad (unless the non-resident parent is within one of the excepted categories under s 44(2A)).[96]

(b)   Cases where what is sought is 'top-up' maintenance: this only arises where the NRP has an income of more than £2,000 net per week and the court regards a 'top-up' as appropriate: s 8(6).

(c)   Cases where what is sought is the payment of school fees or other expenses associated with 'instruction at an educational establishment or undergoing training for a trade, profession or vocation': s 8(7).

(d)   Cases where the child is disabled and the person with care seeks payment solely to meet 'any expenses attributable to the child's disability': s 8(8). A broad view is taken of what constitutes expenses.[97]

(e)   Where an order is sought against the person with care of the child: s 8(10).

(f)   If the parties reach a written agreement that child maintenance should be paid, the court may make an order for such maintenance to be paid: s 8(5).[98] A maintenance calculation can be made under the Act however once the order has been in force for a year.

---

[96]   The main excepted categories are servants of the Crown, including members of the diplomatic corps, and members of the armed forces serving abroad.
[97]   *C v F (Disabled Child: Maintenance Orders)* [1998] 2 FLR 1.
[98]   And CSA 1991, s 4(10)(aa).

The court may revoke or vary an order made under s 8(5).

The formula

10.117 The current child support formula is straightforward in relation to calculation of the basic rate. The non-resident parent (NRP) pays 15% of net[99] income for the first child, 20% for two children, and 25% for three or more. If the NRP is in a new household with other children living under the same roof,[100] the amount taken into consideration as income is reduced by 15% for the first child living under the same roof, 20% for the second, and 25% for three or more. This reduction applies if there any children for whom the NRP or his new partner receive child benefit. The fact that the children may be receiving child support payments from another parent is irrelevant. 'Partner' is defined as 'if they are a couple, the other member of that couple' and the definition of couple includes 'two people of the same sex who are not civil partners of each other but are living together as if they were civil partners'.[101]

10.118 If the NRP's net income is less than £200 per week, a reduced rate is payable.

Number of qualifying children	1	2	3+
No 'relevant' children	25%	35%	45%
1 relevant child	20.5%	29%	37.5%
2 relevant children	19%	27%	35%
3+ relevant children	17.5%	25%	32.5%

10.119 If the NRP earns less than £100 per week, or he or his partner is in receipt of income support or job-seeker's allowance, or he is in receipt of incapacity benefit, the state pension, or certain other benefits, a flat rate of £5 per week is payable. Nothing is payable if the NRP is in prison, a student or living in residential care.

10.120 In addition, if the NRP looks after a qualifying child for 52 to 103 nights per annum, the payments are reduced by 1/7th; if for 104 to 155 nights, 2/7th; if 156 to 174 nights, 3/7ths; if 175 nights or more, one half plus £7. If there are several qualifying children and they stay for different periods, an average has to be taken.

---

[99] Net income is defined as income after tax, pension contributions and National Insurance. Investment income is not normally included in net income.

[100] There is no requirement that the children are biologically related to the NRP. As long as they are under the same roof and the NPR or his partner receive child benefit for the child (or would do but for the fact that a member of the family is living abroad).

[101] CSA 1991, Sch 1, para 10C.

10.121   The state is seeking to discourage parents from using CMEC as a mechanism for collecting child support. Parents are now encouraged to make their own arrangements.

Proposals for change

10.122   The formula by which child support is calculated is planned to change and will become based on gross rather than net income. It is also likely that those cases where CMEC has to become involved to calculate and collect the child support will involve payment of a fee by the person making the application of up to £100 (£50 for those on benefits).

Schedule 1 Children Act 1989

10.123   Schedule 1 of the Children Act 1989 provides a statutory scheme whereby financial provision for children can be sought outside the schemes which exist for such provision on the breakdown of marriage or civil partnership.

10.124   An application under Sch 1 can be made by a parent, guardian, special guardian, or any person in whose favour a residence order is in force in relation to a child.

10.125   Orders can be made against either or both parents of a child. 'Parent' is defined as including: 'any party to a marriage (whether or not subsisting) in relation to whom the child concerned is a child of the family' and 'any civil partner in a civil partnership (whether or not subsisting) in relation to whom the child concerned is a child of the family'.[102] This definition includes step-parents (a person married to or in a civil partnership with the legal parent) but does not include unmarried partners. In *J v J (A Minor: Property Transfer)*[103] a female cohabitant sought an order transferring a tenancy in the joint names of the parties into her sole name for the benefit of their child.[104] The application was refused: the male cohabitant was not a party to a marriage.

10.126   The High Court has considered the effect of the definition of parent in Sch 1 in the case of a same sex couple in detail in the case of *T v B*.[105] A female partner had conceived a child by an anonymous donor and, on the breakdown of the relationship, her partner had gone to court to obtain a residence order and parental responsibility for the child. The biological mother then sought financial provision under Sch 1. Moylan J observed:

> '[54] It is clear to me that the respondent is a parent of the child in this case in the third way identified by Baroness Hale in *Re G (children) (residence: same sex partner)*, namely as a social and psychological parent. She is a social and

---

[102]   Schedule 1, para 16.
[103]   [1993] 2 FLR 56.
[104]   This case precedes the introduction of the power to transfer tenancies between cohabitants.
[105]   [2010] EWHC 1444 (Fam). Also referred to in chapter 1.

psychological parent as a result of her relationship with the child and the child's relationship with her. However, as Baroness Hale also notes, there is a difference between a 'natural' parent, as defined by her, and a legal parent.

[55] The question I have to answer is whether, as a matter of statutory interpretation, a parent against whom an order for financial provision for a child can be made under Sch 1 is:

(a)   confined to legal parents – ie biological parents and those who have become a parent by operation of law such as by adoption, under the 1990 Act or under the 2008 Act – and those otherwise included by para 16; or,

(b)   whether it extends, as submitted by Mr Goldrein, to include any person who has acquired parental responsibility (by virtue of an order) or who is a social and psychological parent, a 'natural parent' as described by Baroness Hale in *Re G (Children) (Residence: Same-sex Partner)*.

[56] There are clearly advantages to each outcome …

[57] I have come to the clear conclusion that those against whom orders can be made under Sch 1 are confined to those who are a parent in the legal meaning of that word. I have come to that conclusion because in my view, as a matter of statutory interpretation, Sch 1 is confined to those who have the status of parent (as expressly extended by para 16). It is not in my view a discretionary welfare-informed decision … but a matter of status …

[58] First, I am not aware of, and I have not been referred to, any criticism of the decision of *J v J (Property Transfer Application)* [1993] 1 FCR 471 … I accept [the] submission that there have been significant social advances since 1992 but these do not in my view undermine the effect of this decision. The attribution of legal parentage has not changed since 1992 save as a result of statutory reform.

[60] … [I]n my view Sch 1 is not using the word "parent" in a broad welfare-informed sense but is confined to legal parent. I agree with Bracewell J, when she said in *Re B (Minors) (Parentage)* [1996] 3 FCR 697, that if Parliament had intended to alter or amend the general principles as to parenthood, specific enactment would have been made.

[61] This conclusion is supported by the approach taken by the Court of Appeal to the determination of the issue of parenthood in *J v C (Void Marriage: Status of Children)* [2008] 1 FCR 368, [2006] 3 WLR 876. The issue was determined by reference to the statutes which define parenthood in the context of AID, not by a broad factual analysis as proposed by Mr Goldrein in the present case. In order to determine whether the applicant was a parent for the purposes of s 10 of the 1989 Act, Wall LJ determined whether he was within the relevant statutory definition of parent as contained in the '[t]wo Acts of Parliament which define parenthood in the context of AID' (at [18]). In my view, I should apply the same approach to the determination of whether the respondent in this case is a parent within the meaning of Sch 1. Adopting this approach, it is not contended that the respondent is a parent.'

10.127 Orders can only be made against:

(a) legal parents (including those who have acquired parental status under HFEA 2008);

(b) step-parents who have married to or are in a civil partnership with a legal parent of the child.

10.128 The court can make any of the orders set out in para 1(2) of Sch 1:

'(2) The orders referred to in sub-paragraph (1) are –

(a) an order requiring either or both parents of a child –
  (i)   to make to the applicant for the benefit of the child; or
  (ii) to make to the child himself,
  such periodical payments, for such term, as may be specified in the order;

(b) an order requiring either or both parents of a child –
  (i)   to secure to the applicant for the benefit of the child; or
  (ii) to secure to the child himself,
  such periodical payments, for such term, as may be so specified;

(c) an order requiring either or both parents of a child –
  (i)   to pay to the applicant for the benefit of the child; or
  (ii) to pay to the child himself,
  such lump sum as may be so specified;

(d) an order requiring a settlement to be made for the benefit of the child, and to the satisfaction of the court, of property –
  (i)   to which either parent is entitled (either in possession or in reversion); and
  (ii) which is specified in the order;

(e) an order requiring either or both parents of a child –
  (i)   to transfer to the applicant, for the benefit of the child; or
  (ii) to transfer to the child himself,
  such property to which the parent is, or the parents are, entitled (either in possession or in reversion) as may be specified in the order.'

10.129 An order can be made at any time before the child reaches the age of eighteen. Once the child reaches eighteen, he can make his own application for provision against either or both of his parents. The only provision which can be made at this stage is provision by way of periodical payments or by payment of a lump sum, and the applicant must show either that he is 'receiving instruction at an educational establishment or undergoing training for a trade, profession or vocation, whether or not while in gainful employment' or would be, if an order were made, or that 'there are special circumstances which justify the making of an order'. In addition, such an order can only be made if the parents of the applicant are not living in the same household.

10.130 In all applications under Sch 1 the court is required to take into account all the circumstances including:

'(a)   the income, earning capacity, property and other financial resources which each person mentioned in sub-paragraph (4) has or is likely to have in the foreseeable future;

(b)   the financial needs, obligations and responsibilities which each person mentioned in sub-paragraph (4) has or is likely to have in the foreseeable future;

(c)   the financial needs of the child;

(d)   the income, earning capacity (if any), property and other financial resources of the child;

(e)   any physical or mental disability of the child;

(f)   the manner in which the child was being, or was expected to be, educated or trained.'

10.131   The persons mentioned in sub-para (4) are:

'(a)   in relation to a decision whether to exercise its powers under paragraph 1, any parent of the child;

(b)   in relation to a decision whether to exercise its powers under paragraph 2, the mother and father of the child;

(c)   the applicant for the order;

(d)   any other person in whose favour the court proposes to make the order.'

10.132   In deciding whether or not to make an order against a person who is not the mother or father of the child the court is in addition required to consider:

'(a)   whether that person has assumed responsibility for the maintenance of the child and, if so, the extent to which and basis on which he assumed that responsibility and the length of the period during which he met that responsibility;

(b)   whether he did so knowing that the child was not his child;

(c)   the liability of any other person to maintain the child.'

There is no express requirement that first consideration is given to the welfare of the child who is the subject of the application.

Property transfer orders

10.133   An order for the transfer of property can be made in favour of the child or in favour of the applicant for the benefit of the child. 'Property' in this sense includes an interest under a tenancy, which will normally be transferred to the applicant. Some caution must be exercised in relation to this if the potentially valuable right of a local authority right to buy will be lost by the party against whom the order was made. This arose in *K v K (Minors; Property Transfer)*[106] where an order for transfer of a council tenancy to a mother was made in circumstances where the father would lose his right to buy and, it was argued, would have difficulty getting back into local authority housing.[107] The judge was found to have failed to consider properly the matters which the court

---

[106]   [1992] 2 FLR 220.
[107]   This was a claim under the Guardianship of Minors Act 1971, which contained provision in similar terms to that now found in Sch 1.

is required to take into account and in particular had not attached sufficient weight to the impact on the father of losing the tenancy. If property is transferred to the applicant for the benefit of the child, the child does not acquire a beneficial interest in it.[108]

10.134   The usual provision in the case of a property transfer order is for the property to be transferred to the applicant on the basis that it reverts back to the transferor when the child reaches a certain age. The statute itself does not require this, but it is the approach usually taken by the courts: in *Phillips v Peace*[109] the mother obtained an order for payment of a lump sum of £90,000 for the purchase of a property for herself and the child, which would eventually revert to the father. Similarly in *Re P (Child: Financial Provision)*[110] the mother of the child of a 'fabulously wealthy' Iranian was awarded a £450,000 housing fund, increased to £1 million on appeal, on similar terms. And in *F v G (Child: Financial Provision)*[111] a sum of £900,000 was awarded for the purchase of a property on the basis that it would be held on trust and the mother would be required to leave it when the child was eighteen, even though that might put the mother in a vulnerable position in her fifties.

10.135   The court may not make more than one property settlement or property transfer order against the same person.[112]

Lump sum provision

10.136   The court can make a lump sum order to enable the applicant to meet expenditure:

> '(a)   incurred in connection with the birth of the child or in maintaining the child; and
> (b)   reasonably incurred before the making of the order.'

More than one lump sum order can be made.

Periodical payments

10.137   The court may make an order for periodical payments extending up to the child's seventeenth birthday 'unless the court thinks it right to specify a later date' and in any event not beyond his eighteen birthday. The child can apply himself for an order beyond that date as set out in **10.129**.

10.138   The court will however only have jurisdiction in cases where CMEC does not. Those circumstances would include: payment of top-up maintenance where a non-resident parent has a net weekly income in excess of £2,000; payment of maintenance for the purpose of meeting expenses attributable to a

---

[108]   *Re B (Child: Property Transfer)* [1999] 2 FLR 418.
[109]   [2005] 2 FLR 1212.
[110]   [2003] EWCA Civ 837.
[111]   [2004] EWHC 1848 (Fam).
[112]   Schedule 1, para 5(b).

child's disability; payment of maintenance where there is an agreement as to maintenance and the parties wish to have it included in an order.

10.139 Once made, periodical payments orders can be varied on more than one occasion.[113] Once the child has reached the age of sixteen, he can apply himself for a variation.

Big money cases

10.140 The courts have shown a willingness in recent years to make large awards in cases where one parent is wealthy. In *Re P* the 'fabulously wealthy' father indicated that he could pay £10 million if required to do so. The mother of his child was awarded a housing fund of £1 million, a lump for internal decoration of £100,000, and periodical payments of £70,000 per annum until the child reached eighteen.

10.141 In *F v G* the mother received accommodation at a cost of £900,000 plus £60,000 per annum. These cases demonstrate that although lifestyle/ standard of living is not one of the criteria referred to in the schedule it is highly relevant in cases where one of the parents is wealthy and there is a reasonable expectation that the child, and the child's carer during the child's minority, should not have to live a lifestyle which is wholly different from that of the wealthy parent.

Procedure

10.142 The procedure for making a claim under Sch 1 has recently been simplified and brought into line with other claims for a financial remedy under the Family Procedure Rules 2010. The application form is Form A1 and both parties are required to file a Form E1 setting out in detail their financial circumstances. Application can be made in the High Court, county court or magistrates' court. In the case of the magistrates court however the court's powers are limited to the making of lump sum and periodical payments orders, and the maximum lump sum order which can be made is £1,000. The majority of applications start their life in the county court.

---

[113] Paragraph 6 of Sch 1.

Chapter 11

SUCCESSION

INTRODUCTION

11.1 This chapter deals with the passing of property assets on death.

11.2 There is no doubt that the simplest and recommended method for any person to ensure that when they die their property passes to those they wish to benefit is to make a will. In the absence of a will their property will be distributed in accordance with the Intestacy Rules (see **11.46** below) or, if there is no relative who falls within those rules, it will be treated as what is known as *bona vacantia*[1] and becomes the property of the state. Although making a will is a relatively simple process, and many solicitors offer a streamlined and cheap service for straightforward wills, large numbers of people die intestate,[2] causing significant problems for their friends and relatives.

PROPERTY WHICH DOES NOT PASS UNDER A WILL

11.3 Certain types of property pass to another person on the death of the owner even if there is no will in place. They fall into the following principal categories.

Interests in real property held on a joint tenancy

11.4 'Tenancy' in this context refers to the ownership of property, not to the tenancy of property rented on a short term basis. 'Real property' is land and the buildings which stand on it.

11.5 As has been explained in chapter 10 above, the majority of houses purchased jointly in the UK are purchased by the owners as 'joint tenants in equity'.[3] On the death of one of two or more joint tenants of property, the share of the deceased person passes to the survivor. If there is more than one survivor, it passes to them in equal shares. So if a house is owned by four

---

[1] Literally, 'vacant goods'; more accurately, ownerless property.
[2] The number of intestate deaths is not known, but around 500,000 people die each year in the UK. 280,000 of those deaths result in formal steps being taken to administer the estate of the deceased, of which about one-third relate to intestate estates. Of the remaining 220,000 deaths where no formal steps are taken, it is likely that many are intestate. (Source: Law Commission Consultation Paper no 191 – Intestacy and Family Provisions Claims on Death pub 2010.)
[3] The distinction between equitable joint tenancy and equitable tenancy in common is explained in chapter 10.

people as tenants in common and one dies, the remaining three acquire one-third each of his one-quarter share, and as a result have a one-third share each. This long-established doctrine of English law is known as the right of survivorship.[4] The deceased's share passes to the other owners seamlessly, without ever becoming a part of the deceased's estate (the assets which are dealt with by his will, or if there is no will by the Intestacy Rules).

11.6   There is however as was discussed in chapter 10 another method whereby joint owners can hold a property, that is, on trust for themselves as tenants in common. This may be in equal or unequal shares. This is an extremely important distinction because there is no right of survivorship if a property is held in this way.

11.7   It is relatively easy for one owner unilaterally to sever an equitable joint tenancy by giving notice.[5] If this occurs, the tenancy ceases to be joint and the property is held by the owners as tenants in common. The notice of severance must be in writing and must be served on the other owner. The courts have been prepared to interpret this in a fairly technical sense: in *Kinch v Bullard*[6] a wife arranged for her solicitors to serve a notice of severance on her husband. It was duly sent by first class post to him at the home they still shared. The wife intercepted the letter on receipt because she had second thoughts. Subsequently the husband died. It was held that the notice was effective even though not physically received by him, because it had been sent to a property at which he might ordinarily be expected to receive it, and his half share did not pass to the wife by survivorship.

11.8   It is also possible for a joint tenancy to be severed by 'by any course of dealing sufficient to intimate that the interests of all were mutually treated as constituting a tenancy in common'.[7] In practice this means that if a co-owner deals with his share as if it were entirely his own property to dispose of without reference to the other owner, severance is likely to occur. An oral agreement by one co-owner to sell his share to the other is sufficient to bring about a severance, even though the agreement would not have been enforceable:[8] see *Burgess v Rawnsley*. However written discussions between the solicitors of two separating co-owners that the joint property should be put on the market were not sufficient to sever a tenancy.[9] If co-owners make separate wills leaving their share in the joint property to third parties, thus showing that they do not intend the share to pass by survivorship, and communicate this fact to each other, severance will occur.[10]

---

[4]   Or *jus accrescendi* for those who prefer Latin.
[5]   Law of Property Act 1925, s 36(2).
[6]   [1998] 3 EGLR 112.
[7]   *Burgess v Rawnsley* [1975] Ch 429, [1975] 3 All ER 142 and *Wallbank and another v Price* [2007] EWHC 3001 (Ch).
[8]   Because contracts for the sale of land are not enforceable unless in writing: Law of Property (Miscellaneous Provisions) Act 1989, s 2.
[9]   *Marshall v Marshall* 1998 All England Official Transcript.
[10]   *Carr v Isard* [2006] EWHC 2095 (Ch).

11.9 If severance occurs, the owners cease to be equitable joint tenants, and become equitable tenants in common. From the point of view of succession on death this is a fundamental change as the right of survivorship no longer applies and the deceased's interest will form part of his estate. It will not automatically pass to his co-owner(s). It will pass under his will, or under the Intestacy Rules if he is intestate.

11.10 The bankruptcy of one of two or more joint tenants has the effect of severing the joint tenancy from the date and time at which the bankruptcy order is made.[11]

11.11 If one joint tenant causes the other's death, the tenancy is severed so as to prevent the guilty party succeeding to the other's share.[12] However the court has the power under s 7 of the Forfeiture Act 1982 enables the court to modify this rule if the survivor's culpability is limited.[13]

11.12 The legal position is broadly the same if property which is subject to a long leasehold is owned jointly.

Payments made by pension schemes and under insurance policies

11.13 Each pension scheme operates under its own rules and reference must be had to those for precisely what will occur if a scheme member dies. Money held in pension funds is usually held for the members of the scheme under a trust, and the participant is invited to nominate beneficiaries to receive any death benefit which may become payable. When such a payment is made, it is paid direct to the beneficiary and does not form part of the estate of the deceased. If no beneficiary has been nominated, the scheme rules usually make provision for the trustees to select a person to whom to pay the death benefit.

11.14 Life insurance policies taken out for the benefit of a third party are usually written under trust and the sum payable on death is paid out to the person for whose benefit the policy was taken out. It does not form part of the deceased's estate.

Personal property

11.15 Joint bank accounts and other accounts with financial institutions are usually subject to a written agreement signed at the time the parties opened the account (or, if the account started life in the sole name of one party, at the time the other was added). The contractual terms vary from institution but many of such contracts will contain a provision that, on the death of one account holder, the interest in the funds held in the account will become the sole property of the other account holder. If parties to a bank account wish some

---

[11]   *Re Palmer* [1994] Ch 316.
[12]   *Re K* [1985] Ch 85 and the Forfeiture Act 1982, s 2.
[13]   *Gray v Barr* [1971] 2 All ER 949.

other arrangement to apply, they should make it clear to the institution and request that the account is not held on this basis.

Chattels

11.16 The ownership of chattels, as discussed in chapter 10 above, is not a straightforward question. The starting point is to consider whether the chattel was owned solely by the deceased, or jointly by the deceased and former partner. If owned solely by the deceased, it will pass under his will. If he is intestate, see below in **11.50**. If they are owned jointly, the question will be whether the intention of the owners at the time of purchase was for the survivor to take the whole chattel on death, or for the chattel to fall into the deceased's estate. In the case of ordinary household effects the former is likely to be the case, but this may not be the case in relation to more valuable items. Some parallel can perhaps be drawn with the approach taken in the Administration of Estates Act 1925 (see **11.50**) which makes provision for those chattels which would pass to a spouse or civil partner on intestacy. Even relatively large items such as motor cars are covered. If the deceased and his partner were cohabitants however there is no legislative framework for the division of chattels (save for the general provisions of the Inheritance (Provision for Family and Dependants) Act 1975) and the survivor may, if faced with unco-operative relatives, have to rely on property law to assist him. It will rarely be worth the cost of litigating about chattels: in the case of any chattel in relation to which the survivor believes he has a share the most effective course is likely to be to retain possession and let any would-be claimant assert a case to a share.

The body of the deceased

11.17 Under English law there is no property in the body of a deceased person. If the deceased has made a will, his executor is entitled to possession of the body, and is under a duty to bury or otherwise dispose of it. If the deceased dies intestate, the persons having priority under r 22 of the Non-contentious Probate Rules 1987 are in the same position as the executors.[14] In the case of a child this will usually be the father and mother of the deceased, who will have equal priority.

INHERITANCE UNDER A WILL

Is the will valid?

11.18 In order for a will to be valid the testator has to have capacity, a subject which is outside the scope of this work.

---

[14] See **11.33** for discussion as to who those persons are.

11.19   There are also certain formalities which have to be complied with in the execution of the will by the testator. These are again outside the scope of this work.

11.20   More important for those who enter into civil partnerships is that doing so has the effect of revoking any will already made.[15] There is an exception to this rule if a will is made in contemplation of entering into a civil partnership with a particular person; in this case, the will is not revoked. Section 18B(3) of the Wills Act 1837 provides:

'(3) If it appears from a will –

   (a)   that at the time it was made the testator was expecting to form a civil partnership with a particular person, and
   (b)   that he intended that the will should not be revoked by the formation of the civil partnership,

the will is not revoked by its formation.'

The will must therefore include wording which indicates the testator's intentions. It must state that he intends to form a civil partnership with a particular person and that he intends that the formation of the partnership should not have the effect of revoking the will.

11.21   Entering into a civil partnership which is voidable on any of the grounds set out in s 50 of the Civil Partnership Act 2004, and which is subsequently annulled, falls within s 18B(1) of the Wills Act, and the will is revoked unless s 18B(3) is complied with.[16] Entering into a void civil partnership within the meaning of s 49 of the 2004 Act however does not have this effect, because the civil partnership is treated for the purposes of the Act as having never come into existence.

11.22   Dissolution[17] or annulment of a civil partnership also has an effect on any will. Section 18C of the Wills Act 1837 as amended provides:

18C   Effect of dissolution or annulment of civil partnership on wills

'(1) This section applies if, after a testator has made a will –

   (a)   a court of civil jurisdiction in England and Wales dissolves his civil partnership or makes a nullity order in respect of it, or
   (b)   his civil partnership is dissolved or annulled and the dissolution or annulment is entitled to recognition in England and Wales by virtue of Chapter 3 of Part 5 of the Civil Partnership Act 2004.

(2) Except in so far as a contrary intention appears by the will –

   (a)   provisions of the will appointing executors or trustees or conferring a power of appointment, if they appoint or confer the power on the

---

15   Wills Act 1837, s 18B(1), as amended by the CPA 2004.
16   *Re Roberts deceased* [1978] 1 WLR 653.
17   The same principles apply in the case of annulment.

former civil partner, take effect as if the former civil partner had died on the date on which the civil partnership is dissolved or annulled, and

(b)   any property which, or an interest in which, is devised or bequeathed to the former civil partner shall pass as if the former civil partner had died on that date.'

Thus, if the former civil partner of the testator was appointed an executor or trustee, that appointment takes effect as if the former partner had died on the date of the dissolution or annulment. If the will contains any provision whereby property passes to the former civil partner, it takes effect as if the civil partner had died at the date of dissolution or annulment.

11.23   This provision does not eliminate the right of the former civil partner to apply for provision under the Inheritance (Provision for Family and Dependants) Act 1975.[18]

11.24   The effect of the failure of a disposition because of dissolution or annulment is that the gift becomes part of the residuary estate of the deceased, and will pass under any gift of residue. If there is no gift of residue, it passes on intestacy.

11.25   It is important to note that s 18C only comes into effect when a final order of dissolution or annulment is made. A conditional order does not have this effect. If a civil partner on the breakdown of a relationship wishes to change the provisions of his will to avoid a gift to the estranged partner taking effect, the will must be altered either by making a new will or executing a codicil.

GIFTS BY WILL TO CHILDREN

11.26   There are no restrictions on gifts by will to children. Such gifts can be made by way of legacy (a gift of a specific sum of money or specific piece of property) or by gift of residue whereby the child receives the balance of the deceased's estate after any legacies have been paid out and after deduction of the funeral and testamentary expenses of the deceased. A child cannot give a valid receipt for monies due to him under a will[19] unless the will contains a provision permitting him to do so. Alternatively, the will may provide for another person, usually a parent, to give such a receipt. If there is no such provision, the executor or personal representative must either pay the money into court, or establish a trust under s 42 of the Administration of Estates Act 1925 whereby the money or property will be held on trust for the child until he reaches his majority.

11.27   A will may make provision for children by referring to them in a number of different ways. A testator may make provision for 'my issue'

---

[18]   Wills Act 1837, s 18C(3).
[19]   *Harvell v Foster* [1954] 2 QB 367.

although this wording is probably relatively uncommon in recent times. Potentially use of that expression includes all descendants: children, grandchildren, great grandchildren and so on, and any gift to 'issue' will be divided equally between them. A will making provision for the residue of the testator's estate to be divided between 'my issue' would therefore, in the case of a testator with two children and four grandchildren result in the residue being divided six ways. However, if it is clear from the wording otherwise used the will that the testator intends the property to pass to his children, the use of the expression will be restricted to them.[20] Whether the wording of the will justifies this conclusion depends on technical rules relating to the construction of wills which are outside the scope of this work. It is worth noting that:

(a) 'Issue by our marriage' has been construed as referring only to children and not other descendants.[21] The same would apply to 'issue by our civil partnership'.

(b) If a will refers to 'issue' and 'children' interchangeably it will generally be construed as referring to children.[22]

11.28 More commonly a will includes provision for a 'child' or 'children'. This will be interpreted in accordance with the provisions of the common law and subsequent legislation as discussed in more detail in chapter 1. It is likely that the courts will interpret 'child' to include a child of parent who has gained that status under the Human Fertilisation and Embryology Act 2008.

11.29 As is pointed out in chapter 1 the majority of children being brought up in a family by same sex partners will not have two legal parents of the same sex. If this is the case any partner who is not a legal parent but who wishes to benefit a child of the relationship should ensure that any will makes reference to that child by name and does not simply make provision for 'children'.

11.30 At common law since the coming into effect of the Family Law Act 1969 on 1 January 1970 there is no bar on illegitimate children inheriting under a will and any reference to 'children' will include illegitimate children.

11.31 A reference to 'children' will also include a child who has been adopted. Since the coming into force of the Adoption Act 1976 on 1 January 1976 (the provisions of which have been replaced by the Adoption and Children Act 2004) an adopted child is treated as if born as the child of the adopter or adopters and any gift to 'children' by will made after 1 January 1976 will include adopted children.

---

[20] This is known as the rule in *Sibley v Perry* (1802) 7 Ves 522.
[21] *Re Noad* [1951] Ch 553.
[22] *Benn v Dixon* (1847) 16 Sim 21.

11.32 Only legal adoption has this effect. The fact that a child of a partner is regarded informally as a 'stepchild' will not in itself bring them within the class of 'children' described in a will.[23]

INTESTATE SUCCESSION

11.33 The first consideration for a person living in a same sex relationship whose partner dies without having made a will is likely to be who is entitled to deal with funeral arrangements, and the second, who is to deal with their property and sort out their affairs. The question of who is entitled to make funeral arrangements can be one which causes particular difficulty where the deceased was in a same sex relationship which his relatives did not acknowledge or accept. In the case of both questions the answer is: the person who is entitled to a grant of administration (often referred to as letters of administration.) As discussed above in **11.17** the question of who is entitled to possession of the body of the deceased is governed by the r 22 of the Non-Contentious Probate Rules 1987. Rule 22 provides the following order of priority for relatives of the deceased:

'**22 Order of priority for grant in case of intestacy**

(1) Where the deceased died on or after 1st January 1926, wholly intestate, the person or persons having a beneficial interest in the estate shall be entitled to a grant of administration in the following classes in order of priority, namely –

    (a)   the surviving spouse or civil partner;

    (b)   the children of the deceased[24] and the issue of any deceased child who died before the deceased;

    (c)   the father and mother of the deceased;

    (d)   brothers and sisters of the whole blood and the issue of any deceased brother or sister of the whole blood who died before the deceased;

    (e)   brothers and sisters of the half blood and the issue of any deceased brother or sister of the half blood who died before the deceased;

    (f)   grandparents;

    (g)   uncles and aunts of the whole blood and the issue of any deceased uncle or aunt of the whole blood who died before the deceased;

    (h)   uncles and aunts of the half blood and the issue of any deceased uncle or aunt of the half blood who died before the deceased.

(2) In default of any person having a beneficial interest in the estate, the Treasury Solicitor shall be entitled to a grant if he claims bona vacantia on behalf of the Crown.'

---

[23] *Re Davison* [1949] Ch 670 suggests that if the wording of the will can only be understood as including a stepchild, they will not be excluded, but this will only apply in a case where the will permits such an interpretation.

[24] 'Children' for this purpose includes illegitimate children and a child of a parent who has acquired that status by virtue of s 42 or 43 of the HFEA 2008, but does not include 'children of the family' or children informally referred to as 'stepchildren'.

It will be seen that a surviving cohabitant does not have any place in this list. Cohabitation without civil partnership, no matter how long its duration, is not recognised by the Non-Contentious Probate Rules.

11.34 The High Court has power under s 116 of the Senior Courts Act 1981 to appoint another person as administrator. Section 116 provides:

> **'116 Power of court to pass over prior claims to grant.**
>
> (1) If by reason of any special circumstances it appears to the High Court to be necessary or expedient to appoint as administrator some person other than the person who, but for this section, would in accordance with probate rules have been entitled to the grant, the court may in its discretion appoint as administrator such person as it thinks expedient.
>
> (2) Any grant of administration under this section may be limited in any way the court thinks fit.'

11.35 It is only in exceptional circumstances that the court will exercise this power. The position was considered in the case of *Burrows v HM Coroner for Preston*[25] in relation to the question of who was entitled to make funeral arrangements. The deceased was a 15-year-old boy, Liam, who had committed suicide in a young offender's institution. Both his parents were heroin addicts from the time of his birth, and were never able to look after him (his father died when he was a few years old). A paternal uncle, the claimant, came forward to offer care and Liam lived with his uncle and aunt for the last eight years of his life. A residence order was made in their favour. There was no provision for any contact with his mother. Cranston J observed that:

> 'the Burrows were, as Baroness Hale of Richmond describes it in *Re G (Children)* [2006] UKHL 43, [2006] 4 All ER 241, [2006] 1 WLR 2305 at 2316 F-G, the psychological parents of Liam. As she analyses it, these are parents who are neither genetic nor gestational, but who have become in effect parents of a child and thus have an important contribution to make to its welfare. As I say, despite the trouble that Liam got into the Burrows were still his mum and dad. Mr Burrows told me in evidence that he did not claim to be Liam's father, but that he had a sense of responsibility towards him.'

In the last year of his life Liam decided to trace his mother and succeeded in making contact both with her and with his sister, who lived with her. It was apparent that there was a bond with his mother and they began to make plans for a possible future together, but his death occurred before they could be realised. The claimant began to make plans for Liam's funeral, but his mother then sought to claim his body, and a dispute arose. The claimant wished to arrange for cremation, to take place in St Helens, where Liam had spent most of his life, although he was content for Liam's mother then to dispose of his ashes. Liam's mother wanted him to be buried in a family plot in Liverpool. There was evidence that, in the context of a discussion which followed the

---

[25]   [2008] EWHC 1387 (QB).

death of another family member some time before, Liam had expressed a clear wish that he would not wish to be buried.

11.36   Cranston J expressed the view that, in the light of the earlier decision in *Buchanan v Milton*,[26] the law was clear:

> 'If there are no personal representatives, then it must be asked: who has the best claim to be appointed as administrator of a deceased person's estate. Rule 22 lays down the order of priority. If there is a dispute, then s 116 may come into play if no compromise is possible. That requires an answer to two questions. First, are there special circumstances which may displace the order of priority set out in r 22; secondly, is it necessary or expedient by reason of those special circumstances to displace the normal order of priority. As demonstrated by the result in Buchanan, the situations where the order of priority will be varied will be rare indeed.'

11.37   He noted that the domestic authorities however gave no consideration to the effect of the Human Rights Act 1998. Previous cases heard by the European Court of Human Rights indicated that potentially Art 8 (right to family life) was engaged. In *X v The Federal Republic of Germany*[27] the applicant wished to have his ashes scattered in his own garden. The administrative authorities in his home city of Hamburg refused. The ECHR took the view that Art 8 was engaged but that the interference by the public authorities was justified under Art 8.2. Similarly in *Dödsbo v Sweden*,[28] there was agreement that Art 8 was engaged in a case where a wife wished to disinter her late husband's ashes so that they could be buried in a family plot elsewhere; the court held that the authorities' refusal to permit a move was a justified interference. Part of the reasoning was based on the apparent preference of the deceased for burial of his ashes in their original location, situated in a town he had lived in for many years.

11.38   Cranston J expressed a clear opinion that previous case law regarding the irrelevance of the deceased's wishes to the question of disposal of their body is no longer valid in the light of decisions of the ECtHR:

> 'One thing is clear, that in as much as our domestic law says that the views of a deceased person can be ignored it is no longer good law. That rule of common law can be traced back to *Williams v Williams*, where it was said that directions given by a deceased as to the disposal of his body were not enforceable as a matter of law. It is quite clear from the jurisprudence of the European Courts of Human Rights that the views of a deceased person as to funeral arrangements and the disposal of his or her body must be taken into account. However, this aspect of Strasbourg jurisprudence is easily accommodated within domestic law: in this type of case a person's wishes can be regarded as a special circumstance in terms of s 116 of the [Senior Courts] Act. Otherwise, the jurisprudence of the European Court of Human Rights does not cast doubt on the domestic law. Rule 22 [of the

---

26   [1999] 2 FLR 844.
27   Application No 8741/79, decided on 10 March 1981, DR 24, 137.
28   ECHR 2006 No 5.

Non-Contentious Probate Rules] can still apply. Special circumstances may displace the order of priority set out there although a high test has to be satisfied, whether it is necessary or expedient to do so.'

11.39 He found that:

'the approach to be adopted is to consider whether, in light of the factors set out earlier, the court should exercise its discretion to vary the order of priority set out in r 22. The first stage involves identifying any special circumstances including, in accordance with art 8 jurisprudence, the wishes of the deceased. The second stage is to decide whether, in the light of those special circumstances weighing in favour of varying the order of priority, if it is necessary or expedient to do so.'

11.40 On this basis the judge found that there were special circumstances which involved displacing the priority under r 22 and that it was necessary and expedient to do so. On the facts of this case those circumstances included the inability of Liam's mother to organise a funeral herself, Liam's own wishes regarding disposal of his body, and the fact that the Burrows were his psychological parents, their daughter having a particularly close relationship with him. There were also people in the St Helens area who would wish to pay their respects at a funeral there rather than in Liverpool.

11.41 Cranston J also sought to provide some guidance for coroners in this difficult area:

'[28] Coroners need have no fear of the ruling in this case. Coroners need certainty but there is no uncertainty in what has been said. At the present, where there is no executor or administrator, they will simply apply the order of priority set out in r 22 of the Non Contentious Probate Rules to decide who has the right to claim the body of a deceased person. However, if someone lower in that order of priority, or not there at all, advances a claim, they will need to consider it. It may be that in those cases they will be able to effect a compromise. Mediation will often resolve the issue, for example, as to how the funeral will be conducted. A compromise is the most desirable outcome. Such disputes are not really matters for the courts.

[29] In those cases, however, where a compromise is not possible, coroners need to make a decision. They do this by asking themselves two questions, first, are there any special circumstances which weigh in favour of varying the order of priority set out in r 22. Consistently with the jurisprudence of the European Court of Human Rights, special circumstances include the wishes of the deceased person, if there is clear evidence of those wishes. Given that there are special circumstances and these weigh in favour of varying the order of priority in r 22, a second question they need to ask is whether it is necessary or expedient to do so. Cases such as the present, where both questions can be answered affirmatively, will be very unusual. The courts will be slow to interfere, although if it appears that there may be a legal challenge to their decision coroners will need to delay releasing the body for a short time so that parties can apply for urgent relief. If cases are brought to the High Court, they can be and will be handled expeditiously.'

11.42 Similar considerations arose in the case of *Scotching v Birch*.[29] The deceased was a child. His parents had separated when he was only a few years old and contact with his father had ceased; the father subsequently issued an application for contact. The mother alleged repeated violence towards herself on the part of the father. On 2 August 2007, the day after she had failed to attend a hearing in relation to the contact application, the mother killed Jay and attempted to kill herself. She was charged with murder, and entered a plea to manslaughter, which was not accepted by the Crown. While she was in custody awaiting trial litigation began between the father and her in relation to arrangements for the disposal of Jay's body and to determine the question of who should administer his estate. There was no money in the estate: the issue was about funeral arrangements. The father wished him to be buried in Leighton Buzzard, the father's home but not a place with which Jay had any real connection. The mother's older children from a previous relationship also joined in the proceedings on the basis that they had an entitlement, under Art 8, to have their views as to the disposal of their sibling's body taken into account. It was clear on the basis of r 22 of the Non-Contentious Probate Rules that both parents were entitled to a grant of letters of administration, and both sought such a grant. Patten J found that the public policy rules which prevents a person who has unlawfully killed another from benefiting from his estate applied, and that the mother was therefore excluded as a beneficiary of Jay's estate. Rule 22 of the Non-Contentious Probate Rules (see **11.33** above) limits the class of persons entitled to apply for a grant to those having a beneficial interest in the estate, and, as the mother was excluded from having such an interest, she had no standing to apply for a grant.

11.43 Patten J also had to consider the position of Jay's siblings, who wished him to be buried near their home so that they would be able to visit his grave. He observed that:

> 'Without necessarily deciding the matter, it seems to me that the right to organise a funeral and to stipulate the place of burial is probably sufficient to engage Art 8, at least in respect of the more fundamental aspects of the decision which would include the determination of the place of burial and the right to attend the funeral service.'

11.44 He noted however that both the claimant father and the mother had Art 8 rights and indicated that in his view Art 8 was only of significance if it enabled the mother to overcome the hurdle posed by r 22 of the Non-Contentious Probate Rules and enabled her to obtain a grant despite the public policy rule preventing her from benefiting from her son's estate. It did not do so: the public policy rule arose from an accepted moral and legal framework that a person should not be allowed to benefit from his own wrong. He concluded that in the absence of any standing on the part of the mother the position of the children was of little relevance, and on this basis he declined to make any order under s 116 of the Senior Courts Act 1981. The father was

---

[29] [2008] EWHC 844 (Ch).

therefore entitled to apply for a grant and to arrange the funeral on the basis of his standing under r 22 of the Non-Contentious Probate Rules.

11.45 Both cases referred to above are principally disputes related to disposal of a body rather than disposal of assets, although the relevant legislation is the same in both cases. A case where the disposal of a body was not the principal issue is *Khan v Crossland*.[30] The claimant (K) sought the removal of the defendants (C) as executors of the estate of his late step-father. The defendants operated a will-writing service and in 1999 had drafted a will for the deceased in which they were appointed as executors and permitted to charge for their services. The beneficiaries of the will were K and his sister. The deceased died in 2008, and no will was found. K and his sister reached an informal agreement as to how to deal with his estate. In 2009 the will was found, and C was invited to withdraw as an executor. They declined to do so although they did offer to reduce their fees. K applied for their removal under s 116 on the Senior Courts Act 1980 on the basis that there had been a complete loss of confidence in them. He succeeded: the judge took the view that the court's discretion under s 116 was a wide one and that it was not necessary for an executor to be discredited before he could be removed[31]. The combination of the breakdown in the relationship between the beneficiaries and C, together with the fact that the beneficiaries were in agreement about what should happen to the estate, were sufficient to justify the making of an order. If beneficiaries of full age and with full mental capacity were united in the view that an executor should be removed, this could be a special circumstance under s 116.

11.46 Cohabitants who are not in a civil partnership do not have any standing under r 22 of the Non-Contentious Probate Rules. There is a risk if the family of a person in a same sex relationship are not accepting of that relationship they will, following a death, be reluctant to let the deceased's partner participate in arrangements arising out of the death. A cohabitant who wants his partner to be able to make funeral arrangements for him, but who for other reasons does not wish to make a will and appoint that partner his executor, should ensure that he leaves clear signed written instructions setting out his intentions. If this step is taken the bereaved partner is in a strong negotiating position to make funeral arrangements and the family would be advised that to seek to override the deceased's firmly expressed wishes would be to interfere with his rights under Art 8.

11.47 A similar document could be used to express a wish that a partner should be entitled to apply for letters of administration where there is no will. A will of course avoids any complications, but circumstances can arise in which a choice is made not to make one or where sudden ill-health makes the practicalities of having one drafted difficult to arrange.

---

[30] Unreported, 25 November 2011, HH Judge Behrens.
[31] This appears to imply disapproval of the approach taken in *AB v Dobbs* [2010] EWHC 497 (Fam).

11.48 Likewise if a person wishes arrangements to be made on his death by a person who has been regarded by him as a child of the family or stepchild but who is not a child within the meaning of the Non-Contentious Probate Rules, a signed written direction would assist the child in establishing a right to make those arrangements.

Inheritance on intestacy

11.49 Section 46 of the Administration of Estates Act 1925 sets out the division of the property of a deceased person who has died intestate in all cases after 1996:

> (1) The residuary estate of an intestate shall be distributed in the manner or be held on the trusts mentioned in this section, namely –
>
>> (i)   If the intestate leaves a spouse or civil partner, then in accordance with the following Table:
>>
>> TABLE
>>
>> If the intestate –

(1)	leaves –	the residuary estate shall be held in trust for the surviving spouse or civil partner absolutely.
	(a) no issue, and	
	(b) no parent, or brother or sister of the whole blood, or issue of a brother or sister of the whole blood	
(2)	leaves issue (whether or not persons mentioned in sub-paragraph (b) above also survive)	the surviving spouse or civil partner shall take the personal chattels absolutely and, in addition, the residuary estate of the intestate (other than the personal chattels) shall stand charged with the payment of a fixed net sum, free of death duties and costs, to the surviving spouse or civil partner with interest thereon from the date of the death . . . at such rate as the Lord Chancellor may specify by order until paid or appropriated, and, subject to providing for that sum and the interest thereon, the residuary estate (other than the personal chattels) shall be held—
		(a) as to one half upon trust for the surviving spouse or civil partner during his or her life, and, subject to such life interest, on the statutory trusts for the issue of the intestate, and
		(b) as to the other half, on the statutory trusts for the issue of the intestate.

(3) leaves one or more of the following, that is to say, a parent, a brother or sister of the whole blood, or issue of a brother or sister of the whole blood, but leaves no issue

the surviving spouse or civil partner shall take the personal chattels absolutely and, in addition, the residuary estate of the intestate (other than the personal chattels) shall stand charged with the payment of a fixed net sum, free of death duties and costs, to the surviving spouse or civil partner with interest thereon from the date

of the death . . . at such rate as the Lord Chancellor may specify by order until paid or appropriated, and, subject to providing for that sum and the interest thereon, the residuary estate (other than the personal chattels) shall be held—

(a) as to one half in trust for the surviving spouse or civil partner absolutely, and

(b) as to the other half –

   (i) where the intestate leaves one parent or both parents (whether or not brothers or sisters of the intestate or their issue also survive) in trust for the parent absolutely or, as the case may be, for the two parents in equal shares absolutely

   (ii) where the intestate leaves no parent, on the statutory trusts for the brothers and sisters of the whole blood of the intestate.

The fixed net sums referred to in paragraphs (2) and (3) of this Table shall be of the amounts provided by or under section 1 of the Family Provision Act 1966

(ii) If the intestate leaves issue but no spouse or civil partner, the residuary estate of the intestate shall be held on the statutory trusts for the issue of the intestate;

(iii) If the intestate leaves no spouse or civil partner and no issue but both parents, then . . . the residuary estate of the intestate shall be held in trust for the father and mother in equal shares absolutely;

(iv) if the intestate leaves no spouse or civil partner and no issue but one parent, then . . . the residuary estate of the intestate shall be held in trust for the surviving father or mother absolutely;

(v) If the intestate leaves no spouse or civil partner and no issue and no parent, then . . . the residuary estate of the intestate shall be held in trust for the following persons living at the death of the intestate, and in the following order and manner, namely –

First, on the statutory trusts for the brothers and sisters of the whole blood of the intestate; but if no person takes an absolutely vested interest under such trusts; then
Secondly, on the statutory trusts for the brothers and sisters of the half blood of the intestate; but if no person takes an absolutely vested interest under such trusts; then

Thirdly, for the grandparents of the intestate and, if more than one survive the intestate, in equal shares; but if there is no member of this class; then Fourthly, on the statutory trusts for the uncles and aunts of the intestate (being brothers or sisters of the whole blood of a parent of the intestate); but if no person takes an absolutely vested interest under such trusts; then Fifthly, on the statutory trusts for the uncles and aunts of the intestate (being brothers or sisters of the half blood of a parent of the intestate) . . .

(vi)   In default of any person taking an absolute interest under the foregoing provisions, the residuary estate of the intestate shall belong to the Crown or to the Duchy of Lancaster or to the Duke of Cornwall for the time being, as the case may be, as bona vacantia, and in lieu of any right to escheat.

The Crown or the said Duchy or the said Duke may (without prejudice to the powers reserved by section nine of the Civil List Act 1910, or any other powers), out of the whole or any part of the property devolving on them respectively, provide, in accordance with the existing practice, for dependents, whether kindred or not, of the intestate, and other persons for whom the intestate might reasonably have been expected to make provision.

(1A) The power to make orders under subsection (1) above shall be exercisable by statutory instrument subject to annulment in pursuance of a resolution of either House of Parliament; and any such order may be varied or revoked by a subsequent order made under the power.]

(2) A husband and wife shall for all purposes of distribution or division under the foregoing provisions of this section be treated as two persons.

(2A) Where the intestate's spouse or civil partner survived the intestate but died before the end of the period of 28 days beginning with the day on which the intestate died, this section shall have effect as respects the intestate as if the spouse or civil partner had not survived the intestate.

(3) Where the intestate and the intestate's spouse or civil partner have died in circumstances rendering it uncertain which of them survived the other and the intestate's spouse or civil partner is by virtue of section one hundred and eighty-four of the Law of Property Act 1925, deemed to have survived the intestate, this section shall, nevertheless, have effect as respects the intestate as if the spouse or civil partner had not survived the intestate.

(4) The interest payable on the fixed net sum payable to a surviving spouse or civil partner shall be primarily payable out of income.

11.50   The effect of this can be summarised as follows:

(a)   If the deceased is in a civil partnership (or married) has no children[32], no parents, no full siblings, no nieces and nephews who are the children of full siblings, the whole of the deceased's residuary estate is held on trust for the surviving civil partner provided that the civil partner survives him

---

[32]   The expression used in the legislation is 'issue'. This includes illegitimate issue where the death occurs after 4 April 1988; in cases where the death occurred before that date but after 1969, illegitimate children are included as next of kin but their children are not included in the statutory trusts (see below) . Issue also include the child of a parent who has acquired that status by virtue of s 42 or 43 of the HFEA 2008. It also includes adopted children.

for twenty-eight days. If he does not, the estate is distributed as if the death of the survivor had occurred before the death of the deceased.

(b) If the deceased was in a civil partnership and has no children, but has parents, full siblings, or nephews and nieces who are the children of full siblings, the surviving partner receives the following:

(i) the deceased's personal chattels;
(ii) a fixed net sum outright, free of taxes, currently £450,000;
(iii) a half interest in the remaining estate outright.

(c) If the deceased was in a civil partnership and has children, the surviving partner receives the following:

(i) the deceased's personal chattels;
(ii) a fixed net sum outright, free of taxes, currently £450,000;
(iii) a life interest in half of the remaining estate.

(d) If the deceased was in a civil partnership but there was a separation order in force in relation to that partnership (pursuant to s 56 of the Civil Partnership Act 2004) the estate of the deceased passes on intestacy as if the other civil partner were dead.

(e) 'Chattels' are defined by the Administration of Estates Act 1925, s 55(1)(x) as:

'(x) carriages, horses, stable furniture and effects (not used for business purposes), motor cars and accessories (not used for business purposes), garden effects, domestic animals, plate, plated articles, linen, china, glass, books, pictures, prints, furniture, jewellery, articles of household or personal use or ornament, musical and scientific instruments and apparatus, wines, liquors and consumable stores, but do not include any chattels used at the death of the intestate for business purposes nor money or securities for money.'

Collections of items, even of some value, such as clocks and watches, or antiques, are chattels for this purpose.[33]

(f) The fixed net sum is increased periodically by statutory instrument. From 1 February 2009 it has been £450,000. Prior to that from 1 December 1993 it was £200,000.

(g) Where there is no surviving civil partner, the children take the whole of the residuary estate on the statutory trusts (see below). If there is a surviving civil partner, they take whatever is left of the estate after the survivor has received the provision set out in (c) above, again on the statutory trusts.

---

[33] *Re Collins's Settlement Trusts, Donne v Hewetson* [1971] 1 All ER 283.

(h)   The statutory trusts are the following:

  (1)   all members of a class take equally;
  (2)   shares of members under 18 are contingent on the attaining of that age or marrying or forming a civil partnership under that age;
  (3)   the share of any member who predeceases the testator is taken by his children or remoter issue equally among them per stirpes,[34] but contingently upon attaining 18 or marrying or forming a civil partnership under that age.

(i)   If the deceased leaves a surviving civil partner, and no children, but has a parent or parents still living, the parents take half the residuary estate, less the fixed sum, and the chattels, and it is divided between them equally.

(j)   If the deceased leaves a surviving civil partner, no children, no parents, but has siblings living, those siblings will receive a half share in the residuary estate, less the fixed sum, and the chattels, and it is divided between them equally.

(k)   If there is no civil partner, but there are parents and siblings, the parents will receive the whole of the residuary estate which, if there are two parents, will be divided equally between them. The siblings do not receive anything.

11.51   It can be seen that the Intestacy Rules can have outcomes which may be highly undesirable. In particular:

(a)   there is no provision for cohabitants;

(b)   there is no provision for children of the family (who are not the deceased's own children), however long they may have been treated in that way.

11.52   A parent who dies intestate leaving four children, some of whom are regarded as children under the Intestacy Rules and some who are not, leaves the children who are not so regarded without any provision. They will have a right to apply for provision under the Inheritance (Provision for Family and Dependants) Act 1975 (see below) but as will be seen that is not a straightforward process, particularly in the case of an adult child.

11.53   A cohabitant who dies intestate leaves his partner with no more than a right to apply under the 1975 Act and the same observations apply.

11.54   There are other potentially arbitrary outcomes. If the deceased has no children, but has parents and siblings surviving, the parents will receive the

---

[34]   Where the testator has two children both of whom have two children, one of whom predeceases the testator, survived by his two children, a distribution of the residue per stirpes will give an equal share to each family. The surviving child takes the whole of his family's share and the children of the predeceasing child take that family's share equally between them.

entirety of his estate and the siblings nothing, although their financial positions and/or the nature of family relationships may make that far from a fair outcome. It cannot be emphasised too strongly that the way in which to avoid these difficulties is to make a will.

SUCCESSION TO TENANCIES

11.55 If a same sex couple hold the tenancy of a property in their joint names, on the death of one of them the survivor becomes the sole tenant. The position is more complicated if the tenancy is in the name of only one partner, but some protection is given to the survivor. The mechanism is different for different types of tenancy.

Rent Act tenancies

11.56 Schedule 1 of the Rent Act 1977 sets out the scheme for succession to tenancies under the Act (most residential tenancies created between 1977 and January 1989). Paragraph 1 of the Schedule provides that a civil partner 'if residing in the dwelling-house immediately before the death of the original tenant' will become the statutory tenant of the property. Paragraph 1(2)(b) extends this right to a person who was 'living with the original tenant as if they were civil partners' immediately prior to his death.

11.57 In considering whether or not the deceased and the would-be successor were living together as if they were civil partners at the time of the death, the court will consider the nature of the relationship and in particular: whether a lifetime commitment has been made; whether the relationship is acknowledged openly by the parties; whether the parties have a common life together; and whether the perception of the outside world would be that this was a committed emotional relationship. Living together out of convenience, or friendship, or as lovers without an enduring commitment will not suffice.[35]

11.58 The situation might arise where two people are eligible to succeed under this provision: for example, if the tenant prior to death was living in a same sex relationship with a partner who resided with him, but had a spouse still living in the same dwelling house. In that case, the eligible survivors can agree who succeeds; in default of agreement, application can be made to the county court for a decision as to who should succeed. If such an application is necessary, the court will consider all the circumstances of the case. It has no power however to grant a joint tenancy to the competing survivors.

11.59 In the event of such a succession occurring, the survivor receives a statutory Rent Act tenancy of the property.

---

[35] *Southern Housing Group Ltd v Nutting* [2004] EWHC 2982 (Ch) discussed in more detail at **11.84–11.85**.

11.60 It should be noted that prior to the coming into force of the Civil Partnership Act 2004, which amended the Rent Act to permit succession by a civil partner or a person living with the tenant as a civil partner, the courts had ruled that, in order to avoid discrimination which would be unlawful under Art 14 of the European Convention on Human Rights, the existing provisions of the Act as to succession should be construed as applying to same sex couples.[36] The survivor of a same sex couple where the deceased was the original tenant where the death occurred before the CPA took effect will have succeeded to a Rent Act statutory tenancy, even though he and his landlord may have been unaware of that fact. However, this is only the case if the death occurred on or after 15 January 1989. Prior to that date, only the survivor of a valid marriage could succeed to a tenancy.

11.61 If there is no spouse, civil partner, or person who was living with the deceased as such to succeed, any member of the original tenant's family who was residing with the tenant in the property for a period of two years up to and including the time of the tenant's death will succeed: however that person will acquire only an assured tenancy. This reduces the tenant's security of tenure; additionally, if the Rent Act tenancy was subject to a registered fair rent, it will no longer be so restricted and the landlord can increase the rent to a market rent.[37] If more than one person is entitled to succeed, and they cannot agree between themselves who should succeed, the county court can determine the issue.

11.62 Temporary absences do not prevent a family member from residing with the tenant. If the family member has work obligations which require him to spend time away from the property, this will not undermine the fact of residence.

11.63 In certain limited circumstances a second succession can occur. The second successor has to show that he was a member of the original tenant's family, and has lived with the successor for two years up to and including the date of the successor's death. An adult child, living with a surviving civil partner (or person who has lived as a civil partner), would qualify for such a succession provided that he has fulfilled the 2 years residence requirement.

11.64 Whether or not a person is a member of the original tenant's family for the purposes of determining entitlement to succeed is not the subject of any statutory definition. The test has been said to be whether an ordinary person, at the date of the relevant death, looking at the question of whether or not a particular person was a member of the tenant's family, would have taken a positive or negative view.[38] On this basis children of the deceased, including illegitimate children, and step-children, have been held to be members of the deceased's family. Decisions of the court on this issue reflect changing social attitudes. The child of one of two civil partners would be regarded as a

---

[36]　*Ghaidan v Godin-Mendoza* [2003] 2 WLR 478.
[37]　Rent Act 1977, Sch 1, para 6.
[38]　*Brock v Wollams* [1949] 2 KB 388.

stepchild and entitled to succeed. It is likely that the child of one of two people living together as civil partners would also be treated as a member of the family of the non-parent.

11.65 A child, even though a minor, is probably entitled to succeed to a Rent Act statutory tenancy.[39] This arises because a statutory tenancy is not an interest in land (which a minor cannot hold).

Assured tenancies

11.66 One succession to an assured tenancy is permitted under the Housing Act 1988. The only persons entitled to succeed are the deceased tenant's spouse or civil partner or a person living with him as his spouse or civil partner.[40] The successor must have been occupying the property as his only or principal home at the time of the death. There is no requirement that he was also residing with the deceased, so it would be possible for a succession to occur if the two separate households were operating within the same property.[41] Because only one succession is permitted, the deceased must not have been a successor. The deceased will be treated as a successor if he had previously held the tenancy jointly with another person, that person had died, and the deceased had therefore succeeded to the tenancy not under the Act but by survivorship.

11.67 Children, whether of the deceased or of the family, have no succession rights.

11.68 The above principles apply only where the assured tenancy is a periodic tenancy. It is possible for an assured tenancy to be granted for a fixed term; in the case of such a tenancy, there are no succession rights, but the remaining part of the term can be the subject of provision under a will, or will devolve on intestacy.

Secure tenancies

11.69 A person may succeed to a secure tenancy if at the time of the tenant's death the successor occupied the property as his only or principal home and he was the tenant's spouse or civil partner. There is no specific provision for persons living with the deceased as if they were husband and wife or civil partners.

11.70 In addition a member of tenant's family who has resided with the tenant for a period of twelve months ending with the tenant's death is entitled to succeed. If a person claims the right to succeed on the basis that he was living with the deceased as if they were civil partners, he will have to claim under this provision, and will need to show twelve months residence.

---

[39] *Portman Registrars & Nominees v Mohammed Latif* (1987) 6 CL 217.
[40] Housing Act 1988, s 17.
[41] The tenancy will only be an assured tenancy if the tenant was occupying it as his only or principal home at the time of his death.

11.71   These principles only apply if the tenant was not himself a successor. If he was a successor, there can be no further succession. The tenant will be treated as a successor in most circumstances where the tenancy began as a joint tenancy and became a sole tenancy, but not if the tenancy was assigned pursuant to a property adjustment order in connection with civil partnership proceedings (eg on dissolution). If civil partners or persons living together in a same sex relationship hold a secure joint tenancy, and on the breakdown of the relationship one partner assigns his interest under the tenancy to the other,[42] this will be treated as a succession and no further succession will be possible. If the transfer of tenancy on relationship breakdown is effected by surrender of the original tenancy and grant of a new tenancy to the remaining party (a procedure which requires the co-operation of the landlord) this will not constitute a succession.

INHERITANCE AND FAMILY PROVISION

11.72   The Inheritance (Provision for Family and Dependants) Act 1975 provides those who have had a significant relationship with a deceased person but who have not been provided for adequately, or have been left without any provision, either by the deceased's will, or by the operation of the Intestacy Rules, with the possibility of a claim against the estate. The Act has been amended on a number of occasions to take into account changing social attitudes, and in particular to make provision for civil partners and for same sex couples who live together as if they were civil partners (but who have not entered into any formal civil partnership). It also enables provision to be made not only for children but for someone who has been treated as 'child of the family' in relation to a civil partnership.

11.73   In the late nineteenth century, one could find a clear and unmistakable approach by the courts to challenges to the wishes of testators: a man could leave his assets to whomsoever he might wish. The legal position was very clearly stated by the President of the Probate and Divorce Division, Sir James Hannen, in *Boughton v Knight*:[43]

> 'By the law of England everyone is left free to choose the person upon whom he will bestow his property after death entirely unfettered in the selection he may think proper to make. He may disinherit, either wholly or partially, his children, and leave his property to strangers to gratify his spite, or to charities to gratify his pride, and we must give effect to his will, however much we may condemn the course he has pursued.'

---

[42]   Permitted under Housing Act 1985, s 91(3)(c) – the assignee must have been in a position to succeed if the assignor had died rather than departed.

[43]   (1873) LR 3 P&D 64.

In that quotation one can see both a statement of the law as it then stood and the growth of a feeling that this situation required reform and it was not tolerable in a caring society for a father to cut off his wife or his children with a penny.

11.74   The move to change the law came from the other side of the world. In 1900 the New Zealand Parliament passed the Family Protection Act which enabled the court to overturn wills so far as was necessary to provide for the proper maintenance and support of spouses and children. A favourable reaction to the New Zealand Act led over the next twenty years or so to every state in Australia making its own Family Protection Act. The proper interpretation of such legislation finally came before the Privy Council in 1938 in the case of *Bosch v Perpetual Trustee Co Ltd*.[44] This was an appeal from the Supreme Court of New South Wales. The dispute was concerned with the two infant children of the deceased. Their case was that the sums that the deceased had left them in his will were not adequate provision for their proper maintenance. The Privy Council approved the principles which had been applied in relation to such claims, in particular in the case of *Re Allardice*[45] where the New Zealand Court of Appeal laid down the principles that:

(a)   The Act did not empower the Court to make a new will for the testator.

(b)   The Court is allowed to alter a testator's disposition of his property only so far as it is necessary to provide for the proper maintenance and support of wife, husband or children where adequate provision has not been made for this purpose.

(c)   In the case of a widow, the Court would make more ample provision than in the case of children, if the children are physically and mentally able to maintain and support themselves.

(d)   The whole circumstances have to be considered.

> 'Even in money cases where the Court comes to a decision that the will is most unjust from a moral point of view, that is not enough to make the Court alter the testator's disposition of his property. The first inquiry in every case must be "Who is the need of maintenance and support"; and the second, "What property has the testator left".'

One can see those principles appearing in the subsequent English decisions.

11.75   *Bosch* was decided whilst the Inheritance (Family Provision) Act 1938 was proceeding through the UK Parliament. It made provision for a spouse of the deceased or a daughter who had not married or who was by reason of some mental or physical disability incapable of maintaining herself, or a son under the age of 21 or who by reason of some mental and physical disability was

---

[44]   [1938] AC 463.
[45]   (1910) 29 NZLR 959.

incapable of maintaining himself. It will thus be seen that from the start, adult daughters were able to make a claim, so long as they had not married. The court was given the power to make provision out of the net estate for the maintenance of dependants within those categories providing that the court was of the opinion that the will did not make reasonable provision for the maintenance of that dependant. Among other things, the court was obliged to have regard to the testator's reasons for the provision.

11.76   The new Act was greeted with mixed feelings. In Halsbury's Statutes, it was commented that it 'marked a notable departure from one of the most cherished principles of English law by enabling the court to make provision for maintenance for dependants of a testator out of his estate in defiance of his will'. Indeed, the perceptive comment was also made that it imposed, albeit indirectly, a duty upon testators to provide for their dependants. In 1952 the Act was amended so as to include the situation where the deceased died intestate and the effect of the law as to intestacy was not to make reasonable provision for the dependant.

11.77   Over the thirty or more years of its operation, the 1938 Act did enable the courts to make provision for the limited category of beneficiaries included in the Act. However, the provision was frequently far from generous. For example in *Re Ducksbury*,[46] the deceased, a hotelier, had married twice By his first marriage he had two daughters. On his divorce from his first wife, he settled a sum of money to provide for the maintenance of his daughters. They had on separation remained with their mother and relations with their father had broken down. The elder daughter wished to become an artist and so by the time of her father's death she was 30, a student, working part time and earning little. She had unsuccessfully tried to mend her relationship with her father before his death. He left everything to his second wife. Buckley J came to the conclusion that although the daughter was not suffering from any kind of mental or physical disability, the court must look at all the circumstances and consider whether it was reasonable to make provision for her maintenance. He came to the conclusion that it was. He laid down (at 1230) the legal position:

> 'It is for the Court to decide upon such evidence as it has before it, whether or not the testator has made reasonable provision for the maintenance of the applicants, and I do not think the Court should start with a leaning one way or another either in favour of the view or against the view that the testator had some sort of moral duty to provide for any particular applicant.'

Later he went on (at 1233):

> 'I have to consider what is reasonable in the circumstances of this case to Order that she should receive, having first of all satisfied myself that the deceased had failed to make reasonable provision for her. He has, in fact, made no provision for her, and for the reasons I have indicated, I think that he was under a moral obligation to make some provision for her.'

---

[46]   [1966] 1WLR 1226.

Accordingly, he awarded her £2 per week until death or earlier marriage. Even in 1966 £2 per week was a very modest amount. The observations of Buckley J about 'moral duty' cast a long shadow over the subsequent development of the law.

11.78 In the late 1960s and early 1970s matrimonial law in England and Wales was the subject of major reform. This reform included a significant extension of the requirement on a spouse to make financial provision for the other on divorce. Those reforms reflected changes in society and a growing belief that the richer spouse, usually the husband, should be expected to do more than provide simply basic maintenance for his former wife and children, and that the wife should have a right to a share of any capital which the family had accumulated, even if it was in the husband's name. Similar considerations resulted in the introduction of the Inheritance (Provision for Family and Dependants) Act 1975. That Act extended the categories of possible claimants to include all adult children, former spouses and other persons who were dependants of the deceased at the time of his or her death. The duty to have regard to the reasons given by the deceased was abolished and the powers of the court were greatly extended.

11.79 The Act has been amended on more than one occasion. In 1995 a further category of claimant was added: persons who had lived with the deceased as husband and wife for 2 years preceding the death of the deceased. In 2005 following the coming into force of the Civil Partnership Act, the 1975 Act was again amended to add as potential claimants civil partners, former civil partners, and persons who had lived with the deceased as a civil partner for 2 years before the death of the deceased.

11.80 Section 1 of the 1975 Act as amended provides as follows:

'(1) Where after the commencement of this Act a person dies domiciled in England and Wales and is survived by any of the following persons –

(a)   the spouse or civil partner of the deceased;

(b)   a former spouse or former civil partner of the deceased, but not one who has formed a subsequent marriage or civil partnership;

(ba)   any person (not being a person included in paragraph (a) or (b) above) to whom subsection (1A) or (1B) below applies;

(c)   a child of the deceased;

(d)   any person (not being a child of the deceased) who, in the case of any marriage or civil partnership to which the deceased was at any time a party, was treated by the deceased as a child of the family in relation to that marriage or civil partnership;

(e)   any person (not being a person included in the foregoing paragraphs of this subsection) who immediately before the death of the deceased was being maintained, either wholly or partly, by the deceased;

that person may apply to the court for an order under section 2 of this Act on the ground that the disposition of the deceased's estate effected by his will or the law relating to intestacy, or the combination of his will and that law, is not such as to make reasonable financial provision for the applicant.

(1A) This subsection applies to a person if the deceased died on or after 1st January 1996 and, during the whole of the period of two years ending immediately before the date when the deceased died, the person was living –

(a)   in the same household as the deceased, and
(b)   as the husband or wife of the deceased.

(1B) This subsection applies to a person if for the whole of the period of two years ending immediately before the date when the deceased died the person was living –

(a)   in the same household as the deceased, and
(b)   as the civil partner of the deceased.'

Civil partners

11.81   The expression 'civil partner' is not defined in the 1975 Act and its meaning is therefore as defined in the Civil Partnership Act 2004. 'Former civil partner' is defined in s 25 of the Act as:

a person whose civil partnership with the deceased was during the lifetime of the deceased either –

(a)   dissolved or annulled by an order made under the law of any part of the British Islands, or
(b)   dissolved or annulled in any country or territory outside the British Islands by a dissolution or annulment which is entitled to be recognised as valid by the law of England and Wales.

Living 'in the same household as the deceased and . . . as the civil partner of the deceased'

'Living in the same household'

11.82   The meaning of this expression was considered by the court in *Churchill v Roach* where HH Judge Norris QC said:[47]

'It is, of course, dangerous to try and define what "living in the same household" means. It seems to me to have elements of permanence, to involve a consideration of the frequency and intimacy of contact, to contain an element of mutual support, to require some consideration of the degree of voluntary restraint upon personal freedom which each party undertakes, and to involve an element of community of resources. None of these factors of itself is sufficient, but each may provide an indicator.'

Applying that approach he went on to find that a couple who spent many long weekends together, but who maintained separate households, were not living in the same household.

---

[47]   [2004] 3 FCR 744, [2004] 2 FLR 989.

'As the civil partner'

11.83 Some guidance can also be obtained from *Crake v Supplementary Benefits Commission*[48] where the court had to consider the meaning of the same wording when used in social security legislation. Woolf LJ found that the following signposts should be used to indicate whether a couple were living together as husband and wife:

'They are: whether they are members of the same household; then there is a reference to stability; then there is a question of financial support; then there is the question of sexual relationship; the question of children; and public acknowledgement.'

11.84 In *Southern Housing Group Ltd v Nutting*[49] the court considered whether, for the purposes of succession to a tenancy, a couple were living together in a same sex relationship which was akin to living as husband and wife. At first instance the Recorder hearing the case applied the following test:

'(a) Have the parties openly set up home together?
(b) Is the relationship an emotional one of mutual lifetime commitment rather than simply one of convenience, friendship, companionship or the living together of lovers?
(c) Is the relationship one which has been presented to the outside world openly and unequivocally so that society considers it to be of permanent intent – the words 'till death us do part' being apposite?
(d) Do the parties have a common life together, both domestically (in relation to the household) and externally (in relation to family and friends)?'

11.85 On appeal Evans-Lombe J was not enthusiastic about this approach. His view was:

'Having regard to the authorities it does not seem to me, with respect, that the fact that question (a) can be answered in the affirmative is indicative of a 'spousal' relationship. That answer could have been given in relation to students sharing lodgings. The recorder himself did not treat an affirmative answer to question (d) as being so indicative. I agree with him. Without a lifetime commitment at least at some point in the relationship there is no sufficient similarity to marriage. There are many ways in which a marriage relationship can be described but it seems to me that the test prescribed by the recorder at paragraph (b) subject to the qualification in paragraph (c), that the relationship must be openly and unequivocally displayed to the outside world, is an entirely adequate test and one which is consistent with the authorities.'

11.86 In *Baynes v Hedger*[50] Lewison J agreed with that view and particularly stressed the need for the relationship to be openly and unequivocally displayed. In that case a female couple had enjoyed an intimate relationship for many years but had maintained separate households and had, save in relation to close

---

[48] [1982] 1 All ER 498.
[49] [2004] EWHC 2982 (Ch).
[50] [2008] EWHC 1587 (Ch).

friends and family, kept their relationship covert. The judge found that this did not constitute living together as civil partners.

11.87 The 1975 Act as amended does not prescribe any starting date for the application of the amendment which enabled persons living as civil partners to bring a claim. Lewison J in *Baynes v Hedger* suggests that it is unlikely that a period of living together as civil partners could predate the point at which it was possible to form a civil partnership (5 December 2005). He observed however that for periods of such cohabitation prior to that date the Act can be read (in accordance with the reasoning of the House of Lords in *Ghaidan v Godin-Mendoza*[51]) on the basis that the expression 'living together as husband and wife' covers same sex relationships, so in practice this should not give rise to any difficulty.

11.88 Temporary separation caused by illness or relationship problems does not prevent partners living in the same household, provided the relationship has not broken down irretrievably. In *Gully v Dix*[52] an unmarried couple lived together from about 1974 to 2001. There were a number of separations caused by the male cohabitant's drunken violence. In 2001 he threatened the female cohabitant with a knife, and she left. There were some negotiations, carried out through the woman's daughter, about a possible return, but the deceased was found dead in his garden around three months after the separation. Ward LJ, giving judgment in the Court of Appeal, stated that:

> 'Subsection (1A) [of section 1 of the 1975 Act] requires that during the whole of the two-year period, two elements be present. First, that the claimant was living in the same household as the deceased and, secondly, that she lived in a relationship which can be categorised as living as the wife of the deceased. The concept of parties living together in the same household is a familiar one in other areas of statutory law.'

11.89 He referred to the case of *Santos v Santos*[53] in which the court had to consider the meaning of s 1(6) of the Matrimonial Causes Act 1973 which provides that: 'a husband and wife shall be treated as living apart unless they are living with each other in the same household.' In *Santos* Sachs LJ observed that:

> 'use is again made of words with a well settled matrimonial meaning – "living together", a phrase which is simply the antithesis of living apart, and "household", a word which essentially refers to people held together by a particular kind of tie, even if temporarily separated "living apart" is a state of affairs to establish which it is in the vast generality of cases arising under those heads necessary to prove something more than that the husband and wife were physically separated. For the purpose of that vast generality, it is sufficient to say that the relevant state of affairs does not exist while both parties recognise the

---

[51]   [2004] UKHL 30.
[52]   [2004] 1 FCR 453.
[53]   [1972] 2 All ER 246.

marriage as subsisting. That involves considering attitudes of mind; and naturally the difficulty of judicially determining that attitude in a particular case may on occasions be great.'

11.90 Following on from that Ward LJ commented:

'The relevant word is 'household' not 'house', and 'household' bears the meaning given to it by Sachs LJ. Thus they will be in the same household if they are tied by their relationship. The tie of that relationship may be made manifest by various elements, not simply their living under the same roof, but the public and private acknowledgment of their mutual society, and the mutual protection and support that binds them together. In former days one would possibly say one should look at the whole consortium vitae. For present purposes it is sufficient to ask whether either has demonstrated a settled acceptance or recognition that the relationship is in truth at an end. If the circumstances show an irretrievable breakdown of the relationship, then they no longer live in the same household and the Act is not satisfied. If, however, the interruption is transitory, serving as a pause for reflection about the future of a relationship going through difficult times but still recognised to be subsisting, then they will be living in the same household and the claim will lie. Just as the arrangements for maintenance may fluctuate ... so the steadfastness of a commitment to live together may wax and wane, but so long as it is not extinguished, it survives. These notions are succinctly encapsulated in the judge's test, which was to ask whether the relationship was merely suspended, and I see no error in his approach.'

Thus it is not necessary for a cohabitant seeking to rely on s 1(1B) of the Act to demonstrate continuous cohabitation up to the death of the deceased. If the relationship is ongoing, a separation, even if brought about by difficulties within the relationship, will not bring to an end for the purposes of the Act their cohabitation in the same household.

'Child of the deceased'

11.91 Section 25(1) of the Act provides that 'child' includes 'an illegitimate child and a child en ventre sa mere[54] at the death of the deceased'. An adopted child is treated as a 'child' for the purposes of the Act.[55] Similarly a child in relation to whom a parental order has been made will be treated as a child for the purposes of the Act.[56]

'Child of the family'

11.92 'Child' in this context denotes only the relationship, not the age, of the potential applicant.

---

[54] Conceived but not yet born.
[55] ACA 2002, s 67.
[56] Section 67 of the Act and the Human Fertilisation and Embryology (Parental Orders) Regulations 2010, reg 2 and Sch 1.

11.93 'Child of the family' includes a person who has been treated as a child in adulthood rather than while a minor. In *Re Callaghan deceased*[57] the court considered a claim by an adult child who had been treated as the son of the deceased since he was about sixteen years of age. The deceased lived with this claimant's mother and supported the claimant financially and emotionally while he still lived at home. When the claimant became financially independent, he remained on close terms with his mother and the deceased and his children, when born, treated the deceased as their grandfather. The deceased and the claimant's mother eventually married, but not until the claimant was thirty-five years of age. It was argued that the words 'treated by the deceased as a child of the family' must refer to such treatment when the child is a minor and dependent on others, including the deceased. Booth J rejected this submission: in his view treatment of the claimant as a child of the family when an adult sufficed. After the deceased had married he treated the claimant's children as his grandchildren, reposed confidence in the claimant in relation to his property and financial affairs, and depended on the claimant to care for him during his last illness. These were all matters which indicated that the claimant was treated as a child of the family.

11.94 A child can only be treated as a 'child of the family' if there is an existing civil partnership. A child who is treated as a child of the family by a same sex couple who live together as if they were civil partners is not a child of the family for the purposes of s 1(1)(d).

11.95 Claims by adult children have provided the courts with particular problems. Five years after the 1975 Act was passed, the case of *Re Coventry*[58] was decided in the High Court. It concerned a claim by an adult son for provision. His deceased father had been estranged from his wife, and father and son had lived together. His estate (worth only £7,000) went in its entirety to his widow under the Intestacy Rules. She was relatively elderly and living on state benefits. The son, who was working and in good health, sought provision. He was awarded £2,000 in the lower court. The widow appealed, and succeeded in the High Court. Oliver J, giving judgment said:

> 'In regarding the circumstances and applying the guidelines set out in section 3, it always has to be borne in mind that the Act, so far as it relates to applicants other than spouses, is an Act whose purpose is limited to the provision of reasonable maintenance. It is not the purpose of the Act to provide legacies or rewards for meritorious conduct. Subject to the Court's powers under the Act and to fiscal demands, an Englishman still remains at liberty at his death to dispose of his own property in whatever way he pleases or, if he chooses to do so, to leave that disposition to be regulated by the laws of intestate succession. In order to enable the Courts to interfere with and reform those dispositions it must, in my judgement, be shown, not that the deceased acted unreasonably, but that, looked at objectively, his disposition or lack of disposition produces an unreasonable result in that it does not make any or any greater provision for the applicant – and

57   [1985] Fam 1.
58   [1980] Ch 461.

that means, in the case of an applicant other than a spouse, for that applicant's maintenance. It clearly cannot be enough to say that the circumstances are such that if the deceased had made a particular provision for the applicant, that would not have been an unreasonable thing for him to do and therefore it now ought to be done ... It cannot be enough to say "Here is the son of the deceased, he is in necessitous circumstances; there is property of the deceased which could be made available to assist him but which is not available if the deceased's dispositions stand; therefore those dispositions do not make reasonable provision for the applicant". There must, as it seems to me, be established some sort of moral claim by the applicant to be maintained by the deceased or at the expense of his estate beyond the mere fact of a blood relationship, some reason why it can be said that, in the circumstances, it is unreasonable that no or no greater provision was in fact made.'

11.96 The son appealed unsuccessfully to the Court of Appeal, where Oliver J's judgment met with approval. The Court of Appeal did not however expressly approve of his suggestion that it was necessary to establish a moral claim. Buckley LJ said:

'Oliver J. is said to have treated the existence of a moral obligation as a condition precedent to the exercise of this jurisdiction – a moral obligation resting upon the deceased to make some provision for the plaintiff. On a correct reading of the judge's judgment, I do not think that he did so. His approach was that where an applicant is an adult male in employment, and so capable of earning his own living, some special circumstance is required to make a failure on the part of the deceased to make some financial provision for the applicant unreasonable.'

A similar observation was made by Goff LJ.

11.97 It is the judgment of Oliver J which has been more frequently relied on in subsequent cases and which brought about the development of an approach to claims by adult children which suggested that it was necessary for the claimant to show a moral obligation on the part of the deceased in order to succeed.[59] This was a reading of the 1975 Act which is not justified by the text of the Act itself.

11.98 However the recent decision of the Court of Appeal in *Ilott v Mitson*[60] suggests that this arguably incorrect interpretation of the Act will no longer be adopted. Mrs Jackson, the deceased, was the mother of one daughter, Mrs Ilott. Her husband, the father of her child, died before the child was born. She brought her daughter up alone, but their relationship deteriorated during her teens, and major problems arose when she took up with a young man who did not meet with her mother's approval. Eventually she left home and moved in with him; they subsequently married. They had five children but did not prosper financially. On a number of occasions the daughter sought a reconciliation with her mother, but these attempts foundered on her mother's antipathy to the daughter's husband and her unforgiving nature. Attempts by

---

[59] Eg *Re Jennings* [1994] Ch 286.
[60] [2011] EWCA Civ 346.

the children of Mrs Ilott to heal the rift were also unsuccessful. Mrs Jackson had said that she would leave her daughter nothing, and she kept her word. She divided her estate (worth just under £500,000) by will between a number of charities, in none of which she had shown the slightest interest during her lifetime. Mrs Ilott, who remained impecunious, sought provision for herself. She succeeded before a District Judge, but was awarded only £50,000. She appealed against that figure and the charities who stood to benefit cross-appealed on that basis that she should receive no provision at all. The High Court judge agreed with the charities. Mrs Ilott then appealed to the Court of Appeal. Sir Nicholas Wall, President of the Family Division, commented that in relation to *Re Coventry*:

> 'In my judgment, this case bears careful examination both for what it says and, as importantly, for what it is believed to say, but does in fact not say.'

This passage of his judgment is followed by a summary of the relevant case law during the course of which he makes it clear that he does not accept that either *Re Coventry* or the cases which follow it should be interpreted as indicating that a moral claim must be asserted. Arden LJ takes a similar approach.

11.99   *Ilott* was an unusual case in that there were no completing claims from other relatives or dependents and the beneficiaries of Mrs Jackson's will were wealthy charities. However it seems clear following that decision that if an impecunious adult child is disinherited by a parent they will have a potential claim under the Act, unless that parent has excluded them in favour of someone with a greater claim. To exclude a child in favour of a civil partner will often be justified, unless the estate is so large that ample provision could have been made for both, but if the parent has no surviving civil partner or long term cohabitant, the impecunious adult child will be difficult to disregard."

'Any person ... who immediately before the death of the deceased was being maintained, either wholly or partly, by the deceased'

11.100   Section 1(3) of the Act adds to this provision:

> '(3) For the purposes of subsection (1)(e) above, a person shall be treated as being maintained by the deceased, either wholly or partly, as the case may be, if the deceased, otherwise than for full valuable consideration, was making a substantial contribution in money or money's worth towards the reasonable needs of that person.'

11.101   A family member who is not a child and has not been treated as a child of the family may be able to use this part of the Act to get a claim off the ground; in particular, the sub-section may assist a cohabitant who cannot show the required two years living in the same household as a civil partner. Two factors must be present for an applicant to succeed on this ground: first, the applicant must demonstrate maintenance; second, he must show an assumption of responsibility on the part of the deceased.

11.102 Section 1(3) qualifies s 1(1)(e): it does not provide an alternative to it. 'Maintenance' in this context therefore means 'a substantial contribution in money or money's worth' to the needs of the applicant.

11.102 In *Re Beaumont*[61] Megarry VC considered the issues which arise when the deceased (or the survivor) spends time out of a joint home in the period before death being cared for in hospital, and his needs were fully met there: if the deceased was not maintaining the applicant, because the applicant was being looked after in hospital, or for some other reason a temporary separation has occurred, so that day to day maintenance ceases, does the applicant lose the ability to make a claim? The clear answer is that he does not:

> 'The question is what that something is. If at the moment before the death of the deceased there is some settled basis or arrangement between the parties as regards maintenance, then I think that s 1 should be applied to this rather than to any de facto variation in the actual maintenance that may happen to exist at that moment. If the general arrangement between the parties is that D is substantially maintaining C, then matters ought to be decided on that basis. This should be so even if, at the moment before D dies, C is in fact making such contributions, whether in personal services such as nursing or in the provision of money or goods, that on balance C is substantially maintaining D. The word 'immediately' plainly confines the court to the basis or arrangement subsisting at the moment before death, and excludes whatever previously subsisted but has ended, and the state of affairs under it. The nature or the quality of the basis or arrangement in question is a matter that I shall consider in due course. At this stage I shall only add that under all the other heads of s 1(1) the qualification is of an enduring nature. There must be a past or present marriage, paternity or maternity, or the treatment of the claimant as a child of the marriage of the deceased. If para (e) made no more than a transient and fluctuating requirement, it would be strikingly out of line with the other paragraphs.'

The fact that both parties to a relationship were caring for and maintaining each other does not prevent a claim under this part of the Act.

11.104 Provided actual maintenance can be shown, the court is likely to infer an assumption of responsibility on the part of the deceased: *Re B*.[62] In that case a daughter had received a large sum in damages following a birth injury leaving her with significant mental and physical disabilities. Her mother was appointed her receiver by the Court of Protection and received regular payments which were used by her for the daughter's maintenance. She lived in a property with the daughter purchased mainly by the daughter's fund. The daughter died intestate, with the result that her estate would be divided equally between her parents, and the mother made a claim under s 1(1)(e). At first instance the court took the view that it did not have jurisdiction but this decision was overturned by the Court of Appeal: the father contended that the payments made to the mother were solely to meet the daughter's needs, and that the daughter had not maintained the mother. The Court of Appeal found

---

[61] [1980] 1 All ER 266.
[62] [2000] 1 All ER 665.

that for the purposes of deciding whether a claim arose under s 1(1)(e) the motives of the deceased person in maintaining the other were of limited relevance: the fact that one person made a substantial contribution to the needs of the other in itself gave rise to an inference that responsibility had been assumed.

What provision can be made?

11.105   Section 2 of the Act gives the court wide powers to make provision from the deceased's estate. This can be in the form of an order for periodical payments from the estate, for the payment of a lump sum, or for the transfer of particular property contained within the estate. The court can also order the settlement of property (for example, by giving an applicant a life interest in a dwelling) and can vary a settlement made by civil partners during their lifetime in such a way as to benefit the surviving civil partner, or a child of the civil partnership, or a person treated as a child of the civil partnership.

'Reasonable financial provision'

11.106   The test for a claim under the Act is whether the deceased's will, or the effect of his intestacy, has failed to make 'reasonable financial provision' for the applicant. If the claim is by a civil partner, this means:[63]

> 'such financial provision as it would be reasonable in all the circumstances of the case for a civil partner to receive, whether or not that provision is required for his or her maintenance.'

11.107   In the case of any other applicant, it means:[64]

> 'such financial provision as it would be reasonable in all the circumstances of the case for the applicant to receive for his maintenance.'

Matters to which the court is to have regard

11.108   These are set out in detail in s 3 of the Act. They are:

'(a)   the financial resources and financial needs which the applicant has or is likely to have in the foreseeable future;

(b)   the financial resources and financial needs which any other applicant for an order under section 2 of this Act has or is likely to have in the foreseeable future;

(c)   the financial resources and financial needs which any beneficiary of the estate of the deceased has or is likely to have in the foreseeable future;

(d)   any obligations and responsibilities which the deceased had towards any applicant for an order under the said section 2 or towards any beneficiary of the estate of the deceased;

(e)   the size and nature of the net estate of the deceased;

(f)   any physical or mental disability of any applicant for an order under the said section 2 or any beneficiary of the estate of the deceased;

---

[63]   Section 1(2)(aa) of the Inheritance (Provision for Family and Dependants) Act 1975.
[64]   Section 1(2)(b) of the 1975 Act.

(g)   any other matter, including the conduct of the applicant or any other
person, which in the circumstances of the case the court may consider
relevant.'

11.109 The court therefore has to balance the needs of the applicant, other
applicants, and the beneficiaries under the will (or on the intestacy). It will have
regard to any particular obligations the deceased had to the applicant, to other
applicants, and to the beneficiaries. It will also consider the size and nature of
the estate.

11.110 In considering whether to make an order under the Act, and what
order to make, the court has a wide discretion. The first stage of the process,
the decision as to whether or not there has been a failure to make 'reasonable
financial provision' under the Act has been described as the exercise of a 'value
judgment' by the court and as such particularly difficult to challenge.[65]

The approach in civil partnership cases

11.111 If the applicant was the civil partner of the deceased, the court is
additionally required to take into account the following matters:

(a)   the age of the applicant and the duration of the civil partnership;

(b)   the contribution made by the applicant to the welfare of the family of the
deceased, including any contribution made by looking after the home or
caring for the family.

11.112 In the case of an application by the civil partner of the deceased, the
court shall also, unless at the date of the death a separation order under
Chapter 2 of Part 2 of the Civil Partnership Act 2004 was in force and the
separation was continuing, have regard to the provision which the applicant
might reasonably have expected to receive if on the day on which the deceased
died the civil partnership, instead of being terminated by death, had been
terminated by a dissolution order.[66]

11.113 This test in the context of matrimonial cases is often referred to as the
'deemed divorce' test. In civil partnership cases the approach will be one of
'deemed dissolution'.[67] The court will consider what approach would have been
taken if the civil partnership had been ended by dissolution[68] rather than by
death.

11.114 It should be noted however that on dissolution the court is required to
consider the needs of both parties to the civil partnership. Where a civil
partnership has been ended by death, the deceased has no 'needs' and the

---

[65]   *Ilott v Mitson* [2011] EWCA Civ 346.
[66]   Section 3(2) of the 1975 Act.
[67]   Consideration of the financial aspect of dissolution is dealt with in chapter 9.
[68]   See chapter 9.

entirety of his assets is available for distribution. If the estate is modest, the needs of the surviving partner are likely to result in a significant departure from equality of distribution.

Other points in relation to the 1975 Act

11.115   Claims under the Act are subject to a statutory time limit imposed by s 3 of the 1975 Act. Claims must be made within six months of the taking out of a grant of probate or letters of administration. The court has a discretion to extend the time for the a claim and in considering an application to do so will have regard to the following matters:[69]

(a)   the court has an unfettered discretion to extend time;

(b)   the burden of showing that an extension is justified falls on the applicant;

(c)   the circumstances and how promptly the applicant has sought an extension of time;

(d)   whether or not the parties have been engaged in negotiations: if they have, this is a point in the applicant's favour;

(e)   whether or not the estate had been distributed to its beneficiaries;

(f)   whether a refusal to extend time will leave the applicant without redress against anyone else (for example, a solicitor or other legal advisor).

11.116   Section 9 of the 1975 Act gives the court the following power:

'(1) Where a deceased person was immediately before his death beneficially entitled to a joint tenancy of any property, then, if, before the end of the period of six months from the date on which representation with respect to the estate of the deceased was first taken out, an application is made for an order under section 2 of this Act, the court for the purpose of facilitating the making of financial provision for the applicant under this Act may order that the deceased's severable share of that property, at the value thereof immediately before his death, shall, to such extent as appears to the court to be just in all the circumstances of the case, be treated for the purposes of this Act as part of the net estate of the deceased.'

11.117   This provision permits the court to treat the deceased's share of a property held on a joint tenancy as if it were part of his estate. This is an exceptional provision which in effect permits retrospective severance of a property held on a joint tenancy. It can only be used if the application for relief under the Act is made within the statutory time limit.

11.118   A claim under the 1975 Act can only be made if the deceased was domiciled in the UK at the time of his death.

---

[69]   *Re Salmon* [1981] Ch 167.

Proposals for reform

11.119 In December 2011 the Law Commission published detailed proposals for reform of the law in relation to intestacy and family provision on death. Those proposals included a draft bill which the government may or may not choose to take up. A number of the proposals are relevant to same sex families and their children:

(a) Where the deceased has no issue, the surviving civil partner shall take the whole estate outright.

(b) The expression 'child of the family' should be widened to include take into account situations where the deceased was not a party to a civil partnership. The relevant factor should be the quality of the relationship rather than whether or not the deceased was in a civil partnership;

(c) The scope of claims by dependants will be widened.

(d) Cohabitants (same sex or heterosexual) will have rights on intestacy if they have lived together for 5 years (or for 2 years if there is a child of the relationship).[70] They will, if they qualify on the basis of having lived together for the requisite period as if they were civil partners, to the same entitlement on intestacy as if they had been civil partners.

(e) There will be scope for a claim against assets held in the UK, even if the deceased was not domiciled in the UK.

If the Law Commmission proposals are accepted there will be a notable distinction on the position on death for cohabitants and that which currently exists (or rather, does not exist) on separation during their lifetime.

---

[70] The Law Commission's research indicates that there are about 2.3 million cohabiting couples (heterosexual and same sex) in the UK. Their recommendations are based on research which suggests that number will increase to nearly 4 million by 2033.

Chapter 12

WELFARE BENEFITS[1]

INTRODUCTION

12.1 This chapter is not a comprehensive guide to social security or welfare benefits; it is merely aimed at pointing out the differences, if any, when civil partners[2] or same sex couples apply for benefits. It is important to understand how government departments with responsibility for social security benefits,[3] tax credits,[4] housing benefit (HB) and council tax benefit (CTB)[5] consider applications from civil partners, cohabiting same sex couples and couples who are not living together for the purpose of social security benefits. The government departments will be referred to as the administering agency (agencies) or decision makers in this chapter.

BACKGROUND

12.2 Apart from the area of statutory paternity pay and statutory adoption pay,[6] which became payable to partners in same sex couples from April 2003,

---

[1]   In writing this chapter, the author has made use of the following: Welfare Benefits and Tax Credits Handbook 2011/2012 – Child Poverty Action Group; Civil Partnership, the New Law 2005 – Family Law (New Law series); The Blue Book – The Law relating to Social Security (www.dwp.uk/publications/specialist-guide/law-volumes); The Civil Partnership Act 2004, s 254 and Sch 24; Guidance from the Department of Work and Pensions (http://search2.openobjects.com/kbroker/dwp/dwp/search/search.lsim?sr=0&nh=10&cs=iso-8859-1&sc=dwp&sm=0&mt=1&to=0&ha=1092&qt=same+sex+partners+interdependence) and HMRC (http://search.hmrc.gov.uk/kb5/hmrc/hmrc/results.page?qt=same+sex+couples).

[2]   In this chapter, 'civil partners' is used to mean same sex couples registered or recognised under the Civil Partnership Act. 'Same sex couple' is used to mean a couple who may or may not be registered.

[3]   The Department for Work and Pensions (DWP). (Welfare Benefits and Tax Credits Handbook 2011/2012).

[4]   Tax Credits, child benefits and guardian's allowance are administered by Her Majesty's Revenue and Customs (HMRC).

[5]   HB and CTB are administered by the local authorities.

[6]   The European Union passed the Employment Framework Directive (2000/78/EC), which prohibits discrimination in employment and training on grounds including sexual orientation, with a view to putting into effect the principle of equal treatment. This was the first European measure which gave legal protection on grounds of sexual orientation. The UK government implemented these measures through the Employment Act 2002, which introduced the statutory right to paid Paternity Leave to all qualifying employees and detail of the rights, were contained in the Paternity and Adoption Leave Regulations 2002, SI 2002/2788 and the Statutory Paternity Pay and Statutory Adoption Pay (General) Regulations 2002, SI 2002/2822. The majority of the provisions in the Act came into force on 6th April 2003. The Employment Equality (Sexual Orientation) Regulations 2003, SI 2003/1661 became law on 1

same sex couples were not recognised by the social security system, prior to the enactment of the Civil Partnership Act 2004.[7] This meant that no matter how close and permanent a same sex relationship was, whether they lived together, whether or not they had children within the relationship and whether or not they regarded themselves as a family, the benefits system treated them as two single people. An example of this could be found in the then existing legislation in social security[8] and tax credits[9] which recognised two different types of opposite sex couples, 'married' and 'unmarried'.

12.3   In relation to means-tested benefits (income support (IS), income-based jobseeker's allowance (JSA), pension credit (PC), housing benefit (HB), council tax benefit (CT)), s 137(1) of the Social Security Contributions and Benefits Act 1992 (SSCBA) defines couples as follows:[10]

> '"married couple" means a man and a woman who are married to each other and are members of the same household, or
>
> "unmarried couple" means a man and a woman who are not married to each other but are "living together" as husband and wife otherwise than in prescribed circumstances.'

12.4   The meaning of 'family' has been interpreted under s 35(1) of the Jobseekers Act 1995 as:

> '"family" means –
>
> (a)   a married or unmarried couple;
> (b)   a married or unmarried couple and a member of the same household for whom one of them is, or both are, responsible and who is a child or a person of a prescribed description;
> (c)   except in prescribed circumstances, a person who is not a member of a married or unmarried couple and a member of the same household for whom that person is responsible and who is a child or a person of a prescribed description;
>
> "married couple" means a man and woman who are married to each other and are members of the same household;
>
> "unmarried couple" means a man and woman who are not married to each other but are living together as husband and wife otherwise than in prescribed circumstances;'

December 2003 making it unlawful to discriminate in employment on grounds of sexual orientation. These Regulations have since been replaced by the Equality Act 2010, although the legal protection remains the same.

[7]   The Act received Royal Assent on 18 November 2004, and it was brought fully into force on 5 December 2005.

[8]   The Social Security Contributions and Benefits Act 1992 (SSCBA) in England and Wales and Scotland, the Social Security Contributions and Benefits (Northern Ireland) Act 1992 in Northern Ireland and the Social Security Administration Act 1992 in England and Wales and Scotland, and the Social Security Administration (Northern Ireland) Act 1992 in Northern Ireland.

[9]   Tax Credits Act 2002.

[10]   A similar definition in relation to the meaning of 'family' can be found under Jobseekers Act 1995, s 35(1).

12.5 In relation to tax credits,[11] the definition of unmarried couple is almost the same as the one above:

> '"unmarried couple" means a man and a woman who are not a married couple but are living together as husband and wife'

12.6 However, with tax credits there was a different approach to defining a married couple:

> '"married couple" means a man and a woman who are married to each other and are neither
>
> (a)   separated under a court order nor
> (b)   separated in circumstances in which the separation is likely to be permanent.'

12.7 The enactment of the Human Rights Act 1998 which came into force on 2 October 2000, enabled same sex couples to challenge the definition of 'unmarried couple', the 'living together test' and family. Although international human rights law does not yet require that the English prohibition of same sex marriage be lifted,[12] it is established in the case-law of the European Court of Human Rights that a difference in treatment based on sexual orientation is covered by Art 14 of the European Convention on Human Rights and Fundamental Freedoms, 'the Convention' (which guarantees enjoyment of the other rights secured by the Convention without discrimination on any ground) and that where sexual orientation is the ground for different treatment, there is a need for particularly weighty justification.

12.8 In the case of *Ghaidan v Godin-Mendoza*[13] the House of Lords considered the implications of these developments under the Human Rights Act 1998. In that case the original tenant died after the HRA 1998 came into force on 2 October 2000. In April 1983 Mr Hugh Wallwyn-James was granted an oral residential tenancy of the basement flat at 17 Cresswell Gardens, London SW5. Until his death on 5 January 2001 he lived there in a stable and monogamous same sex relationship with the defendant Mr Juan Godin-Mendoza. Mr Godin-Mendoza continued to live in the property after his partner's death. Following the death of Mr Wallwyn-James the landlord, Mr Ahmad Ghaidan, brought proceedings in the West London county court claiming possession of the flat. Judge Cowell held that on the death of Hugh Wallwyn-James, Mr Godin-Mendoza did not succeed to the tenancy of the flat as the surviving spouse of Hugh Wallwyn-James within the meaning of para 2 of Sch 1 to the Rent Act 1977, but that he did become entitled to an assured tenancy of the flat by succession as a member of the original tenant's 'family' under para 3(1) of that Schedule.

---

[11]   Tax Credits Act 2002, s 3(5) and 3(6).
[12]   See cases of *Wilkinson v Kitzinger and Attorney General and Lord Chancellor intervening* [2006] EWHC 2022 (Fam) and of *Schalk and Kopf v Austria* (Application No 30141/04) as discussed in chapter 8.
[13]   *Mendoza Ghaidan v Godin-Mendoza* (FC) [2004] UKHL 30 (21 June 2004).

12.9   Mr Godin-Mendoza appealed, and the Court of Appeal, allowed the appeal.[14] The court held he was entitled to succeed to a tenancy of the flat as a statutory tenant under para 2. From that decision Mr Ghaidan, the landlord, appealed to the House of Lords. Before their Lordships, Mr Godin-Mendoza submitted that the distinction drawn by para 2 of Sch 1 to the Rent Act 1977 is made on the grounds of sexual orientation and that this difference in treatment lacked justification.

12.10   The Law Lords decided that the phrase in the Rent Act 1977[15] 'living together as husband and wife', in relation to succeeding to a statutory tenancy on the death of a partner, must be interpreted to include same sex couples in order to be compatible with Convention rights. They found that as same sex couples can have exactly the same sort of interdependent relationship that heterosexuals can, they should be treated in a comparable way. The Law Lords pointed out that affording heterosexual couples alone more favourable treatment did not serve the aim of protecting the family or encouraging stable relationships. Excluding same sex couples from the protection given to the security of tenure of heterosexual couples failed to serve any legitimate aim and was incompatible with Art 14.

12.11   At para 24 of the judgment, Lord Nicholls stated:

> 'In my view, therefore, Mr Godin-Mendoza makes good the first step in his argument: paragraph 2 of Schedule 1 to the Rent Act 1977, construed without reference to section 3 of the Human Rights Act, violates his Convention right under article 14 taken together with Article 8.'

The government recognised that there was significant unfairness and inequality caused by the fact that, although many committed same sex couples lived, to all intents and purposes, as families, they experienced serious social disadvantages. For example, their family status was not recognised for the purposes of welfare benefits. Unlike unmarried opposite couples, many have been refused a hospital visit to see their seriously ill partner or, on the death of their partner, have been denied financial or property rights despite having supported their partner for many years.

12.12   This situation could not continue and as a result the Civil Partnership Bill 2002[16] proposed a new legislative scheme for the recognition of the relationships of unmarried couples and provided for a package of benefits and responsibilities for registered couples. Amongst other far reaching proposals, the Bill also had provisions to treat same sex couples and civil partners as a

---

[14]   *Mendoza Ghaidan v Godin-Mendoza* [2002] EWCA Civ 1533, [2003] Ch 380.

[15]   Rent Act 1977, Sch 1, para 2(2).

[16]   The Civil Partnerships Bill 2002 was the joint initiative of the Odysseus Trust and Stonewall. The Bill sought to enable unmarried couples, both same and opposite sex, living in a mutually supportive relationship to make legal provision for their joint protection.

single family unit for the purpose of assessing certain means-tested benefits. The government's policy intention[17] was:

> 'that civil partners should be treated as a single family unit for income-related benefits purposes. In addition, where appropriate, unregistered cohabiting same sex couples should also be assessed as a single family unit as is the case for unmarried cohabiting opposite sex couples. The Government will ensure that this matter is handled sensitively.'

Treating same sex couples (whether registered or unregistered), in the same way as opposite sex couples (whether married or unmarried) in relation to income-related benefits is the best way to ensure fairness in this area and ensure that same sex couples who wish to register a civil partnership would not be financially worse off than they would be if they chose not to register their partnership.

12.13 A number of other factors also brought about positive changes in attitudes towards gay and lesbian couples, notably: the work over the years of campaigning organisations such as *Stonewall* and *Outrage!*; the higher profile accorded to the LGB community following the onset of AIDS; greater prominence of lesbian and gay people in the media and in soap opera plots; government ministers having been open about their sexual orientation; breakdown of more traditional concepts of marriage in the 1960s and 1970s; the rise of individual consumerism; decriminalisation;[18] the lowering of the age of consent; and the removal of s 28 of the Local Government Act 1988.[19]

RELEVANT LEGISLATION AND EFFECTS ON SOCIAL SECURITY AND TAX CREDITS

12.14 The enactment of the Civil Partnership Act 2004[20] brought about profound effects on social security and tax credits for same sex couples. Despite the fact that this legislation was undoubtedly significant in bringing about

---

[17] The Department of Trade and Industries (DTI) Consultation Paper 'Civil Partnership: a framework for the legal recognition of same sex couples' June 2003 (http://www.dti/consultations/pdf/consult-civil.pdf)See also Government's Report on Responses:http://www.womenandequalityunit.gov.uk/research/index.htm#cp-responses; 'Civil Partnership Registration: A Legal Status for Committed Same Sex Couples in Scotland' (http://www.scotland.gov.uk/consultations/justice/cprs-00.asp); 'Civil Partnership: A legal Status for committed Same Sex Couples in Northern Ireland (http://www.dfpni.gov.uk/samesexconsult.pdf).

[18] National Centre for Social Research – Same Sex Couples and the Impact of Legislative Changes 2009 by Martin Mitchell, Sarah Dickens and William O'Connor, prepared for: Economic and Social Research Council.

[19] The Local Government Act 1988 prohibited local authorities to (a) 'intentionally promote homosexuality or publish material with the intention of promoting homosexuality'; (b) 'promote the teaching in any maintained school of the acceptability of homosexuality as a protected family relationship'. The Act was repealed in Scotland in 2000 and in England and Wales in 2003.

[20] Amendments to welfare legislation became effective from 5 December 2005.

changes to lesbian and gay members of our society, it could be said that the civil partnership legislation had ridden on the back of other more significant changes and was more of an indicator than trigger of attitudinal changes.[21]

12.15 Nevertheless, s 254 of the CPA 2004 introduced Sch 24, which makes amendments to legislation governing social security, child support and tax credits.[22] Schedule 24 deals in detail with amendments relating to social security, child support and tax credits. Subsections (2) and (3)[23] extend the general power to make further provision in connection with civil partnership which is contained in s 259. Therefore legislation, which in respect of welfare benefits/social security, child support and tax credits, referred to persons living together as husband and wife is amended so as to refer to persons who are living together as if they were civil partners. The amended legislation under Sch 24 is as follows:

Part 1   Amendments of the Child Support Act 1991 (c 48)

Part 2   Amendments of the Child Support (Northern Ireland) Order 1991 (SI 1991/2628 (NI 23))

Part 3   Amendments of the Social Security Contributions and Benefits Act 1992 (c 4)

Part 4   Amendments of the Social Security Administration Act 1992 (c 5)

Part 5   Amendments of the Social Security Contributions and Benefits (Northern Ireland) Act 1992 (c 7)

Part 6   Amendments of the Social Security Administration (Northern Ireland) Act 1992 (c 8)

Part 7   Amendments of the Jobseekers Act 1995 (c 18)

Part 8   Amendments of the Child Support Act 1991 (c 34)

Part 9   Amendments of the Child Support (Northern Ireland) Order 1995 (SI 1995/2702 (NI 13))

Part 10   Amendments of the Jobseekers (Northern Ireland) Order 1995 (SI 1995/2705 (NI 15))

Part 11   Amendments of the Social Security Act 1998 (c 14)

Part 12   Amendments of the Social Security (Northern Ireland) Order 1998 (SI 1998/1506 (NI 10))

Part 13   Amendments of the State Pension Credit Act 2002 (c 16)

Part 14   Amendments of the Tax Credits Act 2002 (c 21)

Part 15   Amendments of the State Pension Credit Act (Northern Ireland) 2002 (c 14)

---

[21] National Centre for Social Research – Same Sex Couples and the Impact of Legislative Changes 2009.

[22] The provisions under CPA 2004, s 254 also came into force on 5 December 2005.

[23] CPA 2004, Sch 24.

Whilst every single amendment made by the CPA 2004 will not be detailed in this chapter, in general, the changes mean that for the purposes of benefit claims, whether they are 'Means-tested' or 'Non-means-tested', civil partners will be treated in the same way as spouses, and people living together as if they were civil partners will be treated in the same way as people living together as husband and wife.

Means-tested benefits and non-means-tested benefits

Means-tested benefits

12.16 These are benefits which are paid only if a claimant has limited income or capital. Means-tested benefits are: income support, income-based jobseeker's allowance, pension credit, income-related employment support allowance, housing benefit, council tax benefit, social fund payments, child tax credit and working tax credit. The agencies responsible for administering the said benefits would investigate the financial situation of a claimant and decide if they are entitled to be paid the benefits. A claimant does not have to satisfy the National Insurance (NI) contribution conditions to obtain the benefit.

Non-means-tested benefits

12.17 These are benefits which are paid without a detailed financial investigation of the claimant's means. However, certain conditions must be satisfied, for example, a claimant can only claim child benefit if they have a child or disability living allowance if disabled etc. Non-means-tested benefits are: attendance allowance, bereavement benefits, carer's allowance, child benefit, disability living allowance, contributory employment and support allowance, guardian's allowance, short term incapacity benefit, long term incapacity benefit, contribution-based jobseeker's allowance, maternity allowance, statutory maternity/paternity and adoption pay, statutory sick pay, retirement pension and severe disablement allowance. A claimant does not have to satisfy the National Insurance contribution conditions to obtain most of these benefits. However, benefits such as pension credit may be affected if a claimant is in receipt of maintenance payment[24] from a liable relative.[25]

---

[24] Means: payments made towards the maintenance of the claimant by his spouse, civil partner, former spouse or former civil partner or towards the maintenance of the claimant's partner by his spouse, civil partner, former spouse or former civil partner, including payments made: (i) under a court order; (ii) under an agreement for maintenance; or (iii) voluntarily. the State Pension Credit Regulations 2002 (SPC Regs 2002), SI 2002/1792, reg 15(5)(d).

[25] The Words 'civil partner' or 'former civil partner' of a claimant or of a member of the claimant's family have been added in definition of 'liable relative' by para 26(6)(a) of Sch 3 to SI 2005/2877 as from 5 December 2005. 'liable relative' means: (a) a spouse, former spouse, civil partner or former civil partner of a claimant or of a member of the claimant's family in the Income Support (General) Regulations 1987 (IS Regs 1987), reg 54; Jobseeker's Allowance Regulations 1996, SI 1996/207 (JSA Regs 1996), reg 117; and Employment Support and Allowance Regulations 2008, SI 2008/794 (ESA Regs 2008), reg 119.

Social security benefits and definitions of same sex couple

12.18 So as to accomplish the notion of 'fairness', as was proposed in the Civil Partnership Bill, the Civil Partnership Act 2004 amended the definition of 'a couple' for welfare benefits/social security purposes. The changes are extensive, as can be seen by the amount of amended legislation referred to above. The CPA 2004 created a four part definition for 'couple', labelling the existing opposite sex ones above in SSCBA s 137(1) as (a) and (b) and inserting two new definitions:[26]

> '(c)   two people of the same sex who are civil partners of each other and are members of the same household, or
>
> (d)   two people of the same sex who are not civil partners of each other but are living together as if they were civil partners.
>
> For the purposes of this paragraph, two adults of the same sex are to be regarded as living together in the same household as if they were civil partners if, but only if, they would be regarded as living together as husband and wife were they instead two adults of the opposite sex.'[27]

Tax credits and definitions of same sex couple

12.19 The Tax Credits Act 2002[28] was also amended by the CPA 2004 in order to define 'civil partner couples' as:[29]

> 'Two people of the same sex who are civil partners of each other and are neither –
>
> (a)   separated under a court order nor
>
> (b)   separated in circumstances in which the separation is likely to be permanent.'

The meaning of couple

12.20 Under subsequent legislation enacted after the CPA 2004, for example the Welfare Reform Act 2007,[30] which refers to the assessment of income-related allowance, the definition of 'couple' is very similar to the Civil Partnership Act 2004. In Sch 1, para 6(5):

> '"couple" means –
>
> (a)   a man and woman who are married to each other and are members of the same household;
>
> (b)   a man and woman who are not married to each other, but are living together as husband and wife otherwise than in prescribed circumstances;
>
> (c)   two people of the same sex who are civil partners of each other and are members of the same household; or

---

[26]   CPA 2004, Sch 24, para 46(3).
[27]   CPA 2004, Sch 24, para 46(5) and s 137(1A) SSCBA.
[28]   CPA 2004, Sch 24, para 144.
[29]   New subsection (5A) Tax Credits Act 2002, s 3.
[30]   Enacted on 3 May 2007.

  (d) two people of the same sex who are not civil partners of each other, but are living together as if they were civil partners otherwise than in prescribed circumstances.

(6) For the purposes of this paragraph, two people of the same sex are to be regarded as living together as if they were civil partners if, but only if, they would be regarded as living together as husband and wife were they instead two people of the opposite sex.'

THE LIVING TOGETHER TEST

What is meant by 'living together'

12.21 This is known as the old cohabitation rule for the purpose of social security benefits. The income and capital of a member of the claimant's family is treated as that of the claimant for the purposes of a claim for benefit.[31] The 'living together' test for the purposes of welfare or social security benefits is applied if two adults reside in the same household, irrespective of sexual orientation. Essentially the treatment of any couple who share a household is the same, or can be, regardless of sex, marital or civil partnership status. The situation is considered by decision makers on the basis of information relating to the relationship of the individuals concerned and the circumstances in which they live.[32]

Meaning of living together as husband and wife ('LTAHAW')

12.22 If two people of the opposite sex live together and share their lives in the same way as a married couple, the administering agency consider that they are living together as husband and wife, even though they are not married. Therefore when claiming benefits or tax credits couples living under these circumstances are expected to inform the decision maker that they are living together as if they are husband and wife so that any benefits they may be entitled to, are worked out correctly. Those living together as if they are husband and wife are referred to as 'partners' for the purposes of claiming benefits.[33]

The meaning of partner

12.23 The agencies responsible for welfare benefits use the term *partner* to mean – a person 'you are married to or a person you live with as if you are married to them, **or**, a civil partner or a person you live with as if you are civil partners'.[34]

---

[31] Social Security Contributions and Benefits Act 1992, s 136.
[32] DWP IS20 – A guide to Income Support September 2011.
[33] Information Sheet (Leaflet INF3 10/08) – Living together as husband and wife or civil partner by the Social Security Agency.
[34] Information Sheet (Leaflet INF3 10/08) – Living together as husband and wife or civil partner by the Social Security Agency.

Meaning of living together as civil partners ('LTACP')

12.24 Same sex couples who form civil partnerships have many of the same rights as married couples, including equal treatment for social security benefits and entitlements. If two people of the same sex live together and share their lives in the same way as civil partners, the benefits agencies consider that they are living together as civil partners, even though they have not legally registered their partnership. Therefore when claiming benefits same sex couples living under these circumstances are expected to inform the administering agencies that they are living together as if they are civil partners so that any benefits that they may be entitled to are worked out correctly. As above, those living together as if they are civil partners, are referred to as living with 'partners' for the purposes of claiming benefits.

The 'living together' cohabiting same sex couples (couples who are unmarried and not civil partners)

12.25 Before the passage of the Civil Partnership Act 2004, the test was only applied to couples of opposite sex and was not applied to same sex couples. This was because there was no legal basis for such an 'association' to exist. However, since the passage of the CPA it has been possible for same–sex couples to be treated as a couple, regardless of whether or not they have registered a civil partnership.

12.26 The changes to include civil partners and those living together as if they were civil partners under s 137 of SSCBA have been described above. This means that same sex couples who are not registered civil partners and are living together will be regarded as living together as if they are civil partners if they would have been regarded as living together as husband and wife had they been opposite sex partners.

12.27 The effect of this is that one member of the same sex couple would make a claim for both of them, and the needs and income of both will be taken into account in the same way as previously applied to opposite sex couples. This would be the case where same sex couples have entered into a civil partnership or where the couple are living together as if they were civil partners. Comparable rules apply to couples whose partnership is registered but who separate, to those which apply to married couples who separate.[35]

---

[35] Regulation 2(1) of the IS Regs 1987; s 35(1A) of the Jobseekers Act 1995 (JSA 1995); reg 1(3) of the JSA Regs 1996; Sch 1 para 6(6) of the Welfare Reform Act 2007 (WRA 2007); reg 2(1) of the ESA Regs 2008; s 17(1A) of the State Pension Credit Act 2002 (SPCA 2002); reg 1(2) of the SPC Regs 2002, reg 2(1) of the Housing Benefit Regulations 2006, SI 2006/213 (HB Regs 2006); reg 2(1) of the Housing Benefit (Persons who have attained the qualifying age for state pension credit) Regulations 2006, SI 2006/214 (HB (SPC) Regs 2006); reg 2(1) of the Council Tax Benefit Regulations 2006, SI 2006/215; reg 2(1) of the Council Tax Benefit (Persons who have attained the qualifying age for state pension credit) Regulations 2006, SI 2006/216 (CTB (SPC) Regs 2006) and IS/HB/CTB s 137(1A) of the SSCBA 1992.

12.28 The legislation does not indicate what conditions must exist before the agencies responsible for administering welfare benefits would conclude that a couple is living together as husband and wife (LTAHAW). As far as welfare benefits law is concerned, there is also no case law established which tests the living together test in respect of same sex couples. HMRC and local authorities have therefore adopted the approach used by the Department for Work and Pensions (DWP). Using the same approach for same sex couples means they are not treated any more or less favourably.[36]

12.29 Since 1977 the DPW[37] has followed a standard approach to the question of whether a man and woman are living together based on a list of criteria to be considered both individually and as a whole. Local authorities have adopted the same criteria to make decisions about housing benefits and council tax benefit and HMRC have also adopted the same criteria to make assessments in relation to working families' tax credit (WFTC) and child tax credit (CTC). This approach ensures unmarried couples are not treated any more or less favourably than married couples. Therefore the way in which the living together test is phrased ensures that existing case law on opposite sex cohabitation would apply.

12.30 Although the term 'living together as husband and wife' has its normal meaning in everyday language, the courts and administrative practice have developed a number of criteria to help apply that meaning to everyday situations. The criteria were established in the cases of *Crake v Supplementary Benefits Commission, Butterworth v Supplementary Benefits Commission*[38] which suggested factors which determine whether or not a couple is cohabiting. They are:

• whether the parties are living in the same household;

• the stability of the relationship;

• financial support;

• sexual relationship;

• children;

• public acknowledgment.

12.31 As there is currently no corresponding case law for same sex couples in welfare benefits law, the living together test for same sex couples would be much the same as the test for opposite sex couples as found in the cases of *Crake v Supplementary Benefits Commission, Butterworth v Supplementary*

---

[36] HMRC guide: CCM15040 – Undisclosed Partners: Couples who are Unmarried and Not Civil Partners.

[37] Formerly the Benefits Agency.

[38] *Crake and Butterworth v Supplementary Benefits Commission*, [1982] 1 All ER 498.

Benefits Commission[39] where the claimants lived in the same house. In that case the woman had severe injuries. Her male friend had at some point moved into the house to assist with her care. She later moved to live with him, leaving her husband. There was no sexual relationship. The commissioner treated them as living together as husband and wife. They appealed. It was held that the absence of reasons in the decision did not necessarily constitute an error of law. In the absence of other explanations, the fact that a man and a woman lived in the same house was strong evidence that they lived together as husband and wife. Here the tribunal had addressed the correct issues, and had evidence upon which the finding was based.

The case of *T and M v OCC and C (A Child)*[40] is a same sex couple adoption case which considered: (i) the recognition of an adoption order in Nicaragua; (ii) whether the same sex couple who were, unusually, living separately should be regarded as a couple within the meaning of the Adoption and Children Act 2002; and (iii) whether the adoption was justified by the criteria of s 1 of the ACA 2002.

Section 144(4) of the Adoption and Children Act 2002 provides:

'(4) In this Act, a couple means –

  (a)   a married couple, or
  (aa)   two people who are civil partners of each other, or
  (b)   two people (whether of different sexes or the same sex) living as partners
         in an enduring family relationship.'

In considering whether T and M were in fact a couple within the meaning of s 50 of the 2002 Act, the court held that the background to the case and the shared care arrangement was entirely consistent with the concept of a family of four people and thus within the ambit of s 144(4)(b). Hedley J at paras 16–17 said:

'Clearly the crucial words are "living as partners in an enduring family relationship." These words are no doubt chosen so as not to require the residence of both in the same property. That is not surprising as historically many a parent has had to work abroad whilst the family remained at home without in anyway imperilling an enduring family relationship. Nor is that unusual today with people having to move jobs often at short notice. What is required is: first, an unambiguous intention to create and maintain family life, and secondly, a factual matrix consistent with that intention. That is clearly a question of fact and degree in each case.'

Here the parties live in a committed and exclusive relationship recognised by our family law and spend significant time as a unit of four. The background to the case and the shared care arrangement is entirely consistent with the concept of a family

---

[39]   *Crake and Butterworth v Supplementary Benefits Commission*, [1982] 1 All ER 498 (concerned
       with Supplementary Benefits Act 1976, Sch 1, para 3(1)(b)).
[40]   [2010] EWHC 964.

of four. In my judgment, the parties in this case bring themselves within the ambit of s 144 (b) and thus s 50 of the 2002 Act. They are thus entitled to make a joint application to adopt C."

Living in the same household

12.32 The same considerations apply for married couples and civil partners. The relevant factors considered by decision makers when determining whether a couple are living in the same household may be:

- How/why the couple came together.

- Is rent received or paid? If so the income will (unless it is exempt under the rent a room scheme) be treated as income in the hands of the recipient.

- What kind of accommodation they share.

- If there is no formal rent agreement how are costs shared? How would exceptional expenditure be met? For example, if major unexpected repairs had to be carried out or home improvements made.

- Any absences from the household – factors to be considered include: why, how often, the length of the absence, how much longer it is expected to last, to what extent the couple have maintained contact, the couple's future intentions (the common feature of all of these reasons for absence is their temporary nature. There is no specific period of time after which an absence ceases to be temporary and the administering agencies' conclusions will be based on the particular facts of each case).

- Any other reasons for them living in the same household.

Even if it is established that a couple are living in the same house this does not necessarily mean they are LTAHAW or LTACP. The claimant may admit they live in the same household as the partner but that does not automatically mean they are LTAHAW or LTACP.[41]

12.33 There are a number of reasons why a same sex couple may share accommodation, an example would be a separated couple living at the same address. Separated same sex couples may sometimes continue to live at the same address for financial reasons. Usually this is because one or both of them would be unable to buy or rent suitable accommodation or they cannot sell their old property or there would be a significant penalty to pay if they redeemed their mortgage. In such circumstances the administering agency will consider what aspects of their financial or domestic circumstances have

---

[41] HMRC – Decision Makers Guide – DMG11055 and CCM15070 – Undisclosed Partners: Living in the Same Household at http://search.hmrc.gov.uk/kb5/hmrc/hmrc/results. page?qt=same+sex+couples.

changed when a claim for benefits or tax credit is made. Although this type of situation is difficult and may bring about sensitive issues, the relevant administering agency's aim would be to establish whether the civil partners are separated in such circumstances as to be permanent or whether they are still living together as civil partners.[42]

Stability of relationship

12.34 Although the administering agency may consider the stability of the relationship, the length of time a couple has been together does not necessarily indicate how stable the relationship is. However the relevant factors considered may be:

- on what basis they split household chores and responsibilities, such as cooking, cleaning and paying bills;

- whether they are both involved in caring for any children who live in the household;

- whether they tend to spend their leisure time together or separately;

- whether they normally take joint holidays;

- whether they plan any future activities or responsibilities jointly or separately;

- whether they intend to get engaged or married or enter into a civil partnership;

- whether the relationship has a volatile history; ie the couple is known to have had several splits and reconciliations.

An established pattern of domestic or financial activity will usually indicate an established relationship.[43]

Financial support

12.35 How a couple manage their financial affairs will vary from couple to couple. The administering agency will attempt to establish the claimant's incomings and outgoings so that they can establish if he or she could exist on their own income or whether there is a financial dependency. They would gather information from bank statements, look to the extent to which money and other financial resources are pooled and household bills etc. Therefore if

---

[42]   HMRC – Decision Makers Guide – DMG11055 and CCM15395 – Undisclosed Partners: Separated couple living at the same address. Web link as above.
[43]   HMRC Guide: CCM15080 – Undisclosed Partners: Stability of Relationship.

one partner is supported by the other and household expenses are shared this could be treated as evidence of LTACP.

Sexual relationship

12.36 The existence of a sexual relationship may be a relevant factor but it is not an absolute determinative. As this is seen as a sensitive subject, administering agencies are reluctant to ask questions about a couples's sexual relationship because of its intrusive nature. It is therefore left to the claimant to volunteer this information if they so wish.

Dependent children

12.37 Joint responsibility for a child or children (who may belong to either or both of the couple) may be an indication that the couple is LTACP, but it is not conclusive proof. Other factors that may be considered may be the parentage of the child or children and whether, and how, the couple exercises joint responsibility in the day-to-day care of the children. An intention to adopt by the non-birth partner could be a particularly telling indication of the couple's long term view of the family unit.[44]

Public acknowledgement

12.38 Whilst this may be a straightforward factor when considering opposite sex couples, it may present administering agencies with some difficulties in relation to same sex couples. This is because some same sex couples may present separate identities in public and in private due to fears of homophobia. Therefore how a couple presents in private amongst friends and family may not necessarily match how the outside world perceives a couple. The National Centre for Social Research Report on Same Sex Couples and the Impact of Legislative Changes[45] found that same sex couples feel that the legislation had made no difference to their reluctance to be open about one's sexual orientation in some settings, because of the fear of discrimination or hostile responses in public. This response was evident amongst both civil partners and non-civil partners. It was also evident amongst some of those who spoke about having been confident for a long time about being open in different settings. For example, people spoke in this context about continuing to feel reservations about displaying affection in public places, or indicating their sexual orientation to certain colleagues or acquaintances who they feared might react negatively – for example 'other mums in the playground'. Participants who felt like this had experienced what they had perceived to have been discrimination against or negative responses towards their sexual orientation in the past in

---

[44] HMRC Guide: CCM15100 – Undisclosed Partners: Dependent Children.
[45] National Centre for Social Research – Same Sex Couples and the Impact of Legislative Changes 2009 by Martin Mitchell, Sarah Dickens and William O'Connor, prepared for: Economic and Social Research Council.

these settings, sometimes after they had become civil partners. This was what seemed to have had a formative effect on their continued lack of comfort about being open in these settings.

12.39 Despite the above, agencies may use third party information powers to obtain information from persons other than the claimant(s) to progress the examination of the claim.[46]

12.40 It is not possible to lay down any rules about the weight and worth of the various criteria in establishing that a couple are living together because the weight and worth of each indicator will vary from relationship to relationship. The criteria referred to above are just indicators helping the decision maker to form a sustainable view of whether a couple is living together as civil partner for the purposes of determining their entitlement to welfare benefits and tax credit. Therefore every case has to be decided on its own merits and on the balance of evidence. The administering agencies or decision maker would then arrive at conclusions based on the balance of evidence.

12.41 However, without the living together test unmarried couples or same sex couples who have not registered a civil partnership, would be treated more favourably than married couples or civil partners, because they would receive more benefit as two individuals. It could be argued that the effect of these benefit rules is often to treat all couples less favourably than individuals, and the effect of this rule in particular is to treat unmarried couples or same sex couples who have not registered a civil partnership less favourably than married couples and civil partners. This is because a finding that a couple is living together as husband and wife, or as civil partners, does not mean that they are entitled to claim bereavement benefits, dependants' additions, or enjoy any of the other advantages that married couples and civil partners benefit from.

12.42 The list below shows a breakdown of the main differences in the welfare benefits and tax credits system as they may affect same sex couples who live with a partner or are registered as civil partners.[47]

Civil partners

12.43

- State pension benefits, for example civil partners will be able to claim a state pension based on their partner's NI contributions.

- Civil partners will be able to claim bereavement benefits when their partner dies.

---

[46]   Tax Credit Act 2002, ss 14(2)(b), 15(2)(b) and 16(3)(b).
[47]   For further information on welfare benefits and taxes visit: www.jobcentreplus.gov.uk, www.direct.gov.uk and www.dwp.gov.uk.

- Civil partners will become eligible for 'adult dependant additions' on certain benefits – an extra amount paid with some benefits, including carer's allowance, for individuals who support their spouse/civil partner.

- Same sex couples, including civil partners, who live together will be jointly assessed for means tested benefits such as income support, income based jobseeker's allowance, pension credit, housing benefit and council tax benefit.

- Same sex couples, including civil partners, who live together, will have to make joint claims for tax credits. For claimants who get working tax credit they will start to qualify for the 'couple element', an increase in their maximum award. Some couples will lose out as a result of having both incomes taken into account.

Same sex couples who live together but are not registered as civil partners

12.44

- State pension benefits not affected – for example, they will not be able to claim a state pension based on their partner's NI contributions.

- Not able to claim bereavement benefits when a partner dies.

- Adult dependant additions on benefits like carer's allowance not usually payable.

- Same sex couples who live together will be jointly assessed for means tested benefits such as income support, income based jobseeker's allowance, pension credit, housing benefit and council tax benefit. Many same sex couples may find they are worse off as a result of this change.

- Same sex couples who live together will have to make joint claims for tax credits. For claimants who get working tax credit they will qualify as a couple, with an increase in their maximum award. Some couples will lose out as a result of having both incomes taken into account.

Same sex co-parents not living together

12.45 Just because co-parents may share financial responsibilities for children with one another, this does not necessarily mean that they are living together as husband and wife or as civil partners. The situation is considered by decision-makers on the basis of information relating to the relationship of the individuals concerned and the circumstances in which they live. If a same sex co-parent seeks a dissolution of a civil partnership or is no longer in a relationship with his or her partner and has ceased living together with their partner, any claim they make for benefits would be on an individual basis.

12.46   Section 254 of the CPA has therefore put same sex couples in the same position as opposite sex couples for the purposes of welfare benefit and tax credit claims. Civil partners are now able to claim means-tested and non-means-tested benefits in the same way as married couples and same sex couples who do not register a civil partnership will be treated in the same way as opposite sex couples who are unmarried. However, the consequence is that same sex couples will share the same disadvantages as opposite sex couples. They are no longer treated as single individuals for the purpose of benefit and tax credit claims. The amount of benefits awarded to a couple is usually less than that for two single people. This means that as a result of the change in legislation, couples in same sex relationships wishing to claim benefits will be financially worse off than they were previously. Those who were claiming as single individuals are now under a duty to report a change in their circumstance if they are living together. A failure to report a change in circumstances would result in overpayments which are recoverable. It is also an offence to fail to disclose a change in circumstances and administering agencies often prosecute for such failures.[48]

GENDER RECOGNITION AND IMPLICATIONS FOR WELFARE BENEFITS

12.47   The Gender Recognition Act 2004 also allows anyone who has been granted a full gender recognition certificate to receive state benefits appropriate to his or her acquired gender, not those payable to his or her birth gender. Once an individual has been legally recognised the Act describes how this will affect entitlement to certain state benefits.

12.48   Provisions for social security benefits, pensions and tax are governed by the Social Security Contributions and Benefits Act 1992 (SSCBA)[49] in England and Wales and Scotland, the Social Security Contributions and Benefits (Northern Ireland) Act 1992[50] in Northern Ireland and the Social Security Administration Act 1992[51] in England and Wales and Scotland, and the Social Security Administration (Northern Ireland) Act 1992 in Northern Ireland[52].

Gender recognition and the 'living together test'

12.49   The 'living together' test as explored above is also applicable if two adults reside in the same household, irrespective of their acquired gender.[53] Before the passage of the CPA 2004, the test was not applied to individuals of the same sex. This was because there was no legal basis for such an 'association' to exist. However, since the passage of that Act it has been possible for two

[48]   Social Security Contributions and Benefits Act 1992, ss 111 and 112.
[49]   GRA 2004, Sch 5, para 2(1)(a).
[50]   GRA 2004, Sch 5, para 2(1)(b).
[51]   GRA 2004, Sch 5, para 2(2)(a).
[52]   GRA 2004, Sch 5, para 2(2)(b).
[53]   See chapter 6 on gender recognition.

people of the same gender to be treated as a couple, regardless of whether or not they have registered a civil partnership.

12.50 The test is applied equally to a married couple who divorce and form a civil partnership following the granting of a GRC, to one or both members, where they continue to live in the same household.[54] Essentially the treatment of any couple who share a household is the same, regardless of sex, marital or civil partnership status. The test of whether or not a couple is living together is subjective and is based on a number of criteria discussed above. There would be no presumption that because a married couple have divorced but continue to share the same household they continue to live as if they were a married, unmarried or civil partnership couple. This situation is likely to happen in acquired gender cases especially in circumstances were the couple choose to remain together but do not wish to register a civil partnership.[55] The decision makers in welfare benefit claims will consider whether or not the couple can establish a valid legal relationship ie marry or form a civil partnership. So, for example, the test would not be applied to a person who lives with their sibling or child, as the test looks to treat people who are not married or in a civil partnership in the same way as those who are. Leaflet INF3 is issued to people subject to the test. It sets out what issues are considered when applying the test and the reasons for looking at their domestic arrangements.[56]

State pensions, benefits and tax issues

12.51 When an individual obtains a full Gender Recognition Certificate, there is likely to be an impact on the assessment of their NI contributions and on the benefits or State Pension to which they are entitled. The Gender Recognition Panel has produced '*The Guidance on Benefits and Pensions ('Benefit Note'[57])* which contains a detailed explanation of the likely consequences on pensions, benefits and tax issues when an individual acquires a gender recognition certificate. As discussed in chapter 6 on gender recognition, if a person is married or in a civil partnership and then ends the marriage or civil partnership in order to obtain a full Gender Recognition Certificate, the assessment of his spouse's NI Contributions and benefit entitlement may also be affected. Under these circumstances, the person who has been granted a GRC should notify HMRC and DWP and any other relevant administering agencies immediately of when the marriage or civil partnership has ended to ensure that his or her and their partner's NI Contributions and benefits are reassessed correctly. The amount of tax paid is likely to be affected if an individual is married, as they would be required to end the marriage in order to get a full Gender

---

[54] Gender Identity Research and Education Society (GIRES), State Pensions.

[55] See chapter 6 on gender recognition.

[56] Info from Leaflet INF3 – Living together as husband and wife or as civil partners – Social Security Agency 10/08.http://www.gires.org.uk/assets/Legal-Assets/inf3.pdf.

[57] Tribunals Services – Gender Recognition Panel: How getting a full Gender Recognition Certificate may affect a transsexual man's or transsexual woman's National Insurance, benefits and pensions at http://www.justice.gov.uk/downloads/guidance/courts-and-tribunals/tribunals/gender-recognition-panel/other-guidance-and-information/GuideBenefitsPension.pdf.

Recognition Certificate. When an individual is divorced, the amount of income tax, capital gains tax and inheritance tax they pay may be affected. This could happen, for example, as a result of financial arrangements they have made with their former husband or wife or civil partner when ending their marriage or civil partnership.

Disagreement with decision maker

12.52 Once a decision maker has decided whether or not a couple is living together as husband and wife or as civil partners, they will decide how this affects their benefit. The decision maker must write and inform them about their decision. If a couple or an individual disagrees with their decision they may have a right to appeal against the DWP, the local authority and the HMRC. There are strict time limits for appealing, normally one month. The appeal must be in writing and in a prescribed form if stipulated and it must contain all the necessary information, otherwise it may be invalid. Appeal rights are vast and may be complicated and they are beyond the scope of this chapter. It is important to seek legal advice if you are thinking about appealing.

OTHER BENEFITS ISSUES RELATING TO SAME SEX COUPLES

Pensions provisions

12.53 Sections 140, 142 and 143 of the State Pension Credit Act 2002 have been amended so that registered civil partners have the same pension rights as married couples.[58] Widowers of civil partners can access survivor pensions in public service schemes and contracted-out pension schemes from 1988.[59]

Tax

12.54 Civil partners are treated in the same way as spouses for tax purposes. The HM Revenue and Customs Department have produced a booklet for lesbian, gay, bisexual and transgender people on taxes and benefits issues.[60] They can also be contacted for specific queries about taxation law.[61] They also have produced a booklet for lesbian, gay, bisexual and transgender people on taxes and benefits issues.[62]

---

[58] SPCA 2002, ss 140, 142 and 143.
[59] SPCA 2002, ss 142 and 143. For further details, contact the Pension Service: www.thepensionservice.gov.uk.
[60] http://www.hmrc.gov.uk/leaflets/Pride1.pdf.
[61] www.hmrc.gov.uk.
[62] http://www.hmrc.gov.uk/leaflets/Pride1.pdf.

SUMMARY

12.55

- Same sex couples who are civil partners are treated similarly to a married couple and must claim benefits together.

- Same sex couples who do not register as civil partners will have the rules applied to them in the same way as opposite sex couples who live together but are not married to each other and may be treated as a couple and have to claim benefits together.

- The incomes of both partners are taken into account when calculating entitlement to Tax Credits.

- Since the change in law on 5 December 2005 same sex couples 'living together' (whether or not they register a civil partnership) have been under an obligation to notify the Tax Credits Office of their change in circumstances.

- There is no single factor that will show that a couple is living together as husband and wife or as civil partners.

- The living together test is equally applicable to couples who have been granted a gender recognition certificate.

Appendix 1

FLOWCHARTS TRACING LEGAL AND GENETIC PARENTAGE

A1.1

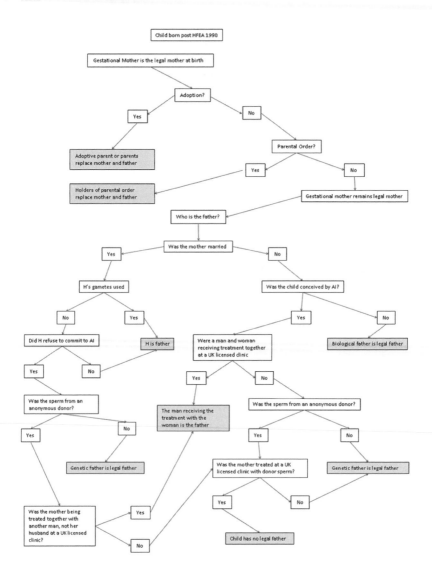

A1.2

Appendix 2

FORMS

A2.1

Particulars of Birth

BIRTH		Entry No.
Registration district		Administrative
area		
Sub-district		
1. Date and place of birth **CHILD**		
2. Name and surname		3. Sex
4. Name and surname **FATHER/PARENT**		
5. Place of birth	6. Occupation	
7. Name and surname **MOTHER**		
8.(a) Place of birth	8. (b) Occupation	
9.(a) Maiden surname	9. (b) Surname at marriage/civil partnership if different from maiden surname	
10. Usual address (if different from place of child's birth)		
11. Name and surname (if not the mother or father/parent) **INFORMANT**	12. Qualification	
13. Usual address (if different from that in 10 above)		
14. I certify that the particulars entered above are true to the best of my knowledge and belief Signature of informant		
15. Date of registration	16. Signature of registrar	
17. Name given after registration, and surname		

A2.2

Form of Entry in the Parental Order Register

BIRTH			Entry No.
Registration district		**Administrative area**	
Sub-district			
1. Date and place of birth	**CHILD**		
2. Name and surname			3. Sex
4. Name and surname	**PARENT**		
5. Place of birth		6. Occupation	
7 Name and surname	**PARENT**		
8 Place of birth		9 Occupation	
10 Parents' address			
11 Date of registration		12 Signature of registering officer	
13 Name given after registration, and surname			

A2.3

Form C(PRA1) – Parental Responsibility Agreement

Parental Responsibility Agreement
Section 4(1)(b) Children Act 1989

Keep this form in a safe place
Date recorded at the Principal Registry of the Family Division:

**Read the notes on the other side
before you make this agreement.**

This is a Parental Responsibility Agreement regarding

the Child   *Full Name* _____

Gender   *Date of birth*   *Date of 18th birthday*

Between
the Mother *Name*

Address

and the Father *Name*

Address

We declare that   we are the mother and father of the above child and we agree that the child's father shall have parental responsibility for the child (in addition to the mother having parental responsibility).

Signed **(Mother)**   Signed **(Father)**

Date   Date

**Certificate
of witness**

The following evidence of identity was produced by the person signing above: The following evidence of identity was produced by the person signing above:

Signed in the presence of:
Name of Witness   Signed in the presence of:
Name of Witness

Address   *Address*

Signature of Witness   *Signature of Witness*

[A Justice of the Peace] [Justices' Clerk] [An assistant to a justices' clerk] [An officer of the court authorised by the judge to administer oaths]   [A Justice of the Peace] [Justices' Clerk] [An assistant to a justices' clerk] [An Officer of the Court authorised by the judge to administer oaths]

C(PRA1) (09.09)

Notes about the Parental Responsibility Agreement

Read these notes before you make the agreement.

About the Parental Responsibility Agreement

The making of this agreement will affect the legal position of the mother and the father. You should both seek legal advice before you make the Agreement. You can obtain the name and address of a solicitor from the Children Panel (020 7242 1222)

or from
- your local family proceedings court, or county court
- a Citizens Advice Bureau
- a Law Centre
- a local library.

You may be eligible for public funding.

When you fill in the Agreement

Please use black ink (the Agreement will be copied). Put the name of one child only. If the father is to have parental responsibility for more than one child, fill in a separate form for each child. **Do not sign the Agreement.**

When you have filled in the Agreement

Take it to a local family proceedings court, or county court, or the Principal Registry of the Family Division (the address is below).

A justice of the peace, a justices' clerk, an assistant to a justices' clerk, or a court official who is authorised by the judge to administer oaths, will witness your signature and he or she will sign the certificate of the witness. **A solicitor cannot witness your signature.**

To the mother: When you make the declaration you will have to prove that you are the child's mother so take to the court the child's full birth certificate.

You will also need evidence of your identity showing a photograph and signature (for example, a photocard, official pass or passport). **Please note that the child's birth certificate cannot be accepted as sufficient proof of your identity.**

To the father: You will need evidence of your identity showing a photograph and signature (for example, a photocard, official pass or passport).

When the Certificate has been signed and witnessed

Make 2 copies of the Agreement form. You do not need to copy these notes.

Take, or send, this form and the copies to **The Principal Registry of the Family Division, First Avenue House, 42-49 High Holborn, London, WC1V 6NP.**

The Registry will record the Agreement and keep this form. The copies will be stamped and sent back to each parent at the address on the Agreement. The Agreement will not take effect until it has been received and recorded at the Principal Registry of the Family Division.

Ending the Agreement

Once a parental responsibility agreement has been made it can only end
- by an order of the court made on the application of any person who has parental responsibility for the child
- by an order of the court made on the application of the child with permission of the court
- when the child reaches the age of 18.

C(PRA1) (Notes) (12.05)

A2.4

Form C(PRA2) – Step-Parent Parental Responsibility Agreement

**Step-Parent Parental
Responsibility Agreement**
Section 4A(1)(a) Children Act 1989

Keep this form in a safe place
*Date recorded at the Principal Registry
of the Family Division:*

Read the notes on the other side before you make this agreement.

This is a Step-Parent Parental Responsibility Agreement regarding

the Child	*Full Name*		
	Gender	*Date of birth*	*Date of 18th birthday*

Between
Parent A   *Name*

Address

and
*the other parent   *Name*
(with parental
responsibility)   *Address*

and
the step-parent   *Name*

Address

**We declare
that**   we are the parents and step-parent of the above child and we agree that the above mentioned step-parent shall have parental responsibility for the child (in addition to those already having parental responsibility).

Signed **(Parent A)**	*Signed **(Other Parent)**	Signed **(Step-Parent)**
Date	Date	Date
Certificate of witness The following evidence of identity was produced by the person signing above:	The following evidence of identity was produced by the person signing above:	The following evidence of identity was produced by the person signing above:
Signed in the presence of: *Name of Witness*	Signed in the presence of: *Name of Witness*	Signed in the presence of: *Name of Witness*
Address	*Address*	*Address*
Signature of Witness	*Signature of Witness*	*Signature of Witness*
[A Justice of the Peace] [Justices' Clerk] [An assistant to a justices' clerk] [An Officer of the Court authorised by the judge to administer oaths]	[A Justice of the Peace] [Justices' Clerk] [An assistant to a justices' clerk] [An Officer of the Court authorised by the judge to administer oaths]	[A Justice of the Peace] [Justices' Clerk] [An assistant to a justices' clerk] [An Officer of the Court authorised by the judge to administer oaths]

*If there is only one parent with parental responsibility, please delete this section.

C(PRA2) (09.09)

Notes about the Step-Parent Parental Responsibility Form

Read these notes before you make the Agreement

About the Step-Parent Parental Responsibility Agreement

The making of this agreement will affect the legal position of the parent(s) and the step-parent. You should seek legal advice before you make the Agreement. You can obtain the name and address of a solicitor from the Children Panel (020 7242 1222) or from:

- your local family proceedings court, or county court,
- a Citizens Advice Bureau,
- a Law Centre,
- a local library.

You may be eligible for public funding.

When you fill in the Agreement

Please use black ink (the Agreement will be copied). Put the name of one child only. If the step-parent is to have parental responsibility for more than one child, fill in a separate form for each child. **Do not sign the Agreement.**

When you have filled in the Agreement

Take it to a local family proceedings court, or county court, or the Principal Registry of the Family Division (the address is below).

A justice of the peace, a justices' clerk, an assistant to a justices' clerk, or a court official who is authorised by the judge to administer oaths, will witness your signature and he or she will sign the certificate of the witness. **A solicitor cannot witness your signature.**

To Parent A and the Other Parent with parental responsibility:

When you make the declaration you will have to prove that you have parental responsibility for the child. You should therefore take with you to the court one of the following documents:

- the child's full birth certificate and a marriage certificate or civil partnership certificate to show that the parents were married to each other or were in a civil partnership with each other at the time of birth or subsequently,
- a court order granting parental responsibility,
- a registered Parental Responsibility Agreement Form between the child's mother and father or other parent

- if the birth was registered after the 1 December 2003, the child's full birth certificate showing that the parents jointly registered the child's birth.

You will also require evidence of your (both parents') identity showing a photograph and signature (for example, a photocard, official pass or passport) **(Please note that the child's birth certificate cannot be accepted as sufficient proof of your identity.)**

To the step-parent: When you make the declaration you will have to prove that you are married to, or the civil partner of, a parent of the child so take to the court your marriage certificate or certificate of civil partnership.

You will also need evidence of your identity showing a photograph and signature (for example, a photocard, official pass or passport).

When the Certificate has been signed and witnessed

Make sufficient copies of the Agreement Form for each person who has signed the form. You do not need to copy these notes.

Take, or send, the original form and the copies to: **The Principal Registry of the Family Division, First Avenue House, 42-49 High Holborn, London, WC1V 6NP.**

The Registry will record the Agreement and retain the original form. The copies will be stamped with the seal of the court and sent back to every person with parental responsibility who has signed the Agreement Form and to the step-parent. The Agreement will not take effect until it has been received and recorded at the Principal Registry of the Family Division.

Ending the Agreement

Once a step-parent parental responsibility agreement has been made it can only end:

- by an order of the court made on the application of any person who has parental responsibility for the child,
- by an order of the court made on the application of the child with permission of the court,
- when the child reaches the age of 18.

A2.5

Form C(PRA3) – Parental Responsibility Agreement (Second Female Parent)

Parental Responsibility Agreement
Section 4ZA Children Act 1989 (Acquisition of parental
responsibility by second female parent)

Keep this form in a safe place
*Date recorded at the Principal Registry
of the Family Division:*

**Read the notes on the other side before
you make this agreement.**

This is a Parental Responsibility Agreement regarding

the Child	*Full Name*

| *Gender* | *Date of birth* | *Date of 18th birthday* |

Between

the Mother   *Name*

Address

and   other parent   *Name*
(*Second female
parent*)   *Address*

We declare that   that we are the parents of the above child and we agree that the above mentioned parent shall
have parental responsibility for the child (in addition to the mother having parental responsibility
for the child).

Signed **(Mother)**   Signed **(Other parent)**

Date   Date

**Certificate
of witness**

The following evidence of identity
was produced by the person signing above:

The following evidence of identity
was produced by the person signing above:

Signed in the presence of:
Name of Witness

Signed in the presence of:
Name of Witness

Address   *Address*

Signature of Witness   *Signature of Witness*

[A Justice of the Peace] [Justices' Clerk]
[An assistant to a justices' clerk] [An officer
of the court authorised by the judge to
administer oaths]

[A Justice of the Peace] [Justices' Clerk]
[An assistant to a justices' clerk] [An Officer
of the Court authorised by the judge to
administer oaths]

C(PRA3) (09.09)   © Crown copyright 2009

Notes about the Parental Responsibility Agreement

Read these notes before you make the agreement.

This form is for use by **a mother** and **a woman** who is a parent of the child by virtue of section 43 of the Human Fertilisation and Embryology Act 2008 (the 'other parent').

About the Parental Responsibility Agreement

The making of this agreement will affect the legal position of the mother and other parent. You should both seek legal advice before you make the Agreement. You can obtain the name and address of a solicitor from the Children Panel (020 7242 1222)

or from
- your local family proceedings court, or county court
- a Citizens Advice Bureau
- a Law Centre
- a local library.

You may be eligible for public funding.

When you fill in the Agreement

Please use black ink (the Agreement will be copied). Put the name of one child only. If the other parent is to have parental responsibility for more than one child, fill in a separate form for each child. **Do not sign the Agreement.**

When you have filled in the Agreement

Take it to a local family proceedings court, or county court, or the Principal Registry of the Family Division (the address is below).

A justice of the peace, a justices' clerk, an assistant to a justices' clerk, or a court official who is authorised by the judge to administer oaths, will witness your signature and he or she will sign the certificate of the witness. **A solicitor cannot witness your signature.**

To the mother: When you make the declaration you will have to prove that you are the child's mother so take to the court the child's full birth certificate.

You will also need evidence of your identity showing a photograph and signature (for example, a photocard, official pass or passport). **Please note that the child's birth certificate cannot be accepted as sufficient proof of your identity.**

To the other parent: You will need evidence of your identity showing a photograph and signature (for example, a photocard, official pass or passport).

When the Certificate has been signed and witnessed

Make 2 copies of the Agreement form. You do not need to copy these notes, please send a copy of the child's full birth certificate with the two copies of the Agreement.

Take, or send, this form and the copies to **The Principal Registry of the Family Division, First Avenue House, 42-49 High Holborn, London, WC1V 6NP.**

The Registry will record the Agreement and keep this form. The copies will be stamped and sent back to each parent at the address on the Agreement. The Agreement will not take effect until it has been received and recorded at the Principal Registry of the Family Division.

Ending the Agreement

Once a parental responsibility agreement has been made it can only end
- by an order of the court made on the application of any person who has parental responsibility for the child
- by an order of the court made on the application of the child with permission of the court
- When the child reaches the age of 18.

C(PRA3) (Notes) (09.09)

A2.6

Notice of Civil Partnership

| Regulation 3 | | | | Form 1 | | | Civil Partnership Act 2004, s.8(2) |

NOTICE OF CIVIL PARTNERSHIP

PARTICULARS RELATING TO THE PERSONS FORMING A CIVIL PARTNERSHIP

Name and surname (1)	Date of birth (2)	Sex (3)	Condition (4)	Occupation (5)	Period of residence (6)	Venue in which civil partnership is to be formed (7)	Nationality and registration authority of residence (8)

To the Registration Authority of ....

I, the above-named ....*(name and surname)*

of ....*(place of residence)*

give you notice that I and ....*(name and surname)*

of ....*(place of residence)*

intend to form a civil partnership on the authority of a schedule within *one month/three months/twelve months from the date this notice is recorded and I declare as follows:

1. I believe that there is no impediment of kindred or affinity or other lawful hindrance to the formation of the civil partnership.

2. I and the other person named above have for the period of seven days immediately before the giving of this notice had our usual places of residence within the areas of the registration authorities named in Column 8 above.

3. In respect of myself, I am eighteen years of age or over.

4. In respect of the said ....*(name and surname)* *he/she is eighteen years of age or over.

5. I further declare that to the best of my knowledge and belief the declarations which I have made above and the particulars relating to the persons forming a civil partnership are true. I understand that if any of the declarations are false I MAY BE LIABLE TO PROSECUTION UNDER SECTION 80(1)(a) OF THE CIVIL PARTNERSHIP ACT 2004.

6. I also understand that if, in fact, there is an impediment of kindred or affinity or other lawful hindrance to the intended civil partnership the civil partnership may be invalid or void.

Signed .... Date ....

In the presence of .... *(name)* ....*(signature)*,

a person authorised for that purpose by the Registration Authority.

Place of residence .... Registration Authority.

* Delete whichever does not apply

A2.7

Civil Partnership Schedule

Regulation 6   Form 9   Civil Partnership Act, s.14(2)

CIVIL PARTNERSHIP SCHEDULE
(Section 14 of the Civil Partnership Act 2004)

1. Civil partnership schedule issued by .... on behalf of
....registration authority on ....
The issue of this schedule has not been forbidden by any person authorised to forbid the issue thereof.
The waiting period in respect of both notices of proposed civil partnership has expired, or has been reduced on the authority of the Registrar General.
The civil partnership must be formed on or before ....
(Signature)

2. Venue for the civil partnership formation

3. Name and surname		
4. Date of birth		
5. Sex		
6. Condition		
7. Occupation		

8. Residence at time of civil partnership formation		
9. Father's name, surname and occupation		
10. Mother's name, surname and occupation		

11.*	*I declare that I know of no legal reason why we may not register as each other's civil partner. I understand that on signing this document we will be forming a civil partnership with each other.*	
12. Civil partner's signature		
13. Witnesses	(name) .... (signature)	(name) .... (signature)
14. Date of formation of civil partnership		15. The civil partnership was formed on this date by these civil partners in the place shown in space 2 above. Signed.. Civil Partnership Registrar

*Civil partners may choose to speak these words to each other, but doing so is not a necessary part of the formation of their civil partnership.

A2.8

Form TR 1

Land Registry
Transfer of whole of registered title(s)

TR1

If you need more room than is provided for in a panel, and your software allows, you can expand any panel in the form. Alternatively use continuation sheet CS and attach it to this form.

Leave blank if not yet registered.	1	Title number(s) of the property:
Insert address including postcode (if any) or other description of the property, for example 'land adjoining 2 Acacia Avenue'.	2	Property:
	3	Date:
Give full name(s).	4	Transferor:
Complete as appropriate where the transferor is a company.		<u>For UK incorporated companies/LLPs</u> Registered number of company or limited liability partnership including any prefix: <u>For overseas companies</u> (a) Territory of incorporation: (b) Registered number in the United Kingdom including any prefix:
Give full name(s).	5	Transferee for entry in the register:
Complete as appropriate where the transferee is a company. Also, for an overseas company, unless an arrangement with Land Registry exists, lodge either a certificate in Form 7 in Schedule 3 to the Land Registration Rules 2003 or a certified copy of the constitution in English or Welsh, or other evidence permitted by rule 183 of the Land Registration Rules 2003.		<u>For UK incorporated companies/LLPs</u> Registered number of company or limited liability partnership including any prefix: <u>For overseas companies</u> (a) Territory of incorporation: (b) Registered number in the United Kingdom including any prefix:
Each transferee may give up to three addresses for service, one of which must be a postal address whether or not in the UK (including the postcode, if any). The others can be any combination of a postal address, a UK DX box number or an electronic address.	6	Transferee's intended address(es) for service for entry in the register:
	7	The transferor transfers the property to the transferee

Place 'X' in the appropriate box. State the currency unit if other than sterling. If none of the boxes apply, insert an appropriate memorandum in panel 11.

8   Consideration

☐ The transferor has received from the transferee for the property the following sum (in words and figures):

☐ The transfer is not for money or anything that has a monetary value

☐ Insert other receipt as appropriate:

Place 'X' in any box that applies.

Add any modifications.

9   The transferor transfers with

☐ full title guarantee

☐ limited title guarantee

Where the transferee is more than one person, place 'X' in the appropriate box.

10   Declaration of trust. The transferee is more than one person and

☐ they are to hold the property on trust for themselves as joint tenants

☐ they are to hold the property on trust for themselves as tenants in common in equal shares

Complete as necessary.

☐ they are to hold the property on trust:

Insert here any required or permitted statement, certificate or application and any agreed covenants, declarations and so on.

11   Additional provisions

The transferor must execute this transfer as a deed using the space opposite. If there is more than one transferor, all must execute. Forms of execution are given in Schedule 9 to the Land Registration Rules 2003. If the transfer contains transferee's covenants or declarations or contains an application by the transferee (such as for a restriction), it must also be executed by the transferee.

12   Execution
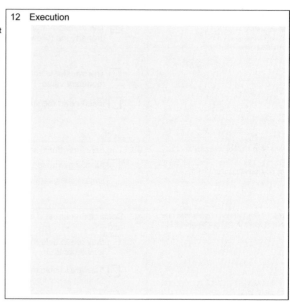

WARNING
If you dishonestly enter information or make a statement that you know is, or might be, untrue or misleading, and intend by doing so to make a gain for yourself or another person, or to cause loss or the risk of loss to another person, you may commit the offence of fraud under section 1 of the Fraud Act 2006, the maximum penalty for which is 10 years' imprisonment or an unlimited fine, or both.

Failure to complete this form with proper care may result in a loss of protection under the Land Registration Act 2002 if, as a result, a mistake is made in the register.

Under section 66 of the Land Registration Act 2002 most documents (including this form) kept by the registrar relating to an application to the registrar or referred to in the register are open to public inspection and copying. If you believe a document contains prejudicial information, you may apply for that part of the document to be made exempt using Form EX1, under rule 136 of the Land Registration Rules 2003.

Appendix 3

MATERIAL RELATING TO GENDER RECOGNITION

A3.1

Gender Recognition (Approved Countries and Territories) Order 2011
SI 2001/1630

1 Citation and commencement

This Order may be cited as the Gender Recognition (Approved Countries and Territories) Order 2011 and comes into force on the day after the day on which it is made.

2 Approved countries and territories

The countries and territories set out in the Schedule are each prescribed as an 'approved country or territory' for the purposes of the Gender Recognition Act 2004.

3 Revocation

The Gender Recognition (Approved Countries and Territories) Order 2005 is revoked.

SCHEDULE
Approved Countries and Territories

Article 2

The Australian territories of Australian Capital Territory and Northern Territory and the states of New South Wales, Queensland, South Australia, Tasmania, Victoria and Western Australia,

Austria,

Belgium,

Bulgaria,

the Canadian provinces of Alberta, British Columbia, Manitoba, New Brunswick, Newfoundland and Labrador, Nova Scotia, Ontario, Prince Edward Island, Quebec and Saskatchewan and the Yukon Territory,

Croatia,

Republic of Cyprus,

Czech Republic,

Denmark,

Estonia,

Finland,

France,

Germany,

Greece,

Iceland,

Italy,

Japan,

Liechtenstein,

Luxembourg,

Malta,

the Federal District of Mexico,

Moldova,

Netherlands,

New Zealand,

Norway,

Poland,

Romania,

Russian Federation,

Serbia,

Singapore,

Slovakia,

Slovenia,

South Africa,

South Korea,

Spain,

Sweden,

Switzerland,

Turkey,

Ukraine,

the District of Columbia and all of the States of the United States of America except for Idaho, Ohio, Tennessee and Texas, and

Uruguay.

A3.2

Application to Gender Recognition Panel

HM Courts
& Tribunals
Service

Application for a
Gender Recognition Certificate

Updated September 2007

This form should be used by applicants for a Gender Recognition Certificate who are not applying using the Overseas Process.

Applicants applying under this process must demonstrate that they have lived in their acquired gender for at least two years.

Before you start, please read the document '**Explanatory Leaflet – a Guide for Users**', which explains the gender recognition process.

If you are married or in a civil partnership, please also read '**Guidance for Married People or those in Civil Partnerships**' and '**Guidance for married couples where one or both partners wish to apply for a Gender Recognition Certificate**'.

We hope we have made this form easy to understand and complete. The guidance notes (see 'Guidance on completing the Application Form for a Gender Recognition Certificate') should answer most of the questions you may have. We recommend that you read the notes before completing each section of the form. If you do find it difficult to complete on your own, you could ask a friend or someone from a support organisation to help you, or you telephone the Gender Recognition Panel on 0300 123 4503 and one of the administrators will be happy to provide support.

You must complete sections 1, 2, 5, 6, 7, 8, 9, 10 and EITHER section 3 OR section 4, which ever applies to you.

Please use black ink when completing this form.

The information in this publication is available in alternative formats on request. Please contact the Gender Recognition Panel on 0300 123 4503 or
grpenquiries@hmcts.gsi.gov.uk

1. Your contact details

The names and title that you provide below will be used in all correspondence relating to your application.

1.1 Preferred Title (Mr, Mrs, Ms, Miss, Dr Etc.)

1.2 Full name you would like us to use when contacting you

1.3 Postal address (for all written correspondence)

1.4 How would you like us to contact you if we have any questions?

Post ☐   Telephone ☐   e-mail ☐

1.5 Daytime contact telephone number and times you will be available on this number (if you would like to be contacted by telephone)

Telephone

Times / days available

1.6 e-mail address (if you would like us to contact you by e-mail)

Please remember that e-mail cannot be guaranteed as secure.

1.7 If possible, please list any dates when you know you will be unavailable for any periods of more than 5 consecutive days over the next 6 months

2. Your personal details

A. The names and title you provided at 1.2 will be used in all future correspondence. Please read the guidance carefully before filling in this section.

2.1 Surname you wish to be recorded on a Gender Recognition Certificate

2.2 First name(s) you wish to be recorded on a Gender Recognition Certificate

B. In order to protect your privacy, you must supply us with a password. If you telephone the Gender Recognition Panel to enquire about your application we will ask you for this password before we give out any personal information. Before choosing a password, please read the guidance to this section.

2.3 Password (between 6 & 10 letters. Numbers must not be used)

2.4 Why is this significant to you?

C. You should read the guidance to the sections below before you decide whether to provide your National Insurance number.

2.5 Please enter your National Insurance number here

2.6 Please tick here if you DO NOT wish the Panel to pass this information to the Inland Revenue if you are granted a full Gender Recognition Certificate *   ☐

* Please note that if you do not want the Gender Recognition Panel to pass on this information then you are legally obliged to pass on this information to the Inland Revenue if your application is successful. This will mean sending your Gender Recognition Certificate and National Insurance number to the Inland Revenue.

This service only applies to UK tax payers. Unfortunately we are not able to inform the authorities in the Isle of Man or Channel Islands.

3. Birth registration information for births registered in the UK

If your birth was registered in the UK you must complete this section. This also applies if you born to a UK citizen abroad but registered by a Forces registering officer, or with the British Consul or High Commission, or born on board a ship, aeroplane or hovercraft and registered under the Merchant Shipping or Civil Aviation provisions.

Please note, if you are adopted we require your adoptive parents' details (as shown on your birth certificate).

3.1 Your surname as recorded on birth or adoption certificate

3.2 Your forename(s) as recorded on birth or adoption certificate

3.3 Gender as stated on birth or adoption certificate

Male/Boy ☐   Female/Girl ☐

3.4 Date of birth   D D   M M   Y YYY

3.5 Place of birth

3.6 Father's Surname (if listed)

3.7 Father's forename(s) (if listed)

3.8 Mother's maiden name (if listed)

3.9 Mother's forename(s) (if listed)

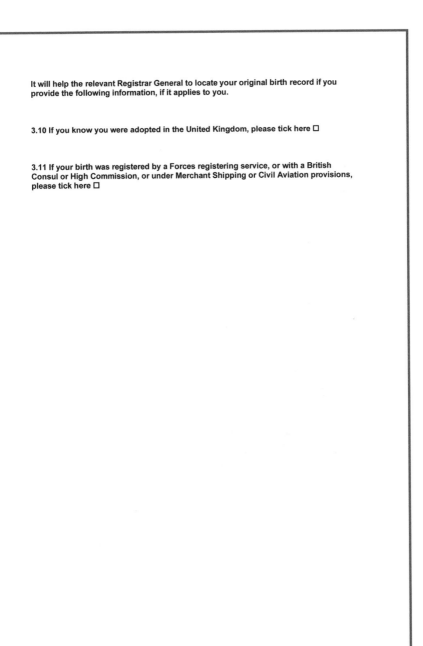

It will help the relevant Registrar General to locate your original birth record if you provide the following information, if it applies to you.

3.10 If you know you were adopted in the United Kingdom, please tick here ☐

3.11 If your birth was registered by a Forces registering service, or with a British Consul or High Commission, or under Merchant Shipping or Civil Aviation provisions, please tick here ☐

4.   Birth registration information for births registered outside the UK

If your birth was registered outside the UK you must complete this section. If not please proceed to section 5.

Please provide your original birth certificate or other official confirmation of your date of birth and birth gender and supply the information requested below.

4.1 Your surname as recorded on birth or adoption certificate

4.2 Your forename(s) as recorded on birth or adoption certificate

4.3 Gender as stated on birth or adoption certificate

Male/Boy ☐   Female/Girl ☐

4.4 Date of birth   D D   M M   Y Y Y Y

4.5 Country where birth is registered

If you are unable to supply certain pieces of information in section 4, above, please use the box below to explain why (continue on additional paper if required and include it on the list of evidence you have supplied in section 9)

5. Time living in your new gender

As part of your application, you must provide evidence to demonstrate that you have lived full time in your new gender for at least two years (up to the date of your application).

The evidence could take the form of letters from official, professional or business organisations or from friends or family; utility bills; copies of official documents (e.g. driving licence, passport). Please see accompanying guidance notice for a fuller list. If the evidence is in a different name to the one you have used on this form, you will need to prove that it does relate to you.

You must ensure that you provide accurate information.

5.1 Please give the date from which you can provide evidence that you have lived full-time in your new gender for two years.

Please use the box in section 9 of this application form to list the evidence you providing.

6. Medical Reports A

The guidance notes to section 6 explain the nature of the report that is required. Please include the original report (as given to you by your medical practitioner / chartered psychologist; a copy will be accepted for subsequent applications) with your application pack and fill in the panels below.

6A.1 Name of registered medical practitioner or specialist chartered psychologist who provided the report

6A.2 Professional address (if the individual is still practising)

6A.3 Daytime contact number

On occasions the Gender Recognition Panel may wish to check the validity of a report. In such case, it would be quicker for the panel to contact the doctor or psychologist directly, although we will copy any correspondence to you. The panel would need consent to contact your doctor or psychologist.

6A.4 I give my consent to the Gender Recognition Panel contacting the supplier of the medical report to check its validity (please tick box) ☐

6. Medical Reports B

The guidance notes to section 6 explain the nature of the report that is required. Please include the original report (as given to you by your medical practitioner / chartered psychologist; a copy will be accepted for subsequent applications) with your application pack and fill in the panels below.

6B.1 Name of registered medical practitioner or specialist chartered psychologist who provided the report

6B.2 Professional address (if the individual is still practising)

6B.3 Daytime contact number

On occasions the Gender Recognition Panel may wish to check the validity of a report. In such case, it would be quicker for the panel to contact the doctor or psychologist directly, although we will copy any correspondence to you. The panel would need consent to contact your doctor or psychologist.

6B.4 I give my consent to the Gender Recognition Panel contacting the supplier of the medical report to check its validity (please tick box) ☐

7. Statutory Declaration

You are required to provide a 'statutory declaration' making several statements about your circumstances and your application. This is to ensure that you meet the criteria for Gender Recognition. We have provided a general version of this form for you to use as the basis for your Statutory Declaration. You should use this form and follow the instructions contained in the guidance notes.

Once you have filled in the Statutory Declaration and had it witnessed by one of the people listed in the guidance notes, please provide the information requested in the boxes below.

7.1 Date of Statutory Declaration

D D	M M	Y Y Y Y

7.2 Name of witness to Statutory Declaration

7.3 Professional title of witness

7.4 Address of witness

7.5 Daytime contact telephone number of witness

You will have given a Statutory Declaration about whether you are currently married or in a civil partnership. Please also tick the appropriate box below.

7.6 Are you currently married?

Yes ☐   No ☐

Are you currently in a civil partnership in the United Kingdom?

Yes ☐   No ☐

Please include the original Statutory Declaration (the one you actually signed, not a copy) in your application pack.

8. Payment

The fees for applying for a Gender Recognition Certificate are outlined in a separate leaflet *'Fees for Applying to the Gender Recognition Panel'*. You should read the leaflet carefully to see whether you need to pay the full, or any fee. If you qualify for reduction of the fee, you will need to include a statement to that effect your Statutory Declaration. If you qualify for exemption from the fee because you are in receipt of certain entitlements or benefits, you should include evidence of that entitlement and list it in section 9, below.

8.1 Are you required to pay a fee?

YES ☐   Income below threshold ☐

Include evidence with your application

8.2 If yes, how much is the fee?   £ [   ]

8.3 If no, why are you not paying a fee? (please tick one box)

☐ **In receipt of a 'qualifying benefit'**
You will need to supply evidence of entitlement

☐ **Income is below the threshold**
Include evidence with your application

☐ **Type of application does not attract a fee**
Include evidence with your application

Method of Payment

If you are required to pay a fee for your application, you should indicate how you are paying it. If paying by cheque or postal order, you must include this with your application form.

Cheque ☐   **Postal Order** ☐

Debit/Credit card ☐ (please see below)

If you would like to pay by Debit/Credit Card then please contact the GRP administrator on 0300 123 4503 within 10 days of receipt of application acknowledgment. We will then take payment from you over the telephone. For security purposes, please have your GRP reference number and password to hand.

9. Supporting evidence

This checklist will help you and the Gender Recognition Panel to be sure that you have included originals or certified copies of everything that you are required to. Please list every piece of evidence that you are including with your application. We will return any documentation to you when we have verified that it is genuine.

Documents	To be returned
Statutory Declaration	
A copy of you decree absolute, if divorced or evidence that your civil partnership has been dissolved	
Medical Reports A and B If you have not used the medical form provided, please list the document(s) you are supplying	
Evidence of the length of time you have lived in your new gender List documents	
Evidence relating to payment qualifications or exemptions List documents	
Please list any other papers or extra pages you have enclosed with your application pack	

10. Declarations

If your birth was registered in the UK, to process your application, the Gender Recognition Panel needs to pass your details to the relevant Registrar Gender who needs to notify the authority that holds your original birth record that your birth has been re-registered.

If you consent below, the Registrar General will contact you (if your application is successful) to inform you about options for your new birth certificate.

I consent to the Registrar General contacting me in relation to the issuance of a new birth certificate.   ☐

I certify that all the information given in this application is correct to the best of my knowledge. I understand that to make a false application is an offence.

Signature of applicant

Date

DD	MM	YYYY

When you have signed and dated the form, it should be sent, with all supporting documentation including Statutory Declaration and medicals reports to:

GRP
PO Box 9300
Leicester
LE1 8DJ

Section 22 of the Gender Recognition Act 2004 protects the information on your application form and information about your gender history if your application is successful. The data you provide will only be processed as permitted by the Act. It will be processed primarily for the purpose of determining your application (and any related legal proceedings) and for maintaining the Gender Recognition Register. The Guidance to this application form and Explanatory Leaflet contain more information about how your data may be processed. Information about you will not be disclosed except where permitted by law, or where you have consented to it.

The **Ministry of Justice** is the Data Controller for the Gender Recognition Secretariat and Panel for the purposes of the Data Protection Act 1998. If you want to know more about what information we have about you, or the way we use your information, you can find details on the **MoJ** website www.justice.gov.uk/about/datasharingandprotection.htm

**HM Courts
& Tribunals
Service**

**Statutory Declaration
Gender Recognition Act 2004**

"I ▨▨▨▨▨▨▨▨ do solemnly and sincerely declare that:

1. I am over 18 years of age.

2. I have lived as a male / female (delete word that does not apply) throughout the period of ▨▨▨ years since I transitioned in ▨▨▨ (month and year of transition).

3 I intend to live as a male / female (delete word that does not apply) until death.

4a. I hereby declare that I am / am not legally married in my original gender to someone of the opposite sex (delete as appropriate).

4b. I hereby declare that I am / am not in a civil partnership in my original gender to someone of the same sex (delete as appropriate).

4c. I hereby declare that my former marriage or civil partnership was dissolved on ▨▨▨ (Please enter date, or delete if not applicable).

5. I make this solemn declaration conscientiously believing the same to be true and by virtue of the provisions of the Statutory Declarations Act 1835

Declared at ▨▨▨▨▨▨ (insert place)

This ▨▨ day of ▨▨▨▨ 20

▨▨▨▨▨▨ (Signature of applicant)

before me ▨▨▨▨▨▨ (name of witness)

▨▨▨▨▨▨ (Signature of witness)"

A3.3

Application to Gender Recognition Panel – Guidance

HM Courts & Tribunals Service

Guidance on completing the application Form for a Gender Recognition Certificate.

Updated September 2007

This document is designed to assist applicants for a Gender Recognition Certificate. If your acquired gender has been recognised under the law of another country, you should read the Explanatory Leaflet carefully and, if necessary you should complete the Overseas Track Application Form and NOT this application form.

Before completing the form, you should read all the explanatory material carefully, so that you are fully aware of the consequences of applying for gender recognition. Each section indicates what information you should include in the corresponding section on the form.

Applicant under this process must demonstrate that they have lived in their acquired gender for at least two years. Further details can be found in the Explanatory leaflet: A guide to users.

These guidance notes should answer most of the questions you may have regarding the application form. We recommend that you read the relevant notes before completing each section of the form. If you do find the application form difficult to complete on your own, you could ask a friend or someone from a support organisation to help you, or you can telephone the Gender Recognition Panel on 0300 123 4503 and one of the administrators will be happy to provide support.

You must complete sections 1, 2, 5, 6, 7, 8, 9, 10 and EITHER section 3 OR section 4, which ever applies to you.

The information in this publication is available in alternative formats on request. Please contact the Gender Recognition Panel on 0300 123 4503 or
grpenquiries@hmcts.gsi.gov.uk

1. Your contact details

This section asks you to provide the basic information the Gender Recognition Panel and the Registrar General (responsible for the registration of births and issue of birth certificates) will need in order to correspond with you about the progress of your application. The Panel will only contact you when necessary: to acknowledge your application and inform you of a decision and, if necessary, to ask for more information.

We ask you to tell us how you would prefer to be contacted if we do have any questions (eg post, email or telephone). However, even if you choose to be contacted by email or telephone, we will still need a postal address as we will need to return original documents and to send you a Gender Recognition Certificate if your application is successful. Also, if we do need to contact you about your application and we have significant difficulties reached you using your preferred method, we will write to you at your postal address with the relevant information about your application.

Questions	Notes
1.1 Preferred title (Mr, Mrs, Miss, Ms etc)	Please tell us how you wish to be addressed.
1.2 Full name you would like us to use when contacting you	Tell us the name by which you would like to be addressed in all correspondence.
1.3 Postal address (for all written correspondence)	The postal address will be used for all correspondence where we need to send original or official documents to you (eg to return your driving licence or to send you the Panel's decision, including a Gender Recognition Certificate if you are successful). If you wish, it can be used for **all** correspondence. This address does not have to be your home address. You can use any address for postal correspondence, you just need to make sure it is secure and that you will be able to pick up your post regularly (at least twice a week).
1.4 How would you like us to contact you if we have any questions?	Please select your preferred means of contact. Wherever possible, the staff of the Gender Recognition Panel will use this method. If we cannot contact you using this means, we will write to you at the address you have

		supplied.
1.5	Daytime contact telephone number and times you will be available on this number (if you would like us to contact you by telephone)	Please fill this in if you wish us to contact you by telephone. You should give a number on which you are available between 10:00 and 16:00, and let us know when would be the best time to call
1.6	Email address (if you would like us to contact you by email). Please remember that email cannot be guaranteed as secure	If you wish to be contacted by email, please write your email address here. Please remember that email cannot be guaranteed as secure.
1.7	If possible, please list any dates when you know you will be unavailable for any periods of more than 5 consecutive days over the next 6 months	In general, the staff of the Gender Recognition Panel will require a response to queries within 28 days. However, we appreciate that this will not be possible if you are away. Therefore, we would like you to make a note in this box of any periods of more than five consecutive days when you know that you will be available over the six months after you submit your application form.

If, after you have submitted your application, you have to go away for more than five working days at a time, please contact the Gender Recognition Panel to let them know. |

2. Your personal details

There are three pieces of information we request

    A. The names you wish to be recorded on your Gender Recognition Certificate if you are successful.

    B. A password for your application to help us to protect your privacy.

    C. Your National Insurance number if you wish us to inform the relevant authorities if your application is successful.

A.   **The names you wish to be recorded on your Gender Recognition Certificate if you are successful**

We ask you to tell us what names you would want recorded on your Gender Recognition Certificate as these could be different to the names you have given in Section 1 above.

The key points to bear in mind when confirming the names you want to appear on your Gender Recognition Certificate are:

- The name that you choose should be the one that you wish to be known by permanently in your new gender.

- The forename(s) that appear on your Gender Recognition Certificate will be recorded in the Gender Recognition Register. The surname that appears on your Gender Recognition Certificate may be recorded in the Gender Recognition Register **OR** you may have the surname from your original birth record (or adoption record) recorded in the Gender Recognition Register. This register is held by the Registrar General and is used in the same way as the Adoption Register to enable the Registrar General to issue new Birth Certificates without changing the original entry in the Birth Register. More details about the process for obtaining a new Birth Certificate (including details of the Gender Recognition Register) can be found in the Explanatory Leaflet. Alternatively you can contact the General Registrars Office direct who will be able to assist you with all queries relating to your new birth certificate.

- The forename(s) and surname recorded in the Gender Recognition Register will be the names shown on a new birth certificate. **Upon gaining recognition in your new gender, the relevant General Register Office will contact you and explain the options for your birth certificate and the recording of surnames.**

- If you have already changed your name by statutory declaration or deed poll and you wish to change it *again* as part of the gender recognition process, you will need to complete another statutory declaration of name change or deed poll before you apply for a Gender Recognition Certificate. Your application for gender recognition does not change your name in law.

Questions	Notes
2.1 Surname you wish to be recorded on a Gender Recognition Certificate	This surname will appear on the Gender Recognition Certificate and may be recorded on the Gender Recognition Register and feature on any new Birth Certificate, unless you have the surname from your birth registration recorded
2.2 First name(s) you wish to be recorded on a Gender Recognition Certificate	The first name(s) you record here will be recorded on the Gender Recognition Certificate, the Gender Recognition Register and any new Birth Certificate that is issued to you as a result.

B.   A password for your application to help us to protect your privacy

We know that the information contained in this application is sensitive. If you telephone the Gender Recognition Panel or General Register Office with a query, we will ask for your password before we give out any information.

Questions	Notes
2.3 Password (between 6 & 10 letters)	The password should be any word of between six and ten letters that is easy for you to remember. Our password should not have any numbers, spaces or characters other than letters in it.
2.4 Why is this significant to you?	You need to explain why your chosen password is significant to you so that, if you forget it, we will be able to give you a clue to help you remember it. For example, you may choose 'goldie' as your password. If you forget it, the Gender Recognition Panel will remind you that you wrote 'name of my first pet' in this section.

C.   Your National Insurance number if you wish us to inform the relevant authorities if your application is successful

If your application is successful and you have lived, or paid tax, in the UK, or have claimed benefits, tax credits or pension, you will need to inform the relevant authorities. It is your responsibility to ensure that the Inland Revenue and any organisation that pays you benefits or tax credits (this could be the Department for Work and Pensions, the Social Security Agency in Northern Ireland or the Veterans' Agency) are informed.

If you fail to notify the relevant organisations that you have obtained a full Gender Recognition Certificate the possible consequences are that:

- Your National Insurance records may be incorrect;
- You may get the incorrect amount of benefits, tax credits or pensions;
- You may lose out on benefits, tax credits, pensions or services to which you may be entitled to; or
- You may get benefits, tax credits, pensions or services to which you are not entitled.

Where payments are involved, the relevant organisation may take action to recover any amounts that you owe.

To make it easier for you, if you are successful, the Gender Recognition Panel is happy to inform the Inland Revenue who hold your National Insurance records and will pass the information on to the relevant benefit provider(s). To enable us to do this, we will need your National Insurance number.

Questions	Notes
2.5 Please enter your National Insurance number here:	You will find your National Insurance number on your National Insurance Card, on a payslip or on most tax forms such as a P45 or P60. If you do not know or cannot remember your National Insurance number contact the Inland Revenue on 0845 91 57006. If you do not have a National Insurance number and you would like to get one you should contact your local Jobcentre Plus or social security office.
	Please note that this information will only be provided in order to update your tax, tax credit and benefit records. It will not be used for any other purpose.
2.6 Please tick her if you **do not** wish the Panel to pass on this information*	If you would prefer the Gender Recognition Panel **not to** inform Inland Revenue if you receive a full Gender Recognition Certificate please tick this box.
	Bear in mind that you must let the Inland Revenue know if your application is successful which will mean sending them your Gender Recognition Certificate and National Insurance number.
	If you fail to notify Inland Revenue that you have received a full Gender Recognition Certificate you may be liable for prosecution.

Once the Inland Revenue have been made aware of your successful application, (either by you or by the Gender Recognition panel), you will be sent notification to confirm that your national insurance, tax, tax credits, benefits and pension records have been updated. This confirmation will be sent to you at the address held on the Inland Revenues records. This may be different to the address that you have given at section 1.3. You may wish to contact the Inland Revenue on 02920 325080 to ensure that the name and address that they hold for you are up-to-date. If you have elected for the Gender Recognition Panel to inform Inland Revenue, the letter of confirmation from Inland Revenue will not mention why your records have been updated or refer in any way to your Gender Recognition application or Certificate. If you choose to inform the Inland Revenue yourself, they will of course need to return your Gender Recognition Certificate.

This service only applies to UK residents. Unfortunately we are not able to inform the authorities in the Isle of Man or Channel Islands and residents of these islands will need to inform the relevant authorities directly.

3. Birth registration information for births registered in the UK

If your birth was registered in the UK (or by the Forces registering service, or with a British Consul or High Commission, or under Merchant Shipping or Civil Aviation provisions), you need to provide your birth registration details in this section.

Your birth registration details are required as they will enable the Panel and the Registrar General to validate your application and, if you achieve recognition in your new gender, to create the entry that will enable you to obtain a new Birth Certificate.

Please provide your birth registration details as recorded on your Birth Certificate or Adoption Certificate. Don't worry if you don't have a copy of the relevant document. We do not require you to provide a copy of the Certificate or all the details if you do not have them. However, the more information you provide here, the easier it will be to process your application. Upon receipt of your application, the Panel will check your details with the relevant Registrar General to make sure we have all the information needed for the gender recognition process.

If your birth was registered **outside** the United Kingdom, you should provide your birth registration details in section 4.

Questions	Notes
3.1 Your surname as recorded on birth or adoption certificate	This information, along with the other details that you supply, will assist the Registrar General to find your original birth record. No surname is recorded for a child in some birth records where it was assumed at the time that the parent(s)'s surname would be used. If this is the case, please give the parent(s)'s surname.
3.2 Your forename(s) as recorded on birth or adoption certificate	These will be listed in full on your birth or adoption certificate. Don't worry if you are not sure of **all** your forenames.
	Your original name will not appear on any correspondence or on a Gender Recognition Certificate (unless you have kept your original name). If your application is successful, upon request you will receive a letter stating your original name and that you are now recognised in your new

	gender, with a new name (where relevant). This letter may be useful to you in proving that you are who you say you are, but it will not be the Gender Recognition Certificate. The certificate will be a separate document and will only include the names you have said you want to be used in section 2 above.
3.3 Gender as stated on birth or adoption certificate	Please circle the gender in which you were registered at birth.
3.4 Date of birth	If you are successful, your date of birth and other details from your existing birth certificate will appear on a Gender Recognition Certificate and a new birth certificate. You must state the date of birth as it appears on your Birth or Adoption Certificate. You cannot change this.
3.5 Place of birth	This information will assist the Registrar General in finding your birth record, and will appear on any new Birth Certificate that is issued.

The answers to questions 3.6-3.11 will be helpful, as they may enable the Registrar General to find your birth record more quickly, but are not essential.

Questions	Notes
3.6 Father's surname, if listed	If your father's details are recorded on your birth or adoption certificate, you should fill them in here.
3.7 Father's forenames, if listed	This will enable the Registrar General to verify that they have the correct birth record.
3.8 Mother's maiden surname, if listed	Your mother's names will appear on all birth and adoption certificates, and will enable the Registrar General to verify that they have located the correct birth or adoption record.
3.9 Mother's forenames, if listed	
3.10 If you know that you were adopted in the United Kingdom, please tick here	The birth entries of individuals who have been adopted, or whose births were registered overseas by a Forces registering service, or with a British Consul or High Commission, or under Merchant Shipping or Civil Aviation provisions, appear on separate registers.

| 3.11 | If your birth was registered by a Forces registering service, or with a British Consul or High Commission, or under Merchant Shipping or Civil Aviation provisions, please tick here | It will help the relevant Registrar General to locate your birth record if you indicate by ticking the appropriate boxes whether either or both condition applies to you. |

4.   Birth registration information for births registered outside the UK

If your birth was registered outside the UK (in other words, if your birth was registered in any country that is **not** part of the UK and was **not** registered by the Forces registering service, or with a British Consul or High Commission, or under Merchant Shipping or Civil Aviation provisions), you must complete this section if you want to apply for a Gender Recognition Certificate in the UK.

You must supply an original birth certificate or other official confirmation of your date of birth and birth gender, in addition to the information requested in the boxes below.

Anyone whose application is granted by a UK Gender Recognition Panel can receive a full or interim UK Gender Recognition Certificate. However, if your birth was not registered in the United Kingdom, an entry will not be made in the Gender Recognition Register and you will not be entitled to a UK birth certificate.

In order to grant a Gender Recognition Certificate, the Gender Recognition Panel must be satisfied that you are who you say you are and that the information that you have given in this part of the form is accurate. This is why we ask you to provide your original birth certificate or other official confirmation of your date of birth and birth gender.

Questions	Notes
4.1 Your surname as recorded on birth or adoption certificate	The Gender Recognition Panel needs to record your name as originally registered.
4.2 Your forename(s) as recorded on birth or adoption certificate	These will be listed in full on your birth or adoption certificate. Don't worry if you are not sure of **all** your forenames.
	Your original name will not appear in any correspondence or on a Gender Recognition Certificate (unless you have kept your original name). If your application is successful, upon request you will receive a letter stating your original name and that you are now recognised in your new gender, with a new name (where relevant). This letter may be useful to you in proving that you are who you say you are, but it will not be the Gender Recognition Certificate. The certificate will be a separate

		document and will only include the names you have said you want to be used in section 2 above.
4.3	Gender as stated on or adoption birth certificate	You should tick the gender in which you were registered at birth.
4.4	Date of birth	If you are successful, your date of birth and other details from your existing birth certificate will appear on a Gender Recognition Certificate. You must state the date of birth as it appears on your Birth or Adoption Certificate. You cannot change this.
4.5	Country where birth is registered	You should give the name of the country where your birth was registered.

If you are unable to supply certain pieces of information or official documentation of your date of birth and birth gender you should use the box at the end of section 4 to explain why. For example, where relevant, use this box to explain your asylum status. If you need more space please continue on a separate sheet and send it with your application pack.

5. Time living in your new gender

To qualify for recognition under this provision you must be able to prove that you have lived full time in your new gender for two years before the dater of your application. Therefore, in this section, we ask you to tell us the date from which you can demonstrate that you have been living in your new gender and we ask you to provide supporting evidence.

You must provide either original documentation, which we will return to you, or certified copies of original documentation.

Questions	Notes
5.1 Please give the date from which you can provide evidence that you have lived full-time in your new gender role for two years	You should enter the date from which you can prove that you have been living **full time** in your acquired gender. To meet the requirements, this date must be at least two years prior to the date that you submit your application.

We need you to provide evidence in the form of documents that include your name in your new gender and relevant dates. If the evidence is in a different name to the one you have used on the application form, you will need to prove that it does relate to you.

Evidence could take a variety of forms, below are some examples:

- Letters from official, professional or business organisations or from friends or family **that is dated from 2 years ago or more**.

- Utility bills;

- Official documentation (eg driving licence **both the counterpart and photo ID** passport);

- A statutory declaration or deed poll registering a change of name;

- Academic documentation (if you were a student during the relevant period);

- An official letter from your employer or from an individual in a professional role (eg a solicitor, doctor, dentist, MP, etc ...) who knows you on a personal basis.

This is not exhaustive but is just intended as a guideline.

If you have paid tax or claimed benefits, tax credits or pensions in the UK since you transitioned, you may already have informed one of the providers (eg the Department of Work and Pensions, Northern Ireland's Social Security Agency or the Inland Revenue) that you are living in a new gender. If you did this more than two years ago, they could provide evidence to support your application. If you feel that further evidence is necessary, please contact Inland Revenue, Special Section D, Prudhoe House, Room BP9207, Benton Park View, Longbenton, Newcastle, NE98 1ZZ. You will need to provide your current name, date of birth and National Insurance number. Please note that a response may take a number of weeks.

Please gather your evidence and then list all the documents you are sending in the relevant table in section 9 of this form. Please do not send large quantities of documents unless absolutely necessary. The Panel only wishes to see two different documents that demonstrate that you have been living in your new gender full time for two years prior to the date of your application.

Should you wish to provide evidence for your application that requires translation into English the panel will require you to provide translated documents to support your application.

If you have any concerns about your evidence please contact the Gender Recognition Panel and they will be able to advise you. Contact details are given at the end of this guidance.

6. Medical reports

In addition to proving that you have lived fro two years in your acquired gender, you must provide medical evidence that you have been treated in relation to your gender identity. Evidence must come from either a doctor or a chartered psychologist, who is registered with the General Medical Council (GMC), the British Psychological Society (BPS) and the Royal College of Psychiatrists (RCP).

Since you are applying on the basis of having lived for two years or more in your acquired gender, you need to provide two reports with your application pack. You should list the reports in the table at section 9 of the application form, along with the other evidence that you are submitting.

Report A

Report A must be made by a registered medical practitioner or a chartered psychologist practising in the field of gender dysphoria. A list of doctors and chartered psychologists who are specialists in the field of gender dysphoria is held on the Gender Recognition website at **www.grp.gov.uk/forms**. Alternatively if you do not have access to the website you can contact the panel direct.

This report must be made by a registered medical practitioner or a chartered psychologist practising in the field of gender dysphoria and **must include details of a diagnosis of gender dysphoria**.

Report B

Report B must be made by a registered medical practitioner (who may, but need not, practise in the field of gender dysphoria). For example, this report could be made by your GP.

This report must include specific details of treatment ie whether you have undergone, are undergoing or are planning to undergo surgery for the purpose of modifying sexual characteristics.

If you have not undergone surgery the report must explain why not.

We have provided a general version of the form for medical reports for you and your medical practitioner/chartered psychologist to use if you both wish. Alternatively, your medical practitioner/chartered psychologist may prefer to give you copies of his/her notes and/or letters about your case. Please provide whichever is easier for you and your medical practitioner or chartered psychologist to produce.

If you already have a report from a suitable person that satisfies the criteria above, you can submit it as the medical report for this application if it is on official paper or has an official stamp on it. You should bear in mind that your doctor or psychologist may charge you for providing a report. Please do not worry if you do not have a report from the time of your treatment. The form that we have provided will be easy for your doctor or chartered psychologist to fill in.

Please keep a copy of the report (or papers you are submitting) for yourself (a copy would be accepted if you needed to make a subsequent application) send the original with your application pack and include it (and/or any other relevant papers) in the list in section 9.

Questions		Notes
6A.1 & 6B.1	Name of registered medical practitioner or specialist chartered psychologist who provided the report	Please provide the name and qualification (if you know it) of the registered medical practitioner or specialist chartered psychologist who provided the report to you.
6A.2 & 6B.2	Professional address (if the individual is still practising)	Please provide the contact details of the person who has supplied the evidence only if he or she continues to practise. The Panel may check that individuals meet the required criteria to provide a valid report.
6A.3 & 6B.3	Daytime contact telephone number	Please provide a daytime contact telephone number of the registered medical practitioner or chartered psychologist.

The Gender Recognition Panel may wish to clarify some aspects of your evidence. In such a case, it would be quicker for the Panel to contact your doctor or psychologist directly. In addition, if there is concern about the validity of a report, the Panel will need to contact the person who supplied the report before your application can proceed. The Panel cannot contact your doctor or psychologist to check the validity of a report without your consent. Any correspondence with your doctor or psychologist will be copied to you.

Questions		Notes
6A.4 & 6B.4	If you give consent to the Gender Recognition Panel contacting the suppliers of the report(s) above, please tick here	Please tick this box to give your consent to the Gender Recognition Panel contacting your doctor or psychologist, where required, to check the validity of the report they have provided on your case and treatment.

If you do not give your consent on the application form, in the event of a query, the Panel will contact you to discuss the issue and agree the way to resolve it. This may delay your application.

7. Statutory Declaration

A 'Statutory Declaration' is a written statement of facts which the person making it signs and solemnly declares to be true before a witness. You are required to provide a Statutory Declaration making several statements about your circumstances and your application. This is to ensure that you meet the criteria for Gender Recognition.

You are required to state that:

- You are over 18 years of age.
- You intend to live in your acquired gender until death
- You have lived in your acquired gender continuously for a period of two years or more (as you stated in section 5) before the date of your application
- You are or are not married in your original gender to someone of the opposite sex
- You are or are not in a civil partnership in your original gender to someone of the same sex.

Please ensure you complete or delete, as appropriate section 4c of the statutory declaration with a dissolvement date of your former marriage or civil partner.

If you have been in a former marriage or Civil Partnership it is important to give us the correct date it was dissolved so that your pension benefits can be calculated correctly, you must include a copy of your decree absolute or evidence that your Civil Partnership has been dissolved with your application.

We have provided a standard template for the statutory declaration. It includes all the statements that you may need to make. You may add to it to meet your personal needs.

When you have filled in the Statutory Declaration and you are content that it represents the truth, you need to take it to an officer authorised to administer an oath. You will then need to read and sign the Statutory Declaration in front of the witness who will sign the document to witness it.

The Statutory Declaration must be made before a person who is authorised to attest an oath. Examples of people who would be acceptable: a Justice of peace, a magistrate, a commissioner for oaths, a practising solicitor, a notary public, a licensed conveyancer, an authorised advocate or an authorised litigator.

You will normally be charged for drawing up and witnessing statutory declarations. You should find out the likely costs in advance. In order to get it witnessed by a magistrate/JP you must go to the magistrate's court. To find out when they hear applications for declarations you should contact your local magistrates' court. They will also be able to tell you how much the fee will be or whether it can be waived.

In section 7 of the application form, you should provide details of the statutory declaration and the witness before whom the declaration was made.

Questions	Notes
7.6 Are you currently married in your original gender to someone of the opposite sex or in a civil partnership in your original gender to someone of the same sex?	Please tick any box that is relevant to you. This will determine whether you are issued with a full or an interim Gender Recognition Certificate. If you are married you should read the special guidance for married people before applying.

8. Payment

Details about the fees payable for an application for a Gender Recognition Certificate can be found in the separate leaflet *Fees for Applying to the Gender Recognition Panel*. You should read this carefully as it will tell you whether you need to pay a fee for your application and, if so, how much the fee is. There are also details about how to pay the fee.

You will find answers to all the questions on the application form in this leaflet. If you are not required to pay a fee you should answer questions 8.1 and 8.3. If you are paying a fee you should answer questions 8.1, 8.2, 8.4 and, if paying by credit or debit card 8.5.

Please remember that you will need to provide evidence if you are paying a reduced fee or no fee at all. The evidence is explained in the fees leaflet. If you fail to provide evidence, or the correct fee, your application will not be processed until the Gender Recognition Panel receives the correct documentation or payment.

Please make cheques and postal orders payable to **HM Courts and Tribunals Service**.

9. Supporting evidence

As well as the completed application form, Medical Reports and Statutory Declaration, you have been asked to provide other pieces of evidence to support your application.

If you were previously married and have been divorced please enclose a copy of the decree absolute. Or if you have been in Civil Partnership evidence that this has been dissolved.

Please ensure that you submit any change of name documents with your application, these need not be over two years but must contain an accurate trail of any name changes you have been through. If you do not have any please provide an explanation as to why not.

Please use section 9 to list all the pieces of evidence that you are submitting in support of the answers that you have given on the application for. This will help the staff of the Panel to ensure that everything that you intend to go before the Panel will be seen by it.

Please DO NOT send large quantities of documents unless absolutely necessary. The Panel normally only wishes to see **two different documents** that demonstrate that you have been living in your new gender full time for two years prior to the date of your application.

To qualify as evidence, documents must include your name (in your new gender) and relevant dates. If the evidence is in a different name to the one you have used on the application form, you will need to prove that it does relate to you.

In addition to a medical report and statutory declaration, please list the items of supporting evidence you are providing with your application in the box provided, such as:

- Letters from official, professional or business organisations or from friends or family **that is dated from 2 years ago or more**;
- Utility bills;
- Official documentation (eg driving licence **both the counterpart and photo ID**, passport);
- A statutory declaration or deed poll registering a change of name;
- Academic documentation (if you were a student during the relevant period);
- An official letter from your employer or from an individual in a professional role (eg a solicitor, doctor, dentist, MP, etc …) who knows you on a personal basis.

You should also list evidence relating to your qualification for a reduced, or exemption from, fee payment.

To avoid any confusion, please tick the box on the right of the table if you want the original document returned to you.

If you have any concerns about the evidence you are providing, please contact the Panel for clarification.

10. Declarations

It is necessary to sign and date your application to verify that all the information that you have given is, to the best of your knowledge, true. It is an offence to apply fraudulently for a Gender Recognition Certificate.

If your birth was originally registered in the UK, the Panel will contact the Registrar General upon receipt of your application to confirm that your birth registration details are correct and to verify your application. If you consent to an application for a new birth certificate to be made on your behalf to the Registrar General, please tick the appropriate box on the form.

A checklist is provided to help you ensure that you have remembered to include everything and to enable you to keep a record of all the documents you send. Please place all documentation, including the application form and cheque, if applicable, into one envelope and post it to the address supplied.

Your application will be acknowledged within two working days of receipt.

If there are any problems we will contact you to ensure that your application is dealt with as quickly as possible.

When your application has been determined, you will receive a letter from the Panel informing you of its decision and providing guidance on what you may wish to do next. If you are successful, this letter will include your Gender Recognition Certificate.

A3.4

Table of gender recognition schemes in countries and territories that have been approved by the Secretary of State

April 2005

Country or Territory	Outline of recognition process
Australia Capital Territory	The Births, Deaths and Marriages Registration Act 1997 allows for a person who is not married and who has undergone sexual reassignment surgery to apply to alter the record of that person's sex in the registration of the persons birth. The application to alter the register must be accompanied by a statutory declaration from each of two Doctors verifying that the person has undergone gender reassignment surgery.
Australia Northern Territory	The Births, Deaths and Marriages Registration Act 1996 allows for the registration of a change of sex. The provisions in law are substantially the same as those for Australia Capital Territory and New South Wales.
Australia New South Wales	The Births, Deaths and Marriages Registration Act 1995 allows for the alteration of birth registers and the issuing of new birth certificates to record a change of sex. The provisions are substantively the same as those in Australia Capital Territory.
Australia Queensland	The Births, Deaths and Marriages Registration Act 1962 provides that a transsexual person may apply to the registrar-general to enter a change of sex in the register of births or adopted children register and to re-register the person's birth or adoption. The transsexual person must have undergone sexual reassignment surgery and must not be married. Applications must be accompanied by either statutory declarations by two Doctors verifying that the person has undergone sexual reassignment surgery, or by a recognition certificate issued under the law of another state, and any other documents prescribed by regulations.
Australia South Australia	The Specific Sexual Reassignment Act 1988 provides for application to an authorised magistrate for the issue of a recognition certificate. The individual must have had a reassignment procedure carried out in South Australia, and the magistrate must be satisfied that the person believes that his or her true sex is the sex to which the person has been reassigned, and has received proper counselling in relation to his/her sexual identity. The person must not be married. 'Reassignment procedure' means a medical or surgical procedure (or a combination of both) to alter genitals and other sexual characteristics of a person identified by birth certificate as male or female so that the person will be identified as a person of the opposite sex.
Australia Tasmania	The Births, Deaths and Marriages Registration Act 1999 refers. An unmarried adult born in Tasmania who has undergone sexual reassignment surgery may apply to the Registrar to register a change of the person's sex. Applications must be accompanied by statutory declarations from two Doctors verifying that the person has undergone sexual reassignment surgery. The Registrar may request further and better particulars before agreeing to do so.
Australia Victoria	The Births, Deaths and Marriages Registration (Amendment) Act 2004 refers. An unmarried person who is 18 years or older and whose birth is registered in Victoria and who has undergone sex affirmation surgery may apply to the Registrar for the record of his/her birth registration to be altered. An application must include Statutory Declarations that the applicant has undergone such surgery, by –

  • two Doctors; or

  • two medical practitioners registered under the law of the place where the sex affirmation surgery was performed -

who performed the surgery or provided other medical treatment to the applicant in connection with the applicant's transsexualism. |
| **Australia** Western Australia | The Gender Reassignment Act 2000 provided for a Gender Reassignment Board with the power to issue recognition certifcates.

Applications are made to the Board for such a certificate following reassignment procedure. The applicant must be unmarried.

'Reassignment procedure' means a medical or surgical procedure (or a combination of both) to alter genitals and other sexual characteristics of a person identified by birth certificate as male or female so that the person will be identified as a person of the opposite sex. The Board must be satisfied that the person believes his/her true gender is the gender to which they have been reassigned, has adopted the lifestyle and has the gender characteristics of the gender to which they have been reassigned and has received proper counselling in relation to his/her gender identity. |

Country or Territory	Outline of recognition process
Austria EU	Whilst there is no specific legislation, Austria has a formal recognition system. In order to gain recognition of acquired gender the person must be diagnosed as transsexual and must then undergo psychotherapy treatment for a year. They must also have started hormone treatment at that time and take a 'real life' test which considers the social aspects of living in their newly acquired gender. This is followed by a psychotherapeutic assessment which, if positive, leads to a decision by the Vienna Medical Examiner (ME) as to whether treatment can be suspended and gender reassignment surgery performed. Before surgery it is necessary to obtain the expert opinion of the ME in order to apply for recognition of the gender change. The ME must be satisfied that: • the applicant has lived for a long time with the compulsive idea of belonging to the opposite sex, and that it has caused him/her to undergo measures of sex reassignment • these measures have led to a visible approach to the appearance of the opposite sex • it is probable that his/her feeling of belonging to the opposite sex will not change • any pre existing marriage has been dissolved. A trans person will be issued with an amended birth certificate in their acquired gender. Following recognition a trans person may marry in their acquired gender.
Belgium EU	There is no specific legislation but applications are dealt with on a case by case basis in the courts. The criteria are: ''a regular, durable and irreversible possession of the new state following medical treatment (hormonal, surgical, psychological) prescribed for therapeutic reasons, preferably after a multi-disciplinary diagnosis'. A note of the legal decision modifying the sex and, if need be, a change of first name(s) is written in the margin of the birth certificate. Following the legal decision the trans person belongs to the recognised sex and can marry in the acquired gender. As at March 2002, in principle, any pre existing marriage must be dissolved (by annulment or divorce) before the change of sex will be recognised. However, in January 2003 a law was passed which provided for recognition of same-sex marriage.
Bulgaria	The alteration of gender will pass through a court procedure. In order to rule in favour of a gender change, the court requires medical papers showing that an operation has been made or hormone tests proving the change of sexual characteristics (More information can be taken from the court decisions on a case-by-case basis. There is no unified court practice yet). There are no requirements for the trans persons to be unmarried before being accepted for gender change. If he/she is married, the court applies the rules for divorce. A person with legally recognised gender can marry in the acquired gender. This comes from the prohibition of discrimination rules in the Constitution of the Republic of Bulgaria. When the court rules in favour of a gender change, it also rules in its decision whether the birth certificate should be amended or a new one should be issued, depending on the facts of the case.
Canada	
Canada Alberta	The Vital Statistics Act section 22 refers. Where a person has had his/her anatomical sex structure changed to a sex other than on the birth certificate, on production of affidavits from two physicians and evidence of identity the Director of Vital Statistics shall cause a notation to be made to that person's registration. If registered outside Alberta a copy of the proof of change will be sent the official in charge of registration in the other province. Once the sex has been legally changed on a birth certificate, that person is legally deemed to be of that sex. Every birth (or marriage) certificate issued after the making of a notation is issued as if the registration had been made with the sex as changed. A trans person is not allowed to marry in their acquired gender. [Although the Province includes a provision with regard to changing the designation of sex on marriage certificates, they do not have the constitutional jurisdiction to overrule the *Corbett* and *Cossey* cases – they still apply to determine the legal validity of any marriage.]
Canada British Columbia	The Vital Statistics Act section 27 refers. An unmarried transsexual who has undergone surgery may apply to the chief executive officer of vital statistics to have his/her change of gender recorded on their birth registration document. The officer will require a certificate from a qualified and licensed medical practitioner explaining the procedurescarried out and certifying that the medical practitioner performed the surgery. If the surgery was carried out outside of Canada the officer will still need to be satisfied that the person who performed the surgery was qualified to do so and will require a statement as above, and another medical practitioner will examine the applicant to confirm surgery has been carried out and is complete by accepted medical standards. A birth certificate issued after the registration of birth is changed must be issued as if the original registration had been made showing the sex designation as changed. A trans person is not allowed to marry in their acquired gender.

Country or Territory	Outline of recognition process
Canada Manitoba	The Vital Statistics Act section 25 refers. Once the transsexual has undergone surgery he/she may apply to the Director of Vital Statistics to make a notation of gender change on their registration of birth. The Director will require two medical certificates signed by legally qualified medical practitioners stating that they performed or assisted in the surgery and that as a result of the surgical procedures the gender should be changed. Where two statements cannot be obtained, the director may require such other evidence of the matters contained in those certificates as the director considers necessary. Every birth certificate (or marriage certificate) issued after the making of a notation shall be issued as if the original registration had been made with the sex as changed. A trans person is not allowed to marry in their acquired gender. [Although the Province includes a provision with regard to changing the designation of sex on marriage certificates, they do not have the constitutional jurisdiction to overrule the *Corbett* and *Cossey* cases – they still apply to determine the legal validity of any marriage.]
Canada New Brunswick	The Vital Statistics Act section 34 refers. An unmarried transsexual who has undergone surgery may apply to the Registrar General for a notation to be made on the birth registration so that the registration of sex is consistent with the perceived results of the surgery. The Registrar General will require a certificate signed by a qualified medical practitioner explaining the surgical procedures carried out and certifying that he/she performed transsexual surgery on the applicant, and that as a result of that surgery the designation of sex on the registration of birth should be changed. If this is unavailable the Registrar General will require other evidence confirming the surgery. The Registrar will also require a certificate of a qualified medical practitioner who did not perform the surgery stating that he/she can substantiate transsexual surgery was performed and that as a result the birth registration should be changed. The Registrar will also require evidence if identity and a statutory declaration (of what is unclear). Every birth certificate issued after the making of a notation shall be issued as if the registration had been made with the sex as changed. A trans person is not allowed to marry in their acquired gender.
Canada Newfoundland and Labrador	The Vital Statistics Act section 19 refers. A person wishing to change information related to his/her birth, sex or marriage, shall submit proof or supporting documents as may be required by the appropriate Government Minister. The proof or supporting documents consists of three forms, one completed by the applicant, one by the physician who performed the surgery and one by a physician who has examined the applicant post surgery. The applicant must be single or divorced. Where successful, the applicant may then have the birth certificate changed and is recognised in the acquired gender thereafter. He or she can marry in their acquired gender.
Canada Nova Scotia	The Vital Statistics Act section 25 refers. An application can be made to the Registrar General for a notation to be made on the registry where a person has had his/her birth certificate changed to a sex other than that which appears on his birth certificate. The Registrar will require two affidavits from qualified medical practitioners, each deposing that the anatomical sex has changed, and evidence of identity. If the sex of the person is registered outside the Province, the Registrar will transmit a copy of proof of change to the other Registrar. Every birth (or marriage certificate) issued after the making of a notation shall be issued as if the registration had been made of the sex as changed. A trans person is not allowed to marry in their acquired gender. [Although the Province includes a provision with regard to changing the designation of sex on marriage certificates, they do not have the constitutional jurisdiction to overrule the *Corbett* and *Cossey* cases – they still apply to determine the legal validity of any marriage.]
Canada Ontario	The Vital Statistics Act section 36 refers. Where the anatomical sex structure of a person is changed to a sex other than that which appears on the registration of birth, the person may apply to the Registrar General to have the designation of sex on the registration changed so that it is consistent with the results of the transsexual surgery. The Registrar General would require a signed certificate from a qualified medical practitioner stating they performed the surgery on the applicant and that as a result the gender of the applicant should be changed on the birth registration, a certificate of a qualified medical practitioner licensed to practice medicine in Canada, who did not perform the surgery but examined the applicant after the operation to confirm the surgery was performed and therefore the gender of the applicant should be changed on the birth registration. If such medical certificates are unavailable the Registrar may ask for alternative evidence. Satisfactory evidence confirming the identity of the applicant is also a requirement. Every birth certificate issued after the making of a notation shall be issued as if the original registration had been made with the sex as changed. A trans person is not allowed to marry in their acquired gender.
Canada Quebec	In Quebec, the Civil Code recognises the legal status of a transsexual person by granting them the right to change their name and acquired gender on the act of birth provided the person has undergone reassignment surgery and other medical treatment, he/she is unmarried and of full age and is a Canadian citizen resident in Quebec for at least one year. The Registrar of Civil Status will require a certificate from the attending physician and another physician practising in Quebec confirming that the medical treatments and surgical operations involving a structural modification of the sexual organs have been successful. The new designation of sex is entered only in the act of birth of the person concerned. Any decision of the Registrar relating to the assignment of a name or to a change of name or designation of sex may be reviewed by the court, on the application of an interested person.

Country or Territory	Outline of recognition process
Canada Saskatchewan	The Vital Statistics Act sections 29 and 31 refer. A person who has undergone gender reassignment surgery may apply to the Director of Vital Statistics to have the gender changed on their birth registration The director requires a signed certificate by a qualified medical practitioner, licensed to practice medicine in the jurisdiction that the surgery was performed, certifying that he/she performed the surgery on the applicant and as a result the birth registration should be changed to reflect their acquired gender. Where such a certificate is unobtainable, the Director may request any other medical evidence that gender reassignment surgery was performed. The Director will also require a certificate signed by a qualified medical practitioner who did not perform the surgery but examined the applicant after the operation to confirm the surgery was carried out and that the birth registration should be changed to reflect the acquired gender. The Director may ask for any other evidence he/she considers necessary. Every birth certificate issued after registration of birth has been changed is to be issued as if the original registration had been made showing the designation of sex as changed. A trans person is not allowed to marry in the acquired gender.
Canada Yukon Territory	The Vital Statistics Act section 12 refers. An application can be made to the Registrar of Vital Statistics for a notation to be made on the registry where a person has had his/her anatomical sex structure changed to a sex other than that which appears on his birth certificate. The Registrar requires affidavits of two medical practitioners stating the applicant has undergone gender reassignment surgery and evidence of the applicant's identity. If the birth was registered in Yukon the Registrar will make a notation on the original birth registration stating the change of gender, but if the applicant was registered in another Province he/she would transmit a copy of the proof of the change of sex to the appropriate Registrar. Every birth (or marriage) certificate issued after the making of a notation shall be issued as if the registration had been made with the sex as changed. A trans person is not allowed to marry in the acquired gender. [Although the Province includes a provision with regard to changing the designation of sex on marriage certificates, they do not have the constitutional jurisdiction to overrule the *Corbett* and *Cossey* cases – they still apply to determine the legal validity of any marriage.]
(Republic of) Cyprus **EU**	There is some provision for changes to entries in the Population Records (counterpart to UK's Public Records). Although very few and far between, gender changes have been known to have been entered in the Population Record under the administrative regulations governed by the Population Record Law. These regulations in substance gave power of discretion to the Permanent Secretary of the Ministry of the Interior to approve changes (of general nature, without specific reference to gender change) to entries in the Population Record according to individual circumstance. This provision was used as the step on which to base cases for gender change entries. The process followed was one that involved certification of the gender change from the medical authorities, and an application for an amendment to be made to the particular entry in the Population Record.
Denmark EU	Anyone seeking to undergo gender reassignment surgery must notify the Civil Law Division of Ministry of Justice prior to the operation. The CLD authorise the operation to take place. The applicant must be unmarried, be suffering considerably mentally, and supply medical diagnosis of being a transsexual before CLD will 'authorise'. The CLD will inform the Civil Registry who will amend the birth certificate. The original entry in the Registry will be struck out and will refer to the new entry giving the new gender. The fact that this was as a result of gender reassignment surgery will be noted in the observations. A person is deemed to have acquired the new gender after gender reassignment surgery. The trans person can marry in their acquired gender. Denmark grants legal recognition to same-sex couples but limits marriage to opposite-sex couples.
Estonia EU	The main legislation on gender change is the "General Requirements on Medical Procedures of the Change of Gender" issued by the Minister of Social Affairs. This sets out the sequence of action needed to change the gender:- • application to the Ministry of Social Affairs • seeing the medical expert committee who will make a decision about changing the gender, after which the medical (hormonal and surgical) treatment may start • after two years of treatment the expert committee makes a decision on gender change • the person may change all legal documents e.g. birth certificates, ID etc. The change of gender is also mentioned in the Vital Statistics Registration Act which sets out the rules for changing birth certificate, passport and ID card after changing gender and name. Estonian legislation does not set any restrictions on foreigners who have changed their gender and recognises them if their current ID proves that. After the documents have been changed there is no restriction on marrying in acquired gender.
Finland EU	Legislation was introduced in January 2003. Applicants must produce as evidence a medical statement signed by two psychiatrists (from the 2 treating university hospitals). This statement has to include the following: the person permanently believes that he/she belongs to the other gender, and he/she leads a life in this gender role, and he/she is sterilized or is for some other reason not able to conceive. Criteria applied: • is legally of age • sterile (see above)

Country or Territory	Outline of recognition process

- is not married or living in a registered partnership. However, it can be determined that the person who is married or lives in a registered partnership has a different gender to the one indicated in the population-datasystem, if the spouse or other partner in the registered partnership gives his or her consent after being informed of the consequences. In these instances, a marriage is transformed without special measures into a registered partnership, and a registered partnership into a marriage.

- is a Finnish citizen or a citizen of another country living permanently in Finland. Formal gender changes made in another country are accepted in Finland without any Finnish procedures.

The trans person applies to the Local Register Office, who will, having confirmed a person's sex, update the Population Information System to take account of the change including name change. This means that the person will be given a new PIN number. Following issue of a new PIN number the trans person holds equal status of other persons of the same gender.
Any person can, on payment of a fee, obtain from the Local Register Office a certificate showing name, PIN number, address and marital status.
In Finland, birth certificates are hardly ever used – nationals are rarely asked to produce one.

France
EU

There is no statute; only case law codified by two rulings delivered by the Cour de Cassation (the British equivalent of the High Court) in 1992. These provide that when an individual has undergone suitable medical treatment, no longer possesses all the characteristics of original sex and has taken on appearance and social behaviour of the other sex, the individual's civil status should henceforth correspond to the sex of his/her appearance. Legal recognition depends upon medically verified evidence of a transsexual syndrome and treatment (hormone therapy and a surgical operation leading to an artificial change of appearance) modifying the physical appearance to the assumed sex.
Trans people may alter their civil status by amending their birth certificate on application to the county court where birth originally registered. The legal decision to alter an individual's sex and the change of name which this implies, are recorded in the margin of the birth certificate.
An official change of sex does not call into question previous sexual identity i.e. a previous marriage is not retrospectively annulled upon change of sex. This means a French couple can stay married although the gender change is a ground for nullity if the parties request it. It us up to them to decide. The Civil Code refers.
A trans person may marry in their acquired gender but a pre-operative transsexual may not legally marry because marriage in France is only possible with a member of the opposite sex to that which appears on the person's original birth certificate.

Germany
EU

Legislation exists for recognition of acquired gender. A court can decide that a person should belong to the opposite sex where:

- the applicant must has lived for three years in opposite gender

- is unmarried

- of age

- permanently sterile, and

- has undergone surgical operation to obtain reasonable appearance of opposite sex.

They must also provide reports from two experts stating that their feeling of belonging to opposite gender will not change. Surgical operation is the imperative condition for a change of sex.
A note is made in the margin of the birth record and the civil status record is noted with details of the court's decision. if a new birth certificate is issued following legal recognition, this will show only the acquired gender.
Full legal recognition is achieved for all purposes including marriage. Pre-operative transsexuals are not able to marry in their new gender.
Under current legislation pre-operative transsexuals may only marry in the original gender to a person of the opposite sex. But as those undergoing an official name/sex change must be single or divorced at the time, there is no provision for a pre-operative marriage to continue. The Federal Government was (in March 2002) considering updating the legislation of 1980 and amongst the reforms they will consider whether a marriage can, after change of gender by one of the parties, be re-registered as a same-sex partnership (a measure introduced in August 2001). A communication in January 2004 from a member of the Commission Internationale De L'Etat Civil/
International Commission on Civil Status, indicates that the 1980 legislation was still in force at that time.
Germany gives legal recognition to same-sex couples but limits marriage to opposite-sex couples.

Greece
EU

No legislation but transsexual people can change name and identity papers following surgical operation. According to jurisprudence, it is necessary that this operation is imposed because of therapeutic needs (psychological, hermaphrodism or predisposition towards the other sex). The judgement orders the modification of the birth certificate, which involves modification of all the administrative documents.
There are no legal provisions relating to marriage.

Country or Territory	Outline of recognition process
Iceland EEA	No provisions in legislation or administrative rules concerning gender change per se. However, Icelandic Health Service Act states in Article 1 that everybody is entitled to the best health service possible for the protection of their mental, physical and social health and it is in accordance with this Article that procedures have been carried out. Directorate of Health decides whether an operation to change gender is permitted or not. In practice all applications are directed to The Board of Gender Operations which consists of two psychiatrists, one plastic surgeon, one gynaecologist and one urological surgeon. Process is lengthy, involving direct interviews with applicants, physical examination and interviews with psychiatrists. The Board looks at medical records and focuses on medical symptoms and gender identity disorder. The Board then gives its opinion on whether permission is granted to have an operation to change gender. Medical Director of Health takes final decision and is there is an appeals process. All expenses paid for by The National Health Service, including hormone treatment. Birth certificate is issued (which includes a comment that the gender has been changed), and the new gender is registered following surgical intervention. Original gender registration cannot be changed. Even though there is no special legislation it is considered that if the registration of gender has changed the person gains most of the legal standards of persons of the acquired gender inter alia concerning marriage, inheritance law and right to adopt.
Italy EU	A change of sex is recognised after due legal process. Legislation was introduced in 1982 stipulating an operation had to be authorised by a court, which also authorises the register of population to rectify the birth certificate. The law does not distinguish between hormonal treatment or surgery – it considers the sexual-psychological characteristics to be most significant, and provides for the court to authorise the medical-surgical treatment which will bring the individual anatomically into line with these characteristics. The amendment of the individual's civil status is subordinated to subsequent verification that the treatment has been carried out. The law does not clarify the nature or extent of the reassignment required for recognition in the acquired gender – in practice it is considered sufficient for the individual's physical appearance to correspond overall with that of the new sex. Once the birth record has been altered as a result of the court's authorisation, all civil status certificates will bear the new name and sex, including the birth certificate. Full legal recognition is given for all purposes, including marriage. Change of sex can be recognised even if individual is married. However, spouse can have marriage impugned if they have been misled provided action is taken within 12 months of discovering the 'error'. A change of gender is also grounds for divorce.
Japan	Law 111 July 16th 2003 refers. The law came into force in July 2004. In this law a person suffering from gender identity disorder means a person who, against his/her defined biological sex, has persistent conviction that he/she belongs to the opposite sex and has a will to make himself/herself into physical and social conformity with the opposite sex; provided that two or more physicians who have experience and expertise required to properly make such a diagnosis, should make such a diagnosis on the subject concerned based upon accepted medical standards. Applicants • should be of or above age 20 • should be unmarried at present • should not have a child • should not have gonad or should be in permanent loss of gonadal function • should have a part of body which assumes the external genital features of the opposite sex. Applicant with GID must submit medical certificate by the physicians which details progress of treatments, results of treatments and other prescribed matters. Upon approval from Family Court, the registry can be changed with respect to sex.
Latvia EU	No legislation but medical institution will make necessary medical changes. Afterwards, commission of Doctors state gender changes have been made and make a separate note of this. On the basis of the note the regional registry office changes gender of person.
Luxembourg EU	No legislation but changes of sex admitted by jurisprudence. The court only rules in favour if they are deeply convinced the individual is the victim of an error of nature and they come to this conclusion after examining several medical certificates or a complete medical file reflecting various stages of treatment. The court often names a Doctor to make psychological evaluation too. Change of sex not recognised except after an operation which has involved a complete assimilation of the genitals to the sex organs to which the individual wants to belong. This operation is preceded by psychological analysis and hormonal treatment, etc. Given complete assimilation sterility is not an issue. The judgement recognising the change of sex allows the applicant to obtain an amended birth certificate in the new gender. [Case law on the question of birth certificates is not however consistent: some judgements have resulted in the acquired gender being added to the birth certificates with mention that the birth gender is to be replaced by the new gender, whilst other judgements have stated that a new birth certificate in the acquired gender should be provided.] The right of a trans person to marry in their acquired gender and the recognition of a change of gender have, as of March 2002, not been tested.

Country or Territory	Outline of recognition process
Malta **EU**	No legislation. However, two judgements of the Constitutional Court resulted in changes to birth certificates following surgical intervention.

> (1)   *Cassar vs. Hon. Prime Minister et* [decided 14/7/1995] – The Court ordered the Director of Public Registry to add to the birth certificate of the person in question a declaration stating that as from the date of the surgical intervention 'A' changed to the female sex and is to be known as 'B'.

> (2)   *Gilford vs Director of Public Registry* [decided 9/10/2001] – The Court of First Instance ordered as a remedy that the Director is to change the birth certificate and instead of 'boy' writes 'girl' and changes the name 'A' to 'B' whilst noting that this change took place in execution of this judgement and after the applicant had undergone a surgical intervention of 'gender reassignment' on the {date}. The applicant had appealed against the last annotation whereby there is mentioned that the change in the public act was made after surgical intervention. The Constitutional Court finally ordered that such annotation be removed so as not to prejudice the applicant any further.

Thus, whilst there is no statute which governs gender recognition, Maltese Courts have recognised gender changes and allowed amendments to birth certificates. Maltese law does not allow that new birth certificates be issued and all amendments are to be reflected on the original birth certificate. There is no law that regulates marriage between homosexuals.

Moldova	Moldova's recognition process is almost identical to that for transsexuals in the Ukraine and Russian Federation. In the Ukraine once gender reassignment surgery has occurred an individual may change all of his/her documents which state sex and name to a new gender and set of names / patronymic / surnames. The procedure for this is as follows: the individual gives the authorities a 'resolution' from the medical commission along with a petition, the original birth certificate and a small payment. All this is done at the registry office of the place where the trans person is currently living (as opposed to place of birth). The registry office sends this information to the registry office of the applicant's place of birth. At this stage the registrar crosses out the old name, patronymic and surname in the book of registration of births, writes in the new details, makes a new birth certificate and sends it to the registry office that originally dealt with the case. The applicant is then given the new birth certificate and a certificate of change of name / patronymic / surname. The new birth certificate of a transgendered person will be no different to that of a pre-op transsexual apart from the fact that it will convey the correct gender. Any non-primary birth certificate will have duplicate stamp marks on them, distinguishing them from other birth certificates.
Netherlands EU	Legislation exists. Individual must be sterile and have undergone full gender reassignment surgery or at least partial reassignment surgery if the person concerned is convinced, to the satisfaction of a team of medical and psychiatric experts, that the wish to change is permanent. If the court orders a change of gender, the registrar makes an entry on the birth certificate record of the order. Any change to the sex stated on the birth certificate does not affect family law relationships. There are no restrictions on the right of the trans person to marry in their acquired gender. Same sex marriages are now allowed. Therefore the requirement under the 1985 law to be single to qualify for legal recognition of their new gender is abolished but the Civil Code was modified, and the condition imposed is that transsexual people should not be married until he/she presents the request for modification of his/her birth certificate to the court and it is crossed out.
New Zealand	The Births, Deaths and Marriages Act 1995 refers. An application is made to the Family Court for a declaration as to the appropriate sex to be shown on the birth certificate. The court will issue such a declaration if the applicant is over 18 years of age and unmarried. If lawfully married, the Act prohibits a new registration since this would result in same-sex marriage. Such applicants therefore face a choice of not having their new gender registered or having to dissolve their marriage. The court must also be satisfied by evidence that the applicant:

- has assumed (or has always had) the gender identity of a person of the nominated sex, and

- has undergone such medical treatment as is usually regarded by medical experts as desirable to enable persons of the genetic and physical conformation that accords with the gender identity of a person of the nominated sex, and

- will, as a result of the medical treatment undertaken, maintain a gender identity of a person of the nominated sex.

Country or Territory	Outline of recognition process
	Documents presented to the court will include affidavits by the applicant describing their personal background and their intention to continue to function as a person of their nominated sex, supported by statements by medical professionals which state that the applicant has had irreversible gender re-assignment surgery, and is undertaking ongoing/has completed hormone treatment etc. and any other relevant documentation. In the case of a child under 18 who has never married, the child's guardian may make an application to the court. Where the issue of marriage is not involved, and no contrary medical evidence has been presented, the effect of a successful sex change re-registration is that applicants create for themselves a new identity. However, the Act also states that the sex of every person shall continue to be determined by reference to the general law in NZ. Although the expectation is that registration of the new gender will be recognised for all legal purposes this has, with the exception of marriage, largely been untested. Where a person has undergone surgical and medical procedures that have effectively given that person the physical conformation of a person of a specified sex, there is no lawful impediment to that person marrying as a person of that sex.
Norway **EEA**	No specific legislation. Treatment (psychological and hormonal) and operations available on the equivalent of NHS. National ID numbers are changed. A name change in the Population Register can be effected before operation with approval of County Governor or Ministry of Justice, but after surgery it can be done by direct notification to the Population Register.
Poland **EU**	Polish nationals can be granted legal recognition of their gender change by a civil court. Following such a decision, applicants can apply to a borough-equivalent local authority (Starosta) for a change of name. The Starosta then decides whether to approve the change of name on grounds of gender change, and if so it forwards the decision to the Birth Certificate Registrar. The birth certificate remains unchanged, but information about the gender change is appended. According to the Supreme Court, a change in civil status is in principle justified only after surgery. An applicant is entitled to apply for a new ID on grounds of significant changes of personal data and thereby gets a new Personal Identification Number. He/she is entitled to apply for a new passport in his/her new name. He/she has a right to get married with the same legal provisions as for all other citizens.
Romania	Legal provisions on gender change are in Article 44 of Law no. 119 of 1996 on the civil status documents and in Article 4 of Government Ordinance no. 41 of 2003 which provides that a person can request the competent administrative bodies (i.e. the president of the county council) to approve modification of first name following a court decision. To that end applicant has to provide a copy of a court decision that ruled on the gender change (a gender change can only be recognised by a final and irrevocable decision of the court), along with a copy of a forensic medical document which shows current gender. Neither of the above articles contain rules on criteria to be satisfied before a court could give a positive ruling. (There is no published case law either.) In the opinion of the Professor of Law and former Chief Justice the court would use medical criteria involving a forensic medical report prepared by licensed doctors upon the request of the court. Although there are no explicit legal provisions in this respect, the Professor's advice is that such a person would be able to marry in the acquired gender.
Russian Federation	Once gender reassignment surgery has occurred an individual may change all of his/her documents which state sex and name to a new gender and set of names / patronymic / surnames. The procedure for this is as follows: the individual gives the authorities a 'resolution' from the medical commission along with a petition, the original birth certificate and a small payment. All this is done at the registry office of the place where the trans person is currently living (as opposed to place of birth). The registry office sends this information to the registry office of the applicant's place of birth. At this stage the registrar crosses out the old name, patronymic and surname in the book of registration of births, writes in the new details, makes a new birth certificate and sends it to the registry office that originally dealt with the case. The applicant is then given the new birth certificate and a certificate of change of name / patronymic / surname. The new birth certificate of a transgendered person will be no different to that of a pre-op transsexual apart from the fact that it will convey the correct gender. (Birth certificates in the former USSR did not have a column for "sex" but had in particular a patronymic column which in the case of the Russian language indicates a specific gender.) Any non-primary birth certificate will have duplicate stamp marks on them, distinguishing them from other birth certificates.
Serbia and Montenegro	No legislation but once the final medical procedures (surgical, hormonal therapy etc.) are over, a medical certificate is issued confirming the gender process has been completed. After that, the transsexual submits a request for a name and gender change to the Local Registrar Office. In addition to the request form, the trans person will have to present all the relevant medical records, together with numerous other types of certificates (e.g. that the individual does not have a criminal record, parents' birth/death certificates etc.). Once the trans person receives the new birth certificate (with the new name and gender) all the details in the birth certificate (including the gender) will be automatically legally valid and recognised.

Country or Territory	Outline of recognition process
Slovakia EU	The law provides for official administrative recognition. Birth numbers will be changed on basis of official medical statement evidencing change of gender. [An Amicus Brief from Liberty indicates that administrators will allow a transsexual to change their name and birth certificate if a Doctor can issue a letter stating that gender reassignment surgery has been successfully completed. The surgery is legally available.]
Slovenia EU	If person submits a Doctor's certificate on change of gender the Register of Civil Status Act will fully recognise the change of gender and issue applicant with a birth certificate accordingly.
Spain EU	Spanish legislature legalised transsexual surgical operations in reformation of penal code. Before the creation of new administrative documents in favour of the transsexual person, it is necessary for the individual to pursue the following process: • to adapt his/her sex and anatomical-morphologic to his/her behaviour psychical and social sex by means of surgicalintervention, completed with corresponding medical hormonal treatment • to obtain a firm judicial judgement recognising the sex change • to modify the birth entry to show the acquired sex and birth forename. Sterility is not envisaged as a condition. The change of sex and forename is proved by means of the certification of the Civil Register and national identity document delivered after the change. Legally, transsexual people keep the sex they had at birth even though documents can be issued in the new name and gender. Neither pre nor post operative transsexuals are allowed to marry.
Sweden EU	Legislation is contained in the Determination of Gender in Certain Cases Act 1972. Applications made to the Legal Council of the National Board of Health and Welfare. There is an authorising panel consisting of a judge, 2/3 physicians, one social scientist and one lay person. Applicant must be a Swedish citizen, at least 18 years old, sterile, unmarried, must feel they were born into wrong gender since youth, have lived in this situation for a long time and expect to continue doing so for foreseeable future and completed a one year life test and at least a two year consultation period. The Council will in practice recognise change of gender after completion of a 'one year life test' but the person must also have been in contact with a psychiatrist and Legal Council evaluation team for at least two years before lodging an application. Hormonal treatment can be started after 9 months of consultation. Legally the change of gender is recognised only after the new national identity number is obtained following the ruling of the National Board of Health and Welfare. Following a Board ruling, a trans person has legal recognition in the new gender for all purposes, including marriage. Sweden grants legal recognition to same-sex couples but limits marriage to opposite-sex couples.
Switzerland	Each case subject to Court decision. Irreversible surgery required and must be sterile. Doctor's certificate required confirming surgery has taken place. Inscription in the registry of new name and sex. Existing marriages must be ended.
Turkey	Applications are made to the Court. The individual must not be married. He/she should have a transsexual outlook, and should prove by an official health committee report from an education and research hospital, that a sex change is absolutely necessary for his/her mental health, and that he/she is completely deprived of fecundity. Those changing their sex can get an identity card recognising their acquired gender after applying to the Civil Court and providing physical/medical evidence that confirms their change of sex. After Court approval of their acquired gender, they can apply to the Directorate of Birth Records to change the sex registered on their birth certificates. Once this is done they can be legally recognised in their acquired gender.
Ukraine	The Ministry of Justice of Ukraine gave instructions to all registry offices in Ukraine to authorise the change of names of transsexuals only after reassignment surgery was completed. Surgery will only be completed after at least one year of full psychological and social adaptation in the desired gender. Once gender reassignment surgery has occurred an individual may change all of his/her documents which state sex and name to a new gender and set of names / patronymic / surnames. The procedure for this is as follows: the individual gives the authorities a 'resolution' from the medical commission along with a petition, the original birth certificate and a small payment. All this is done at the registry office of the place the trans person is currently living (as opposed to place of birth). The registry office sends this information to the registry office of the applicant's place of birth. At this stage the registrar crosses out the old name, patronymic and surname in the book of registration of births, writes in the new details, makes a new birth certificate and sends it to the registry office that originally dealt with the case. The applicant is then given the new birth certificate and a certificate of change of name / patronymic / surname. The new birth certificate of a transgendered person will be no different to that of a pre-op transsexual apart from the fact that it will convey the correct gender. Any non-primary birth certificate will have duplicate stamp marks on them, distinguishing them from other birth certificates.
United States of America	

Country or Territory	Outline of recognition process
Alabama	Specific statute: Ala. Code § 229A-19(d) Alabama will issue an 'amended' birth certificate noting change of name and sex, but will not issue a new birth certificate replacing the original. Court Order required for name change and Doctor's letter verifying SRS for gender change on birth certificate.
Alaska	General Statute: Ala Stat. § 18.50.320 Alaska will issue an amended birth certificate noting change of name and sex. Court Order required for name change and Doctor's letter verifying SRS for gender change on birth certificate.
Arizona	Specific Statute: Ariz. Rev. Stat. § 36-326 (A)(4) Arizona will change both name and sex, and will issue a new birth certificate rather than amend the old one. The original certificate is 'closed' to further inspection. Court Order required for name change and Doctor's letter verifying SRS for gender change (along with current identification) on birth certificate.
Arkansas	Specific Statute: Ark. Code Ann. § 20-18-307 Arkansas will change both name and sex, and will issue a new birth certificate if the Court Order so specifies. Court Order required for name change and Doctor's letter verifying SRS for gender change on birth certificate.
California	Specific Statute: Cal. Health and Safety Code § 103425 California will change both name and sex, and will issue new birth certificate rather than amend the old one. For name change on birth certificate a Court Order is required but if applicant has no Court Order he/she may petition the court for change of name at the same time as they petition for a new birth certificate. A Doctor's letter verifying SRS required. Hysterectomy/orchidectomy required.
Colorado	Specific Statute: Colo. Rev. Stat. 25-2-115 Colorado will change both name and sex, and will issue a new birth certificate rather than amend the old one. For the birth certificate a certified copy of name change Order, signed by the Judge, along with a notarised letter from the surgeon verifying SRS and a notarised letter from trans person asking for the change in information, is required.
Connecticut	Specific Statute: Conn. Gen. Stat. § 19a-42 Connecticut will change both name and sex. The birth certificate is marked 'amended,' but the item(s) amended are not specified. (New law passed on October 1st 2001 means birth certificates are now amended without the asterisks that were previously used.) A Court Order is not required but documentation from SRS surgeon is.
Delaware	General Statute: Del. Code Ann. Tit. 16 § 3131 Delaware will change both name and sex, and will issue a new birth certificate rather than amend the old one. Court Order required for name change on birth certificate plus Doctor's letter that SRS is completed.
District of Columbia (Washington DC)	Specific Statute: D.C. Code Ann. § 7-217(d) The District of Columbia will NOT issue a new birth certificate, but will amend the original birth certificate. Court Order required for name change and letter from surgeon who performed SRS.
Florida	General Statute: Fla. Stat. Ch. 29, § 382.016 Birth records can now be changed. (Until recently the Department of Vital Statistics would not change the gender but if presented with Court Order for a name change they may have done so.) A statement from any licensed physician (that the sex-change was completed or that the original certificate is in fact in error), and a Court Order for name change required.
Georgia	Specific Statute: Ga. Code Ann. § 31-10-23(e) Georgia will change both name and sex, and will issue a new birth certificate rather than amend the old one. Court Order required for name change on birth certificate and letter from Doctor verifying SRS for gender change.
Hawaii	Specific Statute: Haw. Rev. Stat. 338-17.7(4) Hawaii will change both name and sex, and will issue a new birth certificate rather than amend the old one. One source of information indicates a Court Order is required for name change on birth certificate but another source indicates it's not. Both however state a letter from Doctor verifying SRS for gender change is necessary.
Illinois	Specific Statute: 410 Ill. Comp. Stat. 535/17(d) Illinois will change both name and sex, and will issue a new birth certificate rather than amend. Birth certificates can be changed via certified copy of Court Order for name change plus original letter from SRS surgeon.

Country or Territory	Outline of recognition process
Indiana	General Statute: Ind. Code § 16-37-2-10 Indiana will issue a new birth certificate with your new name. Indiana does not include the sex on a birth certificate. The original letter from the SRS surgeon required plus copy of Court Order for name change and copy of old birth certificate.
Iowa	General Statute: Iowa Code IV § 144.38 Iowa will change both name and sex, and will issue a new birth certificate rather than amend the old one. Name change on birth certificate via Court Order. Gender change requires original letter from SRS surgeon.
Kansas	Kan. Admin. Regs. 28-17-20(b)(1)(A)(i) permits amendment in the event of sex reassignment. This is done through an administrative process. An affidavit is required from applicant documenting dressing and living in new gender. One source indicates for a name change a Court Order is required and the same source states a gender change requires Doctor's certification verifying SRS whilst another indicates documentation of hormone treatment and surgery (physiological or hormonal change) is required.
Kentucky	Specific Statute: Ky. Rev. Stat. Ann. § 213.121 (5) Kentucky will change both name and sex, and will issue a new birth certificate rather than amend the old one. Name change on birth certificate via Court Order. Gender change requires doctor's original letter verifying SRS.
Louisiana	Specific Statute: La. Rev. Stat. Ann. 40:62 Louisiana will change both name and sex, and will issue a new birth certificate rather than amend the old one. An original letter from SRS surgeon required along with an original or copy of the order for a name change which must be approved by the District Attorney. If married, the spouse must give written consent for the changes.
Maine	Code Me. R. § 10-146 Chpt. 2 refers. Maine will change both name and sex and issue a new birth certificate but it is done through an administrative process. An original letter from SRS surgeon plus Court Order for name change required.
Maryland	Specific Statute: Md. Code Ann., Health-General § 4-214 refers. The Division of Vital Records can change sex and name on birth certificate. Court Orders required for name and gender change on the birth certificate. The old birth record simply has a line drawn through the information unless the trans person has the Court Order direct the department to issue a new birth record.
Massachusetts	Specific Statute: Mass. Gen. Laws ch. 46. § 13(e) Massachusetts will issue an amended birth certificate. A copy of the court-ordered name change and a notarised copy of proof of the completed SRS are required.
Michigan	Specific Statute: Mich. Comp. Law S. § 333.283(c) Michigan will change both name and sex, and will issue a new birth certificate rather than amend the old one. Michigan law also provides for 'sealing' of the old record – see Michigan Compiled Law 333.2831. For name change a Court Order is required and for gender change the original letter from SRS surgeon.
Minnesota	General Statute: Minn. Stat. § 144.218(4) Minnesota will issue an amended birth certificate. A Court Order for name change is not required but original letter from SRS surgeon is for gender change. Only an amended birth certificate can be issued. However the Department of Vital Statistics will provide an abstract of the certificate which does not have any of the old information on it.
Mississippi	General Statute: Miss. Code Ann. § 41-57-21 With a Court Order an amended birth certificate can be issued with the new name and gender typed in the margin. The old name and gender remain unchanged. Trans person required to provide letter requesting change to birth certificate, a certified copy of a name change Order and a letter from a Doctor confirming SRS.
Missouri	Specific Statute: Mo. Rev. Stat. § 193.215 Missouri will issue an amended birth certificate. Upon receipt of a certified copy of an order of a court of competent jurisdiction changing the name of a person born in this state and upon request of such person or such person's parents, guardian or legal representative, the state registrar shall amend the certificate of birth to show the new name. Upon receipt of a certified copy of an order of a court of competent jurisdiction indicating the sex of an individual born in this state has been changed by surgical procedure and that such individual's name has been changed, the certificate of birth of such individual shall be amended.

Country or Territory	Outline of recognition process
Montana	General Statute: Mont. Code Ann. § 50-15 Name change on birth certificate requires Court Order if last name changed. If only the first name has changed than an affidavit is required. If the first name change is a gender change name then an affidavit is needed saying a correction is required. This affidavit must be signed by a psychiatrist who indicates that the trans person is and has been living in the acquired gender. They redline the incorrect information and type in the correct information. Another source states that this State will issue an amended birth certificate, but that what can be amended in unclear. This source goes on to say an original letter from SRS surgeon required along with original or copy of the Court Order for the name change.
Nebraska	Specific Statute: Neb. Rev. Stat. § 71-604.01 Nebraska will change both name and sex, and will issue a new birth certificate rather than amend the old one. For a name change on the birth certificate a Court Order of name change is required and a Doctor's affidavit (or one source indicates the original letter from the surgeon) of SRS.
Nevada	Nev. Admin. Code 440.130 applies. Nevada will change both name and sex, and will issue a new birth certificate rather than amend the old one. An original letter from SRS surgeon plus an original or certified copy of the Court Order for the name change. [Another source indicates a Court Order is required specifically directing the Department of Vital Statistics to issue a new birth certificate.]
New Hampshire	General Statute: N.H. Rev. Stat. Ann. 126:23-a New Hampshire will change both name and sex, and will issue a new birth certificate rather than amend the old one. The same source indicates a Court Order is only required for the name change along with an original letter from the SRS surgeon. However, another (older) source indicates that for both name and gender change on birth certificate a Court Order is required.
New Jersey	Specific Statute: N.J. Stat. Ann. 26:8-40.12 New Jersey will change both name and sex, and will issue a new birth certificate rather than amend the old one. An original or certified copy of a name change Order, a copy of the original birth record and a notarised statement from the surgeon confirming SRS are required.
New Mexico	Specific Statute: N.M. Stat. Ann. § 24-14-25(D) New Mexico will change both name and sex, and will issue a new birth certificate rather than amend the old one. The old information will be 'sealed' and cannot be opened without a Court Order. An original letter from the SRS surgeon and an original or certified copy of the Court Order for name change required.
New York	**New York City** – see 24 R.C.N.Y. Hlth. Code § 207.01 New York City has its own separate Bureau of Vital Statistics. New York City will issue a new birth certificate rather than amend the old one. The new birth certificate will list the new name but will not have a listing for sex at all; that section is omitted. An original or certified copy of the Court Order for the name change plus original letters from the SRS surgeon and the psychiatrist/psychologist required. **New York State** New York State will change both name and sex, and will issue a new birth certificate. New York requires more documentation than most States. The applicant must first complete an application form available from the State of New York Department of Health, Vital Records Section. The application must include the following documents: 1 a Court Order for name change, bearing the court seal, certified by the clerk of the court is required. The Court Order must include original name, date and place of birth. 2 a certified proof of publication 3 a letter from the SRS surgeon, specifying date, place, and type of procedure 4 an operative report from the SRS 5 a letter from the primary therapist documenting 'true transsexualism or inappropriate sexual identification', as set by the guidelines of the State of New York 6 a letter from the endocrinologist or other medical physician 'concerning hormonal, chromosomal or endocrinological information.' Once these documents are received, a 'medical review' will be performed, and a new certificate issued.
North Carolina	Specific Statute: N.C. Gen. Stat. § 130A-118 North Carolina will change both name and sex, and will issue a new birth certificate rather than amend the old one. An original letter from the SRS surgeon plus an original or certified copy of the Court Order for the name change required.

Country or Territory	Outline of recognition process
North Dakota	General Statute: N.D. Cent. Code § 23-02.1-25 North Dakota will issue an amended birth certificate. An original or certified copy of the Court Order for the name change plus an original letter from the SRS surgeon.
Oklahoma	General Statute: Okla. Stat. Tit. 63, § 1-321 Oklahoma will issue an amended birth certificate. Name change on birth certificate can be effected by Court Order (another source states Court Order not required), along with original letter from doctor confirming completion of SRS.
Oregon	Specific Statute: Or. Rev. Stat. § 432.235 Oregon will change both name and sex, and will issue an amended birth certificate, without any designation of what has been amended. An original or certified copy of the Court Order for the name change and an original letter from the SRS surgeon (or an original Court Order for the change of sex designation) required.
Pennsylvania	General Statute: 35 Pa. Cons. Stat. § 450.603 Pennsylvania will change both name and sex, and will issue a new birth certificate with no mention of being amended. The original birth certificate is amended and 'sealed' so that it is unavailable to the public. An original letter from the SRS surgeon and an original or certified copy of the Court Order for the name change required. [Another source indicates the surgery must be irreversible.]
Rhode Island	General Statute: R.I. Gen. Laws § 23-3-21 Rhode Island will issue an amended birth certificate, with a note designating the change of name. The change of sex is not marked as a change on the amended certificate. An original letter from the SRS surgeon required. A Court Order is not. Another (older source) however states birth certificates can be easily changed as no gender appears on them. Court Order required.
South Carolina	General Statute: S.C. Code Ann. § 44-63-150 South Carolina will NOT issue a new birth certificate. They will send a 'card' that can be attached to the old birth certificate, indicating change of name and sex. An original Court Order for the name change is required and a letter from the SRS surgeon.
South Dakota	General Statute: S.D. Codified Laws § 35-25-51 Court Order required to change both name and gender on the birth certificate.
Utah	Specific Statute: Utah Code Ann. § 26-2-11 Utah will issue an amended certificate, changing both name and sex, and the certificate will not reveal which items were changed. An original or certified copy of a Court Order for the name change and a Court Order for the change of sex designation required. (These Court Orders can be from any U.S. State or from Canada.)
Vermont	General Statute: Vt. Stat. Ann. tit. 18 § 5075 Vermont will issue an amended certificate, changing both name and sex. An original or certified copy of a Court Order for the name change and a Court Order for the change of sex designation required. The court will (probably) require documentation from the SRS surgeon.
Virginia	Specific Statute: Va. Code Ann. § 32.1-269 Virginia will change both name and sex, and will issue a new birth certificate rather than amend the old one. An original letter from the SRS surgeon and an original or certified copy of the Court Order for the name change required. Another (older) source indicates certified copies of the name change and gender change required for birth certificate change, or the trans person may also submit a notarised statement from the surgeon or copies of medical records confirming SRS.
Washington	Washington will issue an amended certificate, changing both name and sex. No statute, but issues amended birth certificates through an administrative process. An original or certified copy of a Court Order for the name change and a Court Order for the change of sex designation (or a letter from the SRS surgeon).
West Virginia	General Statute: W. Va. Code § 16-5-24 West Virginia will change both name and sex, and will issue a new birth certificate rather than amend the old one. An original or certified copy of the Court Order for the name change and an original letter from the SRS surgeon required.

Country or Territory	Outline of recognition process
Wisconsin	Specific Statute: Wis. Stat. § 69.15 Wisconsin will change both name and sex, and will issue a new birth certificate. (If applicants check the box on the application form to 'IMPOUND' the original this will cause the original certificate to be closed to further inspection.) An original letter from the SRS surgeon should include the name, date of birth, date of surgery, type of surgery i.e.male-to-female required along with an original or certified copy of the Court Order for the name change.
Wyoming	General Statute: Wyo. Stat. Ann. § 35-1-424 Wyoming will issue an amended certificate. The certificate will specify the birth name and the birth gender, unless a Court Order is obtained mandating a new certificate be created. (Whilst the indication of medical criteria applicable is not clear, reg. 10-5 states "when the sex change of an individual has been changed, a court order shall be required to amend the birth certificate.")

A3.5

Glossary[1]

Acquired gender

The new gender of a person who has undergone gender reassignment and/or legally recognised. It is possible for an individual to transition fully without surgical intervention.

Cross-dresser

The term refers to a person who wears the clothing of the opposite sex because it is the clothing of the opposite sex. This excludes people who wear opposite sex clothing for other reasons. Cross-dressers may not identify with, or want to be the opposite gender, nor adopt the behaviours or practices of the opposite gender, and generally do not want to change their bodies. This term is associated with transvestite, though some cross-dressers would not identify as such.

FtM

Female to male trans person. A person who is changing, or has changed, their gender role from female to male. Also described as a 'trans man'.

Gender

Gender refers to socially constructed roles, behaviours, activities, and attributes. The terms 'man', 'masculine', 'woman', and 'feminine' denote gender.

Gender dysphoria

Gender dysphoria is the medical term for the condition in which a person assigned one gender (usually at birth on the basis of their sex), identifies as belonging to another gender, or does not conform with the gender role their respective society prescribes to them.

Gender identity

The way in which an individual identifies with a gender category,

Gender reassignment

The term 'gender reassignment' applies to the process of transitioning from one gender to another. The term used in the Equality Act to describe people who intend to transition, are transitioning or have transitioned is 'transsexual'. So, a person who intends to undergo, is undergoing or has undergone a process of gender reassignment (which may or may not involve hormone therapy or surgery) is a transsexual person.

---

[1] Our gratitude goes to the Equality and Human Rights Commission (EHRC) for allowing us to use this glossary from their publications on Trans Research Review (November 2011) and Collecting Information on Gender Identity (December 2011).

GRA

Gender Recognition Act 2004.

GRC

Gender Recognition Certificate. A full Gender Recognition Certificate shows that a person has satisfied the criteria for legal recognition in the acquired gender. It makes the recipient of the certificate, for all intents and purposes, the sex listed on the certificate from that moment onward. The legal basis for creating a Gender Recognition Certificate is found in the Gender Recognition Act 2004.

GRS

Gender reassignment surgery.

Intersex

There are a number of intersex conditions (recently renamed Disorders of Sex Development), some of which lead to physical genital anomalies. Those born with them may experience inconsistency between their gender identity and the gender role assigned at birth.

LGBT

Lesbian, Gay, Bisexual and Transgender. Where this group does not include trans people it is referred to as LGB.

MtF

Male to female trans person. A person who is changing, or has changed, their gender role from male to female. Also described as a 'trans woman'.

Sex

Sex refers to biological and physiological characteristics. In Britain, the terms 'male' and 'female' are used in birth certificates to denote the sex of children. Sex and gender, and the terms, 'male/female' and 'man/woman' are often used and understood interchangeably. However, in the research literature, sex and gender are considered separately.

Trans

The terms 'trans people' and 'transgender people' are both often used as umbrella terms for people whose gender identity and/or gender expression differs from their birth sex, including transsexual people (those who intend to undergo, are undergoing or have undergone a process of gender reassignment to live permanently in their acquired gender), transvestite/cross-dressing people (those who wear clothing traditionally associated with the other gender either occasionally or more regularly), androgyne/polygender people (those who do not identify with male or female identities and do not identify as male or female), and others who define as gender variant.

Transgender

An umbrella term for people whose gender identity and/or gender expression differs from their birth sex. They may or may not seek to undergo gender reassignment hormonal treatment/surgery. Often used interchangeably with trans.

Transsexual

The term used in the Equality Act to describe people who intend to transition, are transitioning or have transitioned is 'transsexual'. So, a person who intends to undergo, is undergoing or has undergone a process of gender reassignment (which may or may not involve hormone therapy or surgery) is a transsexual person.

Transvestite

The term used to describe a person who dresses in the clothing of the opposite sex. Generally, transvestites do not wish to alter their body and do not necessarily experience gender dysphoria.

EqA 2010

The Equality Act 2010

Appendix 4

STATUTORY MATERIALS

Statutory Provisions

A4.1   Children Act 1989

A4.2   Civil Partnership Act 2004

A4.3   Family Law Act 1996

A4.4   Gender Recognition Act 2004

A4.5   Housing Act 1985

A4.6   Housing Act 1988

A4.7   Human Fertilisation and Embryology Act 2008

A4.8   Inheritance (Provision for Family and Dependants) Act 1975

A4.9   Rent Act 1977

A4.10   Surrogacy Arrangements Act 1985

A4.11   Trusts of Land and Appointment of Trustees Act 1996

A4.1

CHILDREN ACT 1989

ARRANGEMENT OF SECTIONS

PART I
INTRODUCTORY

Section		*Page*
1	Welfare of the child	461
2	Parental responsibility for children	461
3	Meaning of 'parental responsibility'	462
4	Acquisition of parental responsibility by father	463
4ZA	Acquisition of parental responsibility by second female parent	463
4A	Acquisition of parental responsibility by step-parent	464
5	Appointment of guardians	464
6	Guardians: revocation and disclaimer	465
7	Welfare reports	466

PART II
ORDERS WITH RESPECT TO CHILDREN IN FAMILY PROCEEDINGS

General

8	Residence, contact and other orders with respect to children	467
9	Restrictions on making section 8 orders	468
10	Power of court to make section 8 orders	468
11	General principles and supplementary provisions	470
11A	Contact activity directions	470
11B	Contact activity directions: further provision	471
11C	Contact activity conditions	472
11D	Contact activity conditions: further provision	472
11E	Contact activity directions and conditions: making	473
11F	Contact activity directions and conditions: financial assistance	473
11G	Contact activity directions and conditions: monitoring	474
11H	Monitoring contact	474
11I	Contact orders: warning notices	475
11J	Enforcement orders	475
11K	Enforcement orders: further provision	476
11L	Enforcement orders: making	476
11M	Enforcement orders: monitoring	477
11N	Enforcement orders: warning notices	477
11O	Compensation for financial loss	477
11P	Orders under section 11O(2): further provision	478
12	Residence orders and parental responsibility	479
13	Change of child's name or removal from jurisdiction	479
14	Enforcement of residence orders	479

Special guardianship

14A	Special guardianship orders	480
14B	Special guardianship orders: making	481
14C	Special guardianship orders: effect	481
14D	Special guardianship orders: variation and discharge	482
14E	Special guardianship orders: supplementary	482
14F	Special guardianship support services	483
14G		484

Financial relief

15	Orders for financial relief with respect to children	484

Family assistance orders

16	Family assistance orders	484
16A	Risk assessments	485

Schedule 1 – Financial Provision for Children   486

PART I
INTRODUCTORY

1 Welfare of the child

(1) When a court determines any question with respect to–

(a) the upbringing of a child; or

(b) the administration of a child's property or the application of any income arising from it,

the child's welfare shall be the court's paramount consideration.

(2) In any proceedings in which any question with respect to the upbringing of a child arises, the court shall have regard to the general principle that any delay in determining the question is likely to prejudice the welfare of the child.

(3) In the circumstances mentioned in subsection (4), a court shall have regard in particular to–

(a) the ascertainable wishes and feelings of the child concerned (considered in the light of his age and understanding);

(b) his physical, emotional and educational needs;

(c) the likely effect on him of any change in his circumstances;

(d) his age, sex, background and any characteristics of his which the court considers relevant;

(e) any harm which he has suffered or is at risk of suffering;

(f) how capable each of his parents, and any other person in relation to whom the court considers the question to be relevant, is of meeting his needs;

(g) the range of powers available to the court under this Act in the proceedings in question.

(4) The circumstances are that–

(a) the court is considering whether to make, vary or discharge a special guardianship order or a section 8 order, and the making, variation or discharge of the order is opposed by any party to the proceedings; or

(b) the court is considering whether to make, vary or discharge an order under Part IV.

(5) Where a court is considering whether or not to make one or more orders under this Act with respect to a child, it shall not make the order or any of the orders unless it considers that doing so would be better for the child than making no order at all.

Amendments—Adoption and Children Act 2002, s 115(2), (3).

2 Parental responsibility for children

(1) Where a child's father and mother were married to each other at the time of his birth, they shall each have parental responsibility for the child.

(1A) Where a child –

(a) has a parent by virtue of section 42 of the Human Fertilisation and Embryology Act 2008; or

(b) has a parent by virtue of section 43 of that Act and is a person to whom section 1(3) of the Family Law Reform Act 1987 applies,

the child's mother and the other parent shall each have parental responsibility for the child.

(2) Where a child's father and mother were not married to each other at the time of his birth–

(a) the mother shall have parental responsibility for the child;

(b) the father shall have parental responsibility for the child if he has acquired it (and has not ceased to have it) in accordance with the provisions of this Act.

(2A) Where a child has a parent by virtue of section 43 of the Human Fertilisation and Embryology Act 2008 and is not a person to whom section 1(3) of the Family Law Reform Act 1987 applies –

    (a)   the mother shall have parental responsibility for the child;

    (b)   the other parent shall have parental responsibility for the child if she has acquired it (and has not ceased to have it) in accordance with the provisions of this Act.

(3)   References in this Act to a child whose father and mother were, or (as the case may be) were not, married to each other at the time of his birth must be read with section 1 of the Family Law Reform Act 1987 (which extends their meaning).

(4)   The rule of law that a father is the natural guardian of his legitimate child is abolished.

(5)   More than one person may have parental responsibility for the same child at the same time.

(6)   A person who has parental responsibility for a child at any time shall not cease to have that responsibility solely because some other person subsequently acquires parental responsibility for the child.

(7)   Where more than one person has parental responsibility for a child, each of them may act alone and without the other (or others) in meeting that responsibility; but nothing in this Part shall be taken to affect the operation of any enactment which requires the consent of more than one person in a matter affecting the child.

(8)   The fact that a person has parental responsibility for a child shall not entitle him to act in any way which would be incompatible with any order made with respect to the child under this Act.

(9)   A person who has parental responsibility for a child may not surrender or transfer any part of that responsibility to another but may arrange for some or all of it to be met by one or more persons acting on his behalf.

(10)   The person with whom any such arrangement is made may himself be a person who already has parental responsibility for the child concerned.

(11)   The making of any such arrangement shall not affect any liability of the person making it which may arise from any failure to meet any part of his parental responsibility for the child concerned.

Amendments—Adoption and Children Act 2002, s 111(5); Human Fertilisation and Embryology Act 2008, s 56, Sch 6, Pt 1, para 26.

3 Meaning of 'parental responsibility'

(1)   In this Act 'parental responsibility' means all the rights, duties, powers, responsibilities and authority which by law a parent of a child has in relation to the child and his property.

(2)   It also includes the rights, powers and duties which a guardian of the child's estate (appointed, before the commencement of section 5, to act generally) would have had in relation to the child and his property.

(3)   The rights referred to in subsection (2) include, in particular, the right of the guardian to receive or recover in his own name, for the benefit of the child, property of whatever description and wherever situated which the child is entitled to receive or recover.

(4)   The fact that a person has, or does not have, parental responsibility for a child shall not affect–

    (a)   any obligation which he may have in relation to the child (such as a statutory duty to maintain the child); or

    (b)   any rights which, in the event of the child's death, he (or any other person) may have in relation to the child's property.

(5)   A person who–

    (a)   does not have parental responsibility for a particular child; but

    (b)   has care of the child,

may (subject to the provisions of this Act) do what is reasonable in all the circumstances of the case for the purpose of safeguarding or promoting the child's welfare.

4 Acquisition of parental responsibility by father

(1) Where a child's father and mother were not married to each other at the time of his birth , the father shall acquire parental responsibility for the child if–

(a) he becomes registered as the child's father under any of the enactments specified in subsection (1A);

(b) he and the child's mother make an agreement (a 'parental responsibility agreement') providing for him to have parental responsibility for the child; or

(c) the court, on his application, orders that he shall have parental responsibility for the child.

(1A) The enactments referred to in subsection (1)(a) are–

(a) paragraphs (a), (b) and (c) of section 10(1) and of section 10A(1) of the Births and Deaths Registration Act 1953;

(b) paragraphs (a), (b)(i) and (c) of section 18(1), and sections 18(2)(b) and 20(1)(a) of the Registration of Births, Deaths and Marriages (Scotland) Act 1965; and

(c) sub-paragraphs (a), (b) and (c) of Article 14(3) of the Births and Deaths Registration (Northern Ireland) Order 1976.

(1B) The Secretary of State may by order amend subsection (1A) so as to add further enactments to the list in that subsection.

(2) No parental responsibility agreement shall have effect for the purposes of this Act unless–

(a) it is made in the form prescribed by regulations made by the Lord Chancellor; and

(b) where regulations are made by the Lord Chancellor prescribing the manner in which such agreements must be recorded, it is recorded in the prescribed manner.

(2A) A person who has acquired parental responsibility under subsection (1) shall cease to have that responsibility only if the court so orders.

(3) The court may make an order under subsection (2A) on the application–

(a) of any person who has parental responsibility for the child; or

(b) with the leave of the court, of the child himself,

subject, in the case of parental responsibility acquired under subsection (1)(c), to section 12(4).

(4) The court may only grant leave under subsection (3)(b) if it is satisfied that the child has sufficient understanding to make the proposed application.

Amendments—Adoption and Children Act 2002, s 111(1), (2), (3), (4), (7); SI 2003/3191.

4ZA Acquisition of parental responsibility by second female parent

(1) Where a child has a parent by virtue of section 43 of the Human Fertilisation and Embryology Act 2008 and is not a person to whom section 1(3) of the Family Law Reform Act 1987 applies, that parent shall acquire parental responsibility for the child if –

(a) she becomes registered as a parent of the child under any of the enactments specified in subsection (2);

(b) she and the child's mother make an agreement providing for her to have parental responsibility for the child; or

(c) the court, on her application, orders that she shall have parental responsibility for the child.

(2) The enactments referred to in subsection (1)(a) are –

(a)   paragraphs (a), (b) and (c) of section 10(1B) and of section 10A(1B) of the Births and Deaths Registration Act 1953;

(b)   paragraphs (a), (b) and (d) of section 18B(1) and sections 18B(3)(a) and 20(1)(a) of the Registration of Births, Deaths and Marriages (Scotland) Act 1965; and

(c)   sub-paragraphs (a), (b) and (c) of Article 14ZA(3) of the Births and Deaths Registration (Northern Ireland) Order 1976.

(3) The Secretary of State may by order amend subsection (2) so as to add further enactments to the list in that subsection.

(4) An agreement under subsection (1)(b) is also a "parental responsibility agreement", and section 4(2) applies in relation to such an agreement as it applies in relation to parental responsibility agreements under section 4.

(5) A person who has acquired parental responsibility under subsection (1) shall cease to have that responsibility only if the court so orders.

(6) The court may make an order under subsection (5) on the application –

(a)   of any person who has parental responsibility for the child; or

(b)   with the leave of the court, of the child himself,

subject, in the case of parental responsibility acquired under subsection (1)(c), to section 12(4).

(7) The court may only grant leave under subsection (6)(b) if it is satisfied that the child has sufficient understanding to make the proposed application.

Amendments—Inserted by Human Fertilisation and Embryology Act 2008, s 56, Sch 6, Pt 1, para 27.

4A   Acquisition of parental responsibility by step-parent

(1)   Where a child's parent ('parent A') who has parental responsibility for the child is married to, or a civil partner of, a person who is not the child's parent ('the step-parent') –

(a)   parent A or, if the other parent of the child also has parental responsibility for the child, both parents may by agreement with the step-parent provide for the step-parent to have parental responsibility for the child; or

(b)   the court may, on the application of the step-parent, order that the step-parent shall have parental responsibility for the child.

(2)   An agreement under subsection (1)(a) is also a 'parental responsibility agreement', and section 4(2) applies in relation to such agreements as it applies in relation to parental responsibility agreements under section 4.

(3)   A parental responsibility agreement under subsection (1)(a), or an order under subsection (1)(b), may only be brought to an end by an order of the court made on the application –

(a)   of any person who has parental responsibility for the child; or

(b)   with the leave of the court, of the child himself.

(4)   The court may only grant leave under subsection (3)(b) if it is satisfied that the child has sufficient understanding to make the proposed application.

Amendments—Adoption and Children Act 2002, s 112(7); Civil Partnership Act 2004, s 75(1), (2).

5   Appointment of guardians

(1)   Where an application with respect to a child is made to the court by any individual, the court may by order appoint that individual to be the child's guardian if–

(a)   the child has no parent with parental responsibility for him; or

(b)   a residence order has been made with respect to the child in favour of a parent, guardian or special guardian of his who has died while the order was in force; or

(c)   paragraph (b) does not apply, and the child's only or last surviving special guardian dies.

(2)   The power conferred by subsection (1) may also be exercised in any family proceedings if the court considers that the order should be made even though no application has been made for it.

(3)   A parent who has parental responsibility for his child may appoint another individual to be the child's guardian in the event of his death.

(4)   A guardian of a child may appoint another individual to take his place as the child's guardian in the event of his death;and a special guardian of a child may appoint another individual to be the child's guardian in the event of his death.

(5)   An appointment under subsection (3) or (4) shall not have effect unless it is made in writing, is dated and is signed by the person making the appointment or–

(a)   in the case of an appointment made by a will which is not signed by the testator, is signed at the direction of the testator in accordance with the requirements of section 9 of the Wills Act 1837; or

(b)   in any other case, is signed at the direction of the person making the appointment, in his presence and in the presence of two witnesses who each attest the signature.

(6)   A person appointed as a child's guardian under this section shall have parental responsibility for the child concerned.

(7)   Where–

(a)   on the death of any person making an appointment under subsection (3) or (4), the child concerned has no parent with parental responsibility for him; or

(b)   immediately before the death of any person making such an appointment, a residence order in his favour was in force with respect to the child, or he was the child's only (or last surviving) special guardian

the appointment shall take effect on the death of that person.

(8)   Where, on the death of any person making an appointment under subsection (3) or (4)–

(a)   the child concerned has a parent with parental responsibility for him; and

(b)   subsection (7)(b) does not apply,

the appointment shall take effect when the child no longer has a parent who has parental responsibility for him.

(9)   Subsections (1) and (7) do not apply if the residence order referred to in paragraph (b) of those subsections was also made in favour of a surviving parent of the child.

(10)   Nothing in this section shall be taken to prevent an appointment under subsection (3) or (4) being made by two or more persons acting jointly.

(11)   Subject to any provision made by rules of court, no court shall exercise the High Court's inherent jurisdiction to appoint a guardian of the estate of any child.

(12)   Where the rules of court are made under subsection (11) they may prescribe the circumstances in which, and conditions subject to which, an appointment of such a guardian may be made.

(13)   A guardian of a child may only be appointed in accordance with the provisions of this section.

Amendments—Adoption and Children Act 2002, s 115(2), (4)(a), (b), (c).

6   Guardians: revocation and disclaimer

(1)   An appointment under section 5(3) or (4) revokes an earlier such appointment (including one made in an unrevoked will or codicil) made by the same person in respect of the same child, unless it is clear (whether as the result of an express provision in the later appointment or by any necessary implication) that the purpose of the later appointment is to appoint an additional guardian.

(2)   An appointment under section 5(3) or (4) (including one made in an unrevoked will or codicil) is revoked if the person who made the appointment revokes it by a written and dated instrument which is signed–

(a)   by him; or
(b)   at his direction, in his presence and in the presence of two witnesses who each attest the signature.

(3)   An appointment under section 5(3) or (4) (other than one made in a will or codicil) is revoked if, with the intention of revoking the appointment, the person who made it–

(a)   destroys the instrument by which it was made; or
(b)   has some other person destroy that instrument in his presence.

(3A)   An appointment under section 5(3) or (4) (including one made in an unrevoked will or codicil) is revoked if the person appointed is the spouse of the person who made the appointment and either–

(a)   a decree of a court of civil jurisdiction in England and Wales dissolves or annuls the marriage, or.
(b)   the marriage is dissolved or annulled and the divorce or annulment is entitled to recognition in England and Wales by virtue of Part II of the Family Law Act 1986,

unless a contrary intention appears by the appointment.

(3B)   An appointment under section 5(3) or (4) (including one made in an unrevoked will or codicil) is revoked if the person appointed is the civil partner of the person who made the appointment and either –

(a)   an order of a court of civil jurisdiction in England and Wales dissolves or annuls the civil partnership, or
(b)   the civil partnership is dissolved or annulled and the dissolution or annulment is entitled to recognition in England and Wales by virtue of Chapter 3 of Part 5 of the Civil Partnership Act 2004,

unless a contrary intention appears by the appointment.

(4)   For the avoidance of doubt, an appointment under section 5(3) or (4) made in a will or codicil is revoked if the will or codicil is revoked.

(5)   A person who is appointed as a guardian under section 5(3) or (4) may disclaim his appointment by an instrument in writing signed by him and made within a reasonable time of his first knowing that the appointment has taken effect.

(6)   Where regulations are made by the Lord Chancellor prescribing the manner in which such disclaimers must be recorded, no such disclaimer shall have effect unless it is recorded in the prescribed manner.

(7)   Any appointment of a guardian under section 5 may be brought to an end at any time by order of the court–

(a)   on the application of any person who has parental responsibility for the child;
(b)   on the application of the child concerned, with leave of the court; or
(c)   in any family proceedings, if the court considers that it should be brought to an end even though no application has been made.

Amendments—Law Reform (Succession) Act 1995, s 4(1); Civil Partnership Act 2004, s 76. Prospectively amended by Family Law Act 1996, s 66(1), Sch 8, para 41(2).

7   Welfare reports

(1)   A court considering any question with respect to a child under this Act may–

(a)   ask an officer of the Serviceor a Welsh family proceedings officer; or
(b)   ask a local authority to arrange for–

(i)   an officer of the authority; or

(ii)   such other person (other than an officer of the Service or a Welsh family proceedings officer) as the authority considers appropriate,

to report to the court on such matters relating to the welfare of that child as are required to be dealt with in the report.

(2) The Lord Chancellor may, after consulting the Lord Chief Justice, make regulations specifying matters which, unless the court orders otherwise, must be dealt with in any report under this section.

(3) The report may be made in writing, or orally, as the court requires.

(4) Regardless of any enactment or rule of law which would otherwise prevent it from doing so, the court may take account of–

(a)   any statement contained in the report; and

(b)   any evidence given in respect of the matters referred to in the report,

in so far as the statement or evidence is, in the opinion of the court, relevant to the question which it is considering.

(5) It shall be the duty of the authority or officer of the Service or a Welsh family proceedings officer to comply with any request for a report under this section.

(6) The Lord Chief Justice may nominate a judicial office holder (as defined in section 109(4) of the Constitutional Reform Act 2005) to exercise his functions under subsection (2).

Amendments—Criminal Justice and Court Services Act 2000, s 74, Sch 7, paras 87, 88; Children Act 2004, s 40, Sch 3, paras 5, 6; Constitutional Reform Act 2005, s 15(1), Sch 4, Pt 1, paras 203, 204(1), (2), (3).

PART II
ORDERS WITH RESPECT TO CHILDREN IN FAMILY PROCEEDINGS

General

8 Residence, contact and other orders with respect to children

(1) In this Act–

'a contact order' means an order requiring the person with whom a child lives, or is to live, to allow the child to visit or stay with the person named in the order, or for that person and the child otherwise to have contact with each other;

'a prohibited steps order' means an order that no step which could be taken by a parent in meeting his parental responsibility for a child, and which is of a kind specified in the order, shall be taken by any person without the consent of the court;

'a residence order' means an order settling the arrangements to be made as to the person with whom a child is to live; and

'a specific issue order' means an order giving directions for the purpose of determining a specific question which has arisen, or which may arise, in connection with any aspect of parental responsibility for a child.

(2) In this Act 'a section 8 order' means any of the orders mentioned in subsection (1) and any order varying or discharging such an order.

(3) For the purposes of this Act 'family proceedings' means any proceedings–

(a)   under the inherent jurisdiction of the High Court in relation to children; and

(b)   under the enactments mentioned in subsection (4),

but does not include proceedings on an application for leave under section 100(3).

(4) The enactments are–

(a)   Parts I, II and IV of this Act;

 (b) the Matrimonial Causes Act 1973;
 (ba) Schedule 5 to the Civil Partnership Act 2004;
 (c) *(repealed)*
 (d) the Adoption and Children Act 2002;
 (e) the Domestic Proceedings and Magistrates' Courts Act 1978;
 (ea) Schedule 6 to the Civil Partnership Act 2004;
 (f) *(repealed)*
 (g) Part III of the Matrimonial and Family Proceedings Act 1984;
 (h) the Family Law Act 1996;
 (i) sections 11 and 12 of the Crime and Disorder Act 1998.

Amendments—Family Law Act 1996, s 66(1), Sch 8, Pt III, para 60; Crime and Disorder Act 1998, s 119, Sch 8, para 68; Adoption and Children Act 2002, s 139(1), Sch 3, paras 54, 55; Civil Partnership Act 2004, s 261(1), Sch 27, para 129(1), (2), (3). Prospectively amended by Family Law Act 1996, s 66(1), Sch 8, para 41(3).

9 Restrictions on making section 8 orders

(1) No court shall make any section 8 order, other than a residence order, with respect to a child who is in the care of a local authority.

(2) No application may be made by a local authority for a residence order or contact order and no court shall make such an order in favour of a local authority.

(3) A person who is, or was at any time within the last six months, a local authority foster parent of a child may not apply for leave to apply for a section 8 order with respect to the child unless–

 (a) he has the consent of the authority;
 (b) he is relative of the child; or
 (c) the child has lived with him for at least one year preceding the application.

(4) *(repealed)*

(5) No court shall exercise its powers to make a specific issue order or prohibited steps order–

 (a) with a view to achieving a result which could be achieved by making a residence or contact order; or
 (b) in any way which is denied to the High Court (by section 100(2)) in the exercise of its inherent jurisdiction with respect to children.

(6) No court shall make a specific issue order, contact order or prohibited steps order is to have effect for a period which will end after the child has reached the age of sixteen unless it is satisfied that the circumstances of the case are exceptional.

(7) No court shall make any section 8 order, other than one varying or discharging such an order, with respect to a child who has reached the age of sixteen unless it is satisfied that the circumstances of the case are exceptional.

Amendments—Adoption and Children Act 2002, ss 113(a), (b), 114(2), 139(3), Sch 5; Children and Young Persons Act 2008, s 37(1).

10 Power of court to make section 8 orders

(1) In any family proceedings in which a question arises with respect to the welfare of any child, the court may make a section 8 order with respect to the child if–

 (a) an application for the order has been made by a person who–
   (i) is entitled to apply for a section 8 order with respect to the child; or
   (ii) has obtained the leave of the court to make the application; or
 (b) the court considers that the order should be made even though no such application has been made.

(2) The court may also make a section 8 order with respect to any child on the application of a person who–

 (a) is entitled to apply for a section 8 order with respect to the child; or

    (b)   has obtained the leave of the court to make the application.

(3)   This section is subject to the restrictions imposed by section 9.

(4)   The following persons are entitled to apply to the court for any section 8 order with respect to a child–

    (a)   any parent, guardian or special guardian of the child;
    (aa)   any person who by virtue of section 4A has parental responsibility for the child;
    (b)   any person in whose favour a residence order is in force with respect to the child.

(5)   The following persons are entitled to apply for a residence or contact order with respect to a child–

    (a)   any party to a marriage (whether or not subsisting) in relation to whom the child is a child of the family;
    (aa)   any civil partner in a civil partnership (whether or not subsisting) in relation to whom the child is a child of the family;
    (b)   any person with whom the child has lived for a period of at least three years;
    (c)   any person who–
        (i)   in any case where a residence order is in force with respect to the child, has the consent of each of the persons in whose favour the order was made;
        (ii)   in any case where the child is in the care of a local authority, has the consent of that authority; or
        (iii)   in any other case, has the consent of each of those (if any) who have parental responsibility for the child.

(5A) A local authority foster parent is entitled to apply for a residence order with respect to a child if the child has lived with him for a period of at least one year immediately preceding the application.

(5B) A relative of a child is entitled to apply for a residence order with respect to the child if the child has lived with the relative for a period of at least one year immediately preceding the application.

(6)   A person who would not otherwise be entitled (under the previous provisions of this section) to apply for the variation or discharge of a section 8 order shall be entitled to do so if–

    (a)   the order was made on his application; or
    (b)   in the case of a contact order, he is named in the order.

(7)   Any person who falls within a category of person prescribed by rules of court is entitled to apply for any such section 8 order as may be prescribed in relation to that category of person.

(7A) If a special guardianship order is in force with respect to a child, an application for a residence order may only be made with respect to him, if apart from this subsection the leave of the court is not required, with such leave.

(8)   Where the person applying for leave to make an application for a section 8 order is the child concerned, the court may only grant leave if it is satisfied that he has sufficient understanding to make the proposed application for the section 8 order.

(9)   Where the person applying for leave to make an application for a section 8 order is not the child concerned, the court shall, in deciding whether or not to grant leave, have particular regard to–

    (a)   the nature of the proposed application for the section 8 order;
    (b)   the applicant's connection with the child;
    (c)   any risk there might be of that proposed application disrupting the child's life to such an extent that he would be harmed by it; and
    (d)   where the child is being looked after by a local authority–
        (i)   the authority's plans for the child's future; and
        (ii)   the wishes and feelings of the child's parents.

(10)   The period of three years mentioned in subsection (5)(b) need not be continuous but must not have begun more than five years before, or ended more than three months before, the making of the application.

Amendments—Adoption and Children Act 2002, s 139(1), Sch 3, paras 54, 56; Civil Partnership Act 2004, s 77; Children and Young Persons Act 2008, s 36.

11   General principles and supplementary provisions

(1)   In proceedings in which any question of making a section 8 order, or any other question with respect to such an order, arises, the court shall (in the light of any rules made by virtue of subsection (2))–

  (a)   draw up a timetable with a view to determining the question without delay; and

  (b)   give such directions as it considers appropriate for the purpose of ensuring, so far as is reasonably practicable, that that timetable is adhered to.

(2)   Rules of court may–

  (a)   specify periods within which specified steps must be taken in relation to proceedings in which such questions arise; and

  (b)   make other provision with respect to such proceedings for the purpose of ensuring, so far as is reasonably practicable, that such questions are determined without delay.

(3)   Where a court has power to make a section 8 order, it may do so at any time during the course of the proceedings in question even though it is not in a position to dispose finally of those proceedings.

(4)   Where a residence order is made in favour of two or more persons who do not themselves all live together, the order may specify the periods during which the child is to live in the different households concerned.

(5)   Where–

  (a)   a residence order has been made with respect to a child; and

  (b)   as a result of the order the child lives, or is to live, with one of two parents who each have parental responsibility for him,

the residence order shall cease to have effect if the parents live together for a continuous period of more than six months.

(6)   A contact order which requires the parent with whom a child lives to allow the child to visit, or otherwise have contact with, his other parent shall cease to have effect if the parents live together for a continuous period of more than six months.

(7)   A section 8 order may–

  (a)   contain directions about how it is to be carried into effect;

  (b)   impose conditions which must be complied with by any person–

    (i)   in whose favour the order is made;

    (ii)   who is a parent of the child concerned;

    (iii) who is not a parent of his but who has parental responsibility for him; or

    (iv)   with whom the child is living,

    and to whom the conditions are expressed to apply;

  (c)   be made to have effect for a specified period, or contain provisions which are to have effect for a specified period;

  (d)   make such incidental, supplemental or consequential provision as the court thinks fit.

11A Contact activity directions

(1)   This section applies in proceedings in which the court is considering whether to make provision about contact with a child by making –

  (a)   a contact order with respect to the child, or

(b)   an order varying or discharging a contact order with respect to the child.

(2) The court may make a contact activity direction in connection with that provision about contact.

(3) A contact activity direction is a direction requiring an individual who is a party to the proceedings to take part in an activity that promotes contact with the child concerned.

(4) The direction is to specify the activity and the person providing the activity.

(5) The activities that may be so required include, in particular –

(a)   programmes, classes and counselling or guidance sessions of a kind that –
  (i)   may assist a person as regards establishing, maintaining or improving contact with a child;
  (ii)   may, by addressing a person's violent behaviour, enable or facilitate contact with a child;
(b)   sessions in which information or advice is given as regards making or operating arrangements for contact with a child, including making arrangements by means of mediation.

(6) No individual may be required by a contact activity direction –

(a)   to undergo medical or psychiatric examination, assessment or treatment;
(b)   to take part in mediation.

(7) A court may not on the same occasion –

(a)   make a contact activity direction, and
(b)   dispose finally of the proceedings as they relate to contact with the child concerned.

(8) Subsection (2) has effect subject to the restrictions in sections 11B and 11E.

(9) In considering whether to make a contact activity direction, the welfare of the child concerned is to be the court's paramount consideration.

Amendments—Inserted by Children and Adoption Act 2006, s 1

11B Contact activity directions: further provision

(1) A court may not make a contact activity direction in any proceedings unless there is a dispute as regards the provision about contact that the court is considering whether to make in the proceedings.

(2) A court may not make a contact activity direction requiring an individual who is a child to take part in an activity unless the individual is a parent of the child in relation to whom the court is considering provision about contact.

(3) A court may not make a contact activity direction in connection with the making, variation or discharge of a contact order, if the contact order is, or would if made be, an excepted order.

(4) A contact order with respect to a child is an excepted order if –

(a)   it is made in proceedings that include proceedings on an application for a relevant adoption order in respect of the child; or
(b)   it makes provision as regards contact between the child and a person who would be a parent or relative of the child but for the child's adoption by an order falling within subsection (5).

(5) An order falls within this subsection if it is –

(a)   a relevant adoption order;
(b)   an adoption order, within the meaning of section 72(1) of the Adoption Act 1976, other than an order made by virtue of section 14 of that Act on the application of a married couple one of whom is the mother or the father of the child;

(c)   a Scottish adoption order, within the meaning of the Adoption and Children Act 2002, other than an order made –

         (i)   by virtue of section 14 of the Adoption (Scotland) Act 1978 on the application of a married couple one of whom is the mother or the father of the child, or

         (ii)   by virtue of section 15(1)(aa) of that Act; or

         (iii)   by virtue of an application under section 30 of the Adoption and Children (Scotland) Act 2007 where subsection (3) of that section applies; or

(d)   a Northern Irish adoption order, within the meaning of the Adoption and Children Act 2002, other than an order made by virtue of Article 14 of the Adoption (Northern Ireland) Order 1987 on the application of a married couple one of whom is the mother or the father of the child.

(6) A relevant adoption order is an adoption order, within the meaning of section 46(1) of the Adoption and Children Act 2002, other than an order made –

(a)   on an application under section 50 of that Act by a couple (within the meaning of that Act) one of whom is the mother or the father of the person to be adopted, or

(b)   on an application under section 51(2) of that Act.

(7) A court may not make a contact activity direction in relation to an individual unless the individual is habitually resident in England and Wales; and a direction ceases to have effect if the individual subject to the direction ceases to be habitually resident in England and Wales.

Amendments—Children and Adoption Act 2006, s 1; SI 2011/1740.

11C   Contact activity conditions

(1) This section applies if in any family proceedings the court makes –

(a)   a contact order with respect to a child, or

(b)   an order varying a contact order with respect to a child.

(2) The contact order may impose, or the contact order may be varied so as to impose, a condition (a "contact activity condition") requiring an individual falling within subsection (3) to take part in an activity that promotes contact with the child concerned.

(3) An individual falls within this subsection if he is –

(a)   for the purposes of the contact order so made or varied, the person with whom the child concerned lives or is to live;

(b)   the person whose contact with the child concerned is provided for in that order; or

(c)   a person upon whom that order imposes a condition under section 11(7)(b).

(4) The condition is to specify the activity and the person providing the activity.

(5) Subsections (5) and (6) of section 11A have effect as regards the activities that may be required by a contact activity condition as they have effect as regards the activities that may be required by a contact activity direction.

(6) Subsection (2) has effect subject to the restrictions in sections 11D and 11E.

Amendments—Inserted by Children and Adoption Act 2006, s 1.

11D   Contact activity conditions: further provision

(1) A contact order may not impose a contact activity condition on an individual who is a child unless the individual is a parent of the child concerned.

(2) If a contact order is an excepted order (within the meaning given by section 11B(4)), it may not impose (and it may not be varied so as to impose) a contact activity condition.

(3) A contact order may not impose a contact activity condition on an individual unless the individual is habitually resident in England and Wales; and a condition ceases to have effect if the individual subject to the condition ceases to be habitually resident in England and Wales.

Amendments—Inserted by Children and Adoption Act 2006, s 1.

11E Contact activity directions and conditions: making

(1) Before making a contact activity direction (or imposing a contact activity condition by means of a contact order), the court must satisfy itself as to the matters falling within subsections (2) to (4).

(2) The first matter is that the activity proposed to be specified is appropriate in the circumstances of the case.

(3) The second matter is that the person proposed to be specified as the provider of the activity is suitable to provide the activity.

(4) The third matter is that the activity proposed to be specified is provided in a place to which the individual who would be subject to the direction (or the condition) can reasonably be expected to travel.

(5) Before making such a direction (or such an order), the court must obtain and consider information about the individual who would be subject to the direction (or the condition) and the likely effect of the direction (or the condition) on him.

(6) Information about the likely effect of the direction (or the condition) may, in particular, include information as to –

    (a)   any conflict with the individual's religious beliefs;

    (b)   any interference with the times (if any) at which he normally works or attends an educational establishment.

(7) The court may ask an officer of the Service or a Welsh family proceedings officer to provide the court with information as to the matters in subsections (2) to (5); and it shall be the duty of the officer of the Service or Welsh family proceedings officer to comply with any such request.

(8) In this section 'specified' means specified in a contact activity direction (or in a contact activity condition).

Amendments—Inserted by Children and Adoption Act 2006, s 1.

11F Contact activity directions and conditions: financial assistance

(1) The Secretary of State may by regulations make provision authorising him to make payments to assist individuals falling within subsection (2) in paying relevant charges or fees.

(2) An individual falls within this subsection if he is required by a contact activity direction or condition to take part in an activity that promotes contact with a child, not being a child ordinarily resident in Wales.

(3) The National Assembly for Wales may by regulations make provision authorising it to make payments to assist individuals falling within subsection (4) in paying relevant charges or fees.

(4) An individual falls within this subsection if he is required by a contact activity direction or condition to take part in an activity that promotes contact with a child who is ordinarily resident in Wales.

(5) A relevant charge or fee, in relation to an activity required by a contact activity direction or condition, is a charge or fee in respect of the activity payable to the person providing the activity.

(6) Regulations under this section may provide that no assistance is available to an individual unless –

    (a)   the individual satisfies such conditions as regards his financial resources as may be set out in the regulations;

    (b)   the activity in which the individual is required by a contact activity direction or condition to take part is provided to him in England or Wales;

    (c)   where the activity in which the individual is required to take part is provided to him in England, it is provided by a person who is for the time being approved by the Secretary of State as a provider of activities required by a contact activity direction or condition;

    (d)   where the activity in which the individual is required to take part is provided to him in Wales, it is provided by a person who is for the time being approved by the National Assembly for Wales as a provider of activities required by a contact activity direction or condition.

(7) Regulations under this section may make provision –

    (a)   as to the maximum amount of assistance that may be paid to or in respect of an individual as regards an activity in which he is required by a contact activity direction or condition to take part;

    (b)   where the amount may vary according to an individual's financial resources, as to the method by which the amount is to be determined;

    (c)   authorising payments by way of assistance to be made directly to persons providing activities required by a contact activity direction or condition.

Amendments—Inserted by Children and Adoption Act 2006, s 1.

11G Contact activity directions and conditions: monitoring

(1) This section applies if in any family proceedings the court –

    (a)   makes a contact activity direction in relation to an individual, or

    (b)   makes a contact order that imposes, or varies a contact order so as to impose, a contact activity condition on an individual.

(2) The court may on making the direction (or imposing the condition by means of a contact order) ask an officer of the Service or a Welsh family proceedings officer –

    (a)   to monitor, or arrange for the monitoring of, the individual's compliance with the direction (or the condition);

    (b)   to report to the court on any failure by the individual to comply with the direction (or the condition).

(3) It shall be the duty of the officer of the Service or Welsh family proceedings officer to comply with any request under subsection (2).

Amendments—Inserted by Children and Adoption Act 2006, s 1.

11H Monitoring contact

(1) This section applies if in any family proceedings the court makes –

    (a)   a contact order with respect to a child in favour of a person, or

    (b)   an order varying such a contact order.

(2) The court may ask an officer of the Service or a Welsh family proceedings officer –

    (a)   to monitor whether an individual falling within subsection (3) complies with the contact order (or the contact order as varied);

    (b)   to report to the court on such matters relating to the individual's compliance as the court may specify in the request.

(3) An individual falls within this subsection if the contact order so made (or the contact order as so varied) –

    (a)   requires the individual to allow contact with the child concerned;

    (b)   names the individual as having contact with the child concerned; or

    (c)   imposes a condition under section 11(7)(b) on the individual.

(4) If the contact order (or the contact order as varied) includes a contact activity condition, a request under subsection (2) is to be treated as relating to the provisions of the order other than the contact activity condition.

(5) The court may make a request under subsection (2) –

(a)   on making the contact order (or the order varying the contact order), or

(b)   at any time during the subsequent course of the proceedings as they relate to contact with the child concerned.

(6) In making a request under subsection (2), the court is to specify the period for which the officer of the Service or Welsh family proceedings officer is to monitor compliance with the order; and the period specified may not exceed twelve months.

(7) It shall be the duty of the officer of the Service or Welsh family proceedings officer to comply with any request under subsection (2).

(8) The court may order any individual falling within subsection (3) to take such steps as may be specified in the order with a view to enabling the officer of the Service or Welsh family proceedings officer to comply with the court's request under subsection (2).

(9) But the court may not make an order under subsection (8) with respect to an individual who is a child unless he is a parent of the child with respect to whom the order falling within subsection (1) was made.

(10) A court may not make a request under subsection (2) in relation to a contact order that is an excepted order (within the meaning given by section 11B(4)).

Amendments—Inserted by Children and Adoption Act 2006, s 2.

11I Contact orders: warning notices

Where the court makes (or varies) a contact order, it is to attach to the contact order (or the order varying the contact order) a notice warning of the consequences of failing to comply with the contact order.

Amendments—Inserted by Children and Adoption Act 2006, s 3.

11J Enforcement orders

(1) This section applies if a contact order with respect to a child has been made.

(2) If the court is satisfied beyond reasonable doubt that a person has failed to comply with the contact order, it may make an order (an 'enforcement order') imposing on the person an unpaid work requirement.

(3) But the court may not make an enforcement order if it is satisfied that the person had a reasonable excuse for failing to comply with the contact order.

(4) The burden of proof as to the matter mentioned in subsection (3) lies on the person claiming to have had a reasonable excuse, and the standard of proof is the balance of probabilities.

(5) The court may make an enforcement order in relation to the contact order only on the application of –

(a)   the person who is, for the purposes of the contact order, the person with whom the child concerned lives or is to live;

(b)   the person whose contact with the child concerned is provided for in the contact order;

(c)   any individual subject to a condition under section 11(7)(b) or a contact activity condition imposed by the contact order; or

(d)   the child concerned.

(6) Where the person proposing to apply for an enforcement order in relation to a contact order is the child concerned, the child must obtain the leave of the court before making such an application.

(7) The court may grant leave to the child concerned only if it is satisfied that he has sufficient understanding to make the proposed application.

(8) Subsection (2) has effect subject to the restrictions in sections 11K and 11L.

(9) The court may suspend an enforcement order for such period as it thinks fit.

(10) Nothing in this section prevents a court from making more than one enforcement order in relation to the same person on the same occasion.

(11) Proceedings in which any question of making an enforcement order, or any other question with respect to such an order, arises are to be regarded for the purposes of section 11(1) and (2) as proceedings in which a question arises with respect to a section 8 order.

(12) In Schedule A1 –

    (a)   Part 1 makes provision as regards an unpaid work requirement;
    (b)   Part 2 makes provision in relation to the revocation and amendment of enforcement orders and failure to comply with such orders.

(13) This section is without prejudice to section 63(3) of the Magistrates' Courts Act 1980 as it applies in relation to contact orders.

Amendments—Inserted by Children and Adoption Act 2006, s 4(1).

11K Enforcement orders: further provision

(1) A court may not make an enforcement order against a person in respect of a failure to comply with a contact order unless it is satisfied that before the failure occurred the person had been given (in accordance with rules of court) a copy of, or otherwise informed of the terms of –

    (a)   in the case of a failure to comply with a contact order that was varied before the failure occurred, a notice under section 11I relating to the order varying the contact order or, where more than one such order has been made, the last order preceding the failure in question;
    (b)   in any other case, a notice under section 11I relating to the contact order.

(2) A court may not make an enforcement order against a person in respect of any failure to comply with a contact order occurring before the person attained the age of 18.

(3) A court may not make an enforcement order against a person in respect of a failure to comply with a contact order that is an excepted order (within the meaning given by section 11B(4)).

(4) A court may not make an enforcement order against a person unless the person is habitually resident in England and Wales; and an enforcement order ceases to have effect if the person subject to the order ceases to be habitually resident in England and Wales.

Amendments—Inserted by Children and Adoption Act 2006, s 4(1).

11L Enforcement orders: making

(1) Before making an enforcement order as regards a person in breach of a contact order, the court must be satisfied that –

    (a)   making the enforcement order proposed is necessary to secure the person's compliance with the contact order or any contact order that has effect in its place;
    (b)   the likely effect on the person of the enforcement order proposed to be made is proportionate to the seriousness of the breach of the contact order.

(2) Before making an enforcement order, the court must satisfy itself that provision for the person to work under an unpaid work requirement imposed by an enforcement order can be made in the local justice area in which the person in breach resides or will reside.

(3) Before making an enforcement order as regards a person in breach of a contact order, the court must obtain and consider information about the person and the likely effect of the enforcement order on him.

(4) Information about the likely effect of the enforcement order may, in particular, include information as to –

  (a)   any conflict with the person's religious beliefs;
  (b)   any interference with the times (if any) at which he normally works or attends an educational establishment.

(5) A court that proposes to make an enforcement order may ask an officer of the Service or a Welsh family proceedings officer to provide the court with information as to the matters in subsections (2) and (3).

(6) It shall be the duty of the officer of the Service or Welsh family proceedings officer to comply with any request under this section.

(7) In making an enforcement order in relation to a contact order, a court must take into account the welfare of the child who is the subject of the contact order.

Amendments—Inserted by Children and Adoption Act 2006, s 4(1).

11M Enforcement orders: monitoring

(1) On making an enforcement order in relation to a person, the court is to ask an officer of the Service or a Welsh family proceedings officer –

  (a)   to monitor, or arrange for the monitoring of, the person's compliance with the unpaid work requirement imposed by the order;
  (b)   to report to the court if a report under paragraph 8 of Schedule A1 is made in relation to the person;
  (c)   to report to the court on such other matters relating to the person's compliance as may be specified in the request;
  (d)   to report to the court if the person is, or becomes, unsuitable to perform work under the requirement.

(2) It shall be the duty of the officer of the Service or Welsh family proceedings officer to comply with any request under this section.

Amendments—Inserted by Children and Adoption Act 2006, s 4(1).

11N Enforcement orders: warning notices

Where the court makes an enforcement order, it is to attach to the order a notice warning of the consequences of failing to comply with the order.

Amendments—Inserted by Children and Adoption Act 2006, s 4(1).

11O Compensation for financial loss

(1) This section applies if a contact order with respect to a child has been made.

(2) If the court is satisfied that –

  (a)   an individual has failed to comply with the contact order, and
  (b)   a person falling within subsection (6) has suffered financial loss by reason of the breach,

it may make an order requiring the individual in breach to pay the person compensation in respect of his financial loss.

(3) But the court may not make an order under subsection (2) if it is satisfied that the individual in breach had a reasonable excuse for failing to comply with the contact order.

(4) The burden of proof as to the matter mentioned in subsection (3) lies on the individual claiming to have had a reasonable excuse.

(5) An order under subsection (2) may be made only on an application by the person who claims to have suffered financial loss.

(6) A person falls within this subsection if he is –

    (a)   the person who is, for the purposes of the contact order, the person with whom the child concerned lives or is to live;

    (b)   the person whose contact with the child concerned is provided for in the contact order;

    (c)   an individual subject to a condition under section 11(7)(b) or a contact activity condition imposed by the contact order; or

    (d)   the child concerned.

(7) Where the person proposing to apply for an order under subsection (2) is the child concerned, the child must obtain the leave of the court before making such an application.

(8) The court may grant leave to the child concerned only if it is satisfied that he has sufficient understanding to make the proposed application.

(9) The amount of compensation is to be determined by the court, but may not exceed the amount of the applicant's financial loss.

(10) In determining the amount of compensation payable by the individual in breach, the court must take into account the individual's financial circumstances.

(11) An amount ordered to be paid as compensation may be recovered by the applicant as a civil debt due to him.

(12) Subsection (2) has effect subject to the restrictions in section 11P.

(13) Proceedings in which any question of making an order under subsection (2) arises are to be regarded for the purposes of section 11(1) and (2) as proceedings in which a question arises with respect to a section 8 order.

(14) In exercising its powers under this section, a court is to take into account the welfare of the child concerned.

Amendments—Inserted by Children and Adoption Act 2006, s 5.

11P Orders under section 11O(2): further provision

(1) A court may not make an order under section 11O(2) requiring an individual to pay compensation in respect of a failure by him to comply with a contact order unless it is satisfied that before the failure occurred the individual had been given (in accordance with rules of court) a copy of, or otherwise informed of the terms of –

    (a)   in the case of a failure to comply with a contact order that was varied before the failure occurred, a notice under section 11I relating to the order varying the contact order or, where more than one such order has been made, the last order preceding the failure in question;

    (b)   in any other case, a notice under section 11I relating to the contact order.

(2) A court may not make an order under section 11O(2) requiring an individual to pay compensation in respect of a failure by him to comply with a contact order where the failure occurred before the individual attained the age of 18.

(3) A court may not make an order under section 11O(2) requiring an individual to pay compensation in respect of a failure by him to comply with a contact order that is an excepted order (within the meaning given by section 11B(4)).

Amendments—Inserted by Children and Adoption Act 2006, s 5.

12 Residence orders and parental responsibility

(1) Where the court makes a residence order in favour of the father of a child it shall, if the father would not otherwise have parental responsibility for the child, also make an order under section 4 giving him that responsibility.

(1A) Where the court makes a residence order in favour of a woman who is a parent of a child by virtue of section 43 of the Human Fertilisation and Embryology Act 2008 it shall, if that woman would not otherwise have parental responsibility for the child, also make an order under section 4ZA giving her that responsibility.

(2) Where the court makes a residence order in favour of any person who is not the parent or guardian of the child concerned that person shall have parental responsibility for the child while the residence order remains in force.

(3) Where a person has parental responsibility for a child as a result of subsection (2), he shall not have the right–

  (a) *(repealed)*
  (b) to agree, or refuse to agree, to the making of an adoption order, or an order under section 84 of the Adoption and Children Act 2002, with respect to the child; or
  (c) to appoint a guardian for the child.

(4) Where subsection (1) or (1A) requires the court to make an order under section 4 or 4ZA in respect of the parent of a child, the court shall not bring that order to an end at any time while the residence order concerned remains in force.

(5) *(repealed)*

(6) *(repealed)*

Amendments—Adoption and Children Act 2002, ss 114(1), 139(1), (3), Sch 3, paras 54, 57(a), (b), Sch 5; Human Fertilisation and Embryology Act 2008, s 56, Sch 6, Pt 1, para 28; Children and Young Persons Act 2008, ss 37(2), 42, Sch 4.

13 Change of child's name or removal from jurisdiction

(1) Where a residence order is in force with respect to a child, no person may–

  (a) cause the child to be known by a new surname; or
  (b) remove him from the United Kingdom;

without either the written consent of every person who has parental responsibility for the child or the leave of the court.

(2) Subsection (1)(b) does not prevent the removal of a child, for a period of less than one month, by the person in whose favour the residence order is made.

(3) In making a residence order with respect to a child the court may grant the leave required by subsection (1)(b), either generally or for specified purposes.

14 Enforcement of residence orders

(1) Where–

  (a) a residence order is in force with respect to a child in favour of any person; and
  (b) any other person (including one in whose favour the order is also in force) is in breach of the arrangements settled by that order,

the person mentioned in paragraph (a) may, as soon as the requirement in subsection (2) is complied with, enforce the order under section 63(3) of the Magistrates' Courts Act 1980 as if it were an order requiring the other person to produce the child to him.

(2) The requirement is that a copy of the residence order has been served on the other person.

(3)   Subsection (1) is without prejudice to any other remedy open to the person in whose favour the residence order is in force.

Special guardianship

14A   Special guardianship orders

(1)   A 'special guardianship order' is an order appointing one or more individuals to be a child's 'special guardian' (or special guardians).

(2)   A special guardian –

  (a)   must be aged eighteen or over; and
  (b)   must not be a parent of the child in question,

and subsections (3) to (6) are to be read in that light.

(3)   The court may make a special guardianship order with respect to any child on the application of an individual who –

  (a)   is entitled to make such an application with respect to the child; or
  (b)   has obtained the leave of the court to make the application,

or on the joint application of more than one such individual.

(4)   Section 9(3) applies in relation to an application for leave to apply for a special guardianship order as it applies in relation to an application for leave to apply for a section 8 order.

(5)   The individuals who are entitled to apply for a special guardianship order with respect to a child are –

  (a)   any guardian of the child;
  (b)   any individual in whose favour a residence order is in force with respect to the child;
  (c)   any individual listed in subsection (5)(b) or (c) of section 10 (as read with subsection (10) of that section);
  (d)   a local authority foster parent with whom the child has lived for a period of at least one year immediately preceding the application;
  (e)   a relative with whom the child has lived for a period of at least one year immediately preceding the application.

(6)   The court may also make a special guardianship order with respect to a child in any family proceedings in which a question arises with respect to the welfare of the child if –

  (a)   an application for the order has been made by an individual who falls within subsection (3)(a) or (b) (or more than one such individual jointly); or
  (b)   the court considers that a special guardianship order should be made even though no such application has been made.

(7)   No individual may make an application under subsection (3) or (6)(a) unless, before the beginning of the period of three months ending with the date of the application, he has given written notice of his intention to make the application –

  (a)   if the child in question is being looked after by a local authority, to that local authority, or
  (b)   otherwise, to the local authority in whose area the individual is ordinarily resident.

(8)   On receipt of such a notice, the local authority must investigate the matter and prepare a report for the court dealing with –

  (a)   the suitability of the applicant to be a special guardian;
  (b)   such matters (if any) as may be prescribed by the Secretary of State; and
  (c)   any other matter which the local authority consider to be relevant.

(9)   The court may itself ask a local authority to conduct such an investigation and prepare such a report, and the local authority must do so.

(10)   The local authority may make such arrangements as they see fit for any person to act on their behalf in connection with conducting an investigation or preparing a report referred to in subsection (8) or (9).

(11)   The court may not make a special guardianship order unless it has received a report dealing with the matters referred to in subsection (8).

(12)   Subsections (8) and (9) of section 10 apply in relation to special guardianship orders as they apply in relation to section 8 orders.

(13)   This section is subject to section 29(5) and (6) of the Adoption and Children Act 2002.

Amendments—Adoption and Children Act 2002, s 115(1); Children and Young Persons Act 2008, s 38.

14B   Special guardianship orders: making

(1)   Before making a special guardianship order, the court must consider whether, if the order were made –

(a)   a contact order should also be made with respect to the child,
(b)   any section 8 order in force with respect to the child should be varied or discharged.
(c)   where a contact order made with respect to the child is not discharged, any enforcement order relating to that contact order should be revoked, and
(d)   where a contact activity direction has been made as regards contact with the child and is in force, that contact activity direction should be discharged.

(2)   On making a special guardianship order, the court may also –

(a)   give leave for the child to be known by a new surname;
(b)   grant the leave required by section 14C(3)(b), either generally or for specified purposes.

Amendments—Adoption and Children Act 2002, s 115(1); Children and Adoption Act 2006, s 15, Sch 2, paras 7, 8(a), Sch 3.

14C   Special guardianship orders: effect

(1)   The effect of a special guardianship order is that while the order remains in force –

(a)   a special guardian appointed by the order has parental responsibility for the child in respect of whom it is made; and
(b)   subject to any other order in force with respect to the child under this Act, a special guardian is entitled to exercise parental responsibility to the exclusion of any other person with parental responsibility for the child (apart from another special guardian).

(2)   Subsection (1) does not affect –

(a)   the operation of any enactment or rule of law which requires the consent of more than one person with parental responsibility in a matter affecting the child; or
(b)   any rights which a parent of the child has in relation to the child's adoption or placement for adoption.

(3)   While a special guardianship order is in force with respect to a child, no person may –

(a)   cause the child to be known by a new surname; or
(b)   remove him from the United Kingdom,

without either the written consent of every person who has parental responsibility for the child or the leave of the court.

(4)   Subsection (3)(b) does not prevent the removal of a child, for a period of less than three months, by a special guardian of his.

(5)   If the child with respect to whom a special guardianship order is in force dies, his special guardian must take reasonable steps to give notice of that fact to –

(a)   each parent of the child with parental responsibility; and

(b)   each guardian of the child,

but if the child has more than one special guardian, and one of them has taken such steps in relation to a particular parent or guardian, any other special guardian need not do so as respects that parent or guardian.

(6)   This section is subject to section 29(7) of the Adoption and Children Act 2002.

Amendments—Inserted by Adoption and Children Act 2002, s 115(1).

14D   Special guardianship orders: variation and discharge

(1)   The court may vary or discharge a special guardianship order on the application of –

    (a)   the special guardian (or any of them, if there are more than one);

    (b)   any parent or guardian of the child concerned;

    (c)   any individual in whose favour a residence order is in force with respect to the child;

    (d)   any individual not falling within any of paragraphs (a) to (c) who has, or immediately before the making of the special guardianship order had, parental responsibility for the child;

    (e)   the child himself; or

    (f)   a local authority designated in a care order with respect to the child.

(2)   In any family proceedings in which a question arises with respect to the welfare of a child with respect to whom a special guardianship order is in force, the court may also vary or discharge the special guardianship order if it considers that the order should be varied or discharged, even though no application has been made under subsection (1).

(3)   The following must obtain the leave of the court before making an application under subsection (1)   –

    (a)   the child;

    (b)   any parent or guardian of his;

    (c)   any step-parent of his who has acquired, and has not lost, parental responsibility for him by virtue of section 4A;

    (d)   any individual falling within subsection (1)(d) who immediately before the making of the special guardianship order had, but no longer has, parental responsibility for him.

(4)   Where the person applying for leave to make an application under subsection (1) is the child, the court may only grant leave if it is satisfied that he has sufficient understanding to make the proposed application under subsection (1).

(5)   The court may not grant leave to a person falling within subsection (3)(b)(c) or (d) unless it is satisfied that there has been a significant change in circumstances since the making of the special guardianship order.

Amendments—Inserted by Adoption and Children Act 2002, s 115(1).

14E   Special guardianship orders: supplementary

(1)   In proceedings in which any question of making, varying or discharging a special guardianship order arises, the court shall (in the light of any rules made by virtue of subsection (3)) –

    (a)   draw up a timetable with a view to determining the question without delay; and

    (b)   give such directions as it considers appropriate for the purpose of ensuring, so far as is reasonably practicable, that the timetable is adhered to.

(2)   Subsection (1) applies also in relation to proceedings in which any other question with respect to a special guardianship order arises.

(3)   The power to make rules in subsection (2) of section 11 applies for the purposes of this section as it applies for the purposes of that.

(4) A special guardianship order, or an order varying one, may contain provisions which are to have effect for a specified period.

(5) Section 11(7) (apart from paragraph (c)) applies in relation to special guardianship orders and orders varying them as it applies in relation to section 8 orders.

Amendments—Inserted by Adoption and Children Act 2002, s 115(1).

14F Special guardianship support services

(1) Each local authority must make arrangements for the provision within their area of special guardianship support services, which means –

    (a) counselling, advice and information; and

    (b) such other services as are prescribed,

in relation to special guardianship.

(2) The power to make regulations under subsection (1)(b) is to be exercised so as to secure that local authorities provide financial support.

(3) At the request of any of the following persons –

    (a) a child with respect to whom a special guardianship order is in force;

    (b) a special guardian;

    (c) a parent;

    (d) any other person who falls within a prescribed description,

a local authority may carry out an assessment of that person's needs for special guardianship support services (but, if the Secretary of State so provides in regulations, they must do so if he is a person of a prescribed description, or if his case falls within a prescribed description, or if both he and his case fall within prescribed descriptions).

(4) A local authority may, at the request of any other person, carry out an assessment of that person's needs for special guardianship support services.

(5) Where, as a result of an assessment, a local authority decide that a person has needs for special guardianship support services, they must then decide whether to provide any such services to that person.

(6) If –

    (a) a local authority decide to provide any special guardianship support services to a person, and

    (b) the circumstances fall within a prescribed description,

the local authority must prepare a plan in accordance with which special guardianship support services are to be provided to him, and keep the plan under review.

(7) The Secretary of State may by regulations make provision about assessments, preparing and reviewing plans, the provision of special guardianship support services in accordance with plans and reviewing the provision of special guardianship support services.

(8) The regulations may in particular make provision –

    (a) about the type of assessment which is to be carried out, or the way in which an assessment is to be carried out;

    (b) about the way in which a plan is to be prepared;

    (c) about the way in which, and the time at which, a plan or the provision of special guardianship support services is to be reviewed;

    (d) about the considerations to which a local authority are to have regard in carrying out an assessment or review or preparing a plan;

(e)   as to the circumstances in which a local authority may provide special guardianship support services subject to conditions (including conditions as to payment for the support or the repayment of financial support);

(f)   as to the consequences of conditions imposed by virtue of paragraph (e) not being met (including the recovery of any financial support provided);

(g)   as to the circumstances in which this section may apply to a local authority in respect of persons who are outside that local authority's area;

(h)   as to the circumstances in which a local authority may recover from another local authority the expenses of providing special guardianship support services to any person.

(9)   A local authority may provide special guardianship support services (or any part of them) by securing their provision by –

(a)   another local authority; or

(b)   a person within a description prescribed in regulations of persons who may provide special guardianship support services,

and may also arrange with any such authority or person for that other authority or that person to carry out the local authority's functions in relation to assessments under this section.

(10)   A local authority may carry out an assessment of the needs of any person for the purposes of this section at the same time as an assessment of his needs is made under any other provision of this Act or under any other enactment.

(11)   Section 27 (co-operation between authorities) applies in relation to the exercise of functions of a local authority under this section as it applies in relation to the exercise of functions of a local authority under Part 3.

Amendments—Inserted by Adoption and Children Act 2002, s 115(1).

14G

(repealed)

Amendments—Repealed by Health and Social Care (Community Health and Standards) Act 2003, ss 117(2), 196, Sch 14, Pt 2.

Financial relief

15   Orders for financial relief with respect to children

(1)   Schedule 1 (which consists primarily of the re-enactment, with consequential amendments and minor modifications, of provisions of section 6 of the Family Law Reform Act 1969, the Guardianship of Minors Acts 1971 and 1973, the Children Act 1975 and of sections 15 and 16 of the Family Law Reform Act 1987) makes provision in relation to financial relief for children.

(2)   The powers of a magistrates' court under section 60 of the Magistrates' Courts Act 1980 to revoke, revive or vary an order for the periodical payment of money and the power of a clerk of a magistrates' court to vary such an order shall not apply in relation to an order made under Schedule 1.

Amendments—Courts and Legal Services Act 1990, s 116, Sch 16, para 10(1); Maintenance Enforcement Act 1991, s 11(1), Sch 2, para 10.

Family assistance orders

16   Family assistance orders

(1)   Where, in any family proceedings, the court has power to make an order under this Part with respect to any child, it may (whether or not it makes such an order) make an order requiring–

(a)   an officer of the Service or a Welsh family proceedings officer to be made available; or

(b)   a local authority to make an officer of the authority available,

to advise, assist and (where appropriate) befriend any person named in the order.

(2)   The persons who may be named in an order under this section ('a family assistance order') are–

(a)   any parent, guardian or special guardian of the child;

(b)   any person with whom the child is living or in whose favour a contact order is in force with respect to the child;

(c)   the child himself.

(3)   No court may make a family assistance order unless–

(a)   *(repealed)*

(b)   it has obtained the consent of every person to be named in the order other than the child.

(4)   A family assistance order may direct–

(a)   the person named in the order; or

(b)   such of the persons named in the order as may be specified in the order,

to take such steps as may be so specified with a view to enabling the officer concerned to be kept informed of the address of any person named in the order and to be allowed to visit any such person.

(4A)   If the court makes a family assistance order with respect to a child and the order is to be in force at the same time as a contact order made with respect to the child, the family assistance order may direct the officer concerned to give advice and assistance as regards establishing, improving and maintaining contact to such of the persons named in the order as may be specified in the order.

(5)   Unless it specifies a shorter period, a family assistance order shall have effect for a period of twelve months beginning with the day on which it is made.

(6)   If the court makes a family assistance order with respect to a child and the order is to be in force at the same time as a section 8 order made with respect to the child, the family assistance order may direct the officer concerned to report to the court on such matters relating to the section 8 order as the court may require (including the question whether the section 8 order ought to be varied or discharged).

(7)   A family assistance order shall not be made so as to require a local authority to make an officer of theirs available unless–

(a)   the authority agree; or

(b)   the child concerned lives or will live within their area.

(8), (9)   *(repealed)*

Amendments—Criminal Justice and Court Services Act 2000, s 74, Sch 7, paras 87, 89, Sch 8; Adoption and Children Act 2002, s 139(1), Sch 3, paras 54, 58; Children Act 2004, s 40, Sch 3, paras 5, 7; Children and Adoption Act 2006, ss 6, 15(2), Sch 3.

16A   Risk assessments

(1)   This section applies to the following functions of officers of the Service or Welsh family proceedings officers –

(a)   any function in connection with family proceedings in which the court has power to make an order under this Part with respect to a child or in which a question with respect to such an order arises;

(b)   any function in connection with an order made by the court in such proceedings.

(2)   If, in carrying out any function to which this section applies, an officer of the Service or a Welsh family proceedings officer is given cause to suspect that the child concerned is at risk of harm, he must –

(a)   make a risk assessment in relation to the child, and

(b)   provide the risk assessment to the court.

(3)   A risk assessment, in relation to a child who is at risk of suffering harm of a particular sort, is an assessment of the risk of that harm being suffered by the child.

Amendments—Inserted by Children and Adoption Act 2006, s 7.

****

Schedule 1
Financial Provision for Children

Section 15(1)

1   Orders for financial relief against parents

(1)   On an application made by a parent, guardian or special guardian of a child, or by any person in whose favour a residence order is in force with respect to a child, the court may–

    (a)   in the case of an application to the High Court or a county court, make one or more of the orders mentioned in sub-paragraph (2);

    (b)   in the case of an application to a magistrates' court, make one or both of the orders mentioned in paragraphs (a) and (c) of that sub-paragraph.

(2)   The orders referred to in sub-paragraph (1) are–

    (a)   an order requiring either or both parents of a child–

        (i)   to make to the applicant for the benefit of the child; or

        (ii)   to make to the child himself,

    such periodical payments, for such term, as may be specified in the order;

    (b)   an order requiring either or both parents of a child–

        (i)   to secure to the applicant for the benefit of the child; or

        (ii)   to secure to the child himself,

    such periodical payments, for such term, as may be so specified;

    (c)   an order requiring either or both parents of a child–

        (i)   to pay to the applicant for the benefit of the child; or

        (ii)   to pay to the child himself,

    such lump sum as may be so specified;

    (d)   an order requiring a settlement to be made for the benefit of the child, and to the satisfaction of the court, of property–

        (i)   to which either parent is entitled (either in possession or in reversion); and

        (ii)   which is specified in the order;

    (e)   an order requiring either or both parents of a child–

        (i)   to transfer to the applicant, for the benefit of the child; or

        (ii)   to transfer to the child himself,

    such property to which the parent is, or the parents are, entitled (either in possession or in reversion) as may be specified in the order.

(3)   The powers conferred by this paragraph may be exercised at any time.

(4)   An order under sub-paragraph (2)(a) or (b) may be varied or discharged by a subsequent order made on the application of any person by or to whom payments were required to be made under the previous order.

(5)   Where a court makes an order under this paragraph–

    (a)   it may at any time make a further such order under sub-paragraph (2)(a), (b) or (c) with respect to the child concerned if he has not reached the age of eighteen;

    (b)   it may not make more than one order under sub-paragraph (2)(d) or (e) against the same person in respect of the same child.

(6)   On making, varying or discharging a residence order or a special guardianship order the court may exercise any of its powers under this Schedule even though no application has been made to it under this Schedule.

(7)   Where a child is a ward of court, the court may exercise any of its powers under this Schedule even though no application has been made to it.

2   Orders for financial relief for persons over eighteen

(1)   If, on an application by a person who has reached the age of eighteen, it appears to the court–

(a)   that the applicant is, will be or (if an order were made under this paragraph) would be receiving instruction at an educational establishment or undergoing training for a trade, profession or vocation, whether or not while in gainful employment; or

(b)   that there are special circumstances which justify the making of an order under this paragraph,

the court may make one or both of the orders mentioned in sub-paragraph (2).

(2)   The orders are–

(a)   an order requiring either or both of the applicant's parents to pay to the applicant such periodical payments, for such term, as may be specified in the order;

(b)   an order requiring either or both of the applicant's parents to pay to the applicant such lump sum as may be so specified.

(3)   An application may not be made under this paragraph by any person if, immediately before he reached the age of sixteen, a periodical payments order was in force with respect to him.

(4)   No order shall be made under this paragraph at a time when the parents of the applicant are living with each other in the same household.

(5)   An order under sub-paragraph (2)(a) may be varied or discharged by a subsequent order made on the application of any person by or to whom payments were required to be made under the previous order.

(6)   In sub-paragraph (3) 'periodical payments order' means an order made under–

(a)   this Schedule;

(b)   *(repealed)*

(c)   section 23 or 27 of the Matrimonial Causes Act 1973;

(d)   Part I of the Domestic Proceedings and Magistrates' Courts Act 1978,

(e)   Part 1 or 9 of Schedule 5 to the Civil Partnership Act 2004 (financial relief in the High Court or a county court etc);

(f)   Schedule 6 to the 2004 Act (financial relief in the magistrates' courts etc),

for the making or securing of periodical payments.

(7)   The powers conferred by this paragraph shall be exercisable at any time.

(8)   Where the court makes an order under this paragraph it may from time to time while that order remains in force make a further such order.

Amendments—CSA 1991, s58(14); CPA 2004, s 78(1), (2).

3   Duration of orders for financial relief

(1)   The term to be specified in an order for periodical payments made under paragraph 1(2)(a) or (b) in favour of a child may begin with the date of the making of an application for the order in question or any later date or a date ascertained in accordance with sub-paragraph (5) or (6) but–

(a)   shall not in the first instance extend beyond the child's seventeenth birthday unless the court thinks it right in the circumstances of the case to specify a later date; and

(b)   shall not in any event extend beyond the child's eighteenth birthday.

(2)   Paragraph (b) of sub-paragraph (1) shall not apply in the case of a child if it appears to the court that–

(a)   the child is, or will be (if an order were made without complying with that paragraph) would be receiving instruction at an educational establishment or undergoing training for a trade, profession or vocation, whether or not while in gainful employment; or

(b)   there are special circumstances which justify the making of an order without complying with that paragraph.

(3)   An order for periodical payments made under paragraph 1(2)(a) or 2(2)(a) shall, notwithstanding anything in the order, cease to have effect on the death of the person liable to make payments under the order.

(4)   Where an order is made under paragraph 1(2)(a) or (b) requiring periodical payments to be made or secured to the parent of a child, the order shall cease to have effect if–

(a)   any parent making or securing the payments; and

(b)   any parent to whom the payments are made or secured,

live together for a period of more than six months.

(5)   Where–

(a)   a maintenance calculation- ('the current calculation -') is in force with respect to a child; and

(b)   an application is made for an order under paragraph 1(2)(a) or (b) of this Schedule for periodical payments in favour of that child–
        (i)   in accordance with section 8 of the Child Support Act 1991; and
        (ii)   before the end of the period of 6 months beginning with the making of the current calculation-,

the term to be specified in any such order made on that application may be expressed to begin on, or at any time after, the earliest permitted date.

(6)   For the purposes of subsection (5) above, 'the earliest permitted date' is whichever is the later of–

(a)   the date 6 months before the application is made; or

(b)   the date on which the current calculation- took effect or, where successive maintenance calculations – have been continuously in force with respect to a child, on which the first of those calculations – took effect.

(7)   Where–

(a)   a maintenance calculation- ceases to have effect by or under any provision of the Child Support Act 1991, and

(b)   an application is made, before the end of the period of 6 months beginning with the relevant date, for an order for periodical payments under paragraph 1(2)(a) or (b) in favour of a child with respect to whom that maintenance calculation was in force immediately before it ceased to have effect,

the term to be specified in any such order, or in any interim order under paragraph 9, made on that application may begin with the date on which that maintenance calculation ceased to have effect, or any later date.

(8)   In sub-paragraph (7)(b)–

(a)   where the maintenance calculation ceased to have effect, the relevant date is the date on which it so ceased; and
        (b)   *(repealed)*

Amendments—SI 19933/623; CSPSSA 2000, SS 26, 85, SCH 3,para 10, Sch 9.

4   Matters to which court is to have regard in making orders for financial relief

(1)   In deciding whether to exercise its powers under paragraph 1 or 2, and if so in what manner, the court shall have regard to all the circumstances including–

(a)   the income, earning capacity, property and other financial resources which each person mentioned in sub-paragraph (4) has or is likely to have in the foreseeable future;

(b)   the financial needs, obligations and responsibilities which each person mentioned in sub-paragraph (4) has or is likely to have in the foreseeable future;

(c)   the financial needs of the child;

(d)   the income, earning capacity (if any), property and other financial resources of the child;

(e)   any physical or mental disability of the child;

(f)   the manner in which the child was being, or was expected to be, educated or trained.

(2)   In deciding whether to exercise its powers under paragraph 1 against a person who is not the mother or father of the child, and if so in what manner, the court shall in addition have regard to–

(a)   whether that person had assumed responsibility for the maintenance of the child, and, if so, the extent to which and basis on which he assumed that responsibility and the length of the period during which he met that responsibility;

(b)   whether he did so knowing that the child was not his child;

(c)   the liability of any other person to maintain the child.

(3)   Where the court makes an order under paragraph 1 against a person who is not the father of the child, it shall record in the order that the order is made on the basis that the person against whom the order is made is not the child's father.

(4)   The persons mentioned in sub-paragraph (1) are–

(a)   in relation to a decision whether to exercise its powers under paragraph 1, any parent of the child;

(b)   in relation to a decision whether to exercise its powers under paragraph 2, the mother and father of the child;

(c)   the applicant for the order;

(d)   any other person in whose favour the court proposes to make the order.

(5) In the case of a child who has a parent by virtue of section 42 or 43 of the Human Fertilisation and Embryology Act 2008, any reference in sub-paragraph (2), (3) or (4) to the child's father is a reference to the woman who is a parent of the child by virtue of that section.

Amendments—HFEA 2008, s 56, Sch 6, Pt 1, para 32(1),(2).

5 Provisions relating to lump sums

(1) Without prejudice to the generality of paragraph 1, an order under that paragraph for the payment of a lump sum may be made for the purpose of enabling any liabilities or expenses–

(a)   incurred in connection with the birth of the child or in maintaining the child; and

(b)   reasonably incurred before the making of the order,

to be met.

(2)   The amount of any lump sum required to be paid by an order made by a magistrates' court under paragraph 1 or 2 shall not exceed £1000 or such larger amount as the Lord Chancellor may, after consulting the Lord Chief Justice, from time to time by order fix for the purposes of this sub-paragraph.

(3)   The power of the court under paragraph 1 or 2 to vary or discharge an order for the making or securing of periodical payments by a parent shall include power to make an order under that provision for the payment of a lump sum by that parent.

(4)   The amount of any lump sum which a parent may be required to pay by virtue of sub-paragraph (3) shall not, in the case of an order made by a magistrates' court, exceed the maximum amount that may at the time of the making of the order be required to be paid under sub-paragraph (2), but a magistrates' court may make an order for the payment of a lump sum not exceeding that amount even though the parent was required to pay a lump sum by a previous order under this Act.

(5)   An order made under paragraph 1 or 2 for the payment of a lump sum may provide for the payment of that sum by instalments.

(6)   Where the court provides for the payment of a lump sum by instalments the court, on an application made either by the person liable to pay or the person entitled to receive that sum, shall have power to vary that order by varying–

    (a)   the number of instalments payable;

    (b)   the amount of any instalment payable;

    (c)   the date on which any instalment becomes payable.

(7)   The Lord Chief Justice may nominate a judicial office holder (as defined in section 109(4) of the Constitutional Reform Act 2005) to exercise his functions under this paragraph.

Amendments—SI 1992/709; CRA 2005, s 15(1), Sch 4, Pt 1, paras 203, 209.

6   Variation etc of orders for periodical payments

(1)   In exercising its powers under paragraph 1 or 2 to vary or discharge an order for the making or securing of periodical payments the court shall have regard to all the circumstances of the case, including any change in any of the matters to which the court was required to have regard when making the order.

(2)   The power of the court under paragraph 1 or 2 to vary an order for the making or securing of periodical payments shall include power to suspend any provision of the order temporarily and to revive any provision so suspended.

(3)   Where on an application under paragraph 1 or 2 for the variation or discharge of an order for the making or securing of periodical payments the court varies the payments required to be made under that order, the court may provide that the payments as so varied shall be made from such date as the court may specify except that, subject to sub-paragraph (9), the date shall not be earlier than the date of the making of the application.

(4)   An application for the variation of an order made under paragraph 1 for the making or securing of periodical payments to or for the benefit of a child may, if the child has reached the age of sixteen, be made by the child himself.

(5)   Where an order for the making or securing of periodical payments made under paragraph 1 ceases to have effect on the date on which the child reaches the age of sixteen, or at any time after that date but before or on the date on which he reaches the age of eighteen, the child may apply to the court which made the order for an order for its revival.

(6)   If on such an application it appears to the court that–

    (a)   the child is, will be or (if an order were made under this sub-paragraph) would be receiving instruction at an educational establishment or undergoing training for a trade, profession or vocation, whether or not while in gainful employment; or

    (b)   there are special circumstances which justify the making of an order under this paragraph,

the court shall have power by order to revive the order from such date as the court may specify, not being earlier than the date of the making of the application.

(7)   Any order which is revived by an order under sub-paragraph (5) may be varied or discharged under that provision, on the application of any person by whom or to whom payments are required to be made under the revived order.

(8)   An order for the making or securing of periodical payments made under paragraph 1 may be varied or discharged, after the death of either parent, on the application of a guardian or special guardian of the child concerned.

(9)   Where–

(a)   an order under paragraph 1(2)(a) or (b) for the making or securing of periodical payments in favour of more than one child ('the order') is in force;

(b)   the order requires payments specified in it to be made to or for the benefit of more than one child without apportioning those payments between them;

(c)   a maintenance calculation ('the calculation') is made with respect to one or more, but not all, of the children with respect to whom those payments are to be made; and

(d)   an application is made, before the end of the period of 6 months beginning with the date on which the calculation was made, for the variation or discharge of the order,

the court may, in exercise of its powers under paragraph 1 to vary or discharge the order, direct that the variation or discharge shall take effect from the date on which the calculation took effect or any later date.

Amendments—SI 1992/709; CRA 2005, s 15(1), Sch 4, Pt 1, paras 203, 209.

6A   Variation of orders for periodical payments etc made by magistrates' courts

(1)   Subject to sub-paragraphs (7) and (8), the power of a magistrates' court–

(a)   under paragraph 1 or 2 to vary an order for the making of periodical payments, or

(b)   under paragraph 5(6) to vary an order for the payment of a lump sum by instalments,

shall include power, if the court is satisfied that payment has not been made in accordance with the order, to exercise one of its powers under paragraphs (a) to (d) of section 59(3) of the Magistrates' Courts Act 1980.

(2)   In any case where–

(a)   a magistrates' court has made an order under this Schedule for the making of periodical payments or for the payment of a lump sum by instalments, and

(b)   payments under the order are required to be made by any method of payment falling within section 59(6) of the Magistrates' Courts Act 1980 (standing order, etc),

any person entitled to make an application under this Schedule for the variation of the order (in this paragraph referred to as 'the applicant') may apply to a magistrates' court acting in the same local justice area as the court which made the order for the order to be varied as mentioned in sub-paragraph (3).

(3)   Subject to sub-paragraph (5), where an application is made under sub-paragraph (2), a justices clerk, after giving written notice (by post or otherwise) of the application to any interested party and allowing that party, within the period of 14 days beginning with the date of the giving of that notice, an opportunity to make written representations, may vary the order to provide that payments under the order shall be made to the designated officer for the court.

(4)   The clerk may proceed with an application under sub-paragraph (2) notwithstanding that any such interested party as is referred to in sub-paragraph (3) has not received written notice of the application.

(5)   Where an application has been made under sub-paragraph (2), the clerk may, if he considers it inappropriate to exercise his power under sub-paragraph (3), refer the matter to the court which, subject to sub-paragraphs (7) and (8), may vary the order by exercising one of its powers under paragraphs (a) to (d) of section 59(3) of the Magistrates' Courts Act 1980.

(6)   Subsection (4) of section 59 of the Magistrates' Courts Act 1980 (power of court to order that account be opened) shall apply for the purposes of sub-paragraphs (1) and (5) as it applies for the purposes of that section.

(7)   Before varying the order by exercising one of its powers under paragraphs (a) to (d) of section 59(3) of the Magistrates' Courts Act 1980, the court shall have regard to any representations made by the parties to the application.

(8)   If the court does not propose to exercise its power under paragraph (c), (cc) or (d) of subsection (3) of section 59 of the Magistrates' Courts Act 1980, the court shall, unless upon

representations expressly made in that behalf by the applicant for the order it is satisfied that it is undesirable to do so, exercise its power under paragraph (b) of that subsection.

(9)   None of the powers of the court, or of a justices clerk, conferred by this paragraph shall be exercisable in relation to an order under this Schedule for the making of periodical payments, or for the payment of a lump sum by instalments, which is not a qualifying maintenance order (within the meaning of section 59 of the Magistrates' Courts Act 1980).

(10)   In sub-paragraphs (3) and (4) 'interested party', in relation to an application made by the applicant under sub-paragraph (2), means a person who would be entitled to be a party to an application for the variation of the order made by the applicant under any other provision of this Schedule if such an application were made.

7   Variation of orders for secured periodical payments after death of parent

(1)   Where the parent liable to make payments under a secured periodical payments order has died, the persons who may apply for the variation or discharge of the order shall include the personal representatives of the deceased parent.

(2)   No application for the variation of the order shall, except with the permission of the court, be made after the end of the period of six months from the date on which representation in regard to the estate of that parent is first taken out.

(3)   The personal representatives of a deceased person against whom a secured periodical payments order was made shall not be liable for having distributed any part of the estate of the deceased after the end of the period of six months referred to in sub-paragraph (2) on the ground that they ought to have taken into account the possibility that the court might permit an application for variation to be made after that period by the person entitled to payments under the order.

(4)   Sub-paragraph (3) shall not prejudice any power to recover any part of the estate so distributed arising by virtue of the variation of an order in accordance with this paragraph.

(5)   Where an application to vary a secured periodical payments order is made after the death of the parent liable to make payments under the order, the circumstances to which the court is required to have regard under paragraph 6(1) shall include the changed circumstances resulting from the death of the parent.

(6)   In considering for the purposes of sub-paragraph (2) the question when representation was first taken out, a grant limited to settled land or to trust property shall be left out of account and a grant limited to real estate or to personal estate shall be left out of account unless a grant limited to the remainder of the estate has previously been made or is made at the same time.

(7)   In this paragraph 'secured periodical payments order' means an order for secured periodical payments under paragraph 1(2)(b).

8   Financial relief under other enactments

(1)   This paragraph applies where a residence order or a special guardianship order is made with respect to a child at a time when there is in force an order ('the financial relief order') made under any enactment other than this Act and requiring a person to contribute to the child's maintenance.

(2)   Where this paragraph applies, the court may, on the application of–

  (a)   any person required by the financial relief order to contribute to the child's maintenance; or
  (b)   any person in whose favour a residence order or a special guardianship order with respect to the child is in force,

make an order revoking the financial relief order, or varying it by altering the amount of any sum payable under that order or by substituting the applicant for the person to whom any such sum is otherwise payable under that order.

Amendments—ACA 2002,s 139(1),Sch 3, para 71.

9 Interim orders

(1) Where an application is made under paragraph 1 or 2 the court may, at any time before it disposes of the application, make an interim order–

    (a)   requiring either or both parents to make such periodical payments, at such times and for such term as the court thinks fit; and

    (b)   giving any direction which the court thinks fit.

(2) An interim order made under this paragraph may provide for payments to be made from such date as the court may specify except that, subject to paragraph 3(5) and (6), the date shall not be earlier than the date of the making of the application under paragraph 1 or 2.

(3) An interim order made under this paragraph shall cease to have effect when the application is disposed of or, if earlier, on the date specified for the purposes of this paragraph in the interim order.

(4) An interim order in which a date has been specified for the purposes of sub-paragraph (3) may be varied by substituting a later date.

Amendments—SI 1993/623.

Alteration of maintenance agreements

10

(1) In this paragraph and in paragraph 11 'maintenance agreement' means any agreement in writing made with respect to a child, whether before or after the commencement of this paragraph, which–

    (a)   is or was made between the father and mother of the child; and

    (b)   contains provision with respect to the making or securing of payments, or the disposition or use of any property, for the maintenance or education of the child,

and any such provisions are in this paragraph, and paragraph 11, referred to as 'financial arrangements'.

(2) Subject to sub-paragraph (2A), where a maintenance agreement is for the time being subsisting and each of the parties to the agreement is for the time being either domiciled or resident in England and Wales, then, either party may apply for an order under this paragraph.

(2A) If an application or part of an application relates to a matter where jurisdiction falls to be determined by reference to the jurisdictional requirements of the Maintenance Regulation and Schedule 6 to the Civil Jurisdiction and Judgments (Maintenance) Regulations 2011 –

    (a)   the requirement as to domicile or residence in sub-paragraph (2) does not apply to the application or that part of it, but

    (b)   the court may not entertain the application or that part of it unless it has jurisdiction to do so by virtue of that Regulation and that Schedule.

(2B) In sub-paragraph (2A), "the Maintenance Regulation" means Council Regulation (EC) No 4/2009 including as applied in relation to Denmark by virtue of the Agreement made on 19th October 2005 between the European Community and the Kingdom of Denmark.

(3) If the court to which the application is made is satisfied either–

    (a)   that, by reason of a change in the circumstances in the light of which any financial arrangements contained in the agreement were made (including a change foreseen by the parties when making the agreement), the agreement should be altered so as to make different financial arrangements; or

    (b)   that the agreement does not contain proper financial arrangements with respect to the child, then that court may by order make such alterations in the agreement by varying or revoking any financial arrangements contained in it as may appear to it to be just having regard to all the circumstances.

(4)   If the maintenance agreement is altered by an order under this paragraph, the agreement shall have effect thereafter as if the alteration had been made by agreement between the parties and for valuable consideration.

(5)   Where a court decides to make an order under this paragraph altering the maintenance agreement–

(a)   by inserting provision for the making or securing by one of the parties to the agreement of periodical payments for the maintenance of the child; or

(b)   by increasing the rate of periodical payments required to be made or secured by one of the parties for the maintenance of the child,

then, in deciding the term for which under the agreement as altered by the order the payments or (as the case may be) the additional payments attributable to the increase are to be made or secured for the benefit of the child, the court shall apply the provisions of sub-paragraphs (1) and (2) of paragraph 3 as if the order were an order under paragraph 1(2)(a) or (b).

(6)   A magistrates' court shall not entertain an application under sub-paragraph (2) unless both the parties to the agreement are resident in England and Wales and at least one of the parties is resident in the commission area ... the court acts in, or is authorised by the Lord Chancellor to act for, a local justice area in which at least one of the parties is resident, and shall not have power to make any order on such an application except–

(a)   in a case where the agreement contains no provision for periodical payments by either of the parties, an order inserting provision for the making by one of the parties of periodical payments for the maintenance of the child;

(b)   in a case where the agreement includes provision for the making by one of the parties of periodical payments, an order increasing or reducing the rate of, or terminating, any of those payments.

(7)   For the avoidance of doubt it is hereby declared that nothing in this paragraph affects any power of a court before which any proceedings between the parties to a maintenance agreement are brought under any other enactment to make an order containing financial arrangements or any right of either party to apply for such an order in such proceedings.

(8)   In the case of a child who has a parent by virtue of section 42 or 43 of the Human Fertilisation and Embryology Act 2008, the reference in sub-paragraph (1)(a) to the child's father is a reference to the woman who is a parent of the child by virtue of that section.

Amendments—Justices of the Peace Act 1997, s 73(2), Sch 5, para 27; AJA 1999, s 106, Sch 15; Courts Act 2003, s 109(1), Sch 8, para339; HFEA 2008,s 56, Sch 6, Pt 1, para 32(1),(3); SI 2011/1484.

11

(1)   Where a maintenance agreement provides for the continuation, after the death of one of the parties, of payments for the maintenance of a child and that party dies domiciled in England and Wales, the surviving party or the personal representatives of the deceased party may apply to the High Court or a county court for an order under paragraph 10.

(2)   If a maintenance agreement is altered by a court on an application under this paragraph, the agreement shall have effect thereafter as if the alteration had been made, immediately before the death, by agreement between the parties and for valuable consideration.

(3)   An application under this paragraph shall not, except with leave of the High Court or a county court, be made after the end of the period of six months beginning with the day on which representation in regard to the estate of the deceased is first taken out.

(4)   In considering for the purposes of sub-paragraph (3) the question when representation was first taken out, a grant limited to settled land or to trust property shall be left out of account and a

grant limited to real estate or to personal estate shall be left out of account unless a grant limited to the remainder of the estate has previously been made or is made at the same time.

(5) A county court shall not entertain an application under this paragraph, or an application for leave to make an application under this paragraph, unless it would have jurisdiction to hear and determine proceedings for an order under section 2 of the Inheritance (Provision for Family and Dependants) Act 1975 in relation to the deceased's estate by virtue of section 25 of the County Courts Act 1984 (jurisdiction under the Act of 1975).

(6) The provisions of this paragraph shall not render the personal representatives of the deceased liable for having distributed any part of the estate of the deceased after the expiry of the period of six months referred to in sub-paragraph (3) on the ground that they ought to have taken into account the possibility that a court might grant leave for an application by virtue of this paragraph to be made by the surviving party after that period.

(7) Sub-paragraph (6) shall not prejudice any power to recover any part of the estate so distributed arising by virtue of the making of an order in pursuance of this paragraph.

12 Enforcement of orders for maintenance

(1) Any person for the time being under an obligation to make payments in pursuance of any order for the payment of money made by a magistrates' court under this Act shall give notice of any change of address to such person (if any) as may be specified in the order.

(2) Any person failing without reasonable excuse to give such a notice shall be guilty of an offence and liable on summary conviction to a fine not exceeding level 2 on the standard scale.

(3) An order for the payment of money made by a magistrates' court under this Act shall be enforceable as a magistrates' court maintenance order within the meaning of section 150(1) of the Magistrates' Courts Act 1980.

13 Direction for settlement of instrument by conveyancing counsel

Where the High Court or a county court decides to make an order under this Act for the securing of periodical payments or for the transfer or settlement of property, it may direct that the matter be referred to one of the conveyancing counsel of the court to settle a proper instrument to be executed by all necessary parties.

14

(1) If an application under paragraph 1 or 2, or part of such an application, relates to a matter where jurisdiction falls to be determined by reference to the jurisdictional requirements of the Maintenance Regulation and Schedule 6 to the Civil Jurisdiction and Judgments (Maintenance) Regulations 2011, the court may not entertain the application or that part of it unless it has jurisdiction to do so by virtue of that Regulation and that Schedule.

(2) In sub-paragraph (1), "the Maintenance Regulation" means Council Regulation (EC) No 4/2009 including as applied in relation to Denmark by virtue of the Agreement made on 19th October 2005 between the European Community and the Kingdom of Denmark.

Amendments—Substituted by SI 2011/1484.

15 Local authority contribution to child's maintenance

(1) Where a child lives, or is to live, with a person as the result of a residence order, a local authority may make contributions to that person towards the cost of the accommodation and maintenance of the child.

(2) Sub-paragraph (1) does not apply where the person with whom the child lives, or is to live, is a parent of the child or the husband or wife or civil partner of a parent of the child.

Amendments—CPA 2004, s 78(1), (3).

16   Interpretation

(1)   In this Schedule 'child' includes, in any case where an application is made under paragraph 2 or 6 in relation to a person who has reached the age of eighteen, that person.

(2)   In this Schedule, except paragraphs 2 and 15, 'parent' includes –

   (a)   any party to a marriage (whether or not subsisting) in relation to whom the child concerned is a child of the family, and
   (b)   any civil partner in a civil partnership (whether or not subsisting) in relation to whom the child concerned is a child of the family;

and for this purpose any reference to either parent or both parents shall be read as a reference to any parent of his and to all of his parents.

(3)   In this Schedule, 'maintenance calculation' has the same meaning as it has in the Child Support Act 1991 by virtue of section 54 of that Act as read with any regulations in force under that section.

Amendments—SI 1993/623; CSPSSA 2000, s 26, Sch 3, para 10; CPA, s 78(1), (4).

****

A4.2

CIVIL PARTNERSHIP ACT 2004

ARRANGEMENT OF SECTIONS

PART 1

INTRODUCTION

Section		*Page*
1	Civil partnership	500

PART 2

CIVIL PARTNERSHIP: ENGLAND AND WALES

Formation, eligibility and parental etc consent

2	Formation of civil partnership by registration	500
3	Eligibility	501
4	Parental etc consent where proposed civil partner under 18	501

Registration procedure: general

5	Types of pre-registration procedure	501
6	Place of registration	501
6A	Power to approve premises	502
7	The civil partnership document	503

The standard procedure

8	Notice of proposed civil partnership and declaration	503
9	Power to require evidence of name etc	504
10	Proposed civil partnership to be publicised	504
11	Meaning of 'the waiting period'	505
12	Power to shorten the waiting period	505
13	Objection to proposed civil partnership	505
14	Issue of civil partnership schedule	505
15	Appeal against refusal to issue civil partnership schedule	506
16	Frivolous objections and representations: liability for costs etc	506
17	Period during which registration may take place	506

The procedures for house-bound and detained persons

18	House-bound persons	507
19	Detained persons	507

Modified procedures for certain non-residents

20	Modified procedures for certain non-residents	508

The special procedure

21	Notice of proposed civil partnership	509
22	Evidence to be produced	509
23	Application to be reported to Registrar General	509
24	Objection to issue of Registrar General's licence	509
25	Issue of Registrar General's licence	509
26	Frivolous objections: liability for costs	510
27	Period during which registration may take place	510

Supplementary

28	Registration authorities	510
29	Civil partnership registrars	511
30	The Registrar General and the register	511
31	Offences relating to civil partnership schedule	511
32	Offences relating to Registrar General's licence	512
33	Offences relating to the recording of civil partnerships	512
34	Fees	513
35	Power to assimilate provisions relating to civil registration	513
36	Regulations and orders	513

Introduction

37	Powers to make orders and effect of orders	514
38	The period before conditional orders may be made final	514
39	Intervention of the Queen's Proctor	515
40	Proceedings before order has been made final	515
41	Time bar on applications for dissolution orders	516
42	Attempts at reconciliation of civil partners	516
43	Consideration by the court of certain agreements or arrangements	516

Dissolution of civil partnership

44	Dissolution of civil partnership which has broken down irretrievably	517
45	Supplemental provisions as to facts raising presumption of breakdown	517
46	Dissolution order not precluded by previous separation order etc	518
47	Refusal of dissolution in 5 year separation cases on ground of grave hardship	519
48	Proceedings before order made final: protection for respondent in separation cases	519

Nullity

49	Grounds on which civil partnership is void	520
50	Grounds on which civil partnership is voidable	520
51	Bars to relief where civil partnership is voidable	521
52	Proof of certain matters not necessary to validity of civil partnership	521
53	Power to validate civil partnership	521
54	Validity of civil partnerships registered outside England and Wales	522

Presumption of death orders

55	Presumption of death orders	523

Separation orders

56	Separation orders	523
57	Effect of separation order	523

Declarations

58	Declarations	524
59	General provisions as to making and effect of declarations	524
60	The Attorney General and proceedings for declarations	524
61	Supplementary provisions as to declarations	525

General provisions

62	Relief for respondent in dissolution proceedings	525
63	Restrictions on making of orders affecting children	525
64	Parties to proceedings under this Chapter	526
65	Contribution by civil partner to property improvement	526
66	Disputes between civil partners about property	526
67	Applications under section 66 where property not in possession etc	526
68	Applications under section 66 by former civil partners	527
69	Actions in tort between civil partners	527
70	Assurance policy by civil partner for benefit of other civil partner etc	528
70A	Money and property derived from housekeeping allowance	528
71	Wills, administration of estates and family provision	528
72	Financial relief for civil partners and children of family	528
73	Civil partnership agreements unenforceable	528
74	Property where civil partnership agreement is terminated	529

Chapter 5
Children

75	Parental responsibility, children of the family and relatives	529
76	Guardianship	529
77	Entitlement to apply for residence or contact order	530
78	Financial provision for children	530
79	Adoption	530
80	False statements etc with reference to civil partnerships	531
81	Housing and tenancies	532
82	Family homes and domestic violence	532
83	Fatal accidents claims	532
84	Evidence	532

PART 5

CIVIL PARTNERSHIP FORMED OR DISSOLVED ABROAD ETC

Chapter 1

Registration Outside Uk Under Order in Council

210	Registration at British consulates etc.	533
211	Registration by armed forces personnel	533
212	Meaning of 'overseas relationship'	534
213	Specified relationships	534
214	The general conditions	535
215	Overseas relationships treated as civil partnerships: the general rule	535
216	The same-sex requirement	536
217	Person domiciled in a part of the United Kingdom	536
218	The public policy exception	537

Introduction

219	Power to make provision corresponding to EC Regulation 2201/2003	537

Jurisdiction of courts in England and Wales

220	Meaning of 'the court'	538
221	Proceedings for dissolution, separation or nullity order	538
222	Proceedings for presumption of death order	539
223	Proceedings for dissolution, nullity or separation order: supplementary	539
224	Applications for declarations as to validity etc	539

Recognition of dissolution, annulment and separation

233	Effect of dissolution, annulment or separation obtained in the UK	539
234	Recognition in the UK of overseas dissolution, annulment or separation	540
235	Grounds for recognition	540
236	Refusal of recognition	541
237	Supplementary provisions relating to recognition of dissolution etc	541
238	Non-recognition elsewhere of dissolution or annulment	542

Chapter 4

Miscellaneous and Supplementary

239	Commanding officers' certificates for Part 2 purposes	542
240	Certificates of no impediment to overseas relationships	543
241	Transmission of certificates of registration of overseas relationships	543
242	Power to make provision relating to certain Commonwealth forces	543
243	Fees	544
244	Orders in Council: supplementary	544
245	Interpretation	544

Schedule 1 – Prohibited degrees of relationship: England and Wales	545
Part 1 – The Prohibitions	545
Part 2 – Special Provisions Relating to Qualified Prohibitions	546
Schedule 5 – Financial Relief in the High Court or a County Court etc	547
Part 1 – Financial Provision in Connection With Dissolution, Nullity or Separation	547
Part 2 – Property Adjustment on or After Dissolution, Nullity or Separation	549
Part 3 – Sale of Property Orders	550
Part 4 – Pension Sharing Orders on or After Dissolution or Nullity Order	551
Part 4A – Pension Compensation Sharing Orders on or after Dissolution or Nullity Order	552
Part 5 – Matters to Which Court is to Have Regard Under Parts 1 to 4A	554
Part 6 – Making of Part 1 Orders Having Regard to Pension Benefits	557
Part 7 – Pension Protection Fund Compensation etc	559
Part 8 – Maintenance Pending Outcome of Dissolution, Nullity or Separation Proceedings	562
Part 9 – Failure to Maintain: Financial Provision (and Interim Orders)	562
Part 10 – Commencement of Certain Proceedings and Duration of Certain Orders	564
Part 11 – Variation, Discharge etc of Certain Orders for Financial Relief	567
Part 12 – Arrears and Repayments	572
Part 13 – Consent Orders and Maintainence Agreements	574
Part 14 – Miscellaneous and Supplementary	578
Schedule 7 – Financial Relief in England and Wales after Overseas Dissolution etc of a Civil Partnership	581
Part 1 – Financial Relief	581
Part 2 – Steps to Prevent Avoidance Prior to Application for Leave Under Paragraph 4	589
Part 3 – Supplementary	590
Schedule 9 – Family Homes and Domestic Violence	590
Part 1 – Amendments of the Family Law Act 1996 (c 27)	590

PART 1
INTRODUCTION

1 Civil partnership

(1) A civil partnership is a relationship between two people of the same sex ('civil partners') –

    (a)   which is formed when they register as civil partners of each other –

        (i)   in England or Wales (under Part 2),

        (ii)   in Scotland (under Part 3),

        (iii)   in Northern Ireland (under Part 4), or

        (iv)   outside the United Kingdom under an Order in Council made under Chapter 1 of Part 5 (registration at British consulates etc or by armed forces personnel), or

    (b)   which they are treated under Chapter 2 of Part 5 as having formed (at the time determined under that Chapter) by virtue of having registered an overseas relationship.

(2) Subsection (1) is subject to the provisions of this Act under or by virtue of which a civil partnership is void.

(3) A civil partnership ends only on death, dissolution or annulment.

(4) The references in subsection (3) to dissolution and annulment are to dissolution and annulment having effect under or recognised in accordance with this Act.

(5) References in this Act to an overseas relationship are to be read in accordance with Chapter 2 of Part 5.

PART 2
CIVIL PARTNERSHIP: ENGLAND AND WALES

Formation, eligibility and parental etc consent

2 Formation of civil partnership by registration

(1) For the purposes of section 1, two people are to be regarded as having registered as civil partners of each other once each of them has signed the civil partnership document –

    (a)   at the invitation of, and in the presence of, a civil partnership registrar, and

    (b)   in the presence of each other and two witnesses.

(2) Subsection (1) applies regardless of whether subsections (3) and (4) are complied with.

(3) After the civil partnership document has been signed under subsection (1), it must also be signed, in the presence of the civil partners and each other, by –

    (a)   each of the two witnesses, and

    (b)   the civil partnership registrar.

(4) After the witnesses and the civil partnership registrar have signed the civil partnership document, the relevant registration authority must ensure that –

    (a)   the fact that the two people have registered as civil partners of each other, and

    (b)   any other information prescribed by regulations,

is recorded in the register as soon as is practicable.

(5) No religious service is to be used while the civil partnership registrar is officiating at the signing of a civil partnership document.

(6) 'The civil partnership document' has the meaning given by section 7(1).

(7) 'The relevant registration authority' means the registration authority in whose area the registration takes place.

3 Eligibility

(1) Two people are not eligible to register as civil partners of each other if –

(a)   they are not of the same sex,
(b)   either of them is already a civil partner or lawfully married,
(c)   either of them is under 16, or
(d)   they are within prohibited degrees of relationship.

(2) Part 1 of Schedule 1 contains provisions for determining when two people are within prohibited degrees of relationship.

4 Parental etc consent where proposed civil partner under 18

(1) The consent of the appropriate persons is required before a child and another person may register as civil partners of each other.

(2) Part 1 of Schedule 2 contains provisions for determining who are the appropriate persons for the purposes of this section.

(3) The requirement of consent under subsection (1) does not apply if the child is a surviving civil partner.

(4) Nothing in this section affects any need to obtain the consent of the High Court before a ward of court and another person may register as civil partners of each other.

(5) In this Part 'child', except where used to express a relationship, means a person who is under 18.

Registration procedure: general

5 Types of pre-registration procedure

(1) Two people may register as civil partners of each other under –

(a)   the standard procedure;
(b)   the procedure for house-bound persons;
(c)   the procedure for detained persons;
(d)   the special procedure (which is for cases where a person is seriously ill and not expected to recover).

(2) The procedures referred to in subsection (1)(*a*) to (*c*) are subject to –

(a)   section 20 (modified procedures for certain non-residents);
(b)   Schedule 3 (former spouses one of whom has changed sex).

(3) The procedures referred to in subsection (1) (including the procedures as modified by section 20 and Schedule 3) are subject to –

(a)   Part 2 of Schedule 1 (provisions applicable in connection with prohibited degrees of relationship), and
(b)   Parts 2 and 3 of Schedule 2 (provisions applicable where proposed civil partner is under 18).

(4) This section is also subject to section 249 and Schedule 23 (immigration control and formation of civil partnerships).

6 Place of registration

(1) The place at which two people may register as civil partners of each other –

(a)   must be in England or Wales,
(b)   (*repealed*)

    (c)   must be specified in the notices, or notice, of proposed civil partnership required by this Chapter.

(2) *(repealed)*

(3) Subsections (3A) and (3B) apply in the case of registration under the standard procedure (including that procedure modified as mentioned in section 5).

(3A) The place must be —

    (a)   on approved premises, or
    (b)   in a register office.

(3B) If it is in a register office, the place must be open to any person wishing to attend the registration.

(3C) In this Chapter 'register office' means a register office provided under section 10 of the Registration Service Act 1953.

(4), (5) *(repealed)*

Amendments—Equality Act 2010, ss 202(1), (2), 211(2), Sch 27, Pt 1; SI 2005/2000.

6A Power to approve premises

(1) The Secretary of State may by regulations make provision for and in connection with the approval by registration authorities of premises for the purposes of section 6(3A)(a).

(2) The matters dealt with by regulations may include –

    (a)   the kind of premises in respect of which approvals may be granted;
    (b)   the procedure to be followed in relation to applications for approval;
    (c)   the considerations to be taken into account by a registration authority in determining whether to approve any premises;
    (d)   the duration and renewal of approvals;
    (e)   the conditions that must or may be imposed by a registration authority on granting or renewing an approval;
    (f)   the determination and charging by registration authorities of fees in respect of applications for the approval of premises and in respect of the renewal of approvals;
    (g)   the circumstances in which a registration authority must or may revoke an approval;
    (h)   the review of any decision to refuse an approval or the renewal of an approval, to impose conditions on granting or renewing an approval or to revoke an approval;
    (i)   the notification to the Registrar General of all approvals granted, renewed or revoked;
    (j)   the keeping by registration authorities of registers of approved premises;
    (k)   the issue by the Registrar General of guidance supplementing the provision made by the regulations.

(2A) Regulations under this section may provide that premises approved for the registration of civil partnerships may differ from those premises approved for the registration of civil marriages.

(2B) Provision by virtue of subsection (2)(b) may, in particular, provide that applications for approval of premises may only be made with the consent (whether general or specific) of a person specified, or a person of a description specified, in the provision.

(2C) The power conferred by section 258(2), in its application to the power conferred by this section, includes in particular –

    (a)   power to make provision in relation to religious premises that differs from provision in relation to other premises;
    (b)   power to make different provision for different kinds of religious premises.

(3) Without prejudice to the width of subsection (2)(e), the Secretary of State must exercise his power to provide for the imposition of conditions as mentioned there so as to secure that members

of the public are permitted to attend when two people sign the civil partnership schedule on approved premises in accordance with section 6(3A)(a).

(3A) For the avoidance of doubt, nothing in this Act places an obligation on religious organisations to host civil partnerships if they do not wish to do so.

(3B) "Civil marriage" means marriage solemnised otherwise than according to the rites of the Church of England or any other religious usages.

(3C) "Religious premises" means premises which–

(a)   are used solely or mainly for religious purposes, or

(b)   have been so used and have not subsequently been used solely or mainly for other purposes.

Amendments—Equality Act 2010, s 202(1), (3); SI 2005/2000; SI 2008/678.

7 The civil partnership document

(1) In this Part 'the civil partnership document' means –

(a)   in relation to the special procedure, a Registrar General's licence, and

(b)   in relation to any other procedure, a civil partnership schedule.

(2) Before two people are entitled to register as civil partners of each other –

(a)   the civil partnership document must be delivered to the civil partnership registrar, and

(b)   the civil partnership registrar may then ask them for any information required (under section 2(4)) to be recorded in the register.

The standard procedure

8 Notice of proposed civil partnership and declaration

(1) For two people to register as civil partners of each other under the standard procedure a notice of proposed civil partnership must be given –

(a)   if the proposed civil partners have resided in the area of the same registration authority for the period of 7 days immediately before the giving of the notice, by each of them to that registration authority;

(b)   if the proposed civil partners have not resided in the area of the same registration authority for that period, by each of them to the registration authority in whose area he or she has resided for that period.

(2) A notice of proposed civil partnership must contain such information as may be prescribed by regulations.

(3) A notice of proposed civil partnership must also include the necessary declaration, made and signed by the person giving the notice –

(a)   at the time when the notice is given, and

(b)   in the presence of an authorised person;

and the authorised person must attest the declaration by adding his name, description and place of residence.

(4) The necessary declaration is a solemn declaration in writing –

(a)   that the proposed civil partner believes that there is no impediment of kindred or affinity or other lawful hindrance to the formation of the civil partnership;

(b)   that the proposed civil partners have for the period of 7 days immediately before the giving of the notice had their usual places of residence in the area of the registration authority, or in the areas of the registration authorities, to which notice is given.

(5) Where a notice of proposed civil partnership is given to a registration authority in accordance with this section, the registration authority must ensure that the following information is recorded in the register as soon as possible –

(a)   the fact that the notice has been given and the information in it;

(b)   the fact that the authorised person has attested the declaration.

(6) 'Authorised person' means an employee or officer or other person provided by a registration authority who is authorised by that authority to attest notices of proposed civil partnership.

(7) For the purposes of this Chapter, a notice of proposed civil partnership is recorded when subsection (5) is complied with.

Amendments—SI 2005/2000.

9 Power to require evidence of name etc

(1) The registration authority to which a notice of proposed civil partnership is given may require the person giving the notice to provide it with specified evidence –

(a)   relating to that person, or

(b)   if the registration authority considers that the circumstances are exceptional, relating not only to that person but also to that person's proposed civil partner.

(2) Such a requirement may be imposed at any time before the registration authority issues the civil partnership schedule under section 14.

(3) 'Specified evidence', in relation to a person, means such evidence as may be specified in guidance issued by the Registrar General –

(a)   of the person's name and surname,

(b)   of the person's age,

(c)   as to whether the person has previously formed a civil partnership or a marriage and, if so, as to the ending of the civil partnership or marriage and,

(d)   of the person's nationality.

(e)   (*repealed*)

Amendments—SI 2005/2000.

10 Proposed civil partnership to be publicised

(1) Where a notice of proposed civil partnership has been given to a registration authority, the registration authority must keep the relevant information on public display during the waiting period,

(a)   by that registration authority,

(b)   by any registration authority in whose area the person giving the notice has resided during the period of 7 days preceding the giving of the notice,

(c)   by any registration authority in whose area the proposed civil partner of the person giving the notice has resided during the period of 7 days preceding the giving of that notice,

(d)   by the registration authority in whose area the place specified in the notice as the place of proposed registration is located, and

(e)   by the Registrar General.

(2) 'The relevant information' means –

(a)   the name of the person giving the notice,

(b)   the name of that person's proposed civil partner, and

(c)   such other information included in the notice of proposed civil partnership as may be prescribed by regulations.

(3) All information that a registration authority is required for the time being to keep on public display under subsection (1) must be kept on display by it at one register office provided for a district within its area.

Amendments—SI 2005/2000.

11 Meaning of 'the waiting period'

In this Chapter the waiting period', in relation to a notice of proposed civil partnership, means the period –

(a)   beginning the day after the notice is recorded, and
(b)   subject to section 12, ending at the end of the period of 15 days beginning with that day.

12 Power to shorten the waiting period

(1) If the Registrar General, on an application being made to him, is satisfied that there are compelling reasons because of the exceptional circumstances of the case for shortening the period of 15 days mentioned in section 11(*b*), he may shorten it to such period as he considers appropriate.

(2) Regulations may make provision with respect to the making, and granting, of applications under subsection (1).

(3) Regulations under subsection (2) may provide for –

(a)   the power conferred by subsection (1) to be exercised by a registration authority on behalf of the Registrar General in such classes of case as are prescribed by the regulations;
(b)   the making of an appeal to the Registrar General against a decision taken by a registration authority in accordance with regulations made by virtue of paragraph (a).

13 Objection to proposed civil partnership

(1) Any person may object to the issue of a civil partnership schedule under section 14 by giving any registration authority notice of his objection.

(2) A notice of objection must –

(a)   state the objector's place of residence and the ground of objection, and
(b)   be signed by or on behalf of the objector.

(3) If a notice of objection is given to a registration authority, it must ensure that the fact that it has been given and the information in it are recorded in the register as soon as possible.

14 Issue of civil partnership schedule

(1) As soon as the waiting period in relation to each notice of proposed civil partnership has expired, the registration authority in whose area it is proposed that the registration take place is under a duty, at the request of one or both of the proposed civil partners, to issue a document to be known as a 'civil partnership schedule'.

(2) Regulations may make provision as to the contents of a civil partnership schedule.

(3) The duty in subsection (1) does not apply if the registration authority is not satisfied that there is no lawful impediment to the formation of the civil partnership.

(4) If an objection to the issue of the civil partnership schedule has been recorded in the register, no civil partnership schedule is to be issued until –

(a)   the relevant registration authority has investigated the objection and is satisfied that the objection ought not to obstruct the issue of the civil partnership schedule, or
(b)   the objection has been withdrawn by the person who made it.

(5) 'The relevant registration authority' means the authority which first records that a notice of proposed civil partnership has been given by one of the proposed civil partners.

15 Appeal against refusal to issue civil partnership schedule

(1) If the registration authority refuses to issue a civil partnership schedule –

(a)   because an objection to its issue has been made under section 13, or
(b)   in reliance on section 14(3),

either of the proposed civil partners may appeal to the Registrar General.

(2) On an appeal under this section the Registrar General must either confirm the refusal or direct that a civil partnership schedule be issued.

16 Frivolous objections and representations: liability for costs etc

(1) Subsection (3) applies if –

(a)   a person objects to the issue of a civil partnership schedule, but
(b)   the Registrar General declares that the grounds on which the objection is made are frivolous and ought not to obstruct the issue of the civil partnership schedule.

(2) Subsection (3) also applies if –

(a)   in reliance on section 14(3), the registration authority refuses to issue a civil partnership schedule as a result of a representation made to it, and
(b)   on an appeal under section 15 against the refusal, the Registrar General declares that the representation is frivolous and ought not to obstruct the issue of the civil partnership schedule.

(3) The person who made the objection or representation is liable for –

(a)   the costs of the proceedings before the Registrar General, and
(b)   damages recoverable by the proposed civil partner to whom the objection or representation relates.

(4) For the purpose of enabling any person to recover any such costs and damages, a copy of a declaration of the Registrar General purporting to be sealed with the seal of the General Register Office is evidence that the Registrar General has made the declaration.

17 Period during which registration may take place

(1) The proposed civil partners may not register as civil partners of each other on the production of the civil partnership schedule until the waiting period in relation to each notice of proposed civil partnership has expired.

(2) Subject to subsection (1), under the standard procedure, they may register as civil partners by signing the civil partnership schedule on any day in the applicable period between 8 o'clock in the morning and 6 o'lock in the evening (3) If they do not register as civil partners by signing the civil partnership schedule before the end of the applicable period –

(a)   the notices of proposed civil partnership and the civil partnership schedule are void, and
(b)   no civil partnership registrar may officiate at the signing of the civil partnership schedule by them.

(4) The applicable period, in relation to two people registering as civil partners of each other, is the period of 12 months beginning with –

(a)   the day on which the notices of proposed civil partnership are recorded, or
(b)   if the notices are not recorded on the same day, the earlier of those days.

Amendments—SI 2005/2000.

The procedures for house-bound and detained persons

18 House-bound persons

(1) This section applies if two people wish to register as civil partners of each other at the place where one of them is house-bound.

(2) person is house-bound at any place if, in relation to that person, a statement is made by a registered medical practitioner that, in his opinion –

(a)   because of illness or disability, that person ought not to move or be moved from the place where he is at the time when the statement is made, and

(b)   it is likely to be the case for at least the following 3 months that because of the illness or disability that person ought not to move or be moved from that place.

(3) The procedure under which the two people concerned may register as civil partners of each other is the same as the standard procedure, except that –

(a)   each notice of proposed civil partnership must be accompanied by a statement under subsection (2) ('a medical statement'), which must have been made not more than 14 days before the day on which the notice is recorded,

(b)   the fact that the registration authority to whom the notice is given has received the medical statement must be recorded in the register, and

(c)   the applicable period (for the purposes of section 17) is the period of 3 months beginning with –

   (i)   the day on which the notices of proposed civil partnership are recorded, or

   (ii)   if the notices are not recorded on the same day, the earlier of those days.

(4) A medical statement must contain such information and must be made in such manner as may be prescribed by regulations.

(5) A medical statement may not be made in relation to a person who is detained as described in section 19(2).

(6) For the purposes of this Chapter, a person in relation to whom a medical statement is made is to be treated, if he would not otherwise be so treated, as resident and usually resident at the place where he is for the time being.

19 Detained persons

(1) This section applies if two people wish to register as civil partners of each other at the place where one of them is detained.

(2) 'Detained' means detained –

(a)   as a patient in a hospital (but otherwise than by virtue of section 2, 4, 5, 35, 36 or 136 of the Mental Health Act 1983 (c. 20) (short term detentions)), or

(b)   in a prison or other place to which the Prison Act 1952 (c. 52) applies.

(3) The procedure under which the two people concerned may register as civil partners of each other is the same as the standard procedure, except that –

(a)   each notice of proposed civil partnership must be accompanied by a supporting statement, which must have been made not more than 21 days before the day on which the notice is recorded,

(b)   the fact that the registration authority to whom the notice is given has received the supporting statement must be recorded in the register, and

(c)   the applicable period (for the purposes of section 17) is the period of 3 months beginning with –

   (i)   the day on which the notices of proposed civil partnership are recorded, or

   (ii)   if the notices are not recorded on the same day, the earlier of those days.

(4) A supporting statement, in relation to a detained person, is a statement made by the responsible authority which –

(a)   identifies the establishment where the person is detained, and

(b)   states that the responsible authority has no objection to that establishment being specified in a notice of proposed civil partnership as the place at which the person is to register as a civil partner.

(5) A supporting statement must contain such information and must be made in such manner as may be prescribed by regulations.

(6) 'The responsible authority' means –

(a)   if the person is detained in a hospital, the hospital's managers;

(b)   if the person is detained in a prison or other place to which the 1952 Act applies, the governor or other officer for the time being in charge of that prison or other place.

(7) 'Patient' and 'hospital' have the same meaning as in Part 2 of the 1983 Act and 'managers', in relation to a hospital, has the same meaning as in section 145(1) of the 1983 Act.

(8) For the purposes of this Chapter, a detained person is to be treated, if he would not otherwise be so treated, as resident and usually resident at the place where he is for the time being.

Modified procedures for certain non-residents

20 Modified procedures for certain non-residents

(1) Subsection (5) applies in the following two cases.

(2) The first is where –

(a)   two people wish to register as civil partners of each other in England and Wales, and

(b)   one of them ('A') resides in Scotland and the other ('B') resides in England or Wales.

(3) *(repealed)*

(4) The second is where –

(a)   two people wish to register as civil partners of each other in England and Wales, and

(b)   one of them ('A') is an officer, seaman or marine borne on the books of one of Her Majesty's ships at seaand the other ('B') resides in England or Wales.

(5) For the purposes of the standard procedure, the procedure for house-bound persons and the procedure for detained persons –

(a)   A is not required to give a notice of proposed civil partnership under this Chapter;

(b)   B may make the necessary declaration without reference to A's usual place of residence for any period;

(c)   the waiting period is calculated by reference to the day on which B's notice is recorded;

(d)   the civil partnership schedule is not to be issued by a registration authority unless A or B produces to that registration authority a certificate of no impediment issued to A under the relevant provision;

(e)   the applicable period is calculated by reference to the day on which B's notice is recorded and, where the standard procedure is used in the first case, is the period of 3 months beginning with that day;

(f)   section 31 applies as if in subsections (1)(a) and (2)(c) for 'each notice' there were substituted 'B's notice'.

(6) 'The relevant provision' means –

(a)   if A resides in Scotland, section 97;

(b)   *(repealed)*

(c)   if A is a an officer, seaman or marine borne on the books of one of Her Majesty's ships at sea, section 239.

(7) *(repealed)*

Amendments—SI 2005/2000.

The special procedure

21 Notice of proposed civil partnership

(1) For two people to register as civil partners of each other under the special procedure, one of them must –

    (a)   give a notice of proposed civil partnership to the registration authority for the area in which it is proposed that the registration take place, and

    (b)   comply with any requirement made under section 22.

(2) The notice must contain such information as may be prescribed by regulations.

(3) Subsections (3) to (6) of section 8 (necessary declaration etc), apart from paragraph (*b*) of subsection (4), apply for the purposes of this section as they apply for the purposes of that section.

22 Evidence to be produced

(1) The person giving a notice of proposed civil partnership to a registration authority under the special procedure must produce to the authority such evidence as the Registrar General may require to satisfy him –

    (a)   that there is no lawful impediment to the formation of the civil partnership,

    (b)   that the conditions in subsection (2) are met, and

    (c)   that there is sufficient reason why a licence should be granted.

(2) The conditions are that one of the proposed civil partners—

    (a)   is seriously ill and not expected to recover,

    (b)   cannot be moved to a place where they could be registered as civil partners of each other under the standard procedure, and

    (c)   understands the nature and purport of signing a Registrar General's licence.

(3) The certificate of a registered medical practitioner is sufficient evidence of any or all of the matters referred to in subsection (2).s

Amendments—SI 2005/2000.

23 Application to be reported to Registrar General

On receiving a notice of proposed civil partnership under section 21 and any evidence under section 22, the registration authority must –

    (a)   inform the Registrar General, and

    (b)   comply with any directions the Registrar General may give for verifying the evidence given.

24 Objection to issue of Registrar General's licence

(1) Any person may object to the Registrar General giving authority for the issue of his licence by giving the Registrar General or any registration authority notice of his objection.

(2) A notice of objection must –

    (a)   state the objector's place of residence and the ground of objection, and

    (b)   be signed by or on behalf of the objector.

(3) If a notice of objection is given to a registration authority, it must ensure that the fact that it has been given and the information in it are recorded in the register as soon as possible.

25 Issue of Registrar General's licence

(1) This section applies where a notice of proposed civil partnership is given to a registration authority under section 21.

(2) The registration authority may issue a Registrar General's licence if, and only if, given authority to do so by the Registrar General.

(3) The Registrar General –

    (a)   may not give his authority unless he is satisfied that one of the proposed civil partners is seriously ill and not expected to recover, but

    (b)   if so satisfied, must give his authority unless a lawful impediment to the issue of his licence has been shown to his satisfaction to exist.

(4) A licence under this section must state that it is issued on the authority of the Registrar General.

(5) Regulations may (subject to subsection (4)) make provision as to the contents of a licence under this section.

(6) If an objection has been made to the Registrar General giving authority for the issue of his licence, he is not to give that authority until –

    (a)   he has investigated the objection and decided whether it ought to obstruct the issue of his licence, or

    (b)   the objection has been withdrawn by the person who made it.

(7) Any decision of the Registrar General under subsection (6)(*a*) is final.

26   Frivolous objections: liability for costs

(1) This section applies if –

    (a)   a person objects to the Registrar General giving authority for the issue of his licence, but

    (b)   the Registrar General declares that the grounds on which the objection is made are frivolous and ought not to obstruct the issue of his licence.

(2) The person who made the objection is liable for –

    (a)   the costs of the proceedings before the Registrar General, and

    (b)   damages recoverable by the proposed civil partner to whom the objection relates.

(3) For the purpose of enabling any person to recover any such costs and damages, a copy of a declaration of the Registrar General purporting to be sealed with the seal of the General Register Office is evidence that the Registrar General has made the declaration.

27   Period during which registration may take place

(1) If a Registrar General's licence has been issued under section 25, the proposed civil partners may register as civil partners by signing it at any time within 1 month from the day on which the notice of proposed civil partnership was given.

(2) If they do not register as civil partners by signing the licence within the 1 month period –

    (a)   the notice of proposed civil partnership and the licence are void, and

    (b)   no civil partnership registrar may officiate at the signing of the licence by them.

Supplementary

28   Registration authorities

In this Chapter 'registration authority' means –

    (a)   in relation to England, a county council, the council of any district comprised in an area for which there is no county council, a London borough council, the Common Council of the City of London or the Council of the Isles of Scilly;

    (b)   in relation to Wales, a county council or a county borough council.

29   Civil partnership registrars

(1) A civil partnership registrar is an individual who is designated by a registration authority as a civil partnership registrar for its area.

(2) It is the duty of each registration authority to ensure that there is a sufficient number of civil partnership registrars for its area to carry out in that area the functions of civil partnership registrars.

(3) Each registration authority must inform the Registrar General as soon as is practicable –

   (a)   of any designation it has made of a person as a civil partnership registrar, and
   (b)   of the ending of any such designation.

(4) (*repealed*)

Amendments—SI 2005/2000.

30   The Registrar General and the register

(1) In this Chapter 'the Registrar General' means the Registrar General for England and Wales.

(2) The Registrar General must provide a system for keeping any records that relate to civil partnerships and are required by this Chapter to be made.

(3) The system may, in particular, enable those records to be kept together with other records kept by the Registrar General.

(4) In this Chapter 'the register' means the system for keeping records provided under subsection (2).

31   Offences relating to civil partnership schedule

(1) A person commits an offence if he issues a civil partnership schedule knowing that he does so –

   (a)   before the waiting period in relation to each notice of proposed civil partnership has expired,
   (b)   after the end of the applicable period, or
   (c)   at a time when its issue has been forbidden under Schedule 2 by a person entitled to forbid its issue.

(2) A person commits an offence if, in his actual or purported capacity as a civil partnership registrar, he officiates at the signing of a civil partnership schedule by proposed civil partners knowing that he does so –

   (a)   at a place other than the place specified in the notices of proposed civil partnership and the civil partnership schedule,
   (aa) on premises that are not approved premises although the signing is purportedly in accordance with section 6(3A)(a),
   (ab) at any other time other than between 8 o'clock in the morning and 6 o'clock in the evening,
   (b)   in the absence of a civil partnership registrar,
   (c)   before the waiting period in relation to each notice of proposed civil partnership has expired, or
   (d)   even though the civil partnership is void under section 49(b) or (c).

(3) A person guilty of an offence under subsection (1) or (2)(a), (aa), (b), (c) or (d) is liable on conviction on indictment to imprisonment for a term not exceeding 5 years or to a fine (or both).

(3A) A person guilty of an offence under subsection (2)(ab) is liable on conviction on indictment to imprisonment for a term not exceeding 14 years or to a fine or both.

(4) A prosecution under this section may not be commenced more than 3 years after the commission of the offences

Amendments—SI 2005/2000.

32   Offences relating to Registrar General's licence

(1) A person commits an offence if –

    (a)   he gives information by way of evidence in response to a requirement under section 22(1), knowing that the information is false;

    (b)   he gives a certificate as provided for by section 22(3), knowing that the certificate is false.

(2) A person commits an offence if, in his actual or purported capacity as a civil partnership registrar, he officiates at the signing of a Registrar General's licence by proposed civil partners knowing that he does so –

    (a)   at a place other than the place specified in the licence,

    (b)   in the absence of a civil partnership registrar,

    (c)   after the end of 1 month from the day on which the notice of proposed civil partnership was given, or

    (d)   even though the civil partnership is void under section 49(b) or (c).

(3) A person guilty of an offence under subsection (1) or (2) is liable –

    (a)   on conviction on indictment, to imprisonment not exceeding 3 years or to a fine (or both);

    (b)   on summary conviction, to a fine not exceeding the statutory maximum.

(4) A prosecution under this section may not be commenced more than 3 years after the commission of the offence.

33   Offences relating to the recording of civil partnerships

(1) A civil partnership registrar commits an offence if he refuses or fails to comply with the provisions of this Chapter or of any regulations made under section 36.

(2) A civil partnership registrar guilty of an offence under subsection (1) is liable –

    (a)   on conviction on indictment, to imprisonment for a term not exceeding 2 years or to a fine (or both);

    (b)   on summary conviction, to a fine not exceeding the statutory maximum;

and on conviction shall cease to be a civil partnership registrar.

(3) A person commits an offence if –

    (a)   under arrangements made by a registration authority for the purposes of section 2(4), he is under a duty to record information required to be recorded under section 2(4), but

    (b)   he refuses or without reasonable cause omits to do so.

(4) A person guilty of an offence under subsection (3) is liable on summary conviction to a fine not exceeding level 3 on the standard scale.

(5) A person commits an offence if he records in the register information relating to the formation of a civil partnership by the signing of a civil partnership schedule, knowing that the civil partnership is void under section 49(*b*) or (*c*).

(6) A person guilty of an offence under subsection (5) is liable on conviction on indictment, to imprisonment for a term not exceeding 5 years or to a fine (or both).

(7) A person commits an offence if he records in the register information relating to the formation of a civil partnership by the signing of a Registrar General's licence, knowing that the civil partnership is void under section 49(*b*) or (*c*).

(8) A person guilty of an offence under subsection (7) is liable –

   (a)   on conviction on indictment, to imprisonment for a term not exceeding 3 years or to a fine (or both);

   (b)   on summary conviction, to a fine not exceeding the statutory maximum.

(9) A prosecution under subsection (5) or (7) may not be commenced more than 3 years after the commission of the offence.

34 Fees

(1) The Secretary of State may by order provide for fees, of such amounts as may be specified in the order, to be payable to such persons as may be prescribed by the order in respect of –

   (a)   the giving of a notice of proposed civil partnership and the attestation of the necessary declaration;

   (b)   the making of an application under section 12(1) (application to reduce waiting period);

   (c)   the issue of a Registrar General's licence;

   (d)   the attendance of the civil partnership registrar when two people sign the civil partnership document;

   (e)   such other services provided in connection with civil partnerships either by registration authorities or by or on behalf of the Registrar General as may be prescribed by the order.

(2) The Registrar General may remit the fee for the issue of his licence in whole or in part in any case where it appears to him that the payment of the fee would cause hardship to the proposed civil partners.s

(3) Where a civil partnership registrar for any area attends when two people sign the civil partnership schedule on approved premises, in accordance with section 6(3A)(a)—

   (a)   subsection (1)(d) does not apply, but

   (b)   the registration authority for that area is entitled from those people a fee of an amount determined by the authority in accordance with regulations under section 6A.

Amendments—SI 2005/2000; Si 2008/678.

35 Power to assimilate provisions relating to civil registration

(1) The Secretary of State may by order make –

   (a)   such amendments of this Act as appear to him appropriate for the purpose of assimilating any provision connected with the formation or recording of civil partnerships in England and Wales to any provision made ... in relation to civil marriage in England and Wales, and

   (b)   such amendments of other enactments and of subordinate legislation as appear to him appropriate in consequence of any amendments made under paragraph (a).

(2) 'Civil marriage' means marriage solemnised otherwise than according to the rites of the Church of England or any other religious usages.

(3) 'Amendment' includes repeal or revocation.

(4) 'Subordinate legislation' has the same meaning as in the Interpretation Act 1978 (c. 30).

Amendments—Legislative and Regulatory Reform Act 2006, s 30(1), Sch; SI 2008/678.

36 Regulations and orders

(1) Regulations may make provision supplementing the provisions of this Chapter.

(2) Regulations may in particular make provision –

   (a)   relating to the use of Welsh in documents and records relating to civil partnerships;

   (b)   with respect to the retention of documents relating to civil partnerships;

   (c)   prescribing the duties of civil partnership registrars;

(d)   prescribing the duties of persons in whose presence any declaration is made for the purposes of this Chapter;

(e)   for the issue by the Registrar General of guidance supplementing any provision made by the regulations.

(f)   for the issue by registration authorities or the Registrar General of certified copies of entries in the register and for such copies to be received in evidence.

(3) In this Chapter, except in section 6A, 'regulations' means regulations made by the Registrar General with the approval of the Secretary of State.

(4) Any power to make regulations or an order under this Chapter is exercisable by statutory instrument.

(5) A statutory instrument containing regulations under section 6A or an order under section 34 is subject to annulment in pursuance of a resolution of either House of Parliament.

(6) No order may be made under section 35 unless a draft of the statutory instrument containing the order has been laid before, and approved by a resolution of, each House of Parliaments

Amendments—SI 2005/2000; SI 2008/678.

Introduction

37   Powers to make orders and effect of orders

(1) The court may, in accordance with this Chapter –

(a)   make an order (a 'dissolution order') which dissolves a civil partnership on the ground that it has broken down irretrievably;

(b)   make an order (a 'nullity order') which annuls a civil partnership which is void or voidable;

(c)   make an order (a 'presumption of death order') which dissolves a civil partnership on the ground that one of the civil partners is presumed to be dead;

(d)   make an order (a 'separation order') which provides for the separation of the civil partners.

(2) Every dissolution, nullity or presumption of death order –

(a)   is, in the first instance, a conditional order, and

(b)   may not be made final before the end of the prescribed period (see section 38);

and any reference in this Chapter to a conditional order is to be read accordingly.

(3) A nullity order made where a civil partnership is voidable annuls the civil partnership only as respects any time after the order has been made final, and the civil partnership is to be treated (despite the order) as if it had existed up to that time.

(4) In this Chapter, other than in sections 58 to 61, 'the court' means –

(a)   the High Court, or

(b)   if a county court has jurisdiction by virtue of Part 5 of the Matrimonial and Family Proceedings Act 1984 (c. 42), a county court.

(5) This Chapter is subject to sections 219 to 224 (jurisdiction of the court).

38   The period before conditional orders may be made final

(1) Subject to subsections (2) to (4), the prescribed period for the purposes of section 37(2)(*b*) is –

(a)   6 weeks from the making of the conditional order, or

(b)   if the 6 week period would end on a day on which the office or registry of the court dealing with the case is closed, the period of 6 weeks extended to the end of the first day on which the office or registry is next open.

(2) The Lord Chancellor may by order amend this section so as to substitute a different definition of the prescribed period for the purposes of section 37(2)(*b*).

(3) But the Lord Chancellor may not under subsection (2) provide for a period longer than 6 months to be the prescribed period.

(4) In a particular case the court dealing with the case may by order shorten the prescribed period.

(5) The power to make an order under subsection (2) is exercisable by statutory instrument.

(6) An instrument containing such an order is subject to annulment in pursuance of a resolution of either House of Parliament.

39 Intervention of the Queen's Proctor

(1) This section applies if an application has been made for a dissolution, nullity or presumption of death order.

(2) The court may, if it thinks fit, direct that all necessary papers in the matter are to be sent to the Queen's Proctor who must under the directions of the Attorney General instruct counsel to argue before the court any question in relation to the matter which the court considers it necessary or expedient to have fully argued.

(3) If any person at any time –

  (a)   during the progress of the proceedings, or
  (b)   before the conditional order is made final,

gives information to the Queen's Proctor on any matter material to the due decision of the case, the Queen's Proctor may take such steps as the Attorney General considers necessary or expedient.

(4) If the Queen's Proctor intervenes or shows cause against the making of the conditional order in any proceedings relating to its making, the court may make such order as may be just as to –

  (a)   the payment by other parties to the proceedings of the costs incurred by him in doing so, or
  (b)   the payment by the Queen's Proctor of any costs incurred by any of those parties because of his doing so.

(5) The Queen's Proctor is entitled to charge as part of the expenses of his office –

  (a)   the costs of any proceedings under subsection (2);
  (b)   if his reasonable costs of intervening or showing cause as mentioned in subsection (4) are not fully satisfied by an order under subsection (4)(a), the amount of the difference;
  (c)   if the Treasury so directs, any costs which he pays to any parties under an order made under subsection (4)(b).

40 Proceedings before order has been made final

(1) This section applies if –

  (a)   a conditional order has been made, and
  (b)   the Queen's Proctor, or any person who has not been a party to proceedings in which the order was made, shows cause why the order should not be made final on the ground that material facts have not been brought before the court.

(2) This section also applies if –

  (a)   a conditional order has been made,
  (b)   3 months have elapsed since the earliest date on which an application could have been made for the order to be made final,
  (c)   no such application has been made by the civil partner who applied for the conditional order, and
  (d)   the other civil partner makes an application to the court under this subsection.

(3) The court may –

(a)   make the order final,
(b)   rescind the order,
(c)   require further inquiry, or
(d)   otherwise deal with the case as it thinks fit.

(4) Subsection (3)(*a*) –

(a)   applies despite section 37(2) (period before conditional orders may be made final), but
(b)   is subject to section 48(4) (protection for respondent in separation cases) and section 63 (restrictions on making of orders affecting children).

41 Time bar on applications for dissolution orders

(1) No application for a dissolution order may be made to the court before the end of the period of 1 year from the date of the formation of the civil partnership.

(2) Nothing in this section prevents the making of an application based on matters which occurred before the end of the 1 year period.

42 Attempts at reconciliation of civil partners

(1) This section applies in relation to cases where an application is made for a dissolution or separation order.

(2) Rules of court must make provision for requiring the legal representative acting for the applicant to certify whether he has –

(a)   discussed with the applicant the possibility of a reconciliation with the other civil partner, and
(b)   given the applicant the names and addresses of persons qualified to help effect a reconciliation between civil partners who have become estranged.

(3) If at any stage of proceedings for the order it appears to the court that there is a reasonable possibility of a reconciliation between the civil partners, the court may adjourn the proceedings for such period as it thinks fit to enable attempts to be made to effect a reconciliation between them.

(4) The power to adjourn under subsection (3) is additional to any other power of adjournment.

Amendments—Legal Services Act 2007, s 208(1), Sch 21, para 150.

43 Consideration by the court of certain agreements or arrangements

(1) This section applies in relation to cases where –

(a)   proceedings for a dissolution or separation order are contemplated or have begun, and
(b)   an agreement or arrangement is made or proposed to be made between the civil partners which relates to, arises out of, or is connected with, the proceedings.

(2) Rules of court may make provision for enabling –

(a)   the civil partners, or either of them, to refer the agreement or arrangement to the court, and
(b)   the court –
    (i)   to express an opinion, if it thinks it desirable to do so, as to the reasonableness of the agreement or arrangement, and
    (ii)   to give such directions, if any, in the matter as it thinks fit.

Dissolution of civil partnership

44 Dissolution of civil partnership which has broken down irretrievably

(1) Subject to section 41, an application for a dissolution order may be made to the court by either civil partner on the ground that the civil partnership has broken down irretrievably.

(2) On an application for a dissolution order the court must inquire, so far as it reasonably can, into –

    (a)   the facts alleged by the applicant, and
    (b)   any facts alleged by the respondent.

(3) The court hearing an application for a dissolution order must not hold that the civil partnership has broken down irretrievably unless the applicant satisfies the court of one or more of the facts described in subsection (5)(*a*), (*b*), (*c*) or (*d*).

(4) But if the court is satisfied of any of those facts, it must make a dissolution order unless it is satisfied on all the evidence that the civil partnership has not broken down irretrievably.

(5) The facts referred to in subsections (3) and (4) are –

    (a)   that the respondent has behaved in such a way that the applicant cannot reasonably be expected to live with the respondent;
    (b)   that –
        (i)   the applicant and the respondent have lived apart for a continuous period of at least 2 years immediately preceding the making of the application ('2 years' separation'), and
        (ii)   the respondent consents to a dissolution order being made;
    (c)   that the applicant and the respondent have lived apart for a continuous period of at least 5 years immediately preceding the making of the application ('5 years' separation');
    (d)   that the respondent has deserted the applicant for a continuous period of at least 2 years immediately preceding the making of the application.

45 Supplemental provisions as to facts raising presumption of breakdown

(1) Subsection (2) applies if –

    (a)   in any proceedings for a dissolution order the applicant alleges, in reliance on section 44(5)(a), that the respondent has behaved in such a way that the applicant cannot reasonably be expected to live with the respondent, but
    (b)   after the date of the occurrence of the final incident relied on by the applicant and held by the court to support his allegation, the applicant and the respondent have lived together for a period (or periods) which does not, or which taken together do not, exceed 6 months.

(2) The fact that the applicant and respondent have lived together as mentioned in subsection (1)(*b*) must be disregarded in determining, for the purposes of section 44(5)(*a*), whether the applicant cannot reasonably be expected to live with the respondent.

(3) Subsection (4) applies in relation to cases where the applicant alleges, in reliance on section 44(5)(*b*), that the respondent consents to a dissolution order being made.

(4) Rules of court must make provision for the purpose of ensuring that the respondent has been given such information as will enable him to understand –

    (a)   the consequences to him of consenting to the making of the order, and
    (b)   the steps which he must take to indicate his consent.

(5) For the purposes of section 44(5)(*d*) the court may treat a period of desertion as having continued at a time when the deserting civil partner was incapable of continuing the necessary intention, if the evidence before the court is such that, had he not been so incapable, the court would have inferred that the desertion continued at that time.

(6) In considering for the purposes of section 44(5) whether the period for which the civil partners have lived apart or the period for which the respondent has deserted the applicant has been continuous, no account is to be taken of –

(a)   any one period not exceeding 6 months, or
(b)   any two or more periods not exceeding 6 months in all,

during which the civil partners resumed living with each other.

(7) But no period during which the civil partners have lived with each other counts as part of the period during which the civil partners have lived apart or as part of the period of desertion.

(8) For the purposes of section 44(5)(*b*) and (*c*) and this section civil partners are to be treated as living apart unless they are living with each other in the same household, and references in this section to civil partners living with each other are to be read as references to their living with each other in the same household.

46   Dissolution order not precluded by previous separation order etc

(1) Subsections (2) and (3) apply if any of the following orders has been made in relation to a civil partnership –

(a)   a separation order;
(b)   an order under Schedule 6 (financial relief in magistrates' courts etc);
(c)   an order under section 33 of the Family Law Act 1996 (c. 27) (occupation orders);
(d)   an order under section 37 of the 1996 Act (orders where neither civil partner entitled to occupy the home).

(2) Nothing prevents –

(a)   either civil partner from applying for a dissolution order, or
(b)   the court from making a dissolution order,

on the same facts, or substantially the same facts, as those proved in support of the making of the order referred to in subsection (1).

(3) On the application for the dissolution order, the court –

(a)   may treat the order referred to in subsection (1) as sufficient proof of any desertion or other fact by reference to which it was made, but
(b)   must not make the dissolution order without receiving evidence from the applicant.

(4) If –

(a)   the application for the dissolution order follows a separation order or any order requiring the civil partners to live apart,
(b)   there was a period of desertion immediately preceding the institution of the proceedings for the separation order, and
(c)   the civil partners have not resumed living together and the separation order has been continuously in force since it was made,

the period of desertion is to be treated for the purposes of the application for the dissolution order as if it had immediately preceded the making of the application.

(5) For the purposes of section 44(5)(*d*) the court may treat as a period during which the respondent has deserted the applicant any period during which there is in force –

(a)   an injunction granted by the High Court or a county court which excludes the respondent from the civil partnership home, or
(b)   an order under section 33 or 37 of the 1996 Act which prohibits the respondent from occupying a dwelling-house in which the applicant and the respondent have, or at any time have had, a civil partnership home.

47 Refusal of dissolution in 5 year separation cases on ground of grave hardship

(1) The respondent to an application for a dissolution order in which the applicant alleges 5 years' separation may oppose the making of an order on the ground that –

(a) the dissolution of the civil partnership will result in grave financial or other hardship to him, and

(b) it would in all the circumstances be wrong to dissolve the civil partnership.

(2) Subsection (3) applies if –

(a) the making of a dissolution order is opposed under this section,

(b) the court finds that the applicant is entitled to rely in support of his application on the fact of 5 years' separation and makes no such finding as to any other fact mentioned in section 44(5), and

(c) apart from this section, the court would make a dissolution order.

(3) The court must –

(a) consider all the circumstances, including the conduct of the civil partners and the interests of the civil partners and of any children or other persons concerned, and

(b) if it is of the opinion that the ground mentioned in subsection (1) is made out, dismiss the application for the dissolution order.

(4) 'Hardship' includes the loss of the chance of acquiring any benefit which the respondent might acquire if the civil partnership were not dissolved.

48 Proceedings before order made final: protection for respondent in separation cases

(1) The court may, on an application made by the respondent, rescind a conditional dissolution order if –

(a) it made the order on the basis of a finding that the applicant was entitled to rely on the fact of 2 years' separation coupled with the respondent's consent to a dissolution order being made,

(b) it made no such finding as to any other fact mentioned in section 44(5), and

(c) it is satisfied that the applicant misled the respondent (whether intentionally or unintentionally) about any matter which the respondent took into account in deciding to give his consent.

(2) Subsections (3) to (5) apply if –

(a) the respondent to an application for a dissolution order in which the applicant alleged –

(i) 2 years' separation coupled with the respondent's consent to a dissolution order being made, or

(ii) 5 years' separation,

has applied to the court for consideration under subsection (3) of his financial position after the dissolution of the civil partnership, and

(b) the court –

(i) has made a conditional dissolution order on the basis of a finding that the applicant was entitled to rely in support of his application on the fact of 2 years' or 5 years' separation, and

(ii) has made no such finding as to any other fact mentioned in section 44(5).

(3) The court hearing an application by the respondent under subsection (2) must consider all the circumstances, including –

(a) the age, health, conduct, earning capacity, financial resources and financial obligations of each of the parties, and

(b) the financial position of the respondent as, having regard to the dissolution, it is likely to be after the death of the applicant should the applicant die first.

(4) Subject to subsection (5), the court must not make the order final unless it is satisfied that –

    (a)   the applicant should not be required to make any financial provision for the respondent, or

    (b)   the financial provision made by the applicant for the respondent is –

        (i)   reasonable and fair, or

        (ii)   the best that can be made in the circumstances.

(5) The court may if it thinks fit make the order final if –

    (a)   it appears that there are circumstances making it desirable that the order should be made final without delay, and

    (b)   it has obtained a satisfactory undertaking from the applicant that he will make such financial provision for the respondent as it may approve.

Nullity

49 Grounds on which civil partnership is void

Where two people register as civil partners of each other in England and Wales, the civil partnership is void if –

    (a)   at the time when they do so, they are not eligible to register as civil partners of each other under Chapter 1 (see section 3),

    (b)   at the time when they do so they both know –

        (i)   that due notice of proposed civil partnership has not been given,

        (ii)   that the civil partnership document has not been duly issued,

        (iii)   that the civil partnership document is void under section 17(3) or 27(2) (registration after end of time allowed for registering),

        (iv)   that the place of registration is a place other than that specified in the notices (or notice) of proposed civil partnership and the civil partnership document,

        (v)   that a civil partnership registrar is not present, or

        (vi)   that the place of registration is on premises that are not approved premises although the registration is purportedly in accordance with section 6(3A)(a), or

    (c)   the civil partnership document is void under paragraph 6(5) of Schedule 2 (civil partnership between child and another person forbidden).

Amendments—SI 2005/2000.

50   Grounds on which civil partnership is voidable

(1) Where two people register as civil partners of each other in England and Wales, the civil partnership is voidable if –

    (a)   either of them did not validly consent to its formation (whether as a result of duress, mistake, unsoundness of mind or otherwise);

    (b)   at the time of its formation either of them, though capable of giving a valid consent, was suffering (whether continuously or intermittently) from mental disorder of such a kind or to such an extent as to be unfitted for civil partnership;

    (c)   at the time of its formation, the respondent was pregnant by some person other than the applicant;

    (d)   an interim gender recognition certificate under the Gender Recognition Act 2004 (c. 7) has, after the time of its formation, been issued to either civil partner;

    (e)   the respondent is a person whose gender at the time of its formation had become the acquired gender under the 2004 Act.

(2) In this section and section 51 'mental disorder' has the same meaning as in the Mental Health Act 1983 (c. 20).

51 Bars to relief where civil partnership is voidable

(1) The court must not make a nullity order on the ground that a civil partnership is voidable if the respondent satisfies the court –

   (a)   that the applicant, with knowledge that it was open to him to obtain a nullity order, conducted himself in relation to the respondent in such a way as to lead the respondent reasonably to believe that he would not seek to do so, and

   (b)   that it would be unjust to the respondent to make the order.

(2) Without prejudice to subsection (1), the court must not make a nullity order by virtue of section 50(1)(*a*), (*b*), (*c*) or (*e*) unless –

   (a)   it is satisfied that proceedings were instituted within 3 years from the date of the formation of the civil partnership, or

   (b)   leave for the institution of proceedings after the end of that 3 year period has been granted under subsection (3).

(3) A judge of the court may, on an application made to him, grant leave for the institution of proceedings if he –

   (a)   is satisfied that the applicant has at some time during the 3 year period suffered from mental disorder, and

   (b)   considers that in all the circumstances of the case it would be just to grant leave for the institution of proceedings.

(4) An application for leave under subsection (3) may be made after the end of the 3 year period.

(5) Without prejudice to subsection (1), the court must not make a nullity order by virtue of section 50(1)(*d*) unless it is satisfied that proceedings were instituted within the period of 6 months from the date of issue of the interim gender recognition certificate.

(6) Without prejudice to subsections (1) and (2), the court must not make a nullity order by virtue of section 50(1)(*c*) or (*e*) unless it is satisfied that the applicant was at the time of the formation of the civil partnership ignorant of the facts alleged.

52 Proof of certain matters not necessary to validity of civil partnership

(1) Where two people have registered as civil partners of each other in England and Wales, it is not necessary in support of the civil partnership to give any proof –

   (a)   that any person whose consent to the civil partnership was required by section 4 (parental etc consent) had given his consent, or

   (aa) that before the registration either of the civil partners resided, or resided for any period, in the area stated in the notices of proposed civil partnership to be the area of that person's place of residence;

   (b)   (*repealed*)

and no evidence is to be given to prove the contrary in any proceedings touching the validity of the civil partnership.

(2) Subsection (1)(*a*) is subject to section 49(*c*) (civil partnership void if forbidden).

Amendments—SI 2005/2000.

53 Power to validate civil partnership

(1) Where two people have registered as civil partners of each other in England and Wales, the Lord Chancellor may by order validate the civil partnership if it appears to him that it is or may be void under section 49(*b*).

(2) An order under subsection (1) may include provisions for relieving a person from any liability under section 31(2), 32(2) or 33(5) or (7).

(3) The draft of an order under subsection (1) must be advertised, in such manner as the Lord Chancellor thinks fit, not less than one month before the order is made.

(4) The Lord Chancellor must –

    (a)   consider all objections to the order sent to him in writing during that month, and

    (b)   if it appears to him necessary, direct a local inquiry into the validity of any such objections.

(5) An order under subsection (1) is subject to special parliamentary procedure.

54 Validity of civil partnerships registered outside England and Wales

(1) Where two people register as civil partners of each other in Scotland, the civil partnership is –

    (a)   void, if it would be void in Scotland under section 123, and

    (b)   voidable, if the circumstances fall within section 50(1)(d).

(2) Where two people register as civil partners of each other in Northern Ireland, the civil partnership is –

    (a)   void, if it would be void in Northern Ireland under section 173, and

    (b)   voidable, if the circumstances fall within any paragraph of section 50(1).

(3) Subsection (4) applies where two people register as civil partners of each other under an Order in Council under –

    (a)   section 210 (registration at British consulates etc), or

    (b)   section 211 (registration by armed forces personnel),

('the relevant section').

(4) The civil partnership is –

    (a)   void, if –

        (i)   the condition in subsection (2)(*a*) or (*b*) of the relevant section is not met, or

        (ii)   a requirement prescribed for the purposes of this paragraph by an Order in Council under the relevant section is not complied with, and

    (b)   voidable, if –

        (i)   the appropriate part of the United Kingdom is England and Wales or Northern Ireland and the circumstances fall within any paragraph of section 50(1), or

        (ii)   the appropriate part of the United Kingdom is Scotland and the circumstances fall within section 50(1)(*d*).

(5) The appropriate part of the United Kingdom is the part by reference to which the condition in subsection (2)(*b*) of the relevant section is met.

(6) Subsections (7) and (8) apply where two people have registered an apparent or alleged overseas relationship.

(7) The civil partnership is void if –

    (a)   the relationship is not an overseas relationship, or

    (b)   (even though the relationship is an overseas relationship) the parties are not treated under Chapter 2 of Part 5 as having formed a civil partnership.

(8) The civil partnership is voidable if –

    (a)   the overseas relationship is voidable under the relevant law,

    (b)   the circumstances fall within section 50(1)(d), or

    (c)   where either of the parties was domiciled in England and Wales or Northern Ireland at the time when the overseas relationship was registered, the circumstances fall within section 50(1)(a), (b), (c) or (e).

(9) Section 51 applies for the purposes of –

(a)   subsections (1)(b), (2)(b) and (4)(b),

(b)   subsection (8)(a), in so far as applicable in accordance with the relevant law, and

(c)   subsection (8)(b) and (c).

(10) In subsections (8)(*a*) and (9)(*b*) 'the relevant law' means the law of the country or territory where the overseas relationship was registered (including its rules of private international law).

(11) For the purposes of subsections (8) and (9)(*b*) and (*c*), references in sections 50 and 51 to the formation of the civil partnership are to be read as references to the registration of the overseas relationship.

Presumption of death orders

55   Presumption of death orders

(1) The court may, on an application made by a civil partner, make a presumption of death order if it is satisfied that reasonable grounds exist for supposing that the other civil partner is dead.

(2) In any proceedings under this section the fact that –

(a)   for a period of 7 years or more the other civil partner has been continually absent from the applicant, and

(b)   the applicant has no reason to believe that the other civil partner has been living within that time,

is evidence that the other civil partner is dead until the contrary is proved.

Separation orders

56   Separation orders

(1) An application for a separation order may be made to the court by either civil partner on the ground that any such fact as is mentioned in section 44(5)(*a*), (*b*), (*c*) or (*d*) exists.

(2) On an application for a separation order the court must inquire, so far as it reasonably can, into –

(a)   the facts alleged by the applicant, and

(b)   any facts alleged by the respondent,

but whether the civil partnership has broken down irretrievably is irrelevant.

(3) If the court is satisfied on the evidence of any such fact as is mentioned in section 44(5)(*a*), (*b*), (*c*) or (*d*) it must, subject to section 63, make a separation order.

(4) Section 45 (supplemental provisions as to facts raising presumption of breakdown) applies for the purposes of an application for a separation order alleging any such fact as it applies in relation to an application for a dissolution order alleging that fact.

57   Effect of separation order

If either civil partner dies intestate as respects all or any of his or her real or personal property while –

(a)   a separation order is in force, and

(b)   the separation is continuing,

the property as respects which he or she died intestate devolves as if the other civil partner had then been dead.

Declarations

58   Declarations

(1) Any person may apply to the High Court or a county court for one or more of the following declarations in relation to a civil partnership specified in the application –

(a)   a declaration that the civil partnership was at its inception a valid civil partnership;

(b)   a declaration that the civil partnership subsisted on a date specified in the application;

(c)   a declaration that the civil partnership did not subsist on a date so specified;

(d)   a declaration that the validity of a dissolution, annulment or legal separation obtained outside England and Wales in respect of the civil partnership is entitled to recognition in England and Wales;

(e)   a declaration that the validity of a dissolution, annulment or legal separation so obtained in respect of the civil partnership is not entitled to recognition in England and Wales.

(2) Where an application under subsection (1) is made to a court by a person other than a civil partner in the civil partnership to which the application relates, the court must refuse to hear the application if it considers that the applicant does not have a sufficient interest in the determination of that application.

59   General provisions as to making and effect of declarations

(1) Where on an application for a declaration under section 58 the truth of the proposition to be declared is proved to the satisfaction of the court, the court must make the declaration unless to do so would be manifestly contrary to public policy.

(2) Any declaration under section 58 binds Her Majesty and all other persons.

(3) The court, on the dismissal of an application for a declaration under section 58, may not make any declaration for which an application has not been made.

(4) No declaration which may be applied for under section 58 may be made otherwise than under section 58 by any court.

(5) No declaration may be made by any court, whether under section 58 or otherwise, that a civil partnership was at its inception void.

(6) Nothing in this section affects the powers of any court to make a nullity order in respect of a civil partnership.

60   The Attorney General and proceedings for declarations

(1) On an application for a declaration under section 58 the court may at any stage of the proceedings, of its own motion or on the application of any party to the proceedings, direct that all necessary papers in the matter be sent to the Attorney General.

(2) The Attorney General, whether or not he is sent papers in relation to an application for a declaration under section 58, may –

(a)   intervene in the proceedings on that application in such manner as he thinks necessary or expedient, and

(b)   argue before the court dealing with the application any question in relation to the application which the court considers it necessary to have fully argued.

(3) Where any costs are incurred by the Attorney General in connection with any application for a declaration under section 58, the court may make such order as it considers just as to the payment of those costs by parties to the proceedings.

61   Supplementary provisions as to declarations

(1) Any declaration made under section 58, and any application for such a declaration, must be in the form prescribed by rules of court.

(2) Rules of court may make provision –

    (a)   as to the information required to be given by any applicant for a declaration under section 58;

    (b)   requiring notice of an application under section 58 to be served on the Attorney General and on persons who may be affected by any declaration applied for.

(3) No proceedings under section 58 affect any final judgment or order already pronounced or made by any court of competent jurisdiction.

(4) The court hearing an application under section 58 may direct that the whole or any part of the proceedings must be heard in private.

(5) An application for a direction under subsection (4) must be heard in private unless the court otherwise directs.

General provisions

62   Relief for respondent in dissolution proceedings

(1) If in any proceedings for a dissolution order the respondent alleges and proves any such fact as is mentioned in section 44(5)(*a*), (*b*), (*c*) or (*d*) the court may give to the respondent the relief to which he would have been entitled if he had made an application seeking that relief.

(2) When applying subsection (1), treat –

    (a)   the respondent as the applicant, and

    (b)   the applicant as the respondent,

for the purposes of section 44(5).

63   Restrictions on making of orders affecting children

(1) In any proceedings for a dissolution, nullity or separation order, the court must consider –

    (a)   whether there are any children of the family to whom this section applies, and

    (b)   if there are any such children, whether (in the light of the arrangements which have been, or are proposed to be, made for their upbringing and welfare) it should exercise any of its powers under the Children Act 1989 (c. 41) with respect to any of them.

(2) If, in the case of any child to whom this section applies, it appears to the court that –

    (a)   the circumstances of the case require it, or are likely to require it, to exercise any of its powers under the 1989 Act with respect to any such child,

    (b)   it is not in a position to exercise the power or (as the case may be) those powers without giving further consideration to the case, and

    (c)   there are exceptional circumstances which make it desirable in the interests of the child that the court should give a direction under this section,

it may direct that the order is not to be made final, or (in the case of a separation order) is not to be made, until the court orders otherwise.

(3) This section applies to –

    (a)   any child of the family who has not reached 16 at the date when the court considers the case in accordance with the requirements of this section, and

    (b)   any child of the family who has reached 16 at that date and in relation to whom the court directs that this section shall apply.

64 Parties to proceedings under this Chapter

(1) Rules of court may make provision with respect to –

(a) the joinder as parties to proceedings under sections 37 to 56 of persons involved in allegations of improper conduct made in those proceedings,

(b) the dismissal from such proceedings of any parties so joined, and

(c) the persons who are to be parties to proceedings on an application under section 58.

(2) Rules of court made under this section may make different provision for different cases.

(3) In every case in which the court considers, in the interest of a person not already a party to the proceedings, that the person should be made a party, the court may if it thinks fit allow the person to intervene upon such terms, if any, as the court thinks just.

65 Contribution by civil partner to property improvement

(1) This section applies if –

(a) a civil partner contributes in money or money's worth to the improvement of real or personal property in which or in the proceeds of sale of which either or both of the civil partners has or have a beneficial interest, and

(b) the contribution is of a substantial nature.

(2) The contributing partner is to be treated as having acquired by virtue of the contribution a share or an enlarged share (as the case may be) in the beneficial interest of such an extent –

(a) as may have been then agreed, or

(b) in default of such agreement, as may seem in all the circumstances just to any court before which the question of the existence or extent of the beneficial interest of either of the civil partners arises (whether in proceedings between them or in any other proceedings).

(3) Subsection (2) is subject to any agreement (express or implied) between the civil partners to the contrary.

66 Disputes between civil partners about property

(1) In any question between the civil partners in a civil partnership as to title to or possession of property, either civil partner may apply to –

(a) the High Court, or

(b) such county court as may be prescribed by rules of court.

(2) On such an application, the court may make such order with respect to the property as it thinks fit (including an order for the sale of the property).

(3) Rules of court made for the purposes of this section may confer jurisdiction on county courts whatever the situation or value of the property in dispute.

67 Applications under section 66 where property not in possession etc

(1) The right of a civil partner ('A') to make an application under section 66 includes the right to make such an application where A claims that the other civil partner ('B') has had in his possession or under his control –

(a) money to which, or to a share of which, A was beneficially entitled, or

(b) property (other than money) to which, or to an interest in which, A was beneficially entitled,

and that either the money or other property has ceased to be in B's possession or under B's control or that A does not know whether it is still in B's possession or under B's control.

(2) For the purposes of subsection (1)(*a*) it does not matter whether A is beneficially entitled to the money or share –

  (a)   because it represents the proceeds of property to which, or to an interest in which, A was beneficially entitled, or
  (b)   for any other reason.

(3) Subsections (4) and (5) apply if, on such an application being made, the court is satisfied that B –

  (a)   has had in his possession or under his control money or other property as mentioned in subsection (1)(a) or (b), and
  (b)   has not made to A, in respect of that money or other property, such payment or disposition as would have been appropriate in the circumstances.

(4) The power of the court to make orders under section 66 includes power to order B to pay to A –

  (a)   in a case falling within subsection (1)(a), such sum in respect of the money to which the application relates, or A's s share of it, as the court considers appropriate, or
  (b)   in a case falling within subsection (1)(b), such sum in respect of the value of the property to which the application relates, or A's interest in it, as the court considers appropriate.

(5) If it appears to the court that there is any property which –

  (a)   represents the whole or part of the money or property, and
  (b)   is property in respect of which an order could (apart from this section) have been made under section 66,

the court may (either instead of or as well as making an order in accordance with subsection (4)) make any order which it could (apart from this section) have made under section 66.

(6) Any power of the court which is exercisable on an application under section 66 is exercisable in relation to an application made under that section as extended by this section.

68   Applications under section 66 by former civil partners

(1) This section applies where a civil partnership has been dissolved or annulled.

(2) Subject to subsection (3), an application may be made under section 66 (including that section as extended by section 67) by either former civil partner despite the dissolution or annulment (and references in those sections to a civil partner are to be read accordingly).

(3) The application must be made within the period of 3 years beginning with the date of the dissolution or annulment.

69   Actions in tort between civil partners

(1) This section applies if an action in tort is brought by one civil partner against the other during the subsistence of the civil partnership.

(2) The court may stay the proceedings if it appears –

  (a)   that no substantial benefit would accrue to either civil partner from the continuation of the proceedings, or
  (b)   that the question or questions in issue could more conveniently be disposed of on an application under section 66.

(3) Without prejudice to subsection (2)(*b*), the court may in such an action –

  (a)   exercise any power which could be exercised on an application under section 66, or
  (b)   give such directions as it thinks fit for the disposal under that section of any question arising in the proceedings.

70   Assurance policy by civil partner for benefit of other civil partner etc

Section 11 of the Married Women's Property Act 1882 (c. 75) (money payable under policy of assurance not to form part of the estate of the insured) applies in relation to a policy of assurance –

(a)   effected by a civil partner on his own life, and

(b)   expressed to be for the benefit of his civil partner, or of his children, or of his civil partner and children, or any of them,

as it applies in relation to a policy of assurance effected by a husband and expressed to be for the benefit of his wife, or of his children, or of his wife and children, or of any of them.

70A   Money and property derived from housekeeping allowance

Section 1 of the Matrimonial Property Act 1964 (money and property derived from housekeeping allowance to be treated as belonging to husband and wife in equal shares) applies in relation to—

(a)   money derived from any allowance made by a civil partner for the expenses of the civil partnership home or for similar purposes, and

(b)   any property acquired out of such money,

as it applies in relation to money derived from any allowance made by a husband or wife for the expenses of the matrimonial home or for similar purposes, and any property acquired out of such money.

Amendments—Section prospectively inserted by Equality Act 2010, s 2011 with effect from a date to be appointed.

71   Wills, administration of estates and family provision

Schedule 4 amends enactments relating to wills, administration of estates and family provision so that they apply in relation to civil partnerships as they apply in relation to marriage.

Amendments—Section prospectively inserted by SI 2005/3175.

72   Financial relief for civil partners and children of family

(1) Schedule 5 makes provision for financial relief in connection with civil partnerships that corresponds to provision made for financial relief in connection with marriages by Part 2 of the Matrimonial Causes Act 1973 (c 18).

(2) Any rule of law under which any provision of Part 2 of the 1973 Act is interpreted as applying to dissolution of a marriage on the ground of presumed death is to be treated as applying (with any necessary modifications) in relation to the corresponding provision of Schedule 5.

(3) Schedule 6 makes provision for financial relief in connection with civil partnerships that corresponds to provision made for financial relief in connection with marriages by the Domestic Proceedings and Magistrates' Courts Act 1978 (c 22).

(4) Schedule 7 makes provision for financial relief in England and Wales after a civil partnership has been dissolved or annulled, or civil partners have been legally separated, in a country outside the British Islands.

73   Civil partnership agreements unenforceable

(1) A civil partnership agreement does not under the law of England and Wales have effect as a contract giving rise to legal rights.

(2) No action lies in England and Wales for breach of a civil partnership agreement, whatever the law applicable to the agreement.

(3) In this section and section 74 'civil partnership agreement' means an agreement between two people –

(a)   to register as civil partners of each other –

(i)   in England and Wales (under this Part),
(ii)   in Scotland (under Part 3),
(iii) in Northern Ireland (under Part 4), or
(iv)   outside the United Kingdom under an Order in Council made under Chapter 1 of
       Part 5 (registration at British consulates etc or by armed forces personnel), or
(b)   to enter into an overseas relationship.

(4) This section applies in relation to civil partnership agreements whether entered into before or after this section comes into force, but does not affect any action commenced before it comes into force.

74 Property where civil partnership agreement is terminated

(1) This section applies if a civil partnership agreement is terminated.

(2) Section 65 (contributions by civil partner to property improvement) applies, in relation to any property in which either or both of the parties to the agreement had a beneficial interest while the agreement was in force, as it applies in relation to property in which a civil partner has a beneficial interest.

(3) Sections 66 and 67 (disputes between civil partners about property) apply to any dispute between or claim by one of the parties in relation to property in which either or both had a beneficial interest while the agreement was in force, as if the parties were civil partners of each other.

(4) An application made under section 66 or 67 by virtue of subsection (3) must be made within 3 years of the termination of the agreement.

(5) A party to a civil partnership agreement who makes a gift of property to the other party on the condition (express or implied) that it is to be returned if the agreement is terminated is not prevented from recovering the property merely because of his having terminated the agreement.

Chapter 5
Children

75 Parental responsibility, children of the family and relatives

(1) Amend the Children Act 1989 (c 41) ("the 1989 Act") as follows.

(2) In section 4A(1) (acquisition of parental responsibility by step-parent) after "is married to" insert ", or a civil partner of,".

(3) In section 105(1) (interpretation), for the definition of "child of the family" (in relation to the parties to a marriage) substitute—

> ""child of the family", in relation to parties to a marriage, or to two people who are civil partners of each other, means—
>
> (a)   a child of both of them, and
> (b)   any other child, other than a child placed with them as foster parents by a local authority or voluntary organisation, who has been treated by both of them as a child of their family."

(4) In the definition of "relative" in section 105(1), for "by affinity)" substitute "by marriage or civil partnership)".

Amendments—Section prospectively inserted by SI 2005/3175.

76 Guardianship

In section 6 of the 1989 Act (guardians: revocation and disclaimer) after subsection (3A) insert—

> "(3B) An appointment under section 5(3) or (4) (including one made in an unrevoked will or codicil) is revoked if the person appointed is the civil partner of the person who made the appointment and either—

(a)   an order of a court of civil jurisdiction in England and Wales dissolves or annuls the civil partnership, or

(b)   the civil partnership is dissolved or annulled and the dissolution or annulment is entitled to recognition in England and Wales by virtue of Chapter 3 of Part 5 of the Civil Partnership Act 2004,

unless a contrary intention appears by the appointment

Amendments—Section prospectively inserted by SI 2005/3175.

77 Entitlement to apply for residence or contact order

In section 10(5) of the 1989 Act (persons entitled to apply for residence or contact order) after paragraph (a) insert—

"(aa)   any civil partner in a civil partnership (whether or not subsisting) in relation to whom the child is a child of the family;" .

Amendments—Section prospectively inserted by SI 2005/3175.

78 Financial provision for children

(1) Amend Schedule 1 to the 1989 Act (financial provision for children) as follows.

(2) In paragraph 2(6) (meaning of "periodical payments order") after paragraph (d) insert—

"(e)   Part 1 or 9 of Schedule 5 to the Civil Partnership Act 2004 (financial relief in the High Court or a county court etc);

(f)   Schedule 6 to the 2004 Act (financial relief in the magistrates' courts etc)," .

(3) In paragraph 15(2) (person with whom a child lives or is to live) after "husband or wife" insert "or civil partner".

(4) For paragraph 16(2) (extended meaning of "parent") substitute—

"(2) In this Schedule, except paragraphs 2 and 15, "parent" includes—

(a)   any party to a marriage (whether or not subsisting) in relation to whom the child concerned is a child of the family, and

(b)   any civil partner in a civil partnership (whether or not subsisting) in relation to whom the child concerned is a child of the family;

and for this purpose any reference to either parent or both parents shall be read as a reference to any parent of his and to all of his parents."

Amendments—Section prospectively inserted by SI 2005/3175.

79 Adoption

(1) Amend the Adoption and Children Act 2002 (c 38) as follows.

(2) In section 21 (placement orders), in subsection (4)(c), after "child marries" insert ", forms a civil partnership".

(3) In section 47 (conditions for making adoption orders), after subsection (8) insert—

"(8A) An adoption order may not be made in relation to a person who is or has been a civil partner."

(4) In section 51 (adoption by one person), in subsection (1), after "is not married" insert "or a civil partner".

(5) After section 51(3) insert—

"(3A) An adoption order may be made on the application of one person who has attained the age of 21 years and is a civil partner if the court is satisfied that—

(a)   the person's civil partner cannot be found,

(b)   the civil partners have separated and are living apart, and the separation is likely to be permanent, or

(c)   the person's civil partner is by reason of ill-health, whether physical or mental, incapable of making an application for an adoption order."

(6) In section 64 (other provision to be made by regulations), in subsection (5) for "or marriage" substitute ", marriage or civil partnership".

(7) In section 74(1) (enactments for whose purposes section 67 does not apply), for paragraph (a) substitute—

> "(a)   section 1 of and Schedule 1 to the Marriage Act 1949 or Schedule 1 to the Civil Partnership Act 2004 (prohibited degrees of kindred and affinity)," .

(8) In section 79 (connections between the register and birth records), in subsection (7)—

> (a)   in paragraph (b), after "intends to be married" insert "or form a civil partnership", and
> (b)   for "the person whom the applicant intends to marry" substitute "the intended spouse or civil partner".

(9) In section 81 (Adoption Contact Register: supplementary), in subsection (2) for "or marriage" substitute ", marriage or civil partnership".

(10) In section 98 (pre-commencement adoptions: information), in subsection (7), in the definition of "relative" for "or marriage" substitute ", marriage or civil partnership".

(11) In section 144 (interpretation), in the definition of "relative" in subsection (1), after "by marriage" insert "or civil partnership".

(12) In section 144(4) (meaning of "couple"), after paragraph (a) insert—

> "(aa)   two people who are civil partners of each other, or" .

Amendments—Section prospectively inserted by SI 2005/3175.

80   False statements etc with reference to civil partnerships

(1) A person commits an offence if –

> (a)   for the purpose of procuring the formation of a civil partnership, or a document mentioned in subsection (2), he –
> > (i)   makes or signs a declaration required under this Part or Part 5, or
> > (ii)   gives a notice or certificate so required,
> > knowing that the declaration, notice or certificate is false,
> (b)   for the purpose of a record being made in any register relating to civil partnerships, he –
> > (i)   makes a statement as to any information which is required to be registered under this Part or Part 5, or
> > (ii)   causes such a statement to be made,
> > knowing that the statement is false,
> (c)   he forbids the issue of a document mentioned in subsection (2)(a) or (b) by representing himself to be a person whose consent to a civil partnership between a child and another person is required under this Part or Part 5, knowing the representation to be false, or
> (d)   with respect to a declaration made under paragraph 5(1) of Schedule 1 he makes a statement mentioned in paragraph 6 of that Schedule which he knows to be false in a material particular.

(2) The documents are –

> (a)   a civil partnership schedule or a Registrar General's licence under Chapter 1;
> (b)   a document required by an Order in Council under section 210 or 211 as an authority for two people to register as civil partners of each other;
> (c)   a certificate of no impediment under section 240.

(3) A person guilty of an offence under subsection (1) is liable –

> (a)   on conviction on indictment, to imprisonment for a term not exceeding 7 years or to a fine (or both);
> (b)   on summary conviction, to a fine not exceeding the statutory maximum.

(4) The Perjury Act 1911 (c. 6) has effect as if this section were contained in it.

81 Housing and tenancies

Schedule 8 amends certain enactments relating to housing and tenancies.

Amendments—Section prospectively inserted by SI 2005/3175.

82 Family homes and domestic violence

Schedule 9 amends Part 4 of the Family Law Act 1996 (c 27) and related enactments so that they apply in relation to civil partnerships as they apply in relation to marriages

Amendments—Section prospectively inserted by SI 2005/3175.

83 Fatal accidents claims

(1) Amend the Fatal Accidents Act 1976 (c 30) as follows.

(2) In section 1(3) (meaning of "dependant" for purposes of right of action for wrongful act causing death), after paragraph (a) insert –

"(aa) the civil partner or former civil partner of the deceased;" .

(3) In paragraph (b)(iii) of section 1(3), after "wife" insert "or civil partner".

(4) After paragraph (f) of section 1(3) insert –

"(fa)   any person (not being a child of the deceased) who, in the case of any civil partnership in which the deceased was at any time a civil partner, was treated by the deceased as a child of the family in relation to that civil partnership;" .

(5) After section 1(4) insert –

"(4A) The reference to the former civil partner of the deceased in subsection (3)(aa) above includes a reference to a person whose civil partnership with the deceased has been annulled as well as a person whose civil partnership with the deceased has been dissolved."

(6) In section 1(5)(a), for "by affinity" substitute "by marriage or civil partnership".

(7) In section 1A(2) (persons for whose benefit claim for bereavement damages may be made)—

(a)   in paragraph (a), after "wife or husband" insert "or civil partner", and
(b)   in paragraph (b), after "was never married" insert "or a civil partner".

(8) In section 3 (assessment of damages), in subsection (4), after "wife" insert "or civil partner".

Amendments—Section prospectively inserted by SI 2005/3175.

84   Evidence

(1) Any enactment or rule of law relating to the giving of evidence by a spouse applies in relation to a civil partner as it applies in relation to the spouse.

(2) Subsection (1) is subject to any specific amendment made by or under this Act which relates to the giving of evidence by a civil partner.

(3) For the avoidance of doubt, in any such amendment, references to a person's civil partner do not include a former civil partner.

(4) References in subsections (1) and (2) to giving evidence are to giving evidence in any way (whether by supplying information, making discovery, producing documents or otherwise).

(5) Any rule of law –

(a)   which is preserved by section 7(3) of the Civil Evidence Act 1995 (c. 38) or section 118(1) of the Criminal Justice Act 2003 (c. 44), and

(b)   under which in any proceedings evidence of reputation or family tradition is admissible for the purpose of proving or disproving the existence of a marriage,

is to be treated as applying in an equivalent way for the purpose of proving or disproving the existence of a civil partnership.

***

PART 5
CIVIL PARTNERSHIP FORMED OR DISSOLVED ABROAD ETC

Chapter 1
Registration Outside Uk Under Order in Council

210 Registration at British consulates etc.

(1) Her Majesty may by Order in Council make provision for two people to register as civil partners of each other –

(a)   in prescribed countries or territories outside the United Kingdom, and

(b)   in the presence of a prescribed officer of Her Majesty's Diplomatic Service,

in cases where the officer is satisfied that the conditions in subsection (2) are met.(2) The conditions are that –

(a)   at least one of the proposed civil partners is a United Kingdom national,

(b)   the proposed civil partners would have been eligible to register as civil partners of each other in such part of the United Kingdom as is determined in accordance with the Order,

(c)   the authorities of the country or territory in which it is proposed that they register as civil partners will not object to the registration, and

(d)   insufficient facilities exist for them to enter into an overseas relationship under the law of that country or territory.

(3) An officer is not required to allow two people to register as civil partners of each other if in his opinion the formation of a civil partnership between them would be inconsistent with international law or the comity of nations.

(4) An Order in Council under this section may make provision for appeals against a refusal, in reliance on subsection (3), to allow two people to register as civil partners of each other.

(5) An Order in Council under this section may provide that two people who register as civil partners of each other under such an Order are to be treated for the purposes of sections 221(1)(c)(i) and (2)(c)(i), 222(c), 224(b), 225(1)(c)(i) and (3)(c)(i), 229(1)(c)(i) and (2)(c)(i), 230(c) and 232(b) and section 1(3)(c)(i) of the Presumption of Death (Scotland) Act 1977 (c. 27) as if they had done so in the part of the United Kingdom determined as mentioned in subsection (2)(b).

211 Registration by armed forces personnel

(1) Her Majesty may by Order in Council make provision for two people to register as civil partners of each other   –

(a)   in prescribed countries or territories outside the United Kingdom, and

(b)   in the presence of an officer appointed by virtue of the Registration of Births, Deaths and Marriages (Special Provisions) Act 1957 (c. 58),

in cases where the officer is satisfied that the conditions in subsection (2) are met.

(2) The conditions are that –

(a)   at least one of the proposed civil partners –

(i)   is a member of a part of Her Majesty's forces serving in the country or territory,

      (ii)   is employed in the country or territory in such other capacity as may be prescribed, or

      (iii)   is a child of a person falling within sub-paragraph (i) or (ii) and has his home with that person in that country or territory,

(b)   the proposed civil partners would have been eligible to register as civil partners of each other in such part of the United Kingdom as is determined in accordance with the Order, and

(c)   such other requirements as may be prescribed are complied with.

(3) In determining for the purposes of subsection (2) whether one person is the child of another, a person who is or was treated by another as a child of the family in relation to –

(a)   a marriage to which the other is or was a party, or

(b)   a civil partnership in which the other is or was a civil partner,

is to be regarded as the other's child.

(4) An Order in Council under this section may provide that two people who register as civil partners of each other under such an Order are to be treated for the purposes of section 221(1)(c)(i) and (2)(c)(i), 222(c), 224(b), 225(1)(c)(i) and (3)(c)(i), 229(1)(c)(i) and (2)(c)(i), 230(c) and 232(b) and section 1(3)(c)(i) of the Presumption of Death (Scotland) Act 1977 (c. 27) as if they had done so in the part of the United Kingdom determined in accordance with subsection (2)(b).

(5) Any references in this section –

(a)   to a country or territory outside the United Kingdom,

(b)   to forces serving in such a country or territory, and

(c)   to persons employed in such a country or territory,

include references to ships which are for the time being in the waters of a country or territory outside the United Kingdom, to forces serving in any such ship and to persons employed in any such ship.

212 Meaning of 'overseas relationship'

(1) For the purposes of this Act an overseas relationship is a relationship which –

(a)   is either a specified relationship or a relationship which meets the general conditions, and

(b)   is registered (whether before or after the passing of this Act) with a responsible authority in a country or territory outside the United Kingdom, by two people –

      (i)   who under the relevant law are of the same sex at the time when they do so, and

      (ii)   neither of whom is already a civil partner or lawfully married.

(2) In this Chapter, 'the relevant law' means the law of the country or territory where the relationship is registered (including its rules of private international law).

213 Specified relationships

(1) A specified relationship is a relationship which is specified for the purposes of section 212 by Schedule 20.

(2) The Secretary of State may by order amend Schedule 20 by –

(a)   adding a relationship,

(b)   amending the description of a relationship, or

(c)   omitting a relationship.

(3) No order may be made under this section without the consent of the Scottish Ministers and the Department of Finance and Personnel.

(4) The power to make an order under this section is exercisable by statutory instrument.

(5) An order which contains any provision (whether alone or with other provisions) amending Schedule 20 by –

(a)   amending the description of a relationship, or

(b)   omitting a relationship,

may not be made unless a draft of the statutory instrument containing the order is laid before, and approved by a resolution of, each House of Parliament.

(6) A statutory instrument containing any other order under this section is subject to annulment in pursuance of a resolution of either House of Parliament.

Amendments—SI 2010/1839.

214 The general conditions

The general conditions are that, under the relevant law –

(a)   the relationship may not be entered into if either of the parties is already a party to a relationship of that kind or lawfully married,

(b)   the relationship is of indeterminate duration, and

(c)   the effect of entering into it is that the parties are –

   (i)   treated as a couple either generally or for specified purposes, or

   (ii)   treated as married.

215 Overseas relationships treated as civil partnerships: the general rule

(1) Two people are to be treated as having formed a civil partnership as a result of having registered an overseas relationship if, under the relevant law, they –

(a)   had capacity to enter into the relationship, and

(b)   met all requirements necessary to ensure the formal validity of the relationship.

(2) Subject to subsection (3), the time when they are to be treated as having formed the civil partnership is the time when the overseas relationship is registered (under the relevant law) as having been entered into.

(3) If the overseas relationship is registered (under the relevant law) as having been entered into before this section comes into force, the time when they are to be treated as having formed a civil partnership is the time when this section comes into force.

(4) But if –

(a)   before this section comes into force, a dissolution or annulment of the overseas relationship was obtained outside the United Kingdom, and

(b)   the dissolution or annulment would be recognised under Chapter 3 if the overseas relationship had been treated as a civil partnership at the time of the dissolution or annulment,

subsection (3) does not apply and subsections (1) and (2) have effect subject to subsection (5).

(5) The overseas relationship is not to be treated as having been a civil partnership for the purposes of any provisions except –

(a)   Schedules 7, 11 and 17 (financial relief in United Kingdom after dissolution or annulment obtained outside the United Kingdom);

(b)   such provisions as are specified (with or without modifications) in an order under section 259;

(c)   Chapter 3 (so far as necessary for the purposes of paragraphs (a) and (b)).

(6) This section is subject to sections 216, 217 and 218.

216 The same-sex requirement

(1) Two people are not to be treated as having formed a civil partnership as a result of having registered an overseas relationship if, at the critical time, they were not of the same sex under United Kingdom law.

(2) But if a full gender recognition certificate is issued under the 2004 Act to a person who has registered an overseas relationship which is within subsection (4), after the issue of the certificate the relationship is no longer prevented from being treated as a civil partnership on the ground that, at the critical time, the parties were not of the same sex.

(3) However, subsection (2) does not apply to an overseas relationship which is within subsection (4) if either of the parties has formed a subsequent civil partnership or lawful marriage.

(4) An overseas relationship is within this subsection if (and only if), at the time mentioned in section 215(2) –

    (a)   one of the parties ('A') was regarded under the relevant law as having changed gender (but was not regarded under United Kingdom law as having done so), and

    (b)   the other party was (under United Kingdom law) of the gender to which A had changed under the relevant law.

(5) In this section –

'the critical time' means the time determined in accordance with section 215(2) or (as the case may be) (3);

'the 2004 Act' means the Gender Recognition Act 2004 (c. 7);

'United Kingdom law' means any enactment or rule of law applying in England and Wales, Scotland and Northern Ireland.

(6) Nothing in this section prevents the exercise of any enforceable EU right.

Amendments—SI 2011/1043.

217 Person domiciled in a part of the United Kingdom

(1) Subsection (2) applies if an overseas relationship has been registered by a person who was at the time mentioned in section 215(2) domiciled in England and Wales.

(2) The two people concerned are not to be treated as having formed a civil partnership if, at the time mentioned in section 215(2) –

    (a)   either of them was under 16, or

    (b)   they would have been within prohibited degrees of relationship under Part 1 of Schedule 1 if they had been registering as civil partners of each other in England and Wales.

(3) Subsection (4) applies if an overseas relationship has been registered by a person who at the time mentioned in section 215(2) was domiciled in Scotland.

(4) The two people concerned are not to be treated as having formed a civil partnership if, at the time mentioned in section 215(2), they were not eligible by virtue of paragraph (*b*), (*c*) or (*e*) of section 86(1) to register in Scotland as civil partners of each other.

(5) Subsection (6) applies if an overseas relationship has been registered by a person who at the time mentioned in section 215(2) was domiciled in Northern Ireland.

(6) The two people concerned are not to be treated as having formed a civil partnership if, at the time mentioned in section 215(2) –

    (a)   either of them was under 16, or

    (b)   they would have been within prohibited degrees of relationship under Schedule 12 if they had been registering as civil partners of each other in Northern Ireland.

218 The public policy exception

Two people are not to be treated as having formed a civil partnership as a result of having entered into an overseas relationship if it would be manifestly contrary to public policy to recognise the capacity, under the relevant law, of one or both of them to enter into the relationship.

Introduction

219 Power to make provision corresponding to EC Regulation 2201/2003

(1) The Lord Chancellor may by regulations make provision –

    (a)   as to the jurisdiction of courts in England and Wales in proceedings for the dissolution or annulment of a civil partnership or for legal separation of the civil partners in cases where a civil partner –
        (i)   is or has been habitually resident in a member State,
        (ii)   is a national of a member State, or
        (iii)   is domiciled in a part of the United Kingdom or the Republic of Ireland, and
    (b)   as to the recognition in England and Wales . . . of any judgment of a court of another member State which orders the dissolution or annulment of a civil partnership or the legal separation of the civil partners.

(1A) The Department of Justice in Northern Ireland may by regulations make provision –

    (a)   as to the jurisdiction of courts in Northern Ireland in proceedings for the dissolution or annulment of a civil partnership or for legal separation of the civil partners in such cases as are mentioned in subsection (1)(a), and
    (b)   as to the recognition in Northern Ireland of any such judgment as is mentioned in subsection (1)(b).

(2) The Scottish Ministers may by regulations make provision –

    (a)   as to the jurisdiction of courts in Scotland in proceedings for the dissolution or annulment of a civil partnership or for legal separation of the civil partners in such cases as are mentioned in subsection (1)(a), and
    (b)   as to the recognition in Scotland of any such judgment as is mentioned in subsection (1)(b).

(3) The regulations may in particular make provision corresponding to that made by Council Regulation (EC) No 2201/2003 of 27th November 2003 in relation to jurisdiction and the recognition and enforcement of judgments in matrimonial matters.

(4) The regulations may provide that for the purposes of this Part and the regulations 'member State' means –

    (a)   all member States with the exception of such member States as are specified in the regulations, or
    (b)   such member States as are specified in the regulations.

(5) The regulations may make provision under subsections (1)(*b*), (1A)(b) and (2)(*b*) which applies even if the date of the dissolution, annulment or legal separation is earlier than the date on which this section comes into force.

(6) Regulations under subsection (1) are to be made by statutory instrument and may only be made if a draft has been laid before and approved by resolution of each House of Parliament.

(6A) Regulations under subsection (1A) are to be made by statutory rule for the purposes of the Statutory Rules (Northern Ireland) Order 1979.

(6B) No regulations shall be made under subsection (1A) unless a draft has been laid before and approved by resolution of the Northern Ireland Assembly.

(6C) Section 41(3) of the Interpretation Act (Northern Ireland) 1954 applies for the purposes of subsection (6B) in relation to the laying of a draft as it applies in relation to the laying of a statutory document under an enactment.

(7) Regulations under subsection (2) are to be made by statutory instrument and may only be made if a draft has been laid before and approved by resolution of the Scottish Parliament.

(8) In this Part 'section 219 regulations' means regulations made under this section.

Amendments—SI 2010/976.

Jurisdiction of courts in England and Wales

220 Meaning of 'the court'

In sections 221 to 224 'the court' means –

(a)   the High Court, or
(b)   if a county court has jurisdiction by virtue of Part 5 of the Matrimonial and Family Proceedings Act 1984 (c. 42), a county court.

221 Proceedings for dissolution, separation or nullity order

(1) The court has jurisdiction to entertain proceedings for a dissolution order or a separation order if (and only if) –

(a)   the court has jurisdiction under section 219 regulations,
(b)   no court has, or is recognised as having, jurisdiction under section 219 regulations and either civil partner is domiciled in England and Wales on the date when the proceedings are begun, or
(c)   the following conditions are met –
    (i)   the two people concerned registered as civil partners of each other in England or Wales,
    (ii)   no court has, or is recognised as having, jurisdiction under section 219 regulations, and
    (iii)   it appears to the court to be in the interests of justice to assume jurisdiction in the case.

(2) The court has jurisdiction to entertain proceedings for a nullity order if (and only if) –

(a)   the court has jurisdiction under section 219 regulations,
(b)   no court has, or is recognised as having, jurisdiction under section 219 regulations and either civil partner –
    (i)   is domiciled in England and Wales on the date when the proceedings are begun, or
    (ii)   died before that date and either was at death domiciled in England and Wales or had been habitually resident in England and Wales throughout the period of 1 year ending with the date of death, or
(c)   the following conditions are met –
    (i)   the two people concerned registered as civil partners of each other in England or Wales,
    (ii)   no court has, or is recognised as having, jurisdiction under section 219 regulations, and
    (iii)   it appears to the court to be in the interests of justice to assume jurisdiction in the case.

(3) At any time when proceedings are pending in respect of which the court has jurisdiction by virtue of subsection (1) or (2) (or this subsection), the court also has jurisdiction to entertain other proceedings, in respect of the same civil partnership, for a dissolution, separation or nullity order, even though that jurisdiction would not be exercisable under subsection (1) or (2).

222 Proceedings for presumption of death order

The court has jurisdiction to entertain proceedings for a presumption of death order if (and only if) –

(a) the applicant is domiciled in England and Wales on the date when the proceedings are begun,

(b) the applicant was habitually resident in England and Wales throughout the period of 1 year ending with that date, or

(c) the two people concerned registered as civil partners of each other in England and Wales and it appears to the court to be in the interests of justice to assume jurisdiction in the case.

223 Proceedings for dissolution, nullity or separation order: supplementary

(1) Rules of court may make provision in relation to civil partnerships corresponding to the provision made in relation to marriages by Schedule 1 to the Domicile and Matrimonial Proceedings Act 1973 (c. 45).

(2) The rules may in particular make provision –

(a) for the provision of information by applicants and respondents in proceedings for dissolution, nullity or separation orders where proceedings relating to the same civil partnership are continuing in another jurisdiction, and

(b) for proceedings before the court to be stayed by the court where there are concurrent proceedings elsewhere in respect of the same civil partnership.

224 Applications for declarations as to validity etc

The court has jurisdiction to entertain an application under section 58 if (and only if) –

(a) either of the civil partners in the civil partnership to which the application relates –

(i) is domiciled in England and Wales on the date of the application,

(ii) has been habitually resident in England and Wales throughout the period of 1 year ending with that date, or

(iii) died before that date and either was at death domiciled in England and Wales or had been habitually resident in England and Wales throughout the period of 1 year ending with the date of death, or

(b) the two people concerned registered as civil partners of each other in England and Wales and it appears to the court to be in the interests of justice to assume jurisdiction in the case.

****

Recognition of dissolution, annulment and separation

233 Effect of dissolution, annulment or separation obtained in the UK

(1) No dissolution or annulment of a civil partnership obtained in one part of the United Kingdom is effective in any part of the United Kingdom unless obtained from a court of civil jurisdiction.

(2) Subject to subsections (3) and (4), the validity of a dissolution or annulment of a civil partnership or a legal separation of civil partners which has been obtained from a court of civil jurisdiction in one part of the United Kingdom is to be recognised throughout the United Kingdom.

(3) Recognition of the validity of a dissolution, annulment or legal separation obtained from a court of civil jurisdiction in one part of the United Kingdom may be refused in any other part if the dissolution, annulment or separation was obtained at a time when it was irreconcilable with a decision determining the question of the subsistence or validity of the civil partnership –

(a)   previously given by a court of civil jurisdiction in the other part, or
(b)   previously given by a court elsewhere and recognised or entitled to be recognised in the other part.

(4) Recognition of the validity of a dissolution or legal separation obtained from a court of civil jurisdiction in one part of the United Kingdom may be refused in any other part if the dissolution or separation was obtained at a time when, according to the law of the other part, there was no subsisting civil partnership.

234 Recognition in the UK of overseas dissolution, annulment or separation

(1) Subject to subsection (2), the validity of an overseas dissolution, annulment or legal separation is to be recognised in the United Kingdom if, and only if, it is entitled to recognition by virtue of sections 235 to 237.

(2) This section and sections 235 to 237 do not apply to an overseas dissolution, annulment or legal separation as regards which provision as to recognition is made by section 219 regulations.

(3) For the purposes of subsections (1) and (2) and sections 235 to 237, an overseas dissolution, annulment or legal separation is a dissolution or annulment of a civil partnership or a legal separation of civil partners which has been obtained outside the United Kingdom (whether before or after this section comes into force).

235 Grounds for recognition

(1) The validity of an overseas dissolution, annulment or legal separation obtained by means of proceedings is to be recognised if –

(a)   the dissolution, annulment or legal separation is effective under the law of the country in which it was obtained, and
(b)   at the relevant date either civil partner –
       (i)   was habitually resident in the country in which the dissolution, annulment or legal separation was obtained,
       (ii)   was domiciled in that country, or
       (iii) was a national of that country.

(2) The validity of an overseas dissolution, annulment or legal separation obtained otherwise than by means of proceedings is to be recognised if –

(a)   the dissolution, annulment or legal separation is effective under the law of the country in which it was obtained,
(b)   at the relevant date –
       (i)   each civil partner was domiciled in that country, or
       (ii)   either civil partner was domiciled in that country and the other was domiciled in a country under whose law the dissolution, annulment or legal separation is recognised as valid, and
(c)   neither civil partner was habitually resident in the United Kingdom throughout the period of 1 year immediately preceding that date.

(3) In this section 'the relevant date' means –

(a)   in the case of an overseas dissolution, annulment or legal separation obtained by means of proceedings, the date of the commencement of the proceedings;
(b)   in the case of an overseas dissolution, annulment or legal separation obtained otherwise than by means of proceedings, the date on which it was obtained.

(4) Where in the case of an overseas annulment the relevant date fell after the death of either civil partner, any reference in subsection (1) or (2) to that date is to be read in relation to that civil partner as a reference to the date of death.

236 Refusal of recognition

(1) Recognition of the validity of an overseas dissolution, annulment or legal separation may be refused in any part of the United Kingdom if the dissolution, annulment or separation was obtained at a time when it was irreconcilable with a decision determining the question of the subsistence or validity of the civil partnership –

    (a)   previously given by a court of civil jurisdiction in that part of the United Kingdom, or

    (b)   previously given by a court elsewhere and recognised or entitled to be recognised in that part of the United Kingdom.

(2) Recognition of the validity of an overseas dissolution or legal separation may be refused in any part of the United Kingdom if the dissolution or separation was obtained at a time when, according to the law of that part of the United Kingdom, there was no subsisting civil partnership.

(3) Recognition of the validity of an overseas dissolution, annulment or legal separation may be refused if –

    (a)   in the case of a dissolution, annulment or legal separation obtained by means of proceedings, it was obtained –
        (i)   without such steps having been taken for giving notice of the proceedings to a civil partner as, having regard to the nature of the proceedings and all the circumstances, should reasonably have been taken, or
        (ii)   without a civil partner having been given (for any reason other than lack of notice) such opportunity to take part in the proceedings as, having regard to those matters, he should reasonably have been given, or

    (b)   in the case of a dissolution, annulment or legal separation obtained otherwise than by means of proceedings –
        (i)   there is no official document certifying that the dissolution, annulment or legal separation is effective under the law of the country in which it was obtained, or
        (ii)   where either civil partner was domiciled in another country at the relevant date, there is no official document certifying that the dissolution, annulment or legal separation is recognised as valid under the law of that other country, or

    (c)   in either case, recognition of the dissolution, annulment or legal separation would be manifestly contrary to public policy.

(4) In this section –

    'official', in relation to a document certifying that a dissolution, annulment or legal separation is effective, or is recognised as valid, under the law of any country, means issued by a person or body appointed or recognised for the purpose under that law;
    'the relevant date' has the same meaning as in section 235.

237 Supplementary provisions relating to recognition of dissolution etc

(1) For the purposes of sections 235 and 236, a civil partner is to be treated as domiciled in a country if he was domiciled in that country –

    (a)   according to the law of that country in family matters, or

    (b)   according to the law of the part of the United Kingdom in which the question of recognition arises.

(2) The Lord Chancellor, the Department of Justice in Northern Ireland or the Scottish Ministers may by regulations make provision –

    (a)   applying sections 235 and 236 and subsection (1) with modifications in relation to any country whose territories have different systems of law in force in matters of dissolution, annulment or legal separation;

    (b)   applying sections 235 and 236 with modifications in relation to –
        (i)   an overseas dissolution, annulment or legal separation in the case of an overseas relationship (or an apparent or alleged overseas relationship);

       (ii)   any case where a civil partner is domiciled in a country or territory whose law does not recognise legal relationships between two people of the same sex;

(c)   with respect to recognition of the validity of an overseas dissolution, annulment or legal separation in cases where there are cross-proceedings;

(d)   with respect to cases where a legal separation is converted under the law of the country or territory in which it is obtained into a dissolution which is effective under the law of that country or territory;

(e)   with respect to proof of findings of fact made in proceedings in any country or territory outside the United Kingdom.

(3) The power of the Lord Chancellor or the Scottish Ministers to make regulations under subsection (2) is exercisable by statutory instrument.

(4) A statutory instrument containing such regulations –

(a)   if made by the Lord Chancellor, is subject to annulment in pursuance of a resolution of either House of Parliament;

(b)   if made by the Scottish Ministers, is subject to annulment in pursuance of a resolution of the Scottish Parliament.

(4A) The power of the Department of Justice in Northern Ireland to make regulations under subsection (2) is exercisable by statutory rule for the purposes of the Statutory Rules (Northern Ireland) Order 1979.

(4B) Regulations made by the Department of Justice under subsection (2) are subject to negative resolution within the meaning of section 41(6) of the Interpretation Act (Northern Ireland) 1954.

(5) In this section (except subsection (4)) and sections 233 to 236 and 238 –

'annulment' includes any order annulling a civil partnership, however expressed;
'part of the United Kingdom' means England and Wales, Scotland or Northern Ireland;
'proceedings' means judicial or other proceedings.

(6) Nothing in this Chapter is to be read as requiring the recognition of any finding of fault made in proceedings for dissolution, annulment or legal separation or of any maintenance, custody or other ancillary order made in any such proceedings.

Amendments—SI 2010/976.

238 Non-recognition elsewhere of dissolution or annulment

(1) This section applies where, in any part of the United Kingdom –

(a)   a dissolution or annulment of a civil partnership has been granted by a court of civil jurisdiction, or

(b)   the validity of a dissolution or annulment of a civil partnership is recognised by virtue of this Chapter.

(2) The fact that the dissolution or annulment would not be recognised outside the United Kingdom does not –

(a)   preclude either party from forming a subsequent civil partnership or marriage in that part of the United Kingdom, or

(b)   cause the subsequent civil partnership or marriage of either party (wherever it takes place) to be treated as invalid in that part.

Chapter 4
Miscellaneous and Supplementary

239 Commanding officers' certificates for Part 2 purposes

(1) Her Majesty may by Order in Council make provision in relation to cases where-

(a)   two people wish to register as civil partners of each other in England and Wales (under Chapter 1 of Part 2), and

(b)   one of them ('A') is an officer, seaman or marine borne on the books of one of Her Majesty's ships at sea and the other is resident in England and Wales,

for the issue to A, by the captain or other officer in command of the ship, of a certificate of no impediment.

(2) The Order may provide for the issue of the certificate to be subject to the giving of such notice and the making of such declarations as may be prescribed.

(3) A certificate of no impediment is a certificate that no legal impediment to the formation of the civil partnership has been shown to the ... officer issuing the certificate to exist.

(4) *(repealed)*

Amendments—SI 2005/2000.

240   Certificates of no impediment to overseas relationships

(1) Her Majesty may by Order in Council make provision for the issue of certificates of no impediment to –

(a)   United Kingdom nationals, and

(b)   such other persons falling within subsection (2) as may be prescribed,

who wish to enter into overseas relationships in prescribed countries or territories outside the United Kingdom with persons who are not United Kingdom nationals and who do not fall within subsection (2).

(2) A person falls within this subsection if under any enactment for the time being in force in any country mentioned in Schedule 3 to the British Nationality Act 1981 (c. 61) (Commonwealth countries) that person is a citizen of that country.

(3) A certificate of no impediment is a certificate that, after proper notices have been given, no legal impediment to the recipient entering into the overseas relationship has been shown to the person issuing the certificate to exist.

241   Transmission of certificates of registration of overseas relationships

(1) Her Majesty may by Order in Council provide –

(a)   for the transmission to the Registrar General, by such persons or in such manner as may be prescribed, of certificates of the registration of overseas relationships entered into by United Kingdom nationals in prescribed countries or territories outside the United Kingdom,

(b)   for the issue by the Registrar General of a certified copy of such a certificate received by him, and

(c)   for such certified copies to be received in evidence.

(2) 'The Registrar General' means –

(a)   in relation to England and Wales, the Registrar General for England and Wales,

(b)   in relation to Scotland, the Registrar General of Births, Deaths and Marriages for Scotland, and

(c)   in relation to Northern Ireland, the Registrar General for Northern Ireland.

242   Power to make provision relating to certain Commonwealth forces

(1) This section applies if it appears to Her Majesty that any law in force in Canada, the Commonwealth of Australia or New Zealand (or in a territory of either of the former two countries) makes, in relation to forces raised there, provision similar to that made by section 211 (registration by armed forces personnel).

(2) Her Majesty may by Order in Council make provision for securing that the law in question has effect as part of the law of the United Kingdom.

243 Fees

(1) The power to make an order under section 34(1) (fees) includes power to make an order prescribing fees in respect of anything which, by virtue of an Order in Council under this Part, is required to be done by registration authorities in England and Wales or by or on behalf of the Registrar General for England and Wales.

(2) Regulations made by the Registrar General of Births, Deaths and Marriages for Scotland may prescribe fees in respect of anything which, by virtue of an Order in Council under this Part, is required to be done by him or on his behalf.

(3) Subsections (3) and (4) of section 126 apply to regulations made under subsection (2) as they apply to regulations under Part 3.

(4) The power to make an order under section 157(1) includes power to make an order prescribing fees in respect of anything which, by virtue of an Order in Council under this Part, is required to be done by or on behalf of the Registrar General for Northern Ireland.

244 Orders in Council: supplementary

(1) An Order in Council under section 210, 211, 239, 240, 241 or 242 may make –

    (a)   different provision for different cases, and

    (b)   such supplementary, incidental, consequential, transitional, transitory or saving provision as appears to Her Majesty to be appropriate.

(2) The provision that may be made by virtue of subsection (1)(b) includes in particular provision corresponding to or applying with modifications any provision made by or under

    (a)   this Act, or

    (b)   any Act relating to marriage outside the United Kingdom.

(3) A statutory instrument containing an Order in Council under section 210, 211, 239, 240, 241 or 242 is subject to annulment in pursuance of a resolution of either House of Parliament.

(4) Subsection (3) applies whether or not the Order also contains other provisions made by Order in Council under –

the Foreign Marriage Act 1892 (c. 23),
section 3 of the Foreign Marriage Act 1947 (c. 33), or
section 39 of the Marriage Act 1949 (c. 76).

(5) In sections 210, 211, 239, 240 and 241 'prescribed' means prescribed by an Order in Council under the section in question.

245 Interpretation

(1) In this Part 'United Kingdom national' means a person who is

    (a)   a British citizen, a British overseas territories citizen, a British Overseas citizen or a British National (Overseas),

    (b)   a British subject under the British Nationality Act 1981 (c. 61), or

    (c)   a British protected person, within the meaning of that Act.

(2) In this Part 'Her Majesty's forces' has the same meaning as in the Armed Forces Act 2006.

Amendments—Armed Forces Act 2006, s 378(1), Sch 16, para 243.

****

Schedule 1
Prohibited degrees of relationship: England and Wales

Sections 3(2) and 5(3)

PART 1
THE PROHIBITIONS

Absolute prohibitions

1

(1) Two people are within prohibited degrees of relationship if one falls within the list below in relation to the other.

Adoptive child
Adoptive parent
Child
Former adoptive child
Former adoptive parent
Grandparent
Grandchild
Parent
Parent's sibling
Sibling
Sibling's child

(2) In the list 'sibling' means a brother, sister, half-brother or half-sister.

Qualified prohibitions

2

(1) Two people are within prohibited degrees of relationship if one of them falls within the list below in relation to the other, unless –

(a) both of them have reached 21 at the time when they register as civil partners of each other, and
(b) the younger has not at any time before reaching 18 been a child of the family in relation to the other.
Child of former civil partner
Child of former spouse
Former civil partner of grandparent
Former civil partner of parent
Former spouse of grandparent
Former spouse of parent
Grandchild of former civil partner
Grandchild of former spouse

(2) 'Child of the family', in relation to another person, means a person who –

(a) has lived in the same household as that other person, and
(b) has been treated by that other person as a child of his family.

3

Two people are within prohibited degrees of relationship if one falls within column 1 of the table below in relation to the other, unless –

(a) both of them have reached 21 at the time when they register as civil partners of each other, and
(b) the persons who fall within column 2 are dead.

Relationship	Relevant deaths
Former civil partner of child	The child
	The child's other parent
Former spouse of child	The child
	The child's other parent
Parent of former civil partner	The former civil partner
	The former civil partner's other parent
Parent of former spouse	The former spouse
	The former spouse's other parent

PART 2
SPECIAL PROVISIONS RELATING TO QUALIFIED PROHIBITIONS

Provisions relating to paragraph 24

Paragraphs 5 to 7 apply where two people are subject to paragraph 2 but intend to register as civil partners of each other by signing a civil partnership schedule.

5

(1) The fact that a notice of proposed civil partnership has been given must not be recorded in the register unless the registration authority –

    (a)   is satisfied by the production of evidence that both the proposed civil partners have reached 21, and

    (b)   has received a declaration made by each of the proposed civil partners –

        (i)   specifying their affinal relationship, and

        (ii)   declaring that the younger of them has not at any time before reaching 18 been a child of the family in relation to the other.

(2) Sub-paragraph (1) does not apply if a declaration is obtained under paragraph 7.

(3) A declaration under sub-paragraph (1)(b) must contain such information and must be signed and attested in such manner as may be prescribed by regulations.

(4) The fact that a registration authority has received a declaration under sub-paragraph (1)(b) must be recorded in the register.

(5) A declaration under sub-paragraph (1)(b) must be filed and kept by the registration authority.

6

(1) Sub-paragraph (2) applies if –

    (a)   a registration authority receives from a person who is not one of the proposed civil partners a written statement signed by that person which alleges that a declaration made under paragraph 5 is false in a material particular, and

    (b)   the register shows that such a statement has been received.

(2) The registration authority in whose area it is proposed that the registration take place must not issue a civil partnership schedule unless a High Court declaration is obtained under paragraph 7.

7

(1) Either of the proposed civil partners may apply to the High Court for a declaration that, given that –

    (a)   both of them have reached 21, and

(b)   the younger of those persons has not at any time before reaching 18 been a child of the family in relation to the other,

there is no impediment of affinity to the formation of the civil partnership.

(2) Such an application may be made whether or not any statement has been received by the registration authority under paragraph 6.

8

Section 13 (objection to proposed civil partnership) does not apply in relation to a civil partnership to which paragraphs 5 to 7 apply, except so far as an objection to the issue of a civil partnership schedule is made under that section on a ground other than the affinity between the proposed civil partners.

Provisions relating to paragraph 3

9

(1) This paragraph applies where two people are subject to paragraph 3 but intend to register as civil partners of each other by signing a civil partnership schedule.

(2) The fact that a notice of proposed civil partnership has been given must not be recorded in the register unless the registration authority is satisfied by the production of evidence –

(a)   that both the proposed civil partners have reached 21, and
(b)   that the persons referred to in paragraph 3(b) are dead.

Amendments—SI 2005/2000.

****

Schedule 5
Financial Relief in the High Court or a County Court etc

PART 1
FINANCIAL PROVISION IN CONNECTION WITH DISSOLUTION, NULLITY OR SEPARATION

1   Circumstances in which orders under this Part may be made

(1) The court may make any one or more of the orders set out in paragraph 2(1) –

(a)   on making a dissolution, nullity or separation order, or
(b)   at any time afterwards.

(2) The court may make any one or more of the orders set out in paragraph 2(1)(*d*), (*e*) and (*f*) –

(a)   in proceedings for a dissolution, nullity or separation order, before making the order;
(b)   if proceedings for a dissolution, nullity or separation order are dismissed after the beginning of the trial, either straightaway or within a reasonable period after the dismissal.

(3) The power of the court to make an order under sub-paragraph (1) or (2) (*a*) in favour of a child of the family is exercisable from time to time.

(4) If the court makes an order in favour of a child under sub-paragraph (2)(*b*), it may from time to time make a further order in the child's favour of any of the kinds set out in paragraph 2(1)(*d*), (*e*) or (*f*).

2   The orders: periodical and secured periodical payments and lump sums

(1) The orders are –

(a)   an order that either civil partner must make to the other such periodical payments for such term as may be specified;

(b)   an order that either civil partner must secure to the other, to the satisfaction of the court, such periodical payments for such term as may be specified;

(c)   an order that either civil partner must pay to the other such lump sum or sums as may be specified;

(d)   an order that one of the civil partners must make –

    (i)   to such person as may be specified for the benefit of a child of the family, or

    (ii)   to a child of the family,

such periodical payments for such term as may be specified;

(e)   an order that one of the civil partners must secure –

    (i)   to such person as may be specified for the benefit of a child of the family, or

    (ii)   to a child of the family,

to the satisfaction of the court, such periodical payments for such term as may be specified;

(f)   an order that one of the civil partners must pay such lump sum as may be specified –

    (i)   to such person as may be specified for the benefit of a child of the family, or

    (ii)   to a child of the family.

(2) 'Specified' means specified in the order.

3   Particular provision that may be made by lump sum orders

(1) An order under this Part requiring one civil partner to pay the other a lump sum may be made for the purpose of enabling the other civil partner to meet any liabilities or expenses reasonably incurred by the other in maintaining –

(a)   himself or herself, or

(b)   a child of the family,

before making an application for an order under this Part in his or her favour.

(2) An order under this Part requiring a lump sum to be paid to or for the benefit of a child of the family may be made for the purpose of enabling any liabilities or expenses reasonably incurred by or for the benefit of the child before making an application for an order under this Part to be met.

(3) An order under this Part for the payment of a lump sum may –

(a)   provide for its payment by instalments of such amount as may be specified, and

(b)   require the payment of the instalments to be secured to the satisfaction of the court.

(4) Sub-paragraphs (1) to (3) do not restrict the powers to make the orders set out in paragraph 2(1)(*c*) and (*f*).

(5) If the court –

(a)   makes an order under this Part for the payment of a lump sum, and

(b)   directs that –

    (i)   payment of the sum or any part of it is to be deferred, or

    (ii)   the sum or any part of it is to be paid by instalments,

it may provide for the deferred amount or the instalments to carry interest at such rate as may be specified from such date as may be specified until the date when payment of it is due.

(6) A date specified under sub-paragraph (5) must not be earlier than the date of the order.

(7) 'Specified' means specified in the order.

4   When orders under this Part may take effect

(1) If an order is made under paragraph 2(1)(*a*), (*b*) or (*c*) on or after making a dissolution or nullity order, neither the order nor any settlement made in pursuance of it takes effect unless the dissolution or nullity order has been made final.

(2) This paragraph does not affect the power of the court to give a direction under paragraph 76 (settlement of instrument by conveyancing counsel).

5   Restrictions on making of orders under this Part

The power to make an order under paragraph 2(1)(*d*), (*e*) or (*f*) is subject to paragraph 49(1) and (5) (restrictions on orders in favour of children who have reached 18).

PART 2
PROPERTY ADJUSTMENT ON OR AFTER DISSOLUTION, NULLITY OR SEPARATION

6   Circumstances in which property adjustment orders may be made

(1) The court may make one or more property adjustment orders –

    (a)   on making a dissolution, nullity or separation order, or
    (b)   at any time afterwards.

(2) In this Schedule 'property adjustment order' means a property adjustment order under this Part.

7   Property adjustment orders

(1) The property adjustment orders are –

    (a)   an order that one of the civil partners must transfer such property as may be specified, being property to which he is entitled –
        (i)   to the other civil partner,
        (ii)   to a child of the family, or
        (iii)   to such person as may be specified for the benefit of a child of the family;
    (b)   an order that a settlement of such property as may be specified, being property to which one of the civil partners is entitled, be made to the satisfaction of the court for the benefit of –
        (i)   the other civil partner and the children of the family, or
        (ii)   either or any of them;
    (c)   an order varying for the benefit of –
        (i)   the civil partners and the children of the family, or
        (ii)   either or any of them,
        a relevant settlement;
    (d)   an order extinguishing or reducing the interest of either of the civil partners under a relevant settlement.

(2) The court may make a property adjustment order under sub-paragraph (1)(*c*) even though there are no children of the family.

(3) In this paragraph –

    'entitled' means entitled in possession or reversion,
    'relevant settlement' means, in relation to a civil partnership, a settlement made, during its subsistence or in anticipation of its formation, on the civil partners including one made by will or codicil, but not including one in the form of a pension arrangement (within the meaning of Part 4), and
    'specified' means specified in the order.

8   When property adjustment orders may take effect

(1) If a property adjustment order is made on or after making a dissolution or nullity order, neither the property adjustment order nor any settlement made under it takes effect unless the dissolution or nullity order has been made final.

(2) This paragraph does not affect the power to give a direction under paragraph 76 (settlement of instrument by conveyancing counsel).

9   Restrictions on making property adjustment orders

The power to make a property adjustment order under paragraph 7(1)(*a*) is subject to paragraph 49(1) and (5) (restrictions on making orders in favour of children who have reached 18).

PART 3
SALE OF PROPERTY ORDERS

10   Circumstances in which sale of property orders may be made

(1) The court may make a sale of property order –

   (a)   on making –
         (i)   under Part 1, a secured periodical payments order or an order for the payment of a lump sum, or
         (ii)   a property adjustment order, or
   (b)   at any time afterwards.

(2) In this Schedule 'sale of property order' means a sale of property order under this Part.

11   Sale of property orders

(1) A sale of property order is an order for the sale of such property as may be specified, being property in which, or in the proceeds of sale of which, either or both of the civil partners has or have a beneficial interest, either in possession or reversion.

(2) A sale of property order may contain such consequential or supplementary provisions as the court thinks fit.

(3) A sale of property order may in particular include –

   (a)   provision requiring the making of a payment out of the proceeds of sale of the property to which the order relates, and
   (b)   provision requiring any property to which the order relates to be offered for sale to a specified person, or class of persons.

(4) 'Specified' means specified in the order.

12   When sale of property orders may take effect

(1) If a sale of property order is made on or after the making of a dissolution or nullity order, it does not take effect unless the dissolution or nullity order has been made final.

(2) Where a sale of property order is made, the court may direct that –

   (a)   the order, or
   (b)   such provision of it as the court may specify,

is not to take effect until the occurrence of an event specified by the court or the end of a period so specified.

13   When sale of property orders cease to have effect

If a sale of property order contains a provision requiring the proceeds of sale of the property to which the order relates to be used to secure periodical payments to a civil partner, the order ceases to have effect –

(a)   on the death of the civil partner, or
(b)   on the formation of a subsequent civil partnership or marriage by the civil partner.

14   Protection of third parties

(1) Sub-paragraphs (2) and (3) apply if –

(a)   a civil partner has a beneficial interest in any property, or in the proceeds of sale of any property, and
(b)   another person ('A') who is not the other civil partner also has a beneficial interest in the property or the proceeds.

(2) Before deciding whether to make a sale of property order in relation to the property, the court must give A an opportunity to make representations with respect to the order.

(3) Any representations made by A are included among the circumstances to which the court is required to have regard under paragraph 20.

PART 4
PENSION SHARING ORDERS ON OR AFTER DISSOLUTION OR NULLITY ORDER

15   Circumstances in which pension sharing orders may be made

(1) The court may make a pension sharing order –

(a)   on making a dissolution or nullity order, or
(b)   at any time afterwards.

(2) In this Schedule 'pension sharing order' means a pension sharing order under this Part.

16   Pension sharing orders

(1) A pension sharing order is an order which –

(a)   provides that one civil partner's –
    (i)   shareable rights under a specified pension arrangement, or
    (ii)   shareable state scheme rights,
    are to be subject to pension sharing for the benefit of the other civil partner, and
(b)   specifies the percentage value to be transferred.

(2) Shareable rights under a pension arrangement are rights in relation to which pension sharing is available under –

(a)   Chapter 1 of Part 4 of the Welfare Reform and Pensions Act 1999 (c. 30), or
(b)   corresponding Northern Ireland legislation.

(3) Shareable state scheme rights are rights in relation to which pension sharing is available under –

(a)   Chapter 2 of Part 4 of the 1999 Act, or
(b)   corresponding Northern Ireland legislation.

(4) In this Part 'pension arrangement' means –

(a)   an occupational pension scheme,
(b)   a personal pension scheme,
(c)   a retirement annuity contract,
(d)   an annuity or insurance policy purchased, or transferred, for the purpose of giving effect to rights under –

(i)   an occupational pension scheme, or

(ii)   a personal pension scheme, and

(e)   an annuity purchased, or entered into, for the purpose of discharging liability in respect of a pension credit under –

(i)   section 29(1)(*b*) of the 1999 Act, or

(ii)   corresponding Northern Ireland legislation.

(5) In sub-paragraph (4) –

'occupational pension scheme' has the same meaning as in the Pension Schemes Act 1993 (c. 48);

'personal pension scheme' has the same meaning as in the 1993 Act;

'retirement annuity contract' means a contract or scheme approved under Chapter 3 of Part 14 of the Income and Corporation Taxes Act 1988 (c. 1).

17   Pension sharing orders: apportionment of charges

If a pension sharing order relates to rights under a pension arrangement, the court may include in the order provision about the apportionment between the civil partners of any charge under –

(a)   section 41 of the 1999 Act (charges in respect of pension sharing costs), or

(b)   corresponding Northern Ireland legislation.

18   Restrictions on making of pension sharing orders

(1) A pension sharing order may not be made in relation to a pension arrangement which –

(a)   is the subject of a pension sharing order in relation to the civil partnership, or

(b)   has been the subject of pension sharing between the civil partners.

(2) A pension sharing order may not be made in relation to shareable state scheme rights if –

(a)   such rights are the subject of a pension sharing order in relation to the civil partnership, or

(b)   such rights have been the subject of pension sharing between the civil partners.

(3) A pension sharing order may not be made in relation to the rights of a person under a pension arrangement if there is in force a requirement imposed by virtue of Part 6 which relates to benefits or future benefits to which that person is entitled under the pension arrangement.

19   When pension sharing orders may take effect

(1) A pension sharing order is not to take effect unless the dissolution or nullity order on or after which it is made has been made final.

(2) No pension sharing order may be made so as to take effect before the end of such period after the making of the order as may be prescribed by regulations made by the Lord Chancellor.

(3) The power to make regulations under sub-paragraph (2) is exercisable by statutory instrument which is subject to annulment in pursuance of a resolution of either House of Parliament.

PART 4A
PENSION COMPENSATION SHARING ORDERS ON OR AFTER DISSOLUTION OR NULLITY ORDER

19A   Circumstances in which pension compensation sharing orders may be made

(1) The court may make a pension compensation sharing order –

(a)   on making a dissolution or nullity order, or

(b)   at any time afterwards.

(2) In this Schedule "pension compensation sharing order" means a pension compensation sharing order under this Part.

Amendments—Inserted by the Pensions Act 2008, s 120, Sch 6, Pt 3.

19B Pension compensation sharing orders

(1) A pension compensation sharing order is an order which –

    (a)   provides that one civil partner's shareable rights to PPF compensation that derive from rights under a specified pension scheme are to be subject to pension compensation sharing for the benefit of the other civil partner, and

    (b)   specifies the percentage value to be transferred.

(2) Shareable rights to PPF compensation are rights in relation to which pension compensation sharing is available under –

    (a)   Chapter 1 of Part 3 of the Pensions Act 2008, or

    (b)   corresponding Northern Ireland legislation.

(3) In sub-paragraph (1) "specified" means specified in the order.

Amendments—Inserted by the Pensions Act 2008, s 120, Sch 6, Pt 3.

19C Pension compensation sharing orders: apportionment of charges

The court may include in a pension compensation sharing order provision about the apportionment between the civil partners of any charge under –

    (a)   section 117 of the Pensions Act 2008 (charges in respect of pension compensation sharing costs), or

    (b)   corresponding Northern Ireland legislation.

Amendments—Inserted by the Pensions Act 2008, s 120, Sch 6, Pt 3.

19D Restrictions on making pension compensation sharing orders

(1) A pension compensation sharing order may not be made in relation to rights to PPF compensation that –

    (a)   are the subject of pension attachment,

    (b)   derive from rights under a pension scheme that were the subject of pension sharing between the civil partners,

    (c)   are the subject of pension compensation attachment, or

    (d)   are or have been the subject of pension compensation sharing between the civil partners.

(2) For the purposes of sub-paragraph (1)(a), rights to PPF compensation "are the subject of pension attachment" if any of the following three conditions is met.

(3) The first condition is that –

    (a)   the rights derive from rights under a pension scheme in relation to which an order was made under Part 1 imposing a requirement by virtue of paragraph 25(2), and

    (b)   that order, as modified under paragraph 31, remains in force.

(4) The second condition is that –

    (a)   the rights derive from rights under a pension scheme in relation to which an order was made under Part 1 imposing a requirement by virtue of paragraph 25(5), and

    (b)   that order –

        (i)   has been complied with, or

        (ii)   has not been complied with and, as modified under paragraph 32, remains in force.

(5) The third condition is that –

    (a)   the rights derive from rights under a pension scheme in relation to which an order was made under Part 1 imposing a requirement by virtue of paragraph 26, and

    (b)   that order remains in force.

(6) For the purposes of sub-paragraph (1)(b), rights under a pension scheme "were the subject of pension sharing between the civil partners" if the rights were at any time the subject of a pension sharing order in relation to the civil partnership or a previous civil partnership between the same parties.

(7) For the purposes of sub-paragraph (1)(c), rights to PPF compensation "are the subject of pension compensation attachment" if there is in force a requirement imposed by virtue of Part 6 relating to them.

(8) For the purposes of sub-paragraph (1)(d), rights to PPF compensation "are or have been the subject of pension compensation sharing between the civil partners" if they are or have ever been the subject of a pension compensation sharing order in relation to the civil partnership or a previous civil partnership between the same parties.

Amendments—Inserted by the Pensions Act 2008, s 120, Sch 6, Pt 3.

19E When pension compensation sharing orders may take effect

(1) A pension compensation sharing order is not to take effect unless the dissolution or nullity order on or after which it is made has been made final.

(2) No pension compensation sharing order may be made so as to take effect before the end of such period after the making of the order as may be prescribed by regulations made by the Lord Chancellor.

(3) The power to make regulations under sub-paragraph (2) is exercisable by statutory instrument which is subject to annulment in pursuance of a resolution of either House of Parliament.

Amendments—Inserted by the Pensions Act 2008, s 120, Sch 6, Pt 3.

19F Interpretation

In this Schedule –

    "PPF compensation" means compensation payable under the pension compensation provisions;
    "the pension compensation provisions" means–

    (a)   Chapter 3 of Part 2 of the Pensions Act 2004 (pension protection) and any regulations or order made under it,

    (b)   Chapter 1 of Part 3 of the Pensions Act 2008 (pension compensation sharing) and any regulations or order made under it, and

    (c)   any provision corresponding to the provisions mentioned in paragraph (a) or (b) in force in Northern Ireland.

Amendments—Inserted by the Pensions Act 2008, s 120, Sch 6, Pt 3.

PART 5
MATTERS TO WHICH COURT IS TO HAVE REGARD UNDER PARTS 1 TO 4A

20 General

The court in deciding –

    (a)   whether to exercise its powers under –

        (i)   Part 1 (financial provision on dissolution etc),

        (ii)   Part 2 (property adjustment orders),

        (iii)   Part 3 (sale of property orders),

(iv)   any provision of Part 4 (pension sharing orders) other than paragraph 17 (apportionment of charges), or

(v)   any provision of Part 4A (pension compensation sharing orders) other than paragraph 19C (apportionment of charges), and

(b)   if so, in what way,

must have regard to all the circumstances of the case, giving first consideration to the welfare, while under 18, of any child of the family who has not reached 18.

Amendments—Pensions Act 2008, s 120, Sch 6, Pt 3.

21 Particular matters to be taken into account when exercising powers in relation to civil partners

(1) This paragraph applies to the exercise by the court in relation to a civil partner of its powers under –

(a)   Part 1 (financial provision on dissolution etc) by virtue of paragraph 2(1)(a), (b) or (c),

(b)   Part 2 (property adjustment orders),

(c)   Part 3 (sale of property orders),

(d)   Part 4 (pension sharing orders), or

(e)   Part 4A (pension compensation sharing orders).

(2) The court must in particular have regard to –

(a)   the income, earning capacity, property and other financial resources which each civil partner –

(i)   has, or

(ii)   is likely to have in the foreseeable future,

including, in the case of earning capacity, any increase in that capacity which it would in the opinion of the court be reasonable to expect a civil partner in the civil partnership to take steps to acquire;

(b)   the financial needs, obligations and responsibilities which each civil partner has or is likely to have in the foreseeable future;

(c)   the standard of living enjoyed by the family before the breakdown of the civil partnership;

(d)   the age of each civil partner and the duration of the civil partnership;

(e)   any physical or mental disability of either of the civil partners;

(f)   the contributions which each civil partner has made or is likely in the foreseeable future to make to the welfare of the family, including any contribution by looking after the home or caring for the family;

(g)   the conduct of each civil partner, if that conduct is such that it would in the opinion of the court be inequitable to disregard it;

(h)   in the case of proceedings for a dissolution or nullity order, the value to each civil partner of any benefit which, because of the dissolution or annulment of the civil partnership, that civil partner will lose the chance of acquiring.

Amendments—Pensions Act 2008, s 120, Sch 6, Pt 3.

22 Particular matters to be taken into account when exercising powers in relation to children

(1) This paragraph applies to the exercise by the court in relation to a child of the family of its powers under –

(a)   Part 1 (financial provision on dissolution etc) by virtue of paragraph 2(1)(d), (e) or (f)),

(b)   Part 2 (property adjustment orders), or

(c)   Part 3 (sale of property orders).

(2) The court must in particular have regard to –

(a)   the financial needs of the child;

(b)   the income, earning capacity (if any), property and other financial resources of the child;

(c)   any physical or mental disability of the child;

(d)   the way in which the child was being and in which the civil partners expected the child to be educated or trained;

(e)   the considerations mentioned in relation to the civil partners in paragraph 21(2)(a), (b), (c) and (e).

(3) In relation to the exercise of any of those powers against a civil partner ('A') in favour of a child of the family who is not A's child, the court must also have regard to –

(a)   whether A has assumed any responsibility for the child's maintenance;

(b)   if so, the extent to which, and the basis upon which, A assumed such responsibility and the length of time for which A discharged such responsibility;

(c)   whether in assuming and discharging such responsibility A did so knowing that the child was not A's child;

(d)   the liability of any other person to maintain the child.

23   Terminating financial obligations

(1) Sub-paragraphs (2) and (3) apply if, on or after the making of a dissolution or nullity order, the court decides to exercise its powers under –

(a)   Part 1 (financial provision on dissolution etc) by virtue of paragraph 2(1)(a), (b) or (c),

(b)   Part 2 (property adjustment orders),

(c)   Part 3 (sale of property orders),

(d)   Part 4 (pension sharing orders), or

(e)   Part 4A (pension compensation sharing orders),

in favour of one of the civil partners.

(2) The court must consider whether it would be appropriate to exercise those powers in such a way that the financial obligations of each civil partner towards the other will be terminated as soon after the making of the dissolution or nullity order as the court considers just and reasonable.

(3) If the court decides to make –

(a)   a periodical payments order, or

(b)   a secured periodical payments order,

in favour of one of the civil partners ('A'), it must in particular consider whether it would be appropriate to require the payments to be made or secured only for such term as would in its opinion be sufficient to enable A to adjust without undue hardship to the termination of A's financial dependence on the other civil partner.

(4) If –

(a)   on or after the making of a dissolution or nullity order, an application is made by one of the civil partners for a periodical payments or secured periodical payments order in that civil partner's favour, but

(b)   the court considers that no continuing obligation should be imposed on either civil partner to make or secure periodical payments in favour of the other,

the court may dismiss the application with a direction that the applicant is not entitled to make any future application in relation to that civil partnership for an order under Part 1 by virtue of paragraph 2(1)(*a*) or (*b*).

Amendments—Pensions Act 2008, s 120, Sch 6, Pt 3, paras 14, 16.

PART 6
MAKING OF PART 1 ORDERS HAVING REGARD TO PENSION BENEFITS

24 Pension benefits to be included in matters to which court is to have regard

(1) The matters to which the court is to have regard under paragraph 21(2)(*a*) include any pension benefits under a pension arrangement or by way of pension which a civil partner has or is likely to have; and, accordingly, in relation to any pension benefits paragraph 21(2)(*a*)(ii) has effect as if 'in the foreseeable future' were omitted.

(2) The matters to which the court is to have regard under paragraph 21(2)(*h*) include any pension benefits which, because of the making of a dissolution or nullity order, a civil partner will lose the chance of acquiring.

(3) 'Pension benefits' means –

    (a)   benefits under a pension arrangement, or
    (b)   benefits by way of pension (whether under a pension arrangement or not).

25 Provisions applying where pension benefits taken into account in decision to make Part 1 order

(1) This paragraph applies if, having regard to any benefits under a pension arrangement, the court decides to make an order under Part 1.

(2) To the extent to which the Part 1 order is made having regard to any benefits under a pension arrangement, it may require the person responsible for the pension arrangement, if at any time any payment in respect of any benefits under the arrangement becomes due to the civil partner with pension rights, to make a payment for the benefit of the other civil partner.

(3) The Part 1 order must express the amount of any payment required to be made by virtue of sub-paragraph (2) as a percentage of the payment which becomes due to the civil partner with pension rights.

(4) Any such payment by the person responsible for the arrangement –

    (a)   discharges so much of his liability to the civil partner with pension rights as corresponds to the amount of the payment, and
    (b)   is to be treated for all purposes as a payment made by the civil partner with pension rights in or towards the discharge of that civil partner's liability under the order.

(5) If the civil partner with pension rights has a right of commutation under the arrangement, the Part 1 order may require that civil partner to exercise it to any extent.

(6) This paragraph applies to any payment due in consequence of commutation in pursuance of the Part 1 order as it applies to other payments in respect of benefits under the arrangement.

(7) The power conferred by sub-paragraph (5) may not be exercised for the purpose of commuting a benefit payable to the civil partner with pension rights to a benefit payable to the other civil partner.

(8) The powers conferred by sub-paragraphs (2) and (5) may not be exercised in relation to a pension arrangement which –

    (a)   is the subject of a pension sharing order in relation to the civil partnership, or
    (b)   has been the subject of pension sharing between the civil partners.

26 Pensions: lump sums

(1) This paragraph applies if the benefits which the civil partner with pension rights has or is likely to have under a pension arrangement include any lump sum payable in respect of that civil partner's death.

(2) The court's power under Part 1 to order a civil partner to pay a lump sum to the other civil partner includes the power to make by the order any provision in sub-paragraph (3) to (5).

(3) If the person responsible for the pension arrangement has power to determine the person to whom the sum, or any part of it, is to be paid, the court may require him to pay the whole or part of that sum, when it becomes due, to the other civil partner.

(4) If the civil partner with pension rights has power to nominate the person to whom the sum, or any part of it, is to be paid, the court may require the civil partner with pension rights to nominate the other civil partner in respect of the whole or part of that sum.

(5) In any other case, the court may require the person responsible for the pension arrangement in question to pay the whole or part of that sum, when it becomes due, for the benefit of the other civil partner instead of to the person to whom, apart from the order, it would be paid.

(6) Any payment by the person responsible for the arrangement under an order made under Part 1 made by virtue of this paragraph discharges so much of his liability in respect of the civil partner with pension rights as corresponds to the amount of the payment.

(7) The powers conferred by this paragraph may not be exercised in relation to a pension arrangement which –

(a)   is the subject of a pension sharing order in relation to the civil partnership, or
(b)   has been the subject of pension sharing between the civil partners.

27   Pensions: supplementary

If –

(a)   a Part 1 order made by virtue of paragraph 25 or 26 imposes any requirement on the person responsible for a pension arrangement ('the first arrangement'),
(b)   the civil partner with pension rights acquires rights under another pension arrangement ('the new arrangement') which are derived (directly or indirectly) from the whole of that civil partner's rights under the first arrangement, and
(c)   the person responsible for the new arrangement has been given notice in accordance with regulations made by the Lord Chancellor,

the Part 1 order has effect as if it had been made instead in respect of the person responsible for the new arrangement.

28   Regulations

(1) The Lord Chancellor may by regulations –

(a)   make provision, in relation to any provision of paragraph 25 or 26 which authorises the court making a Part 1 order to require the person responsible for a pension arrangement to make a payment for the benefit of the other civil partner, as to –
        (i)   the person to whom, and
        (ii)   the terms on which,
        the payment is to be made;
(b)   make provision, in relation to payment under a mistaken belief as to the continuation in force of a provision included by virtue of paragraph 25 or 26 in a Part 1 order, about the rights or liabilities of the payer, the payee or the person to whom the payment was due;
(c)   require notices to be given in respect of changes of circumstances relevant to Part 1 orders which include provision made by virtue of paragraphs 25 and 26;
(d)   make provision for the person responsible for a pension arrangement to be discharged in prescribed circumstances from a requirement imposed by virtue of paragraph 25 or 26;
(e)   make provision about calculation and verification in relation to the valuation of –
        (i)   benefits under a pension arrangement, or
        (ii)   shareable state scheme rights (within the meaning of paragraph 16(3)),

for the purposes of the court's functions in connection with the exercise of any of its powers under this Schedule.

(2) Regulations under sub-paragraph (1)(*e*) may include –

(a)   provision for calculation or verification in accordance with guidance from time to time prepared by a prescribed person, and

(b)   provision by reference to regulations under section 30 or 49(4) of the 1999 Act.

(3) The power to make regulations under paragraph 27 or this paragraph is exercisable by statutory instrument which is subject to annulment in pursuance of a resolution of either House of Parliament.

(4) 'Prescribed' means prescribed by regulations.

29 Interpretation of provisions relating to pensions

(1) In this Part 'the civil partner with pension rights' means the civil partner who has or is likely to have benefits under a pension arrangement.

(2) In this Part 'pension arrangement' has the same meaning as in Part 4.

(3) In this Part, references to the person responsible for a pension arrangement are to be read in accordance with section 26 of the Welfare Reform and Pensions Act 1999 (c. 30).

PART 7
PENSION PROTECTION FUND COMPENSATION ETC

30 PPF compensation to be included in matters to which court is to have regard

(1) The matters to which a court is to have regard under paragraph 21(2)(*a*) include any PPF compensation to which a civil partner is or is likely to be entitled; and, accordingly, in relation to any PPF compensation paragraph 21(2)(*a*)(ii) has effect as if 'in the foreseeable future' were omitted.

(2) The matters to which a court is to have regard under paragraph 21(2)(*h*) include any PPF compensation which, because of the making of a dissolution or nullity order, a civil partner will lose the chance of acquiring entitlement to.

(3) *(repealed)*

31 Assumption of responsibility by PPF Board in paragraph 25(2) cases

(1) This paragraph applies to an order under Part 1 so far as it includes provision made by virtue of paragraph 25(2) which –

(a)   imposed requirements on the trustees or managers of an occupational pension scheme for which the Board has assumed responsibility, and

(b)   was made before the trustees or managers received the transfer notice.

(2) From the time the trustees or managers of the scheme receive the transfer notice, the order has effect –

(a)   except in descriptions of case prescribed by regulations, with the modifications set out in sub-paragraph (3), and

(b)   with such other modifications as may be prescribed by regulations.

(3) The modifications are that –

(a)   references in the order to the trustees or managers of the scheme have effect as references to the Board, and

(b)   references in the order to any pension or lump sum to which the civil partner with pension rights is or may become entitled under the scheme have effect as references to any PPF compensation to which that person is or may become entitled in respect of the pension or lump sum.

32 Assumption of responsibility by PPF Board in paragraph 25(5) cases

(1) This paragraph applies to an order under Part 1 if –

    (a)   it includes provision made by virtue of paragraph 25(5) which requires the civil partner with pension rights to exercise his right of commutation under an occupational pension scheme to any extent, and

    (b)   before the requirement is complied with the Board has assumed responsibility for the scheme.

(2) From the time the trustees or managers of the scheme receive the transfer notice, the order has effect with such modifications as may be prescribed by regulations.

33 Lump sums: power to modify paragraph 26 in respect of assessment period

Regulations may modify paragraph 26 in its application to an occupational pension scheme during an assessment period in relation to the scheme.

34 Assumption of responsibility by the Board not to affect power of court to vary order etc

(1) This paragraph applies where the court makes, in relation to an occupational pension scheme –

    (a)   a pension sharing order, or
    (b)   an order including provision made by virtue of paragraph 25(2) or (5).

(2) If the Board subsequently assumes responsibility for the scheme, that does not affect –

    (a)   the powers of the court under paragraph 51 to vary or discharge the order or to suspend or revive any provision of it;

    (b)   on an appeal, the powers of the appeal court to affirm, reinstate, set aside or vary the order.

34A Attachment of PPF compensation

(1) This paragraph applies if, having regard to any PPF compensation to which a civil partner is or is likely to be entitled, the court decides to make an order under Part 1.

(2) To the extent to which the Part 1 order is made having regard to such compensation, it may require the Board, if at any time any payment in respect of PPF compensation becomes due to the civil partner with compensation rights, to make a payment for the benefit of the other civil partner.

(3) The Part 1 order must express the amount of any payment required to be made by virtue of sub-paragraph (2) as a percentage of the payment which becomes due to the civil partner with compensation rights.

(4) Any such payment by the Board–

    (a)   discharges so much of its liability to the civil partner with compensation rights as corresponds to the amount of the payment, and

    (b)   is to be treated for all purposes as a payment made by the civil partner with compensation rights in or towards the discharge of that civil partner's liability under the order.

(5) If the civil partner with compensation rights has a right to commute any PPF compensation, the Part 1 order may require that civil partner to exercise it to any extent.

(6) This paragraph applies to any payment due in consequence of commutation in pursuance of the Part 1 order as it applies to other payments in respect of PPF compensation.

(7) The power conferred by sub-paragraph (5) may not be exercised for the purpose of commuting a benefit payable to the civil partner with compensation rights to a benefit payable to the other civil partner.

(8) The powers conferred by sub-paragraphs (2) and (5) may not be exercised in relation to rights to PPF compensation that–

(a)   derive from rights under a pension scheme that were at any time the subject of a pension sharing order in relation to the civil partnership or a previous civil partnership between the same parties, or

(b)   are or have ever been the subject of a pension compensation sharing order in relation to the civil partnership or a previous civil partnership between the same parties.

Amendments—Pensions Act 2008, s 120, Sch 6, Pt 3.

34B

(1) Regulations may–

(a)   make provision, in relation to any provision of paragraph 34A which authorises the court making a Part 1 order to require the Board to make a payment for the benefit of the other civil partner, as to the person to whom, and the terms on which, the payment is to be made;

(b)   make provision, in relation to payment under a mistaken belief as to the continuation in force of a provision included by virtue of paragraph 34A in a Part 1 order, about the rights or liabilities of the payer, the payee or the person to whom the payment was due;

(c)   require notices to be given in respect of changes of circumstances relevant to Part 1 orders which include provision made by virtue of paragraph 34A;

(d)   make provision for the Board to be discharged in prescribed circumstances from a requirement imposed by virtue of paragraph 34A;

(e)   make provision about calculation and verification in relation to the valuation of PPF compensation for the purposes of the court's functions in connection with the exercise of any of its powers under this Schedule.

(2) Regulations under sub-paragraph (1)(e) may include–

(a)   provision for calculation or verification in accordance with guidance from time to time prepared by a prescribed person;

(b)   provision by reference to regulations under section 112 of the Pensions Act 2008.

Amendments—Pensions Act 2008, s 120, Sch 6, Pt 3.

Regulations

35

Regulations may make such consequential modifications of any provision of, or made by virtue of, this Schedule as appear to the Lord Chancellor necessary or expedient to give effect to the provisions of this Part.

36

(1) In this Part 'regulations' means regulations made by the Lord Chancellor.

(2) A power to make regulations under this Part is exercisable by statutory instrument which is subject to annulment in pursuance of a resolution of either House of Parliament.

37   Interpretation

(1) In this Part –

'assessment period' means –
(*a*)   an assessment period within the meaning of Part 2 of the Pensions Act 2004 (pension protection), or
(*b*)   an equivalent period under corresponding Northern Ireland legislation;

'the Board' means the Board of the Pension Protection Fund;

'the civil partner with compensation rights' means the civil partner who is or is likely to be entitled to PPF compensation;

'the civil partner with pension rights' has the meaning given by paragraph 29(1);

'occupational pension scheme' has the same meaning as in the Pension Schemes Act 1993 (c. 48);

'prescribed' means prescribed by regulations;

'transfer notice' has the same meaning as in –

    (a)   Chapter 3 of Part 2 of the 2004 Act, or

    (b)   corresponding Northern Ireland legislation.

(2) References in this Part to the Board assuming responsibility for a scheme are to the Board assuming responsibility for the scheme in accordance with –

    (a)   Chapter 3 of Part 2 of the 2004 Act (pension protection), or

    (b)   corresponding Northern Ireland legislation.

Amendments—Pensions Act 2008, ss 120, 148, Sch 6, Pt 3.

PART 8
MAINTENANCE PENDING OUTCOME OF DISSOLUTION, NULLITY OR SEPARATION PROCEEDINGS

38

On an application for a dissolution, nullity or separation order, the court may make an order requiring either civil partner to make to the other for the other's maintenance such periodical payments for such term –

    (a)   beginning no earlier than the date on which the application was made, and

    (b)   ending with the date on which the proceedings are determined,

as the court thinks reasonable.

PART 9
FAILURE TO MAINTAIN: FINANCIAL PROVISION (AND INTERIM ORDERS)

39 Circumstances in which orders under this Part may be made

(1) Either civil partner in a subsisting civil partnership may apply to the court for an order under this Part on the ground that the other civil partner ('the respondent') –

    (a)   has failed to provide reasonable maintenance for the applicant, or

    (b)   has failed to provide, or to make a proper contribution towards, reasonable maintenance for any child of the family.

(2) The court must not entertain an application under this paragraph unless it has jurisdiction to do so by virtue of the Maintenance Regulation and Schedule 6 to the Civil Jurisdiction and Judgments (Maintenance) Regulations 2011.

(3) If, on an application under this paragraph, it appears to the court that –

    (a)   the applicant or any child of the family to whom the application relates is in immediate need of financial assistance, but

    (b)   it is not yet possible to determine what order, if any, should be made on the application,

the court may make an interim order.

(4) If, on an application under this paragraph, the applicant satisfies the court of a ground mentioned in sub-paragraph (1), the court may make one or more of the orders set out in paragraph 41.

(5) In this paragraph, "the Maintenance Regulation" means Council Regulation (EC) No 4/2009 including as applied in relation to Denmark by virtue of the Agreement made on 19th October 2005 between the European Community and the Kingdom of Denmark.

40 Interim orders

An interim order is an order requiring the respondent to make to the applicant, until the determination of the application, such periodical payments as the court thinks reasonable.

41 Orders that may be made where failure to maintain established

(1) The orders are –

    (a)   an order that the respondent must make to the applicant such periodical payments for such term as may be specified;

    (b)   an order that the respondent must secure to the applicant, to the satisfaction of the court, such periodical payments for such term as may be specified;

    (c)   an order that the respondent must pay to the applicant such lump sum as may be specified;

    (d)   an order that the respondent must make such periodical payments for such term as may be specified –

        (i)   to such person as may be specified, for the benefit of the child to whom the application relates, or

        (ii)   to the child to whom the application relates;

    (e)   an order that the respondent must secure –

        (i)   to such person as may be specified for the benefit of the child to whom the application relates, or

        (ii)   to the child to whom the application relates,

to the satisfaction of the court, such periodical payments for such term as may be specified;

    (f)   an order that the respondent must pay such lump sum as may be specified –

        (i)   to such person as may be specified for the benefit of the child to whom the application relates, or

        (ii)   to the child to whom the application relates.

(2) In this Part 'specified' means specified in the order.

42 Particular provision that may be made by lump sum orders

(1) An order under this Part for the payment of a lump sum may be made for the purpose of enabling any liabilities or expenses reasonably incurred in maintaining the applicant or any child of the family to whom the application relates before the making of the application to be met.

(2) An order under this Part for the payment of a lump sum may –

    (a)   provide for its payment by instalments of such amount as may be specified, and

    (b)   require the payment of the instalments to be secured to the satisfaction of the court.

(3) Sub-paragraphs (1) and (2) do not restrict the power to make an order by virtue of paragraph 41(1)(c) or (f).

43 Matters to which the court is to have regard on application under paragraph 39(1)(a)

(1) This paragraph applies if an application under paragraph 39 is made on the ground mentioned in paragraph 39(1)(a).

(2) In deciding –

    (a)   whether the respondent has failed to provide reasonable maintenance for the applicant, and

    (b)   what order, if any, to make under this Part in favour of the applicant, the court must have regard to all the circumstances of the case including the matters mentioned in paragraph 21(2).

(3) If an application is also made under paragraph 39 in respect of a child of the family who has not reached 18, the court must give first consideration to the welfare of the child while under 18.

(4) Paragraph 21(2)(*c*) has effect as if for the reference in it to the breakdown of the civil partnership there were substituted a reference to the failure to provide reasonable maintenance for the applicant.

44　Matters to which the court is to have regard on application under paragraph 39(1)(b)

(1) This paragraph applies if an application under paragraph 39 is made on the ground mentioned in paragraph 39(1)(*b*).

(2) In deciding –

(a)　whether the respondent has failed to provide, or to make a proper contribution towards, reasonable maintenance for the child of the family to whom the application relates, and
(b)　what order, if any, to make under this Part in favour of the child,

the court must have regard to all the circumstances of the case.

(3) Those circumstances include –

(a)　the matters mentioned in paragraph 22(2)(a) to (e), and
(b)　if the child of the family to whom the application relates is not the child of the respondent, the matters mentioned in paragraph 22(3).

(4) Paragraph 21(2)(*c*) (as it applies by virtue of paragraph 22(2)(*e*)) has effect as if for the reference in it to the breakdown of the civil partnership there were substituted a reference to –

(a)　the failure to provide, or
(b)　the failure to make a proper contribution towards,

reasonable maintenance for the child of the family to whom the application relates.

45　Restrictions on making orders under this Part

The power to make an order under paragraph 41(1)(*d*), (*e*) or (*f*) is subject to paragraph 49(1) and (5) (restrictions on orders in favour of children who have reached 18).

Amendments—SI 2011/1484.

PART 10
COMMENCEMENT OF CERTAIN PROCEEDINGS AND DURATION OF CERTAIN ORDERS

46　Commencement of proceedings for ancillary relief, etc

(1) Sub-paragraph (2) applies if an application for a dissolution, nullity or separation order has been made.

(2) Subject to sub-paragraph (3), proceedings for –

(a)　an order under Part 1 (financial provision on dissolution etc),
(b)　a property adjustment order, or
(c)　an order under Part 8 (maintenance pending outcome of dissolution, nullity or separation proceedings),

may be begun (subject to and in accordance with rules of court) at any time after the presentation of the application.

(3) Rules of court may provide, in such cases as may be prescribed by the rules, that –

(a) an application for any such relief as is mentioned in sub-paragraph (2) must be made in the application or response, and

(b) an application for any such relief which –

　　(i) is not so made, or

　　(ii) is not made until after the end of such period following the presentation of the application or filing of the response as may be so prescribed,

may be made only with the leave of the court.

47 Duration of periodical and secured periodical payments orders for a civil partner

(1) The court may specify in a periodical payments or secured periodical payments order in favour of a civil partner such term as it thinks fit, except that the term must not –

(a) begin before the date of the making of an application for the order, or

(b) extend beyond the limits given in sub-paragraphs (2) and (3).

(2) The limits in the case of a periodical payments order are –

(a) the death of either civil partner;

(b) where the order is made on or after the making of a dissolution or nullity order, the formation of a subsequent civil partnership or marriage by the civil partner in whose favour the order is made.

(3) The limits in the case of a secured periodical payments order are –

(a) the death of the civil partner in whose favour the order is made;

(b) where the order is made on or after the making of a dissolution or nullity order, the formation of a subsequent civil partnership or marriage by the civil partner in whose favour the order is made.

(4) In the case of an order made on or after the making of a dissolution or nullity order, sub-paragraphs (1) to (3) are subject to paragraphs 23(3) and 59(4).

(5) If a periodical payments or secured periodical payments order in favour of a civil partner is made on or after the making of a dissolution or nullity order, the court may direct that that civil partner is not entitled to apply under paragraph 51 for the extension of the term specified in the order.

(6) If –

(a) a periodical payments or secured periodical payments order in favour of a civil partner is made otherwise than on or after the making of a dissolution or nullity order, and

(b) the civil partnership is subsequently dissolved or annulled but the order continues in force,

the order ceases to have effect (regardless of anything in it) on the formation of a subsequent civil partnership or marriage by that civil partner, except in relation to any arrears due under it on the date of its formation.

48 Subsequent civil partnership or marriage

If after the making of a dissolution or nullity order one of the civil partners forms a subsequent civil partnership or marriage, that civil partner is not entitled to apply, by reference to the dissolution or nullity order, for –

(a) an order under Part 1 in that civil partner's favour, or

(b) a property adjustment order,

against the other civil partner in the dissolved or annulled civil partnership.

49 Duration of continuing orders in favour of children, and age limit on making certain orders in their favour

(1) Subject to sub-paragraph (5) –

    (a)   no order under Part 1,

    (b)   no property adjustment order made by virtue of paragraph 7(1)(a) (transfer of property), and

    (c)   no order made under Part 9 (failure to maintain) by virtue of paragraph 41,

is to be made in favour of a child who has reached 18.

(2) The term to be specified in a periodical payments or secured periodical payments order in favour of a child may begin with –

    (a)   the date of the making of an application for the order or a later date, or

    (b)   a date ascertained in accordance with sub-paragraph (7) or (8).

(3) The term to be specified in such an order –

    (a)   must not in the first instance extend beyond the date of the birthday of the child next following the child's reaching the upper limit of the compulsory school age unless the court considers that in the circumstances of the case the welfare of the child requires that it should extend to a later date, and

    (b)   must not in any event, subject to sub-paragraph (5), extend beyond the date of the child's 18th birthday.

(4) Sub-paragraph (3)(*a*) must be read with section 8 of the Education Act 1996 (c. 56) (which applies to determine for the purposes of any enactment whether a person is of compulsory school age).

(5) Sub-paragraphs (1) and (3)(*b*) do not apply in the case of a child if it appears to the court that –

    (a)   the child is, or will be, or, if an order were made without complying with either or both of those provisions, would be –

        (i)   receiving instruction at an educational establishment, or

        (ii)   undergoing training for a trade, profession or vocation,

        whether or not the child also is, will be or would be in gainful employment, or

    (b)   there are special circumstances which justify the making of an order without complying with either or both of sub-paragraphs (1) and (3)(b).

(6) A periodical payments order in favour of a child, regardless of anything in the order, ceases to have effect on the death of the person liable to make payments under the order, except in relation to any arrears due under the order on the date of the death.

(7) If –

    (a)   a maintenance calculation ('the current calculation') is in force with respect to a child, and

    (b)   an application is made under this Schedule for a periodical payments or secured periodical payments order in favour of that child –

        (i)   in accordance with section 8 of the Child Support Act 1991 (c. 48), and

        (ii)   before the end of 6 months beginning with the making of the current calculation,

the term to be specified in any such order made on that application may be expressed to begin on, or at any time after, the earliest permitted date.

(8) 'The earliest permitted date' is whichever is the later of –

    (a)   the date 6 months before the application is made, or

    (b)   the date on which the current calculation took effect or, where successive maintenance calculations have been continuously in force with respect to a child, on which the first of those calculations took effect.

(9) If –

    (a)   a maintenance calculation ceases to have effect by or under any provision of the 1991 Act, and

    (b)   an application is made, before the end of 6 months beginning with the relevant date, for a periodical payments or secured periodical payments order in favour of a child with respect to whom that maintenance calculation was in force immediately before it ceased to have effect,

the term to be specified in any such order made on that application may begin with the date on which that maintenance calculation ceased to have effect or any later date.

(10) 'The relevant date' means the date on which the maintenance calculation ceased to have effect.

(11) In this paragraph 'maintenance calculation' has the same meaning as it has in the 1991 Act by virtue of section 54 of the 1991 Act as read with any regulations in force under that section.

PART 11
VARIATION, DISCHARGE ETC OF CERTAIN ORDERS FOR FINANCIAL RELIEF

50 Orders etc to which this Part applies

(1) This Part applies to the following orders –

    (a)   a periodical payments order under Part 1 (financial provision on dissolution etc) or Part 9 (failure to maintain);

    (b)   a secured periodical payments order under Part 1 or 9;

    (c)   an order under Part 8 (maintenance pending outcome of dissolution proceedings etc);

    (d)   an interim order under Part 9;

    (e)   an order made under Part 1 by virtue of paragraph 3(3) or under Part 9 by virtue of paragraph 42(2) (lump sum by instalments);

    (f)   a deferred order made under Part 1 by virtue of paragraph 2(1)(c) (lump sum for civil partner) which includes provision made by virtue of –

        (i)   paragraph 25(2),

        (ii)   paragraph 26, or

        (iii)   paragraph 34A(2),

(provision in respect of pension rights or pension compensation rights);

    (g)   a property adjustment order made on or after the making of a separation order by virtue of paragraph 7(1)(b), (c) or (d) (order for settlement or variation of settlement);

    (h)   a sale of property order;

    (i)   a pension sharing order, or a pension compensation sharing order, made before the dissolution or nullity order has been made final.

(2) If the court has made an order referred to in sub-paragraph (1)(f)(ii), this Part ceases to apply to the order on the death of either of the civil partners.

(3) The powers exercisable by the court under this Part in relation to an order are also exercisable in relation to any instrument executed in pursuance of the order.

Amendments—Pensions Act 2008, s 120, Sch 6, Pt 3.

51 Powers to vary, discharge, suspend or revive order

(1) If the court has made an order to which this Part applies, it may –

    (a)   vary or discharge the order,

    (b)   suspend any provision of it temporarily, or

    (c)   revive the operation of any provision so suspended.

(2) Sub-paragraph (1) is subject to the provisions of this Part and paragraph 47(5).

52 Power to remit arrears

(1) If the court has made an order referred to in paragraph 50(1)(*a*), (*b*), (*c*) or (*d*), it may remit the payment of any arrears due under the order or under any part of the order.

(2) Sub-paragraph (1) is subject to the provisions of this Part.

53 Additional powers on discharging or varying a periodical or secured periodical payments order after dissolution of civil partnership

(1) Sub-paragraph (2) applies if, after the dissolution of a civil partnership, the court –

  (a)   discharges a periodical payments order or secured periodical payments order made in favour of a civil partner, or

  (b)   varies such an order so that payments under the order are required to be made or secured only for such further period as is determined by the court.

(2) The court may make supplemental provision consisting of any of the following –

  (a)   an order for the payment of a lump sum in favour of one of the civil partners;

  (b)   one or more property adjustment orders in favour of one of the civil partners;

  (c)   one or more pension sharing orders;

  (ca) a pension compensation sharing order;

  (d)   a direction that the civil partner in whose favour the original order discharged or varied was made is not entitled to make any further application for –

    (i)   a periodical payments or secured periodical payments order, or

    (ii) an extension of the period to which the original order is limited by any variation made by the court.

(3) The power under sub-paragraph (2) is in addition to any power the court has apart from that sub-paragraph.

Amendments—Pensions Act 2008, s 120, Sch 6, Pt 3.

54

(1) An order for the payment of a lump sum under paragraph 53 may –

  (a)   provide for the payment of it by instalments of such amount as may be specified, and

  (b)   require the payment of the instalments to be secured to the satisfaction of the court.

(2) Sub-paragraphs (5) and (6) of paragraph 3 (interest on deferred instalments) apply where the court makes an order for the payment of a lump sum under paragraph 53 as they apply where it makes such an order under Part 1.

(3) If under paragraph 53 the court makes more than one property adjustment order in favour of the same civil partner, each of those orders must fall within a different paragraph of paragraph 7(1) (types of property adjustment orders).

(4) Part 3 (orders for the sale of property) and paragraph 76 (direction for settlement of instrument) apply where the court makes a property adjustment order under paragraph 53 as they apply where it makes any other property adjustment order.

(5) Paragraph 18 (restrictions on making of pension sharing order) applies in relation to a pension sharing order under paragraph 53 as it applies in relation to any other pension sharing order.

(6) Paragraph 19D (restrictions on making pension compensation sharing orders) applies in relation to a pension compensation sharing order under paragraph 53 as it applies in relation to any other pension compensation sharing order.

Amendments—Pensions Act 2008, s 120, Sch 6, Pt 3.

55 Variation etc of periodical or secured periodical payments orders made in cases of failure to maintain

(1) An application for the variation under paragraph 51 of a periodical payments order or secured periodical payments order made under Part 9 in favour of a child may, if the child has reached 16, be made by the child himself.

(2) Sub-paragraph (3) applies if a periodical payments order made in favour of a child under Part 9 ceases to have effect –

(a)   on the date on which the child reaches 16, or
(b)   at any time after that date but before or on the date on which the child reaches 18.

(3) If, on an application made to the court for an order under this sub-paragraph, it appears to the court that –

(a)   the child is, will be or, if an order were made under this sub-paragraph, would be –
    (i)   receiving instruction at an educational establishment, or
    (ii)   undergoing training for a trade, profession or vocation,
    whether or not the child also is, will be or would be in gainful employment, or
(b)   there are special circumstances which justify the making of an order under this sub-paragraph,

the court may by order revive the order mentioned in sub-paragraph (2) from such date as it may specify.

(4) A date specified under sub-paragraph (3) must not be earlier than the date of the application under that sub-paragraph.

(5) If under sub-paragraph (3) the court revives an order it may exercise its power under paragraph 51 in relation to the revived order.

56 Variation etc of property adjustment and pension sharing orders, pension sharing and pension compensation sharing orders

The court must not exercise the powers conferred by this Part in relation to a property adjustment order falling within paragraph 7(1)(*b*), (*c*) or (*d*) (order for settlement or for variation of settlement) except on an application made in proceedings –

(a)   for the rescission of the separation order by reference to which the property adjustment order was made, or
(b)   for a dissolution order in relation to the civil partnership.

Amendments—Pensions Act 2008, s 120, Sch 6, Pt 3.

57

(1) In relation to a pension sharing order or pension compensation sharing order which is made at a time before the dissolution or nullity order has been made final –

(a)   the powers conferred by this Part (by virtue of paragraph 50(1)(i)) may be exercised –
    (i)   only on an application made before the pension sharing order or pension compensation sharing order has or, but for paragraph (*b*), would have taken effect, and
    (ii)   only if, at the time when the application is made, the dissolution or nullity order has not been made final, and
(b)   an application made in accordance with paragraph (a) prevents the pension sharing order or pension compensation sharing order from taking effect before the application has been dealt with.

(2) No variation of a pension sharing order or pension compensation sharing order is to be made so as to take effect before the order is made final.

(3) The variation of a pension sharing order or pension compensation sharing order prevents the order taking effect before the end of such period after the making of the variation as may be prescribed by regulations made by the Lord Chancellor.

(4) The power to make regulations under sub-paragraph (3) is exercisable by statutory instrument which is subject to annulment in pursuance of a resolution of either House of Parliament.

Amendments—Pensions Act 2008, s 120, Sch 6, Pt 3.

58

(1) Sub-paragraphs (2) and (3) –

    (a)   are subject to paragraphs 53 and 54, and
    (b)   do not affect any power exercisable by virtue of paragraph 50(e), (f), (g) or (i) or otherwise than by virtue of this Part.

(2) No property adjustment order, pension sharing order or pension compensation sharing order may be made on an application for the variation of a periodical payments or secured periodical payments order made (whether in favour of a civil partner or in favour of a child of the family) under Part 1.

(3) No order for the payment of a lump sum may be made on an application for the variation of a periodical payments or secured periodical payments order in favour of a civil partner (whether made under Part 1 or 9).

Amendments—Pensions Act 2008, s 120, Sch 6, Pt 3.

59 Matters to which court is to have regard in exercising powers under this Part

(1) In exercising the powers conferred by this Part the court must have regard to all the circumstances of the case, giving first consideration to the welfare, while under 18, of any child of the family who has not reached 18.

(2) The circumstances of the case include, in particular, any change in any of the matters to which the court was required to have regard when making the order to which the application relates.

(3) Sub-paragraph (4) applies in the case of –

    (a)   a periodical payments order, or
    (b)   a secured periodical payments order,

made on or after the making of a dissolution or nullity order.

(4) The court must consider whether in all the circumstances, and after having regard to any such change, it would be appropriate to vary the order so that payments under the order are required –

    (a)   to be made, or
    (b)   to be secured,

only for such further period as will in the opinion of the court be sufficient to enable the civil partner in whose favour the order was made to adjust without undue hardship to the termination of those payments.

(5) In considering what further period will be sufficient, the court must, if the civil partnership has been dissolved, take into account any proposed exercise by it of its powers under paragraph 53.

(6) If the civil partner against whom the order was made has died, the circumstances of the case also include the changed circumstances resulting from that civil partner's death.

60 Variation of secured periodical payments order where person liable has died

(1) This paragraph applies if the person liable to make payments under a secured periodical payments order has died.

(2) Subject to sub-paragraph (3), an application under this Part relating to the order (and to any sale of property order which requires the proceeds of sale of property to be used for securing those payments) may be made by –

(a)   the person entitled to payments under the periodical payments order, or
(b)   the personal representatives of the deceased person.

(3) No such application may be made without the leave of the court after the end of 6 months from the date on which representation in regard to the estate of that person is first taken out.

(4) The personal representatives of the person who has died are not liable for having distributed any part of the estate of the deceased after the end of the 6 month period on the ground that they ought to have taken into account the possibility that the court might allow an application under this paragraph to be made after that period by the person entitled to payments under the order.

(5) Sub-paragraph (4) does not affect any power to recover any part of the estate so distributed arising by virtue of the making of an order in pursuance of this paragraph.

(6) In considering for the purposes of sub-paragraph (3) the question when representation was first taken out –

(a)   a grant limited to settled land or to trust property is to be disregarded, and
(b)   a grant limited to real estate or to personal estate is to be disregarded unless a grant limited to the remainder of the estate has previously been made or is made at the same time.

61 Power to direct when variation etc is to take effect

(1) If the court, in exercise of its powers under this Part, decides –

(a)   to vary, or
(b)   to discharge,

a periodical payments or secured periodical payments order, it may direct that the variation or discharge is not to take effect until the end of such period as may be specified in the order.

(2) Sub-paragraph (1) is subject to paragraph 47(1) and (6).

62

(1) If –

(a)   a periodical payments or secured periodical payments order in favour of more than one child ('the order') is in force,
(b)   the order requires payments specified in it to be made to or for the benefit of more than one child without apportioning those payments between them,
(c)   a maintenance calculation ('the calculation') is made with respect to one or more, but not all, of the children with respect to whom those payments are to be made, and
(d)   an application is made, before the end of the period of 6 months beginning with the date on which the calculation was made, for the variation or discharge of the order,

the court may, in exercise of its powers under this Part to vary or discharge the order, direct that the variation or discharge is to take effect from the date on which the calculation took effect or any later date.

(2) If –

(a)   an order ('the child order') of a kind prescribed for the purposes of section 10(1) of the Child Support Act 1991 (c. 48) is affected by a maintenance calculation,
(b)   on the date on which the child order became so affected there was in force a periodical payments or secured periodical payments order ('the civil partner's order') in favour of a civil partner having the care of the child in whose favour the child order was made, and

(c)   an application is made, before the end of the period of 6 months beginning with the date on which the maintenance calculation was made, for the civil partner's order to be varied or discharged,

the court may, in exercise of its powers under this Part to vary or discharge the civil partner's order, direct that the variation or discharge is to take effect from the date on which the child order became so affected or any later date.

(3) For the purposes of sub-paragraph (2), an order is affected if it ceases to have effect or is modified by or under section 10 of the 1991 Act.

(4) Sub-paragraphs (1) and (2) do not affect any other power of the court to direct that the variation of discharge of an order under this Part is to take effect from a date earlier than that on which the order for variation or discharge was made.

(5) In this paragraph 'maintenance calculation' has the same meaning as it has in the 1991 Act by virtue of section 54 of the 1991 Act as read with any regulations in force under that section.

PART 12
ARREARS AND REPAYMENTS

63 Payment of certain arrears unenforceable without the leave of the court

(1) This paragraph applies if any arrears are due under –

(a)   an order under Part 1 (financial provision on dissolution etc),
(b)   an order under Part 8 (maintenance pending outcome of dissolution, nullity or separation proceedings), or
(c)   an order under Part 9 (failure to maintain),

and the arrears became due more than 12 months before proceedings to enforce the payment of them are begun.

(2) A person is not entitled to enforce through the High Court or any county court the payment of the arrears without the leave of that court.

(3) The court hearing an application for the grant of leave under this paragraph may –

(a)   refuse leave,
(b)   grant leave subject to such restrictions and conditions (including conditions as to the allowing of time for payment or the making of payment by instalments) as that court thinks proper, or
(c)   remit the payment of the arrears or of any part of them.

(4) An application for the grant of leave under this paragraph must be made in such manner as may be prescribed by rules of court.

64 Orders for repayment in certain cases of sums paid under certain orders

(1) This paragraph applies if –

(a)   a person ('R') is entitled to receive payments under an order listed in sub-paragraph (2), and
(b)   R's circumstances or the circumstances of the person ('P') liable to make payments under the order have changed since the order was made, or the circumstances have changed as a result of P's death.

(2) The orders are –

(a)   any order under Part 8 (maintenance pending outcome of dissolution, nullity or separation proceedings);
(b)   any interim order under Part 9;
(c)   any periodical payments order;

    (d)   any secured periodical payments order.

(3) P or P's personal representatives may (subject to sub-paragraph (7)) apply for an order under this paragraph against R or R's personal representatives.

(4) If it appears to the court that, because of the changed circumstances or P's death, the amount received by R in respect of a relevant period exceeds the amount which P or P's personal representatives should have been required to pay, it may order the respondent to the application to pay to the applicant such sum, not exceeding the amount of the excess, as it thinks just.

(5) 'Relevant period' means a period after the circumstances changed or (as the case may be) after P's death.

(6) An order under this paragraph for the payment of any sum may provide for the payment of that sum by instalments of such amount as may be specified in the order.

(7) An application under this paragraph –

    (a)   may be made in proceedings in the High Court or a county court for –
        (i)   the variation or discharge of the order listed in sub-paragraph (2), or
        (ii)   leave to enforce, or the enforcement of, the payment of arrears under that order, but
    (b)   if not made in such proceedings, must be made to a county court;

and accordingly references in this paragraph to the court are references to the High Court or a county court, as the circumstances require.

(8) The jurisdiction conferred on a county court by this paragraph is exercisable even though, because of the amount claimed in the application, the jurisdiction would not but for this sub-paragraph be exercisable by a county court.

65 Orders for repayment after cessation of order because of subsequent civil partnership etc

(1) Sub-paragraphs (3) and (4) apply if –

    (a)   a periodical payments or secured periodical payments order in favour of a civil partner ('R') has ceased to have effect because of the formation of a subsequent civil partnership or marriage by R, and
    (b)   the person liable to make payments under the order ('P') (or P's personal representatives) has made payments in accordance with it in respect of a relevant period in the mistaken belief that the order was still subsisting.

(2) 'Relevant period' means a period after the date of the formation of the subsequent civil partnership or marriage.

(3) P (or P's personal representatives) is not entitled to bring proceedings in respect of a cause of action arising out of the circumstances mentioned in sub-paragraph (1)(*a*) and (*b*) against R (or R's personal representatives).

(4) But, on an application under this paragraph by P (or P's personal representatives) against R (or R's personal representatives), the court –

    (a)   may order the respondent to pay to the applicant a sum equal to the amount of the payments made in respect of the relevant period, or
    (b)   if it appears to the court that it would be unjust to make that order, may –
        (i)   order the respondent to pay to the applicant such lesser sum as it thinks fit, or
        (ii)   dismiss the application.

(5) An order under this paragraph for the payment of any sum may provide for the payment of that sum by instalments of such amount as may be specified in the order.

(6) An application under this paragraph –

(a)   may be made in proceedings in the High Court or a county court for leave to enforce, or the enforcement of, payment of arrears under the order in question, but

(b)   if not made in such proceedings, must be made to a county court;

and accordingly references in this paragraph to the court are references to the High Court or a county court, as the circumstances require.

(7) The jurisdiction conferred on a county court by this paragraph is exercisable even though, because of the amount claimed in the application, the jurisdiction would not but for this sub-paragraph be exercisable by a county court.

(8) Subject to sub-paragraph (9) –

(a)   the designated officer for a magistrates' court to whom any payments under a payments order are required to be made is not liable for any act done by him in pursuance of the payments order after the date on which that order ceased to have effect because of the formation of a subsequent civil partnership or marriage by the person entitled to payments under it, and

(b)   the collecting officer under an attachment of earnings order made to secure payments under a payments order is not liable for any act done by him after that date in accordance with any enactment or rule of court specifying how payments made to him in compliance with the attachment of earnings order are to be dealt with.

(9) Sub-paragraph (8) applies if (and only if) the act –

(a)   was one which the officer would have been under a duty to do had the payments order not ceased to have effect, and

(b)   was done before notice in writing of the formation of the subsequent civil partnership or marriage was given to him by or on behalf of –

(i)   the person entitled to payments under the payments order,

(ii)   the person liable to make payments under it, or

(iii)   the personal representatives of either of them.

(10) In sub-paragraphs (8) and (9) 'payments order' means a periodical payments order or secured periodical payments order and 'collecting officer', in relation to an attachment of earnings order, means –

(a)   the officer of the High Court,

(b)   the district judge of a county court, or

(c)   the designated officer for a magistrates' court,

to whom a person makes payments in compliance with the order.

PART 13
CONSENT ORDERS AND MAINTAINENCE AGREEMENTS

66 Consent orders for financial relief

(1) Regardless of anything in the preceding provisions of this Schedule, on an application for a consent order for financial relief, the court may, unless it has reason to think that there are other circumstances into which it ought to inquire, make an order in the terms agreed on the basis only of such information supplied with the application as is required by rules of court.

(2) Sub-paragraph (1) applies to an application for a consent order varying or discharging an order for financial relief as it applies to an application for an order for financial relief.

(3) In this paragraph –

'consent order', in relation to an application for an order, means an order in the terms applied for to which the respondent agrees;

'order for financial relief' means an order under any of Parts 1, 2, 3, 4 and 9.

67 Meaning of 'maintenance agreement' and 'financial arrangements'

(1) In this Part 'maintenance agreement' means any agreement in writing between the civil partners in a civil partnership which –

    (a)   is made during the continuance or after the dissolution or annulment of the civil partnership and contains financial arrangements, or

    (b)   is a separation agreement which contains no financial arrangements but is made in a case where no other agreement in writing between the civil partners contains financial arrangements.

(2) In this Part 'financial arrangements' means provisions governing the rights and liabilities towards one another when living separately of the civil partners in a civil partnership (including a civil partnership which has been dissolved or annulled) in respect of –

    (a)   the making or securing of payments, or

    (b)   the disposition or use of any property,

including such rights and liabilities with respect to the maintenance or education of a child (whether or not a child of the family).

(3) 'Education' includes training.

68 Validity of maintenance agreements

If a maintenance agreement includes a provision purporting to restrict any right to apply to a court for an order containing financial arrangements –

    (a)   that provision is void, but

    (b)   any other financial arrangements contained in the agreement –

        (i)   are not void or unenforceable as a result, and

        (ii)   unless void or unenforceable for any other reason, are (subject to paragraphs 69 and 73) binding on the parties to the agreement.

69 Alteration of agreements by court during lives of parties

(1) Subject to sub-paragraph (1A), either party to a maintenance agreement may apply to the court or, subject to sub-paragraph (6), to a magistrates' court for an order under this paragraph if –

    (a)   the maintenance agreement is for the time being subsisting, and

    (b)   each of the parties to the agreement is for the time being domiciled or resident in England and Wales.

(1A) If an application or part of an application relates to a matter where jurisdiction falls to be determined by reference to the jurisdictional requirements of the Maintenance Regulation and Schedule 6 to the Civil Jurisdiction and Judgments (Maintenance) Regulations 2011 –

    (a)   the requirement as to domicile or residence in sub-paragraph (1)(b) does not apply to the application or that part of it, but

    (b)   the court may not entertain the application or that part of it unless it has jurisdiction to do so by virtue of that Regulation and that Schedule.

(2) The court may make an order under this paragraph if it is satisfied that –

    (a)   because of a change in the circumstances in the light of which –

        (i)   any financial arrangements contained in the agreement were made, or

        (ii)   financial arrangements were omitted from it,

        the agreement should be altered so as to make different financial arrangements or so as to contain financial arrangements, or

    (b)   that the agreement does not contain proper financial arrangements with respect to any child of the family.

(3) In sub-paragraph (2)(*a*) the reference to a change in the circumstances includes a change foreseen by the parties when making the agreement.

(4) An order under this paragraph may make such alterations in the agreement –

    (a)   by varying or revoking any financial arrangements contained in it, or

    (b)   by inserting in it financial arrangements for the benefit of one of the parties to the agreement or of a child of the family,

as appear to the court to be just having regard to all the circumstances, including, if relevant, the matters mentioned in paragraph 22(3).

(5) The effect of the order is that the agreement is to be treated as if any alteration made by the order had been made by agreement between the partners and for valuable consideration.

(6) The power to make an order under this paragraph is subject to paragraphs 70 and 71.

(7) In this paragraph, "the Maintenance Regulation" means Council Regulation (EC) No 4/2009 including as applied in relation to Denmark by virtue of the Agreement made on 19th October 2005 between the European Community and the Kingdom of Denmark.

70 Restrictions on applications to and orders by magistrates' courts under paragraph 69

(1) A magistrates' court must not entertain an application under paragraph 69(1) unless –

    (a)   both the parties to the agreement are resident in England and Wales, and

    (b)   the court acts in, or is authorised by the Lord Chancellor to act for, a local justice area in which at least one of the parties is resident.

(2) A magistrates' court must not make any order on such an application other than –

    (a)   if the agreement includes no provision for periodical payments by either of the parties, an order inserting provision for the making by one of the parties of periodical payments for the maintenance of –

        (i)   the other party, or

        (ii)   any child of the family;

    (b)   if the agreement includes provision for the making by one of the parties of periodical payments, an order increasing or reducing the rate of, or terminating, any of those payments.

71 Provisions relating to periodical and secured periodical payments: duration

(1) If a court decides to make an order under paragraph 69 altering an agreement –

    (a)   by inserting provision for the making or securing by one of the parties to the agreement of periodical payments for the maintenance of the other party, or

    (b)   by increasing the rate of the periodical payments which the agreement provides shall be made by one of the parties for the maintenance of the other,

it may specify such term as it thinks fit as the term for which the payments or, as the case may be, the additional payments attributable to the increase are to be made under the altered agreement, except that the term must not extend beyond the limits in sub-paragraphs (2) and (3).

(2) The limits if the payments are not to be secured are –

    (a)   the death of either of the parties to the agreement, or

    (b)   the formation of a subsequent civil partnership or marriage by the party to whom the payments are to be made.

(3) The limits if the payments are to be secured are –

    (a)   the death of the party to whom the payments are to be made, or

    (b)   the formation of a subsequent civil partnership or marriage by that party.

(4) Sub-paragraph (5) applies if a court decides to make an order under paragraph 69 altering an agreement by –

(a)   inserting provision for the making or securing by one of the parties to the agreement of periodical payments for the maintenance of a child of the family, or

(b)   increasing the rate of the periodical payments which the agreement provides shall be made or secured by one of the parties for the maintenance of such a child.

(5) The court, in deciding the term for which under the agreement as altered by the order –

(a)   the payments are to be made or secured for the benefit of the child, or

(b)   the additional payments attributable to the increase are to be made or secured for the benefit of the child,

must apply paragraph 49(2) to (5) (age limits) as if the order in question were a periodical payments or secured periodical payments order in favour of the child.

72 Saving

Nothing in paragraphs 68 to 71 affects –

(a)   any power of a court before which any proceedings between the parties to a maintenance agreement are brought under any other enactment (including a provision of this Schedule) to make an order containing financial arrangements, or

(b)   any right of either party to apply for such an order in such proceedings.

73 Alteration of agreements by court after death of one party

(1) This paragraph applies if –

(a)   a maintenance agreement provides for the continuation of payments under the agreement after the death of one of the parties, and

(b)   that party ('A') dies domiciled in England and Wales.

(2) Subject to sub-paragraph (4), the surviving party or A's personal representatives may apply to the High Court or a county court for an order under paragraph 69.

(3) If a maintenance agreement is altered by a court on an application made under sub-paragraph (2), the same consequences follow as if the alteration had been made immediately before the death by agreement between the parties and for valuable consideration.

(4) An application under this paragraph may not, without the leave of the High Court or a county court, be made after the end of 6 months from the date on which representation in regard to A's estate is first taken out.

(5) A's personal representatives are not liable for having distributed any part of A's estate after the end of the 6 month period on the ground that they ought to have taken into account the possibility that a court might allow an application by virtue of this paragraph to be made by the surviving party after that period.

(6) Sub-paragraph (5) does not affect any power to recover any part of the estate so distributed arising by virtue of the making of an order in pursuance of this paragraph.

(7) Paragraph 60(6) applies for the purposes of sub-paragraph (4) as it applies for the purposes of paragraph 60(3).

Amendments—SI 2011/1484.

PART 14

MISCELLANEOUS AND SUPPLEMENTARY

74 Avoidance of transactions intended to prevent or reduce financial relief

(1) This paragraph applies if proceedings for relief ('financial relief') are brought by one person ('A') against another ('B') under Part 1, 2, 4, 8, 9, or 11 (other than paragraph 60(2)), or paragraph 69.

(2) If the court is satisfied, on an application by A, that B is, with the intention of defeating A's claim for financial relief, about to –

    (a)   make any disposition, or

    (b)   transfer out of the jurisdiction or otherwise deal with any property,

it may make such order as it thinks fit for restraining B from doing so or otherwise for protecting the claim.

(3) If the court is satisfied, on an application by A, that –

    (a)   B has, with the intention of defeating A's claim for financial relief, made a reviewable disposition, and

    (b)   if the disposition were set aside, financial relief or different financial relief would be granted to A,

it make an order setting aside the disposition.

(4) If the court is satisfied, on an application by A in a case where an order has been obtained by A against B under any of the provisions mentioned in sub-paragraph (1), that B has, with the intention of defeating A's claim for financial relief, made a reviewable disposition, it may make an order setting aside the disposition.

(5) An application for the purposes of sub-paragraph (3) must be made in the proceedings for the financial relief in question.

(6) If the court makes an order under sub-paragraph (3) or (4) setting aside a disposition it must give such consequential directions as it thinks fit for giving effect to the order (including directions requiring the making of any payments or the disposal of any property).

75

(1) Any reference in paragraph 74 to defeating A's claim for financial relief is to –

    (a)   preventing financial relief from being granted to A, or to A for the benefit of a child of the family,

    (b)   reducing the amount of any financial relief which might be so granted, or

    (c)   frustrating or impeding the enforcement of any order which might be or has been made at A's instance under any of those provisions.

(2) In paragraph 74 and this paragraph 'disposition' –

    (a)   does not include any provision contained in a will or codicil, but

    (b)   subject to paragraph (a), includes any conveyance, assurance or gift of property of any description (whether made by an instrument or otherwise).

(3) Any disposition made by B (whether before or after the commencement of the proceedings for financial relief) is a reviewable disposition for the purposes of paragraphs 74(3) and (4) unless it was made –

    (a)   for valuable consideration (other than formation of a civil partnership), and

    (b)   to a person who, at the time of the disposition, acted in relation to it in good faith and without notice of any intention on B's part to defeat A's claim for financial relief.

(4) If an application is made under paragraph 74 with respect to a disposition which took place less than 3 years before the date of the application or with respect to a disposition or other dealing with property which is about to take place and the court is satisfied –

    (a)   in a case falling within paragraph 74(2) or (3), that the disposition or other dealing would (apart from paragraph 74) have the consequence of defeating A's claim for financial relief, or

    (b)   in a case falling within paragraph 74(4), that the disposition has had the consequence of defeating A's claim for financial relief,

it is presumed, unless the contrary is shown, that the person who disposed of or is about to dispose of or deal with the property did so or, as the case may be, is about to do so, with the intention of defeating A's claim for financial relief.

76 Direction for settlement of instrument for securing payments or effecting property adjustment

(1) This paragraph applies if the court decides to make –

    (a)   an order under Part 1 or 9 requiring any payments to be secured, or

    (b)   a property adjustment order.

(2) The court may direct that the matter be referred to one of the conveyancing counsel of the court for him to settle a proper instrument to be executed by all necessary parties.

(3) If the order referred to in sub-paragraph (1) is to be made in proceedings for a dissolution, nullity or separation order, the court may, if it thinks fit, defer the making of the dissolution, nullity or separation order until the instrument has been duly executed.

77 Settlement, etc, made in compliance with a property adjustment order may be avoided on bankruptcy of settlor

The fact that –

    (a)   a settlement, or

    (b)   a transfer of property,

had to be made in order to comply with a property adjustment order does not prevent the settlement or transfer from being a transaction in respect of which an order may be made under section 339 or 340 of the Insolvency Act 1986 (c. 45) (transfers at an undervalue and preferences).

78 Payments, etc, under order made in favour of person suffering from mental disorder

(1) This paragraph applies if –

    (a)   the court makes an order under this Schedule requiring –

        (i)   payments (including a lump sum payment) to be made, or

        (ii)   property to be transferred,

to a civil partner, and

    (b)   the court is satisfied that the person in whose favour the order is made is incapable, because of mental disorder, of managing and administering his or her property and affairs.

(2) 'Mental disorder' has the same meaning as in the Mental Health Act 1983 (c. 20).

(3) Subject to any order, direction or authority made or given in relation to that person under Part 8 of the 1983 Act, the court may order the payments to be made or, as the case may be, the property to be transferred to such persons having charge of that person as the court may direct.

79 Appeals relating to pension sharing orders which have taken effect

(1) Sub-paragraphs (2) and (3) apply if an appeal against a pension sharing order is begun on or after the day on which the order takes effect.

(2) If the pension sharing order relates to a person's rights under a pension arrangement, the appeal court may not set aside or vary the order if the person responsible for the pension arrangement has acted to his detriment in reliance on the order taking effect.

(3) If the pension sharing order relates to a person's shareable state scheme rights, the appeal court may not set aside or vary the order if the Secretary of State has acted to his detriment in reliance on the taking effect of the order.

(4) In determining for the purposes of sub-paragraph (2) or (3) whether a person has acted to his detriment in reliance on the taking effect of the order, the appeal court may disregard any detriment which in its opinion is insignificant.

(5) Where sub-paragraph (2) or (3) applies, the appeal court may make such further orders (including one or more pension sharing orders) as it thinks fit for the purpose of putting the parties in the position it considers appropriate.

(6) Paragraph 19 only applies to a pension sharing order under this paragraph if the decision of the appeal court can itself be the subject of an appeal.

(7) In sub-paragraph (2), the reference to the person responsible for the pension arrangement is to be read in accordance with paragraph 29(3).

79A Appeals relating to pension compensation sharing orders which have taken effect

(1) This paragraph applies where an appeal against a pension compensation sharing order is begun on or after the day on which the order takes effect.

(2) If the Board of the Pension Protection Fund has acted to its detriment in reliance on the taking effect of the order the appeal court–

    (a)   may not set aside or vary the order;
    (b)   may make such further orders (including a pension compensation sharing order) as it thinks fit for the purpose of putting the parties in the position it considers appropriate.

(3) In determining for the purposes of sub-paragraph (2) whether the Board has acted to its detriment the appeal court may disregard any detriment which in the court's opinion is insignificant.

(4) Paragraph 19E only applies to a pension compensation sharing order under this paragraph if the decision of the appeal court can itself be the subject of an appeal.

Amendments—Inserted by Pensions Act 2008, s 120, Sch 6, Pt 3.

80 Interpretation

(1) References in this Schedule to –

    (a)   periodical payments orders,
    (b)   secured periodical payments orders, and
    (c)   orders for the payment of a lump sum,

are references to such of the orders that may be made under Parts 1 and 9 (other than interim orders) as are relevant in the context of the reference in question.

(2) In this Schedule 'child of the family', in relation to two people who are civil partners of each other, means –

    (a)   a child of both of them, and

(b) any other child, other than a child placed with them as foster parents by a local authority or voluntary organisation, who has been treated by both the civil partners as a child of their family.

(3) In this Schedule 'the court' (except where the context otherwise requires) means –

(a) the High Court, or

(b) where a county court has jurisdiction by virtue of Part 5 of the Matrimonial and Family Proceedings Act 1984 (c. 42), a county court.

(4) References in this Schedule to a subsequent civil partnership include a civil partnership which is by law void or voidable.

(5) References in this Schedule to a subsequent marriage include a marriage which is by law void or voidable.

Amendments—Pensions Act 2008, s 120, Sch 6, Pt 3.

****

Schedule 7
Financial Relief in England and Wales after Overseas Dissolution etc of a Civil Partnership

PART 1
FINANCIAL RELIEF

1 Part applies where civil partnership has been dissolved etc overseas

(1) This Part of this Schedule applies where –

(a) a civil partnership has been dissolved or annulled, or the civil partners have been legally separated, by means of judicial or other proceedings in an overseas country, and

(b) the dissolution, annulment or legal separation is entitled to be recognised as valid in England and Wales.

(2) This Part of this Schedule applies even if the date of the dissolution, annulment or legal separation is earlier than the date on which the Part comes into force.

(3) In this Schedule 'overseas country' means a country or territory outside the British Islands.

(4) In this Part of this Schedule 'child of the family' means –

(a) a child of both of the civil partners, and

(b) any other child, other than a child placed with them as foster parents or by a local authority or voluntary organisation, who has been treated by both the civil partners as a child of their family.

2 Either civil partner may make application for financial relief

(1) Either of the civil partners may make an application to the court for an order under paragraph 9 or 13.

(2) The rights conferred by sub-paragraph (1) are subject to –

(a) paragraph 3 (civil partner may not apply after forming subsequent civil partnership etc), and

(b) paragraph 4 (application may not be made until leave to make it has been granted).

(3) An application for an order under paragraph 9 or 13 must be made in a manner prescribed by rules of court.

3 No application after formation of subsequent civil partnership or marriage

(1) If –

    (a)   the civil partnership has been dissolved or annulled, and

    (b)   after the dissolution or annulment, one of the civil partners forms a subsequent civil partnership or marriage,

that civil partner shall not be entitled to make, in relation to the civil partnership, an application for an order under paragraph 9 or 13.

(2) The reference in sub-paragraph (1) to the forming of a subsequent civil partnership or marriage includes a reference to the forming of a civil partnership or marriage which is by law void or voidable.

4 Leave of court required for making of application

(1) No application for an order under paragraph 9 or 13 shall be made unless the leave of the court has been obtained in accordance with rules of court.

(2) The court shall not grant leave under this paragraph unless it considers that there is substantial ground for the making of an application for such an order.

(3) The court may grant leave under this paragraph notwithstanding that an order has been made by a court in a country outside England and Wales requiring the other civil partner to make any payment, or transfer any property, to the applicant or to a child of the family.

(4) Leave under this paragraph may be granted subject to such conditions as the court thinks fit.

5 Interim orders for maintenance

(1) Where –

    (a)   leave is granted under paragraph 4, and

    (b)   it appears to the court that the civil partner who applied for leave, or any child of the family, is in immediate need of financial assistance,

the court may, subject to sub-paragraph (4), make an interim order for maintenance.

(2) An interim order for maintenance is one requiring the other civil partner to make –

    (a)   to the applicant, or

    (b)   to the child,

such periodical payments as the court thinks reasonable for such term as the court thinks reasonable.

(3) The term must be one –

    (a)   beginning not earlier than the date of the grant of leave, and

    (b)   ending with the date of the determination of the application made under the leave.

(4) If it appears to the court that the court will, in the event of an application being made under the leave, have jurisdiction to entertain the application only under paragraph 7(4), the court shall not make an interim order under this paragraph.

(5) An interim order under this paragraph may be made subject to such conditions as the court thinks fit.

6 Paragraphs 7 and 8 apply where application made for relief under paragraph 9 or 13

Paragraphs 7 and 8 apply where –

    (a)   one of the civil partners has been granted leave under paragraph 4, and

    (b)   acting under the leave, that civil partner makes an application for an order under paragraph 9 or 13.

7 Jurisdiction of the court

(1) Subject to sub-paragraph (6), the court shall have jurisdiction to entertain the application only if one or more of the following jurisdictional requirements is satisfied.

(2) The first requirement is that either of the civil partners –

(a)   was domiciled in England and Wales on the date when the leave was applied for, or

(b)   was domiciled in England and Wales on the date when the dissolution, annulment or legal separation took effect in the overseas country in which it was obtained.

(3) The second is that either of the civil partners –

(a)   was habitually resident in England and Wales throughout the period of one year ending with the date when the leave was applied for, or

(b)   was habitually resident in England and Wales throughout the period of one year ending with the date on which the dissolution, annulment or legal separation took effect in the overseas country in which it was obtained.

(4) The third is that either or both of the civil partners had, at the date when the leave was applied for, a beneficial interest in possession in a dwelling-house situated in England or Wales which was at some time during the civil partnership a civil partnership home of the civil partners.

(5) In sub-paragraph (4) 'possession' includes receipt of, or the right to receive, rents and profits, but here 'rent' does not include mortgage interest.

(6) If an application or part of an application relates to a matter where jurisdiction falls to be determined by the jurisdictional requirements of the Maintenance Regulation and Schedule 6 to the Civil Jurisdiction and Judgments (Maintenance) Regulations 2011, those requirements are to determine whether the court has jurisdiction to entertain the application or that part of it.

(7) In sub-paragraph (6) "the Maintenance Regulation" means Council Regulation (EC) No 4/2009 including as applied in relation to Denmark by virtue of the Agreement made on 19th October 2005 between the European Community and the Kingdom of Denmark.

8 Duty of the court to consider whether England and Wales is appropriate venue for application

(1) Before deciding the application, the court must consider whether in all the circumstances of the case it would be appropriate for an order of the kind applied for to be made by a court in England and Wales.

(2) Subject to sub-paragraph (4), if the court is not satisfied that it would be appropriate, the court shall dismiss the application.

(3) The court must, in particular, have regard to the following matters –

(a)   the connection which the civil partners have with England and Wales;

(b)   the connection which the civil partners have with the country in which the civil partnership was dissolved or annulled or in which they were legally separated;

(c)   the connection which the civil partners have with any other country outside England and Wales;

(d)   any financial benefit which, in consequence of the dissolution, annulment or legal separation –

(i)   the applicant, or

(ii)   a child of the family,

has received, or is likely to receive, by virtue of any agreement or the operation of the law of a country outside England and Wales;

(e)   in a case where an order has been made by a court in a country outside England and Wales requiring the other civil partner –

(i)   to make any payment, or

(ii)   to transfer any property,

for the benefit of the applicant or a child of the family, the financial relief given by the order and the extent to which the order has been complied with or is likely to be complied with;

(f)   any right which the applicant has, or has had, to apply for financial relief from the other civil partner under the law of any country outside England and Wales and, if the applicant has omitted to exercise that right, the reason for that omission;

(g)   the availability in England and Wales of any property in respect of which an order under this Schedule in favour of the applicant could be made;

(h)   the extent to which any order made under this Schedule is likely to be enforceable;

(i)   the length of time which has elapsed since the date of the dissolution, annulment or legal separation.

(4) If the court has jurisdiction in relation to the application or part of it by virtue of the Maintenance Regulation and Schedule 6 to the Civil Jurisdiction and Judgments (Maintenance) Regulations 2011, the court may not dismiss the application or that part of it on the ground mentioned in sub-paragraph (2) if to do so would be inconsistent with the jurisdictional requirements of that Regulation and that Schedule.

(5) In sub-paragraph (4) "the Maintenance Regulation" means Council Regulation (EC) No 4/2009 including as applied in relation to Denmark by virtue of the Agreement made on 19th October 2005 between the European Community and the Kingdom of Denmark.

9 Orders for financial provision, property adjustment, pension sharing and pension compensation sharing

(1) Sub-paragraphs (2) and (3) apply where one of the civil partners has made an application for an order under this paragraph.

(2) If the civil partnership has been dissolved or annulled, the court may on the application make any one or more of the orders which it could make under Part 1, 2, 4 or 4A of Schedule 5 (financial provision, property adjustment, pension sharing and pension compensation sharing) if a dissolution order or nullity order had been made in respect of the civil partnership under Chapter 2 of Part 2 of this Act.

(3) If the civil partners have been legally separated, the court may on the application make any one or more of the orders which it could make under Part 1 or 2 of Schedule 5 (financial provision and property adjustment) if a separation order had been made in respect of the civil partners under Chapter 2 of Part 2 of this Act.

(4) Where under sub-paragraph (2) or (3) the court makes –

(a)   an order which, if made under Schedule 5, would be a secured periodical payments order,

(b)   an order for the payment of a lump sum, or

(c)   an order which, if made under that Schedule, would be a property adjustment order,

then, on making that order or at any time afterwards, the court may make any order which it could make under Part 3 of Schedule 5 (sale of property) if the order under sub-paragraph (2) or (3) had been made under that Schedule.

(5) The powers under sub-paragraphs (2) to (4) are subject to paragraph 11.

Amendments—Pensions Act 2008, s 120, Sch 6, Pt 3.

10 Matters to which court is to have regard in exercising its powers under paragraph 9

(1) The court, in deciding –

(a)   whether to exercise its powers under paragraph 9, and

(b)   if so, in what way,

must act in accordance with this paragraph.

(2) The court must have regard to all the circumstances of the case, giving first consideration to the welfare, while under 18, of any child of the family who has not reached 18.

(3) The court, in exercising its powers under paragraph 9 in relation to one of the civil partners –

    (a)   must in particular have regard to the matters mentioned in paragraph 21(2) of Schedule 5, and

    (b)   shall be under duties corresponding to those imposed by sub-paragraphs (2) and (3) of paragraph 23 of that Schedule (duties to consider termination of financial obligations) where it decides to exercise under paragraph 9 powers corresponding to the powers referred to in those sub-paragraphs.

(4) The matters to which the court is to have regard under sub-paragraph (3)(*a*), so far as relating to paragraph 21(2)(*a*) of Schedule 5 (regard to be had to financial resources), include –

    (a)   any benefits under a pension arrangement which either of the civil partners has or is likely to have, and

    (b)   any PPF compensation to which a civil partner is or is likely to be entitled,

(whether or not in the foreseeable future).

(5) The matters to which the court is to have regard under sub-paragraph (3)(*a*), so far as relating to paragraph 21(2)(*h*) of Schedule 5 (regard to be had to benefits that cease to be acquirable), include –

    (a)   any benefits under a pension arrangement which, because of the dissolution or annulment of the civil partnership, one of the civil partners will lose the chance of acquiring, and

    (b)   any PPF compensation which, because of the making of the dissolution or nullity order, a civil partner will lose the chance of acquiring entitlement to.

(6) The court, in exercising its powers under paragraph 9 in relation to a child of the family, must in particular have regard to the matters mentioned in paragraph 22(2) of Schedule 5.

(7) The court, in exercising its powers under paragraph 9 against a civil partner ('A') in favour of a child of the family who is not A's child, must also have regard to the matters mentioned in paragraph 22(3) of Schedule 5.

(8) Where an order has been made by a court outside England and Wales for –

    (a)   the making of payments, or

    (b)   the transfer of property,

by one of the civil partners, the court in considering in accordance with this paragraph the financial resources of the other civil partner, or of a child of the family, shall have regard to the extent to which that order has been complied with or is likely to be complied with.

(9) In this paragraph –

    (a)   'pension arrangement' has the same meaning as in Part 4 of Schedule 5,

    (b)   references to benefits under a pension arrangement include any benefits by way of pension, whether under a pension arrangement or not, and

    (c)   'PPF compensation' has the same meaning as in Schedule 5.

Amendments—Pensions Act 2008, s 120, Sch 6, Pt 3.

11 Restriction of powers under paragraph 9 where jurisdiction depends on civil partnership home in England or Wales

(1) Sub-paragraphs (2) to (4) apply where the court has jurisdiction to entertain an application for an order under paragraph 9 only because a dwelling-house which was a civil partnership home of the civil partners is situated in England or Wales.

(2) The court may make under paragraph 9 any one or more of the following orders (but no other) –

    (a)   an order that one of the civil partners shall pay to the other a specified lump sum;

    (b)   an order that one of the civil partners shall pay to a child of the family, or to a specified person for the benefit of a child of the family, a specified lump sum;

    (c)   an order that one of the civil partners shall transfer that civil partner's interest in the dwelling-house, or a specified part of that interest –

        (i)   to the other,

        (ii)   to a child of the family, or

        (iii)   to a specified person for the benefit of a child of the family;

    (d)   an order that a settlement of the interest of one of the civil partners in the dwelling-house, or a specified part of that interest, be made to the satisfaction of the court for the benefit of any one or more of –

        (i)   the other civil partner and the children of the family, or

        (ii)   either or any of them;

    (e)   an order varying for the benefit of any one or more of –

        (i)   the civil partners and the children of the family, or

        (ii)   either or any of them,

    a relevant settlement so far as that settlement relates to an interest in the dwelling-house;

    (f)   an order extinguishing or reducing the interest of either of the civil partners under a relevant settlement so far as that interest is an interest in the dwelling-house;

    (g)   an order for the sale of the interest of one of the civil partners in the dwelling-house.

(3) Where under paragraph 9 the court makes just one order for the payment of a lump sum by one of the civil partners, the amount of the lump sum must not exceed the amount specified in sub-paragraph (5).

(4) Where under paragraph 9 the court makes two or more orders each of which is an order for the payment of a lump sum by the same civil partner, the total of the amounts of the lump sums must not exceed the amount specified in sub-paragraph (5).

(5) That amount is –

    (a)   if the interest of the paying civil partner in the dwelling-house is sold in pursuance of an order made under sub-paragraph (2)(g), the amount of the proceeds of sale of that interest after deducting from those proceeds any costs incurred in the sale of that interest;

    (b)   if that interest is not so sold, the amount which in the opinion of the court represents the value of that interest.

(6) Where the interest of one of the civil partners in the dwelling-house is held jointly or in common with any other person or persons –

    (a)   the reference in sub-paragraph (2)(g) to the interest of one of the civil partners shall be construed as including a reference to the interest of that other person, or the interest of those other persons, in the dwelling-house, and

    (b)   the reference in sub-paragraph (5)(a) to the amount of the proceeds of a sale ordered under sub-paragraph (2)(g) shall be construed as a reference to that part of those proceeds which is attributable to the interest of that civil partner in the dwelling-house.

(7) In sub-paragraph (2) –

'relevant settlement' means a settlement made, during the subsistence of the civil partnership or in anticipation of its formation, on the civil partners, including one made by will or codicil;

'specified' means specified in the order.

12   Consent orders under paragraph 9

(1) On an application for a consent order under paragraph 9, the court may make an order in the terms agreed on the basis only of the prescribed information furnished with the application.

(2) Sub-paragraph (1) does not apply if the court has reason to think that there are other circumstances into which it ought to inquire.

(3) Sub-paragraph (1) applies to an application for a consent order varying or discharging an order under paragraph 9 as it applies to an application for such an order.

(4) Sub-paragraph (1) applies despite paragraph 10.

(5) In this paragraph –

'consent order', in relation to an application for an order, means an order in the terms applied for to which the respondent agrees;
'prescribed' means prescribed by rules of court.

13   Orders for transfers of tenancies of dwelling-houses

(1) This paragraph applies if –

(a)   an application is made by one of the civil partners for an order under this paragraph, and
(b)   one of the civil partners is entitled, either in his own right or jointly with the other civil partner, to occupy a dwelling-house in England or Wales by virtue of a tenancy which is a relevant tenancy within the meaning of Schedule 7 to the Family Law Act 1996 (c. 27).

(2) The court may make in relation to that dwelling-house any order which it could make under Part 2 of that Schedule (order transferring tenancy or switching statutory tenants) if it had power to make a property adjustment order under Part 2 of Schedule 5 to this Act with respect to the civil partnership.

(3) The provisions of paragraphs 10, 11 and 14(1) of Schedule 7 to the Family Law Act 1996 (payments by transferee, pre-transfer liabilities and right of landlord to be heard) apply in relation to any order under this paragraph as they apply to any order under Part 2 of that Schedule.

14   Application to orders under paragraphs 5 and 9 of provisions of Schedule 5

(1) The following provisions of Schedule 5 apply in relation to an order made under paragraph 5 or 9 of this Schedule as they apply in relation to a like order made under that Schedule –

(a)   paragraph 3(1) to (3) and (7) (lump sums);
(b)   paragraph 11(2) to (4), 12(2), 13 and 14 (orders for sale);
(c)   paragraphs 17, 18 and 19(2) and (3) (pension sharing);
(ca)   paragraphs 19C, 19D and 19E(2) and (3) (pension compensation sharing);
(d)   paragraphs 25 and 26 (orders under Part 1 relating to pensions);
(e)   paragraphs 31 to 34 and 35 to 37 (orders under Part 1 relating to pensions where Board has assumed responsibility for scheme);
(ea)   paragraph 34A (orders under Part 1 relating to pension compensation attachment);
(f)   paragraphs 47(1) to (4) and (6) and 49 (duration of orders);
(g)   paragraphs 50 to 54 and 57 to 62, except paragraph 50(1)(g) (variation etc of orders);
(h)   paragraphs 63 to 65 (arrears and repayments);
(i)   paragraphs 76 to 79A (drafting of instruments, bankruptcy, mental disorder, pension-sharing appeals and pension compensation-sharing appeals).

(2) Sub-paragraph (1)(*d*) and (*ea*) does not apply where the court has jurisdiction to entertain an application for an order under paragraph 9 only because a dwelling-house which was a civil partnership home of the civil partners is situated in England or Wales.

(3) Paragraph 27 of Schedule 5 (change of pension arrangement under which rights are shared) applies in relation to an order made under paragraph 9 of this Schedule by virtue of sub-paragraph (1)(*d*) above as it applies to an order made under Part 1 of Schedule 5 by virtue of paragraph 25 or 26 of that Schedule.

(4) The Lord Chancellor may by regulationbs make for the purposes of this Schedule provision corresponding to any provision which may be made by him under paragraph 28(1) to (3) of

Schedule 5 (supplementary provision about orders relating to pensions under Part 1 of that Schedule) or under paragraphs 34B to 36 of that Schedule (supplementary provision about orders relating to pension compensation).

(5) The power to make regulations under this paragraph is exercisable by statutory instrument which is subject to annulment in pursuance of a resolution of either House of Parliament.

Amendments—Pensions Act 2008, s 120, Sch 6, Pt 3.

15 Avoidance of transactions designed to defeat claims under paragraphs 5 and 9

(1) Sub-paragraphs (2) and (3) apply where one of the civil partners ('A') is granted leave under paragraph 4 to make an application for an order under paragraph 9.

(2) If the court is satisfied, on application by A, that the other civil partner ('B') is, with the intention of defeating a claim by A, about to –

(a)   make any disposition, or

(b)   transfer out of the jurisdiction, or otherwise deal with, any property,

it may make such order as it thinks fit for restraining B from doing so or otherwise for protecting the claim.

(3) If the court is satisfied, on application by A –

(a)   that the other civil partner ('B') has, with the intention of defeating a claim by A, made a reviewable disposition, and

(b)   that, if the disposition were set aside –
   (i)   financial relief under paragraph 5 or 9, or
   (ii)   different financial relief under paragraph 5 or 9,
   would be granted to A,

it may make an order setting aside the disposition.

(4) If –

(a)   an order under paragraph 5 or 9 has been made by the court at the instance of one of the civil partners ('A'), and

(b)   the court is satisfied, on application by A, that the other civil partner ('B') has, with the intention of defeating a claim by A, made a reviewable disposition,

the court may make an order setting aside the disposition.

(5) Where the court has jurisdiction to entertain an application for an order under paragraph 9 only under paragraph 7(4), it shall not make any order under sub-paragraph (2), (3) or (4) in respect of any property other than the dwelling-house concerned.

(6) Where the court makes an order under sub-paragraph (3) or (4) setting aside a disposition, it shall give such consequential directions as it thinks fit for giving effect to the order (including directions requiring the making of any payments or the disposal of any property).

(7) For the purposes of sub-paragraphs (3) and (4), but subject to sub-paragraph (8), any disposition made by B is a 'reviewable disposition' (whether made before or after the commencement of A's application under that sub-paragraph).

(8) A disposition made by B is not a reviewable disposition for those purposes if made for valuable consideration (other than formation of a civil partnership) to a person who, at the time of the disposition, acted in relation to it in good faith and without notice of any intention on the part of B to defeat A's claim.

(9) A reference in this paragraph to defeating a claim by one of the civil partners is a reference to –

(a)   preventing financial relief being granted, or reducing the amount of financial relief which might be granted, under paragraph 5 or 9 at the instance of that civil partner, or

(b)   frustrating or impeding the enforcement of any order which might be, or has been, made under paragraph 5 or 9 at the instance of that civil partner.

16 Presumptions for the purposes of paragraph 15

(1) Sub-paragraph (3) applies where –

    (a)   an application is made under paragraph 15(2) or (3) by one of the civil partners with respect to –

        (i)   a disposition which took place less than 3 years before the date of the application, or

        (ii)   a disposition or other dealing with property which is about to take place, and

    (b)   the court is satisfied that the disposition or other dealing would (apart from paragraph 15 and this paragraph of this Schedule) have the consequence of defeating a claim by the applicant.

(2) Sub-paragraph (3) also applies where –

    (a)   an application is made under paragraph 15(4) by one of the civil partners with respect to a disposition which took place less than 3 years before the date of the application, and

    (b)   the court is satisfied that the disposition has had the consequence of defeating a claim by the applicant.

(3) It shall be presumed, unless the contrary is shown, that the person who –

    (a)   disposed of, or

    (b)   is about to dispose of or deal with the property,

did so, or (as the case may be) is about to do so, with the intention of defeating the applicant's claim.

(4) A reference in this paragraph to defeating a claim by one of the civil partners has the meaning given by paragraph 15(9).

PART 2
STEPS TO PREVENT AVOIDANCE PRIOR TO APPLICATION FOR LEAVE UNDER PARAGRAPH 4

17 Prevention of transactions intended to defeat prospective claims under paragraphs 5 and 9

(1) If it appears to the court, on application by one of the persons ('A') who formed a civil partnership –

    (a)   that the civil partnership has been dissolved or annulled, or that the civil partners have been legally separated, by means of judicial or other proceedings in an overseas country,

    (b)   that A intends to apply for leave to make an application for an order under paragraph 9 as soon as he or she has been habitually resident in England and Wales for the period of one year, and

    (c)   that the other civil partner ('B') is, with the intention of defeating A's claim, about to –

        (i)   make any disposition, or

        (ii)   transfer out of the jurisdiction, or otherwise deal with, any property,

the court may make such order as it thinks fit for restraining B from taking such action as is mentioned in paragraph (c).

(2) Sub-paragraph (1) applies even if the date of the dissolution, annulment or legal separation is earlier than the date on which that sub-paragraph comes into force.

(3) Sub-paragraph (4) applies where –

    (a)   an application is made under sub-paragraph (1) with respect to –

        (i)   a disposition which took place less than 3 years before the date of the application, or

(ii)   a disposition or other dealing with property which is about to take place, and

(b)   the court is satisfied that the disposition or other dealing would (apart from this paragraph of this Schedule) have the consequence of defeating a claim by the applicant.

(4) It shall be presumed, unless the contrary is shown, that the person who –

(a)   disposed of, or

(b)   is about to dispose of or deal with the property,

did so, or (as the case may be) is about to do so, with the intention of defeating the applicant's claim.

(5) A reference in this paragraph to defeating a person's claim is a reference to preventing financial relief being granted, or reducing the amount of financial relief which might be granted, under paragraph 5 or 9 at the instance of that person.

PART 3
SUPPLEMENTARY

18 Paragraphs 15 to 17: meaning of 'disposition' and saving

(1) In paragraphs 15 to 17 'disposition' does not include any provision contained in a will or codicil but, with that exception, includes any conveyance, assurance or gift of property of any description, whether made by an instrument or otherwise.

(2) The provisions of paragraphs 15 to 17 are without prejudice to any power of the High Court to grant injunctions under section 37 of the Senior Courts Act 1981 (c. 54).

19 Interpretation of Schedule

In this Schedule –

'the court' means the High Court or, where a county court has jurisdiction by virtue of Part 5 of the Matrimonial and Family Proceedings Act 1984 (c. 42), a county court;

'dwelling-house' includes –

(*a*)   any building, or part of a building, which is occupied as a dwelling, and

(*b*)   any yard, garden, garage or outhouse belonging to, and occupied with, the dwelling-house;

'overseas country' has the meaning given by paragraph 1(3).

Amendments—Constitutional Reform Act 2005, s 59(5), Sch 11, Pt 1, para 1(2).

****

Schedule 9
Family Homes and Domestic Violence

Section 82

PART 1
AMENDMENTS OF THE FAMILY LAW ACT 1996 (C 27)

1

(1) Amend section 30 (rights concerning matrimonial home where one spouse has no estate, etc) as follows.

(2) In subsection (1) –

(a)   in paragraph (a) –

(i)   after "one spouse" insert "or civil partner ("A")", and

(ii)   for "that spouse" substitute "A".

    (b)   in paragraph (b), after "other spouse" insert "or civil partner ("B")".

(3) In subsection (2) –

    (a)   for "the spouse not so entitled" substitute "B",

    (b)   for " ("matrimonial home rights")" substitute " ("home rights")", and

    (c)   in paragraph (a), for "the other spouse" substitute "A".

(4) In subsection (3) –

    (a)   for "a spouse" and for "that spouse" substitute "B", and

    (b)   for "the other spouse" (in both places) substitute "A".

(5) In subsection (4) –

    (a)   for "A spouse's" substitute "B's",

    (b)   in paragraph (a), for "by the other spouse as the other spouse's" substitute "by A as A's", and

    (c)   in paragraph (b) –

        (i)   for "the spouse occupies the dwelling-house as that spouse's" substitute "B occupies the dwelling-house as B's", and

        (ii)   for "by the other spouse as the other spouse's" substitute "by A as A's".

(6) In subsection (5) –

    (a)   for "a spouse ("the first spouse")" substitute "B", and

    (b)   in paragraph (b), for "the other spouse ("the second spouse")" substitute "A",

    (c)   for "the second spouse" substitute "A", and

    (d)   for "the first spouse against the second spouse" substitute "B against A".

(7) In subsection (6) –

    (a)   for "a spouse" substitute "B", and

    (b)   for "the other spouse" (in both places) substitute "A".

(8) In subsection (7), for the words from first "which" to the end substitute

    "which—

        (a)   in the case of spouses, has at no time been, and was at no time intended by them to be, a matrimonial home of theirs; and

        (b)   in the case of civil partners, has at no time been, and was at no time intended by them to be, a civil partnership home of theirs."

(9) In subsection (8) –

    (a)   for "A spouse's matrimonial home rights" substitute "B's home rights",

    (b)   in paragraph (a), after "marriage" insert "or civil partnership", and

    (c)   in paragraph (b), for "the other spouse" substitute "A".

(10) In subsection (9) –

    (a)   for "a spouse" (in both places) substitute "a person", and

    (b)   for "matrimonial home rights" substitute "home rights".

(11) In the heading to section 30, for "matrimonial home where one spouse" substitute "home where one spouse or civil partner" and, in the preceding cross-heading, after "matrimonial" insert "or civil partnership".

2

(1) Amend section 31 (effect of matrimonial home rights as charge on dwelling-house) as follows.

(2) In subsection (1) for "marriage, one spouse" substitute "marriage or civil partnership, A".

(3) In subsection (2) for "The other spouse's matrimonial home rights" substitute "B's home rights".

(4) In subsection (3) –

    (a)   in paragraph (a), for "the spouse so entitled" substitute "A", and

    (b)   in paragraph (b), after "marriage" insert "or of the formation of the civil partnership".

(5) In subsection (4) –

    (a)   for "a spouse's matrimonial home rights" substitute "B's home rights",

    (b)   for "the other spouse" substitute "A", and

    (c)   for "either of the spouses" substitute "A or B".

(6) In subsection (5) for "the other spouse" substitute "A".

(7) In subsection (7) for "the spouses" substitute "A and B".

(8) In subsection (8) –

    (a)   for "a spouse's matrimonial home rights" substitute "B's home rights",

    (b)   in paragraph (a), for "the other spouse" substitute "A", and

    (c)   in paragraph (b), after "marriage" insert "or civil partnership".

(9) In subsection (9)

    (a)   in paragraph (a), for "a spouse's matrimonial home rights" substitute "B's home rights", and

    (b)   for "the other spouse" (in both places) substitute "A".

(10) In subsection (10) –

    (a)   for "a spouse" and for "that spouse" substitute "A", and

    (b)   in paragraph (b), for "a spouse's matrimonial home rights" substitute "B's home rights".

(11) For subsection (12)(a) substitute –

       "(a)   B's home rights are a charge on the estate of A or of trustees of A, and".

(12) In the heading to section 31, for "matrimonial home rights" substitute "home rights".

3

For section 32 (further provisions relating to matrimonial home rights) substitute –

    "32 Further provisions relating to home rights

    Schedule 4 (provisions supplementary to sections 30 and 31) has effect.'

4

(1) Amend section 33 (occupation orders where applicant has estate or interest etc or has matrimonial home rights) as follows.

(2) In subsection (1)(a)(ii), for "matrimonial home rights" substitute "home rights".

(3) After subsection (2) insert –

    "(2A) If a civil partnership agreement (as defined by section 73 of the Civil Partnership Act 2004) is terminated, no application under this section may be made by virtue of section 62(3)(eza) by reference to that agreement after the end of the period of three years beginning with the day on which it is terminated.'

(4) In subsection (3)(e) –

    (a)   for "matrimonial home rights" substitute "home rights", and

    (b)   after "spouse" insert "or civil partner".

(5) In subsection (4), for "matrimonial home rights" substitute "home rights".

(6) In subsection (5) –

(a)   for "matrimonial home rights" substitute "home rights",
(b)   after "is the other spouse" insert "or civil partner",
(c)   after "during the marriage" insert "or civil partnership",
(d)   in paragraph (a), after "spouse" insert "or civil partner", and
(e)   in paragraph (b), after "marriage" insert "or civil partnership".

(7) In the heading to section 33, for "matrimonial home rights" substitute "home rights".

5

In section 34 (effect of order under section 33 where rights are charge on dwelling-house), in subsection (1) –

(a)   for "a spouse's matrimonial home rights" substitute "B's home rights", and
(b)   for "the other spouse" (in each place) substitute "A".

6

(1) Amend section 35 (one former spouse with no existing right to occupy) as follows.

(2) In subsection (1)(a) and (b), after "former spouse" insert "or former civil partner".

(3) For subsection (1)(c) substitute –

"(c)   the dwelling-house—
    (i)   in the case of former spouses, was at any time their matrimonial home or was at any time intended by them to be their matrimonial home, or
    (ii)   in the case of former civil partners, was at any time their civil partnership home or was at any time intended by them to be their civil partnership home.'

(4) In subsection (2), after "former spouse" (in both places) insert "or former civil partner".

(5) In subsection (6)(f), after "marriage" insert "or civil partnership".

(6) After subsection (6)(g)(i), insert –
    "(ia) for a property adjustment order under Part 2 of Schedule 5 to the Civil Partnership Act 2004;".

(7) In subsection (9)(a), after "former spouses" insert "or former civil partners".

(8) In subsections (11) and (12), after "former spouse" insert "or former civil partner".

(9) For subsection (13)(a) and (b) substitute –

"(a)   as if he were B (the person entitled to occupy the dwelling-house by virtue of that section); and
(b)   as if the respondent were A (the person entitled as mentioned in subsection (1)(a) of that section).'

(10) In the heading to section 35, after "former spouse" insert "or former civil partner".

7

In section 36 (one cohabitant or former cohabitant with no existing right to occupy), for subsection (13)(a) and (b) substitute –

"(a)   as if he were B (the person entitled to occupy the dwelling-house by virtue of that section); and
(b)   as if the respondent were A (the person entitled as mentioned in subsection (1)(a) of that section).'

8

(1) Amend section 37 (neither spouse entitled to occupy) as follows.

(2) After subsection (1) insert –

"(1A) This section also applies if –

(a)   one civil partner or former civil partner and the other civil partner or former civil partner occupy a dwelling-house which is or was the civil partnership home; but

(b)   neither of them is entitled to remain in occupation –

(i)   by virtue of a beneficial estate or interest or contract; or

(ii)   by virtue of any enactment giving him the right to remain in occupation.'

(3) in subsection (3)(b), for "spouses" substitute "parties".

(4) in the heading to section 37, after "spouse" insert "or civil partner".

9

In section 42 (non-molestation orders), after subsection (4) insert –

"(4ZA) If a civil partnership agreement (as defined by section 73 of the Civil Partnership Act 2004) is terminated, no application under this section may be made by virtue of section 62(3)(eza) by reference to that agreement after the end of the period of three years beginning with the day on which it is terminated.'

10

(1) In section 44 (evidence of agreement to marry), after subsection (2) insert –

"(3) Subject to subsection (4), the court shall not make an order under section 33 or 42 by virtue of section 62(3)(eza) unless there is produced to it evidence in writing of the existence of the civil partnership agreement (as defined by section 73 of the Civil Partnership Act 2004).

(4) Subsection (3) does not apply if the court is satisfied that the civil partnership agreement was evidenced by –

(a)   a gift by one party to the agreement to the other as a token of the agreement, or

(b)   a ceremony entered into by the parties in the presence of one or more other persons assembled for the purpose of witnessing the ceremony.'

(2) In the heading to section 44, after "marry" insert "or form a civil partnership".

11

In section 49 (variation and discharge of orders), in subsection (3) –

(a)   for "a spouse's matrimonial home rights" substitute "B's home rights are, under section 31,", and

(b)   for "the other spouse" (in each place) substitute "A".

12

(1) Amend section 54 (dwelling-house subject to mortgage) as follows.

(2) In subsections (3)(a) and (4), for "matrimonial home rights" substitute "home rights".

(3) In subsection (5), after "spouse, former spouse" insert ", civil partner, former civil partner".

13

(1) Amend section 62 (meaning of "cohabitants", "relevant child" and "associated persons") as follows.

(2) In subsection (1) –

(a)   in paragraph (a), for "two persons who, although not married to each other, are living together as husband and wife or (if of the same sex) in an equivalent relationship;" substitute "two persons who are neither married to each other nor civil partners of each other but are living together as husband and wife or as if they were civil partners;", and

    (b)   in paragraph (b), after "have subsequently married each other" insert "or become civil partners of each other".

(3) After subsection (3)(a) insert –

> "*(aa)* they are or have been civil partners of each other;".

(4) After subsection (3)(e) insert –

> "*(eza)* they have entered into a civil partnership agreement (as defined by section 73 of the Civil Partnership Act 2004) (whether or not that agreement has been terminated);".

14

(1) Amend section 63 (interpretation of Part 4) as follows.

(2) In subsection (1), after the definition of "health" insert –

> ""home rights" has the meaning given by section 30;".

(3) Omit the definition of "matrimonial home rights" in that subsection.

(4) In the definition of relative in that subsection –

    (a)   in paragraphs (a) and (b), for "spouse or former spouse" substitute "spouse, former spouse, civil partner or former civil partner",
    (b)   in paragraph (b), for "by affinity)" substitute "by marriage or civil partnership)", and
    (c)   after "were married to each other" insert "or were civil partners of each other".

(5) After subsection (2)(i) insert –

> "(j)   Schedules 5 to 7 to the Civil Partnership Act 2004.'

15

(1) Amend Schedule 4 (provisions supplementary to sections 30 and 31) as follows.

(2) In paragraph 2, after "spouse" (in both places) insert "or civil partner".

(3) In paragraph 3(1) and (3), after "spouse" insert "or civil partner".

(4) In paragraph 4(1), for "spouse's matrimonial home rights" substitute "spouse's or civil partner's home rights".

(5) For paragraphs 4(1)(a) to (c) substitute –

> "(a)   in the case of a marriage –
>   (i)   by the production of a certificate or other sufficient evidence, that either spouse is dead,
>   (ii)   by the production of an official copy of a decree or order of a court, that the marriage has been terminated otherwise than by death, or
>   (iii)   by the production of an order of the court, that the spouse's home rights constituting the charge have been terminated by the order, and
> (b)   n the case of a civil partnership –
>   (i)   by the production of a certificate or other sufficient evidence, that either civil partner is dead,
>   (ii)   by the production of an official copy of an order or decree of a court, that the civil partnership has been terminated otherwise than by death, or
>   (iii)   by the production of an order of the court, that the civil partner's home rights constituting the charge have been terminated by the order.'

(6) In paragraph 4(2) –

    (a)   in paragraph (a) –
        (i)   after "marriage" insert "or civil partnership", and
        (ii)   after "spouse" insert "or civil partner", and
    (b)   in paragraph (b), after "spouse" insert "or civil partner".

(7) In paragraph 4(3), after "spouse" insert "or civil partner".

(8) In the heading to paragraph 4, after "marriage" insert "or civil partnership".

(9) In paragraph 5(1), for "spouse entitled to matrimonial home rights" substitute "spouse or civil partner entitled to home rights".

(10) In paragraph 5(2) –

(a)   for "matrimonial home rights" substitute "home rights", and
(b)   in paragraph (a), after "spouse" insert "or civil partner".

(11) In the heading to paragraph 5, for "matrimonial home rights" substitute "home rights".

(12) In paragraph 6, after "spouse" (in both places) insert "or civil partner".

16

(1) Amend Schedule 7 (transfer of certain tenancies on divorce etc or on separation of cohabitants) as follows.

(2) In paragraph 1, before the definition of "cohabitant" insert –

> ""civil partner", except in paragraph 2, includes (where the context requires) former civil partner;".

(3) In paragraph 2(1), after "spouse" (in both places) insert "or civil partner".

(4) For paragraph 2(2) substitute –

> "(2) The court may make a Part II order –
>
> (a)   on granting a decree of divorce, a decree of nullity of marriage or a decree of judicial separation or at any time thereafter (whether, in the case of a decree of divorce or nullity of marriage, before or after the decree is made absolute), or
> (b)   at any time when it has power to make a property adjustment order under Part 2 of Schedule 5 to the Civil Partnership Act 2004 with respect to the civil partnership.'

(5) Omit "or" at the end of paragraph 4(a) and insert –

> "(aa)   in the case of civil partners, a civil partnership home; or".

(6) In paragraph 5(a), after "spouses" insert ", civil partners".

(7) In paragraph 6 –

(a)   after "spouse" (in the first place) insert ", a civil partner", and
(b)   after "spouse" (in the second place) insert ", civil partner".

(8) In paragraph 7(1) and (2), after "spouse" (in each place) insert ", civil partner".

(9) For paragraph 7(3) to (4) substitute –

> "(3) If the spouse, civil partner or cohabitant so entitled is a successor within the meaning of Part 4 of the Housing Act 1985 –
>
> (a)   his former spouse (or, in the case of judicial separation, his spouse),
> (b)   his former civil partner (or, if a separation order is in force, his civil partner), or
> (c)   his former cohabitant,
>
> is to be deemed also to be a successor within the meaning of that Part.
>
> (3A) If the spouse, civil partner or cohabitant so entitled is a successor within the meaning of section 132 of the Housing Act 1996 –
>
> (a)   his former spouse (or, in the case of judicial separation, his spouse),
> (b)   his former civil partner (or, if a separation order is in force, his civil partner), or
> (c)   his former cohabitant,
>
> is to be deemed also to be a successor within the meaning of that section.
>
> (4) If the spouse, civil partner or cohabitant so entitled is for the purposes of section 17 of the Housing Act 1988 a successor in relation to the tenancy or occupancy –

(a)   his former spouse (or, in the case of judicial separation, his spouse),

(b)   his former civil partner (or, if a separation order is in force, his civil partner), or

(c)   his former cohabitant,

is to be deemed to be a successor in relation to the tenancy or occupancy for the purposes of that section.'

(10) In paragraph 7(5)(a), after "spouse" insert ", civil partner".

(11) Omit paragraph 7(6).

(12) In paragraph 8(1) and (2)(a) and (b), after "spouse" insert ", civil partner".

(13) In paragraph 8(3), after "surviving spouse" insert "or surviving civil partner".

(14) In paragraphs 9(1), (2)(a) and (b) and (3) (in both places) and 10(1) (in both places), after "spouse" insert ", civil partner".

(15) In paragraph 11(1), after "spouses" insert ", civil partners".

(16) In paragraph 11(2), after "spouse" insert ", civil partner".

(17) For paragraph 12 and the heading preceding it, substitute –

12 "Date when order made between spouses or civil partners takes effect

The date specified in a Part II order as the date on which the order is to take effect must not be earlier than –

(a)   in the case of a marriage in respect of which a decree of divorce or nullity has been granted, the date on which the decree is made absolute;

(b)   in the case of a civil partnership in respect of which a dissolution or nullity order has been made, the date on which the order is made final.'

(18) For paragraph 13 and the heading preceding it substitute –

13 "Effect of remarriage or subsequent civil partnership

(1) If after the grant of a decree dissolving or annulling a marriage either spouse remarries or forms a civil partnership, that spouse is not entitled to apply, by reference to the grant of that decree, for a Part II order.

(2) If after the making of a dissolution or nullity order either civil partner forms a subsequent civil partnership or marries, that civil partner is not entitled to apply, by reference to the making of that order, for a Part II order.

(3) In sub-paragraphs (1) and (2) –

(a)   the references to remarrying and marrying include references to cases where the marriage is by law void or voidable, and

(b)   the references to forming a civil partnership include references to cases where the civil partnership is by law void or voidable.'

(19) In paragraph 15(1) –

(a)   after "spouse" insert "or civil partner", and

(b)   for "spouse's matrimonial home rights" substitute "spouse's or civil partner's home rights".

(20) In paragraph 15(2), after "spouse" insert ", civil partner".

****

Schedule 20
Meaning of Overseas Relationship: Specified Relationships

A relationship is specified for the purposes of section 213 (meaning of 'overseas relationship') if it is registered in a country or territory given in the first column of the table and fits the description given in relation to that country or territory in the second column –

Country or territory	Description
Andorra	unio estable de parella
Australia: Tasmania	significant relationship
Belgium	the relationship referred to as cohabitation légale, wettelijke samenwoning or gesetzliches zusammenwohnen
Belgium	Marriage
Canada	Marriage
Canada: Nova Scotia	domestic partnership
Canada: Quebec	the relationship referred to as union civile or as civil union
Denmark	registreret partnerskab ...
Finland	the relationship referred to as rekisteröity parisuhde or as registreradpartnerskap
France	pacte civil de solidarité
Germany	Lebenspartnerschaft ...
Iceland	staðfesta samvist ...
Luxembourg	the relationship referred to as partenariat enregistré or eingetragene partnerschaft
Netherlands	geregistreerd partnerschap
Netherlands	Marriage
New Zealand	civil union
Norway	registrert partnerskap ...
Spain	Marriage
Sweden	registrerat partnerskap ...
United States of America: California	domestic partnership
United States of America: Connecticut	civil union
United States of America: Maine	domestic partnership
United States of America: Massachusetts	Marriage
United States of America: New Jersey	domestic partnership

United States of America: Vermont	civil union

Amendments—SI 2005/3129; SI 2005/3135.

****

FAMILY LAW ACT 1996

***

Schedule 7
Transfer of Certain Tenancies on Divorce etc or on Separation of Cohabitants

Section 53

PART I
GENERAL

1 Interpretation

In this Schedule–

> 'civil partner', except in paragraph 2, includes (where the context requires) former civil partner;
> 'cohabitant', except in paragraph 3, includes (where the context requires) former cohabitant;
> 'the court' does not include a magistrates' court,
> 'landlord' includes –

> > (a)   any person from time to time deriving title under the original landlord; and
> > (b)   in relation to any dwelling-house, any person other than the tenant who is, or (but for Part VII of the Rent Act 1977 or Part II of the Rent (Agriculture) Act 1976) would be, entitled to possession of the dwelling-house;

> 'Part II order' means an order under Part II of this Schedule;
> 'a relevant tenancy' means –

> > (a)   a protected tenancy or statutory tenancy within the meaning of the Rent Act 1977;
> > (b)   a statutory tenancy within the meaning of the Rent (Agriculture) Act 1976;
> > (c)   a secure tenancy within the meaning of section 79 of the Housing Act 1985;
> > (d)   an assured tenancy or assured agricultural occupancy within the meaning of Part I of the Housing Act 1988; or
> > (e)   an introductory tenancy within the meaning of Chapter I of Part V of the Housing Act 1996;

> 'spouse', except in paragraph 2, includes (where the context requires) former spouse; and
> 'tenancy' includes sub-tenancy.

Cases in which the court may make an order

2

(1)   This paragraph applies if one spouse or civil partner is entitled, either in his own right or jointly with the other spouse or civil partner, to occupy a dwelling-house by virtue of a relevant tenancy.

(2)   The court may make a Part II order –

> (a)   on granting a decree of divorce, a decree of nullity of marriage or a decree of judicial separation or at any time thereafter (whether, in the case of a decree of divorce or nullity of marriage, before or after the decree is made absolute), or
> (b)   at any time when it has power to make a property adjustment order under Part 2 of Schedule 5 to the Civil Partnership Act 2004 with respect to the civil partnership.

3

(1) This paragraph applies if one cohabitant is entitled, either in his own right or jointly with the other cohabitant, to occupy a dwelling-house by virtue of a relevant tenancy.

(2) If the cohabitants cease to cohabit, the court may make a Part II order.

4

The court shall not make a Part II order unless the dwelling-house is or was –

  (a)   in the case of spouses, a matrimonial home;
  (aa) in the case of civil partners, a civil partnership home; or
  (b)   in the case of cohabitants, a home in which they cohabited.

5   Matters to which the court must have regard

In determining whether to exercise its powers under Part II of this Schedule and, if so, in what manner, the court shall have regard to all the circumstances of the case including –

  (a)   the circumstances in which the tenancy was granted to either or both of the spouses, or civil partners or cohabitants or, as the case requires, the circumstances in which either or both of them became tenant under the tenancy;
  (b)   the matters mentioned in section 33(6)(a), (b) and (c) and, where the parties are cohabitants and only one of them is entitled to occupy the dwelling-house by virtue of the relevant tenancy, the further matters mentioned in section 36(6)(e), (f), (g) and (h); and
  (c)   the suitability of the parties as tenants.

Amendments—SI 1997/74; Civil Partnership Act 2004, ss 82, 261(4), Sch 9, Pt 1, para 16(1)–(6), Sch 30; Domestic Violence, Crime and Victims Act 2004, s 58(1), Sch 10, para 42.

PART II
ORDERS THAT MAY BE MADE

6   References to entitlement to occupy

References in this Part of this Schedule to a spouse, a civil partner or a cohabitant being entitled to occupy a dwelling-house by virtue of a relevant tenancy apply whether that entitlement is in his own right or jointly with the other spouse, civil partner or cohabitant.

7   Protected, secure or assured tenancy or assured agricultural occupancy

(1) If a spouse, civil partner or cohabitant is entitled to occupy the dwelling-house by virtue of a protected tenancy within the meaning of the Rent Act 1977, a secure tenancy within the meaning of the Housing Act 1985, an assured tenancy or assured agricultural occupancy within the meaning of Part I of the Housing Act 1988 or an introductory tenancy within the meaning of Chapter I of Part V of the Housing Act 1996, the court may by order direct that, as from such date as may be specified in the order, there shall, by virtue of the order and without further assurance, be transferred to, and vested in, the other spouse, civil partner or cohabitant–

  (a)   the estate or interest which the spouse, civil partner or cohabitant so entitled had in the dwelling-house immediately before that date by virtue of the lease or agreement creating the tenancy and any assignment of that lease or agreement, with all rights, privileges and appurtenances attaching to that estate or interest but subject to all covenants, obligations, liabilities and incumbrances to which it is subject; and
  (b)   where the spouse, civil partner or cohabitant so entitled is an assignee of such lease or agreement, the liability of that spouse, civil partner or cohabitant under any covenant of indemnity by the assignee express or implied in the assignment of the lease or agreement to that spouse, civil partner or cohabitant.

(2)   If an order is made under this paragraph, any liability or obligation to which the spouse, civil partner or cohabitant so entitled is subject under any covenant having reference to the dwelling-house in the lease or agreement, being a liability or obligation falling due to be discharged or performed on or after the date so specified, shall not be enforceable against that spouse, civil partner or cohabitant.

(3)   If the spouse, civil partner or cohabitant so entitled is a successor within the meaning of Part 4 of the Housing Act 1985 –

    (a)   his former spouse (or, in the case of judicial separation, his spouse),
    (b)   his former civil partner (or, if a separation order is in force, his civil partner), or
    (c)   his former cohabitant,

is to be deemed also to be a successor within the meaning of that Part.

(3A)   If the spouse, civil partner or cohabitant so entitled is a successor within the meaning of section 132 of the Housing Act 1996 –

    (a)   his former spouse (or, in the case of judicial separation, his spouse),
    (b)   his former civil partner (or, if a separation order is in force, his civil partner), or
    (c)   his former cohabitant,

is to be deemed also to be a successor within the meaning of that section.

(4)   If the spouse, civil partner or cohabitant so entitled is for the purposes of section 17 of the Housing Act 1988 a successor in relation to the tenancy or occupancy –

    (a)   his former spouse (or, in the case of judicial separation, his spouse),
    (b)   his former civil partner (or, if a separation order is in force, his civil partner), or
    (c)   his former cohabitant,

is to be deemed to be a successor in relation to the tenancy or occupancy for the purposes of that section.

(5)   If the transfer under sub-paragraph (1) is of an assured agricultural occupancy, then, for the purposes of Chapter III of Part I of the Housing Act 1988 –

    (a)   the agricultural worker condition is fulfilled with respect to the dwelling-house while the spouse, civil partner or cohabitant to whom the assured agricultural occupancy is transferred continues to be the occupier under that occupancy, and
    (b)   that condition is to be treated as so fulfilled by virtue of the same paragraph of Schedule 3 to the Housing Act 1988 as was applicable before the transfer.

8   Statutory tenancy within the meaning of the Rent Act 1977

(1)   This paragraph applies if the spouse, civil partner or cohabitant is entitled to occupy the dwelling-house by virtue of a statutory tenancy within the meaning of the Rent Act 1977.

(2)   The court may by order direct that, as from the date specified in the order –

    (a)   that spouse, civil partner or cohabitant is to cease to be entitled to occupy the dwelling-house; and
    (b)   the other spouse, civil partner or cohabitant is to be deemed to be the tenant or, as the case may be, the sole tenant under that statutory tenancy.

(3)   The question whether the provisions of paragraphs 1 to 3, or (as the case may be) paragraphs 5 to 7 of Schedule 1 to the Rent Act 1977, as to the succession by the surviving spouse or surviving civil partner of a deceased tenant, or by a member of the deceased tenant's family, to the right to retain possession are capable of having effect in the event of the death of the person deemed by an order under this paragraph to be the tenant or sole tenant under the statutory tenancy is to be determined according as those provisions have or have not already had effect in relation to the statutory tenancy.

9 Statutory tenancy within the meaning of the Rent (Agriculture) Act 1976

(1) This paragraph applies if the spouse, civil partner or cohabitant is entitled to occupy the dwelling-house by virtue of a statutory tenancy within the meaning of the Rent (Agriculture) Act 1976.

(2) The court may by order direct that, as from such date as may be specified in the order –

    (a) that spouse, civil partner or cohabitant is to cease to be entitled to occupy the dwelling-house; and

    (b) the other spouse, civil partner or cohabitant is to be deemed to be the tenant or, as the case may be, the sole tenant under that statutory tenancy.

(3) A spouse, civil partner or cohabitant who is deemed under this paragraph to be the tenant under a statutory tenancy is (within the meaning of that Act) a statutory tenant in his own right, or a statutory tenant by succession, according as the other spouse, civil partner or cohabitant was a statutory tenant in his own right or a statutory tenant by succession.

Amendments—SI 1997/74; Civil Partnership Act 2004, s 82, Sch 9, Pt 1, para 16(1), (7)–(14).

PART III
SUPPLEMENTARY PROVISIONS

10 Compensation

(1) If the court makes a Part II order, it may by the order direct the making of a payment by the spouse, civil partner or cohabitant to whom the tenancy is transferred ('the transferee') to the other spouse, civil partner or cohabitant ('the transferor').

(2) Without prejudice to that, the court may, on making an order by virtue of sub-paragraph (1) for the payment of a sum –

    (a) direct that payment of that sum or any part of it is to be deferred until a specified date or until the occurrence of a specified event, or

    (b) direct that that sum or any part of it is to be paid by instalments.

(3) Where an order has been made by virtue of sub-paragraph (1), the court may, on the application of the transferee or the transferor –

    (a) exercise its powers under sub-paragraph (2), or

    (b) vary any direction previously given under that sub-paragraph,

at any time before the sum whose payment is required by the order is paid in full.

(4) In deciding whether to exercise its powers under this paragraph and, if so, in what manner, the court shall have regard to all the circumstances including –

    (a) the financial loss that would otherwise be suffered by the transferor as a result of the order;

    (b) the financial needs and financial resources of the parties; and

    (c) the financial obligations which the parties have, or are likely to have in the foreseeable future, including financial obligations to each other and to any relevant child.

(5) The court shall not give any direction under sub-paragraph (2) unless it appears to it that immediate payment of the sum required by the order would cause the transferee financial hardship which is greater than any financial hardship that would be caused to the transferor if the direction were given.

Amendments—SI 1997/74; Civil Partnership Act 2004, s 82, Sch 9, Pt 1, para 16(1), (7)–(14).

11   Liabilities and obligations in respect of the dwelling-house

(1)   If the court makes a Part II order, it may by the order direct that both spouses, civil partners or cohabitants are to be jointly and severally liable to discharge or perform any or all of the liabilities and obligations in respect of the dwelling-house (whether arising under the tenancy or otherwise) which –

> (a)   have at the date of the order fallen due to be discharged or performed by one only of them; or
> (b)   but for the direction, would before the date specified as the date on which the order is to take effect fall due to be discharged or performed by one only of them.

(2)   If the court gives such a direction, it may further direct that either spouse, civil partner or cohabitant is to be liable to indemnify the other in whole or in part against any payment made or expenses incurred by the other in discharging or performing any such liability or obligation.

Amendments—SI 1997/74; Civil Partnership Act 2004, s 82, Sch 9, Pt 1, para 16(1), (7)–(14).

12   Date when order made between spouses or civil partners takes effect

The date specified in a Part II order as the date on which the order is to take effect must not be earlier than –

> (a)   in the case of a marriage in respect of which a decree of divorce or nullity has been granted, the date on which the decree is made absolute;
> (b)   in the case of a civil partnership in respect of which a dissolution or nullity order has been made, the date on which the order is made final.

Amendments—SI 1997/74; Civil Partnership Act 2004, s 82, Sch 9, Pt 1, para 16(1), (7)–(14).

13   Effect of remarriage or subsequent civil partnership

(1)   If after the grant of a decree dissolving or annulling a marriage either spouse remarries or forms a civil partnership, that spouse is not entitled to apply, by reference to the grant of that decree, for a Part II order.

(2)   If after the making of a dissolution or nullity order either civil partner forms a subsequent civil partnership or marries, that civil partner is not entitled to apply, by reference to the making of that order, for a Part II order.

(3)   In sub-paragraphs (1) and (2) –

> (a)   the references to remarrying and marrying include references to cases where the marriage is by law void or voidable, and
> (b)   the references to forming a civil partnership include references to cases where the civil partnership is by law void or voidable.

Amendments—SI 1997/74; Civil Partnership Act 2004, s 82, Sch 9, Pt 1, para 16(1), (7)–(14).

14   Rules of court

(1)   Rules of court shall be made requiring the court, before it makes an order under this Schedule, to give the landlord of the dwelling-house to which the order will relate an opportunity of being heard.

(2)   Rules of court may provide that an application for a Part II order by reference to an order or decree may not, without the leave of the court by which that order was made or decree was granted, be made after the expiration of such period from the order or grant as may be prescribed by the rules.

15 Saving for other provisions of Act

(1)   If a spouse or civil partner is entitled to occupy a dwelling-house by virtue of a tenancy, this Schedule does not affect the operation of sections 30 and 31 in relation to the other spouse's or civil partner's home rights.

(2)   If a spouse, civil partner or cohabitant is entitled to occupy a dwelling-house by virtue of a tenancy, the court's powers to make orders under this Schedule are additional to those conferred by sections 33, 35 and 36.

Amendments—Civil Partnership Act 2004, s 82, Sch 9, Pt 1, para 16(1), (14)–(20).

****

A4.4

GENDER RECOGNITION ACT 2004

ARRANGEMENT OF SECTIONS

Applications for gender recognition certificate

Section		*Page*
1	Applications	606
2	Determination of applications	606
3	Evidence	607
4	Successful applications	608
5	Issue of full certificates where applicant has been married	608
5A	Issue of full certificates where applicant has been a civil partner	609
6	Errors in certificates	609
7	Applications: supplementary	609
8	Appeals etc	610

Consequences of issue of gender recognition certificate etc.

9	General	610
10	Registration	610
12	Parenthood	611
15	Succession etc	611
17	Trustees and personal representatives	611
18	Orders where expectations defeated	611
21	Foreign gender change and marriage	612

Supplementary

22	Prohibition on disclosure of information	612
25	Interpretation	613
26	Commencement	614

Schedule 1 – Gender Recognition Panels	614
Schedule 3 – Registration	616
Part 1 – England and Wales	616

Applications for gender recognition certificate

1 Applications

(1) A person of either gender who is aged at least 18 may make an application for a gender recognition certificate on the basis of –

    (a)   living in the other gender, or

    (b)   having changed gender under the law of a country or territory outside the United Kingdom.

(2) In this Act "the acquired gender", in relation to a person by whom an application under subsection (1) is or has been made, means –

    (a)   in the case of an application under paragraph (a) of that subsection, the gender in which the person is living, or

    (b)   in the case of an application under paragraph (b) of that subsection, the gender to which the person has changed under the law of the country or territory concerned.

(3) An application under subsection (1) is to be determined by a Gender Recognition Panel.

(4) Schedule 1 (Gender Recognition Panels) has effect.

2 Determination of applications

(1) In the case of an application under section 1(1)(*a*), the Panel must grant the application if satisfied that the applicant –

(a)   has or has had gender dysphoria,

(b)   has lived in the acquired gender throughout the period of two years ending with the date on which the application is made,

(c)   intends to continue to live in the acquired gender until death, and

(d)   complies with the requirements imposed by and under section 3.

(2) In the case of an application under section 1(1)(*b*), the Panel must grant the application if satisfied –

(a)   that the country or territory under the law of which the applicant has changed gender is an approved country or territory, and

(b)   that the applicant complies with the requirements imposed by and under section 3.

(3) The Panel must reject an application under section 1(1) if not required by subsection (1) or (2) to grant it.

(4) In this Act "approved country or territory" means a country or territory prescribed by order made by the Secretary of State after consulting the Scottish Ministers and the Department of Finance and Personnel in Northern Ireland.

3 Evidence

(1) An application under section 1(1)(*a*) must include either –

(a)   a report made by a registered medical practitioner practising in the field of gender dysphoria and a report made by another registered medical practitioner (who may, but need not, practise in that field), or

(b)   a report made by a registered psychologist practising in that field and a report made by a registered medical practitioner (who may, but need not, practise in that field).

(2) But subsection (1) is not complied with unless a report required by that subsection and made by –

(a)   a registered medical practitioner, or

(b)   a registered psychologist,

practising in the field of gender dysphoria includes details of the diagnosis of the applicant's gender dysphoria.

(3) And subsection (1) is not complied with in a case where –

(a)   the applicant has undergone or is undergoing treatment for the purpose of modifying sexual characteristics, or

(b)   treatment for that purpose has been prescribed or planned for the applicant,

unless at least one of the reports required by that subsection includes details of it.

(4) An application under section 1(1)(*a*) must also include a statutory declaration by the applicant that the applicant meets the conditions in section 2(1)(*b*) and (*c*).

(5) An application under section 1(1)(*b*) must include evidence that the applicant has changed gender under the law of an approved country or territory.

(6) Any application under section 1(1) must include –

(a)   a statutory declaration as to whether or not the applicant is married or a civil partner,

(b)   any other information or evidence required by an order made by the Secretary of State, and

(c)   any other information or evidence which the Panel which is to determine the application may require,

and may include any other information or evidence which the applicant wishes to include.

(7) The Secretary of State may not make an order under subsection (6)(*b*) without consulting the Scottish Ministers and the Department of Finance and Personnel in Northern Ireland.

(8) If the Panel which is to determine the application requires information or evidence under subsection (6)(*c*) it must give reasons for doing so.

Amendments—CPA 2004, s 250(1),(2); SI 2009/1182.

4 Successful applications

(1) If a Gender Recognition Panel grants an application under section 1(1) it must issue a gender recognition certificate to the applicant.

(2) Unless the applicant is married or a civil partner, the certificate is to be a full gender recognition certificate.

(3) If the applicant is married or a civil partner, the certificate is to be an interim gender recognition certificate.

(4) Schedule 2 (annulment or dissolution of marriage after issue of interim gender recognition certificate) has effect.

(5) The Secretary of State may, after consulting the Scottish Ministers and the Department of Finance and Personnel in Northern Ireland, specify the content and form of gender recognition certificates.

Amendments—CPA 2004, s 250(1), (2).

5 Issue of full certificates where applicant has been married

(1) A court which –

    (a)   makes absolute a decree of nullity granted on the ground that an interim gender recognition certificate has been issued to a party to the marriage, or

    (b)   (in Scotland) grants a decree of divorce on that ground,

must, on doing so, issue a full gender recognition certificate to that party and send a copy to the Secretary of State.

(2) If an interim gender recognition certificate has been issued to a person and either –

    (a)   the person's marriage is dissolved or annulled (otherwise than on the ground mentioned in subsection (1)) in proceedings instituted during the period of six months beginning with the day on which it was issued, or

    (b)   the person's spouse dies within that period,

the person may make an application for a full gender recognition certificate at any time within the period specified in subsection (3) (unless the person is again married or is a civil partner).

(3) That period is the period of six months beginning with the day on which the marriage is dissolved or annulled or the death occurs.

(4) An application under subsection (2) must include evidence of the dissolution or annulment of the marriage and the date on which proceedings for it were instituted, or of the death of the spouse and the date on which it occurred.

(5) An application under subsection (2) is to be determined by a Gender Recognition Panel.

(6) The Panel –

    (a)   must grant the application if satisfied that the applicant is neither married nor a civil partner, and

    (b)   otherwise must reject it.

(7) If the Panel grants the application it must issue a full gender recognition certificate to the applicant.

Amendments—CPA 2004, s 250(1), (3).

5A Issue of full certificates where applicant has been a civil partner

(1) A court which –

  (a) makes final a nullity order made on the ground that an interim gender recognition certificate has been issued to a civil partner, or
  (b) (in Scotland) grants a decree of dissolution on that ground,

must, on doing so, issue a full gender recognition certificate to that civil partner and send a copy to the Secretary of State.

(2) If an interim gender recognition certificate has been issued to a person and either –

  (a) the person's civil partnership is dissolved or annulled (otherwise than on the ground mentioned in subsection (1)) in proceedings instituted during the period of six months beginning with the day on which it was issued, or
  (b) the person's civil partner dies within that period,

the person may make an application for a full gender recognition certificate at any time within the period specified in subsection (3) (unless the person is again a civil partner or is married).

(3) That period is the period of six months beginning with the day on which the civil partnership is dissolved or annulled or the death occurs.

(4) An application under subsection (2) must include evidence of the dissolution or annulment of the civil partnership and the date on which proceedings for it were instituted, or of the death of the civil partner and the date on which it occurred.

(5) An application under subsection (2) is to be determined by a Gender Recognition Panel.

(6) The Panel –

  (a) must grant the application if satisfied that the applicant is neither a civil partner nor married, and
  (b) otherwise must reject it.

(7) If the Panel grants the application it must issue a full gender recognition certificate to the applicant.

Amendments—Inserted by CPA 2004, s 250(1), (4).

6 Errors in certificates

(1) Where a gender recognition certificate has been issued to a person, the person or the Secretary of State may make an application for a corrected certificate on the ground that the certificate which has been issued contains an error.

(2) If the certificate was issued by a court the application is to be determined by the court but in any other case it is to be determined by a Gender Recognition Panel.

(3) The court or Panel –

  (a) must grant the application if satisfied that the gender recognition certificate contains an error, and
  (b) otherwise must reject it.

(4) If the court or Panel grants the application it must issue a corrected gender recognition certificate to the applicant.

7 Applications: supplementary

(1) An application to a Gender Recognition Panel under section 1(1), 5(2), 5A(2) or 6(1) must be made in a form and manner specified by the Secretary of State after consulting the Scottish Ministers and the Department of Finance and Personnel in Northern Ireland.

(2) The applicant must pay to the Secretary of State a non-refundable fee of an amount prescribed by order made by the Secretary of State unless the application is made in circumstances in which, in accordance with provision made by the order, no fee is payable; and fees of different amounts may be prescribed for different circumstances.

Amendments—CPA 2004, s 250(1), (5).

8 Appeals etc

(1) An applicant to a Gender Recognition Panel under section 1(1), 5(2), 5(A)2 or 6(1) may appeal to the High Court or Court of Session on a point of law against a decision by the Panel to reject the application.

(2) An appeal under subsection (1) must be heard in private if the applicant so requests.

(3) On such an appeal the court must –

(a)   allow the appeal and issue the certificate applied for,
(b)   allow the appeal and refer the matter to the same or another Panel for re-consideration, or
(c)   dismiss the appeal.

(4) If an application under section 1(1) is rejected, the applicant may not make another application before the end of the period of six months beginning with the date on which it is rejected.

(5) If an application under section 1(1), 5(2), 5A(2) or 6(1) is granted but the Secretary of State considers that its grant was secured by fraud, the Secretary of State may refer the case to the High Court or Court of Session.

(6) On a reference under subsection (5) the court –

(a)   must either quash or confirm the decision to grant the application, and
(b)   if it quashes it, must revoke the gender recognition certificate issued on the grant of the application and may make any order which it considers appropriate in consequence of, or otherwise in connection with, doing so.

Amendments—CPA 2004, s 250(1), (5).

Consequences of issue of gender recognition certificate etc.

9 General

(1) Where a full gender recognition certificate is issued to a person, the person's gender becomes for all purposes the acquired gender (so that, if the acquired gender is the male gender, the person's sex becomes that of a man and, if it is the female gender, the person's sex becomes that of a woman).

(2) Subsection (1) does not affect things done, or events occurring, before the certificate is issued; but it does operate for the interpretation of enactments passed, and instruments and other documents made, before the certificate is issued (as well as those passed or made afterwards).

(3) Subsection (1) is subject to provision made by this Act or any other enactment or any subordinate legislation.

10 Registration

(1) Where there is a UK birth register entry in relation to a person to whom a full gender recognition certificate is issued, the Secretary of State must send a copy of the certificate to the appropriate Registrar General.

(2) In this Act "UK birth register entry", in relation to a person to whom a full gender recognition certificate is issued, means –

(a)   an entry of which a certified copy is kept by a Registrar General, or

(b) an entry in a register so kept,

containing a record of the person's birth or adoption (or, if there would otherwise be more than one, the most recent).

(3) "The appropriate Registrar General" means whichever of –

 (a) the Registrar General for England and Wales,
 (b) the Registrar General for Scotland, or
 (c) the Registrar General for Northern Ireland,

keeps a certified copy of the person's UK birth register entry or the register containing that entry.

(4) Schedule 3 (provisions about registration) has effect.

****

12 Parenthood

The fact that a person's gender has become the acquired gender under this Act does not affect the status of the person as the father or mother of a child.

****

15 Succession etc

The fact that a person's gender has become the acquired gender under this Act does not affect the disposal or devolution of property under a will or other instrument made before the appointed day.

****

17 Trustees and personal representatives

(1) A trustee or personal representative is not under a duty, by virtue of the law relating to trusts or the administration of estates, to enquire, before conveying or distributing any property, whether a full gender recognition certificate has been issued to any person or revoked (if that fact could affect entitlement to the property).

(2) A trustee or personal representative is not liable to any person by reason of a conveyance or distribution of the property made without regard to whether a full gender recognition certificate has been issued to any person or revoked if the trustee or personal representative has not received notice of the fact before the conveyance or distribution.

(3) This section does not prejudice the right of a person to follow the property, or any property representing it, into the hands of another person who has received it unless that person has purchased it for value in good faith and without notice.

18 Orders where expectations defeated

(1) This section applies where the disposition or devolution of any property under a will or other instrument (made on or after the appointed day) is different from what it would be but for the fact that a person's gender has become the acquired gender under this Act.

(2) A person may apply to the High Court or Court of Session for an order on the ground of being adversely affected by the different disposition or devolution of the property.

(3) The court may, if it is satisfied that it is just to do so, make in relation to any person benefiting from the different disposition or devolution of the property such order as it considers appropriate.

(4) An order may, in particular, make provision for –

 (a) the payment of a lump sum to the applicant,
 (b) the transfer of property to the applicant,
 (c) the settlement of property for the benefit of the applicant,

(d)   the acquisition of property and either its transfer to the applicant or its settlement for the benefit of the applicant.

(5) An order may contain consequential or supplementary provisions for giving effect to the order or for ensuring that it operates fairly as between the applicant and the other person or persons affected by it; and an order may, in particular, confer powers on trustees.

****

21 Foreign gender change and marriage

(1) A person's gender is not to be regarded as having changed by reason only that it has changed under the law of a country or territory outside the United Kingdom.

(2) Accordingly, a person is not to be regarded as being married by reason of having entered into a foreign post-recognition marriage.

(3) But if a full gender recognition certificate is issued to a person who has entered into a foreign post-recognition marriage, after the issue of the certificate the marriage is no longer to be regarded as being void on the ground that (at the time when it was entered into) the parties to it were not respectively male and female.

(4) However, subsection (3) does not apply to a foreign post-recognition marriage if a party to it has entered into a later (valid) marriage or civil partnership before the issue of the full gender recognition certificate.

(5) For the purposes of this section a person has entered into a foreign post-recognition marriage if (and only if) –

(a)   the person has entered into a marriage in accordance with the law of a country or territory outside the United Kingdom,

(b)   before the marriage was entered into the person had changed gender under the law of that or any other country or territory outside the United Kingdom,

(c)   the other party to the marriage was not of the gender to which the person had changed under the law of that country or territory, and

(d)   by virtue of subsection (1) the person's gender was not regarded as having changed under the law of any part of the United Kingdom.

(6) Nothing in this section prevents the exercise of any enforceable Community right.

Amendments—CPA 2004, s 250(1),(6).

Supplementary

22 Prohibition on disclosure of information

(1) It is an offence for a person who has acquired protected information in an official capacity to disclose the information to any other person.

(2) "Protected information" means information which relates to a person who has made an application under section 1(1) and which –

(a)   concerns that application or any application by the person under section 5(2), 5A(2) or 6(1), or

(b)   if the application under section 1(1) is granted, otherwise concerns the person's gender before it becomes the acquired gender.

(3) A person acquires protected information in an official capacity if the person acquires it –

(a)   in connection with the person's functions as a member of the civil service, a constable or the holder of any other public office or in connection with the functions of a local or public authority or of a voluntary organisation,

(b)   as an employer, or prospective employer, of the person to whom the information relates or as a person employed by such an employer or prospective employer, or

(c)   in the course of, or otherwise in connection with, the conduct of business or the supply of professional services.

(4) But it is not an offence under this section to disclose protected information relating to a person if –

(a)   the information does not enable that person to be identified,

(b)   that person has agreed to the disclosure of the information,

(c)   the information is protected information by virtue of subsection (2)(b) and the person by whom the disclosure is made does not know or believe that a full gender recognition certificate has been issued,

(d)   the disclosure is in accordance with an order of a court or tribunal,

(e)   the disclosure is for the purpose of instituting, or otherwise for the purposes of, proceedings before a court or tribunal,

(f)   the disclosure is for the purpose of preventing or investigating crime,

(g)   the disclosure is made to the Registrar General for England and Wales, the Registrar General for Scotland or the Registrar General for Northern Ireland,

(h)   the disclosure is made for the purposes of the social security system or a pension scheme,

(i)   the disclosure is in accordance with provision made by an order under subsection (5), or

(j)   the disclosure is in accordance with any provision of, or made by virtue of, an enactment other than this section.

(5) The Secretary of State may by order make provision prescribing circumstances in which the disclosure of protected information is not to constitute an offence under this section.

(6) The power conferred by subsection (5) is exercisable by the Scottish Ministers (rather than the Secretary of State) where the provision to be made is within the legislative competence of the Scottish Parliament.

(6A) The power conferred by subsection (5) is exercisable by the Department of Justice in Northern Ireland (rather than the Secretary of State) where the provision to be made could be made by an Act of the Northern Ireland Assembly without the consent of the Secretary of State (see sections 6 to 8 of the Northern Ireland Act 1998).

(7) An order under subsection (5) may make provision permitting –

(a)   disclosure to specified persons or persons of a specified description,

(b)   disclosure for specified purposes,

(c)   disclosure of specified descriptions of information, or

(d)   disclosure by specified persons or persons of a specified description.

(8) A person guilty of an offence under this section is liable on summary conviction to a fine not exceeding level 5 on the standard scale.

Amendments—CPA 2004, s 250(1), (5); SI 2010/976.

****

25 Interpretation

In this Act –

"the acquired gender" is to be construed in accordance with section 1(2),

"approved country or territory" has the meaning given by section 2(4),

"the appointed day" means the day appointed by order under section 26,

"enactment" includes an enactment contained in an Act of the Scottish Parliament or in any Northern Ireland legislation,

"full gender recognition certificate" and "interim gender recognition certificate" mean the certificates issued as such under section 4 or 5 or 5A and "gender recognition certificate" means either of those sorts of certificate,

"gender dysphoria" means the disorder variously referred to as gender dysphoria, gender identity disorder and transsexualism,

"Gender Recognition Panel" (and "Panel") is to be construed in accordance with Schedule 1,
"registered psychologist" means a person registered in the part of the register maintained under the Health Professions Order 2001 which relates to practitioner psychologists,
"subordinate legislation" means an Order in Council, an order, rules, regulations, a scheme, a warrant, bye-laws or any other instrument made under an enactment, and
"UK birth register entry" has the meaning given by section 10(2).

Amendments—CPA 2004, s 250(1), (7); SI 2009/1182.

26 Commencement

Apart from sections 23 to 25, this section and sections 28 and 29, this Act does not come into force until such day as the Secretary of State may appoint by order made after consulting the Scottish Ministers and the Department of Finance and Personnel in Northern Ireland.

****

Schedule 1
Gender Recognition Panels

Section 1

1 List of persons eligible to sit

(1) Subject to sub-paragraph (1A), the Lord Chancellor must, after consulting the Scottish Ministers and the Department of Finance and Personnel in Northern Ireland, make appointments to a list of persons eligible to sit as members of Gender Recognition Panels.

(1A) The Lord Chancellor may appoint a person under sub-paragraph (1) only with the concurrence of all of the following—

  (a)   the Lord Chief Justice of England and Wales;
  (b)   the Lord President of the Court of Session;
  (c)   the Lord Chief Justice of Northern Ireland.

(2) The only persons who may be appointed to the list are persons who—

  (a)   have a relevant legal qualification ("legal members"), or
  (b)   are registered medical practitioners or registered psychologists ("medical members").

(3) The following have a relevant legal qualification—

  (a)   a person who has a 7 year general qualification within the meaning of section 71 of the Courts and Legal Services Act 1990 (c 41),
  (b)   an advocate or solicitor in Scotland of at least seven years' standing, and
  (c)   a member of the Bar of Northern Ireland or solicitor of the Court of Judicature of Northern Ireland of at least seven years' standing.

2 President

(1) Subject to sub-paragraph (1A), the Lord Chancellor must, after consulting the Scottish Ministers and the Department of Finance and Personnel in Northern Ireland—

  (a)   appoint one of the legal members to be the President of Gender Recognition Panels ("the President"), and
  (b)   appoint another of the legal members to be the Deputy President of Gender Recognition Panels ("the Deputy President").

(1A) The Lord Chancellor may appoint a person under sub-paragraph (1) only with the concurrence of all of the following—

  (a)   the Lord Chief Justice of England and Wales;
  (b)   the Lord President of the Court of Session;

    (c)   the Lord Chief Justice of Northern Ireland.

(2) The Deputy President has the functions of the President—

    (a)   if the President is unavailable, and

    (b)   during any vacancy in the office of President.

3 Tenure of persons appointed to list

Persons on the list—

    (a)   hold and vacate their appointments in accordance with the terms on which they are appointed, and

    (b)   are eligible for re-appointment at the end of their period of appointment.

4 Membership of Panels

(1) The President must make arrangements for determining the membership of Panels.

(2) The arrangements must ensure that a Panel determining an application under section 1(1)(a) includes—

    (a)   at least one legal member, and

    (b)   at least one medical member.

5

The arrangements must ensure that a Panel determining an application under section 1(1)(b), 5(2), 5A(2) or 6(1) includes at least one legal member.

6 Procedure

(1) Where a Panel consists of more than one member, either the President or Deputy President or another legal member nominated by the President must preside.

(2) Decisions of a Panel consisting of more than one member may be taken by majority vote (and, if its members are evenly split, the member presiding has a casting vote).

(3) Panels are to determine applications in private.

(4) A Panel must determine an application without a hearing unless the Panel considers that a hearing is necessary.

(5) The President may, after consulting the Administrative Justice and Tribunals Council, give directions about the practice and procedure of Panels.

(6) Panels must give reasons for their decisions.

(7) Where a Panel has determined an application, the Secretary of State must communicate to the applicant the Panel's decision and its reasons for making its decision.

7 Staff and facilities

The Secretary of State may make staff and other facilities available to Panels.

8 Money

(1) The Secretary of State may pay sums by way of remuneration, allowances and expenses to members of Panels.

(2) The Secretary of State may pay compensation to a person who ceases to be on the list if the Secretary of State thinks it appropriate to do so because of special circumstances.

8A Delegation

(1) The Lord Chief Justice of England and Wales may nominate a judicial office holder (as defined in section 109(4) of the Constitutional Reform Act 2005) to exercise any of his functions under this Schedule.

(2) The Lord President of the Court of Session may nominate a judge of the Court of Session who is a member of the First or Second Division of the Inner House of that Court to exercise his functions under this Schedule.

(3) The Lord Chief Justice of Northern Ireland may nominate any of the following to exercise his functions under this Schedule—

- (a)   the holder of one of the offices listed in Schedule 1 to the Justice (Northern Ireland) Act 2002;
- (b)   a Lord Justice of Appeal (as defined in section 88 of that Act).

9 Council on Tribunals

In Schedule 1 to the Tribunals and Inquiries Act 1992 (c 53) (tribunals under supervision of Council on Tribunals), before paragraph 22 insert—

"Gender Recognition

    21AA

    Gender Recognition Panels constituted under Schedule 1 to the Gender Recognition Act 2004 (c 7)."

10 Disqualification

In Part 3 of Schedule 1 to the House of Commons Disqualification Act 1975 (c 24) (offices disqualifying person from membership of House of Commons), at the appropriate place insert—

    "Person on the list of those eligible to sit as members of a Gender Recognition Panel."

11

In Part 3 of Schedule 1 to the Northern Ireland Assembly Disqualification Act 1975 (c 25) (offices disqualifying persons from membership of Northern Ireland Assembly), at the appropriate place insert—

"Person on the list of those eligible to sit as members of a Gender Recognition Panel."

Amendments—CPA 2004, s 250(1), (8); CRA 2005, s 59(5), Sch 11, Pt 3, para 5; TCE 2007, s 48(1), Sch 8, para 60; SI 2006/1016; SI 2009/1182.

****

Schedule 3
Registration

Section 10

PART 1
ENGLAND AND WALES

1 Introductory

In this Part—

    "the Registrar General" means the Registrar General for England and Wales, and
    "the 1953 Act" means the Births and Deaths Registration Act 1953 (c 20).

2 Gender Recognition Register

(1) The Registrar General must maintain, in the General Register Office, a register to be called the Gender Recognition Register.

(2) In this Part "the Gender Recognition Register" means the register maintained under sub-paragraph (1).

(3) The form in which the Gender Recognition Register is maintained is to be determined by the Registrar General.

(4) The Gender Recognition Register is not to be open to public inspection or search.

3 Entries in Gender Recognition Register and marking of existing birth register entries

(1) If the Registrar General receives under section 10(1) a copy of a full gender recognition certificate issued to a person, the Registrar General must—

    (a)   make an entry in the Gender Recognition Register containing such particulars as may be prescribed in relation to the person's birth and any other prescribed matter,

    (b)   secure that the UK birth register entry is marked in such manner as may be prescribed, and

    (c)   make traceable the connection between the entry in the Gender Recognition Register and the UK birth register entry.

(2) Sub-paragraph (1) does not apply if the certificate was issued after an application under section 6(1) and that sub-paragraph has already been complied with in relation to the person.

(3) No certified copy of the UK birth register entry and no short certificate of birth compiled from that entry is to include anything marked by virtue of sub-paragraph (1)(b).

(4) Information kept by the Registrar General for the purposes of sub-paragraph (1)(c) is not to be open to public inspection or search.

(5) "Prescribed" means prescribed by regulations made by the Registrar General with the approval of the Secretary of State.

4 Indexing of entries in Gender Recognition Register

(1) The Registrar General must make arrangements for each entry made in the Gender Recognition Register to be included in the relevant index kept in the General Register Office.

(2) Any right to search the relevant index includes the right to search entries included in it by virtue of sub-paragraph (1).

(3) Where by virtue of sub-paragraph (1) an index includes entries in the Gender Recognition Register, the index must not disclose that fact.

(4) "The relevant index", in relation to an entry made in the Gender Recognition Register in relation to a person, means the index of the certified copies of entries in registers, or of entries in registers, which includes the person's UK birth register entry.

5 Certified copies of entries in Gender Recognition Register

(1) Anyone who may have a certified copy of the UK birth register entry of a person issued with a full gender recognition certificate may have a certified copy of the entry made in relation to the person in the Gender Recognition Register.

(2) Any fee which would be payable for a certified copy of the person's UK birth register entry is payable for a certified copy of the entry made in relation to the person in the Gender Recognition Register.

(3) If the person's UK birth register entry is an entry in the Gender Recognition Register, sub-paragraph (1) applies as if the person's UK birth register entry were the most recent entry within section 10(2)(a) or (b) containing a record of the person's birth or adoption which is not an entry in the Gender Recognition Register.

(4) A certified copy of an entry in the Gender Recognition Register must not disclose the fact that the entry is contained in the Gender Recognition Register.

(5) A certified copy of an entry in the Gender Recognition Register must be sealed or stamped with the seal of the General Register Office.

6 Short certificates of birth compiled from Gender Recognition Register

Where a short certificate of birth under section 33 of the 1953 Act is compiled from the Gender Recognition Register, the certificate must not disclose that fact.

7 Gender Recognition Register: re-registration

(1) Section 10A of the 1953 Act (re-registration where parents not married) applies where an entry relating to a person's birth has been made in the Gender Recognition Register as where the birth of a child has been registered under that Act.

(2) In its application by virtue of sub-paragraph (1) section 10A has effect—

    (a)   as if the reference to the registrar in subsection (1) were to the Registrar General, and
    (b)   with the omission of subsection (2).

(3) Sections 14 and 14A of the 1953 Act (re-registration in cases of legitimation and after declaration of parentage) apply where an entry relating to a person's birth has been made in the Gender Recognition Register as if the references in those sections to the Registrar General authorising re-registration of the person's birth were to the Registrar General's re-registering it.

8 Correction etc of Gender Recognition Register

(1) Any power or duty of the Registrar General or any other person to correct, alter, amend, mark or cancel the marking of a person's UK birth register entry is exercisable, or falls to be performed, by the Registrar General in relation to an entry in the Gender Recognition Register which—

    (a)   relates to that person, and
    (b)   under paragraph 4(1) is included in the index which includes the person's UK birth register entry.

(2) If the person's UK birth register entry is an entry in the Gender Recognition Register, the references in sub-paragraph (1) to the person's UK birth register entry are to the most recent entry within section 10(2)(a) or (b) containing a record of the person's birth or adoption which is not an entry in the Gender Recognition Register.

(3) The Registrar General may correct the Gender Recognition Register by entry in the margin (without any alteration of the original entry) in consequence of the issue of a full gender recognition certificate after an application under section 6(1).

9 Revocation of gender recognition certificate etc

(1) This paragraph applies if, after an entry has been made in the Gender Recognition Register in relation to a person, the High Court or the Court of Session makes an order under section 8(6) quashing the decision to grant the person's application under section 1(1), 5(2) or 5A(2).

(2) The High Court or the Court of Session must inform the Registrar General.

(3) Subject to any appeal, the Registrar General must—

    (a)   cancel the entry in the Gender Recognition Register, and

(b)   cancel, or secure the cancellation, of any marking of an entry relating to the person made by virtue of paragraph 3(1)(b).

10 Evidence

(1) Section 34(5) of the 1953 Act (certified copy of entry in register under that Act deemed to be true copy) applies in relation to the Gender Recognition Register as if it were a register under that Act.

(2) A certified copy of an entry made in the Gender Recognition Register in relation to a person is to be received, without further or other proof, as evidence—

(a)   if the relevant index is the index of the Adopted Children Register, of the matters of which a certified copy of an entry in that Register is evidence,

(b)   if the relevant index is the index of the Parental Order Register, of the matters of which a certified copy of an entry in that Register is evidence, and

(c)   otherwise, of the person's birth.

(3) And any certified copy which is receivable in evidence of any matter in Northern Ireland by virtue of paragraph 31(2)(a) or (b) of this Schedule is also receivable as evidence of that matter in England and Wales.

11

Amendments—CPA 2004, s 250(1), (8); Legislative and Regulatory Reform Act 2006, s 33; SI 2008/678.

****

HOUSING ACT 1985

****

89 Succession to periodic tenancy

(1) This section applies where a secure tenant dies and the tenancy is a periodic tenancy.

(2) Where there is a person qualified to succeed the tenant, the tenancy vests by virtue of this section in that person, or if there is more than one such person in the one to be preferred in accordance with the following rules –

   (a)   the tenant's spouse or civil partner is to be preferred to another member of the tenant's family;

   (b)   of two or more other members of the tenant's family such of them is to be preferred as may be agreed between them or as may, where there is no such agreement, be selected by the landlord.

(3) Where there is no person qualified to succeed the tenant, the tenancy ceases to be a secure tenancy –

   (a)   when it is vested or otherwise disposed of in the course of the administration of the tenant's estate, unless the vesting or other disposal is in pursuance of an order made under –

        (i)   section 24 of the Matrimonial Causes Act 1973 (property adjustment orders made in connection with matrimonial proceedings),

        (ii)   section 17(1) of the Matrimonial and Family Proceedings Act 1984 (property adjustment orders after overseas divorce, &c),

        (iii)   paragraph 1 of Schedule 1 to the Children Act 1989 (orders for financial relief against parents), or

        (iv)   Part 2 of Schedule 5, or paragraph 9(2) or (3) of Schedule 7, to the Civil Partnership Act 2004 (property adjustment orders in connection with civil partnership proceedings or after overseas dissolution of civil partnership, etc); or

   (b)   when it is known that when the tenancy is so vested or disposed of it will not be in pursuance of such an order.

(4) A tenancy which ceases to be a secure tenancy by virtue of this section cannot subsequently become a secure tenancy.

Amendments—Civil Partnership Act 2004, s 81, Sch 8, para 22(1), (3).

****

A4.6

****

HOUSING ACT 1988

MISCELLANEOUS

17 Succession to assured periodic tenancy by spouse

(1) In any case where –

    (a)   the sole tenant under an assured periodic tenancy dies, and

    (b)   immediately before the death, the tenant's spouse or civil partner was occupying the dwelling-house as his or her only or principal home, and

    (c)   the tenant was not himself a successor, as defined in subsection (2) or subsection (3) below,

then, on the death, the tenancy vests by virtue of this section in the spouse or civil partner (and, accordingly, does not devolve under the tenant's will or intestacy).

(2) For the purposes of this section, a tenant is a successor in relation to a tenancy if –

    (a)   the tenancy became vested in him either by virtue of this section or under the will or intestacy of a previous tenant; or

    (b)   at some time before the tenant's death the tenancy was a joint tenancy held by himself and one or more other persons and, prior to his death, he became the sole tenant by survivorship; or

    (c)   he became entitled to the tenancy as mentioned in section 39(5) below.

(3) For the purposes of this section, a tenant is also a successor in relation to a tenancy (in this subsection referred to as "the new tenancy") which was granted to him (alone or jointly with others) if –

    (a)   at some time before the grant of the new tenancy, he was, by virtue of subsection (2) above, a successor in relation to an earlier tenancy of the same or substantially the same dwelling-house as is let under the new tenancy; and

    (b)   at all times since he became such a successor he has been a tenant (alone or jointly with others) of the dwelling-house which is let under the new tenancy or of a dwelling-house which is substantially the same as that dwelling-house.

(4) For the purposes of this section –

    (a)   a person who was living with the tenant as his or her wife or husband shall be treated as the tenant's spouse, and

    (b)   a person who was living with the tenant as if they were civil partners shall be treated as the tenant's civil partner.

(5) If, on the death of the tenant, there is, by virtue of subsection (4) above, more than one person who fulfils the condition in subsection (1)(b) or above, such one of them as may be decided by agreement or, in default of agreement, by the county court shall for the purposes of this section be treated (according to whether that one of them is of the opposite sex to, or of the same sex as, the tenant) as the tenant's spouse or the tenant's civil partner.

Amendments—Civil Partnership Act 2004, s 81, Sch 8, para 41(1), (2).

****

A4.7

HUMAN FERTILISATION AND EMBRYOLOGY ACT 2008

ARRANGEMENT OF SECTIONS

PART 2
PARENTHOOD IN CASES INVOLVING ASSISTED REPRODUCTION

Meaning of "mother"

Section		*Page*
33	Meaning of "mother"	623
34	Application of sections 35 to 47	623
35	Woman married at time of treatment	623
36	Treatment provided to woman where agreed fatherhood conditions apply	623
37	The agreed fatherhood conditions	623
38	Further provision relating to sections 35 and 36	624
39	Use of sperm, or transfer of embryo, after death of man providing sperm	624
40	Embryo transferred after death of husband etc who did not provide sperm	625
41	Persons not to be treated as father	626

Cases in which woman to be other parent

42	Woman in civil partnership at time of treatment	626
43	Treatment provided to woman who agrees that second woman to be parent	626
44	The agreed female parenthood conditions	626
45	Further provision relating to sections 42 and 43	627
46	Embryo transferred after death of civil partner or intended female parent	627
47	Woman not to be other parent merely because of egg donation	628

Effect of sections 33 to 47

| 48 | Effect of sections 33 to 47 | 628 |

References to parties to marriage or civil partnership

| 49 | Meaning of references to parties to a marriage | 629 |
| 50 | Meaning of references to parties to a civil partnership | 629 |

Further provision about registration by virtue of section 39, 40 or 46

| 51 | Meaning of "relevant register of births" | 630 |
| 52 | Late election by mother with consent of Registrar General | 630 |

Interpretation of references to father etc where woman is other parent

| 53 | Interpretation of references to father etc | 630 |

Parental orders

| 54 | Parental orders | 631 |
| 55 | Parental orders: supplementary provision | 632 |

Amendments of enactments

| 56 | Amendments relating to parenthood in cases involving assisted reproduction | 632 |

General

| 57 | Repeals and transitional provision relating to Part 2 | 633 |
| 58 | Interpretation of Part 2 | 633 |

****

PART 2
PARENTHOOD IN CASES INVOLVING ASSISTED REPRODUCTION

Meaning of "mother"

33 Meaning of "mother"

(1) The woman who is carrying or has carried a child as a result of the placing in her of an embryo or of sperm and eggs, and no other woman, is to be treated as the mother of the child.

(2) Subsection (1) does not apply to any child to the extent that the child is treated by virtue of adoption as not being the woman's child.

(3) Subsection (1) applies whether the woman was in the United Kingdom or elsewhere at the time of the placing in her of the embryo or the sperm and eggs.

34 Application of sections 35 to 47

(1) Sections 35 to 47 apply, in the case of a child who is being or has been carried by a woman (referred to in those sections as "W") as a result of the placing in her of an embryo or of sperm and eggs or her artificial insemination, to determine who is to be treated as the other parent of the child.

(2) Subsection (1) has effect subject to the provisions of sections 39, 40 and 46 limiting the purposes for which a person is treated as the child's other parent by virtue of those sections.

35 Woman married at time of treatment

(1) If –

    (a)   at the time of the placing in her of the embryo or of the sperm and eggs or of her artificial insemination, W was a party to a marriage, and

    (b)   the creation of the embryo carried by her was not brought about with the sperm of the other party to the marriage,

then, subject to section 38(2) to (4), the other party to the marriage is to be treated as the father of the child unless it is shown that he did not consent to the placing in her of the embryo or the sperm and eggs or to her artificial insemination (as the case may be).

(2) This section applies whether W was in the United Kingdom or elsewhere at the time mentioned in subsection (1)(a).

36 Treatment provided to woman where agreed fatherhood conditions apply

If no man is treated by virtue of section 35 as the father of the child and no woman is treated by virtue of section 42 as a parent of the child but –

    (a)   the embryo or the sperm and eggs were placed in W, or W was artificially inseminated, in the course of treatment services provided in the United Kingdom by a person to whom a licence applies,

    (b)   at the time when the embryo or the sperm and eggs were placed in W, or W was artificially inseminated, the agreed fatherhood conditions (as set out in section 37) were satisfied in relation to a man, in relation to treatment provided to W under the licence,

    (c)   the man remained alive at that time, and

    (d)   the creation of the embryo carried by W was not brought about with the man's sperm,

then, subject to section 38(2) to (4), the man is to be treated as the father of the child.

37 The agreed fatherhood conditions

(1) The agreed fatherhood conditions referred to in section 36(b) are met in relation to a man ("M") in relation to treatment provided to W under a licence if, but only if, –

(a)   M has given the person responsible a notice stating that he consents to being treated as the father of any child resulting from treatment provided to W under the licence,

(b)   W has given the person responsible a notice stating that she consents to M being so treated,

(c)   neither M nor W has, since giving notice under paragraph (a) or (b), given the person responsible notice of the withdrawal of M's or W's consent to M being so treated,

(d)   W has not, since the giving of the notice under paragraph (b), given the person responsible –

   (i)   a further notice under that paragraph stating that she consents to another man being treated as the father of any resulting child, or

   (ii)   a notice under section 44(1)(b) stating that she consents to a woman being treated as a parent of any resulting child, and

(e)   W and M are not within prohibited degrees of relationship in relation to each other.

(2) A notice under subsection (1)(a), (b) or (c) must be in writing and must be signed by the person giving it.

(3) A notice under subsection (1)(a), (b) or (c) by a person ("S") who is unable to sign because of illness, injury or physical disability is to be taken to comply with the requirement of subsection (2) as to signature if it is signed at the direction of S, in the presence of S and in the presence of at least one witness who attests the signature.

38 Further provision relating to sections 35 and 36

(1) Where a person is to be treated as the father of the child by virtue of section 35 or 36, no other person is to be treated as the father of the child.

(2) In England and Wales and Northern Ireland, sections 35 and 36 do not affect any presumption, applying by virtue of the rules of common law, that a child is the legitimate child of the parties to a marriage.

(3) In Scotland, sections 35 and 36 do not apply in relation to any child who, by virtue of any enactment or other rule of law, is treated as the child of the parties to a marriage.

(4) Sections 35 and 36 do not apply to any child to the extent that the child is treated by virtue of adoption as not being the man's child.

39 Use of sperm, or transfer of embryo, after death of man providing sperm

(1) If –

(a)   the child has been carried by W as a result of the placing in her of an embryo or of sperm and eggs or her artificial insemination,

(b)   the creation of the embryo carried by W was brought about by using the sperm of a man after his death, or the creation of the embryo was brought about using the sperm of a man before his death but the embryo was placed in W after his death,

(c)   the man consented in writing (and did not withdraw the consent)—

   (i)   to the use of his sperm after his death which brought about the creation of the embryo carried by W or (as the case may be) to the placing in W after his death of the embryo which was brought about using his sperm before his death, and

   (ii)   to being treated for the purpose mentioned in subsection (3) as the father of any resulting child,

(d)   W has elected in writing not later than the end of the period of 42 days from the day on which the child was born for the man to be treated for the purpose mentioned in subsection (3) as the father of the child, and

(e)   no-one else is to be treated –

   (i)   as the father of the child by virtue of section 35 or 36 or by virtue of section 38(2) or (3), or

   (ii)   as a parent of the child by virtue of section 42 or 43 or by virtue of adoption,

then the man is to be treated for the purpose mentioned in subsection (3) as the father of the child.

(2) Subsection (1) applies whether W was in the United Kingdom or elsewhere at the time of the placing in her of the embryo or of the sperm and eggs or of her artificial insemination.

(3) The purpose referred to in subsection (1) is the purpose of enabling the man's particulars to be entered as the particulars of the child's father in a relevant register of births.

(4) In the application of this section to Scotland, for any reference to a period of 42 days there is substituted a reference to a period of 21 days.

40 Embryo transferred after death of husband etc who did not provide sperm

(1) If –

   (a)   the child has been carried by W as a result of the placing in her of an embryo,

   (b)   the embryo was created at a time when W was a party to a marriage,

   (c)   the creation of the embryo was not brought about with the sperm of the other party to the marriage,

   (d)   the other party to the marriage died before the placing of the embryo in W,

   (e)   the other party to the marriage consented in writing (and did not withdraw the consent) –

       (i)   to the placing of the embryo in W after his death, and

       (ii)   to being treated for the purpose mentioned in subsection (4) as the father of any resulting child,

   (f)   W has elected in writing not later than the end of the period of 42 days from the day on which the child was born for the man to be treated for the purpose mentioned in subsection (4) as the father of the child, and

   (g)   no-one else is to be treated –

       (i)   as the father of the child by virtue of section 35 or 36 or by virtue of section 38(2) or (3), or

       (ii)   as a parent of the child by virtue of section 42 or 43 or by virtue of adoption,

then the man is to be treated for the purpose mentioned in subsection (4) as the father of the child.

(2) If—

   (a)   the child has been carried by W as a result of the placing in her of an embryo,

   (b)   the embryo was not created at a time when W was a party to a marriage or a civil partnership but was created in the course of treatment services provided to W in the United Kingdom by a person to whom a licence applies,

   (c)   a man consented in writing (and did not withdraw the consent) –

       (i)   to the placing of the embryo in W after his death, and

       (ii)   to being treated for the purpose mentioned in subsection (4) as the father of any resulting child,

   (d)   the creation of the embryo was not brought about with the sperm of that man,

   (e)   the man died before the placing of the embryo in W,

   (f)   immediately before the man's death, the agreed fatherhood conditions set out in section 37 were met in relation to the man in relation to treatment proposed to be provided to W in the United Kingdom by a person to whom a licence applies,

   (g)   W has elected in writing not later than the end of the period of 42 days from the day on which the child was born for the man to be treated for the purpose mentioned in subsection (4) as the father of the child, and

   (h)   no-one else is to be treated –

       (i)   as the father of the child by virtue of section 35 or 36 or by virtue of section 38(2) or (3), or

       (ii)   as a parent of the child by virtue of section 42 or 43 or by virtue of adoption,

then the man is to be treated for the purpose mentioned in subsection (4) as the father of the child.

(3) Subsections (1) and (2) apply whether W was in the United Kingdom or elsewhere at the time of the placing in her of the embryo.

(4) The purpose referred to in subsections (1) and (2) is the purpose of enabling the man's particulars to be entered as the particulars of the child's father in a relevant register of births.

(5) In the application of this section to Scotland, for any reference to a period of 42 days there is substituted a reference to a period of 21 days.

41 Persons not to be treated as father

(1) Where the sperm of a man who had given such consent as is required by paragraph 5 of Schedule 3 to the 1990 Act (consent to use of gametes for purposes of treatment services or non-medical fertility services) was used for a purpose for which such consent was required, he is not to be treated as the father of the child.

(2) Where the sperm of a man, or an embryo the creation of which was brought about with his sperm, was used after his death, he is not, subject to section 39, to be treated as the father of the child.

(3) Subsection (2) applies whether W was in the United Kingdom or elsewhere at the time of the placing in her of the embryo or of the sperm and eggs or of her artificial insemination.

Cases in which woman to be other parent

42 Woman in civil partnership at time of treatment

(1) If at the time of the placing in her of the embryo or the sperm and eggs or of her artificial insemination, W was a party to a civil partnership, then subject to section 45(2) to (4), the other party to the civil partnership is to be treated as a parent of the child unless it is shown that she did not consent to the placing in W of the embryo or the sperm and eggs or to her artificial insemination (as the case may be).

(2) This section applies whether W was in the United Kingdom or elsewhere at the time mentioned in subsection (1).

43 Treatment provided to woman who agrees that second woman to be parent

If no man is treated by virtue of section 35 as the father of the child and no woman is treated by virtue of section 42 as a parent of the child but –

    (a)   the embryo or the sperm and eggs were placed in W, or W was artificially inseminated, in the course of treatment services provided in the United Kingdom by a person to whom a licence applies,

    (b)   at the time when the embryo or the sperm and eggs were placed in W, or W was artificially inseminated, the agreed female parenthood conditions (as set out in section 44) were met in relation to another woman, in relation to treatment provided to W under that licence, and

    (c)   the other woman remained alive at that time,

then, subject to section 45(2) to (4), the other woman is to be treated as a parent of the child.

44 The agreed female parenthood conditions

(1) The agreed female parenthood conditions referred to in section 43(b) are met in relation to another woman ("P") in relation to treatment provided to W under a licence if, but only if, –

    (a)   P has given the person responsible a notice stating that P consents to P being treated as a parent of any child resulting from treatment provided to W under the licence,

    (b)   W has given the person responsible a notice stating that W agrees to P being so treated,

    (c)   neither W nor P has, since giving notice under paragraph (a) or (b), given the person responsible notice of the withdrawal of P's or W's consent to P being so treated,

    (d)   W has not, since the giving of the notice under paragraph (b), given the person responsible –

(i)   a further notice under that paragraph stating that W consents to a woman other than P being treated as a parent of any resulting child, or

(ii)   a notice under section 37(1)(b) stating that W consents to a man being treated as the father of any resulting child, and

(e)   W and P are not within prohibited degrees of relationship in relation to each other.

(2) A notice under subsection (1)(a), (b) or (c) must be in writing and must be signed by the person giving it.

(3) A notice under subsection (1)(a), (b) or (c) by a person ("S") who is unable to sign because of illness, injury or physical disability is to be taken to comply with the requirement of subsection (2) as to signature if it is signed at the direction of S, in the presence of S and in the presence of at least one witness who attests the signature.

45 Further provision relating to sections 42 and 43

(1) Where a woman is treated by virtue of section 42 or 43 as a parent of the child, no man is to be treated as the father of the child.

(2) In England and Wales and Northern Ireland, sections 42 and 43 do not affect any presumption, applying by virtue of the rules of common law, that a child is the legitimate child of the parties to a marriage.

(3) In Scotland, sections 42 and 43 do not apply in relation to any child who, by virtue of any enactment or other rule of law, is treated as the child of the parties to a marriage.

(4) Sections 42 and 43 do not apply to any child to the extent that the child is treated by virtue of adoption as not being the woman's child.

46 Embryo transferred after death of civil partner or intended female parent

(1) If –

(a)   the child has been carried by W as the result of the placing in her of an embryo,

(b)   the embryo was created at a time when W was a party to a civil partnership,

(c)   the other party to the civil partnership died before the placing of the embryo in W,

(d)   the other party to the civil partnership consented in writing (and did not withdraw the consent) –

    (i)   to the placing of the embryo in W after the death of the other party, and

    (ii)   to being treated for the purpose mentioned in subsection (4) as the parent of any resulting child,

(e)   W has elected in writing not later than the end of the period of 42 days from the day on which the child was born for the other party to the civil partnership to be treated for the purpose mentioned in subsection (4) as the parent of the child, and

(f)   no one else is to be treated –

    (i)   as the father of the child by virtue of section 35 or 36 or by virtue of section 45(2) or (3), or

    (ii)   as a parent of the child by virtue of section 42 or 43 or by virtue of adoption,

then the other party to the civil partnership is to be treated for the purpose mentioned in subsection (4) as a parent of the child.

(2) If –

(a)   the child has been carried by W as the result of the placing in her of an embryo,

(b)   the embryo was not created at a time when W was a party to a marriage or a civil partnership, but was created in the course of treatment services provided to W in the United Kingdom by a person to whom a licence applies,

(c)   another woman consented in writing (and did not withdraw the consent)—

    (i)   to the placing of the embryo in W after the death of the other woman, and

    (ii)   to being treated for the purpose mentioned in subsection (4) as the parent of any resulting child,

(d)   the other woman died before the placing of the embryo in W,

(e)   immediately before the other woman's death, the agreed female parenthood conditions set out in section 44 were met in relation to the other woman in relation to treatment proposed to be provided to W in the United Kingdom by a person to whom a licence applies,

(f)   W has elected in writing not later than the end of the period of 42 days from the day on which the child was born for the other woman to be treated for the purpose mentioned in subsection (4) as the parent of the child, and

(g)   no one else is to be treated –

    (i)   as the father of the child by virtue of section 35 or 36 or by virtue of section 45(2) or (3), or

    (ii)   as a parent of the child by virtue of section 42 or 43 or by virtue of adoption,

then the other woman is to be treated for the purpose mentioned in subsection (4) as a parent of the child.

(3) Subsections (1) and (2) apply whether W was in the United Kingdom or elsewhere at the time of the placing in her of the embryo.

(4) The purpose referred to in subsections (1) and (2) is the purpose of enabling the deceased woman's particulars to be entered as the particulars of the child's other parent in a relevant register of births.

(5) In the application of subsections (1) and (2) to Scotland, for any reference to a period of 42 days there is substituted a reference to a period of 21 days.

47 Woman not to be other parent merely because of egg donation

A woman is not to be treated as the parent of a child whom she is not carrying and has not carried, except where she is so treated –

(a)   by virtue of section 42 or 43, or

(b)   by virtue of section 46 (for the purpose mentioned in subsection (4) of that section), or

(c)   by virtue of adoption.

Effect of sections 33 to 47

48 Effect of sections 33 to 47

(1) Where by virtue of section 33, 35, 36, 42 or 43 a person is to be treated as the mother, father or parent of a child, that person is to be treated in law as the mother, father or parent (as the case may be) of the child for all purposes.

(2) Where by virtue of section 33, 38, 41, 45 or 47 a person is not to be treated as a parent of the child, that person is to be treated in law as not being a parent of the child for any purpose.

(3) Where section 39(1) or 40(1) or (2) applies, the deceased man –

(a)   is to be treated in law as the father of the child for the purpose mentioned in section 39(3) or 40(4), but

(b)   is to be treated in law as not being the father of the child for any other purpose.

(4) Where section 46(1) or (2) applies, the deceased woman –

(a)   is to be treated in law as a parent of the child for the purpose mentioned in section 46(4), but

(b)   is to be treated in law as not being a parent of the child for any other purpose.

(5) Where any of subsections (1) to (4) has effect, references to any relationship between two people in any enactment, deed or other instrument or document (whenever passed or made) are to be read accordingly.

(6) In relation to England and Wales and Northern Ireland, a child who –

(a)   has a parent by virtue of section 42, or

(b)   has a parent by virtue of section 43 who is at any time during the period beginning with the time mentioned in section 43(b) and ending with the time of the child's birth a party to a civil partnership with the child's mother,

is the legitimate child of the child's parents.

(7) In relation to England and Wales and Northern Ireland, nothing in the provisions of section 33(1) or sections 35 to 47, read with this section –

(a)   affects the succession to any dignity or title of honour or renders any person capable of succeeding to or transmitting a right to succeed to any such dignity or title, or

(b)   affects the devolution of any property limited (expressly or not) to devolve (as nearly as the law permits) along with any dignity or title of honour.

(8) In relation to Scotland –

(a)   those provisions do not apply to any title, coat of arms, honour or dignity transmissible on the death of its holder or affect the succession to any such title, coat of arms or dignity or its devolution, and

(b)   where the terms of any deed provide that any property or interest in property is to devolve along with a title, coat of arms, honour or dignity, nothing in those provisions is to prevent that property or interest from so devolving.

References to parties to marriage or civil partnership

49 Meaning of references to parties to a marriage

(1) The references in sections 35 to 47 to the parties to a marriage at any time there referred to –

(a)   are to the parties to a marriage subsisting at that time, unless a judicial separation was then in force, but

(b)   include the parties to a void marriage if either or both of them reasonably believed at that time that the marriage was valid; and for the purposes of those sections it is to be presumed, unless the contrary is shown, that one of them reasonably believed at that time that the marriage was valid.

(2) In subsection (1)(a) "judicial separation" includes a legal separation obtained in a country outside the British Islands and recognised in the United Kingdom.

50 Meaning of references to parties to a civil partnership

(1) The references in sections 35 to 47 to the parties to a civil partnership at any time there referred to—

(a)   are to the parties to a civil partnership subsisting at that time, unless a separation order was then in force, but

(b)   include the parties to a void civil partnership if either or both of them reasonably believed at that time that the civil partnership was valid; and for the purposes of those sections it is to be presumed, unless the contrary is shown, that one of them reasonably believed at that time that the civil partnership was valid.

(2) The reference in section 48(6)(b) to a civil partnership includes a reference to a void civil partnership if either or both of the parties reasonably believed at the time when they registered as civil partners of each other that the civil partnership was valid; and for this purpose it is to be presumed, unless the contrary is shown, that one of them reasonably believed at that time that the civil partnership was valid.

(3) In subsection (1)(a), "separation order" means –

(a)   a separation order under section 37(1)(d) or 161(1)(d) of the Civil Partnership Act 2004 (c 33),

(b)   a decree of separation under section 120(2) of that Act, or

(c)   a legal separation obtained in a country outside the United Kingdom and recognised in the United Kingdom.

Further provision about registration by virtue of section 39, 40 or 46

51 Meaning of "relevant register of births"

For the purposes of this Part a "relevant register of births", in relation to a birth, is whichever of the following is relevant –

(a)   a register of live-births or still-births kept under the Births and Deaths Registration Act 1953 (c 20),

(b)   a register of births or still-births kept under the Registration of Births, Deaths and Marriages (Scotland) Act 1965 (c 49), or

(c)   a register of live-births or still-births kept under the Births and Deaths Registration (Northern Ireland) Order 1976 (SI 1976/1041 (NI 14)).

52 Late election by mother with consent of Registrar General

(1) The requirement under section 39(1), 40(1) or (2) or 46(1) or (2) as to the making of an election (which requires an election to be made either on or before the day on which the child was born or within the period of 42 or, as the case may be, 21 days from that day) is nevertheless to be treated as satisfied if the required election is made after the end of that period but with the consent of the Registrar General under subsection (2).

(2) The Registrar General may at any time consent to the making of an election after the end of the period mentioned in subsection (1) if, on an application made to him in accordance with such requirements as he may specify, he is satisfied that there is a compelling reason for giving his consent to the making of such an election.

(3) In this section "the Registrar General" means the Registrar General for England and Wales, the Registrar General of Births, Deaths and Marriages for Scotland or (as the case may be) the Registrar General for Northern Ireland.

Interpretation of references to father etc where woman is other parent

53 Interpretation of references to father etc

(1) Subsections (2) and (3) have effect, subject to subsections (4) and (6), for the interpretation of any enactment, deed or any other instrument or document (whenever passed or made).

(2) Any reference (however expressed) to the father of a child who has a parent by virtue of section 42 or 43 is to be read as a reference to the woman who is a parent of the child by virtue of that section.

(3) Any reference (however expressed) to evidence of paternity is, in relation to a woman who is a parent by virtue of section 42 or 43, to be read as a reference to evidence of parentage.

(4) This section does not affect the interpretation of the enactments specified in subsection (5) (which make express provision for the case where a child has a parent by virtue of section 42 or 43).

(5) Those enactments are –

(a)   the Legitimacy Act (Northern Ireland) 1928 (c 5 (NI)),

(b)   the Schedule to the Population (Statistics) Act 1938 (c 12),

(c)   the Births and Deaths Registration Act 1953 (c 20),

(d)   the Registration of Births, Deaths and Marriages (Special Provisions) Act 1957 (c 58),

(e)   Part 2 of the Registration of Births, Deaths and Marriages (Scotland) Act 1965 (c 49),

(f)   the Congenital Disabilities (Civil Liability) Act 1976 (c 28),

(g)   the Legitimacy Act 1976 (c 31),

(h)   the Births and Deaths Registration (Northern Ireland) Order 1976 (SI 1976/1041 (NI 14)),

(i)   the British Nationality Act 1981 (c 61),
(j)   the Family Law Reform Act 1987 (c 42),
(k)   Parts 1 and 2 of the Children Act 1989 (c 41),
(l)   Part 1 of the Children (Scotland) Act 1995 (c 36),
(m)   section 1 of the Criminal Law (Consolidation) (Scotland) Act 1995 (c 39), and
(n)   Parts 2, 3 and 14 of the Children (Northern Ireland) Order 1995 (SI 1995/755 (NI 2)).

(6) This section does not affect the interpretation of references that fall to be read in accordance with section 1(2)(a) or (b) of the Family Law Reform Act 1987 or Article 155(2)(a) or (b) of the Children (Northern Ireland) Order 1995 (references to a person whose father and mother were, or were not, married to each other at the time of the person's birth).

Parental orders

54 Parental orders

(1) On an application made by two people ("the applicants"), the court may make an order providing for a child to be treated in law as the child of the applicants if –

(a)   the child has been carried by a woman who is not one of the applicants, as a result of the placing in her of an embryo or sperm and eggs or her artificial insemination,
(b)   the gametes of at least one of the applicants were used to bring about the creation of the embryo, and
(c)   the conditions in subsections (2) to (8) are satisfied.

(2) The applicants must be –

(a)   husband and wife,
(b)   civil partners of each other, or
(c)   two persons who are living as partners in an enduring family relationship and are not within prohibited degrees of relationship in relation to each other.

(3) Except in a case falling within subsection (11), the applicants must apply for the order during the period of 6 months beginning with the day on which the child is born.

(4) At the time of the application and the making of the order –

(a)   the child's home must be with the applicants, and
(b)   either or both of the applicants must be domiciled in the United Kingdom or in the Channel Islands or the Isle of Man.

(5) At the time of the making of the order both the applicants must have attained the age of 18.

(6) The court must be satisfied that both –

(a)   the woman who carried the child, and
(b)   any other person who is a parent of the child but is not one of the applicants (including any man who is the father by virtue of section 35 or 36 or any woman who is a parent by virtue of section 42 or 43),

have freely, and with full understanding of what is involved, agreed unconditionally to the making of the order.

(7) Subsection (6) does not require the agreement of a person who cannot be found or is incapable of giving agreement; and the agreement of the woman who carried the child is ineffective for the purpose of that subsection if given by her less than six weeks after the child's birth.

(8) The court must be satisfied that no money or other benefit (other than for expenses reasonably incurred) has been given or received by either of the applicants for or in consideration of –

(a)   the making of the order,
(b)   any agreement required by subsection (6),
(c)   the handing over of the child to the applicants, or
(d)   the making of arrangements with a view to the making of the order,

unless authorised by the court.

(9) For the purposes of an application under this section –

   (a)   in relation to England and Wales, section 92(7) to (10) of, and Part 1 of Schedule 11 to, the Children Act 1989 (c 41) (jurisdiction of courts) apply for the purposes of this section to determine the meaning of "the court" as they apply for the purposes of that Act and proceedings on the application are to be "family proceedings" for the purposes of that Act,

   (b)   in relation to Scotland, "the court" means the Court of Session or the sheriff court of the sheriffdom within which the child is, and

   (c)   in relation to Northern Ireland, "the court" means the High Court or any county court within whose division the child is.

(10) Subsection (1)(a) applies whether the woman was in the United Kingdom or elsewhere at the time of the placing in her of the embryo or the sperm and eggs or her artificial insemination.

(11) An application which –

   (a)   relates to a child born before the coming into force of this section, and

   (b)   is made by two persons who, throughout the period applicable under subsection (2) of section 30 of the 1990 Act, were not eligible to apply for an order under that section in relation to the child as husband and wife,

may be made within the period of six months beginning with the day on which this section comes into force.

55 Parental orders: supplementary provision

(1) The Secretary of State may by regulations provide –

   (a)   for any provision of the enactments about adoption to have effect, with such modifications (if any) as may be specified in the regulations, in relation to orders under section 54, and applications for such orders, as it has effect in relation to adoption, and applications for adoption orders, and

   (b)   for references in any enactment to adoption, an adopted child or an adoptive relationship to be read (respectively) as references to the effect of an order under section 54, a child to whom such an order applies and a relationship arising by virtue of the enactments about adoption, as applied by the regulations, and for similar expressions in connection with adoption to be read accordingly.

(2) The regulations may include such incidental or supplemental provision as appears to the Secretary of State to be necessary or desirable in consequence of any provision made by virtue of subsection (1)(a) or (b).

(3) In this section "the enactments about adoption" means –

   (a)   the Adoption (Scotland) Act 1978 (c 28),
   (b)   the Adoption and Children Act 2002 (c 38),
   (c)   the Adoption and Children (Scotland) Act 2007 (asp 4), and
   (d)   the Adoption (Northern Ireland) Order 1987 (SI 1987/2203 (NI 22)).

Amendments of enactments

56 Amendments relating to parenthood in cases involving assisted reproduction

Schedule 6 contains amendments related to the provisions of this Part.

General

57 Repeals and transitional provision relating to Part 2

(1) Sections 33 to 48 have effect only in relation to children carried by women as a result of the placing in them of embryos or of sperm and eggs, or their artificial insemination (as the case may be), after the commencement of those sections.

(2) Sections 27 to 29 of the 1990 Act (which relate to status) do not have effect in relation to children carried by women as a result of the placing in them of embryos or of sperm and eggs, or their artificial insemination (as the case may be), after the commencement of sections 33 to 48.

(3) Section 30 of the 1990 Act (parental orders in favour of gamete donors) ceases to have effect.

(4) Subsection (3) does not affect the validity of any order made under section 30 of the 1990 Act before the coming into force of that subsection.

58 Interpretation of Part 2

(1) In this Part "enactment" means an enactment contained in, or in an instrument made under –

    (a)   an Act of Parliament,
    (b)   an Act of the Scottish Parliament,
    (c)   a Measure or Act of the National Assembly for Wales, or
    (d)   Northern Ireland legislation.

(2) For the purposes of this Part, two persons are within prohibited degrees of relationship if one is the other's parent, grandparent, sister, brother, aunt or uncle; and in this subsection references to relationships –

    (a)   are to relationships of the full blood or half blood or, in the case of an adopted person, such of those relationships as would subsist but for adoption, and
    (b)   include the relationship of a child with his adoptive, or former adoptive, parents,

but do not include any other adoptive relationships.

(3) Other expressions used in this Part and in the 1990 Act have the same meaning in this Part as in that Act.

****

A4.8

INHERITANCE (PROVISION FOR FAMILY AND DEPENDANTS) ACT 1975

1 Application for financial provision from deceased's estate

(1) Where after the commencement of this Act a person dies domiciled in England and Wales and is survived by any of the following persons –

(a) he spouse or civil partner of the deceased;

(b) a former spouse or former civil partner of the deceased, but not one who has formed a subsequent marriage or civil partnership;

(ba) any person (not being a person included in paragraph (a) or (b) above) to whom subsection (1A) or (1B) below applies;

(c) a child of the deceased;

(d) any person (not being a child of the deceased) who, in the case of any marriage or civil partnership to which the deceased was at any time a party, was treated by the deceased as a child of the family in relation to that marriage or civil partnership;

(e) any person (not being a person included in the foregoing paragraphs of this subsection) who immediately before the death of the deceased was being maintained, either wholly or partly, by the deceased;

that person may apply to the court for an order under section 2 of this Act on the ground that the disposition of the deceased's estate effected by his will or the law relating to intestacy, or the combination of his will and that law, is not such as to make reasonable financial provision for the applicant.

(1A) This subsection applies to a person if the deceased died on or after 1st January 1996 and, during the whole of the period of two years ending immediately before the date when the deceased died, the person was living –

(a) In the same household as the deceased, and

(b) as the husband or wife of the deceased.

(1B) This subsection applies to a person if for the whole of the period of two years ending immediately before the date when the deceased died the person was living –

(a) in the same household as the deceased, and

(b) as the civil partner of the deceased.

(2) In this Act "reasonable financial provision" –

(a) in the case of an application made by virtue of subsection (1)(a) above by the husband or wife of the deceased (except where the marriage with the deceased was the subject of a decree of judicial separation and at the date of death the decree was in force and the separation was continuing), means such financial provision as it would be reasonable in all the circumstances of the case for a husband or wife to receive, whether or not that provision is required for his or her maintenance;

(aa) in the case of an application made by virtue of subsection (1)(a) above by the civil partner of the deceased (except where, at the date of death, a separation order under Chapter 2 of Part 2 of the Civil Partnership Act 2004 was in force in relation to the civil partnership and the separation was continuing), means such financial provision as it would be reasonable in all the circumstances of the case for a civil partner to receive, whether or not that provision is required for his or her maintenance;

(b) in the case of any other application made by virtue of subsection (1) above, means such financial provision as it would be reasonable in all the circumstances of the case for the applicant to receive for his maintenance.

(3) For the purposes of subsection (1)(e) above, a person shall be treated as being maintained by the deceased, either wholly or partly, as the case may be, if the deceased, otherwise than for full valuable consideration, was making a substantial contribution in money or money's worth towards the reasonable needs of that person.

Amendments—Civil Partnership Act 2004, s 71, Sch 4, Pt 2, para 15(1), (2); Law Reform (Succession) Act 1995, s 2(2).

2 Powers of court to make orders

(1) Subject to the provisions of this Act, where an application is made for an order under this section, the court may, if it is satisfied that the disposition of the deceased's estate effected by his will or the law relating to intestacy, or the combination of his will and that law, is not such as to make reasonable financial provision for the applicant, make any one or more of the following orders –

(a)   an order for the making to the applicant out of the net estate of the deceased of such periodical payments and for such term as may be specified in the order;

(b)   an order for the payment to the applicant out of that estate of a lump sum of such amount as may be so specified;

(c)   an order for the transfer to the applicant of such property comprised in that estate as may be so specified;

(d)   an order for the settlement for the benefit of the applicant of such property comprised in that estate as may be so specified;

(e)   an order for the acquisition out of property comprised in that estate of such property as may be so specified and for the transfer of the property so acquired to the applicant or for the settlement thereof for his benefit;

(f)   an order varying any ante-nuptial or post-nuptial settlement (including such a settlement made by will) made on the parties to a marriage to which the deceased was one of the parties, the variation being for the benefit of the surviving party to that marriage, or any child of that marriage, or any person who was treated by the deceased as a child of the family in relation to that marriage;

(g)   an order varying any settlement made –

    (i)   during the subsistence of a civil partnership formed by the deceased, or

    (ii)   in anticipation of the formation of a civil partnership by the deceased,

on the civil partners (including such a settlement made by will), the variation being for the benefit of the surviving civil partner, or any child of both the civil partners, or any person who was treated by the deceased as a child of the family in relation to that civil partnership.

(2) An order under subsection (1)(a) above providing for the making out of the net estate of the deceased of periodical payments may provide for –

(a)   payments of such amount as may be specified in the order,

(b)   payments equal to the whole of the income of the net estate or of such portion thereof as may be so specified,

(c)   payments equal to the whole of the income of such part of the net estate as the court may direct to be set aside or appropriated for the making out of the income thereof of payments under this section,

or may provide for the amount of the payments or any of them to be determined in any other way the court thinks fit.

(3) Where an order under subsection (1)(a) above provides for the making of payments of an amount specified in the order, the order may direct that such part of the net estate as may be so specified shall be set aside or appropriated for the making out of the income thereof of those payments; but no larger part of the net estate shall be so set aside or appropriated than is sufficient, at the date of the order, to produce by the income thereof the amount required for the making of those payments.

(4) An order under this section may contain such consequential and supplemental provisions as the court thinks necessary or expedient for the purpose of giving effect to the order or for the

purpose of securing that the order operates fairly as between one beneficiary of the estate of the deceased and another and may, in particular, but without prejudice to the generality of this subsection –

(a)   order any person who holds any property which forms part of the net estate of the deceased to make such payment or transfer such property as may be specified in the order;

(b)   varying the disposition of the deceased's estate effected by the will or the law relating to intestacy, or by both the will and the law relating to intestacy, in such manner as the court thinks fair and reasonable having regard to the provisions of the order and all the circumstances of the case;

(c)   confer on the trustees of any property which is the subject of an order under this section such powers as appear to the court to be necessary or expedient.

Amendments—Civil Partnership Act 2004, s 71, Sch 4, Pt 2, para 15(1), (2).

3 Matters to which court is to have regard in exercising powers under s 2

(1) Where an application is made for an order under section 2 of this Act, the court shall, in determining whether the disposition of the deceased's estate effected by his will or the law relating to intestacy, or the combination of his will and that law, is such as to make reasonable financial provision for the applicant and, if the court considers that reasonable financial provision has not been made, in determining whether and in what manner it shall exercise its powers under that section, have regard to the following matters, that is to say –

(a)   the financial resources and financial needs which the applicant has or is likely to have in the foreseeable future;

(b)   the financial resources and financial needs which any other applicant for an order under section 2 of this Act has or is likely to have in the foreseeable future;

(c)   the financial resources and financial needs which any beneficiary of the estate of the deceased has or is likely to have in the foreseeable future;

(d)   any obligations and responsibilities which the deceased had towards any applicant for an order under the said section 2 or towards any beneficiary of the estate of the deceased;

(e)   the size and nature of the net estate of the deceased;

(f)   any physical or mental disability of any applicant for an order under the said section 2 or any beneficiary of the estate of the deceased;

(g)   any other matter, including the conduct of the applicant or any other person, which in the circumstances of the case the court may consider relevant.

(2) This subsection applies, without prejudice to the generality of paragraph (g) of subsection (1) above, where an application for an order under section 2 of this Act is made by virtue of section 1(1)(a) or (b) of this Act.

The court shall, in addition to the matters specifically mentioned in paragraphs (a) to (f) of that subsection, have regard to –

(a)   the age of the applicant and the duration of the marriage or civil partnership;

(b)   the contribution made by the applicant to the welfare of the family of the deceased, including any contribution made by looking after the home or caring for the family.

In the case of an application by the wife or husband of the deceased, the court shall also, unless at the date of death a decree of judicial separation was in force and the separation was continuing, have regard to the provision which the applicant might reasonably have expected to receive if on the day on which the deceased died the marriage, instead of being terminated by death, had been terminated by a decree of divorce a divorce order.

In the case of an application by the civil partner of the deceased, the court shall also, unless at the date of the death a separation order under Chapter 2 of Part 2 of the Civil Partnership Act 2004 was in force and the separation was continuing, have regard to the provision which the applicant might reasonably have expected to receive if on the day on which the deceased died the civil partnership, instead of being terminated by death, had been terminated by a dissolution order.

(2A) Without prejudice to the generality of paragraph (g) of subsection (1) above, where an application for an order under section 2 of this Act is made by virtue of section 1(1)(ba) of this Act, the court shall, in addition to the matters specifically mentioned in paragraphs (a) to (f) of that subsection, have regard to –

(a)   the age of the applicant and the length of the period during which the applicant lived as the husband or wife or civil partner of the deceased and in the same household as the deceased;

(b)   the contribution made by the applicant to the welfare of the family of the deceased, including any contribution made by looking after the home or caring for the family.

(3) Without prejudice to the generality of paragraph (g) of subsection (1) above, where an application for an order under section 2 of this Act is made by virtue of section 1(1)(c) or 1(1)(d) of this Act, the court shall, in addition to the matters specifically mentioned in paragraphs (a) to (f) of that subsection, have regard to the manner in which the applicant was being or in which he might expect to be educated or trained, and where the application is made by virtue of section 1(1)(d) the court shall also have regard –

(a)   to whether the deceased had assumed any responsibility for the applicant's maintenance and, if so, to the extent to which and the basis upon which the deceased assumed that responsibility and to the length of time for which the deceased discharged that responsibility;

(b)   to whether in assuming and discharging that responsibility the deceased did so knowing that the applicant was not his own child;

(c)   to the liability of any other person to maintain the applicant.

(4) Without prejudice to the generality of paragraph (g) of subsection (1) above, where an application for an order under section 2 of this Act is made by virtue of section 1(1)(e) of this Act, the court shall, in addition to the matters specifically mentioned in paragraphs (a) to (f) of that subsection, have regard to the extent to which and the basis upon which the deceased assumed responsibility for the maintenance of the applicant, and to the length of time for which the deceased discharged that responsibility.

(5) In considering the matters to which the court is required to have regard under this section, the court shall take into account the facts as known to the court at the date of the hearing.

(6) In considering the financial resources of any person for the purposes of this section the court shall take into account his earning capacity and in considering the financial needs of any person for the purposes of this section the court shall take into account his financial obligations and responsibilities.

Amendments—Civil Partnership Act 2004, s 71, Sch 4, Pt 2, para 17(1), (3); Law Reform (Succession) Act 1995, s 2(4).

****

RENT ACT 1977

****

Schedule 1
Statutory Tenancies

PART I
STATUTORY TENANTS BY SUCCESSION

1

Paragraph 2 below shall have effect, subject to section 2(3) of this Act, for the purpose of determining who is the statutory tenant of a dwelling-house by succession after the death of the person (in this Part of this Schedule referred to as "the original tenant") who, immediately before his death, was a protected tenant of the dwelling-house or the statutory tenant of it by virtue of his previous protected tenancy.

2

(1) The surviving spouse, or surviving civil partner, (if any) of the original tenant, if residing in the dwelling-house immediately before the death of the original tenant, shall after the death be the statutory tenant if and so long as he or she occupies the dwelling-house as his or her residence.

(2) For the purposes of this paragraph –

    (a)   a person who was living with the original tenant as his or her wife or husband shall be treated as the spouse of the original tenant, and

    (b)   a person who was living with the original tenant as if they were civil partners shall be treated as the civil partner of the original tenant.

(3) If, immediately after the death of the original tenant, there is, by virtue of sub-paragraph (2) above, more than one person who fulfils the conditions in sub-paragraph (1) above, such one of them as may be decided by agreement or, in default of agreement, by the county court shall for the purposes of this paragraph be treated (according to whether that one of them is of the opposite sex to, or of the same sex as, the original tenant) as the surviving spouse or the surviving civil partner.

3

(1) Where paragraph 2 above does not apply, but a person who was a member of the original tenant's family was residing with him in the dwelling-house at the time of and for the period of 2 years immediately before his death then, after his death, that person or if there is more than one such person such one of them as may be decided by agreement, or in default of agreement by the county court, shall be entitled to an assured tenancy of the dwelling-house by succession.

(2) If the original tenant died within the period of 18 months beginning on the operative date, then, for the purposes of this paragraph, a person who was residing in the dwelling-house with the original tenant at the time of his death and for the period which began 6 months before the operative date and ended at the time of his death shall be taken to have been residing with the original tenant for the period of 2 years immediately before his death.

4

A person who becomes the statutory tenant of a dwelling-house by virtue of paragraph 2 above is in this Part of this Schedule referred to as "the first successor".

5

If, immediately before his death, the first successor was still a statutory tenant, paragraph 6 below shall have effect, for the purpose of determining who is entitled to an assured tenancy of the dwelling-house by succession.

6

(1) Where a person who –

    (a)   was a member of the original tenant's family immediately before that tenant's death, and

    (b)   was a member of the first successor's family immediately before the first successor's death,

was residing in the dwelling-house with the first successor at the time of, and for the period of 2 years immediately before, the first successor's death, that person or, if there is more than one such person, such one of them as may be decided by agreement or, in default of agreement, by the county court shall be entitled to an assured tenancy of the dwelling-house by succession.

(2) If the first successor died within the period of 18 months beginning on the operative date, then, for the purposes of this paragraph, a person who was residing in the dwelling-house with the first successor at the time of his death and for the period which began 6 months before the operative date and ended at the time of his death shall be taken to have been residing with the first successor for the period of 2 years immediately before his death.

7, 8

repealed

9

Paragraphs 5 to 8 above do not apply where the statutory tenancy of the original tenant arose by virtue of section 4 of the Requisitioned Houses and Housing (Amendment) Act 1955 or section 20 of the Rent Act 1965.

10

(1) Where after a succession the successor becomes the tenant of the dwelling-house by the grant to him of another tenancy, "the original tenant" and "the first successor" in this Part of this Schedule shall, in relation to that other tenancy, mean the persons who were respectively the original tenant and the first successor at the time of the succession, and accordingly—

    (a)   if the successor was the first successor, and, immediately before his death he was still the tenant (whether protected or statutory), paragraph 6 above shall apply on his death,

    (b)   if the successor was not the first successor, no person shall become a statutory tenant on his death by virtue of this Part of this Schedule.

(2) Sub-paragraph (1) above applies –

    (a)   even if a successor enters into more than one other tenancy of the dwelling-house, and

    (b)   even if both the first successor and the successor on his death enter into other tenancies of the dwelling-house.

(3) In this paragraph "succession" means the occasion on which a person becomes the statutory tenant of a dwelling-house by virtue of this Part of this Schedule and "successor" shall be construed accordingly.

(4) This paragraph shall apply as respects a succession which took place before 27th August 1972 if, and only if, the tenancy granted after the succession, or the first of those tenancies, was granted on or after that date, and where it does not apply as respects a succession, no account should be taken of that succession in applying this paragraph as respects any later succession.

11

(1) Paragraphs 5 to 8 above do not apply where –

- (a) the tenancy of the original tenant was granted on or after the operative date within the meaning of the Rent (Agriculture) Act 1976, and
- (b) both that tenancy and the statutory tenancy of the first successor were tenancies to which section 99 of this Act applies.

(2) If the tenants under both of the tenancies falling within sub-paragraph (1)(b) above were persons to whom paragraph 7 of Schedule 9 to the Rent (Agriculture) Act 1976 applies, the reference in sub-paragraph (1)(a) above to the operative date shall be taken as a reference to the date of operation for forestry workers within the meaning of that Act.

11A

In this Part of this Schedule "the operative date" means the date on which Part I of the Housing Act 1988 came into force.

Amendments—Housing Act 1988, ss 39, 140, Sch 4, Pt I, para 1, Sch 18; Civil Partnership Act 2004, s 81, Sch 8, para 13(1), (3).

****

A4.10

SURROGACY ARRANGEMENTS ACT 1985

ARRANGEMENT OF SECTIONS

Section		Page
1	Meaning of "surrogate mother", "surrogacy arrangement" and other terms	641
1A	Surrogacy arrangements unenforceable	641
2	Negotiating surrogacy arrangements on a commercial basis etc	641
3	Advertisements about surrogacy	643
4	Offences	644

1 Meaning of "surrogate mother", "surrogacy arrangement" and other terms

(1) The following provisions shall have effect for the interpretation of this Act.

(2) "Surrogate mother" means a woman who carries a child in pursuance of an arrangement –

  (a) made before she began to carry the child, and

  (b) made with a view to any child carried in pursuance of it being handed over to, and parental responsibility being met (so far as practicable) by, another person or other persons.

(3) An arrangement is a surrogacy arrangement if, were a woman to whom the arrangement relates to carry a child in pursuance of it, she would be a surrogate mother.

(4) In determining whether an arrangement is made with such a view as is mentioned in subsection (2) above regard may be had to the circumstances as a whole (and, in particular, where there is a promise or understanding that any payment will or may be made to the woman or for her benefit in respect of the carrying of any child in pursuance of the arrangement, to that promise or understanding).

(5) An arrangement may be regarded as made with such a view though subject to conditions relating to the handing over of any child.

(6) A woman who carries a child is to be treated for the purposes of subsection (2)(*a*) above as beginning to carry it at the time of the insemination or of the placing in her of an embryo, of an egg in the process of fertilisation or of sperm and eggs as the case may be, that results in her carrying the child.

(7) "Body of persons" means a body of persons corporate or unincorporate.

(7A) "Non-profit making body" means a body of persons whose activities are not carried on for profit.

(8) "Payment" means payment in money or money's worth.

(9) This Act applies to arrangements whether or not they are lawful.

Amendments—CA 1989, s 108(5), Sch 13, para 56; HFEA 1990, s 36; SI 1995/755; HFEA 2008, s 59(2).

1A Surrogacy arrangements unenforceable

No surrogacy arrangement is enforceable by or against any of the persons making it.

Amendments—Inserted by HFEA 1990, s 36.

2 Negotiating surrogacy arrangements on a commercial basis etc

(1) No person shall on a commercial basis do any of the following acts in the United Kingdom, that is –

  (a) initiate any negotiations with a view to the making of a surrogacy arrangement, (aa)   take part in any negotiations with a view to the making of a surrogacy arrangement,

(b)   offer or agree to negotiate the making of a surrogacy arrangement, or

(c)   compile any information with a view to its use in making, or negotiating the making of, surrogacy arrangements;

and no person shall in the United Kingdom knowingly cause another to do any of those acts on a commercial basis.

(2) A person who contravenes subsection (1) above is guilty of an offence; but it is not a contravention of that subsection –

(a)   for a woman, with a view to becoming a surrogate mother herself, to do any act mentioned in that subsection or to cause such an act to be done, or

(b)   for any person, with a view to a surrogate mother carrying a child for him, to do such an act or to cause such an act to be done.

(2A) A non-profit making body does not contravene subsection (1) merely because –

(a)   the body does an act falling within subsection (1)(a) or (c) in respect of which any reasonable payment is at any time received by it or another, or

(b)   it does an act falling within subsection (1)(a) or (c) with a view to any reasonable payment being received by it or another in respect of facilitating the making of any surrogacy arrangement.

(2B) A person who knowingly causes a non-profit making body to do an act falling within subsection (1)(*a*) or (*c*) does not contravene subsection (1) merely because –

(a)   any reasonable payment is at any time received by the body or another in respect of the body doing the act, or

(b)   the body does the act with a view to any reasonable payment being received by it or another person in respect of the body facilitating the making of any surrogacy arrangement.

(2C) Any reference in subsection (2A) or (2B) to a reasonable payment in respect of the doing of an act by a non-profit making body is a reference to a payment not exceeding the body's costs reasonably attributable to the doing of the act.

(3) For the purposes of this section, a person does an act on a commercial basis (subject to subsection (4) below) if –

(a)   any payment is at any time received by himself or another in respect of it, or

(b)   he does it with a view to any payment being received by himself or another in respect of making, or negotiating or facilitating the making of, any surrogacy arrangement.

In this subsection "payment" does not include payment to or for the benefit of a surrogate mother or prospective surrogate mother.

(4) In proceedings against a person for an offence under subsection (1) above, he is not to be treated as doing an act on a commercial basis by reason of any payment received by another in respect of the act if it is proved that –

(a)   in a case where the payment was received before he did the act, he did not do the act knowing or having reasonable cause to suspect that any payment had been received in respect of the act; and

(b)   in any other case, he did not do the act with a view to any payment being received in respect of it.

(5) Where –

(a)   a person acting on behalf of a body of persons takes any part in negotiating or facilitating the making of a surrogacy arrangement in the United Kingdom, and

(b)   negotiating or facilitating the making of surrogacy arrangements is an activity of the body, then, if the body at any time receives any payment made by or on behalf of –

    (i)   a woman who carries a child in pursuance of the arrangement,

    (ii)   the person or persons for whom she carries it, or

    (iii) any person connected with the woman or with that person or those persons, the body is guilty of an offence.

For the purposes of this subsection, a payment received by a person connected with a body is to be treated as received by the body.

(5A) A non-profit making body is not guilty of an offence under subsection (5), in respect of the receipt of any payment described in that subsection, merely because a person acting on behalf of the body takes part in facilitating the making of a surrogacy arrangement.

(6) In proceedings against a body for an offence under subsection (5) above, it is a defence to prove that the payment concerned was not made in respect of the arrangement mentioned in paragraph (*a*) of that subsection.

(7) A person who in the United Kingdom takes part in the management or control –

    (a)   of any body of persons, or

    (b)   of any of the activities of any body of persons,

is guilty of an offence if the activity described in subsection (8) below is an activity of the body concerned.

(8) The activity referred to in subsection (7) above is negotiating or facilitating the making of surrogacy arrangements in the United Kingdom, being –

    (a)   arrangements the making of which is negotiated or facilitated on a commercial basis, or

    (b)   arrangements in the case of which payments are received (or treated for the purposes of subsection (5) above as received) by the body concerned in contravention of subsection (5) above.

(8A) A person is not guilty of an offence under subsection (7) if –

    (a)   the body of persons referred to in that subsection is a non-profit making body, and

    (b)   the only activity of that body which falls within subsection (8) is facilitating the making of surrogacy arrangements in the United Kingdom.

(8B) In subsection (8A)(*b*) "facilitating the making of surrogacy arrangements" is to be construed in accordance with subsection (8).

(9) In proceedings against a person for an offence under subsection (7) above, it is a defence to prove that he neither knew nor had reasonable cause to suspect that the activity described in subsection (8) above was an activity of the body concerned; and for the purposes of such proceedings any arrangement falling within subsection (8)(*b*) above shall be disregarded if it is proved that the payment concerned was not made in respect of the arrangement.

Amendments—HFEA 2008, ss 59(3)–(8).

3 Advertisements about surrogacy

(1) This section applies to any advertisement containing an indication (however expressed) –

    (a)   that any person is or may be willing to enter into a surrogacy arrangement or to negotiate or facilitate the making of a surrogacy arrangement, or

    (b)   that any person is looking for a woman willing to become a surrogate mother or for persons wanting a woman to carry a child as a surrogate mother.

(1A) This section does not apply to any advertisement placed by, or on behalf of, a non-profit making body if the advertisement relates only to the doing by the body of acts that would not contravene section 2(1) even if done on a commercial basis (within the meaning of section 2).

(2) Where a newspaper or periodical containing an advertisement to which this section applies is published in the United Kingdom, any proprietor, editor or publisher of the newspaper or periodical is guilty of an offence.

(3) Where an advertisement to which this section applies is conveyed by means of an electronic communications network so as to be seen or heard (or both) in the United Kingdom, any person who in the United Kingdom causes it to be so conveyed knowing it to contain such an indication as is mentioned in subsection (1) above is guilty of an offence.

(4) A person who publishes or causes to be published in the United Kingdom an advertisement to which this section applies (not being an advertisement contained in a newspaper or periodical or conveyed by means of an electronic communications network) is guilty of an offence.

(5) A person who distributes or causes to be distributed in the United Kingdom an advertisement to which this section applies (not being an advertisement contained in a newspaper or periodical published outside the United Kingdom or an advertisement conveyed by means of an electronic communications network) knowing it to contain such an indication as is mentioned in subsection (1) above is guilty of an offence.

(6) (*repealed*)

Amendments—Communications Act 2003, s 406, Schs 17, 19; HFEA 2008, s 59(7).

4 Offences

(1) A person guilty of an offence under this Act shall be liable on summary conviction –

    (a)   in the case of an offence under section 2 to a fine not exceeding level 5 on the standard scale or to imprisonment for a term not exceeding 3 months or both,
    (b)   in the case of an offence under section 3 to a fine not exceeding level 5 on the standard scale.

(2) No proceedings for an offence under this Act shall be instituted –

    (a)   in England and Wales, except by or with the consent of the Director of Public Prosecutions; and
    (b)   in Northern Ireland, except by or with the consent of the Director of Public Prosecutions for Northern Ireland.

(3) Where an offence under this Act committed by a body corporate is proved to have been committed with the consent or connivance of, or to be attributable to any neglect on the part of, any director, manager, secretary or other similar officer of the body corporate or any person who was purporting to act in any such capacity, he as well as the body corporate is guilty of the offence and is liable to be proceeded against and punished accordingly.

(4) Where the affairs of a body corporate are managed by its members, subsection (3) above shall apply in relation to the acts and defaults of a member in connection with his functions of management as if he were a director of the body corporate.

(5) In any proceedings for an offence under section 2 of this Act, proof of things done or of words written, spoken or published (whether or not in the presence of any party to the proceedings) by any person taking part in the management or control of a body of persons or of any of the activities of the body, or by any person doing any of the acts mentioned in subsection (1)(*a*) to (*c*) of that section on behalf of the body, shall be admissible as evidence of the activities of the body.

(6) In relation to an offence under this Act, section 127(1) of the Magistrates' Courts Act 1980 (information must be laid within six months of commission of offence), section 136(1) of the Criminal Procedure (Scotland) Act 1995 (proceedings must be commenced within that time) and Article 19(1) of the Magistrates' Courts (Northern Ireland) Order 1981 (complaint must be made within that time) shall have effect as if for the reference to six months there were substituted a reference to two years.

Amendments—Statute Law (Repeals) Act 1993; Criminal Procedure (Consequential Provisions) (Scotland) Act 1995, ss 4, 5, Sch 4, para 57.

****

A4.11

TRUSTS OF LAND AND APPOINTMENT OF TRUSTEES ACT 1996

****

Right of beneficiaries to occupy trust land

12 The right to occupy

(1) A beneficiary who is beneficially entitled to an interest in possession in land subject to a trust of land is entitled by reason of his interest to occupy the land at any time if at that time –

    (a)   the purposes of the trust include making the land available for his occupation (or for the occupation of beneficiaries of a class of which he is a member or of beneficiaries in general), or

    (b)   the land is held by the trustees so as to be so available.

(2) Subsection (1) does not confer on a beneficiary a right to occupy land if it is either unavailable or unsuitable for occupation by him.

(3) This section is subject to section 13.

13 Exclusion and restriction of right to occupy

(1) Where two or more beneficiaries are (or apart from this subsection would be) entitled under section 12 to occupy land, the trustees of land may exclude or restrict the entitlement of any one or more (but not all) of them.

(2) Trustees may not under subsection (1) –

    (a)   unreasonably exclude any beneficiary's entitlement to occupy land, or

    (b)   restrict any such entitlement to an unreasonable extent.

(3) The trustees of land may from time to time impose reasonable conditions on any beneficiary in relation to his occupation of land by reason of his entitlement under section 12.

(4) The matters to which trustees are to have regard in exercising the powers conferred by this section include –

    (a)   the intentions of the person or persons (if any) who created the trust,

    (b)   the purposes for which the land is held, and

    (c)   the circumstances and wishes of each of the beneficiaries who is (or apart from any previous exercise by the trustees of those powers would be) entitled to occupy the land under section 12.

(5) The conditions which may be imposed on a beneficiary under subsection (3) include, in particular, conditions requiring him–

    (a)   to pay any outgoings or expenses in respect of the land, or

    (b)   to assume any other obligation in relation to the land or to any activity which is or is proposed to be conducted there.

(6) Where the entitlement of any beneficiary to occupy land under section 12 has been excluded or restricted, the conditions which may be imposed on any other beneficiary under subsection (3) include, in particular, conditions requiring him to –

    (a)   make payments by way of compensation to the beneficiary whose entitlement has been excluded or restricted, or

    (b)   forgo any payment or other benefit to which he would otherwise be entitled under the trust so as to benefit that beneficiary.

(7)   The powers conferred on trustees by this section may not be exercised –

    (a)   so as prevent any person who is in occupation of land (whether or not by reason of an entitlement under section 12) from continuing to occupy the land, or

    (b)   in a manner likely to result in any such person ceasing to occupy the land,

unless he consents or the court has given approval.

(8)   The matters to which the court is to have regard in determining whether to give approval under subsection (7) include the matters mentioned in subsection (4)(a) to (c).

Powers of court

14   Applications for order

(1)   Any person who is a trustee of land or has an interest in property subject to a trust of land may make an application to the court for an order under this section.

(2)   On an application for an order under this section the court may make any such order –

    (a)   relating to the exercise by the trustees of any of their functions (including an order relieving them of any obligation to obtain the consent of, or to consult, any person in connection with the exercise of any of their functions), or

    (b)   declaring the nature or extent of a person's interest in property subject to the trust,

as the court thinks fit.

(3)   The court may not under this section make any order as to the appointment or removal of trustees.

(4)   The powers conferred on the court by this section are exercisable on an application whether it is made before or after the commencement of this Act.

15   Matters relevant in determining applications

(1)   The matters to which the court is to have regard in determining an application for an order under section 14 include –

    (a)   the intentions of the person or persons (if any) who created the trust,

    (b)   the purposes for which the property subject to the trust is held,

    (c)   the welfare of any minor who occupies or might reasonably be expected to occupy any land subject to the trust as his home, and

    (d)   the interests of any secured creditor of any beneficiary.

(2)   In the case of an application relating to the exercise in relation to any land of the powers conferred on the trustees by section 13, the matters to which the court is to have regard also include the circumstances and wishes of each of the beneficiaries who is (or apart from any previous exercise by the trustees of those powers would be) entitled to occupy the land under section 12.

(3)   In the case of any other application, other than one relating to the exercise of the power mentioned in section 6(2), the matters to which the court is to have regard also include the circumstances and wishes of any beneficiaries of full age and entitled to an interest in possession in property subject to the trust or (in case of dispute) of the majority (according to the value of their combined interests).

(4)   This section does not apply to an application if section 335A of the Insolvency Act 1986 (which is inserted by Schedule 3 and relates to applications by a trustee of a bankrupt) applies to it.

****

Appendix 5

USEFUL CONTACTS

Mediation

National Family Mediation
Registered Charity No: 1074796
Margaret Jackson Centre
4 Barnfield Hill
Exeter, Devon, EX1 1SR
Phone: (0300) 4000 636
Fax: (01392) 271945
Website: www.nfm.org.uk

Collaborative Law

Resolution (Solicitors Family Law Association)
PO Box 302
Orpington Sorting Office
Pinson Close
Orpington BR6 0PJ
Website: www.resolution.org.uk – See section of website 'Alternatives to Court'

Domestic abuse

Broken Rainbow UK
www.broken-rainbow.org.uk

0300 999 5428 LGBT DV helpline

Adoption

British Association for Adoption and Fostering (BAAF)
Saffron House,
6-10 Kirby Street,
London,
EC1N 8TS
Phone: 020 7421 2600
Fax: 020 7421 2601
Email: mail@baaf.org.uk

For legal advice direct from the authors contact **clerks@zenithchambers.co.uk** or 0113 245 5438 to make an appointment with Sarah Greenan or Marisa Allman

(subject to the case being suitable for advice on a public access basis – see the Bar Council website **www.barcouncil.org.uk/instructingabarrister/publicaccess** for details)

INDEX

References are to paragraph numbers.

Adoption   5.1–5.33
  agency, duties   5.23
  civil partner   8.13
  Convention conditions   5.18
  delay, reducing   5.4–5.8
  ECHR rights   5.5, 5.6, 5.12–5.17
  historical background   5.1–5.3
  panel
    agency advisor, appointment of   5.28
    constitution   5.26–5.28
    functions   5.25
    medical advisor, appointment of   5.28
    procedure   5.29–5.33
    regulation   5.23
  parental responsibility, and   2.5
  placement   5.24
  procedural rules   5.7
  status conferred by   1.41–1.43
  surrogacy, and   3.40, 3.41, 3.93–3.95
  welfare checklist   5.6
  welfare of child   5.3, 5.5, 5.9, 5.10
Armed forces
  registration of civil partnership   8.39
Artificial insemination *see* Fertility
  services
Assisted reproduction *see* Fertility
  services

Birth certificate
  alteration, gender recognition   6.49–6.57
  form of   A2.1
  parent with no genetic link with
    child   1.29, 1.50
  registration of two female parents   1.30

Child of the family
  family provision   11.92–11.99
  meaning   1.39
  welfare *see* Welfare of child
Child support
  Child Maintenance and
    Enforcement Commission   10.107
  Child Support Agency, abolition   10.107
  court's jurisdiction   10.116
  CSA 1991, aim of   10.106
  formula   10.117–10.120
    changes to   10.122
  maintenance calculation   10.109, 10.110,
                                 10.112

Child support—*continued*
  'non-resident' parent   10.114
  'parent'   10.115
  'person with care'   10.113
  'qualifying child'   10.111
Child tax credit   12.16
Civil partnership
  acquired gender
    eligibility   8.22–8.29
    unknown at time of   6.69–6.72
  assisted conception, child by   1.39
  child of the family   1.39
    treatment on breakdown   1.39
  cross border recognition   8.69, 8.72–8.75
    property consequences on
      dissolution   8.75
  declaration application   8.76–8.90
    case management directions   8.90
    procedure   8.83–8.90
    respondent   8.84
    written evidence   8.87, 8.89
  definition, CPA 2004   8.1
  dissolution order   8.109
    conditional   8.119–8.122
    court, jurisdiction   8.124–8.129
    cross application   8.118
    dispositions under will, effect of 11.22
    final   8.123
    grounds for   8.110–8.112
    overseas, granted, financial
      provision   8.153–8.165
    procedure   8.113–8.123
    proceedings issued in more than
      one country   8.130–8.136
    recognition overseas   8.137–8.145
    recogntion within UK   8.146–8.152
  family provision on death   1.39, 8.13,
                              11.81–11.90
    matters to which the court must
      have regard   11.111–11.114
  financial provision   8.13, 9.1–9.67
    applications, court's
      approach   9.15–9.30
    'big money cases'   9.18–9.28
    child over 18, for   9.34, 9.35
    child, for   9.11, 9.31
    consent order   9.58
    court powers   9.3–9.5
    dissolution/annulment etc
      overseas   9.63–9.67

Civil partnership—*continued*
  financial provision—*continued*
    duration of partnership 9.37, 9.38
    equality principle 9.24
    existing civil partnership 9.6
    factors for consideration 9.12–9.14
    family business 9.19–9.21
    family home 9.45–9.48
    former civil partnership 9.5
    inherited property 9.43, 9.44
    length of marriage 9.23, 9.24
    magistrates' court 9.59
    mediation 9.60–9.62
    orders, for 9.7–9.10
    partnership assets 9.39–9.55
    pensions 9.49–9.55
      earmarking order 9.50, 9.52
      sharing order 9.51–9.55
  home *see* Family home
  home rights (FLA 1996) 8.13
  importance of 8.13, 8.14
  legitimacy 1.45, 1.46
  marriage, distinguished from 8.6–8.12
  notice, form of A2.6
  nullity order 8.109
    conditional 8.119–8.122
    court, jurisdiction 8.124–8.129
    cross application 8.118
    dispositions under will, effect of 11.22
    final 8.123
    interim gender recognition
      certificate 6.58–6.66
    overseas, granted, financial
      provision 8.153–8.165
    procedure 8.113–8.123
    proceedings issued in more than
      one country 8.130–8.136
    recognition overseas 8.137–8.145
    recogntion within UK 8.146–8.152
  overseas relationship treated as 8.4, 8.5,
      8.40–8.66
    capacity 8.57–8.63
    checklist 8.66
    effect of 8.64, 8.65
    general conditions 8.45
    meeting of formalities 8.53–8.56
    registration requirements 8.50–8.52
    same sex requirement 8.40, 8.45
    'specified relationships' (CPA,
      Sch 20) 8.41–8.44
    validity 8.95
  presumption of death order 8.109
    conditional 8.119–8.122
    final 8.123
  procedure 9.56, 9.57
  property rights 8.13
  recognition overseas 8.67–8.71
    BIIR 8.67
    freedom of movement 8.69
  registration (England and
    Wales) 8.15–8.39
    armed forces 8.39
    British consulate, at 8.36–8.38
    ceremony 8.16, 8.17

Civil partnership—*continued*
  registration (England and
    Wales)—*continued*
    eligibility 8.21
      acquired gender 8.22–8.29
    location 8.16, 8.17
    pre-registration procedure 8.30–8.35
      alternative procedure 8.34
      standard procedure 8.31–8.33
    restricitons, gender
      reassignment 8.18–8.20
  right to marry, consultation 8.3
  schedule, form of A2.7
  separation order 8.109
    court, jurisdiction 8.124–8.129
    cross application 8.118
    overseas, granted, financial
      provision 8.153–8.165
    procedure 8.113–8.123
    proceedings issued in more than
      one country 8.130–8.136
    recognition overseas 8.137–8.145
    recogntion within UK 8.146–8.152
  status, restrictions 8.2
  validity 8.91–8.108
  void 8.93, 8.97–8.101
  voidable 8.94, 8.102–8.108
  dispositions under will, effect of 11.21
Cohabitant
  child, financial provision for *see*
    also Child support 10.5,
      10.106–10.122
    CA 1989, Sch 1, under 10.123–10.132
    'big money' cases 10.140, 10.141
    child as applicant 10.129
    lump sum payment 10.128, 10.136
    parent/guardian as
      applicant 10.124
    periodical payments 10.128,
      10.137–10.139
    procedure 10.142
    property transfer order 10.128,
      10.133–10.135
  death of
    family provision application 10.5
  definition 10.1
  family home, rights in *see* Family
    home
  financial relief 10.1–10.142
    court, no power to grant 10.6
    generally 10.1–10.10
    joint bank account 10.96–10.98
    personal bank account 10.99
    personal possessions/
      chattels 10.100–10.105
    protection, proposals for
      reform 10.76–10.78
    written cohabitation agreement 10.10
Contact
  child, with
    biological father 4.36–4.44
    breakdown of transgender
      relationship 6.88–6.99

Contact order *see also* Prohibited steps
order; Residence order; Section
8 order; Special guardianship;
Specific issue order
best interests of child   4.28, 4.35
biological father, with   4.36–4.44
breach
committal   4.49
enforcement order   4.48
breakdown of relationship   4.29–4.35
contact activity condition   4.27
contact activity direction   4.27, 4.47
direct contact   4.25
domestic violence cases, Practice
Direction   4.35
enforcement   4.45–4.49
family assitance order, interation
with   4.47
indirect contact   4.25
meaning   4.24
Council tax benefit   12.3, 12.16
Court
scientific tests, power to direct   1.10, 1.11

Discrimination
prohibition, ECHR   5.12–5.17, 6.21, 6.99,
11.60, 12.7, 12.10, 12.11
sexual orientation   4.13, 6.10, 6.11
transgendered people   6.9, 6.13
Domestic violence
definitions   7.1–7.12
protection, FLA 1996 *see also*
Non-molestation order;
Forced marriage protection
order; Occupation order   7.13–7.15
'associated persons'   7.15
'cohabitants'   7.15
'relevant children'   7.15

Emergency protection order
parental responsibility, and   2.5
Employment support allowance 12.16
**European Convention of Human Rights
and Fundamental Freedoms**
family life, right to   4.13, 5.5, 5.12–5.17,
6.15–6.25, 6.89, 6.99, 12.11
prohibition of discrimination   5.12–5.17,
6.21, 6.99, 11.60, 12.7, 12.10, 12.11
right to an effective remedy   6.21
right to fair trial
adoption, reducing delays   5.6
right to marry   6.15–6.18, 8.7–8.9
**European Convention on the Adoption
of Children 1967 (revised 2008)**
conditions for adoption   5.18

Family home
beneficial interests   10.24, 10.25
constructive trust   10.54

Family home—*continued*
declaration of trust/Form
TR1   10.28–10.36, A2.8
agreement to vary   10.52, 10.53
engaged couples, rights of   10.63, 10.64
home rights   7.16–7.18
charge as   7.18
inadequate declaration of trust   10.50,
10.51
joint ownership in law/tenancy in
common in equity in equal
shares   10.33
joint tenancy   10.32
no declaration of trust/Form
TR1   10.37–10.49
Stack v Dowden   10.37–10.42
non-owner, rights   10.54–10.62
occupation
rights under FLA 1996 *see*
Occupation order
occupation, cohabitant, by   10.11–10.18
ownership   10.21–10.78
ownership in one name   10.54–10.62
two legal owners   10.26–10.53
proprietary estoppel   10.62
regulation, order by   7.19
resulting trust   10.60
tenancy in common   10.34
TLATA 1996, orders under   10.65–10.75
transfer of tenancy   7.36, 10.84–10.92
Family life
adoption, and   1.4
family relationships, new forms of   1.1,
1.2
fertility treament, effect of   1.4
gender recognition, and   5.12–5.17, 6.1,
6.15–6.25, 6.89, 6.99
right to   4.13, 5.5, 5.12–5.17, 6.15–6.25,
6.89, 6.99, 12.11
social and psychological role,
importance of   1.3, 1.103
surrogacy, and   1.4
Family provision *see also*
Succession   11.72–11.102,
11.104–11.119
adult children   11.95–11.99
application for   11.80
'child of the deceased'   11.91
'child of the family'   11.92–11.99
civil partner   11.81–11.90
legislative background   11.72–11.79
lump sum payment   11.105
'maintained by deceased'   11.100–11.102,
11.104
matters to which the court must
have regard   11.108–11.110
civil partnership cases   11.111–11.114
periodical payments   11.105
proposals for reform   11.119
'reasonable financial provision'   11.106,
11.107
settlement, order for   11.105
time limit on claims   11.115

Family provision —*continued*
transfer of property   11.105
Fatal accident claims
civil partner, rights as   8.13
Father *see also* Unmarried father
assisted reproduction
consent and withdrawal   1.69–1.75
involvement in parenting   1.37
legal parent   1.31, 1.47
parental responsibility   1.31
contact, with   4.36–4.44
meaning   1.26, 1.32, 1.34, 1.53–1.58, 1.67,
                                                          1.68
GRA 2004, effect on   1.38
Fertility services
'father'   1.32, 1.34
gamete, use of   1.47
known father   1.31
legal parentage, effect on   1.47–1.50
'mother'   1.32, 1.34
'parent'   1.4, 1.28–1.32, 1.34
post HFEA 1990   1.51–1.60
'father'   1.52–1.58
'mother'   1.51
'parent'   1.59
post HFEA 2008   1.61–1.76
'father'   1.67–1.75
'mother'   1.62
'other female parent'   1.63–1.66
'parent'   1.59
Financial provision
civil partnership, breakdown of *see*
Civil partnership
cohabiting couples
breakdown of relationship *see*
Cohabitant
Forced marriage protection order   7.51–7.57
application   7.54
third party, by   7.54
circumstances for   7.52
contempt of court   7.57
definitions   7.53
power of arrest, attachment of   7.57
scope of   7.56
without notice   7.57
Freedom of movement
civil partner, rights as   8.13
cross border recognition   8.69

Gender identity
meaning   6.3
Gender recognition   6.1–6.117
acquired gender
eligibility for civil
partnership   8.22–8.29
approved countries   6.29, 6.33, A3.1
background   6.8–6.26
certificate *see* Gender recognition
certificate
definition of parent, and   1.38
family relationships, and   6.1

Gender recognition—*continued*
human rights *see also* European
Convention of Human
Rights and Fundamental
Freedoms   6.9, 6.15–6.26
legislation, development of   6.13–6.26
meaning   6.27
overseas schemes, aproved by
Secretary of State   A3.4
P v S and Cornwall County Council,
effect of   6.10–6.12
proposals for change   6.112–6.117
social security benefits, and   12.47–12.52
terminology   A3.5
test cases   6.14–6.26
trans(sexual)/transgender,
meanings   6.4–6.7
Gender recognition certificate   6.1–6.117
applications procedure   6.27–6.30
civil partner   6.58–6.86
determination rules   6.31–6.33
evidence   6.34–6.39
form of   A3.2
guidance   A3.3
married applicant   6.58–6.86
birth certificate, alteration of   6.49–6.57
form of   6.27
full, effect of   6.46–6.48, 6.67
Gender Recognition Panel   6.27–6.30
interim certificate, effect of   6.58–6.66
overseas applications   6.40–6.45
parenthood, effect on   6.87–6.99
registration   6.49–6.86
Gender Recognition
Register   6.51–6.56
Genetic parentage
best interests of the child   1.103, 1.104
determination by court   1.14
generally   1.8–1.14
meaning   1.8
'natural parent'   1.9
scientific tests to determine   1.10
bodily samples, refusal to give   1.12
court's power to direct   1.10
significance   1.9
tracing   A1.1, A1.2

Housing benefit   12.3, 12.16
Human rights
transgendered people   6.9, 6.15–6.26

Immigration
civil partner, rights as   8.13
Income support   12.3, 12.16
Inheritance *see* Succession

Jobseeker's allowance   12.3, 12.4, 12.16

Legal parentage
ACA 2002, effect of   1.28
acquisition of   1.40–1.50
adoption (UK)   1.41–1.43

Legal parentage—*continued*
  acquisition of—*continued*
    assisted reproduction   1.47–1.50
  civil partership   1.36, 8.13
  determination by court   1.14
  legitimacy   1.44–1.46
  meaning   1.19–1.38
  natural parent   1.19
  parental order, effect on   1.100–1.102
  parental responsibility, and   1.20
  post HFEA 1990   1.29, 1.51–1.60, A1.1
    'father'   1.52–1.58
    'mother'   1.51
    'parent'   1.59
  post HFEA 2008   1.28, 1.61–1.76, A1.2
    'father'   1.67–1.75
    'mother'   1.62
    'other female parent'   1.63–1.66
    'parent'   1.59
  statute, governed by   1.13
  surrogacy effect of   1.86–1.98
  surrogacy issues   1.36
  transfer, of   1.35
  two female parents   1.36
  two male parents   1.36
Legitimacy
  presumption of   1.44
    assisted reproduction   1.45, 1.46
    civil partnership   1.45

Marriage
  acquired gender unknown at time
    of   6.69–6.72
  nullity
    interim gender recognition
      certificate   6.58–6.66
    restricitons, gender
      reassignment   6.73–6.86
Matrimonial home *see* Family home
Mother
  meaning   1.27, 1.32, 1.34, 1.52, 1.62
  GRA 2004, effect on   1.38
  surrogacy   1.27

Non-molestation order
  arrest, no power attachable   7.41–7.50
  breach, committal   7.44
  child application   7.42
  child, protection of   7.41–7.43
  contempt proceedings   7.45
  court power   7.43
  criminal offence   7.44
  duration   7.49, 7.50
  undertaking   7.45, 7.46
  variation or discharge   7.50
  violence threatened or used   7.43
  without notice order   7.47
Nullity
  acquired gender unknown at time
    of marriage/civil
      partnership   6.69–6.72

Nullity—*continued*
  interim gender recognition
    certificate
      ground, for   6.58–6.66

Occupation order
  applicant with interest   7.20–7.22
  applicant with no right to
    occupy   7.23–7.25
  applications   7.19–7.28
  breach   7.37–7.40
  child, protection of   7.31
  comittal for breach   7.37
  court's consideration when
    making   7.29–7.34
  duration   7.49, 7.50
  neither cohabitant right to occupy   7.26,
                                       7.28
  neither spouse/civil partner right to
    occupy   7.27
  power of arrest, attached to   7.38–7.40
  respondent entitled to occupy   7.27
  variation or discharge   7.50
  without notice order   7.35

Parent *see also* Father; Mother;
    Parenthood; Parentage
  CA 1989, under   1.21–1.23
  CSA 1991, under   1.24
  genetic *see* Genetic parentage
  legal *see* Legal parentage
  meaning   1.1–1.7, 1.32, 1.34, 1.59, 1.60
  GRA 2004, effect on   1.38
  'natural parent'   1.3, 1.9
  'other female parent'   1.63
  social and psychological role,
    importance of   1.3, 1.103
  unrelated genetically   1.6
Parentage
  declaration   1.13, 1.15–1.18
    application, for   1.15–1.18
      CMEC, by   1.16
      court directions   1.18
      hearing   1.18
      notice   1.15
      procedure   1.15
      request for scitentific tests   1.15
      respondent   1.15, 1.17
      'sufficient personal interest'
        requirement   1.16
      who can apply   1.16, 1.17
  determination by court   1.14
  genetic *see* Genetic parentage
  legal *see* Legal parentage
  meaning   1.14
Parental order
  civil partners   1.84
  legal parentage, effect on   1.100–1.102
  parental responsibility, and   2.5
  refusal to make   3.57
  register, form of entry   A2.2

Parental order—*continued*
surrogacy, following 1.35, 1.77–1.98, 3.19,
               3.22, 3.25–3.30, 3.51–3.81
  agreement of parties   3.64–3.70
  applicant, married/civil partners
      etc   3.58
  application for, procedure   3.82–3.91
    acknowledgment of service   3.85
    directions hearing   3.88
    notice of proceedings   3.85
    parental order reporter   3.88
    refusal   3.91
    respondents   3.85–3.87
    rules for   3.82, 3.83
  assisted conception   3.59
  criteria for making   3.58–3.80
  domicile of applicants   3.62, 3.63
  enduring relationship   1.96–1.98
  form of agreement   3.67–3.70
  one parent is genetic parent   3.60
  party incapable of agreement,
    to   3.74–3.79
  reasonable expenses   3.80
  registration   3.92
  single applicant not allowed   3.58
  status of genetic mother   1.86
  timing of application   3.61
  use of applicant's gamete   1.87
  welfare of child 2.5, 3.56, 3.57, 3.75, 3.88
Parental responsibility   3.56
  acquisition, of
    limitations   2.4
  adoptor   2.5
  agreement *see* Parental
    responsibility agreement
  best interests of child   1.5
  biological father, commitment of 1.5
  child of the family, and   1.39
  civil partner   2.5, 8.13
  definition   2.1–2.6
  emergency protection order   2.5
  father, of *see* Unmarried father
  female couple parenting child   1.5
  legal parent, and   1.20
  mother   2.5
  parental order   2.5
  person who has   2.2, 2.3
  residence order   2.5, 2.20–2.26
  significance in private law
    proceedings   4.21
  special guardian   2.5, 3.96, 3.97
  step-parent   2.5
  surrogacy, following   3.35–3.38
Parental responsibility agreement
  application for   2.9–2.12
  civil partner   2.7
  disputes   2.13–2.19
  effect of   2.12
  form of   2.8, A2.3
  second female parent
    form of   A2.5
  step-parent   2.7
    form of   A2.4

Parental responsibility agreement—*continued*
  welfare of child   2.14, 2.16
Parenthood
  adoption, effect on   1.28, 1.33
  fertility treatment, effect on   1.28
  gender reassigment, and 6.87–6.99
  HFEA 1990   1.29
  'legal parent'   1.28
  terminology   1.26–1.38
Parenting roles
  biological father   1.2
  'principal parenting' 1.2, 4.43, 4.44
  'secondary parenting'   1.2, 4.44
  two females   1.2, 1.5
Partner, civil *see* Civil partnership
Pension rights
  acquired gender, effect on 6.100–6.111
  civil partner   8.13, 12.53
Personal protection *see* Domestic
  violence; Forced marriage
  protection order; Occupation
  order; Protection from
  harassment
Private law proceedings *see also*
  Contact order; Prohibited steps
  order; Residence order; Section
  8 order; Special guardianship;
  Specific issue order
  meaning   4.1
  parties to   4.96, 4.97
  same sex couple, development of
    law   4.3–4.15
  types of order, under   4.2
Prohibited steps order *see also* Contact
  order; Residence order; Section
  8 order; Special guardianship;
  Specific issue order
  meaning   4.68
  use of   4.69, 4.70
Protection from harrassment 7.58–7.64
  civil claim   7.58, 7.59
  'course of conduct'   7.63
  'harrassment'   7.58
  remedies   7.62

Residence order *see also* Contact order;
  Prohibited steps order; Section
  8 order; Special guardianship;
  Specific issue order   4.50–4.58
  application   2.20
    leave for   2.25
  best interests of child   4.52
  change of name, and   4.64
  conditions   4.59–4.62
  couple living together 2.20, 4.54
  duration   2.26
  effect of   4.63
  father, and   2.21, 4.58
  joint   2.20, 4.54
  meaning   4.50
  parental responsibility, and 2.5, 2.26, 4.53

Residence order —*continued*
removal of child from
jurisdiction 4.65–4.67
shared 2.22–2.24, 4.54, 4.56, 4.57
surrogacy, following 3.45–3.50
effect of 3.50
welfare of child 4.51

Scientific tests
parentage, establishing 1.10–1.13
Section 8 order *see also* Contact order;
Prohibited steps order;
Residence order; Special
guardianship; Specific issue
order
application 4.82
child, by 4.95
leave for 4.83–4.95
Mediation, Information and
Assessment, Protocol 4.82
types of 4.23
welfare of child 4.22
Sexual orientation
meaning 6.2
Social security benefits 12.1–12.55
acquired gender, effect on 6.100–6.111
civil partner 8.13, 12.24, 12.43
cohabiting couples, 'living
together' 12.25–12.44
dependent children 12.37
financial suuport 12.35
living in the same household 12.32,
12.33
public acknowledgement 12.38
sexual relationship 12.36
stability of relationship 12.34
co-parents not living together 12.45,
12.46
CPA 2004, effect on 12.14–12.20
definition of couple 12.18, 12.20
gender recognition, and 12.47–12.52
inequality, historical background
of 12.2–12.13
'living together' 12.21
'living together as civil partners' 12.24
'living together as husband and
wife' 12.22
means tested benefits 12.16
non-means tested benefits 12.17
'partner' 12.23
Special guardianship
order *see also* Contact order;
Prohibited steps order;
Residence order; Section 8
order; Specific issue
order 4.78–4.81
application 4.78
court's power to make 4.81
effect 4.79, 4.81
eligibility 4.78
use of 4.78–4.81
parental responsibility, and 2.5, 3.96, 3.97

Special guardianship—*continued*
surrogacy, and 3.96–3.100
Specific issue order *see also* Contact
order; Prohibited steps order;
Residence order; Section 8
order; Special guardianship
change of gender, and 4.76
disclosure of parentage, and 4.74–4.76
meaning 4.71
removal of child from jurisdiction 4.77
use of 4.72–4.77
Stalking
protection from *see* Protection
from harassment
State pension credit 12.3, 12.16
Statutory adoption pay 12.2
Statutory paternity pay 12.2
Succession *see also* Family provision
children, gifts to 11.26–11.32
intestacy 11.33–11.54
division of property 11.49–11.54
grant of administration
court's power to
change 11.34–11.36
order of priority 11.33
property not passing under
will 11.3–11.17
bank accounts 11.15
body of deceased 11.17
chattels 11.16
life insurance policies 11.14
pension scheme payments 11.13
real property, joint
tenancy 11.4–11.12
tenancies 11.55–11.71
assured tenancies 11.66–11.68
Rent Act 1977, under 11.56–11.65
secure tenancies 11.69–11.71
will, dispositions under 11.18–11.25
civil partnership
annulment 11.22
dissolution 11.22
voidable 11.21
Surrogacy 3.1–3.106
adoption, and 3.40, 3.41, 3.93–3.95
agencies 3.31–3.34
commercial surrogacy 3.12–3.34
agencies advertising 3.14
arrangement made outside UK 3.18,
3.19
commercial negotiation 3.13
illegality 3.12
non-profit organisations 3.15, 3.31
'reasonable expenses' 3.20–3.30
proof of 3.29
welfare of child 3.3, 3.23, 3.24, 3.28
commissioning parents 3.2, 3.6
financial stability 3.34
legal status of 3.35–3.44
screening of 3.34
criminal offences 3.12, 3.39, 3.40
international surrogacy 3.101–3.106
legal parentage, effect on 1.86–1.98

Surrogacy—*continued*
meaning	3.2–3.11
mother	1.27
no parental order	
effect on legal parentage	1.99
parental order	1.35, 1.77–1.98, 3.19, 3.22,
	3.25–3.30, 3.51–3.81
agreement of parties	3.64–3.70
applicant, married/civil partners	
etc	3.58
application for, procedure	3.82–3.91
acknowledgment of service	3.85
directions hearing	3.88
notice of proceedings	3.85
parental order reporter	3.88
refusal	3.91
respondents	3.85–3.87
rules for	3.82, 3.83
assisted conception	3.59
criteria for making	3.58–3.80
domicile of applicants	3.62, 3.63
form of agreement	3.67–3.70
one parent is genetic parent	3.60
party incapable of agreement,	
to	3.74–3.79
reasonable expenses	3.80
registration	3.92
single applicant not allowed	3.58
timing of application	3.61
welfare of child	3.56, 3.57
parental responsibility,	
following	3.35–3.38
private fostering arrangement	3.42–3.44
regulation of, problems	3.16
residence order	3.45–3.50
effect of	3.50
special guardiansip	3.96–3.100
surrogacy arrangements	3.9, 3.10
key factors	3.3
meaning of	1.78
unenforceability	1.82, 1.83, 3.9

Surrogacy—*continued*
surrogacy mother	3.6, 3.7
'reasonable expenses', for	3.20–3.30
screening of	3.34

Tax
acquired gender, effect on	6.100–6.111
civil partner	8.13, 12.54

Tax credits
definition of couple	12.19

Tenancy
agreement	10.83
agricultural	10.81
assured or assured shorthold	
tenancy	10.80, 11.66–11.68
cohabitants, rights of	10.79–10.95
non-tenant cohabitant	10.85, 10.94
Rent Act 1977, under	10.80, 11.56–11.65
secure tenancy	10.80, 10.82, 11.69–11.71
succession rights	11.55–11.71
transfer of	7.35, 10.84–10.92

Transgendered person *see* Gender
  recognition

Unmarried father
parental responsibility	2.2

Welfare benefits *see* Social security
  benefits

Welfare of child
adoption	5.3, 5.5
reducing delays	5.9, 5.10
paramountcy principle	1.104, 1.105, 2.16,
	3.23, 4.16, 5.3, 5.5, 6.88, 6.89
parental order, and	3.56, 3.75, 3.88
parental responsibility, and	2.14, 2.16
surrogacy arrangements	3.3, 3.23, 3.24,
	3.28
welfare checklist	4.17–4.20

Working tax credit
	12.16